Java^{TM} I/O

THE JAVA SERIES

Exploring Java™

Java™ Threads

Java™ Network Programming

Java™ Virtual Machine

Java™ AWT Reference

Java™ Language Reference

Java™ Fundamental Classes Reference

Database Programming with JDBC™ and Java™

Java™ Distributed Computing

Developing Java Beans™

Java™ Security

Java™ Cryptography

Java™ Swing

Java™ Servlet Programming

Java™ I/O

Also from O'Reilly

Java™ in a Nutshell

Java™ in a Nutshell, Deluxe Edition

Java™ Examples in a Nutshell

Java™ I/O

Elliotte Rusty Harold

O'REILLY®

Beijing · Cambridge · Köln · Paris · Sebastopol · Taipei · Tokyo

Java™ I/O
by Elliotte Rusty Harold

Copyright © 1999 O'Reilly & Associates, Inc. All rights reserved.
Printed in the United States of America.

Published by O'Reilly & Associates, Inc., 101 Morris Street, Sebastopol, CA 95472.

Editor: Mike Loukides

Production Editor: Clairemarie Fisher O'Leary

Printing History:

March 1999:   First Edition

ISBN: 1-56592-485-1

To Lynn, the best aunt a boy could ask for.

Table of Contents

Preface

In many ways this book is a prequel to my previous book, *Java Network Programming* (O'Reilly & Associates). When writing that book, I more or less assumed that readers were familiar with basic input and output in Java™—that they knew how to use input streams and output streams, convert bytes to characters, connect filter streams to each other, and so forth.

However, after that book was published, I began to notice that a lot of the questions I got from readers of the book and students in my classes weren't so much about network programming itself as they were about input and output (I/O in programmer vernacular). When Java 1.1 was released with a vastly expanded `java.io` package and many new I/O classes spread out across the rest of the class library, it became obvious that a book that specifically addressed I/O was required. This is that book.

Java I/O endeavors to show you how to really use Java's I/O classes, allowing you to quickly and easily write programs that accomplish many common tasks. Some of these include:

- Reading and writing files
- Communicating over network connections
- Filtering data
- Interpreting a wide variety of formats for integer and floating-point numbers
- Passing data between threads
- Encrypting and decrypting data
- Calculating digital signatures for streams
- Compressing and decompressing data

- Writing objects to streams

- Copying, moving, renaming, and getting information about files and directories

- Letting users choose files from a GUI interface

- Reading and writing non-English text in a variety of character sets

- Formatting integer and floating-point numbers as strings

- Talking directly to modems and other serial port devices

- Talking directly to printers and other parallel port devices

Java is the first language to provide a cross-platform I/O library that is powerful enough to handle all these diverse tasks. *Java I/O* is the first book to fully expose the power and sophistication of this library.

Correcting Misconceptions

Java is the first programming language with a modern, object-oriented approach to input and output. Java's I/O model is more powerful and more suited to real-world tasks than any other major language used today. Surprisingly, however, I/O in Java has a bad reputation. It is widely believed (falsely) that Java I/O can't handle basic tasks that are easily accomplished in other languages like C, C++, and Pascal. In particular, it is commonly said that:

- I/O is too complex for introductory students; or, more specifically, there's no good way to read a number from the console.

- Java can't handle basic formatting tasks like printing π with three decimal digits of precision.

This book will show you that not only can Java handle these two tasks with relative ease and grace; it can do anything C and C++ can do, and a whole lot more. Java's I/O capabilities not only match those of classic languages like C and Pascal, they vastly surpass them.

The most common complaint about Java I/O among students, teachers, authors of textbooks, and posters to *comp.lang.java* is that there's no simple way to read a number from the console (System.in). Many otherwise excellent introductory Java books repeat this canard. Some textbooks go to great lengths to reproduce the behavior they're accustomed to from C or Pascal, apparently so teachers don't have to significantly rewrite the tired Pascal exercises they've been using for the last 20 years. However, new books that aren't committed to the old ways of doing things generally use command-line arguments for basic exercises, then rapidly introduce the graphical user interfaces any real program is going to use anyway. Apple wisely abandoned the command-line interface back in 1984, and the rest of the world is slowly catching up.* Although `System.in` and `System.out` are certainly convenient for teaching and debugging, in 1999 no completed, cross-platform program should even assume the existence of a console for either input or output.

The second common complaint about Java I/O is that it can't handle formatted output; that is, that there's no equivalent of `printf()` in Java. In a very narrow sense, this is true because Java does not support the variable length argument lists a function like `printf()` requires. Nonetheless, a number of misguided souls (your author not least among them) have at one time or another embarked on futile efforts to reproduce `printf()` in Java. This may have been necessary in Java 1.0, but as of Java 1.1, it's no longer needed. The `java.text` package, discussed in Chapter 16, provides complete support for formatting numbers. Furthermore, the `java.text` package goes way beyond the limited capabilities of `printf()`. It supports not only different precisions and widths, but also internationalization, currency formats, percentages, grouping symbols, and a lot more. It can easily be extended to handle Roman numerals, scientific or exponential notation, or any other number format you may require.

The underlying flaw in most people's analysis of Java I/O is that they've confused input and output with the formatting and interpreting of data. Java is the first major language to cleanly separate the classes that read and write bytes (primarily, various kinds of input streams and output streams) from the classes that interpret this data. You often need to format strings without necessarily writing them on the console. You may also need to write large chunks of data without worrying about what they represent. Traditional languages that connect formatting and interpretation to I/O and hard-wire a few specific formats are extremely difficult to extend to other formats. In essence, you have to give up and start from scratch every time you want to process a new format.

Furthermore, C's `printf()`, `fprintf()`, and `sprintf()` family only really works well on Unix (where, not coincidentally, C was invented). On other platforms, the underlying assumption that every target may be treated as a file fails, and these standard library functions must be replaced by other functions from the host API.

Java's clean separation between formatting and I/O allows you to create new formatting classes without throwing away the I/O classes, and to write new I/O classes while still using the old formatting classes. Formatting and interpreting strings are fundamentally different operations from moving bytes from one device to another. Java is the first major language to recognize and take advantage of this.

---

* MacOS X will reportedly add a real command-line shell to the Mac for the first time ever. Mainly, this is because MacOS X has Unix at its heart. However, Apple at least has the good taste to hide the shell so it won't confuse end users and tempt developers away from the righteous path of graphical user interfaces.

Organization of the Book

This book has 17 chapters that are divided into four parts, plus two appendixes.

Part I: Basic I/O

Chapter 1, Introducing I/O

Chapter 1 introduces the basic architecture and design of the `java.io` package, including the reader/stream dichotomy. Some basic preliminaries about the `int`, `byte`, and `char` data types are discussed. The `IOException` thrown by many I/O methods is introduced. The console is introduced, along with some stern warnings about its proper use. Finally, I offer a cautionary message about how the security manager can interfere with most kinds of I/O, sometimes in unexpected ways.

Chapter 2, Output Streams

Chapter 2 teaches you the basic methods of the `java.io.OutputStream` class you need to write data onto any output stream. You'll learn about the three overloaded versions of `write()`, as well as `flush()` and `close()`. You'll see several examples, including a simple subclass of `OutputStream` that acts like */dev/null* and a `TextArea` component that gets its data from an output stream.

Chapter 3, Input Streams

The third chapter introduces the basic methods of the `java.io.Input-Stream` class you need to read data from a variety of sources. You'll learn about the three overloaded variants of the `read()` method and when to use each. You'll see how to skip over data and check how much data is available, as well as how to place a bookmark in an input stream, then reset back to that point. You'll learn how and why to close input streams. This will all be drawn together with a `StreamCopier` program that copies data read from an input stream onto an output stream. This program will be used repeatedly over the next several chapters.

Part II: Data Sources

Chapter 4, File Streams

The majority of I/O involves reading or writing files. Chapter 4 introduces the `FileInputStream` and `FileOutputStream` classes, concrete subclasses of `InputStream` and `OutputStream` that let you read and write files. These classes have all the usual methods of their superclasses, such as `read()`, `write()`, `available()`, `flush()`, and so on. Also in this chapter, development of a File Viewer program commences. You'll see how to inspect the raw bytes in a file in both decimal and hexadecimal format. This example will be progressively expanded throughout the rest of the book.

Chapter 5, Network Streams

From its first days, Java has always had the network in mind, more so than any other common programming language. Java is the first programming language to provide as much support for network I/O as it does for file I/O, perhaps even more. Chapter 5 introduces Java's URL, URLConnection, Socket, and ServerSocket classes, all fertile sources of streams. Typically the exact type of the stream used by a network connection is hidden inside the undocumented sun classes. Thus network I/O relies primarily on the basic InputStream and OutputStream methods. Examples in this chapter include several simple web and email clients.

Part III: Filter Streams

Chapter 6, Filter Streams

Chapter 6 introduces filter streams. Filter input streams read data from a preexisting input stream like a FileInputStream, and have an opportunity to work with or change the data before it is delivered to the client program. Filter output streams write data to a preexisting output stream such as a FileOutputStream, and have an opportunity to work with or change the data before it is written onto the underlying stream. Multiple filters can be chained onto a single underlying stream to provide the functionality offered by each filter. Filters streams are used for encryption, compression, translation, buffering, and much more. At the end of this chapter, the File Viewer program is redesigned around filter streams to make it more extensible.

Chapter 7, Data Streams

Chapter 7 introduces data streams, which are useful for writing strings, integers, floating-point numbers, and other data that's commonly presented at a level higher than mere bytes. The DataInputStream and DataOutputStream classes read and write the primitive Java data types (boolean, int, double, etc.) and strings in a particular, well-defined, platform-independent format. Since DataInputStream and DataOutputStream use the same formats, they're complementary. What a data output stream writes, a data input stream can read, and vice versa. These classes are especially useful when you need to move data between platforms that may use different native formats for integers or floating-point numbers. Along the way, you'll develop classes to read and write little-endian numbers, and you'll extend the File Viewer program to handle big- and little-endian integers and floating-point numbers of varying widths.

Chapter 8, Streams in Memory

Chapter 8 shows you how streams can move data from one part of a running Java program to another. There are three main ways to do this. Sequence input streams chain several input streams together so that they appear as a single stream. Byte array streams allow output to be stored in byte arrays and input to be read from byte arrays. Finally, piped input and output streams allow output from one thread to become input for another thread.

Chapter 9, Compressing Streams

Chapter 9 explores the `java.util.zip` and `java.util.jar` packages. These packages contain assorted classes that read and write data in zip, gzip, and inflate/deflate formats. Java uses these classes to read and write JAR archives and to display PNG images. However, the `java.util.zip` classes are more general than that, and can be used for general-purpose compression and decompression. Among other things, they make it trivial to write a simple compressor or decompressor program, and several will be demonstrated. In the final example, support for compressed files is added to the File Viewer program.

Chapter 10, Cryptographic Streams

The Java core API contains two cryptography-related filter streams in the `java.security` package, `DigestInputStream` and `DigestOutputStream`. There are two more in the `javax.crypto` package, `CipherInputStream` and `CipherOutputStream`, available in the Java Cryptography Extension™ (JCE for short). Chapter 10 shows you how to use these classes to encrypt and decrypt data using a variety of algorithms, including DES and Blowfish. You'll also learn how to calculate message digests for streams that can be used for digital signatures. In the final example, support for encrypted files is added to the File Viewer program.

Part IV: Advanced and Miscellaneous Topics

Chapter 11, Object Serialization

The first 10 chapters showed you how to read and write various primitive data types to many different kinds of streams. Chapter 11 shows you how to write everything else. Object serialization, first used in the context of remote method invocation (RMI) and later for JavaBeans™, lets you read and write almost arbitrary objects onto a stream. The `ObjectOutputStream` class provides a `writeObject()` method you can use to write a Java object onto a stream. The `ObjectInputStream` class has a `readObject()` method you can use to read an object from a stream. In this chapter, you'll learn how to use these two classes to read and write objects, as well as how to customize the format used for serialization.

Chapter 12, Working with Files

Chapter 12 shows you how to perform operations on files other than simply reading or writing them. Files can be moved, deleted, renamed, copied, and manipulated without respect to their contents. Files are also often associated with meta-information that's not strictly part of the contents of the file, such as the time the file was created, the icon for the file, or the permissions that determine which users can read or write to the file.

The `java.io.File` class attempts to provide a platform-independent abstraction for common file operations and meta-information. Unfortunately, this class really shows its Unix roots. It works fine on Unix, reasonably well on Windows—with a few caveats—and fails miserably on the Macintosh. File manipulation is thus one of the real bugbears of cross-platform Java programming. Therefore, this chapter shows you not only how to use the `File` class, but also the precautions you need to take to make your file code portable across all major platforms that support Java.

Chapter 13, File Dialogs and Choosers

Filenames are problematic, even if you don't have to worry about cross-platform idiosyncrasies. Users forget filenames, mistype them, can't remember the exact path to files they need, and more. The proper way to ask a user to choose a file is to show them a list of the files and let them pick one. Most graphical user interfaces provide standard graphical widgets for selecting a file. In Java, the platform's native file selector widget is exposed through the `java.awt.FileDialog` class. Like many native peer-based classes, however, `FileDialog` doesn't behave the same or provide the same services on all platforms. Therefore, the Java Foundation Classes™ 1.1 (Swing) provide a pure Java implementation of a file dialog, the `javax.swing.JFileChooser` class. Chapter 13 shows you how to use both these classes to provide a GUI file selection interface. In the final example, you'll add a Swing-based GUI to the File Viewer program.

Chapter 14, Multilingual Character Sets and Unicode

We live on a planet where many languages are spoken, yet most programming languages still operate under the assumption that everything you need to say can be expressed in English. Java is starting to change that by adopting the multinational Unicode as its native character set. All Java chars and strings are given in Unicode. However, since there's also a lot of non-Unicode legacy text in the world, in a dizzying array of encodings, Java also provides the classes you need to read and write this text in these encodings as well. Chapter 14 introduces you to the multitude of character sets used around the world, and develops a simple applet to test which ones your browser/VM combination supports.

Chapter 15, Readers and Writers

A language that supports international text must separate the reading and writing of raw bytes from the reading and writing of characters, since in an international system they are no longer the same thing. Classes that read characters must be able to parse a variety of character encodings, not just ASCII, and translate them into the language's native character set. Classes that write characters must be able to translate the language's native character set into a variety of formats and write those. In Java, this task is performed by the `Reader` and `Writer` classes. Chapter 15 shows you how to use these classes, and adds support for multilingual text to the File Viewer program.

Chapter 16, Formatted I/O with java.text

Java 1.0 did not provide classes for specifying the width, precision, and alignment of numeric strings. Java 1.1 and later make these available as subclasses of `java.text.NumberFormat`. As well as handling the traditional formatting achieved by languages like C and Fortran, `NumberFormat` also internationalizes numbers with different character sets, thousands separators, decimal points, and digit characters. Chapter 16 shows you how to use this class and its subclasses for traditional tasks, like lining up the decimal points in a table of prices, and nontraditional tasks, like formatting numbers in Egyptian Arabic.

Chapter 17, The Java Communications API

Chapter 17 introduces the Java Communications API, a standard extension available for Java 1.1 and later that allows Java applications and trusted applets to send and receive data to and from the serial and parallel ports of the host computer. The Java Communications API allows your programs to communicate with essentially any device connected to a serial or parallel port, like a printer, a scanner, a modem, a tape backup unit, and so on.

Chapters 1 through 3 provide the basic background you'll need to do any sort of work with I/O in Java. After that, you should feel free to jump around as your interests take you. There are, however, some interdependencies between specific chapters. Figure P-1 should allow you to map out possible paths through the book.

A few examples in later chapters depend on material from earlier chapters—for instance, many examples use the `FileInputStream` class discussed in Chapter 4—but they should not be difficult to understand in the large.

Who You Are

This book assumes you have a basic familiarity with Java. You should be thoroughly familiar with the syntax of the language. You should be comfortable with object-oriented programming, including terminology like instances, objects, and classes, and you should know the difference between these terms. You should know what a reference is and what that means for passing arguments to and returning values from methods. You should have written simple applications and applets.

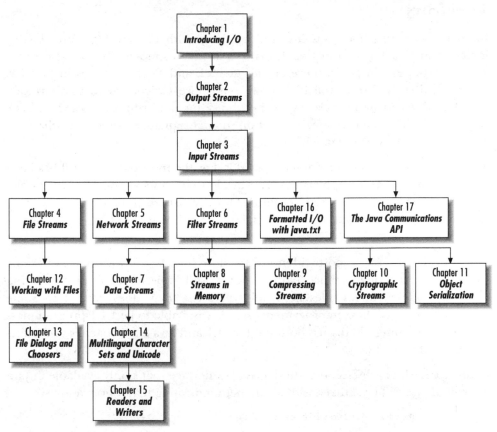

Figure P-1. Chapter prerequisites

For the most part, I try to keep the examples relatively straightforward so that they require a minimum of understanding of other parts of the class library outside the I/O classes. This may lead some to deride these as "toy examples." However, I find that such examples arc far more conducive to understanding and learning than full-blown sophisticated programs that fill page after page with graphical user interface code just to demonstrate a two-line point about I/O. Occasionally, however, a graphical example is simply too tempting to ignore, as in the StreamedTextArea class shown in Chapter 2 or the File Viewer application developed throughout most of the book. I will try to keep the AWT material to a minimum, but a familiarity with 1.1 AWT basics will be assumed.

When you encounter a topic that requires a deeper understanding for I/O than is customary—for instance, the exact nature of strings—I'll cover that topic as well, at least briefly. However, this is not a language tutorial, and the emphasis will always be on the I/O-specific features.

Versions

In many ways, this book was inspired by the wealth of new I/O functionality included in Java 1.1. I/O in Java 1.0 is overall much simpler, though also much less powerful. For instance, there are no Reader and Writer classes in Java 1.0. However, there's also no reliable way to read pure Unicode text. Furthermore, Java 1.1 added many new classes to the library for performing a variety of I/O-related tasks like compression, encryption, digital signatures, object serialization, encoding conversion, and much more.

Therefore, this book assumes at least Java 1.1. For the most part, Java 1.0 has been relegated to developing applets that run inside web browsers. Because the applet security manager severely restricts the I/O an untrusted applet can undertake, most applets do not make heavy use of I/O, and thus it should not be a major concern.

Java 2's I/O classes are mostly identical to those in Java 1.1, with one noticeable exception. Java 2 does a much better (though still imperfect) job of abstracting out platform-dependent filesystem idiosyncrasies than does Java 1.1. Some (though not all) of these improvements are also available to Java 1.1 programmers working with Swing. I'll discuss both the Java 1.1 and Java 2 approaches to the file-system in Chapter 12.

In any case, when I discuss a method, class or interface that's only available in Java 2, its signature will be suffixed with a comment indicating that. For example:

```
public interface Replaceable extends Serializable // Java 2
```

Security Issues

I don't know if there's one most frequently asked question about *Java Network Programming*, but there's definitely a most frequent answer, and it applies to this book too. My mistake in *Java Network Programming* was hiding that answer in the back of a chapter most people didn't read. Since that very same answer should answer an equal number of questions from readers of this book, I want to get it out of the way right up front:

Java's security manager prevents almost all the examples and methods discussed in this book from working in an applet.

This book focuses very much on applications. There is very little that can be done with I/O from an untrusted applet without running afoul of the security manager. The problem may not always be obvious—not all web browsers properly report security exceptions—but it is there.

There are some exceptions. Byte array streams and piped streams work without limitation in applets. Network connections can be made back to the host from whence the applet came (and only to that host). $System.in$ and $System.out$ may be accessible from some, though not all, web browsers. And in Java 2 and later, there are ways to relax the restrictions on applets so they get limited access to the filesystem or unlimited access to the network. However, these are exceptions, not the rule.

If you can make an applet work when run as a standalone application and you cannot get it to work inside a web browser, the problem is almost certainly a conflict with the browser's security manager.

Conventions Used in This Book

Italic is used for:

- Filenames (*readme.txt*)
- Host and domain names (*www.oreilly.com*)
- URLs (*http://metalab.unc.edu/javafaq/*)

Constant width is used for:

- Code examples and fragments
- Class, variable, and method names, and Java keywords used within the text

Significant code fragments and complete programs are generally placed in a separate paragraph like this:

```
InputStream in = new FileInputStream("/etc/mailcap");
```

When code is presented as fragments rather than complete programs, the existence of the appropriate import statements should be inferred. For example, in the previous code fragment you may assume that java.io.InputStream and java.io.FileInputStream were imported.

Some examples intermix user input with program output. In these cases, the user input will be displayed in bold, but otherwise in the same monospaced font, as in this example from Chapter 17:

```
D:\JAVA\16>java PortTyper COM2
at&f
at&f

OK
atdt 321-1444
```

Most of the code examples in this book are optimized for legibility rather than speed. For instance, consider this `getIcon()` method from Chapter 13:

```
public Icon getIcon(File f) {

  if (f.getName().endsWith(".zip")) return zipIcon;
  if (f.getName().endsWith(".gz")) return gzipIcon;
  if (f.getName().endsWith(".dfl")) return deflateIcon;
  return null;
}
```

I invoke the `f.getName()` method three times, when once would do:

```
public Icon getIcon(File f) {

  String name = f.getName();
  if (name.endsWith(".zip")) return zipIcon;
  if (name.endsWith(".gz")) return gzipIcon;
  if (name.endsWith(".dfl")) return deflateIcon;
  return null;
}
```

However, this seemed slightly less obvious than the first example. Therefore, I chose the marginally slower form. Other, still less obvious optimizations are also possible, but would only make the code even more obscure. For example:

```
public Icon getIcon(File f) {

  String name = f.getName();
  String lastDot = name.lastIndexOf('.');
  if (lastDot != -1) {
    String extension = name.substring(lastDot+1);
    if (extension.equals("zip")) return zipIcon;
    if (extension.equals("gz")) return gzipIcon;
    if (extension.equals("dfl")) return deflateIcon;
  }
  return null;
}
```

I might resort to this form if profiling proved that this method was a performance bottleneck in my application, and this revised method was genuinely faster, but I certainly wouldn't use it in my first pass at the problem. In general, I only optimize for speed when similar code seems likely to be a performance bottleneck in situations where it's likely to be used, or when optimizing can be done without negatively affecting the legibility of the code.

Finally, although many of the examples are toys unlikely to be reused, a few of the classes I develop have real value. Please feel free to reuse them or any parts of them in your own code; no special permission is required. Such classes are placed somewhere in the `com.macfaq` package, generally mirroring the `java` package hierarchy. For instance, Chapter 2's `NullOutputStream` class is in the `com.macfaq.io` package; its `StreamedTextArea` class is in the `com.macfaq.awt` package. When working with these classes, don't forget that the compiled *.class* files must reside in directories matching their package structure inside your class path and that you'll have to import them in your own classes before you can use them.* The web page includes a JAR file that can be installed in your class path.

Furthermore, classes not in the default package with `main()` methods are generally run by passing in the full package-qualified name. For example:

```
D:\JAVA\ioexamples\04>java com.macfaq.io.FileCopier oldfile newfile
```

Request for Comments

I enjoy hearing from readers, whether with general comments about how this could be a better book, specific corrections, or other topics you would like to see covered. You can reach me by sending email to *elharo@metalab.unc.edu*. Please realize, however, that I receive several hundred pieces of email a day and cannot personally respond to each one.

I'm especially interested in hearing about mistakes. If you find one, I'll post it on my web page for this book at *http://metalab.unc.edu/javafaq/books/javaio/* and on the O'Reilly web site at *http://www.oreilly.com/catalog/javaio/*. Before reporting errors, please check one of those pages to see if I already know about it and have posted a fix.

Let me also preempt a couple of non-errors that are often mistakenly reported. First, the signatures given in this book don't necessarily match the signatures given in the *javadoc* documentation. I often change method argument names to make them clearer. For instance, Sun documents the `write()` method in `java.io.OutputStream` like this:

```
public void write(byte b[]) throws IOException
public void write(byte b[], int off, int len) throws IOException
```

I've rewritten that in this more intelligible form:

```
public void write(byte[] data) throws IOException
public void write(byte[] data, int offset, int length) throws IOException
```

These are exactly equivalent, however. Method argument names are purely formal and have no effect on client programmer's code that invokes these methods. I could have rewritten them in Latin or Tuvan without really changing anything. The only difference is in their intelligibility to the reader.

---

* See "The Name Space: Packages, Classes, and Members" in the second edition of David Flanagan's *Java in a Nutshell* (O'Reilly & Associates, 1997).

Acknowledgments

Many people were involved in the production of this book. All these people deserve much thanks and credit. My editor, Mike Loukides, got this book rolling and provided many helpful comments that substantially improved it. Clairemarie Fisher O'Leary, Chris Maden, and Robert Romano deserve a special commendation for putting in all the extra effort needed for a book that makes free use of Arabic, Cyrillic, Chinese, and other non-Roman scripts. Tim O'Reilly and the whole crew at O'Reilly deserve special thanks for building a publisher that's willing to give a book the time and support it needs to be a good book rather than rushing it out the door to meet an artificial deadline.

Many people looked over portions of the manuscript and provided helpful comments. These included Scott Bortman, Bob Eckstein, and Avner Gelb. Bruce Schneier and Jan Luehe both lent their expertise to the cryptography chapter. Ian Darwin was invaluable in handling the details of the Java Communications API.

My agent, David Rogelberg, convinced me it was possible to make a living writing books like this rather than working in an office. Finally, I'd like to save my largest thanks for my wife, Beth, without whose support and assistance this book would never have happened.

I

BASIC I/O

1

In this chapter:
- *What Is a Stream?*
- *Numeric Data*
- *Character Data*
- *Readers and Writers*
- *The Ubiquitous IOException*
- *The Console: System. out, System.in, and System.err*
- *Security Checks on I/O*

Introducing I/O

Input and output, I/O for short, are fundamental to any computer operating system or programming language. Only theorists find it interesting to write programs that don't require input or produce output. At the same time, I/O hardly qualifies as one of the more "thrilling" topics in computer science. It's something in the background, something you use every day—but for most developers, it's not a topic with much sex appeal.

There are plenty of reasons for Java programmers to find I/O interesting. Java includes a particularly rich set of I/O classes in the core API, mostly in the `java.io` package. For the most part I/O in Java is divided into two types: byte- and number-oriented I/O, which is handled by input and output streams; and character and text I/O, which is handled by readers and writers. Both types provide an abstraction for external data sources and targets that allows you to read from and write to them, regardless of the exact type of the source. You use the same methods to read from a file that you do to read from the console or from a network connection.

But that's just the tip of the iceberg. Once you've defined abstractions that let you read or write without caring where your data is coming from or where it's going to, you can do a lot of very powerful things. You can define I/O streams that automatically compress, encrypt, and filter from one data format to another, and more. Once you have these tools, programs can send encrypted data or write zip files with almost no knowledge of what they're doing; cryptography or compression can be isolated in a few lines of code that say, "Oh yes, make this an encrypted output stream."

In this book, I'll take a thorough look at all parts of Java's I/O facilities. This includes all the different kinds of streams you can use. We're also going to investigate Java's support for Unicode (the standard multilingual character set). We'll look at Java's powerful facilities for formatting I/O—oddly enough, not part of the

3

`java.io` package proper. (We'll see the reasons for this design decision later.) Finally, we'll take a brief look at the Java Communications API (`javax.comm`), which provides the ability to do low-level I/O through a computer's serial and parallel ports.

I won't go so far as to say, "If you've always found I/O boring, this is the book for you!" I will say that if you do find I/O uninteresting, you probably don't know as much about it as you should. I/O is the means for communication between software and the outside world (including both humans and other machines). Java provides a powerful and flexible set of tools for doing this crucial part of the job.

Having said that, let's start with the basics.

What Is a Stream?

A stream is an ordered sequence of bytes of undetermined length. Input streams move bytes of data into a Java program from some generally external source. Output streams move bytes of data from Java to some generally external target. (In special cases streams can also move bytes from one part of a Java program to another.)

The word *stream* is derived from an analogy with a stream of water. An input stream is like a siphon that sucks up water; an output stream is like a hose that sprays out water. Siphons can be connected to hoses to move water from one place to another. Sometimes a siphon may run out of water if it's drawing from a finite source like a bucket. On the other hand, if the siphon is drawing water from a river, it may well provide water indefinitely. So too an input stream may read from a finite source of bytes like a file or an unlimited source of bytes like `System.in`. Similarly an output stream may have a definite number of bytes to output or an indefinite number of bytes.

Input to a Java program can come from many sources. Output can go to many different kinds of destinations. The power of the stream metaphor and in turn the stream classes is that the differences between these sources and destinations are abstracted away. All input and output are simply treated as streams.

Where Do Streams Come From?

The first source of input most programmers encounter is `System.in`. This is the same thing as `stdin` in C, generally some sort of console window, probably the one in which the Java program was launched. If input is redirected so the program reads from a file, then `System.in` is changed as well. For instance, on Unix, the following command redirects `stdin` so that when the MessageServer program reads from `System.in`, the actual data comes from the file *data.txt* instead of the console:

```
% java MessageServer < data.txt
```

The console is also available for output through the static field `out` in the `java.lang.System` class, that is, `System.out`. This is equivalent to `stdout` in C parlance and may be redirected in a similar fashion. Finally, `stderr` is available as `System.err`. This is most commonly used for debugging and printing error messages from inside `catch` clauses. For example:

```
try {
   //... do something that might throw an exception
}
catch (Exception e) { System.err.println(e); }
```

Both `System.out` and `System.err` are print streams, that is, instances of `java.io.PrintStream`.

Files are another common source of input and destination for output. File input streams provide a stream of data that starts with the first byte in a file and finishes with the last byte in the file. File output streams write data into a file, either by erasing the file's contents and starting from the beginning or by appending data to the file. These will be introduced in Chapter 4, *File Streams*.

Network connections provide streams too. When you connect to a web server or FTP server or something else, you read the data it sends from an input stream connected from that server and write data onto an output stream connected to that server. These streams will be introduced in Chapter 5, *Network Streams*.

Java programs themselves produce streams. Byte array input streams, byte array output streams, piped input streams, and piped output streams all use the stream metaphor to move data from one part of a Java program to another. Most of these are introduced in Chapter 8, *Streams in Memory*.

Perhaps a little surprisingly, AWT (and Swing) components like `TextArea` do not produce streams. The issue here is ordering. Given a group of bytes provided as data, there must be a fixed order to those bytes for them to be read or written as a stream. However, a user can change the contents of a text area or a text field at any point, not just the end. Furthermore, they can delete text from the middle of a stream while a different thread is reading that data. Hence, streams aren't a good metaphor for reading data from graphical user interface (GUI) components. You can, however, always use the strings they do produce to create a byte array input stream or a string reader.

The Stream Classes

Most of the classes that work directly with streams are part of the `java.io` package. The two main classes are `java.io.InputStream` and `java.io.OutputStream`. These are abstract base classes for many different subclasses with more specialized abilities, including:

```
BufferedInputStream           BufferedOutputStream
ByteArrayInputStream          ByteArrayOutputStream
DataInputStream               DataOutputStream
FileInputStream               FileOutputStream
FilterInputStream             FilterOutputStream
LineNumberInputStream         ObjectInputStream
ObjectOutputStream            PipedInputStream
PipedOutputStream             PrintStream
PushbackInputStream           SequenceInputStream
StringBufferInputStream
```

Though I've included them here for completeness, the `LineNumberInputStream` and `StringBufferInputStream` classes are deprecated. They've been replaced by the `LineNumberReader` and `StringReader` classes, respectively.

Sun would also like to deprecate `PrintStream`. In fact, the `PrintStream()` constructors were deprecated in Java 1.1, though undeprecated in Java 2. Part of the problem is that `System.out` is a `PrintStream`; therefore, `PrintStream` is too deeply ingrained in existing Java code to deprecate and is thus likely to remain with us for the foreseeable future.

The `java.util.zip` package contains four input stream classes that read data in a compressed format and return it in uncompressed format and four output stream classes that read data in uncompressed format and write in compressed format. These will be discussed in Chapter 9, *Compressing Streams*.

```
CheckedInputStream            CheckedOutputStream
DeflaterOutputStream          GZIPInputStream
GZIPOutputStream              InflaterInputStream
ZipInputStream                ZipOutputStream
```

The `java.util.jar` package includes two stream classes for reading files from JAR archives. These will also be discussed in Chapter 9.

```
JarInputStream                JarOutputStream
```

The `java.security` package includes a couple of stream classes used for calculating message digests:

```
DigestInputStream             DigestOutputStream
```

The Java Cryptography Extension (JCE) adds two classes for encryption and decryption:

```
CipherInputStream      CipherOutputStream
```

These four streams will be discussed in Chapter 10, *Cryptographic Streams*.

Finally, there are a few random stream classes hiding inside the sun packages—for example, `sun.net.TelnetInputStream` and `sun.net.TelnetOutputStream`. However, these are deliberately hidden from you and are generally presented as instances of `java.io.InputStream` or `java.io.OutputStream` only.

Numeric Data

Input streams read bytes and output streams write bytes. Readers read characters and writers write characters. Therefore, to understand input and output, you first need a solid understanding of how Java deals with bytes, integers, characters, and other primitive data types, and when and why one is converted into another. In many cases Java's behavior is not obvious.

Integer Data

The fundamental integer data type in Java is the `int`, a four-byte, big-endian, two's complement integer. An `int` can take on all values between –2,147,483,648 and 2,147,483,647. When you type a literal integer like 7, –8345, or 3000000000 in Java source code, the compiler treats that literal as an `int`. In the case of 3000000000 or similar numbers too large to fit in an `int`, the compiler emits an error message citing "Numeric overflow."

`long`s are eight-byte, big-endian, two's complement integers with ranges from –9,223,372,036,854,775,808 to 9,223,372,036,854,775,807. `long` literals are indicated by suffixing the number with a lower- or uppercase *L*. An uppercase *L* is preferred because the lowercase *l* is too easily confused with the numeral 1 in most fonts. For example, 7L, –8345L, and 3000000000L are all 64-bit `long` literals.

There are two more integer data types available in Java, the `short` and the `byte`. `short`s are two-byte, big-endian, two's complement integers with ranges from –32,768 to 32,767. They're rarely used in Java and are included mainly for compatibility with C.

`byte`s, however, are very much used in Java. In particular they're used in I/O. A `byte` is an eight-bit, two's complement integer that ranges from –128 to 127. Note that like all numeric data types in Java, a `byte` is signed. The maximum `byte` value is 127. 128, 129, and so on through 255 are not legal values for bytes.

There are no short or byte literals in Java. When you write the literal 42 or 24000, the compiler always reads it as an int, never as a byte or a short, even when used in the right-hand side of an assignment statement to a byte or short, like this:

```
byte b = 42;
short s = 24000;
```

However, in these lines a special *assignment conversion* is performed by the compiler, effectively casting the int literals to the narrower types. Because the int literals are constants known at compile time, this is permitted. However, assignments from int variables to shorts and bytes are not, at least not without an explicit cast. For example, consider these lines:

```
int i = 42;
short s = i;
byte b = i;
```

Compiling these lines produces the following errors:

```
Error:    Incompatible type for declaration.
Explicit cast needed to convert int to short.
ByteTest.java  line 6
Error:    Incompatible type for declaration.
Explicit cast needed to convert int to byte.
ByteTest.java  line 7
```

Note that this occurs even though the compiler is theoretically capable of determining that the assignment does not lose information. To correct this, you must use explicit casts, like this:

```
int i = 42;
short s = (short) i;
byte b = (byte) i;
```

Even simple arithmetic with small, byte-valued constants as follows produces "Explicit cast needed to convert int to byte" errors:

```
byte b = 1 + 2;
```

In fact, even the addition of two byte variables produces an integer result and thus cannot be assigned to a byte variable without a cast; the following code produces that same error:

```
byte b1 = 22;
byte b2 = 23;
byte b3 = b1 + b2;
```

For these reasons, working directly with byte variables is inconvenient at best. Many of the methods in the stream classes are documented as reading or writing bytes. However, what they really return or accept as arguments are ints in the range of an unsigned byte (0–255). This does not match any Java primitive data type. These ints are then converted into bytes internally.

For instance, according to the *javadoc* class library documentation, the read() method of java.io.InputStream returns "the next byte of data, or –1 if the end of the stream is reached." On a little thought, this sounds suspicious. How is a –1 that appears as part of the stream data to be distinguished from a –1 indicating end of stream? In point of fact, the read() method does not return a byte; its signature indicates that it returns an int:

```
public abstract int read() throws IOException
```

This int is not a Java byte with a value between –128 and 127 but a more general unsigned byte with a value between 0 and 255. Hence, –1 can easily be distinguished from valid data values read from the stream.

The write() method in the java.io.OutputStream class is similarly problematic. It returns void, but takes an int as an argument:

```
public abstract void write(int b) throws IOException
```

This int is intended to be an unsigned byte value between 0 and 255. However, there's nothing to stop a careless programmer from passing in an int value outside that range. In this case, the eight low-order bits are written and the top 24 high-order bits are ignored. This is the effect of taking the remainder modulo 256 of the absolute value of the int b; that is:

```
b = Math.abs(b) % 256;
```

Alternately, using bitwise operators:

```
b = b & 0x000000FF;
```

NOTE Although this is the behavior specified by the *Java Language Specification*, since the write() method is abstract, actual implementation of this scheme is left to the subclasses, and a careless programmer could do something different.

On the other hand, real Java bytes are used in those methods that read or write arrays of bytes. For example, consider these two read() methods from java.io.InputStream:

```
public int read(byte[] data) throws IOException
public int read(byte[] data, int offset, int length) throws IOException
```

While the difference between an 8-bit byte and a 32-bit int is insignificant for a single number, it can be very significant when several thousand to several million numbers are read. In fact, a single byte still takes up four bytes of space inside the

Java virtual machine, but a `byte` array only occupies the amount of space it actually needs. The virtual machine includes special instructions for operating on `byte` arrays, but does not include any instructions for operating on single `bytes`. They're just promoted to `ints`.

Although data is stored in the array as signed Java bytes with values between –128 to 127, there's a simple one-to-one correspondence between these signed values and the unsigned bytes normally used in I/O, given by the following formula:

```
int unsignedByte = signedByte > 0 ? signedByte : 256 + signedByte;
```

Conversions and Casts

Since `bytes` have such a small range, they're often converted to `ints` in calculations and method invocations. Often they need to be converted back, generally through a cast. Therefore, it's useful to have a good grasp of exactly how the conversion occurs.

Casting from an `int` to a `byte`—for that matter, casting from any wider integer type to a narrower type—takes place through truncation of the high-order bytes. This means that as long as the value of the wider type can be expressed in the narrower type, the value is not changed. The `int` 127 cast to a `byte` still retains the value 127.

On the other hand, if the `int` value is too large for a `byte`, strange things happen. The `int` 128 cast to a `byte` is not 127, the nearest byte value. Instead, it is –128. This occurs through the wonders of two's complement arithmetic. Written in hexadecimal, 128 is 0x00000080. When that `int` is cast to a `byte`, the leading zeros are truncated, leaving 0x80. In binary this can be written as 10000000. If this were an unsigned number, 10000000 would be 128 and all would be fine, but this isn't an unsigned number. Instead, the leading bit is a sign bit, and that 1 does not indicate 2^7 but a minus sign. The absolute value of the number is found by taking the complement (changing all the 1 bits to 0 bits and vice versa) and adding 1. The complement of 10000000 is 01111111. Adding 1, you have 01111111 + 1 = 10000000 = 128 (decimal). Therefore, the `byte` 0x80 actually represents –128. Similar calculations show that the `int` 129 is cast to the `byte` –127, the `int` 130 is cast to the `byte` –126, the `int` 131 is cast to the `byte` –125, and so on. This continues through the `int` 255, which is cast to the `byte` –1.

When 256 is reached, the low-order bytes of the `int` are now filled with zeros. In other words, 256 is 0x00000100. Thus casting it to a byte produces 0, and the cycle starts over. This behavior can be reproduced algorithmically with this formula, though a cast is obviously simpler:

```
int byteValue;
int temp = intValue % 256;
```

```
if ( intValue < 0) {
  byteValue =  temp < -128 ? 256 + temp : temp;
}
else {
  byteValue =  temp > 127 ? temp - 256 : temp;
}
```

Character Data

Numbers are only part of the data a typical Java program needs to read and write. Most programs also need to handle text, which is composed of characters. Since computers only really understand numbers, characters are encoded by matching each character in a given script to a particular number. For example, in the common ASCII encoding, the character A is mapped to the number 65; the character B is mapped to the number 66; the character C is mapped to the number 67; and so on. Different encodings may encode different scripts or may encode the same or similar scripts in different ways.

Java understands several dozen different character sets for a variety of languages, ranging from ASCII to the Shift Japanese Input System (SJIS) to Unicode. Internally, Java uses the Unicode character set. Unicode is a two-byte extension of the one-byte ISO Latin-1 character set, which in turn is an eight-bit superset of the seven-bit ASCII character set.

ASCII

ASCII, the American Standard Code for Information Interchange, is a seven-bit character set. Thus it defines 2^7 or 128 different characters whose numeric values range from 0 to 127. These characters are sufficient for handling most of American English and can make reasonable approximations to most European languages (with the notable exceptions of Russian and Greek). It's an often used lowest common denominator format for different computers. If you were to read a byte value between 0 and 127 from a stream, then cast it to a char, the result would be the corresponding ASCII character.

ASCII characters 0–31 and character 127 are nonprinting control characters. Characters 32–47 are various punctuation and space characters. Characters 48–57 are the digits 0–9. Characters 58–64 are another group of punctuation characters. Characters 65–90 are the capital letters A–Z. Characters 91–96 are a few more punctuation marks. Characters 97–122 are the lowercase letters a–z. Finally, characters 123 through 126 are a few remaining punctuation symbols. The complete ASCII character set is shown in Table B-1 in Appendix B, *Character Sets*.

All Java programs can be expressed in pure ASCII. Non-ASCII Unicode characters are encoded as Unicode escapes; that is, written as a backslash (\), followed by a *u*, followed by four hexadecimal digits; for example, \u00A9. This is discussed further under the "Unicode" section, later in this chapter.

ISO Latin-1

ISO Latin-1 is an eight-bit character set that's a strict superset of ASCII. It defines 2^8 or 256 different characters whose numeric values range from 0 to 255. The first 128 characters—that is, those numbers with the high-order bit equal to zero—correspond exactly to the ASCII character set. Thus 65 is ASCII A and ISO Latin-1 A; 66 is ASCII B and ISO Latin-1 B; and so on. Where ISO Latin-1 and ASCII diverge is in the characters between 128 and 255 (characters with high bit equal to one). ASCII does not define these characters. ISO Latin-1 uses them for various accented letters like $\ddot{u}$ needed for non-English languages written in a Roman script, additional punctuation marks and symbols like ©, and additional control characters. The upper, non-ASCII half of the ISO Latin-1 character set is shown in Table B-2.

Latin-1 provides enough characters to write most Western European languages (again with the notable exception of Greek). It's a popular lowest common denominator format for different computers. If you were to read an unsigned byte value from a stream, then cast it to a char, the result would be the corresponding ISO Latin-1 character.

Unicode

ISO Latin-1 suffices for most Western European languages, but it doesn't have anywhere near the number of characters required to represent Cyrillic, Greek, Arabic, Hebrew, Persian, or Devanagari, not to mention pictographic languages like Chinese and Japanese. Chinese alone has over 80,000 different characters. To handle these scripts and many others, the Unicode character set was invented. Unicode is a 2-byte, 16-bit character set with 2^{16} or 65,536 different possible characters. (Only about 40,000 are used in practice, the rest being reserved for future expansion.) Unicode can handle most of the world's living languages and a number of dead ones as well.

The first 256 characters of Unicode—that is, the characters whose high-order byte is zero—are identical to the characters of the ISO Latin-1 character set. Thus 65 is ASCII A and Unicode A; 66 is ASCII B and Unicode B and so on.

Java streams do not do a good job of reading Unicode text. (This is why readers and writers were added in Java 1.1.) Streams generally read a byte at a time, but each Unicode character occupies two bytes. Thus, to read a Unicode character, you multiply the first byte read by 256, add it to the second byte read, and cast the result to a char. For example:

```
int b1 = in.read();
int b2 = in.read();
char c = (char) (b1*256 + b2);
```

You must be careful to ensure that you don't inadvertently read the last byte of one character and the first byte of the next, instead. Thus, for the most part, when reading text encoded in Unicode or any other format, you should use a reader rather than an input stream. Readers handle the conversion of bytes in one character set to Java chars without any extra effort. For similar reasons, you should use a writer rather than an output stream to write text.

UTF-8

Unicode is a relatively inefficient encoding when most of your text consists of ASCII characters. Every character requires the same number of bytes—two—even though some characters are used much more frequently than others. A more efficient encoding would use fewer bits for the more common characters. This is what UTF-8 does.

In UTF-8 the ASCII alphabet is encoded using a single byte, just as in ASCII. The next 1,919 characters are encoded in two bytes. The remaining Unicode characters are encoded in three bytes. However, since these three-byte characters are relatively uncommon,* especially in English text, the savings achieved by encoding ASCII in a single byte more than makes up for it.

Java's .class files use UTF-8 internally to store string literals. Data input streams and data output streams also read and write strings in UTF-8. However, this is all hidden from direct view of the programmer, unless perhaps you're trying to write a Java compiler or parse output of a data stream without using the DataInputStream class.

Other encodings

ASCII, ISO Latin-1, and Unicode are hardly the only character sets in common use, though they are the ones handled most directly by Java. There are many other character sets, both that encode different scripts and that encode the same scripts in different ways. For example, IBM mainframes have long used a non-ASCII seven-bit character set called EBCDIC. EBCDIC has most of the same characters as ASCII but assigns them to different numbers. Macintoshes commonly use an eight-bit encoding called MacRoman that matches ASCII in the lower 128 places and has most of the same characters as ISO Latin-1 in the upper 128 characters but in

---

* The vast majority of the characters above 2047 are the pictograms used for Chinese, Japanese, and Korean.

different positions. Big-5 and SJIS are encodings of Chinese and Japanese, respectively, that are designed to allow these large scripts to be input from a standard English keyboard.

Java's `Reader`, `Writer`, and `String` classes understand how to convert these character sets to and from Unicode. This will be the subject of Chapter 14, *Multilingual Character Sets and Unicode*.

The char Data Type

Character-oriented data in Java is primarily composed of the `char` primitive data type, `char` arrays, and `Strings`, which are stored as arrays of `chars` internally. Just as you need to understand `bytes` to really grasp how input and output streams work, so too do you need to understand `chars` to understand how readers and writers work.

In Java, a `char` is a two-byte, unsigned integer, the only unsigned type in Java. Thus, possible `char` values range from 0 to 65,535. Each `char` represents a particular character in the Unicode character set. `chars` may be assigned to by using `int` literals in this range; for example:

```
char copyright = 169;
```

`chars` may also be assigned to by using `char` literals; that is, the character itself enclosed in single quotes:

```
char copyright = '©';
```

Sun's *javac* compiler can translate many different encodings to Unicode by using the −encoding command-line flag to specify the encoding in which the file is written. For example, if you know a file is written in ISO Latin-1, you might compile it as follows:

```
% javac -encoding 8859_1 CharTest.java
```

The complete list of available encodings is given in Table B-4.

With the exception of Unicode itself, most character sets understood by Java do not have equivalents for all the Unicode characters. To encode characters that do not exist in the character set you're programming with, you can use *Unicode escapes*. A Unicode escape sequence is an unescaped backslash, followed by any number of *u* characters, followed by four hexadecimal digits specifying the character to be used. For example:

```
char copyright = '\u00A9';
```

NOTE   The double backslash, \\, is an escaped backslash, which is replaced by a single backslash that only means the backslash character. It is not further interpreted. Thus a Java Compiler interprets the string \u00A9 as © but \\u00A9 as the literal string \u00A9 and the string \\\u00A9 as \©. Whenever an odd number of backslashes precede the four hex digits, they will be interpreted as a single Unicode character. Whenever an even number of backslashes precede the four hex digits, they will be interpreted as four separate characters.

Unicode escapes may be used not just in `char` literals, but also in strings, identifiers, comments, and even in keywords, separators, operators, and numeric literals. The compiler translates Unicode escapes to actual Unicode characters before it does anything else with a source code file. However, the actual use of Unicode escapes inside keywords, separators, operators, and numeric literals is unnecessary and can only lead to obfuscation. With the possible exception of identifiers, comments, and string and `char` literals, Java programs can be expressed in pure ASCII without using Unicode escapes.

A `char` used in arithmetic is promoted to `int`. This presents the same problem as it does for bytes. For instance, the following line causes the compiler to emit an error message: "Incompatible type for declaration. Explicit cast needed to convert `int` to `char`."

```
char c = 'a' + 'b';
```

Admittedly, you rarely need to perform mathematical operations on `chars`.

Readers and Writers

In Java 1.1 and later, streams are primarily intended for data that can be read as pure bytes—basically byte data and numeric data encoded as binary numbers of one sort or another. Streams are specifically not intended for use when reading and writing text, including both ASCII text, like "Hello World," and numbers formatted as text, like "3.1415929." For these purposes, you should use readers and writers.

Input and output streams are fundamentally byte-based. Readers and writers are based on characters, which can have varying widths depending on the character set. For example, ASCII and ISO Latin-1 use one-byte characters. Unicode uses two-byte characters. UTF-8 uses characters of varying width (between one and three bytes). Since characters are ultimately composed of bytes, readers take their input from streams. However, they convert those bytes into `chars` according to a specified encoding format before passing them along. Similarly, writers convert chars to bytes according to a specified encoding before writing them onto some underlying stream.

The `java.io.Reader` and `java.io.Writer` classes are abstract superclasses for classes that read and write character-based data. The subclasses are notable for handling the conversion between different character sets. There are nine reader and eight writer classes in the core Java API, all in the `java.io` package:

```
BufferedReader            BufferedWriter
CharArrayReader           CharArrayWriter
FileReader                FileWriter
FilterReader              FilterWriter
InputStreamReader         LineNumberReader
OutputStreamWriter        PipedReader
PipedWriter               PrintWriter
PushbackReader            StringReader
StringWriter
```

For the most part, these classes have methods that are extremely similar to the equivalent stream classes. Often the only difference is that a `byte` in the signature of a stream method is replaced by a `char` in the signature of the matching reader or writer method. For example, the `java.io.OutputStream` class declares these three `write()` methods:

```
public abstract void write(int i) throws IOException
public void write(byte[] data) throws IOException
public void write(byte[] data, int offset, int length) throws IOException
```

The `java.io.Writer` class, therefore, declares these three `write()` methods:

```
public void write(int i) throws IOException
public void write(char[] data) throws IOException
public abstract void write(char[] data, int offset, int length) throws
IOException
```

As you can see, the six signatures are identical except that in the latter two methods the `byte` array `data` has changed to a `char` array. There's also a less obvious difference not reflected in the signature. While the `int` passed to the `OutputStream write()` method is reduced modulo 256 before being output, the `int` passed to the `Writer write()` method is reduced modulo 65,536. This reflects the different ranges of `chars` and `bytes`.

`java.io.Writer` also has two more `write()` methods that take their data from a string:

```
public void write(String s) throws IOException
public void write(String s, int offset, int length) throws IOException
```

Because streams don't know how to deal with character-based data, there are no corresponding methods in the `java.io.OutputStream` class.

The Ubiquitous IOException

As computer operations go, input and output are unreliable. They are subject to problems completely outside the programmer's control. Disks can develop bad sectors while a file is being read; construction workers drop backhoes through the cables that connect your WAN; users unexpectedly cancel their input; telephone repair crews shut off your modem line while trying to repair someone else's. (This last one actually happened to me while writing this chapter. My modem kept dropping the connection and then not getting a dial tone; I had to hunt down the telephone "repairman" in my building's basement and explain to him that he was working on the wrong line.)

Because of these potential problems and many more, almost every method that performs input or output is declared to throw `IOException`. `IOException` is a checked exception, so you must either declare that your methods throw it or enclose the call that can throw it in a `try/catch` block. The only real exceptions to this rule are the `PrintStream` and `PrintWriter` classes. Because it would be inconvenient to wrap a `try/catch` block around each call to `System.out.println()`, Sun decided to have `PrintStream` (and later `PrintWriter`) catch and eat any exceptions thrown inside a `print()` or `println()` method. If you do want to check for exceptions inside a `print()` or `println()` method, you can call `checkError()`:

```
public boolean checkError()
```

The `checkError()` method returns `true` if an exception has occurred on this print stream, `false` if one hasn't. It only tells you that an error occurred. It does not tell you what sort of error occurred. If you need to know more about the error, you'll have to use a different output stream or writer class.

`IOException` has many subclasses—15 in `java.io`—and methods often throw a more specific exception that subclasses `IOException`. (However, methods usually only declare that they throw an `IOException`.) Here are the subclasses of `IOException` that you'll find in `java.io`:

```
CharConversionException   EOFException
FileNotFoundException     InterruptedIOException
InvalidClassException     InvalidObjectException
NotActiveException        NotSerializableException
ObjectStreamException     OptionalDataException
StreamCorruptedException  SyncFailedException
UTFDataFormatException    UnsupportedEncodingException
WriteAbortedException
```

There are a number of `IOException` subclasses scattered around the other packages, particularly `java.util.zip` (`DataFormatException` and `ZipException`) and `java.net` (`BindException`, `ConnectException`, `MalformedURLException`, `NoRouteToHostException`, `ProtocolException`, `SocketException`, `Unknown HostException`, and `UnknownServiceException`).

The `java.io.IOException` class declares no public methods or fields of significance—just the usual two constructors you find in most exception classes:

```
public IOException()
public IOException(String message)
```

The first constructor creates an `IOException` with an empty message. The second provides more details about what went wrong. Of course, `IOException` has the usual methods inherited by all exception classes such as `toString()` and `printStackTrace()`.

The Console: System.out, System.in, and System.err

The console is the default destination for output written to `System.out` or `System.err` and the default source of input for `System.in`. On most platforms the console is the command-line environment from which the Java program was initially launched, perhaps an *xterm* (Figure 1-1) or a DOS shell window (Figure 1-2). The word *console* is something of a misnomer, since on Unix systems the console refers to a very specific command-line shell, rather than being a generic term for command-line shells overall.

Many common misconceptions about I/O occur because most programmers' first exposure to I/O is through the console. The console is convenient for quick hacks and toy examples commonly found in textbooks, and I will use it for that in this book, but it's really a very unusual source of input and destination for output, and good Java programs avoid it. It behaves almost, but not completely, unlike anything else you'd want to read from or write to. While consoles make convenient examples in programming texts like this one, they're a horrible user interface and really have little place in modern programs. Users are more comfortable with a well-defined graphical user interface. Furthermore, the console is unreliable across platforms. The Mac, for example, has no native console. Macintosh Runtime for Java 2 and earlier has a console window that works only for output, but not for input; that is, `System.out` works but `System.in` does not.* Figure 1-3 shows the Mac console window.

---

* Console input is supported in MRJ 2.1ea2 and presumably later releases.

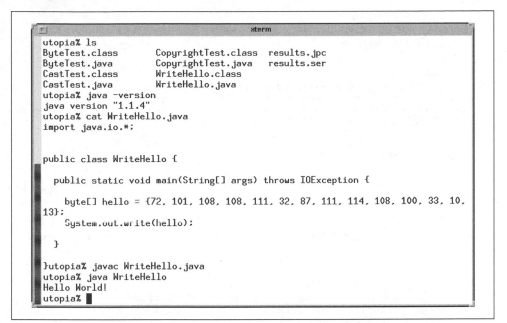

Figure 1-1. Figure 1-1.An xterm console on Unix

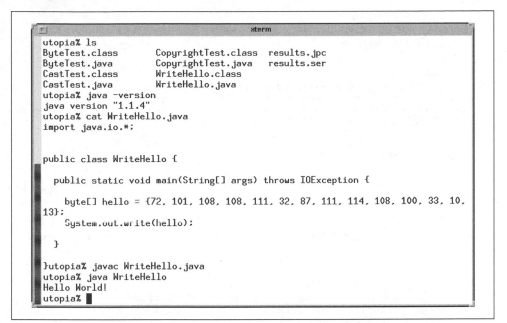

Figure 1-2. A DOS shell console on Windows NT

Personal Digital Assistants (PDAs) and other handheld devices running Personal-Java are equally unlikely to waste their small screen space and low resolution on a 1970s-era interface.

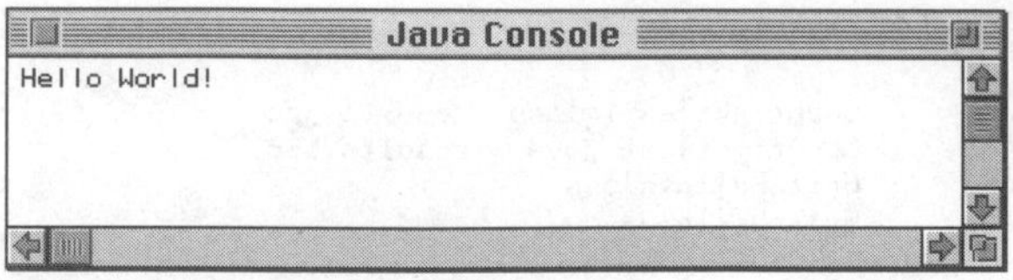

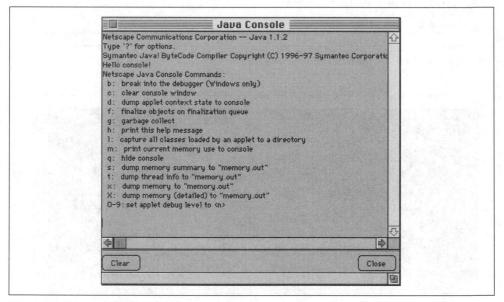

Figure 1-3. The Mac console, used exclusively by Java programs

Consoles in Applets

As well as being unpredictable across platforms, consoles are also unpredictable across web browsers. Netscape provides a "Java console," shown in Figure 1-4, that's used for applets that want to write on System.out. By typing a question mark, you get a list of useful debugging commands that can be executed from the console.

Figure 1-4. Netscape Navigator's Java console window

The console is turned off by default, and users must explicitly request that it be turned on. Therefore, it's a bad idea to use it in production applets, though it's often useful for debugging. Furthermore, mixing and matching a command line and a graphical user interface is generally a bad idea.

Microsoft Internet Explorer does not have a visible console. Instead, data written on System.out appears in a log file. On Windows, this file can be found at

%Windir%\java\javalog.txt. (This probably expands to something like *C:\Windows\ java\javalog.txt*, depending on the exact value of the `%Windir%` environment variable). On the Mac the log file is called *Java Message Log.html* and resides in the same folder as Internet Explorer. To turn this option on, select the `Options...` menu item from the `View` menu, click the `Advanced` tab, then check `Enable Java Logging`.

If you absolutely must use a console in your applet, the following list shows several third-party consoles that work in Internet Explorer. Some provide additional features over the bare-bones implementation of Netscape. Of course, URLs can get stale rather quickly. If for some reason none of these work for you, you can always do what I did to collect them in the first place: go to *http://java.developer. com/* and search for "console."

Arial Bardin's Java Console	*http://www.best.com/~bardin/JavaConsole.html*
Jamie Cansdale's Java Console and Class Flusher	*http://www.obsolete.com/people/cansdale/java/index.htm*
Chuck McManis's Virtual TTY	*http://www.professionals.com/~cmcmanis/java/javaworld/ examples/sept.html*
Trevor Harmon's Java Console for Internet Explorer	*http://vocaro.com/freestuff/javaconsole/main.html*
Frederic Lavigne's Package fr.l2f	*http://www-mips.unice.fr/~flavigne/html/packages.html*

System.out

`System.out` is the first instance of the `OutputStream` class most programmers encounter. In fact, it's often encountered before programmers know what a class or an output stream is. Specifically, `System.out` is the static out field of the `java.lang.System` class. It's an instance of `java.io.PrintStream`, a subclass of `java.io.OutputStream`.

`System.out` corresponds to `stdout` in Unix or C. Normally, output sent to `System.out` appears on the console. As a general rule, the console converts the numeric byte data `System.out` sends to it into ASCII or ISO Latin-1 text. Thus, the following lines write the string "Hello World" on the console:

```
byte[] hello = {72, 101, 108, 108, 111, 32, 87, 111, 114, 108, 100, 33, 10,
                13};
System.out.write(hello);
```

System.err

Unix and C programmers are familiar with `stderr`, which is commonly used for error messages. `stderr` is a separate file pointer from `stdout`, but often means the same thing. Generally, `stderr` and `stdout` both send data to the console, whatever that is. However, `stdout` and `stderr` can be redirected to different places. For instance, output can be redirected to a file while error messages still appear on the console.

`System.err` is Java's version of `stderr`. Like `System.out`, `System.err` is an instance of `java.io.PrintStream`, a subclass of `java.io.OutputStream`. `System.err` is most commonly used inside the catch clause of a `try/catch` block like this:

```
try {
  // Do something that may throw an exception.
}
catch (Exception e) {
  System.err.println(e);
}
```

Finished programs shouldn't have much need for `System.err`, but it is useful while you're debugging.

System.in

`System.in` is the input stream connected to the console, much as `System.out` is the output stream connected to the console. In Unix or C terms, `System.in` is `stdin` and can be redirected from a shell in the same fashion. `System.in` is the static in field of the `java.lang.System` class. It's an instance of `java.io.InputStream`, at least as far as is documented.

Past what's documented, `System.in` is really a `java.io.BufferedInputStream`. `BufferedInputStream` doesn't declare any new methods, just overrides the ones already declared in `java.io.InputStream`. Buffered input streams read data in large chunks into a buffer, then parcel it out in requested sizes. This can be more efficient than reading one character at a time. Otherwise, it's completely transparent to the programmer.

The main significance of this is that each byte is not presented to be read as the user types it on `System.in`. Instead, input enters the program one line at a time. This allows a user typing into the console to backspace over and correct mistakes. Java does not allow you to put the console into "raw mode," where each character becomes available as soon as it's typed, including characters like backspace and delete.

In an application run from the command line, `System.in` is taken from the window where the program was started; that is, the console. In applets, the same console window that's used for `System.out` is also used for `System.in`; however, Internet Explorer has no way to read from `System.in` in an applet. In Netscape, the console is turned off by default, and users must explicitly request that it be turned on.

The user types into the console using the platform's default character set, typically ASCII or some superset thereof. The data is converted into numeric bytes when read. For example, if the user types "Hello World", the following bytes will be read from System.in in this order:

```
72, 101, 108, 108, 111, 32, 87, 111, 114, 108, 100, 33, 10, 13
```

Many programs that run from the command line and read input from System.in require you to enter the "end of stream" character, also known as the "end of file" or EOF character, to terminate a program normally. How this is entered is plat-form-dependent. On Unix and the Mac, Ctrl-D generally indicates end of stream. On Windows, Ctrl-Z does. In some cases it may be necessary to type this character alone on a line. That is, you may need to hit Return/Ctrl-Z or Return/Ctrl-D before Java will recognize the end of stream.

Redirecting System.out, System.in, and System.err

In a shell you often redirect stdout, stdin, or stderr. For example, to specify that output from the Java program OptimumBattingOrder goes into the file *yankees99.out* and that input for that program is read from the file *yankees99.tab*, you might type:

```
% java OptimumBattingOrder < yankees99.tab > yankees99.out
```

Redirection in a DOS shell is the same. It's a little more complicated in graphical environments, but not particularly difficult. To give one example, the JBindery tool included in Apple's Macintosh Runtime for Java, shown in Figure 1-5, provides a simple pop-up menu interface for selecting a file, */dev/null*, or a message window as the target of System.out or source for System.in.

It's sometimes convenient to be able to redirect System.out, System.in, and System.err from inside the running program. The following three static methods in the java.lang.System class do exactly that:

```
public static void setIn(InputStream in)
public static void setOut(PrintStream out)
public static void setErr(PrintStream err)
```

For example, to specify that data written on System.out is sent to the file *yankees99.out* and data read from System.in comes from *yankees99.tab*, you could write:

```
System.setIn(new FileInputStream("yankees99.tab"));
System.setOut(new PrintStream(new FileOutputStream("yankees99.out")));
```

These methods are especially useful when making a quick and dirty port of a program that makes heavy use of System.out, System.in, or System.err from an application to an applet. However, there is no absolute guarantee that console

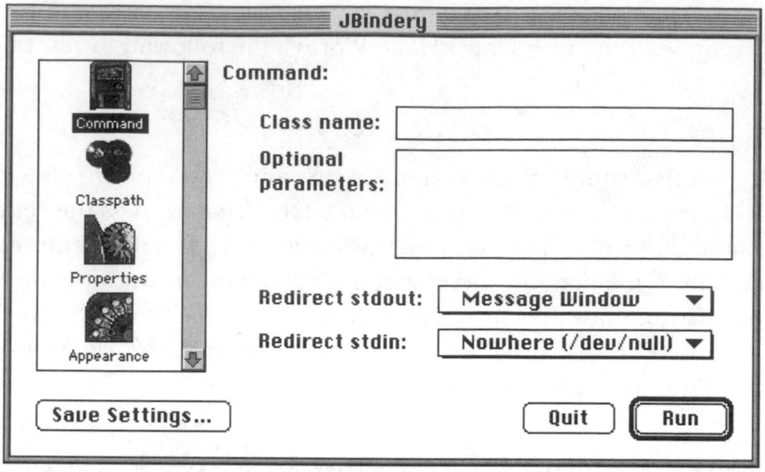

Figure 1-5. Redirecting stdout and stdin from JBindery

redirection will be allowed in all web browsers. Internet Explorer 4.0b2 allowed it, but the released version does not. HotJava 1.1 allows it with the security settings turned down, but not with security at the default level. Netscape Navigator 4.0 and 4.5 and HotJava 1.0 do not allow console redirection.

The `SecurityManager` class does not have a specific method to test whether or not redirecting `System.out` or `System.err` is allowed. However, in Java 1.1 Sun's JDK checks whether this is permitted by calling `checkExec("setIO")`. (The source code contains a comment to the effect that there should be a separate method for this sort of check in future versions of Java.) `checkExec()` determines whether the security manager allows a subprocess called `setio` to be spawned. The `AppletSecurity` security manager used by *appletviewer* in JDK 1.1 always disallows this call.

In Java 2 the security architecture has changed, but the effect is the same. A `RuntimePermission` object with the name `setIO` and no actions is passed to `AccessController.checkPermission()`. This method throws an `Access ControlException`, a subclass of `SecurityException`, if redirection is not allowed.

Security Checks on I/O

One of the original fears about downloading executable content like applets from the Internet was that a hostile applet could erase your hard disk or read your Quicken files. Nothing's happened to change that since Java was introduced. This is why Java applets run under the control of a security manager that checks each operation an applet performs to prevent potentially hostile acts.

The security manager is particularly careful about I/O operations. For the most part, the checks are related to these questions:

- Can an applet read a file?

- Can an applet write a file?

- Can an applet delete a file?

- Can an applet determine whether a file exists?

- Can an applet make a network connection to a particular host?

- Can applet accept an incoming connection from a particular host?

The short answer to all these questions is "No, it cannot." A slightly more elaborate answer would specify a few exceptions. Applets can make network connections to the host they came from; applets can read a few very specific files that contain information about the Java environment; and trusted applets may sometimes run without these restrictions. But for almost all practical purposes, the answer is almost always no.

NOTE   For more exotic situations, such as trusted applets, see *Java Security* by Scott Oaks, (O'Reilly & Associates, 1998). Trusted applets are useful on corporate networks, but you shouldn't waste a lot of time laboring under the illusion that anyone on the Internet at large will trust your applets.

Because of these security issues, you need to be careful when using code fragments and examples from this book in an applet. Everything shown here works when run in an application, but when run in an applet, it may fail with a `SecurityException`. It's not always obvious whether a particular method or class will cause problems. The `write()` method of `BufferedOutputStream`, for instance, is completely safe when the ultimate destination is a `byte` array. However, that same `write()` method will throw an exception when the destination is a file. An attempt to open a connection to a web server may succeed or fail depending on whether or not the web server you're connecting to is the same one the applet came from.

Consequently, this book focuses very much on applications. There is very little I/O that can be done from an applet without running afoul of the security manager. The problem may not always be obvious—not all web browsers properly report security exceptions—but it is there. If you can make an applet work when it's run as a standalone application and you cannot get it to work inside a web browser, the problem is almost certainly a conflict with the browser's security manager.

2

In this chapter:
- *The OutputStream Class*
- *Writing Bytes to Output Streams*
- *Writing Arrays of Bytes*
- *Flushing and Closing Output Streams*
- *Subclassing OutputStream*
- *A Graphical User Interface for Output Streams*

Output Streams

The OutputStream Class

The $java.io.OutputStream$ class declares the three basic methods you need to write bytes of data onto a stream. It also has methods for closing and flushing streams.

```
public abstract void write(int b) throws IOException
public void write(byte[] data) throws IOException
public void write(byte[] data, int offset, int length) throws IOException
public void flush() throws IOException
public void close() throws IOException
```

OutputStream is an abstract class. Subclasses provide implementations of the abstract write(int b) method. They may also override the four nonabstract methods. For example, the FileOutputStream class overrides all five methods with native methods that know how to write bytes into files on the host platform. Although OutputStream is abstract, often you only need to know that the object you have is an OutputStream; the more specific subclass of OutputStream is hidden from you. For example, the getOutputStream() method of java.net. URLConnection has the signature:

```
public OutputStream getOutputStream() throws IOException
```

Depending on the type of URL associated with this URLConnection object, the actual class of the output stream that's returned may be a sun.net. TelnetOutputStream, a sun.net.smtp.SmtpPrintStream, a sun.net.www. http.KeepAliveStream, or something else completely. All you know as a programmer, and all you need to know, is that the object returned is in fact some instance of OutputStream. That's why the detailed classes that handle particular kinds of connections are hidden inside the sun packages.

Furthermore, even when working with subclasses whose types you know, you still need to be able to use the methods inherited from OutputStream. And since methods that are inherited are not included in the online documentation, it's important to remember that they're there. For example, the java.io. DataOutputStream class does not declare a close() method, but you can still call the one it inherits from its superclass.

Writing Bytes to Output Streams

The fundamental method of the OutputStream class is write():

```
public abstract void write(int b) throws IOException
```

This method writes a single unsigned byte of data whose value should be between 0 and 255. If you pass a number larger than 255 or smaller than zero, it's reduced modulo 256 before being written.

Example 2-1, AsciiChart, is a simple program that writes the printable ASCII characters (32 to 126) on the console. The console interprets the numeric values as ASCII characters, not as numbers. This is a feature of the console, not of the OutputStream class or the specific subclass of which System.out is an instance. The write() method merely sends a particular bit pattern to a particular output stream. How that bit pattern is interpreted depends on what's connected to the other end of the stream.

Example 2-1. The AsciiChart Program

```
import java.io.*;

public class AsciiChart {

  public static void main(String[] args) {

    for (int i = 32; i < 127; i++) {
      System.out.write(i);
      // Break line after every eight characters.
      if (i % 8 == 7) System.out.write('\n');
      else System.out.write('\t');
    }
    System.out.write('\n');
  }
}
```

Notice the use of the char literals '\t' and '\n'. The compiler converts these to the numbers 9 and 10, respectively. When these numbers are written on the console, the console interprets those numbers as a linefeed and a tab, respectively. The same effect could have been achieved by writing the if clause like this:

```
if (i % 8 == 7) System.out.write(10);
else System.out.write(9);
```

Here's the output:

```
% java AsciiChart
          !         "         #         $         %         &         '
(         )         *         +         ,         -         .         /
0         1         2         3         4         5         6         7
8         9         :         ;         <         =         >         ?
@         A         B         C         D         E         F         G
H         I         J         K         L         M         N         O
P         Q         R         S         T         U         V         W
X         Y         Z         [         \         ]         ^         _
`         a         b         c         d         e         f         g
h         i         j         k         l         m         n         o
p         q         r         s         t         u         v         w
x         y         z         {         |         }         ~
%
```

The `write()` method can throw an `IOException`, so you'll need to wrap most calls to this method in a `try/catch` block, or declare that your own method throws `IOException`. For example:

```
try {
   for (int i = 32; i <= 127; i++) out.write(i);
}
catch (IOException e) { System.err.println(e); }
```

Astute readers will have noticed that Example 2-1 did not actually catch any `IOExceptions`. The `PrintStream` class, of which `System.out` is an instance, overrides `write()` with a variant that does not throw `IOException`.

Writing Arrays of Bytes

It's often faster to write larger chunks of data than to write byte by byte. Two overloaded variants of the `write()` method do this:

```
public void write(byte[] data) throws IOException
public void write(byte[] data, int offset, int length) throws IOException
```

The first variant writes the entire `byte` array `data`. The second writes only the subarray of `data` starting at `offset` and continuing for `length` bytes. For example, the following code fragment blasts the bytes in a string onto `System.out`:

```
String s = "How are streams treating you?";
byte[] data = s.getBytes();
System.out.write(data);
```

Conversely, you may run into performance problems if you attempt to write too much data at a time. The exact turnaround point depends on the eventual destination of the data. Files are often best written in small multiples of the block size of the disk, typically 512, 1024, or 2048 bytes. Network connections often require smaller buffer sizes, 128 or 256 bytes. The optimal buffer size depends on too many system-specific details for anything to be guaranteed, but I often use 128 bytes for network connections and 1024 bytes for files.

Example 2-2 is a simple program that constructs a byte array filled with an ASCII chart, then blasts it onto the console in one call to write().

Example 2-2. The AsciiArray Program

```java
import java.io.*;

public class AsciiArray {

  public static void main(String[] args) {

    byte[] b = new byte[(127-31)*2];
    int index = 0;
    for (int i = 32; i < 127; i++) {
      b[index++] = (byte) i;
      // Break line after every eight characters.
      if (i % 8 == 7) b[index++] = (byte) '\n';
      else b[index++] = (byte) '\t';
    }
    b[index++] = (byte) '\n';
    try {
      System.out.write(b);
    }
    catch (IOException e) { System.err.println(e); }
  }
}
```

The output is the same as in Example 2-1. Because of the nature of the console, this particular program probably isn't a lot faster than Example 2-1, but it certainly could be if you were writing data into a file rather than onto the console. The difference in performance between writing a byte array in a single call to write() and writing the same array by invoking write() once for each component of the array can easily be a factor of a hundred or more.

Flushing and Closing Output Streams

Many operating systems buffer writes to improve performance. Rather than sending each byte to its destination as it's written, the bytes are accumulated in a memory buffer ranging in size from several bytes to several thousand bytes. When the buffer fills up, all the data is sent at once. The flush() method forces the data to be written whether or not the buffer is full:

```java
public void flush() throws IOException
```

This is not the same as the buffering performed by a `BufferedOutputStream`; that buffering is handled by the Java runtime. This buffering is at the native OS level. However, a call to `flush()` should empty both buffers. For example, assuming `out` is an `OutputStream` of some sort, you would call `out.flush()` to empty the buffers.

If you only use a stream for a short time, you don't need to flush it explicitly. It should be flushed when the stream is closed. This should happen when the program exits or when you explicitly invoke the `close()` method:

```
public void close() throws IOException
```

For example, again assuming `out` is an `OutputStream` of some sort, calling `out.close()` closes the stream and implicitly flushes it. Once you have closed an output stream, you can no longer write to it. Attempting to do so will throw an `IOException`.

NOTE   Again, `System.out` is a partial exception because as a `PrintStream`, all exceptions it throws are eaten. Once you close `System.out`, you can't write to it, but trying to do so won't throw any exceptions. However, your output will not appear on the console.

You only need to flush an output stream explicitly if you want to make sure data is sent before you're through with the stream. For example, a program that sends a burst of data across the network periodically should flush after each burst of data is written to the stream.

Flushing is often important when you're trying to debug a crashing program. All streams flush automatically when their buffers fill up, and all streams should be flushed when a program terminates normally. If a program terminates abnormally, however, buffers may not get flushed. In this case, unless there is an explicit call to `flush()` after each write, you can't be sure the data that appears in the output indicates the point at which the program crashed. In fact, the program may have continued to run for some time past that point before it crashed.

`System.out`, `System.err`, and some (but not all) other print streams automatically flush after each call to `println()` and after each time a new line character (`'\n'`) appears in the string being written. Whether auto-flushing is enabled can be set in the `PrintStream` constructor.

Subclassing OutputStream

OutputStream is an abstract class that mainly describes the operations available with any particular OutputStream object. Specific subclasses know how to write bytes to particular destinations. For instance, a FileOutputStream uses native code to write data in files. A ByteArrayOutputStream uses pure Java to write its output in a potentially expanding byte array.

Recall that there are three overloaded variants of the write() method in OutputStream, one abstract, two concrete:

```
public abstract void write(int b) throws IOException
public void write(byte[] data) throws IOException
public void write(byte[] data, int offset, int length) throws IOException
```

Subclasses must implement the abstract write(int b) method. They often choose to override the third variant, write(byte[], data int offset, int length), for reasons of performance. The implementation of the three-argument version of the write() method in OutputStream simply invokes write(int b) repeatedly; that is:

```
public void write(byte[] data, int offset, int length) throws IOException {
    for (int i = offset; i < offset+length; i++) write(data[i]);
}
```

Most subclasses can provide more efficient implementations of this method. The one-argument variant of write() merely invokes write(data, 0, data.length); if the three-argument variant has been overridden, this method will perform reasonably well. However, a few subclasses may override it anyway.

Example 2-3 is a simple program called NullOutputStream that mimics the behavior of /dev/null on Unix operating systems. Data written into a null output stream is lost.

Example 2-3. The NullOutputStream Class

```
package com.macfaq.io;

import java.io.*;

public class NullOutputStream extends OutputStream {

  public void write(int b) { }
  public void write(byte[] data) { }
  public void write(byte[] data, int offset, int length) { }

}
```

By redirecting System.out and System.err to a null output stream in the shipping version of your program, you can disable any debugging messages that might have slipped through quality assurance. For example:

```
OutputStream out = new NullOutputStream();
PrintStream ps = new PrintStream(out);
System.setOut(ps);
System.setErr(ps);
```

A Graphical User Interface for Output Streams

As a useful example, I'm going to show a subclass of java.awt.TextArea that can be connected to an output stream. As data is written onto the stream, it is appended to the text area in the default character set (generally ISO Latin-1). (This isn't ideal. Since text areas contain text, a writer would be a better source for this data; in later chapters I'll expand on this class to use a writer instead. For now this makes a neat example.) This subclass is shown in Example 2-4.

The actual output stream is contained in an inner class inside the StreamedTextArea class. Each StreamedTextArea component contains a TextAreaOutputStream object in its theOutput field. Client programmers access this object via the getOutputStream() method of the StreamedTextArea class. The StreamedTextArea class has five overloaded constructors that imitate the five constructors in the java.awt.TextArea class, each taking a different combination of text, rows, columns, and scrollbar information. The first four constructors merely pass their arguments and suitable defaults to the most general fifth constructor using this(). The fifth constructor calls the most general superclass constructor, then calls setEditable(false) to ensure that the user doesn't change the text while output is streaming into it.

I've chosen not to override any methods in the TextArea superclass. However, you might want to do so if you feel a need to change the normal abilities of a text area. For example, you could include a do-nothing append() method so that data can only be moved into the text area via the provided output stream or a setEditable() method that doesn't allow the client programmer to make this area editable.

Example 2-4. The StreamedTextArea Component

```
package com.macfaq.awt;

import java.awt.*;
import java.io.*;

public class StreamedTextArea extends TextArea {
```

Example 2-4. The StreamedTextArea Component (continued)

```java
  OutputStream theOutput = new TextAreaOutputStream();

public StreamedTextArea() {
   this("", 0, 0, SCROLLBARS_BOTH);
}

public StreamedTextArea(String text) {
   this(text, 0, 0, SCROLLBARS_BOTH);
}

public StreamedTextArea(int rows, int columns) {
   this("", rows, columns, SCROLLBARS_BOTH);
}

public StreamedTextArea(String text, int rows, int columns) {
   this(text, rows, columns, SCROLLBARS_BOTH);
}

public StreamedTextArea(String text, int rows, int columns, int scrollbars) {
   super(text, rows, columns, scrollbars);
   setEditable(false);
}

public OutputStream getOutputStream() {
   return theOutput;
}

class TextAreaOutputStream extends OutputStream {

  public synchronized void write(int b) {
    // recall that the int should really just be a byte
    b &= 0x000000FF;

    // must convert byte to a char in order to append it
    char c = (char) b;
    append(String.valueOf(c));
  }

  public synchronized void write(byte[] data, int offset, int length) {
    append(new String(data, offset, length));
  }
 }
}
```

The `TextAreaOutputStream` inner class is quite simple. It extends `OutputStream` and thus must implement the abstract method `write()`. It also overrides the primary array `write()` method to provide a more efficient implementation. To use this class, you simply add an instance of it to a container like an applet or a window, much as you'd add a regular text area. Next you invoke its `getOutputStream()` method to get a reference to the output stream for the area, then use the usual `write()` methods to write into the text area. Often these steps will take place at different times in different methods.

Figure 2-1 shows a program using a `StreamedTextArea` to display data downloaded from *http://www.oreilly.com/*. The application in this picture will be developed in Chapter 5, *Network Streams*.

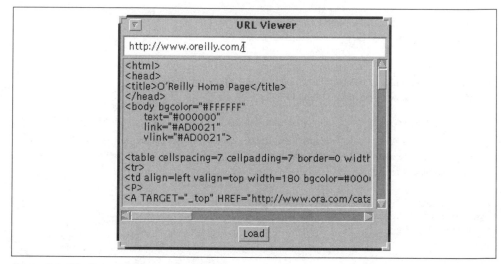

Figure 2-1. The StreamedTextArea component

I'll revisit and improve this class in future chapters using techniques you haven't learned yet. In particular, I'll pay much more attention to the issue of character sets and encodings.

In this chapter:
- *The InputStream Class*
- *The read() Method*
- *Reading Chunks of Data from a Stream*
- *Counting the Available Bytes*
- *Skipping Bytes*
- *Closing Input Streams*
- *Marking and Resetting*
- *Subclassing InputStream*
- *An Efficient Stream Copier*

3

Input Streams

The InputStream Class

The `java.io.InputStream` class is the abstract superclass for all input streams. It declares the three basic methods needed to read bytes of data from a stream. It also has methods for closing and flushing streams, checking how many bytes of data are available to be read, skipping over input, marking a position in a stream and resetting back to that position, and determining whether marking and resetting are supported.

```
public abstract int read() throws IOException
public int read(byte[] data) throws IOException
public int read(byte[] data, int offset, int length) throws IOException
public long skip(long n) throws IOException
public int available() throws IOException
public void close() throws IOException
public synchronized void mark(int readlimit)
public synchronized void reset() throws IOException
public boolean markSupported()
```

The read() Method

The fundamental method of the `InputStream` class is `read()`, which reads a single unsigned byte of data and returns the integer value of the unsigned byte. This is a number between 0 and 255:

```
public abstract int read() throws IOException
```

The following code reads 10 bytes from the System.in input stream and stores them in the int array data:

```
int[] data = new int[10];
for (int i = 0; i < data.length; i++) {
  data[i] = System.in.read();
}
```

Notice that although read() is reading a byte, it returns an int. If you want to store the raw bytes instead, you can cast the int to a byte. For example:

```
byte[] b = new byte[10];
for (int i = 0; i < b.length; i++) {
  b[i] = (byte) System.in.read();
}
```

Of course, this produces a signed byte instead of the unsigned byte returned by the read() method (that is, a byte in the range –128 to 127 instead of 0 to 255). As long as you're clear in your mind and your code about whether you're working with signed or unsigned data, you won't have any trouble. Signed bytes can be converted back to ints in the range 0 to 255 like this:

```
int i = (b >= 0) ? b : 256 + b;
```

When you call read(), you also have to catch the IOException that it might throw. As I've observed, input and output are often subject to problems outside of your control: disks fail, network cables break, and so on. Therefore, virtually any I/O method can throw an IOException, and read() is no exception. You don't get an IOException if read() encounters the end of the input stream; in this case, it returns –1. You use this as a flag to watch for the end of stream. The following code shows how to catch the IOException and test for the end of the stream:

```
try {
  int[] data = new int[10];
  for (int i = 0; i < data.length; i++) {
    int datum = System.in.read();
    if (datum  == -1) break;
    data[i] = datum;
  }
}
catch (IOException e) {System.err.println("Couldn't read from System.in!");}
```

The read() method waits or blocks until a byte of data is available and ready to be read. Input and output can be slow, so if your program is doing anything else of importance, you should try to put I/O in its own thread.

read() is declared abstract; therefore, InputStream is abstract. Hence, you can never instantiate an InputStream directly; you always work with one of its concrete subclasses.

Example 3-1 is a program that reads data from System.in and prints the numeric value of each byte read on the console using System.out.println(). This program could have been written more simply; in particular, I could have put all the logic in the main() method without any trouble. However, this example is the basis for a file-dumping utility that I'll develop throughout the book, and, therefore, I want a flexible design from the start.

Example 3-1. The StreamPrinter Class

```
package com.macfaq.io;
import java.io.*;

public class StreamPrinter {

  InputStream theInput;

  public static void main(String[] args) {
    StreamPrinter sr = new StreamPrinter(System.in);
    sr.print();
  }

  public StreamPrinter(InputStream in) {
    theInput = in;
  }

  public void print() {

    try {
      while (true) {
        int datum = theInput.read();
        if (datum  == -1) break;
        System.out.println(datum);
      }
    }
    catch (IOException e) {System.err.println("Couldn't read from System.in!");}
  }
}
```

Reading Chunks of Data from a Stream

Input and output are often the performance bottlenecks in a program. Reading from or writing to disk can be hundreds of times slower than reading from or writing to memory; network connections and user input are even slower. While disk capacities and speeds have increased over time, they have never kept pace with CPU speeds. Therefore, it's important to minimize the number of reads and writes a program actually performs.

All input streams have overloaded read() methods that read chunks of contiguous data into a byte array. The first variant tries to read enough data to fill the array data. The second variant tries to read length bytes of data starting at position offset into the array data. Neither of these methods is guaranteed to read as many bytes as they want. Both methods return the number of bytes actually read, or –1 on end of stream.

```
public int read(byte[] data) throws IOException
public int read(byte[] data, int offset, int length) throws IOException
```

The default implementation of these methods in the java.io.InputStream class merely calls the basic read() method enough times to fill the requested array or subarray. Thus, reading 10 bytes of data takes 10 times as long as reading one byte of data. However, most subclasses of InputStream override these methods with more efficient methods, perhaps native, that read the data from the underlying source as a block.

For example, to attempt to read 10 bytes from System.in, you could write the following code:

```
try {
  byte[] b = new byte[10];
  System.in.read(b);
}
catch (IOException e) {System.err.println("Couldn't read from System.in!");}
```

Reads don't always succeed in getting as many bytes as you want. Conversely, there's nothing to stop you from trying to read more data into the array than will fit. If you read more data than the array can hold, an ArrayIndexOutOf-BoundsException will be thrown. For example, the following code loops repeatedly until it either fills the array or sees the end of stream:

```
try {
  byte[] b = new byte[100];
  int offset = 0;
  while (offset < b.length) {
    int bytesRead = System.in.read(b, offset, b.length - offset);
    if (bytesRead == -1) break; // end of stream
    offset += bytesRead;
  }
catch (IOException e) {System.err.println("Couldn't read from System.in!");}
```

Counting the Available Bytes

It's sometimes convenient to know how many bytes are available to be read before you attempt to read them. The InputStream class's available() method tells you how many bytes you can read without blocking. It returns 0 if there's no data available to be read.

```
public int available() throws IOException
```

For example:

```
try {
  byte[] b = new byte[100];
  int offset = 0;
  while (offset < b.length) {
    int a = System.in.available();
    int bytesRead = System.in.read(b, offset, a);
    if (bytesRead == -1) break; // end of stream
    offset += bytesRead;
  }
catch (IOException e) {System.err.println("Couldn't read from System.in!");}
```

There's a potential bug in this code. There may be more bytes available than there's space in the array to hold them. One common idiom is to size the array according to the number `available()` returns, like this:

```
try {
  byte[] b = new byte[System.in.available()];
  System.in.read(b);
}
catch (IOException e) {System.err.println("Couldn't read from System.in!");}
```

This works well if you're only going to perform a single read. For multiple reads, however, the overhead of creating multiple arrays is excessive. You should probably reuse the array and only create a new array if more bytes are available than will fit in the array.

The `available()` method in `java.io.InputStream` always returns 0. Subclasses are supposed to override it, but I've seen a few that don't. You may be able to read more bytes from the underlying stream without blocking than `available()` suggests; you just can't guarantee that you can. If this is a concern, you can place input in a separate thread so that blocked input doesn't block the rest of the program.

Skipping Bytes

Although you can just read from a stream and ignore the bytes read, Java provides a `skip()` method that jumps over a certain number of bytes in the input:

```
public long skip(long bytesToSkip) throws IOException
```

The argument to `skip()` is the number of bytes to skip. The return value is the number of bytes actually skipped, which may be less than `bytesToSkip`. −1 is returned if the end of stream is encountered. Both the argument and return value are `longs`, allowing `skip()` to handle extremely long input streams. Skipping is often faster than reading and discarding the data you don't want. For example, when an input stream is attached to a file, skipping bytes just requires that an integer called the file pointer be changed, whereas reading involves copying bytes from the disk into memory. For example, to skip the next 80 bytes of the input stream `in`:

```
try {
  long bytesSkipped = 0;
  long bytesToSkip = 80;
  while (bytesSkipped < bytesToSkip) {
    long n = in.strip(bytesToSkip - bytesSkipped);
    if (n == -1) break;
    bytesSkipped += n;
  }
}
catch (IOException e) {System.err.println(e);}
```

Closing Input Streams

When you're through with a stream, you should close it. This allows the operating system to free any resources associated with the stream; exactly what these resources are depends on your platform and varies with the type of the stream. However, systems only have finite resources. For example, on most personal computer operating systems, no more than several hundred files can be open at once. Multiuser operating systems have larger limits, but limits nonetheless.

To close a stream, you invoke its `close()` method:

```
public void close() throws IOException
```

Not all streams need to be closed—`System.in` generally does not need to be closed, for example. However, streams associated with files and network connections should always be closed when you're done with them. For example:

```
try {
  URL u = new URL("http://www.javasoft.com/");
  InputStream in = u.openStream();
  // Read from the stream...
  in.close();
}
catch (IOException e) {System.err.println(e);}
```

Once you have closed an input stream, you can no longer read from it. Attempting to do so will throw an `IOException`.

Marking and Resetting

It's often useful to be able to read a few bytes and then back up and reread them. For example, in a Java compiler, you don't know for sure whether you're reading the token <, <<, or <<= until you've read one too many characters. It would be useful to be able to back up and reread the token once you know which token you've read. Compiler design and other parsing problems provide many more examples, and this need occurs in other domains as well.

Some (but not all) input streams allow you to mark a particular position in the stream and then return to it. Three methods in the `java.io.InputStream` class handle marking and resetting:

```
public synchronized void mark(int readLimit)
public synchronized void reset() throws IOException
public boolean markSupported()
```

The boolean `markSupported()` method returns `true` if this stream supports marking and `false` if it doesn't. If marking is not supported, `reset()` throws an `IOException` and `mark()` does nothing. Assuming the stream does support marking, the `mark()` method places a bookmark at the current position in the stream. You can rewind the stream to this position later with `reset()` as long as you haven't read more than `readLimit` bytes. There can be only one mark in the stream at any given time. Marking a second location erases the first mark.

The only two input stream classes in `java.io` that always support marking are `BufferedInputStream` (of which `System.in` is an instance) and `ByteArray-InputStream`. However, other input streams, like `DataInputStream`, may support marking if they're chained to a buffered input stream first.

Subclassing InputStream

Immediate subclasses of `InputStream` must provide an implementation of the abstract `read()` method. They may also override some of the nonabstract methods. For example, the default `markSupported()` method returns false, `mark()` does nothing, and `reset()` throws an `IOException`. Any class that allows marking and resetting must override these three methods. Furthermore, they may want to override methods that perform functions like `skip()` and the other two `read()` methods to provide more efficient implementations.

Example 3-2 is a simple class called RandomInputStream that "reads" random bytes of data. This provides a useful source of unlimited data you can use in testing. A java.util.Random object provides the data.

Example 3-2. The RandomInputStream Class

```
package com.macfaq.io;

import java.util.*;
import java.io.*;

public class RandomInputStream extends InputStream {

  private transient Random generator = new Random();

  public int read() {

    int result = generator.nextInt() % 256;
    if (result < 0) result = -result;
    return result;

  }

  public int read(byte[] data, int offset, int length) throws IOException {

    byte[] temp = new byte[length];
    generator.nextBytes(temp);
    System.arraycopy(temp, 0, data, offset, length);
    return length;

  }

  public int read(byte[] data) throws IOException {

    generator.nextBytes(data);
    return data.length;

  }

  public long skip(long bytesToSkip) throws IOException {

    // It's all random so skipping has no effect.
    return bytesToSkip;

  }
}
```

The no-argument read() method returns a random int in the range of an unsigned byte (0 to 255). The other two read() methods fill a specified part of an array with random bytes. They return the number of bytes read (in this case the number of bytes created).

An Efficient Stream Copier

As a useful example of both input and output streams, in Example 3-3 I'll present a StreamCopier class that copies data between two streams as quickly as possible. (I'll reuse this class in later chapters.) An input stream and an output stream are passed to the static copy() method. This method reads from the input stream and writes onto the output stream until the input stream is exhausted. A 256-byte buffer is used to try to make the reads efficient. A main() method provides a simple test for this class by reading from System.in and copying to System.out.

Example 3-3. The StreamCopier Class

```
package com.macfaq.io;
import java.io.*;

public class StreamCopier {

  public static void main(String[] args) {
    try {
      copy(System.in, System.out);
    }
    catch (IOException e) {System.err.println(e);}
  }

  public static void copy(InputStream in, OutputStream out)
   throws IOException {

    // Do not allow other threads to read from the input
    // or write to the output while copying is taking place
    synchronized (in) {
      synchronized (out) {
        byte[] buffer = new byte[256];
        while (true) {
          int bytesRead = in.read(buffer);
          if (bytesRead == -1) break;
          out.write(buffer, 0, bytesRead);
        }
      }
    }
  }
}
```

Here's a simple test run:

```
D:\JAVA\ioexamples\03>java com.macfaq.io.StreamCopier
```

```
this is a test
this is a test
0987654321
0987654321
^Z
```

Input was not fed from the console (DOS prompt) to the StreamCopier program until the end of each line. Since I ran this in Windows, the end-of-stream character is Ctrl-Z. On Unix it would have been Ctrl-D.

The copy() method synchronizes on the in and out variables. This ensures that the copy is faithful by locking out all other possible reads from the input stream and writes to the output stream while the copying is taking place.

II

DATA SOURCES

In this chapter:
- *Reading Files*
- *Writing Files*
- *File Viewer, Part 1*

4

File Streams

Until now, most of the examples in this book have used the streams System.in and System.out. These are convenient for examples, but in real life, you'll more commonly attach streams to data sources like files and network connections. You'll use the java.io.FileInputStream and java.io.FileOutputStream classes, which are concrete subclasses of java.io.InputStream and java.io.Output-Stream, to read and write files. FileInputStream and FileOutputStream provide input and output streams that let you read and write files. We'll discuss these classes in detail in this chapter; they provide the standard methods for reading and writing data. What they don't provide is a mechanism for file-specific operations, like finding out whether a file is readable or writable. For that, you may want to look forward to Chapter 12, *Working with Files*, which talks about the File class itself and the way Java works with files.

Reading Files

java.io.FileInputStream is a concrete subclass of java.io.InputStream. It provides an input stream connected to a particular file.

```
public class FileInputStream extends InputStream
```

FileInputStream has all the usual methods of input streams, such as read(), available(), skip(), and close(), which are used exactly as they are for any other input stream.

```
public native int read() throws IOException
public int read(byte[] data) throws IOException
public int read(byte[] data, int offset, int length) throws IOException
public native long skip(long n) throws IOException
public native int available() throws IOException
public native void close() throws IOException
```

These methods are all implemented in native code, except for the two multibyte `read()` methods. These, however, just pass their arguments on to a private native method called `readBytes()`, so effectively all these methods are implemented with native code. (In Java 2, `read(byte[] data, int offset, int length)` is a native method that `read(byte[] data)` invokes.)

There are three `FileInputStream()` constructors, which differ only in how the file to be read is specified:

```
public FileInputStream(String fileName) throws IOException
public FileInputStream(File file) throws FileNotFoundException
public FileInputStream(FileDescriptor fdObj)
```

The first constructor uses a string containing the name of the file. The second constructor uses a `java.io.File` object. The third constructor uses a `java.io.FileDescriptor` object. Filenames are platform-dependent, so hardcoded file names should be avoided where possible. Using the first constructor violates Sun's rules for "100% Pure Java" immediately. Therefore, the second two constructors are much preferred. Nonetheless, the second two will have to wait until `File` objects and file descriptors are discussed in Chapter 12. For now, I will use only the first.

To read a file, just pass the name of the file into the `FileInputStream()` constructor. Then use the `read()` method as normal. For example, the following code fragment reads the file *README.TXT*, then prints it on `System.out`:

```
try {
  FileInputStream fis = new FileInputStream("README.TXT");
  int n;
  while ((n = fis.available()) > 0) {
    byte[] b = new byte[n];
    int result = fis.read(b);
    if (result == -1) break;
    String s = new String(b);
    System.out.print(s);
  } // End while
} // End try
catch (IOException e) {System.err.println(e);}
System.out.println();
```

Java looks for files in the *current working directory*. Generally, this is the directory you were in when you typed `java program_name` to start running the program. You can open a file in a different directory by passing a full or relative path to the file from the current working directory. For example, to read the file */etc/hosts* no matter which directory is current, you can do this:

```
FileInputStream fis = new FileInputStream("/etc/hosts");
```

Notice that this code depends on Unix-style pathnames. It is not guaranteed to work on Windows or the Mac, though it might; some runtime environments like Apple's Macintosh Runtime for Java include extra code to translate from Unix-style filenames to the native style.

If the file you're trying to read does not exist when the $FileInputStream$ object is constructed, a $FileNotFoundException$ (a subclass of $java.io.IOException$) is thrown. If for some other reason a file cannot be read—for example, the current process does not have read permission for the file—some other kind of $IOException$ is thrown.

Example 4-1 reads filenames from the command line, then copies the named files onto $System.out$. The $StreamCopier.copy()$ method from Example 3-3 in the last chapter does the actual reading and writing. Notice that that method does not care that the input is coming from a file or going to the console. It works regardless of the type of the input and output streams it's copying. It will work equally well for other streams still to be introduced, including ones that did not even exist when $StreamCopier$ was created.

Example 4-1. The FileTyper Program

```java
import java.io.*;
import com.macfaq.io.*;

public class FileTyper {

  public static void main(String[] args) {

    if (args.length == 0) {
      System.err.println("Usage: java FileCopier file1 file2 ...");
      return;
    }

    for (int i = 0; i < args.length; i++) {
      try {
        typeFile(args[i]);
        if (i+1 < args.length) { // more files to type
          System.out.println();
          System.out.println("------------------------------------");
        }
      }
      catch (IOException e) {System.err.println(e);}
    }
  }

  public static void typeFile(String filename) throws IOException {

    FileInputStream fin = new FileInputStream(filename);
```

Example 4-1. The FileTyper Program (continued) (continued)

```
    StreamCopier.copy(fin, System.out);
    fin.close();

  }
}
```

Untrusted applets are not usually allowed to read or write files. If your applet tries to create a `FileInputStream`, the constructor will throw a `SecurityException`.

The `FileInputStream` class has one method that's not declared in the `InputStream` superclass, `getFD()`.

```
    public final FileDescriptor getFD() throws IOException
```

This method returns the `java.io.FileDescriptor` object associated with this stream. File descriptor objects are discussed in Chapter 12. For now, all you can do with this object is use it to create another file stream. `FileInputStream` also has a protected `finalize()` method that's invoked when a `FileInputStream` object is garbage collected. This method ensures that files are properly closed before the file input stream that opened them is garbage-collected:

```
    protected void finalize() throws IOException
```

You don't normally need to invoke this method explicitly, but if you subclass `FileInputStream` (something I've never found a need for), you must invoke `super.finalize()` from your subclass's `finalize()` method.

It is possible to open multiple input streams to the same file at the same time, though it's rarely necessary to do so. Each stream maintains a separate pointer to the current position in the file. Reading from the file does not change the file in any way. Writing to a file is a different story, as you'll see in the next section.

Writing Files

The `java.io.FileOutputStream` class is a concrete subclass of `java.io.OutputStream` that provides output streams connected to files.

```
    public class FileOutputStream extends OutputStream
```

This class has all the usual methods of output streams, such as `write()`, `flush()`, and `close()`, which are used exactly as they are for any other output stream.

```
    public native void write(int b) throws IOException
    public void write(byte[] data) throws IOException
    public void write(byte[] data, int offset, int length) throws IOException
    public native void close() throws IOException
```

These are all implemented in native code except for the two multibyte `write()` methods. These, however, just pass their arguments on to a private native method called `writeBytes()`, so effectively all these methods are implemented with native code.

There are three main `FileOutputStream()` constructors, differing primarily in how the file is specified:

```
public FileOutputStream(String filename) throws IOException
public FileOutputStream(File file) throws IOException
public FileOutputStream(FileDescriptor fd)
```

The first constructor uses a string containing the name of the file; the second constructor uses a `java.io.File` object; the third constructor uses a `java.io.FileDescriptor` object. I will avoid using the second and third constructors until I've discussed `File` objects and file descriptors (Chapter 12). To write data to a file, just pass the name of the file to the `FileOutputStream()` constructor, then use the `write()` methods as normal. If the file does not exist, all three constructors will create it. If the file does exist, any data inside it will be overwritten.

A fourth constructor also lets you specify whether the file's contents should be erased before data is written into it (`append == false`) or whether data is to be tacked onto the end of the file (`append == true`). The other three constructors simply overwrite the file; they do not provide an option to append data to the file.

```
public FileOutputStream(String name, boolean append) throws IOException
```

Java looks for files in the current working directory. You can write to a file in a different directory by passing a full or relative path to the file from the current working directory. For example, to append data to the *\Windows\java\javalog.txt* file no matter which directory is current, you would do this:

```
FileOutputStream fout =
new FileOutputStream("/Windows/java/javalog.txt", true);
```

Although Windows uses a backslash as the directory separator, Java still expects you to use a forward slash as in Unix, at least in Java 1.1. Hardcoded pathnames are dangerously platform-dependent. Using this constructor automatically classifies your program as impure Java. We will take this up in more detail in Chapter 12.

Untrusted applets are normally not allowed to read or write files. If an applet tries to create a `FileOutputStream`, the constructor throws a `SecurityException`.

The `FileOutputStream` class has one method that's not declared in `java.io.OutputStream`, `getFD()`:

```
public final FileDescriptor getFD() throws IOException
```

This method returns the `java.io.FileDescriptor` object associated with this stream.

The `FileOutputStream` class also has a protected `finalize()` method that's invoked before a `FileOutputStream` object is garbage-collected. This method ensures that files are properly flushed and closed before the file output stream that opened them is garbage-collected. You normally don't need to invoke this method explicitly. If you subclass `FileOutputStream` and override `finalize()`, the subclass's `finalize()` method should invoke this `finalize()` method by calling `super.finalize()`.

Example 4-2 reads two filenames from the command line, then copies the first file into the second file. The `StreamCopier` class from Example 3-3 in the last chapter is used to do the actual reading and writing.

Example 4-2. The FileCopier Program

```
import java.io.*;
import com.macfaq.io.*;

public class FileCopier {

  public static void main(String[] args) {

    if (args.length != 2) {
      System.err.println("Usage: java FileCopier infile outfile");
    }
    try {
      copy(args[0], args[1]);
    }
    catch (IOException e) {System.err.println(e);}
  }

  public static void copy(String inFile, String outFile)
   throws IOException {

    FileInputStream fin = null;
    FileOutputStream fout = null;

    try {
      fin  = new FileInputStream(inFile);
      fout = new FileOutputStream(outFile);
      StreamCopier.copy(fin, fout);
    }
    finally {
      try {
        if (fin != null) fin.close();
      }
      catch (IOException e) {
```

Example 4-2. The FileCopier Program (continued)

```
    }
    try {
      if (fout != null) fout.close();
     }
    catch (IOException e) { }
  }
 }
}
```

Since we're no longer writing to System.out and reading from System.in, it's important to make sure the streams are closed when we're done. This is a good use for a finally clause, as we need to make sure the files are closed whether or not the reads and writes succeed.

Java is better about closing files than most languages. As long as the VM doesn't terminate abnormally, the files will be closed when the program exits. Still, if this class is used inside a long-running program like a web server, waiting until the program exits isn't a good idea; other threads and processes may need access to the files.

There is one bug in this program: it does not behave well if the input and output files are the same. While it would be straightforward to compare the two filenames before copying, this is not safe enough. Once aliases, shortcuts, symbolic links, and other factors are taken into account, a single file may have multiple names. The full solution to this problem will have to wait until Chapter 12, when we discuss canonical paths and temporary files.

File Viewer, Part 1

I often find it useful to be able to open an arbitrary file and interpret it in an arbitrary fashion. Most commonly I want to view a file as text, but occasionally it's useful to interpret it as hexadecimal integers, IEEE 754 floating-point data, or something else. In this book, I'm going to develop a program that lets you open any file and view its contents in a variety of different ways. In each chapter, I'll add a piece to the program until it's fully functional. Since this is only the beginning of the program, it's important to keep the code as general and adaptable as possible.

Example 4-3 reads a series of filenames from the command line in the main() method. Each filename is passed to a method that opens the file. The file's data is read and printed on System.out. Exactly how the data is printed on System.out is determined by a command-line switch. If the user selects ASCII format (-a), then the data will be assumed to be ASCII (more properly, ISO Latin-1) text and printed as chars. If the user selects decimal dump (-d), then each byte should be printed as unsigned decimal numbers between 0 and 255, 16 to a line. For example:

```
000 234 127 034 234 234 000 000 000 002 004 070 000 234 127 098
```

Leading zeros are used to maintain a constant width for the printed byte values and for each line. A simple selection algorithm is used to determine how many leading zeros to attach to each number. For hex dump format (-h), each byte should be printed as two hexadecimal digits. For example:

```
CA FE BA BE 07 89 9A 65 45 65 43 6F F6 7F 8F EE E5 67 63 26 98 9E 9C
```

Hexadecimal encoding is easier, because each byte is always exactly two hex digits. The static `Integer.toHexString()` method is used to convert each byte read into two hexadecimal digits.

ASCII format is the default and is the simplest to implement. This conversion can be accomplished merely by copying the input data to the console.

Example 4-3. The FileDumper Program

```java
import java.io.*;
import com.macfaq.io.*;

public class FileDumper {

  public static final int ASC = 0;
  public static final int DEC = 1;
  public static final int HEX = 2;

  public static void main(String[] args) {

    if (args.length < 1) {
      System.err.println("Usage: java FileDumper [-ahd] file1 file2...");
    }

    int firstArg = 0;
    int mode = ASC;

    if (args[0].startsWith("-")) {
      firstArg = 1;
      if (args[0].equals("-h")) mode = HEX;
      else if (args[0].equals("-d")) mode = DEC;
    }

    for (int i = firstArg; i < args.length; i++) {
      if (mode == ASC) dumpAscii(args[i]);
      else if (mode == HEX) dumpHex(args[i]);
      else if (mode == DEC) dumpDecimal(args[i]);
      if (i < args.length-1) {  // more files to dump
        System.out.println("\r\n--------------------------------------\r\n");
```

Example 4-3. The FileDumper Program (continued)

```java
      }
    }
  }

  public static void dumpAscii(String filename) {

    FileInputStream fin = null;
    try {
      fin = new FileInputStream(filename);
      StreamCopier.copy(fin, System.out);
    }
    catch (IOException e) {System.err.println(e);}
    finally {
      try {
        if (fin != null) fin.close();
       }
      catch (IOException e) { }
    }
  }

  public static void dumpDecimal(String filename) {

    FileInputStream fin = null;
    byte[] buffer = new byte[16];
    boolean end = false;
    int bytesRead;

    try {
      fin = new FileInputStream(filename);
      while (!end) {
        bytesRead = 0;
        while (bytesRead < buffer.length) {
          int r = fin.read(buffer, bytesRead, buffer.length - bytesRead);
          if (r == -1) {
            end = true;
            break;
          }
          bytesRead += r;
        }
        for (int i = 0; i < bytesRead; i++) {
          int dec = buffer[i];
          if (dec < 0) dec = 256 + dec;
          if (dec < 10) System.out.print("00" + dec + " ");
          else if (dec < 100) System.out.print("0" + dec + " ");
          else System.out.print(dec + " ");
        }
        System.out.println();
      }
```

Example 4-3. The FileDumper Program (continued)

```java
    }
    catch (IOException e) {System.err.println(e);}
    finally {
      try {
        if (fin != null) fin.close();
        }
      catch (IOException e) { }
    }


  }

  public static void dumpHex(String filename) {

    FileInputStream fin = null;
    byte[] buffer = new byte[24];
    boolean end = false;
    int bytesRead;

    try {
      fin = new FileInputStream(filename);
      while (!end) {
        bytesRead = 0;
        while (bytesRead < buffer.length) {
          int r = fin.read(buffer, bytesRead, buffer.length - bytesRead);
          if (r == -1) {
            end = true;
            break;
          }
          bytesRead += r;
        }
        for (int i = 0; i < bytesRead; i++) {
          int hex = buffer[i];
          if (hex < 0) hex = 256 + hex;
          if (hex >= 16) System.out.print(Integer.toHexString(hex) + " ");
          else System.out.print("0" + Integer.toHexString(hex) + " ");
        }
        System.out.println();
      }
    }
    catch (IOException e) {System.err.println(e);}
    finally {
      try {
        if (fin != null) fin.close();
        }
      catch (IOException e) { }
    }
  }
}
```

When `FileDumper` is used to dump its own *.class* file in hexadecimal format, it produces the following:

```
D:\JAVA\ioexamples\04>java FileDumper -h FileDumper.class
ca fe ba be 00 03 00 2d 00 7e 03 00 00 00 00 03 00 00 00 01 03 00 00 00
02 08 00 43 08 00 44 08 00 52 08 00 53 08 00 54 08 00 55 08 00 56 08 00
63 07 00 5c 07 00 66 07 00 6d 07 00 6e 07 00 6f 07 00 70 07 00 71 07 00
```

In later chapters, I'll add a graphical user interface and many more possible interpretations of the data in the file, including floating-point, big- and little-endian integer, and various text encodings.

5

In this chapter:
- *URLs*
- *URL Connections*
- *Sockets*
- *Server Sockets*
- *URLViewer*

Network Streams

From its first days, Java has had the network in mind, more so than any other common programming language. Java is the first programming language to provide as much support for network I/O as it does for file I/O, perhaps even more—Java's URL, URLConnection, Socket, and ServerSocket classes are all fertile sources of streams. The exact type of the stream used by a network connection is typically hidden inside the undocumented sun classes. Thus, network I/O relies primarily on the basic InputStream and OutputStream methods, which you can wrap with any higher-level stream that suits your needs: buffering, cryptography, compression, or whatever your application requires.

URLs

The java.net.URL class represents a Uniform Resource Locator like *http://metalab.unc.edu/javafaq/*. Each URL unambiguously identifies the location of a resource on the Internet. The URL class has four constructors. All are declared to throw MalformedURLException, a subclass of IOException.

```
public URL(String u) throws MalformedURLException
public URL(String protocol, String host, String file)
  throws MalformedURLException
public URL(String protocol, String host, int port, String file)
  throws MalformedURLException
public URL(URL context, String u) throws MalformedURLException
```

A MalformedURLException is thrown if the constructor's arguments do not specify a valid URL. Often this means a particular Java implementation does not have the right protocol handler installed. Thus, given a complete absolute URL like *http://www.poly.edu/schedule/fall97/bgrad.html#cs*, you construct a URL object like this:

```
URL u = null;
try {
  u = new URL("http://www.poly.edu/schedule/fall97/bgrad.html#cs");
}
catch (MalformedURLException e) { }
```

You can also construct the URL object by passing its pieces to the constructor:

```
URL u = null;
try {
  u = new URL("http", "www.poly.edu", "/schedule/fall97/bgrad.html#cs");
}
catch (MalformedURLException e) { }
```

You don't normally need to specify a port for a URL; most protocols have default ports. For instance, the HTTP port is 80. Sometimes the port used does change, and in that case you can use the third constructor:

```
URL u = null;
try {
  u = new URL("http", "www.poly.edu", 80, "/schedule/fall97/bgrad.html#cs");
}
catch (MalformedURLException e) { }
```

Finally, many HTML files contain relative URLs. The fourth constructor in the previous code creates URLs relative to a given URL and is particularly useful when parsing HTML. For example, the following code creates a URL pointing to the file *08.html*, taking the rest of the URL from u1:

```
URL u1, u2;
try {
  u1 = new URL("http://metalab.unc.edu/javafaq/course/week12/07.html");
  u2 = new URL(u1, "08.html");
}
catch (MalformedURLException e) { }
```

Once a URL object has been constructed, there are two ways to retrieve its data. The openStream() method returns a raw stream of bytes from the source. The getContent() method returns a Java object that represents the data. When you call getContent(), Java looks for a content handler that matches the MIME type of the data. It is the openStream() method that is of concern in this book.

The openStream() method makes a socket connection to the server and port specified in the URL. It returns an input stream from which you can read the data at that URL, allowing you to download data from the server. Any headers that come before the actual data or file requested are stripped off before the stream is opened. You get only raw data.

```
public final InputStream openStream() throws IOException
```

You read from the input stream using an input stream or reader class. For example:

```
try {
 URL u = new URL("http://www.amnesty.org/");
 InputStream in = u.openStream();
 int b;
 while ((b = in.read()) != -1) {
   System.out.write(b);
 }
}
catch (MalformedURLException e) {System.err.println(e);}
catch (IOException e) {System.err.println(e);}
```

Applets running under the control of a security manager—that is, untrusted applets that run inside a web browser—are normally only allowed to connect back to their code base. The code base is the host from which they were downloaded, as returned by the getCodeBase() method of the Applet class. Attempts to connect to other hosts throw security exceptions. You can create URLs that point to other hosts, but you may not download data from them using openStream() or any other method. (This security restriction for applets applies to any network connection, regardless of how you get it.)

Example 5-1 reads a series of URLs from the command line. The program connects to the specified URLs, downloads the data, and copies it to System.out.

Example 5-1. The URLTyper Program

```
import java.net.*;
import java.io.*;
import com.macfaq.io.*;

public class URLTyper {

  public static void main(String[] args) {

    if (args.length == 0) {
      System.err.println("Usage: java URLTyper url1 url2 ...");
      return;
    }

    for (int i = 0; i < args.length; i++) {
      if (args.length > 1) {
        System.out.println(args[i] + ":");
      }
      try {
        URL u = new URL(args[i]);
        InputStream in = u.openStream();
        StreamCopier.copy(in, System.out);
```

Example 5-1. The URLTyper Program (continued)

```
      in.close();
    }
    catch (MalformedURLException e) {System.err.println(e);}
    catch (IOException e) {System.err.println(e);}
  }
 }
}
```

For example, here are the first few lines you see when you connect to *http://www. oreilly.com/*:

```
D:\JAVA\ioexamples\05>java URLTyper http://www.oreilly.com/
<HTML>
<HEAD>
<META name="keywords" content="computer books, technical books, UNIX, unix,
Perl, Java, Linux, Internet, Web, C, C++, Windows, Windows NT, Security,
Sys Admin, System Administration, Oracle, design, graphics, online books,
online courses, Perl Conference, Web-based training, Software, open source,
free software">
<META name="description" content="O'Reilly is a leader in technical and
computer book documentation for UNIX, Perl, Java, Linux, Internet,
Web, C, C++, Windows, Windows NT, Security, Sys Admin, System
Administration, Oracle, Design & Graphics, Online Books, Online Courses,
Perl Conference, Web-based training, and Software">
<TITLE>www.oreilly.com -- Welcome to O'Reilly & Associates!</TITLE>
```

Most network connections, even on LANs, are slower and less reliable sources of data than files. Connections across the Internet are even slower and less reliable, and connections through a modem are slower and less reliable still. One way to enhance performance under these conditions is to buffer the data: to read as much data as you can into a temporary storage array inside the class, then parcel it out as needed. In the next chapter, you'll learn about the `BufferedInputStream` class that does exactly this.

URL Connections

URL connections are closely related to URLs, as their name implies. Indeed, you get a reference to a `URLConnection` by using the `openConnection()` method of a URL object; in many ways, the URL class is only a wrapper around the `URLConnection` class. However, URL connections provide more control over the communication between the client and the server. In particular, URL connections provide not just input streams by which the client can read data from the server, but also output streams to send data from the client to the server. This is essential for protocols like *mailto*.

The `java.net.URLConnection` class is an abstract class that handles communication with different kinds of servers, like FTP servers and web servers. Protocol-specific subclasses of `URLConnection`, hidden inside the sun classes, handle different kinds of servers.

Reading Data from URL Connections

URL connections take place in five steps:

1. The `URL` object is constructed.

2. The `openConnection()` method of the `URL` object creates the `URLConnection` object.

3. The parameters for the connection and the request properties that the client sends to the server are set up.

4. The `connect()` method makes the connection to the server, perhaps using a socket for a network connection or a file input stream for a local connection. The response header information is read from the server.

5. Data is read from the connection by using the input stream returned by `getInputStream()` or through a content handler with `getContent()`. Data can be sent to the server using the output stream provided by `getOutputStream()`.

This scheme is very much based on the HTTP/1.0 protocol. It does not fit other schemes that have a more interactive "request, response, request, response, request, response" pattern instead of HTTP/1.0's "single request, single response, close connection" pattern. In particular, FTP and even HTTP/1.1 aren't well suited to this pattern. I wouldn't be surprised to see this replaced with something more general in a future version of Java.

`URLConnection` objects are not constructed directly in your own programs. Instead, you create a `URL` for the particular resource, and call that `URL`'s `openConnection()` method. This gives you a `URLConnection`. Then the `getInputStream()` method returns an input stream that reads data from the URL. (The `openStream()` method of the `URL` class is just a thin veneer over the `getInputStream()` method of the `URLConnection` class.) For example:

```
try {
  URL u = new URL("http://www.digitalthink.com/");
  URLConnection uc = u.openConnection();
  uc.connect();
  InputStream in = uc.getInputStream();
  //...
}
catch (IOException e) { //...
```

If the connection cannot be opened (possibly because the remote host is unreachable), an $IOException$ is thrown. Example 5-2 reads a URL from the command line, opens a connection to that URL, then prints the data returned by the server at that URL. This is similar to Example 5-1; $WebCat$ differs primarily in that it uses a $URLConnection$ instead of a URL.

Example 5-2. The WebCat Program

```java
import java.net.*;
import java.io.*;
import com.macfaq.io.*;

public class WebCat {

  public static void main(String[] args) {

    if (args.length == 0) {
      System.err.println("Usage: java WebCat url1 url2 ...");
      return;
    }

    for (int i = 0; i < args.length; i++) {
      if (i > 0 && i < args.length) {
        System.out.println();
        System.out.println("---------------------");
        System.out.println();
      }
      System.out.println(args[i] + ":");
      try {
        URL u = new URL(args[i]);
        URLConnection uc = u.openConnection();
        uc.connect();
        InputStream in = uc.getInputStream();
        StreamCopier.copy(in, System.out);
        in.close();
      }
      catch (IOException e) {System.err.println(e);}
    } // end for
  }
}
```

Writing Data on URL Connections

Writing data to a $URLConnection$ is similar to reading data. However, you must first inform the $URLConnection$ that you plan to use it for output, and then, instead of getting the connection's input stream and reading from it, you get the connection's output stream and write to it. This is commonly used to talk to CGIs that use the POST method or to store files on web servers through the PUT method, or to communicate with a Java servlet running on a server. Here are the steps for writing data on a URLConnection:

1. Construct the URL object.

2. Call the openConnection() method of the URL object to create the URLConnection object.

3. Pass true to setDoOutput() to indicate that this URLConnection will be used for output.

4. If you also want to read input from the stream, invoke setDoInput(true) to indicate that this URLConnection will be used for input.

5. Create the data you want to send, preferably as a byte array.

6. Call getOutputStream() to get an output stream object. Write the byte array calculated in step 5 onto the stream.

7. Close the output stream.

8. Call getInputStream() to get an input stream object. Read and write it as usual.

Example 5-3 uses these steps to implement a simple mail client. It forms a *mailto* URL from an email address entered on the command line. Input for the message is copied from System.in onto the output stream of the URLConnection using a StreamCopier. The end of the message is indicated by the end-of-stream character.

Example 5-3. The MailClient Class

```
import java.net.*;
import java.io.*;
import com.macfaq.io.*;

public class MailClient {

  public static void main(String[] args) {

    if (args.length == 0) {
      System.err.println("Usage: java MailClient username@host.com");
      return;
    }

    try {
      URL u = new URL("mailto:" + args[0]);
      URLConnection uc = u.openConnection();
      uc.setDoOutput(true);
      uc.connect();
      OutputStream out = uc.getOutputStream();
      StreamCopier.copy(System.in, out);
```

Example 5-3. The MailClient Class (continued)

```
    out.close();
  }
  catch (IOException e) {System.err.println(e);}
 }
}
```

For example, to send email to the author of this book:

```
% java MailClient elharo@metalab.unc.edu
hi there!
^D
```

MailClient suffers from a few restrictions. The proper way to detect the end of the message is to look for a period on a line by itself. Proper or not, that style of user interface is really antiquated, so I didn't bother to implement it. To do so properly, you'll need to use a Reader or a Writer; they're discussed in Chapter 15, *Readers and Writers*. Furthermore, it only works in Java environments that support the *mailto* protocol; thus, it works under Sun's JDK, but may not work in other environments. It also requires that the local host be running an SMTP server, or that the system property mailhost must contain the name of an accessible SMTP server, or that a machine in the local domain named *mailhost* be running an SMTP server. Finally, the security manager must permit network connections to that server, although this is not normally a problem in an application.

Sockets

Before data is sent across the Internet from one host to another, it is split into packets of varying but finite size called datagrams. Datagrams range in size from a few dozen bytes to about 60,000 bytes. Anything larger, and often things smaller, must be split into smaller pieces before it can be transmitted. The advantage of this scheme is that if one packet is lost, it can be retransmitted without requiring redelivery of all other packets. Furthermore, if packets arrive out of order, they can be reordered at the receiving end of the connection.

Fortunately, packets are invisible to the Java programmer. The host's native networking software splits data into packets on the sending end and reassembles packets on the receiving end. Instead, the Java programmer is presented with a higher-level abstraction called a *socket*. The socket represents a reliable connection for the transmission of data between two hosts. It isolates you from the details of packet encodings, lost and retransmitted packets, and packets that arrive out of order. A socket performs four fundamental operations:

1. Connect to a remote machine

2. Send data

3. Receive data

4. Close the connection

A socket may not be connected to more than one host at a time. However, a socket may both send data to and receive data from the host to which it's connected.

The `java.net.Socket` class is Java's interface to a network socket and allows you to perform all four fundamental socket operations. It provides raw, uninterpreted communication between two hosts. You can connect to remote machines; you can send data; you can receive data; you can close the connection. No part of the protocol is abstracted out, as it is with URL and URLConnection. The programmer is completely responsible for the interaction between the network client and the server. To create a connection, you call one of the Socket constructors, specifying the host you want to connect to. Each Socket object is associated with exactly one remote host. To connect to a different host, you must create a new Socket object:

```
public Socket(String host, int port) throws UnknownHostException, IOException
public Socket(InetAddress address, int port) throws IOException
public Socket(String host, int port, InetAddress localAddr, int localPort)
  throws IOException
public Socket(InetAddress address, int port, InetAddress localAddr, int
localPort) throws IOException
```

The host is a string like `"www.oreilly.com"` or `"metalab.unc.edu"`, which specifies the particular host to connect to. It may even be a numeric, dotted quad string like `"199.1.32.90"`. This argument may also be passed as a `java.net.InetAddress` object.

The `port` argument is the port on the remote host to connect to. A computer's network interface is logically subdivided into 65,536 different ports. As data traverses the Internet in packets, each packet carries not only the address of the host but also the port on that host at which it's aimed. The host is responsible for reading the port number from each packet it receives to decide which program should receive that chunk of data. Many services run on well-known ports. This means that the protocol specifies that the service should or must use a particular port—for example, HTTP servers generally listen on port 80.

The optional `localAddress` and `localPort` arguments specify which address and port on the local host the socket is to connect from, assuming more than one is available. Most hosts have many available ports but only one address. These two arguments are optional. If they're left out, the constructor will choose reasonable values.

Sending and receiving data across a socket is accomplished with output and input streams. These are the methods to get both streams for the socket:

```
public InputStream getInputStream() throws IOException
public OutputStream getOutputStream() throws IOException
```

There's also a method to close a socket:

```
public synchronized void close() throws IOException
```

This effectively closes the socket's input and output streams as well. Any attempt to read from or write to them after the socket is closed will throw an IOException.

Example 5-4 is yet another program that connects to a web server and downloads a specified URL. However, since this one uses raw sockets, it needs to both send the HTTP request and read the headers in the response. These are not parsed away as they are by the URL and URLConnection classes; you use an output stream to send the request explicitly and an input stream to read the data back, including HTTP headers. Only HTTP URLs are supported.

Example 5-4. The SocketTyper Program

```java
import java.net.*;
import java.io.*;
import com.macfaq.io.*;

public class SocketTyper {

  public static void main(String[] args) {

    if (args.length == 0) {
      System.err.println("Usage: java SocketTyper url1 url2 ...");
      return;
    }

    for (int i = 0; i < args.length; i++) {
      if (args.length > 1) {
        System.out.println(args[i] + ":");
      }
      try {
        URL u = new URL(args[i]);
        if (!u.getProtocol().equalsIgnoreCase("http")) {
          System.err.println("Sorry, " + u.getProtocol() +
          " is not yet supported.");
          break;
        }

        String host = u.getHost();
        int port = u.getPort();
        String file = u.getFile();
        // default port
        if (port <= 0) port = 80;
```

Example 5-4. The SocketTyper Program (continued)

```
        Socket s = new Socket(host, port);
        String request = "GET " + file + " HTTP/1.0\r\n"
        + "User-Agent: MechaMozilla\r\nAccept: text/*\r\n\r\n";
        // This next line is problematic on non-ASCII systems
        byte[] b = request.getBytes();

        OutputStream out = s.getOutputStream();
        InputStream in = s.getInputStream();
        out.write(b);
        out.flush();

        StreamCopier.copy(in, System.out);
        in.close();
        out.close();
        s.close();
      }
    catch (MalformedURLException e) {System.err.println(e);}
    catch (IOException e) {System.err.println(e);}
  }
 }
}
```

For example, when SocketTyper connects to *http://www.oreilly.com/*, here is what you see:

```
% java SocketTyper http://www.oreilly.com/
HTTP/1.0 200 OK
Server: WN/1.15.1
Date: Sun, 09 Aug 1998 20:05:03 GMT
Last-modified: Fri, 07 Aug 1998 23:44:36 GMT
Content-type: text/html
Title: www.oreilly.com -- Welcome to O'Reilly & Associates!
Link: <mailto:webmaster@ora.com>; rev="Made"

<HTML>
<HEAD>
<META name="keywords" content="computer books, technical books, UNIX, unix,
Perl, Java, Linux, Internet, Web, C, C++, Windows, Windows NT, Security,
Sys Admin, System Administration, Oracle, design, graphics, online books,
online courses, Perl Conference, Web-based training, Software, open source,
free software">
```

Notice the header lines you didn't see in Example 5-1. When you use the URL class to download a web page, the associated protocol handler never shows you the HTTP header.

Server Sockets

There are two ends to each connection: the client, which initiates the connection, and the server, which responds to the connection. So far, we've only discussed the client side and assumed that a server existed out there for the client to talk to. To implement a server, you need to write a program that waits for other hosts to connect to it. A server socket binds to a particular port on the local machine (the server); once it has successfully bound to a port, it listens for incoming connection attempts from remote machines (the clients). When the server detects a connection attempt, it accepts the connection. This creates a socket between the two machines over which the client and the server communicate.

Many clients can connect to a port on the server simultaneously. Incoming data is distinguished by the port to which it is addressed and the client host and port from which it came. The server can tell for which service (like HTTP or FTP) the data is intended by inspecting the port. It knows where to send any response by looking at the client address and port stored with the data.

No more than one server socket can listen to a particular port at one time. Therefore, since a server may need to handle many connections at once, server programs tend to be heavily multithreaded. Generally, the server socket listening on the port only accepts the connections. It passes off the actual processing of each connection to a separate thread. Incoming connections are stored in a queue until the server can accept them. On most systems, the default queue length is between 5 and 50. Once the queue fills up, further incoming connections are refused until space in the queue opens up.

The `java.net.ServerSocket` class represents a server socket. Three constructors let you specify the port to bind to, the queue length for incoming connections, and the IP address:

```
public ServerSocket(int port) throws IOException
public ServerSocket(int port, int backlog) throws IOException
public ServerSocket(int port, int backlog, InetAddress bindAddr)
  throws IOException
```

Normally, you specify only the port you want to listen on:

```
try {
   ServerSocket ss = new ServerSocket(80);
}
catch (IOException e) {System.err.println(e);}
```

When you create a `ServerSocket` object, it attempts to bind to the port on the local host given by the port argument. If another server socket is already listening to the port, then a `java.net.BindException`, a subclass of `IOException`, is thrown. No more than one process or thread can listen to a particular port at a time. This includes non-Java processes or threads. For example, if there's already an HTTP server running on port 80, you won't be able to bind to port 80. On Unix systems (but not Windows or the Mac) your program must be running as root to bind to a port between 1 and 1023.

0 is a special port number. It tells Java to pick an available port. You can then find out what port it's picked with the getLocalPort() method:

```
public int getLocalPort()
```

This is useful if the client and the server have already established a separate channel of communication over which the chosen port number can be communicated. For example, the FTP protocol uses two sockets. The initial connection is made by the client to the server to send commands. One of the commands sent tells the server the port number on which the client is listening. The server then connects to the client on this port to send data.

Once you have a ServerSocket, you need to wait for incoming connections. You do this by calling the accept() method, which blocks until a connection attempt occurs and then returns a Socket that you can use to communicate with the client. The close() method terminates the ServerSocket.

```
public Socket accept() throws IOException
public void close() throws IOException
```

That's pretty much all there is, except for a few methods dealing with socket options and some other details. In particular, there aren't methods for getting input and output streams. Instead, accept() returns a Socket object: you call the Socket's getInputStream() or getOutputStream() method. For example:

```
try {
  ServerSocket ss = new ServerSocket(2345);
  Socket s = s.accept();
  OutputStream out = s.getOutputStream();
  // Send data to the client.
  s.close();
}
catch (IOException e) {System.err.println(e);}
```

Notice in this example, I closed the Socket s, not the ServerSocket ss. ss is still bound to port 2345. You get a new socket for each connection and reuse the server socket. For example, the next code fragment repeatedly accepts connections:

```
try {
  ServerSocket ss = new ServerSocket(2345);
  while (true) {
    Socket s = s.accept();
    OutputStream out = s.getOutputStream();
```

```
      // send data to the client
      s.close();
    }
  }
  catch (IOException e) {System.err.println(e);}
```

The program in Example 5-5 reads a port number from the command line. It listens on that port for incoming connections. When it detects one, it answers back with the client's address and port and its own. Then it closes the connection.

Example 5-5. The HelloServer Program

```
import java.net.*;
import java.io.*;

public class HelloServer {

  public final static int defaultPort = 2345;

  public static void main(String[] args) {

    int port = defaultPort;

    try {
      port = Integer.parseInt(args[0]);
    }
    catch (Exception e) {}
    if (port <= 0 || port >= 65536) port = defaultPort;

    try {
      ServerSocket ss = new ServerSocket(port);
      while (true) {
        try {
          Socket s = ss.accept();

          String response = "Hello " + s.getInetAddress() + " on port "
           + s.getPort() + "\r\n";
          response += "This is " + s.getLocalAddress() + " on port "
           + s.getLocalPort() + "\r\n";
          OutputStream out = s.getOutputStream();
          out.write(response.getBytes());
          out.flush();
          s.close();
        }
        catch (IOException e) {}
      }
    }
    catch (IOException e) {System.err.println(e);}
  }
}
```

Here's some output from our server. The server is running on *utopia.poly.edu*. The client is connecting from *titan.oit.unc.edu*. Note how the port from which the connection comes changes each time; like most client programs, the telnet program picks a random local port for outgoing connections:

```
% telnet utopia.poly.edu 2545
Trying 128.238.3.21...
Connected to utopia.poly.edu.
Escape character is '^]'.
Hello titan.oit.unc.edu/152.2.22.14 on port 50361
This is utopia.poly.edu/128.238.3.21 on port 2545
Connection closed by foreign host.
% telnet utopia.poly.edu 2545
Trying 128.238.3.21...
Connected to utopia.poly.edu.
Escape character is '^]'.
Hello titan.oit.unc.edu/152.2.22.14 on port 50362
This is utopia.poly.edu/128.238.3.21 on port 2545
Connection closed by foreign host.
```

URLViewer

Example 5-6 is an improved version of the URLViewer you first encountered in Chapter 2. This is a simple application that provides a window in which you can view the contents of a URL. It assumes that those contents are more or less ASCII text. (In future chapters, I'll remove that restriction.) Figure 5-1 shows the result. Our application has a text area in which the user can type a URL, a Load button that the user uses to load the specified URL, and a StreamedTextArea component that displays the text from the URL. Each of these corresponds to a field in the URLViewer class.

Example 5-6. The URLViewer Program

```
import java.awt.*;
import java.awt.event.*;
import java.io.*;
import java.net.*;
import com.macfaq.awt.*;
import com.macfaq.io.*;

public class URLViewer extends Frame
 implements WindowListener, ActionListener {

  TextField theURL = new TextField();
  Button loadButton = new Button("Load");
  StreamedTextArea theDisplay = new StreamedTextArea();

  public URLViewer() {
```

Example 5-6. The URLViewer Program (continued)

```java
    super("URL Viewer");
  }

  public void init() {

    this.add("North", theURL);
    this.add("Center", theDisplay);
    Panel south = new Panel();
    south.add(loadButton);
    this.add("South", south);
    theURL.addActionListener(this);
    loadButton.addActionListener(this);
    this.addWindowListener(this);
    this.setLocation(50, 50);
    this.pack();
    this.show();
  }

  public void actionPerformed(ActionEvent evt) {

    try {
      URL u = new URL(theURL.getText());
      InputStream in = u.openStream();
      OutputStream out = theDisplay.getOutputStream();
      StreamCopier.copy(in, out);
      in.close();
      out.close();
    }
    catch (MalformedURLException ex) {theDisplay.setText("Invalid URL");}
    catch (IOException ex) {theDisplay.setText("Invalid URL");}
  }

  public void windowClosing(WindowEvent e) {

    this.setVisible(false);
    this.dispose();
  }

  public void windowOpened(WindowEvent e) {}
  public void windowClosed(WindowEvent e) {}
  public void windowIconified(WindowEvent e) {}
  public void windowDeiconified(WindowEvent e) {}
  public void windowActivated(WindowEvent e) {}
  public void windowDeactivated(WindowEvent e) {}

  public static void main(String args[]) {

    URLViewer me = new URLViewer();
```

Example 5-6. The URLViewer Program (continued)

```
    me.init();
  }
}
```

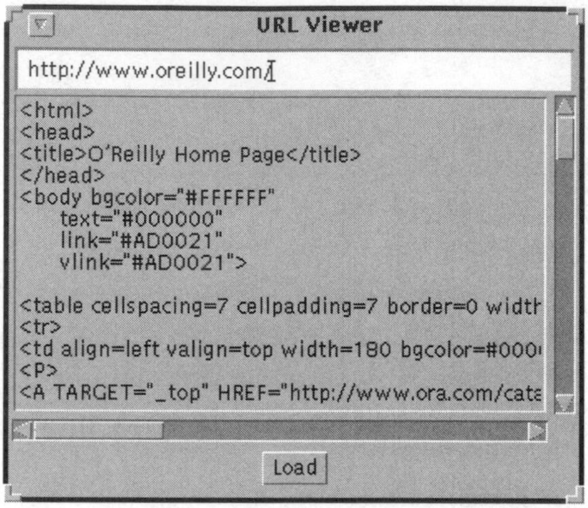

Figure 5-1. The URLViewer

The `URLViewer` class itself extends `Frame`. An alternative would have been to extend `Panel`, which would have allowed `URLViewer` objects to be embedded in other containers. However, this application seemed big enough to justify exclusive use of a window. `URLViewer` implements the `WindowListener` interface to enable the user to close the window by clicking in the close box. Only the `window-Closing()` method is nontrivial. The other six window methods are do-nothing methods required to satisfy the contract of the `WindowListener` interface.

The `init()` method builds the interface and displays the window. This is invoked by the `main()` method, which constructs a new `URLViewer` object. The constructor is quite simple, merely passing the title of the frame to the superclass constructor.

The streamed text area is filled when the user clicks the Load button or hits Return inside the URL text field. The `URLViewer` object listens to both of these components. The `URLViewer`'s `actionPerformed()` method constructs a URL from the text in the text field, then opens an input stream from the URL in the text field. Next, `StreamCopier` from Chapter 3, *Input Streams* pours the data from the URL's input stream into the text area's output stream. When that's finished, both streams are closed.

III

FILTER STREAMS

In this chapter:
- *The Filter Stream Classes*
- *The Filter Stream Subclasses*
- *Buffered Streams*
- *PushbackInputStream*
- *Print Streams*
- *Multitarget Output Streams*
- *File Viewer, Part 2*

6

Filter Streams

Filter input streams read data from a preexisting input stream like a `FileInputStream` and have an opportunity to work with or change the data before it is delivered to the client program. Filter output streams write data to a preexisting output stream such as a `FileOutputStream` and have an opportunity to work with or change the data before it is written onto the underlying stream. Multiple filters can be chained onto a single underlying stream. Filter streams are used for encryption, compression, translation, buffering, and much more.

The word *filter* is derived by analogy from a water filter. A water filter sits between the pipe and faucet, pulling out impurities. A stream filter sits between the source of the data and its eventual destination and applies a specific algorithm to the data. As drops of water are passed through the water filter and modified, so too are bytes of data passed through the stream filter. Of course, there are some big differences—most notably, a stream filter can add data or some other kind of annotation to the stream, in addition to removing things you don't want; it may even produce a stream that is completely different from its original input (for example, by compressing the original data).

The Filter Stream Classes

`java.io.FilterInputStream` and `java.io.FilterOutputStream` are concrete superclasses for input and output stream subclasses that somehow modify or manipulate data of an underlying stream:

```
public class FilterInputStream extends InputStream
public class FilterOutputStream extends OutputStream
```

Each of these classes has a single protected constructor that specifies the underlying stream from which the filter stream reads or writes data:

```
protected FilterInputStream(InputStream in)
protected FilterOutputStream(OutputStream out)
```

These constructors set protected InputStream and OutputStream fields, called in and out, inside the FilterInputStream and FilterOutputStream classes, respectively.

```
protected InputStream in
protected OutputStream out
```

Since the constructors are protected, filter streams may only be created by subclasses. Each subclass implements a particular filtering operation. Normally, such a pattern suggests that polymorphism is going to be used heavily, with subclasses standing in for the common superclass; however, it is uncommon to use filter streams polymorphically as instances of FilterInputStream or FilterOutputStream. Most of the time, references to a filter stream are either references to a more specific subclass like BufferedInputStream or they're polymorphic references to InputStream or OutputStream with no hint of the filter left.

Beyond the constructors, both FilterInputStream and FilterOutputStream declare exactly the methods of their respective superclasses. For FilterInputStream, these are:

```
public int read() throws IOException
public int read(byte[] data) throws IOException
public int read(byte[] data, int offset, int length) throws IOException
public long skip(long n) throws IOException
public int available() throws IOException
public void close() throws IOException
public synchronized void mark(int readlimit)
public synchronized void reset() throws IOException
public boolean markSupported()
```

For FilterOutputStream, these are:

```
public void write(int b) throws IOException
public void write(byte[] data) throws IOException
public void write(byte[] data, int offset, int length) throws IOException
public void flush() throws IOException
public void close() throws IOException
```

Each of these methods merely passes its arguments to the corresponding method in the underlying stream. For example, the skip() method in FilterInputStream behaves like this:

```
  public long skip(long n) throws IOException {
    in.skip(n);
  }
```

The `close()` method in `FilterOutputStream` behaves like this:

```
  public void close() throws IOException {
    out.close();
  }
```

Thus, closing a filter stream closes the underlying stream. You cannot close one filter stream and then open up another on the same underlying stream, nor can you close one filter stream in a chain but still read from the underlying stream or other streams in the chain. Attempts to do so will throw `IOExceptions`. Once a stream is closed—no matter by which filter stream it's chained to—it's closed for good.

Since the constructors are protected, you don't use these classes directly. Instead, you create subclasses and use those. Since `FilterOutputStream` does not have a no-argument constructor, it's essential to give all subclasses explicit constructors and use `super()` to invoke the `FilterOutputStream` constructor. Your subclass will probably also want to override the `write(int b)` and `write(byte[] data, int offset, int length)` methods to perform its filtering. The `write(byte[] data)` method merely invokes `write(data, 0, data.length)`, so if you've overridden the three-argument `write()` method, you probably don't need to also override `write(byte[] data)`. Depending on circumstances, you may or may not need to override some of the other methods.

The `PrintableOutputStream` class shown in Example 6-1 is an example subclass of `FilterOutputStream` that truncates all data to the range of printable ASCII characters: byte values 32–126, plus 9, 10, and 13 (tab, linefeed, and carriage return). Every time a byte in that range is passed to `write()`, it is written onto the underlying output stream, `out`. Every time a byte outside that range is passed to `write()`, a question mark is written onto the underlying output stream, `out`. Among other things, this class provides a quick and dirty way to read ASCII string literals embedded in a *.class* or *.exe* file.

Example 6-1. The PrintableOutputStream Class

```
package com.macfaq.io;

import java.io.*;

public class PrintableOutputStream extends FilterOutputStream {

  public PrintableOutputStream(OutputStream out) {
    super(out);
  }
```

Example 6-1. The PrintableOutputStream Class (continued)

```
public void write(int b) throws IOException {

    // carriage return, linefeed, and tab
    if (b == 10 || b == 13 || b == 9) out.write(b);
    // non-printing characters
    else if (b < 32 || b > 126) out.write('?');
    // printing, ASCII characters
    else out.write(b);
}

public void write(byte[] data, int offset, int length) throws IOException {
    for (int i = offset; i < offset+length; i++) {
        this.write(data[i]);
    }
}
}
```

To use this class, or any other filter output stream, you must chain it to another stream that actually writes the bytes to their eventual target. For example, to chain a `PrintableOutputStream` to `System.out`, you would write:

```
PrintableOutputStream pos = new PrintableOutputStream(System.out);
```

Often, the underlying stream is created directly inside the constructor:

```
PrintableOutputStream pos =
    new PrintableOutputStream(new FileOutputStream("data.txt"));
```

However, the sheer length of the stream class names tends to make this style of coding inconvenient.

Multiple streams can be chained together in sequence to get the benefits of each. For example, to create a buffered printable file output stream, you would chain a file output stream to a buffered output stream, which would then be chained to a printable output stream. For example:

```
FileOutputStream fout = new FileOutputStream("data.txt");
BufferedOutputStream bout = new BufferedOutputStream(fout);
PrintableOutputStream pout = new PrintableOutputStream(bout);
```

Example 6-2 uses the `PrintableOutputStream` class to extract ASCII strings from a file. First it chains either `System.out` or a file output stream to a printable output stream, then it opens a file input stream from a file named on the command line and copies it into the printable output stream, thereby converting it to printable ASCII characters.

Example 6-2. The StringExtractor Class

```java
import com.macfaq.io.*;
import java.io.*;

public class StringExtractor {

  public static void main(String[] args) {

    if (args.length < 1) {
      System.out.println("Usage: java StringExtractor inFile");
      return;
    }
    try {
      FileInputStream fin = new FileInputStream(args[0]);
      OutputStream out;
      if (args.length >= 2) {
        out = new FileOutputStream(args[1]);
      }
      else out = System.out;

      // Here's where the output stream is chained
      // to the ASCII output stream.
      PrintableOutputStream pout = new PrintableOutputStream(out);
      int b;
      while ((b = fin.read()) != -1) pout.write(b);
      // Alternately
      // StreamCopier.copy(fin, pout);
    }
    catch (FileNotFoundException e) {
      System.out.println("Usage: java StringExtractor inFile outFile");
    }
    catch (IOException e) {System.err.println(e);}
  }
}
```

Here's the output produced by running `StringExtractor` on itself in compiled form:

```
% java StringExtractor StringExtractor.class
???????-?=??-??.??+??/??1??2??3??4??5??6??7
?
??
????
????
????    ????    ????
?       ??
?       ??
????
```

```
??????&?
??&?"??&?$??0?)??9?)??:?#??:?$??;????<?!???()I???()V???(I)V???(Ljava/io
/OutputStream;)V???(Ljava/lang/Object;)V???(Ljava/lang/String;)V???([Ljava/
lang/
String;)V???<init>???Code???LineNumberTable???Ljava/io/PrintStream;??
SourceFile???StringExtractor???StringExtractor.java??"Usage: java
StringExtracto
r inFile??*Usage: java StringExtractor inFile outFile??#com/macfaq/io/
PrintableO
utputStream???err???java/io/FileInputStream???java/io/
FileNotFoundException???ja
va/io/FileOutputStream???java/io/IOException???java/io/PrintStream???java/
lang/O
bject???java/lang/System???main???out???println???read???write?!???
?????????&? ???'????????????*?????????(???????????
?8?%???'???????????g*???
N??      -
?????+???Y6????????W??????????L???+?????????O?R?????O?^?????(???J????????
```

Although a lot of information is clearly lost in this translation, a surprising amount is retained—you have every string literal in the file and the names of all the classes and methods invoked by this class.

Filter input streams are created similarly. Since `FilterInputStream` does not have a no-argument constructor, all subclasses require explicit constructors and must use `super()` to invoke the `FilterInputStream` constructor. To do the actual filtering, a subclass overrides the `read()` and `read(byte[] data, int offset, int length)` methods. The `read(byte[] data)` method merely invokes `read(data, 0, data.length)`, so if you've overridden the three-argument `read()` method, you probably don't need to also override `read(byte[] data)`. Depending on circumstances, you may or may not need to override some of the other methods. For example, the `PrintableInputStream` class shown in Example 6-3 truncates all data read to the range of printable ASCII characters. As with `PrintableOutputStream`, any character not in that range is replaced by a question mark.

Example 6-3. The PrintableInputStream Class

```
package com.macfaq.io;

import java.io.*;

public class PrintableInputStream extends FilterInputStream {

  public PrintableInputStream(InputStream in) {
    super(in);
  }
```

Example 6-3. The PrintableInputStream Class (continued)

```
public int read() throws IOException {

    int b = in.read();
    // printing, ASCII characters
    if (b >= 32 && b <= 126) return b;
    else if (b == 10 || b == 13 || b == 9) return b;
    // nonprinting characters
    else return '?';

}

public int read(byte[] data, int offset, int length) throws IOException {

    int result = in.read(data, offset, length);
    for (int i = offset; i < offset+result; i++) {
        // Do nothing with the printing characters.
        if (data[i] == 10 || data[i] == 13 || data[i] == 9) ;
        // nonprinting characters
        else if (data[i] < 32 || data[i] > 126) data[i] = (byte) '?';
    }
    return result;
    }
}
```

The Filter Stream Subclasses

The `java.io` package contains many useful filter stream classes. The `BufferedInputStream` and `BufferedOutputStream` classes buffer reads and writes by first putting data into a buffer (an internal array of bytes). Thus, an application can read or write bytes to the stream without necessarily calling the underlying native methods. The data is read from or written into the buffer in blocks; subsequent accesses go straight to the buffer. This improves performance in many situations. Buffered input streams also allow the reader to back up and reread data.

The `java.io.PrintStream` class, which `System.out` and `System.err` are instances of, allows very simple printing of primitive values, objects, and string literals. It uses the platform's default character encoding to convert characters into bytes. This class traps all `IOExceptions` and is primarily intended for debugging. `System.out` and `System.err` are the most popular examples of the `PrintStream` class, but you can connect a `PrintStream` filter to other output streams as well. For example, you can chain a `PrintStream` to a `FileOutputStream` to easily write text into a file.

The `PushbackInputStream` class has a one-byte pushback buffer so a program can "unread" the last character read. The next time data is read from the stream, the unread character is reread.

The `DataInputStream` and `DataOutputStream` classes read and write primitive Java data types and strings in a machine-independent way. (Big-endian for integer types, IEEE-754 for `floats` and `doubles`, UTF-8 for Unicode.) These are important enough to justify a chapter of their own and will be discussed in the next chapter. The `ObjectInputStream` and `ObjectOutputStream` classes extend `DataInputStream` and `DataOutputStream` with methods to read and write arbitrary Java objects as well as primitive data types. These will be taken up in Chapter 11, *Object Serialization.*

The `java.util.zip` package also includes several filter stream classes. The filter input streams in this package decompress compressed data; the filter output streams compress raw data. These will be discussed in Chapter 9, *Compressing Streams.*

The `java.util.security` package contains the `DigestInputStream` and `DigestOutputStream` filter streams; these calculate message digests of the data that passes through them. Installing the Java Cryptography Extension (JCE) adds two more filter streams to this package, `CipherInputStream` and `CipherOutputStream`, which can encrypt or decrypt data using a variety of algorithms. These will be discussed in Chapter 10, *Cryptographic Streams.*

Buffered Streams

Buffered input streams read more data than they initially need into a buffer (an internal array of bytes). When the stream's `read()` methods are invoked, the data is removed from the buffer rather than the underlying stream. When the buffer runs out of data, the buffered stream refills its buffer from the underlying stream. Likewise, buffered output streams store data in an internal byte array until the buffer is full or the stream is flushed; then the data is written out to the underlying output stream in one swoop. In situations where it's almost as fast to read or write several hundred bytes from the underlying stream as it is to read or write a single byte, a buffered stream can provide a significant performance gain.

There are two `BufferedInputStream` constructors and two `Buffered-OutputStream` constructors:

```
public BufferedInputStream(InputStream in)
public BufferedInputStream(InputStream in, int size)
public BufferedOutputStream(OutputStream out)
public BufferedOutputStream(OutputStream out, int size)
```

The first argument is the underlying stream from which data will be read or to which data will be written. The `size` argument is the number of bytes in the buffer. If a size isn't specified, a 2048-byte buffer is used. The best size for the buffer depends on the platform and is generally related to the block size of the disk (at least for file streams). Less than 512 bytes is probably too small and more than 4096 bytes is probably too large. Ideally, you want an integral multiple of the block size of the disk. However, you might want to use smaller buffer sizes for unreliable network connections. For example:

```
URL u = new URL("http://java.developer.com");
BufferedInputStream bis = new BufferedInputStream(u.openStream(), 256);
```

Example 6-4 copies files named on the command line to `System.out` with buffered reads and writes.

Example 6-4. A BufferedStreamCopier

```
package com.macfaq.io;
import java.io.*;

public class BufferedStreamCopier {

  public static void main(String[] args) {

    try {
      copy(System.in, System.out);
    }
    catch (IOException e) {System.err.println(e);}
  }

  public static void copy(InputStream in, OutputStream out)
   throws IOException {

    // Do not allow other threads to read from the input
    // or write to the output while copying is taking place.
    synchronized (in) {
      synchronized (out) {
        BufferedInputStream bin = new BufferedInputStream(in);
        BufferedOutputStream bout = new BufferedOutputStream(out);

        while (true) {
          int datum = bin.read();
          if (datum == -1) break;
          bout.write(datum);
        }
        bout.flush();
      }
    }
  }
}
```

This `copy()` method copies byte by byte, which is normally not very efficient. However, almost all the copies take place in memory, because the input stream and the output stream are buffered. Therefore, this is reasonably quick.

It wouldn't hurt to read and write byte arrays in the copy method instead of individual bytes, as long as the arrays you were reading and writing were significantly smaller than the buffer size. However, one level of buffering is usually sufficient. Detailed performance calculations depend on the virtual machine and the host OS, so it's hard to make any definite conclusions.

Also note that the output stream is deliberately flushed. The data only reaches its eventual destination in the underlying stream `out` when the stream is flushed or the buffer fills up. Therefore, it's important to call `flush()` explicitly before the method returns.

BufferedInputStream Details

The buffer and the current state of the buffer are stored in protected fields. The buffer itself is a byte array called `buf`; the number of bytes in the buffer is an `int` named `count`; the index of the next byte that will be returned by `read()` is an `int` called `pos`; the mark, if any, is an `int` called `markpos`; the read-ahead limit before the mark is invalidated is an `int` called `marklimit`. Subclasses of `BufferedInputStream` can directly access all these fields, which can be important for performance.

```
protected byte[] buf
protected int count
protected int pos
protected int markpos
protected int marklimit
```

`BufferedInputStream` only overrides methods from `InputStream`. It does not declare any new methods of its own. Marking and resetting are supported.

```
public synchronized int read() throws IOException
public synchronized int read(byte[] data, int offset, int length)
                     throws IOException
public synchronized long skip(long n) throws IOException
public synchronized int available() throws IOException
public synchronized void mark(int readLimit)
public synchronized void reset() throws IOException
public boolean markSupported()
```

In Java 2 and later, the two multibyte `read()` methods try to fill the specified array or subarray completely by reading repeatedly from the underlying input stream. They return only when the requested number of bytes have been read, the end of stream is reached, or the underlying stream would block. This is not the case for most input streams (including buffered input streams in Java 1.1.*x* and earlier), which only attempt one read from the underlying stream or data source before returning.

BufferedOutputStream Details

BufferedOutputStream also stores the buffer in a protected byte array named buf and the index of the next byte that will be returned by read() in an int field named pos. BufferedOutputStream does not expose the number of bytes in the buffer.

```
protected byte buf[]
protected int pos
```

BufferedOutputStream only overrides three methods from OutputStream. It does not declare any new methods.

```
public synchronized void write(int b) throws IOException
public synchronized void write(byte data[], int offset, int length)
                      throws IOException
public synchronized void flush() throws IOException
```

These methods are invoked exactly as they would be for any output stream. The only difference is that writes place data in the buffer rather than directly on the underlying output stream.

PushbackInputStream

The java.io.PushbackInputStream class provides a pushback buffer so a program can "unread" the last several bytes read. The next time data is read from the stream, the unread bytes are reread.

```
public void unread(int b) throws IOException
public void unread(byte[] data, int offset, int length) throws IOException
public void unread(byte[] data) throws IOException
```

By default the buffer is only one byte long, and trying to unread more than one byte throws an IOException. However, you can change the default buffer size with the second constructor:

```
public PushbackInputStream(InputStream in)
public PushbackInputStream(InputStream in, int size)
```

Although both PushbackInputStream and BufferedInputStream use buffers, only a PushbackInputStream allows unreading, and only a BufferedInput-Stream allows marking and resetting. In a PushbackInputStream, markSupported() returns false.

```
public boolean markSupported()
```

The `read()` and `available()` methods work exactly as with normal input streams. However, they first attempt to read from the pushback buffer.

```
public int read() throws IOException
public int read(byte[] data, int offset, int length) throws IOException
public int available() throws IOException
```

Print Streams

`System.out` and `System.err` are instances of the `java.io.PrintStream` class. This is a subclass of `FilterOutputStream` that converts numbers and objects to text. `System.out` is primarily used for simple, character-mode applications and for debugging. Its *raison d'être* is convenience, not robustness; print streams ignore many issues involved in internationalization and error checking. This makes `System.out` easy to use in quick and dirty hacks and simple examples, while simultaneously making it unsuitable for production code, which should use the `java.io.PrintWriter` class (discussed in Chapter 15, *Readers and Writers*) instead.

The `PrintStream` class has `print()` and `println()` methods that handle every Java data type. The `print()` and `println()` methods differ only in that `println()` prints a platform-specific line terminator after printing its arguments and `print()` does not. These methods are:

```
public void print(boolean b)
public void print(char c)
public void print(int i)
public void print(long l)
public void print(float f)
public void print(double d)
public void print(char[] s)
public void print(String s)
public void print(Object o)
public void println()
public void println(boolean b)
public void println(char c)
public void println(int i)
public void println(long l)
public void println(float f)
public void println(double d)
public void println(char[] s)
public void println(String s)
public void println(Object o)
```

Anything at all can be passed to a `print()` method; whatever argument you give is guaranteed to match at least one of these methods. Object types are converted to strings by invoking their `toString()` method. Primitive types are converted with the appropriate `String.valueOf()` method.

One aspect of making `System.out` simple for quick jobs is not in the `PrintStream` class at all but in the compiler. Because Java overloads the + operator to signify concatenation of strings, primitive data types, and objects, you can pass multiple variables to the `print()` and `println()` methods, which are then converted to strings and concatenated . For example, consider the line:

```
System.out.println("As of " + (new Date()) + " there have been over "
 + hits + " hits on the web site." );
```

The compiler rewrites this complicated expression as:

```
StringBuffer sb = new StringBuffer();
sb.append("As of ");
Date d = new Date();
sb.append(d);
sb.append(" there have been over ");
sb.append(hits);
sb.append(" hits on the web site.")
String s = sb.toString();
System.out.println(s);
```

The `StringBuffer append()` method is overloaded in much the same way that the `print()` and `println()` methods are so it can handle any Java data type.

`PrintStream` methods never throw `IOExceptions`. Each method in the class catches `IOExceptions`. When an exception occurs, an internal flag is set to `true`. You test this flag with the `checkError()` method:

```
public boolean checkError()
```

This method returns `true` if this print stream has ever encountered an error during its lifetime. Most of the time, you just ignore this, since print streams are only used in situations where exhaustive error checking is unnecessary.

Besides `System.out` and `System.err`, you can create new print streams with these constructors:

```
public PrintStream(OutputStream out)
public PrintStream(OutputStream out, boolean autoFlush)
```

The `out` argument is just the underlying output stream. The `autoFlush` argument is a `boolean` (`true` or `false`). If it's `true`, then the stream is flushed every time a linefeed (`\n`) character or byte is written, a `println()` method is invoked, or a byte array is written.

The biggest problem with the `PrintStream` class is that it does not properly handle international character sets. In Chapter 15 you'll learn about the

PrintWriter class that has much of the same functionality but can handle international character sets.

Multitarget Output Streams

As a final example, I present two slightly unusual filter output streams that direct their data to multiple underlying streams. The TeeOutputStream class, given in Example 6-5, has not one but two underlying streams. The TeeOutputStream does not modify the data that's written in any way; it merely writes it on both of its underlying streams.

Example 6-5. The TeeOutputStream Class

```java
package com.macfaq.io;

import java.io.*;

public class TeeOutputStream extends FilterOutputStream {

  OutputStream out1;
  OutputStream out2;

  public TeeOutputStream(OutputStream stream1, OutputStream stream2) {
    super(stream1);
    out1 = stream1;
    out2 = stream2;
  }

  public synchronized void write(int b) throws IOException {
    out1.write(b);
    out2.write(b);
  }

  public synchronized void write(byte[] data, int offset, int length)
   throws IOException {
    out1.write(data, offset, length);
    out2.write(data, offset, length);
  }

  public void flush() throws IOException {
    out1.flush();
    out2.flush();
  }

  public void close() throws IOException {
    out1.close();
    out2.close();
  }
}
```

It would be possible to store one of the output streams in `FilterOutputStream`'s protected out field and the other in a field in this class. However, it's simpler and cleaner to maintain the parallelism between the two streams by storing them both in the `TeeOutputStream` class.

I've synchronized the `write()` methods to make sure that two different threads don't try to write to the same `TeeOutputStream` at the same time. Depending on unpredictable thread-scheduling issues, this could lead to data being written out of order or in different orders on different streams. It's important to make sure that one write is completely finished on all streams before the next write begins.

Example 6-6 demonstrates how one might use this class to write a `TeeCopier` program that copies one file into two separate, new files.

Example 6-6. The TeeCopier Program

```java
import java.io.*;
import com.macfaq.io.*;

public class TeeCopier {

  public static void main(String[] args) {

    if (args.length != 3) {
      System.out.println("Usage: java TeeCopier infile outfile1 outfile2");
      return;
    }

    try {
      FileInputStream fin = new FileInputStream(args[0]);
      FileOutputStream fout1 = new FileOutputStream(args[1]);
      FileOutputStream fout2 = new FileOutputStream(args[2]);
      TeeOutputStream tout = new TeeOutputStream(fout1, fout2);
      BufferedStreamCopier.copy(fin, tout);
      fin.close();
      tout.close();
    }
    catch (IOException e) {System.err.println(e);}

  }
}
```

It's not hard to extend this to a `MultiOutputStream` class that handles an arbitrary number of output streams. You simply need to store the list of output streams in a vector and provide an `addStream()` method that adds them to the vector as needed. The methods of the class then simply enumerate the vector, invoking the method on each element of the vector in turn. Example 6-7 demonstrates.

Example 6-7. The MultiOutputStream Class

```java
package com.macfaq.io;
import java.io.*;
import java.util.*;

public class MultiOutputStream extends FilterOutputStream {

  Vector streams = new Vector();

  public MultiOutputStream(OutputStream out) {
    super(out);
    streams.addElement(out);
  }

  public synchronized void addOutputStream(OutputStream out) {
    streams.addElement(out);
  }

  public synchronized void write(int b) throws IOException {

    for (Enumeration e = streams.elements(); e.hasMoreElements();) {
      OutputStream out = (OutputStream) e.nextElement();
      out.write(b);
    }
  }

  public synchronized void write(byte[] data, int offset, int length)
   throws IOException {

    for (Enumeration e = streams.elements(); e.hasMoreElements();) {
      OutputStream out = (OutputStream) e.nextElement();
      out.write(data, offset, length);
    }
  }

  public synchronized void flush() throws IOException {

    for (Enumeration e = streams.elements(); e.hasMoreElements();) {
      OutputStream out = (OutputStream) e.nextElement();
      out.flush();
    }
  }

  public synchronized void close() throws IOException {
```

Example 6-7. The MultiOutputStream Class (continued)

```
    for (Enumeration e = streams.elements(); e.hasMoreElements();) {
      OutputStream out = (OutputStream) e.nextElement();
      out.close();
    }
  }
}
```

This example requires even more synchronization than the `TeeOutputStream`. The concern is that one thread might attempt to add a new stream to the list while the list is being enumerated. Vectors and enumerations are not particularly thread-safe against such actions, so to be on the safe side I've synchronized all the non-constructor methods. This is overkill most of the time, because a typical user will add all the streams they're ever going to add to the list before writing or flushing or closing the stream. Thus, an alternative would be to pass an immutable list of streams to the constructor and not allow the client to add streams to the list from that point forward. You'd still need to synchronize the `write()` methods, however, for the same reasons the `write()` methods in `TeeOutput-Stream` needed to be synchronized.

Example 6-8 is a short program that uses a `MultiOutputStream` to copy the contents of one file into an unlimited number of files named on the command line.

Example 6-8. The MultiCopier Program

```
import java.io.*;
import com.macfaq.io.*;

public class MultiCopier {

  public static void main(String[] args) {

    if (args.length < 2) {
      System.out.println("Usage: java MultiCopier infile outfile1 outfile2...");
      return;
    }

    try {
      FileInputStream fin = new FileInputStream(args[0]);
      FileOutputStream fout1 = new FileOutputStream(args[1]);
      MultiOutputStream mout = new MultiOutputStream(fout1);
      for (int i = 2; i < args.length; i++) {
        mout.addOutputStream(new FileOutputStream(args[i]));
      }
      BufferedStreamCopier.copy(fin, mout);
      fin.close();
      mout.close();
```

Example 6-8. The MultiCopier Program (continued)

```
    }
    catch (IOException e) {System.err.println(e);}
  }
}
```

File Viewer, Part 2

There's a saying among object-oriented programmers that you should create one design just to throw away. Now that we've got filter streams in hand, I'm ready to throw out the monolithic design for the `FileDumper` program used in Chapter 4, *File Streams*. I'm going to rewrite it using a more flexible, extensible, object-oriented approach that relies on multiple chained filters. This allows us to extend the system to handle new formats without rewriting all the old classes. (It also makes some of the examples in subsequent chapters smaller, since I won't have to repeat all the code each time.) The basic idea is to make each interpretation of the data a filter input stream. Bytes from the underlying stream move into the filter; the filter converts the bytes into strings. Since more bytes generally come out of the filter than go into it (for instance, the single byte 32 is replaced by the four bytes "0", "3", "2", " " in decimal dump format), our filter streams buffer the data as necessary.

The architecture revolves around the abstract `DumpFilter` class shown in Example 6-9. The public interface of this class is identical to that of `FilterInputStream`. Internally, a buffer holds the string interpretation of each byte as an array of bytes. The `read()` method returns bytes from this array as long as possible. An `index` field tracks the next available byte. When `index` reaches the length of the array, the abstract `fill()` method is invoked to read from the underlying stream and place data in the buffer. By changing how the `fill()` method translates the bytes it reads into the bytes in the buffer, you can change how the data is interpreted.

Example 6-9. DumpFilter

```
package com.macfaq.io;
import java.io.*;

public abstract class DumpFilter extends FilterInputStream {

  // This is really an array of unsigned bytes.
  protected int[] buf = new int[0];
  protected int index = 0;

  public DumpFilter(InputStream in) {
    super(in);
  }
```

Example 6-9. DumpFilter (continued)

```java
public int read() throws IOException {

  int result;
  if (index < buf.length) {
    result = buf[index];
    index++;
  }  // end if
  else {
    try {
      this.fill();
      // fill is required to put at least one byte
      // in the buffer or throw an EOF or IOException.
      result = buf[0];
      index = 1;
    }
    catch (EOFException e) {result = -1;}
  }  // end else

  return result;
}

protected abstract void fill() throws IOException;

public int read(byte[] data, int offset, int length) throws IOException {

  if (data == null) {
    throw new NullPointerException();
  }
  else if ((offset < 0) || (offset > data.length) || (length < 0)
    || ((offset + length) > data.length) || ((offset + length) < 0)) {
    throw new ArrayIndexOutOfBoundsException();
  }
  else if (length == 0) {
    return 0;
  }

  // Check for end of stream.
  int datum = this.read();
  if (datum == -1) {
    return -1;
  }

  data[offset] = (byte) datum;

  int bytesRead = 1;
  try {
    for (; bytesRead < length ; bytesRead++) {
```

Example 6-9. DumpFilter (continued)

```
      datum = this.read();

      // In case of end of stream, return as much as we've got,
      // then wait for the next call to read to return -1.
      if (datum == -1) break;
      data[offset + bytesRead] = (byte) datum;
    }
  }
  catch (IOException e) {
    // Return what's already in the data array.
  }
  return bytesRead;
}


public int available() throws IOException {
  return buf.length - index;
}


public long skip(long bytesToSkip) throws IOException {

  long bytesSkipped = 0;
  for (; bytesSkipped < bytesToSkip; bytesSkipped++) {
    int c = this.read();
    if (c == -1) break;
  }
  return bytesSkipped;
}


public synchronized void mark(int readlimit) {}

public synchronized void reset() throws IOException {
  throw new IOException("marking not supported");
}


public boolean markSupported() {
  return false;
}
}
```

The `FilterInputStream` class tacitly assumes that the number of bytes of input read from the underlying stream is the same as the number of bytes read from the filter stream. That's not always true, as is the case here. For instance, the `HexFilter` will provide three bytes of data for every byte read from the underlying stream. The `DecimalFilter` will provide four. Therefore, we also have to override `skip()` and `available()`. The `skip()` method simply reads as many bytes as possible, then returns. The `available()` method simply returns the number of bytes remaining in the buffer. For the uses we're putting these classes to, these methods aren't all that important, so I haven't bothered to provide optimal implementations. You can do better in subclasses, if you like.

The same problem applies to the mark() and reset() methods. These will mark and reset the underlying stream, but what's really desired is to mark and reset this stream. The easiest solution here is to deliberately not support marking and resetting. Subclasses can override this if it seems important, or you can simply chain this stream to a buffered stream. However, the buffered stream must follow the dump filter in the chain rather than precede it.

Concrete subclasses need only to implement a constructor or two and fill(). Example 6-10 shows the DecimalFilter class. Example 6-11 shows the HexFilter class. These two classes are very similar. Each implements fill() and overrides available() (the latter mainly because it's straightforward to do). The algorithms for converting bytes to decimal and hexadecimal strings used by the fill() methods are essentially the same as used by the dumpDecimal() and dumpHex() methods back in Chapter 4's FileDumper program.

Example 6-10. DecimalFilter

```
package com.macfaq.io;
import java.io.*;

public class DecimalFilter extends DumpFilter {

  protected int numRead = 0;
  protected int breakAfter = 15;
  protected int ratio = 4; // number of bytes of output per byte of input

  public DecimalFilter(InputStream in) {
    super(in);
  }

  protected void fill() throws IOException {

    buf = new int[ratio];
    int datum = in.read();
    this.numRead++;
    if (datum == -1) {
      // Let read() handle end of stream.
      throw new EOFException();
    }

    String dec = Integer.toString(datum);
    if (datum < 10) { // Add two leading zeros.
      dec = "00" + dec;
    }
    else if (datum < 100) { // Add leading zero.
```

Example 6-10. DecimalFilter (continued)

```
      dec = '0' + dec;
    }
    for (int i = 0; i < dec.length(); i++) {
      buf[i] = dec.charAt(i);
    }
    if (numRead < breakAfter) {
      buf[buf.length - 1] = ' ';
    }
    else {
      buf[buf.length - 1] = '\n';
      numRead = 0;
    }
  }


  public int available() throws IOException {
    return (buf.length - index) + ratio * in.available();
  }


  // With some extra effort, you could provide more efficient
  // implementations of these methods. You could even support
  // marking and resetting.
  /*
    public int read(byte[] data, int offset, int length) throws IOException {}
    public long skip(long bytesToSkip) throws IOException {}
    public synchronized void mark(int readlimit) {}
    public synchronized void reset() throws IOException {}
    public boolean markSupported() {}
  */
}
```

Example 6-11. HexFilter

```
package com.macfaq.io;
import java.io.*;

public class HexFilter extends DumpFilter {

  protected int numRead = 0;
  protected int breakAfter = 24;
  protected int ratio = 3; // Number of bytes of output per byte of input.

  public HexFilter(InputStream in) {
    super(in);
  }

  protected void fill() throws IOException {

    buf = new int[ratio];
```

Example 6-11. HexFilter (continued)

```
    int datum = in.read();
    this.numRead++;
    if (datum == -1) {
      // Let read() handle end of stream.
      throw new EOFException();
    }

    String hex = Integer.toHexString(datum);
    if (datum < 16) { // Add a leading zero.
      hex = '0' + hex;
    }

    for (int i = 0; i < hex.length(); i++) {
      buf[i] = hex.charAt(i);
    }
    if (numRead < breakAfter) {
      buf[buf.length - 1] = ' ';
    }
    else {
      buf[buf.length - 1] = '\n';
      numRead = 0;
    }
  }

  public int available() throws IOException {
    return (buf.length - index) + ratio * in.available();
  }

  // With some extra effort, you could provide more efficient
  // implementations of these methods. You could even support
  // marking and resetting.
  /*
    public int read(byte[] data, int offset, int length) throws IOException {}
    public long skip(long bytesToSkip) throws IOException {}
    public synchronized void mark(int readlimit) {}
    public synchronized void reset() throws IOException {}
    public boolean markSupported() {}
  */
}
```

Another object-oriented maxim is that the generic solution is often simpler than the specific solutions. Looking at these two classes, can you think of a way to create a generic filter that converts to ASCII in an arbitrary base? Would such a class be any simpler than those shown here?

The `main()` method and class in Example 6-12 are similar to what we've had before. However, rather than selecting a method to dump the file, we select a dump filter to use. This allows multiple filters to be used in sequence—a feature that will be important when we want to decompress, decrypt, or perform other transformations on the data, in addition to interpreting it. The program is also easier to read and understand when split across the three classes.

Example 6-12. FileDumper2

```java
import java.io.*;
import com.macfaq.io.*;

public class FileDumper2 {

  public static final int ASC = 0;
  public static final int DEC = 1;
  public static final int HEX = 2;

  public static void main(String[] args) {

    if (args.length < 1) {
      System.err.println("Usage: java FileDumper [-ahd] file1 file2...");
    }

    int firstArg = 0;
    int mode = ASC;

    if (args[0].startsWith("-")) {
      firstArg = 1;
      if (args[0].equals("-h")) mode = HEX;
      else if (args[0].equals("-d")) mode = DEC;
    }

    for (int i = firstArg; i < args.length; i++) {
      try {
        InputStream in = new FileInputStream(args[i]);
        dump(in, System.out, mode);

        if (i < args.length-1) {  // more files to dump
          System.out.println();
          System.out.println("-------------------------------------");
          System.out.println();
        }
      }
      catch (IOException e) {System.err.println(e);}
    }
  }

  public static void dump(InputStream in, OutputStream out, int mode)
    throws IOException {
```

Example 6-12. FileDumper2 (continued)

```
    // The reference variable in may point to several different objects
    // within the space of the next few lines. We can attach
    // more filters here to do decompression, decryption, and more.

    if (mode == ASC) ; // no filter needed, just copy raw bytes
    else if (mode == HEX) in = new HexFilter(in);
    else if (mode == DEC) in = new DecimalFilter(in);

    StreamCopier.copy(in, out);
    in.close();
  }
}
```

The `main()` method is responsible for choosing the file and format to be dumped. The `dump()` method translates an input stream onto an output stream using a particular filter. This allows the `dump()` method to be used by other classes as a more general translation service for streams. An alternative pattern would pass the filter as an argument to `dump()` rather than an integer mode. This might make the program more flexible but would not allow you to easily chain several filters together as we'll do in upcoming chapters.

7

Data Streams

In this chapter:
- *The Data Stream Classes*
- *Reading and Writing Integers*
- *Reading and Writing Floating-Point Numbers*
- *Reading and Writing Booleans*
- *Reading Byte Arrays*
- *Reading and Writing Text*
- *Reading and Writing Little-Endian Numbers*
- *Thread Safety*
- *File Viewer, Part 3*

Data streams read and write strings, integers, floating-point numbers, and other data that's commonly presented at a higher level than mere bytes. The `java.io.DataInputStream` and `java.io.DataOutputStream` classes read and write the primitive Java data types (`boolean`, `int`, `double`, etc.) and strings in a particular, well-defined, platform-independent format. Since `DataInputStream` and `DataOutputStream` use the same formats, they're complementary. What a data output stream writes, a data input stream can read. These classes are especially useful when you need to move data between platforms that may use different native formats for integers or floating-point numbers.

The Data Stream Classes

The `java.io.DataInputStream` and `java.io.DataOutputStream` classes are subclasses of `FilterInputStream` and `FilterOutputStream`, respectively.

```
public class DataInputStream extends FilterInputStream implements DataInput
public class DataOutputStream extends FilterOutputStream
            implements DataOutput
```

They have all the usual methods you've come to associate with input and output stream classes, such as `read()`, `write()`, `flush()`, `available()`, `skip()`, `close()`, `markSupported()`, and `reset()`. (Data input streams support marking

102

if, and only if, their underlying input stream supports marking.) However, the real purpose of DataInputStream and DataOutputStream is not to read and write raw bytes using the standard input and output stream methods. It's to read and interpret multibyte data like ints, floats, doubles, and chars.

The DataInput and DataOutput Interfaces

The java.io.DataInput interface declares 15 methods that read various kinds of data:

```
public abstract boolean readBoolean() throws IOException
public abstract byte readByte() throws IOException
public abstract int readUnsignedByte() throws IOException
public abstract short readShort() throws IOException
public abstract int readUnsignedShort() throws IOException
public abstract char readChar() throws IOException
public abstract int readInt() throws IOException
public abstract long readLong() throws IOException
public abstract float readFloat() throws IOException
public abstract double readDouble() throws IOException
public abstract String readLine() throws IOException
public abstract String readUTF() throws IOException
public void readFully(byte[] data) throws IOException
public void readFully(byte[] data, int offset, int length) throws IOException
public int skipBytes(int n) throws IOException
```

These methods are all available from the DataInputStream class and any other class that implements DataInput. (In the core Java API, this is only DataInputStream and its subclass, ObjectInputStream, which will be discussed in Chapter 11, *Object Serialization*.) Likewise, the java.io.DataOutput interface declares 14 methods, mostly complementary to those in DataInput:

```
public abstract void write(int b) throws IOException
public abstract void write(byte[] data) throws IOException
public abstract void write(byte[] data, int offset, int length)
                      throws IOException
public abstract void writeBoolean(boolean v) throws IOException
public abstract void writeByte(int b) throws IOException
public abstract void writeShort(int s) throws IOException
public abstract void writeChar(int c) throws IOException
public abstract void writeInt(int i) throws IOException
public abstract void writeLong(long l) throws IOException
public abstract void writeFloat(float f) throws IOException
public abstract void writeDouble(double d) throws IOException
public abstract void writeBytes(String s) throws IOException
public abstract void writeChars(String s) throws IOException
public abstract void writeUTF(String s) throws IOException
```

The `writeBytes()` and `writeChars()` methods are not matched by `read Bytes()` and `readChars()` methods in `DataInput`. The format used only writes the actual bytes and chars. It does not write information about the length of the string passed as an argument to `writeBytes()` and `writeChars()`, so the bytes and chars themselves cannot be easily reassembled into a string. It is also unclear why `DataOutput` declares the three common `write()` methods, but `DataInput` does not declare the three common `read()` methods. However, the two `readFully()` methods are actually better matches for `write()`, since, unlike `read()`, they will either fill the array or throw an exception.

Although `DataInput` and `DataOutput` say nothing about the formats in which data is read and written, any class that implements this interface must adhere to an implicit contract, summarized in Table 7-1.

Table 7-1. Formats Used by DataInput and DataOutput

Type	Written by	Read by	Format
`boolean`	`writeBoolean(boolean b)`	`readBoolean()`	One byte, 0 if `false`, 1 if `true`
`byte`	`writeByte(int b)`	`readByte()`	One byte, two's complement
`byte array`	`write(byte[] data)` `write(byte[] data, int offset, int length)`	`readFully(byte[] data)` `readFully(byte[] data, int offset, int length)`	The bytes in the order they appear in the array or subarray
`short`	`writeShort(int s)`	`readShort()`	Two bytes, two's complement, big-endian
`char`	`writeChar(int c)`	`readChar()`	Two bytes, unsigned, big-endian
`int`	`writeInt(int i)`	`readInt()`	Four bytes, two's complement, big-endian
`long`	`writeLong(long l)`	`readLong()`	Eight bytes, two's complement, big-endian
`float`	`writeFloat(float f)`	`readFloat()`	Four bytes, IEEE 754, big-endian
`double`	`writeDouble(double d)`	`readDouble()`	Eight bytes, IEEE 754, big-endian
`unsigned byte`	N/A	`readUnsignedByte()`	One unsigned byte
`unsigned short`	N/A	`readUnsignedShort()`	Two bytes, big-endian, unsigned

Table 7-1. Formats Used by DataInput and DataOutput (continued)

Type	Written by	Read by	Format
String	writeBytes(String s)	N/A	The low-order byte of each character in the string from first to last
String	writeChars(String s)	N/A	Both bytes of each character in the string from first to last
String	writeUTF(String s)	readUTF()	A signed short giving the number of bytes in the UTF-8 encoded string, followed by the UTF-8 encoding of the string

Constructors

The `DataInputStream` and `DataOutputStream` classes have exactly the constructors you would expect:

```
public DataInputStream(InputStream in)
public DataOutputStream(OutputStream out)
```

These chain the data streams to the underlying streams passed as arguments. For example, to read formatted data from a file called *data.txt* and write formatted data to *output.dat*, you would create the two streams `dis` and `dos`:

```
DataInputStream dis = new DataInputStream(new FileInputStream("data.txt"));
DataOutputStream dos = new DataOutputStream(
  new FileOutputStream("output.dat"));
```

We will now take up the data formats used by data streams and the methods used to write data in those formats.

Reading and Writing Integers

The `DataOutputStream` class has methods for writing all of Java's primitive integer data types: `byte`, `short`, `int`, and `long`. The `DataInputStream` class has methods to read these types. It also has methods for reading two integer data types not directly supported by Java or the `DataOutputStream` class: the unsigned `byte` and the unsigned `int`.

Integer Formats

While Java's platform independence guarantees that you don't have to worry about precise data formats when working exclusively in Java, you frequently need to read data created by a program written in another language. Similarly, it's not unusual to have to write data that will be read by a program written in a different language. For example, most Java network clients (like HotJava) talk primarily to servers written in other languages, and most Java network servers (like the Java Web Server) talk primarily to clients written in other languages. You cannot naively assume that the data format Java uses is the data format other programs will understand; you must take care to understand and recognize the data formats being used.

Although other schemes are possible, almost all modern computers have standardized on binary arithmetic performed on integers composed of an integral number of bytes. Furthermore, they've standardized on two's complement arithmetic for signed numbers. In two's complement arithmetic, the most significant bit is 1 for a negative number and 0 for a positive number; the absolute value of a negative number is calculated by taking the complement of the number and adding 1. In Java terms, this means (-n == ~n + 1) is true where n is a negative int.

Regrettably, this is about all that's been standardized. One big difference between computer architectures is the size of an int. Probably the majority of modern computers use four-byte integers that can hold a number between –2,147,483,648 and 2,147,483,647. However, some systems are moving to 64-bit architectures where the native integer ranges from –9,223,372,036,854,775,808 to 9,223,372,036,854,775,807 and takes eight bytes. And many older systems use 16-bit integers that only range from –32,768 to 32,767. Exactly how many bytes a C compiler uses for each int is platform-dependent, which is one of many reasons C code isn't as portable as one might wish. The sizes of C's short and long are even less predictable and may or may not be the same as the size of a C int. Java always uses a two-byte short, a four-byte int, and an eight-byte long, and this is one of the reasons Java code is more portable than C code. However, you must be aware of varying integer widths when your Java code needs to communicate binary numbers with programs written in other languages.

C compilers also allow various unsigned types. For example, an unsigned byte is a binary number between 0 and 255; an unsigned two-byte integer is a number between 0 and 65,535; an unsigned four-byte integer is a number between 0 and 4,294,967,295. Java doesn't have any unsigned numeric data types (unless you count char), but the DataInputStream class does provide two methods to read unsigned bytes and unsigned shorts.

Perhaps worst of all, modern computers are split almost down the middle between those that use a big-endian and a little-endian ordering of the bytes in an integer. In a little-endian architecture, used on Intel (x86, Pentium)-based computers, the most significant byte is at the highest address in memory. On the other hand, on a big-endian system, the most significant byte is at the lowest address in memory.

For example, consider the number 1,108,836,360. In hexadecimal this is written as 0x42178008. On a big-endian system the bytes are ordered much as they are in a hex literal; that is, 42, 17, 80, 08. On the other hand, on a little endian system this is reversed; that is, 08, 80, 17, 42. If 1,108,836,360 is written into a file on a little-endian system, then read on a big-endian system without any special treatment, it comes out as 0x08801742; that is, 142,612,29—not the same thing at all.

Java uses big-endian integers exclusively. Data input streams read and data output streams write big-endian integers. Most Internet protocols that rely on binary numbers such as the time protocol implicitly assume "network byte order," which is a fancy way of saying "big-endian." And finally, almost all computers manufactured today, except those based on the Intel architecture, use big-endian byte orders, so the Intel is really the odd one out. However, the Intel is the 1000-pound gorilla of computer architectures, so it's impossible to ignore it or the data formats it supports. Later in this chapter, I'll develop a class for reading little-endian data.

The Char Format

Unicode characters are two bytes long and are interpreted as an unsigned number between 0 and 65,535. This means they have an "endianness" problem too. The Unicode standard specifically does not require a particular endianness of text written in Unicode; both big- and little-endian encodings are allowed. In my opinion, this is a failing of the specification. The Unicode standard does suggest that character 65,279 (0xFEFF in hex) be placed at the beginning of each file of Unicode text. Thus, by reading the first character, you can determine the endianness of the file and take appropriate action. For example, if you're reading a Unicode file containing little-endian data using big-endian methods, the first character will appear as 0xFFFE (65,534), signaling that something is wrong. Java's data stream classes always write and read Unicode text in a big-endian fashion.

Writing Integers

The `DataOutputStream` class has the usual three `write()` methods you'll find in any output stream class:

```
public synchronized void write(int b) throws IOException
public synchronized void write(byte[] data) throws IOException
public synchronized void write(byte[] data, int offset, int length)
  throws IOException
```

These behave exactly as they do in the superclass, so I won't discuss them further here.

The DataOutputStream class also declares the following void methods that write signed integer types onto its underlying output stream:

```
public final void writeByte(int b) throws IOException
public final void writeShort(int s) throws IOException
public final void writeInt(int i) throws IOException
public final void writeLong(long l) throws IOException
```

Because Java doesn't fully support the byte or short types, the writeByte() and writeShort() methods each take an int as an argument. The excess bytes in the int are ignored before the byte or short is written. Thus writeByte() only writes the low-order byte of its argument. The writeShort() method only writes the low-order two bytes of its argument, higher-order byte first; that is, big-endian order. The writeInt() and writeLong() methods write all the bytes of their arguments in big-endian order. These methods can throw IOExceptions if the underlying stream throws an IOException.

Example 7-1 fills a file called *1000.dat* with the integers between 1 and 1000. This filename is used to construct a FileOutputStream. This stream is then chained to a DataOutputStream whose writeInt() method writes the data into the file.

Example 7-1. One Thousand ints

```
import java.io.*;

public class File1000 {

  public static void main(String args[]) {

    DataOutputStream dos = null;

    try {
      dos = new DataOutputStream(new FileOutputStream("1000.dat"));
      for (int i = 1; i <= 1000; i++) {
        dos.writeInt(i);
      }
    }
    catch (IOException e) {System.err.println(e);}
    finally {
      try { if (dos != null) dos.close(); }
      catch (IOException e) {}
    }
  }
}
```

Let me emphasize that the numbers written by this program or by any other data output stream are *binary numbers*. They are not human-readable text strings like 1, 2, 3, 4, 5, . . . 999, 1000. If you try to open *1000.dat* with a standard text editor, you'll see a lot of gibberish or an error message. The data this program writes is meant to be read by other programs, not by humans.

Reading Integers

`DataInputStream` has the usual three `read()` methods it inherits from its super-class; these methods read a `byte` and return an `int`. These behave exactly as they do in the superclass, so I won't discuss them further:

```
public abstract int read() throws IOException
public int read(byte[] data) throws IOException
public int read(byte[] data, int offset, int length) throws IOException
```

The `DataInputStream` class declares the following methods that return signed integer types:

```
public final byte readByte() throws IOException
public final short readShort() throws IOException
public final char readChar() throws IOException
public final int readInt() throws IOException
public final long readLong() throws IOException
```

Each of the integer `read()` methods reads the necessary number of bytes and converts them into the appropriate integer type. `readByte()` reads a single byte and returns a signed byte between -128 and 127. `readShort()` reads two bytes and returns a `short` between $-32,768$ and $32,767$. `readInt()` reads four bytes and returns an `int` between $-2,147,483,648$ and $2,147,483,647$. `readLong()` reads eight bytes and returns a `long` between $-9,223,372,036,854,775,808$ and $9,223,372,036,854,775,807$. All numbers are read in a big-endian format.

-1 is a valid return value for these methods. Therefore, if the end of stream is encountered while reading, a `java.io.EOFException` is thrown. This is a subclass of `java.io.IOException` and is not separately declared in these methods' `throws` clauses. You should also be aware that an `EOFException` can be thrown while more bytes of data remain in the stream. For example, `readInt()` reads four bytes. If only two bytes are left in the stream, those two bytes will be read and the `EOFException` thrown. However, at this point those two bytes are lost. You can't go back and reread those two bytes as a `short`. If the underlying stream supports marking and resetting, you can mark before each read and reset on an `EOFException`, but that becomes complicated and error-prone.

Example 7-2 interprets a file as four-byte signed integers, reads them, and prints them out. You might use this to read the output of Example 7-1. However, it is not necessary that the program or person who created the file actually intended it to contain 32-bit, two's complement integers. The file contains bytes, and these bytes may be interpreted as `int`s, with the possible exception of one to three bytes at the end of the file (if the file's length is not an even multiple of four bytes). Therefore, it's important to be very careful about what you read.

Example 7-2. The IntReader Program

```java
import java.io.*;

public class IntReader {

  public static void main(String[] args) {

    for (int i = 0; i < args.length; i++) {

      try {
        FileInputStream fin = new FileInputStream(args[i]);
        // Now that we know the file exists, print its name.
        System.out.println("-----------" + args[i] + "-----------");
        DataInputStream din = new DataInputStream(fin);
        while (true) {
          int theNumber = din.readInt();
          System.out.println(theNumber);
        }  // end while
      } // end try
      catch (EOFException e) {
        // normal termination
      }
      catch (IOException e) {
        // abnormal termination
        System.err.println(e);
      }
    }  // end for
  }  // end main
}  // end IntReader
```

This program opens the files named on the command line with a file input stream. The file input stream is chained to a data input stream, which reads successive integers until an `IOException` occurs. Notice that I do not print an error message in the event of an `EOFException`, since that now indicates normal termination.

The `DataInputStream` class also has two methods that read unsigned `bytes` and shorts:

```java
public final int readUnsignedByte() throws IOException
public final int readUnsignedShort() throws IOException
```

Since Java has no unsigned `byte` or unsigned `short` data type, both of these methods return an `int`. `readUnsignedByte()` returns an `int` between 0 and 255, and `readUnsignedShort()` returns an `int` between 0 and 65,535. However, both still indicate end of stream with an EOFException rather than by returning –1. Example 7-3 prints files named on the command line as unsigned shorts.

Example 7-3. The UnsignedShortReader Program

```
import java.io.*;

public class UnsignedShortReader {

  public static void main(String[] args) {

    for (int i = 0; i < args.length; i++) {

      try {
        FileInputStream fin = new FileInputStream(args[i]);
        // Now that we know the file exists, print its name.
        System.out.println("-----------" + args[i] + "-----------");
        DataInputStream din = new DataInputStream(fin);
        while (true) {
          int theNumber = din.readUnsignedShort();
          System.out.println(theNumber);
        }  // end while
      } // end try
      catch (EOFException e) {
        // normal termination
      }
      catch (IOException e) {
        // abnormal termination
        System.err.println(e);
      }
    }  // end for
  }  // end main
}  // end UnsignedShortReader
```

Reading and Writing Floating-Point Numbers

Java understands two floating-point number formats, both specified by the IEEE 754 standard. Floats are stored in four bytes with a 1-bit sign, a 24-bit mantissa, and an 8-bit exponent. Float values range from $1.40129846432481707 \times 10^{-45}$ to $3.40282346638528860 \times 10^{38}$, either positive or negative. Doubles take up eight bytes with a one-bit sign, 11-bit mantissa, and 53-bit exponent. This gives them a range of $4.94065645841246544 \times 10^{-324}$ to $1.79769313486231570 \times 10^{308}$, either positive or negative. Both floats and doubles also have representations of positive and negative zero, positive and negative infinity, and not a number (or NaN).

NOTE   Astute readers will notice that the number of bits given for `floats`
              and `doubles` adds up to 33 and 65 bits, respectively, one too many
              for the width of the number. A trick is used whereby the first bit of
              the mantissa of a nonzero number is assumed to be 1. With this
              trick, it is unnecessary to include the first bit of the mantissa. Thus,
              an extra bit of precision is gained for free.

The details of this format are too complicated to discuss here. You can order the actual specification* from the IEEE for about $29.00. That's approximately $1.50 a page, more than a little steep in my opinion. The specification isn't available online, but it was published in the February 1985 issue of *ACM SIGPLAN Notices* (Volume 22, #2, pp. 9–18), which should be available in any good technical library. The main thing you need to know is that these formats are supported by most modern RISC architectures and by all Pentium and Motorola 680x0 chips with either external or internal floating-point units (FPUs). Nowadays the only chips that don't natively support this format are a few embedded processors and some old 486SX, 68LC040, and other earlier FPU-less chips in legacy hardware. And even these systems are able to emulate IEEE 754 floating-point arithmetic in software.

The `DataInputStream` class reads and the `DataOutputStream` class writes floating-point numbers of either four or eight bytes in length, as specified in the IEEE 754 standard. They do not support the 10-byte and longer long `double`, extended `double`, and double `double` formats supported by some architectures and compilers. If you have to read floating-point data written in some format other than basic IEEE 754 `float` and `double`, you'll need to write your own class to convert the format to four- or eight-byte IEEE 754.

Writing Floating-Point Numbers

There are two methods in the `DataOutputStream` class that write floating-point numbers, `writeFloat()` and `writeDouble()`:

```
public final void writeFloat(float f) throws IOException
public final void writeDouble(double d) throws IOException
```

---

* *IEEE/ANSI Standard for Binary Floating Point Arithmetic*, (Institute of Electrical and Electronics Engineers, 1985), IEEE Std 754-1985. To order, call 1-800-678-IEEE (in the U.S. and Canada) or 1-732-981-0060 (outside the U.S. and Canada), or email *customer.service@ieee.org*. Most of what you need to understand the format can also be found in *The Java Language Specification*, James Gosling, Bill Joy, and Guy Steele, (Addison Wesley, 1996). For a more readable explanation, see Chapter 2 of my book, *Java Secrets* (IDG Books, 1997).

Both of these methods throw an `IOException` if something goes wrong with the underlying stream. Otherwise, they're fairly innocuous and can convert any `float` or `double` to bytes and write it on the underlying stream.

Example 7-4 fills a file called *roots.dat* with the square roots of the numbers 0 to 1000. First a `FileOutputStream` is opened to *roots.dat*. This stream is chained to a `DataOutputStream`, whose `writeDouble()` method writes the data into the file.

Example 7-4. Writing Doubles with a DataOutputStream

```
import java.io.*;

public class RootsFile {

  public static void main(String[] args) {

    try {
      FileOutputStream fout = new FileOutputStream("roots.dat");
      DataOutputStream dout = new DataOutputStream(fout);
      for (int i = 0; i <= 1000; i++) {
        dout.writeDouble(Math.sqrt(i));
      }
      dout.flush();
      dout.close();
    }
    catch (IOException e) {System.err.println(e);}
  }
}
```

Reading Floating-Point Numbers

The `DataInputStream` class has two methods that read floating-point numbers, `readFloat()` and `readDouble()`:

```
public final float readFloat() throws IOException
public final double readDouble() throws IOException
```

The `readFloat()` method reads four bytes, converts the data into an IEEE 754 `float`, and returns it. The `readDouble()` method reads eight bytes, converts the data into an IEEE 754 `double`, and returns that. Both methods will throw an `EOFException`, a subclass of `IOException`, if they can't read enough bytes. In this case data may be lost without careful (and generally unnecessary) marking and resetting.

Example 7-5 reads a file specified on the command line, then prints its contents interpreted as doubles.

Example 7-5. The DoubleReader Program

```java
import java.io.*;

public class DoubleReader {

  public static void main(String[] args) {

    for (int i = 0; i < args.length; i++) {

      try {
        FileInputStream fin = new FileInputStream(args[i]);
        // Now that we know the file exists, print its name.
        System.out.println("-----------" + args[i] + "-----------");
        DataInputStream din = new DataInputStream(fin);
        while (true) {
          double theNumber = din.readDouble();
          System.out.println(theNumber);
        } // end while
      } // end try
      catch (EOFException e) {
        // normal termination
      }
      catch (IOException e) {
        // abnormal termination
        System.err.println(e);
      }
    } // end for
  } // end main
} // end DoubleReader
```

Here are the first few lines produced when this program is used to read the output of Example 7-4, RootsFile. You may recognize this output as the square roots of the integers between 0 and 9.

```
% java DoubleReader roots.dat
-----------roots.dat-----------
0.0
1.0
1.4142135623730951
1.7320508075688772
2.0
2.23606797749979
2.449489742783178
2.6457513110645907
2.8284271247461903
3.0
```

Reading and Writing Booleans

The `DataOutputStream` class has a `writeBoolean()` method and the `DataInput Stream` class has a corresponding `readBoolean()` method:

```
public final void writeBoolean(boolean b) throws IOException
public final boolean readBoolean() throws IOException
```

Although theoretically a single bit could be used to indicate the value of a `boolean`, in practice a whole byte is used. This makes alignment much simpler and doesn't waste enough space to be an issue on modern machines. The `writeBoolean()` method writes a zero byte (0x00) to indicate `false`, a one byte (0x01) to indicate `true`. The `readBoolean()` method interprets 0 as `false` and any positive number as `true`. Negative numbers indicate end of stream and lead to an `EOFException` being thrown.

Reading Byte Arrays

As already mentioned, the `DataInputStream` class has the usual two methods for reading bytes into a `byte` array:

```
public int read(byte[] data) throws IOException
public int read(byte[] data, int offset, int length) throws IOException
```

Neither of these methods guarantees that all the bytes requested will be read. Instead, you're expected to check the number of bytes actually read, then call `read()` again for a different part of the array as necessary. For example, to read 1024 bytes from the `InputStream` in into the `byte` array `data`:

```
int offset = 0;
int bytesRead = 0;
while (true) {
  bytesRead += in.read(data, offset, data.length-offset);
  if (bytesRead == -1 || offset >= data.length) break;
  offset += bytesRead;
}
```

The `DataInputStream` class has two `readFully()` methods that provide this logic. Each reads repeatedly from the underlying input stream until the array `data` or specified portion thereof is filled.

```
public final void readFully(byte[] data) throws IOException
public final void readFully(byte[] data, int offset, int length)
                 throws IOException
```

If the data runs out before the array is filled and no more data is forthcoming, then an `IOException` is thrown.

Reading and Writing Text

Because of the difficulties caused by different character sets, reading and writing text is one of the trickiest things you can do with streams. Most of the time, text should be handled with readers and writers, a subject we'll take up in Chapter 15, *Readers and Writers*. However, the `DataInputStream` and `DataOutputStream` classes do provide methods a Java program can use to read and write text that another Java program will understand. The text format used is a compressed form of Unicode called UTF-8. It's unlikely that other, non-Java programs will understand this format unless they've been specially coded to interoperate with text data written by Java, especially since Java's UTF-8 differs slightly from the standard UTF-8 used in XML and elsewhere.

The UTF-8 Format

Java strings and `chars` are Unicode. However, Unicode isn't particularly efficient. Most files of English text contain almost nothing but ASCII characters. Thus, using two bytes for these characters is really overkill. UTF-8 solves this problem by encoding the ASCII characters in a single byte at the expense of having to use three bytes for many more of the less common characters. For the purposes of this chapter, UTF-8 provides a more efficient way to read and write strings; it is used by the `readUTF()` and `writeUTF()` methods implemented by the `DataInputStream` and `DataOutputStream` classes. For a full description of UTF-8, see Chapter 14, *Multilingual Character Sets and Unicode*.

The variant form of UTF-8 that these classes use is intended for string literals embedded in compiled byte code and serialized Java objects and for communication between two Java programs. It is not intended for reading and writing arbitrary UTF-8 text. To read standard UTF-8, you should use an `InputStreamReader`; to write it, you should use an `OutputStreamWriter`. These classes do not improperly encode the null character and will be discussed in Chapter 15.

Writing Text

The `DataOutputStream` class has four methods that convert text into bytes and write them onto the underlying stream. These are:

```
public final void writeChar(int c) throwsIOException
public final void writeChars(String s) throws IOException
public final void writeBytes(String s) throws IOException
public final void writeUTF(String s) throws IOException
```

The `writeChar()` method writes a single, two-byte Unicode character. This method does not use UTF-8 encoding. It simply writes the two bytes of the character in big-endian order. `writeChars()` writes each character in the `String` argument to the underlying output stream as a two-byte, Unicode character; it also does not use UTF-8 encoding. And the `writeBytes()` method writes the low-order byte of each character in the `String` argument to the underlying output stream. Any information in the high-order byte is lost. In other words, it assumes the string is given in ISO-Latin-1 and contains only characters whose value is between 0 and 255.

The `writeUTF()` method, however, retains the information in the high-order byte as well as the length of the string. First it writes the number of characters in the string onto the underlying output stream as a two-byte unsigned `int` between 0 and 65,535. Next it encodes the string in UTF-8 and writes the bytes of the encoded string to the underlying output stream. This allows a data input stream reading those bytes to completely reconstruct the string. However, strings longer than 65,535 characters are a problem. If you pass a string longer than 65,535 characters to `writeUTF()`, `writeUTF()` throws a `java.io.UTFDataFormat-Exception`, a subclass of `IOException`, and doesn't write any of the data. Although 65,535 characters seems like a large limit, I can imagine reaching it if you're writing a word processor, text editor, or web browser and trying to save your data by writing it out as a single string. If you are writing a program that needs to deal with large blocks of text, you should write your own file format and save routine rather than relying on `writeUTF()`.

Reading Text

The `DataInputStream` class has three methods to read text data. These are:

```
public final char readChar() throws IOException
public final String readUTF() throws IOException
public static final String readUTF(DataInput in) throws IOException
```

The `readChar()` method reads two bytes from the underlying input stream, interprets them as a big-endian Unicode character, and returns that character as a Java `char`. An `IOException` is thrown if the underlying input stream's `read()` method throws an `IOException`. An `EOFException` may be thrown if you're within one byte of the end of the stream and therefore a complete `char` can't be read.

The noargs `readUTF()` method reads and returns a string that was written in Java's pseudo-UTF-8 encoding with a two-byte, unsigned length prefix (in other words, a string written by `writeUTF()` in `DataOutputStream`). An `EOFException` is thrown if the end of the stream is encountered or the stream runs out of data before providing the promised number of characters. A `UTFDataFormat Exception` is thrown if the bytes read do not match the UTF encoding specification; for example, if four bytes in a row begin with the bit sequence 10. An `IOException` is also thrown if the underlying stream throws an `IOException`.

The Deprecated readLine() Method

The `DataInputStream` class also has a widely used but deprecated `readLine()` method:

```
public final String readLine() throws IOException
```

The `readLine()` method reads a single line of text from the underlying input stream and returns it as a string. A line of text is considered to be any number of characters, followed by a carriage return, a linefeed, or a carriage return/linefeed pair. The line terminator (possibly including both a carriage return and a linefeed) is read. However, it is not included in the string returned by `readLine()`. The problem with `readLine()` is that it does not properly handle non-ISO-Latin-1 character sets. In Java 1.1 and later, the `java.io.BufferedReader`'s `readLine()` method is supposed to be used instead. However, much existing code uses `DataInputStream`'s `readLine()` method, and thus it's important to recognize it even if you don't use it yourself.

The Bug in readLine()

There's a nasty bug in the implementation of `readLine()` in most Java VMs, including JDK 1.1 and 1.2. This bug can cause your program to pause or even hang indefinitely. This bug generally doesn't manifest itself when reading from a file, only when you're reading from the network or the console.

The problem is that if `readLine()` sees a carriage return, it waits to see if the next character is a linefeed before returning. If a network client or server on the other end of the connection is only sending carriage returns to end lines, there's a possibility that the remote client or server may wait for a response to the line it's just sent before sending any more data. Most of the time this is a bug, because network protocols like HTTP specify a carriage return/linefeed pair as the end-of-line terminator. However, there are more than a few buggy programs out there that don't adhere to this. What `readLine()` should do (but doesn't) is return as soon as it sees a carriage return *or* a linefeed. Then, if it does see a linefeed and if the previous character was a carriage return, it can ignore the linefeed. Otherwise, it treats the linefeed as a line break.

The undeprecated `readLine()` method in `BufferedReader` has the same problem. Neither should be used for reading from network connections.

Example 7-6 uses `DataInputStream` and `readLine()` to echo what the user types on `System.in` to `System.out`. The program exits on end of stream (Ctrl-D on

Unix or Ctrl-Z on Windows) or when the user types a period on a line by itself. This is a common idiom for character-mode programs that read from System.in.

Example 7-6. The Echo Program

```
import java.io.*;

public class Echo {

  public static void main(String[] args) {

    try {
      DataInputStream din = new DataInputStream(System.in);
      while (true) {
        String theLine = din.readLine();
        if (theLine == null) break;  // end of stream
        if (theLine.equals(".")) break; // . on line by itself
        System.out.println(theLine);
      }
    }
    catch (IOException e) {System.err.println(e);}
  }
}
```

A sample run follows. Notice the deprecation warning when this code is compiled. DataInputStream's readLine() method is one of the most common sources of deprecation warnings in Java 1.1.

```
% javac Echo.java
Note: Echo.java uses a deprecated API.  Recompile with "-deprecation" for
details.
1 warning
% java Echo
This is a test
This is a test
This is another test
This is another test
Hello
Hello
Goodbye Now
Goodbye Now
.
%
```

Although we won't officially take up readers until Chapter 15, it's not very hard to rewrite this program so that it doesn't generate deprecation warnings. All you need to do is replace DataInputStream with BufferedReader chained to an InputStreamReader. Example 7-7 demonstrates.

Example 7-7. The ReaderEcho Program

```
import java.io.*;

public class ReaderEcho {

  public static void main(String[] args) {

    try {
      BufferedReader din = new BufferedReader
        (new InputStreamReader(System.in), 1);
      while (true) {
        String theLine = din.readLine();
        if (theLine == null) break;  // end of stream
        if (theLine.equals(".")) break; // . on line by itself
        System.out.println(theLine);
      }
    }
    catch (IOException e) {System.err.println(e);}
  }
}
```

This only works (and is only needed) for `readLine()`. `BufferedReader` does not have equivalents for the rest of the `DataInputStream` methods like `readFully()`, but more details will wait until Chapter 15.

Miscellaneous Methods

The `DataInputStream` and `DataOutputStream` classes each have one method left to discuss, `skipBytes()` and `size()`, respectively.

Determining the Number of Bytes Written

The `DataOutputStream` class has a protected field called `written` that stores the number of bytes written to the output stream since it was constructed. The value of this field is returned by the public `size()` method:

```
protected int written
public final int size()
```

Every time you invoke `writeInt()`, `writeBytes()`, `writeUTF()`, or some other write method, the `written` field is incremented by the number of bytes written. This might be useful if for some reason you're trying to limit the number of bytes you write. For instance, you may prefer to open a new file when you reach some preset size rather than continuing to write into a very large file.

Skipping Bytes in an Input Stream

The `DataInputStream` class's `skipBytes()` method skips over a specified number of bytes without reading them. Unlike the `skip()` method of `java.io.InputStream` that `DataInputStream` inherits, `skipBytes()` either skips over all the bytes it's asked to skip or it throws an exception:

```
public final int skipBytes(int n) throws IOException
public long skip(long n) throws IOException
```

`skipBytes()` blocks and waits for more data until n bytes have been skipped (successful execution) or an exception is thrown. The method returns the number of bytes skipped, which is always n (because if it's not n, an exception is thrown and nothing is returned). On end of stream, an `EOFException` is thrown. An `IOException` is thrown if the underlying stream throws an `IOException`.

Reading and Writing Little-Endian Numbers

It's likely that at some point in time you'll need to read a file full of little-endian data, especially if you're working on Intel hardware or with data written by native code on such a platform. Java has essentially no support for little-endian numbers. The `LittleEndianOutputStream` class in Example 7-8 and the `LittleEndian InputStream` class in Example 7-9 provide the support you need to do this. These classes are closely modeled on the `java.io.DataInputStream` and `java.io.DataOutputStream` classes. Some of the methods in these classes do exactly the same thing as the same methods in the `DataInputStream` and `DataOutput Stream` classes. After all, a big-endian byte is no different from a little-endian byte. In fact, these two classes come very close to implementing the `java.io.Data Input` and `java.io.DataOutput` interfaces. Actually doing so would have been a bad idea, however, because client programmers will expect objects implementing `DataInput` and `DataOutput` to use big-endian numbers, and it's best not to go against such common assumptions.

I also considered making the little-endian classes subclasses of `DataInputStream` and `DataOutputStream`. While this would have eliminated some duplicated methods like `readBoolean()` and `writeBoolean()`, it would also have required the new, little-endian methods to have unwieldy names like `readLittle EndianInt()` and `writeLittleEndianInt()`. Furthermore, it's unlikely you'll need to read or write both little-endian and big-endian numbers from the same stream. Most streams will contain one or the other but not both.

Example 7-8. A LittleEndianOutputStream Class

```java
/*
 * @(#)LittleEndianOutputStream.java  1.0 98/08/29
 */

package com.macfaq.io;
import java.io.*;

/**
 * A little-endian output stream writes primitive Java numbers
 * and characters to an output stream in a little-endian format.
 * The standard java.io.DataOutputStream class which this class
 * imitates uses big-endian integers.
 *
 * @author  Elliotte Rusty Harold
 * @version 1.0, 29 Aug 1998
 * @see     com.macfaq.io.LittleEndianInputStream
 * @see     java.io.DataOutputStream
 */
public class LittleEndianOutputStream extends FilterOutputStream {

  /**
   * The number of bytes written so far to the little-endian output stream.
   */
  protected int written;

  /**
   * Creates a new little-endian output stream and chains it to the
   * output stream specified by the out argument.
   *
   * @param   out   the underlying output stream.
   * @see     java.io.FilterOutputStream#out
   */
  public LittleEndianOutputStream(OutputStream out) {
    super(out);
  }

  /**
   * Writes the specified byte value to the underlying output stream.
   *
   * @param      b   the <code>byte</code> value to be written.
   * @exception  IOException  if the underlying stream throws an IOException.
   */
  public synchronized void write(int b) throws IOException {
    out.write(b);
    written++;
```

Example 7-8. A LittleEndianOutputStream Class (continued)

```
}

/**
 * Writes <code>length</code> bytes from the specified byte array
 * starting at <code>offset</code> to the underlying output stream.
 *
 * @param      data      the data.
 * @param      offset    the start offset in the data.
 * @param      length    the number of bytes to write.
 * @exception  IOException  if the underlying stream throws an IOException.
 */
public synchronized void write(byte[] data, int offset, int length)
 throws IOException {
  out.write(data, offset, length);
  written += length;
}

/**
 * Writes a <code>boolean</code> to the underlying output stream as
 * a single byte. If the argument is true, the byte value 1 is written.
 * If the argument is false, the byte value <code>0</code> is written.
 *
 * @param      b    the <code>boolean</code> value to be written.
 * @exception  IOException  if the underlying stream throws an IOException.
 */
public void writeBoolean(boolean b) throws IOException {

  if (b) this.write(1);
  else this.write(0);
}

/**
 * Writes out a <code>byte</code> to the underlying output stream
 *
 * @param      b    the <code>byte</code> value to be written.
 * @exception  IOException  if the underlying stream throws an IOException.
 */
public void writeByte(int b) throws IOException {
  out.write(b);
  written++;
}

/**
 * Writes a two byte <code>short</code> to the underlying output stream in
 * little-endian order, low byte first.
 *
 * @param      s    the <code>short</code> to be written.
 * @exception  IOException  if the underlying stream throws an IOException.
```

Example 7-8. A LittleEndianOutputStream Class (continued)

```java
  */
 public void writeShort(int s) throws IOException {

   out.write(s & 0xFF);
   out.write((s >>> 8) & 0xFF);
   written += 2;
 }


 /**
  * Writes a two byte <code>char</code> to the underlying output stream
  * in little-endian order, low byte first.
  *
  * @param       c   the <code>char</code> value to be written.
  * @exception   IOException  if the underlying stream throws an IOException.
  */
 public void writeChar(int c) throws IOException {

   out.write(c & 0xFF);
   out.write((c >>> 8) & 0xFF);
   written += 2;
 }


 /**
  * Writes a four-byte <code>int</code> to the underlying output stream
  * in little-endian order, low byte first, high byte last
  *
  * @param       i   the <code>int</code> to be written.
  * @exception   IOException  if the underlying stream throws an IOException.
  */
 public void writeInt(int i) throws IOException {

   out.write(i & 0xFF);
   out.write((i >>> 8) & 0xFF);
   out.write((i >>> 16) & 0xFF);
   out.write((i >>> 24) & 0xFF);
   written += 4;
 }


 /**
  * Writes an eight-byte <code>long</code> to the underlying output stream
  * in little-endian order, low byte first, high byte last
  *
  * @param       l   the <code>long</code> to be written.
  * @exception   IOException  if the underlying stream throws an IOException.
  */
 public void writeLong(long l) throws IOException {
```

Example 7-8. A LittleEndianOutputStream Class (continued)

```
    out.write((int) l & 0xFF);
    out.write((int) (l >>> 8) & 0xFF);
    out.write((int) (l >>> 16) & 0xFF);
    out.write((int) (l >>> 24) & 0xFF);
    out.write((int) (l >>> 32) & 0xFF);
    out.write((int) (l >>> 40) & 0xFF);
    out.write((int) (l >>> 48) & 0xFF);
    out.write((int) (l >>> 56) & 0xFF);
    written += 8;
  }


  /**
   * Writes a 4 byte Java float to the underlying output stream in
   * little-endian order.
   *
   * @param      f   the <code>float</code> value to be written.
   * @exception  IOException  if an I/O error occurs.
   */
  public final void writeFloat(float f) throws IOException {

    this.writeInt(Float.floatToIntBits(f));
  }


  /**
   * Writes an 8 byte Java double to the underlying output stream in
   * little-endian order.
   *
   * @param      d   the <code>double</code> value to be written.
   * @exception  IOException  if an I/O error occurs.
   */
  public final void writeDouble(double d) throws IOException {

    this.writeLong(Double.doubleToLongBits(d));
  }


  /**
   * Writes a string to the underlying output stream as a sequence of
   * bytes. Each character is written to the data output stream as
   * if by the <code>writeByte()</code> method.
   *
   * @param      s   the <code>String</code> value to be written.
   * @exception  IOException  if the underlying stream throws an IOException.
   * @see        java.io.LittleEndianOutputStream#writeByte(int)
   * @see        java.io.LittleEndianOutputStream#out
   */
  public void writeBytes(String s) throws IOException {

  int length = s.length();
```

Example 7-8. A LittleEndianOutputStream Class (continued)

```java
    for (int i = 0; i < length; i++) {
      out.write((byte) s.charAt(i));
    }
    written += length;
  }


  /**
   * Writes a string to the underlying output stream as a sequence of
   * characters. Each character is written to the data output stream as
   * if by the <code>writeChar</code> method.
   *
   * @param      s  a <code>String</code> value to be written.
   * @exception  IOException  if the underlying stream throws an IOException.
   * @see        java.io.LittleEndianOutputStream#writeChar(int)
   * @see        java.io.LittleEndianOutputStream#out
   */
  public void writeChars(String s) throws IOException {

    int length = s.length();
    for (int i = 0; i < length; i++) {
      int c = s.charAt(i);
      out.write(c & 0xFF);
      out.write((c >>> 8) & 0xFF);
    }
    written += length * 2;
  }


  /**
   * Writes a string of no more than 65,535 characters
   * to the underlying output stream using little-endian UTF-8
   * encoding. This method first writes a two byte short
   * in little-endian order as if by the
   * <code>writeShort()</code> method. This gives the number of bytes in the
   * UTF-8 encoded version of the string, not the number of characters
   * in the string. Next each character of the string is written
   * using the little-endian UTF-8 encoding for the character.
   *
   * @param      s  the string to be written.
   * @exception  UTFDataFormatException if the string is longer than
   *             65,535 characters.
   * @exception  IOException  if the underlying stream throws an IOException.
   */
  public void writeUTF(String s) throws IOException {

    int strlen = s.length();
    int utflen = 0;

    for (int i = 0 ; i < strlen ; i++) {
```

Example 7-8. A LittleEndianOutputStream Class (continued)

```
        int c = s.charAt(i);
        if ((c >= 0x0001) && (c <= 0x007F)) utflen++;
        else if (c > 0x07FF) utflen += 3;
        else utflen += 2;
    }

    if (utflen > 65535) throw new UTFDataFormatException();

    out.write(utflen & 0xFF);
    out.write((utflen >>> 8) & 0xFF);
    for (int i = 0 ; i < strlen ; i++) {
      int c = s.charAt(i);
      if ((c >= 0x0001) && (c <= 0x007F)) {
        out.write(c);
      }
      else if (c > 0x07FF) {
        out.write(0x80 | (c & 0x3F));
        out.write(0x80 | ((c >>  6) & 0x3F));
        out.write(0xE0 | ((c >> 12) & 0x0F));
        written += 2;
      }
      else {
        out.write(0x80 | (c & 0x3F));
        out.write(0xC0 | ((c >>  6) & 0x1F));
        written += 1;
      }
    }
  written += strlen + 2;
}


/**
 * Returns the number of bytes written to this little-endian output stream.
 * (This class is not thread-safe with respect to this method. It is
 * possible that this number is temporarily less than the actual
 * number of bytes written.)
 * @return  the value of the <code>written</code> field.
 * @see     java.io.LittleEndianOutputStream#written
 */
public int size() {
  return this.written;
}
}
```

Notice how all writing is done by passing byte values to the underlying output stream out (set in the constructor and inherited from the superclass, FilterOutputStream). The primary purpose of these methods is to convert the Java data type to bytes and then write them in a little-endian order. In general, the conversions are accomplished by shifting the bits of interest into the low-order eight bits, then masking off the bits of interest. For example, consider the `writeInt()` method:

```
public void writeInt(int i) throws IOException {

  out.write(i & 0xFF);
  out.write((i >>> 8) & 0xFF);
  out.write((i >>> 16) & 0xFF);
  out.write((i >>> 24) & 0xFF);
  written += 4;
}
```

A Java `int` is composed of four bytes in big-endian order. Thus, the low-order byte is in the last eight bits. This byte needs to be written first in a little-endian scheme. The mask `0xFF` has one bit in the low-order eight bits and zero bits everywhere else. By bitwise ANDing `0xFF` with `i`, we select the low-order eight bits of `i`. The second-lowest-order byte—that is, bits 16 to 23—is selected by first shifting the bits right without sign extension into the low-order bits. That's the purpose of (`i >>> 8`). Then this byte can be retrieved with the same `0xFF` mask used before. The same is done for the second-to-lowest-order byte and the highest-order byte. Here, however, it's necessary to shift by 16 and 24 bits, respectively.

`floats` and `doubles` are converted to `ints` and `longs` using `Float.float ToIntBits()` and `Double.longBitsToDouble()`, then invoking `writeInt()` or `writeLong()` to write those bits in little-endian order.

Each method increments the protected field `written` by the number of bytes actually written. This tracks the total number of bytes written onto the output stream at any one time. This incurs a surprising amount of overhead. If this class did not track the number of bytes written, it could be several methods shorter. Furthermore, there is a potential synchronization problem, which happens to be shared by `DataOutputStream`. It is possible for one thread to interrupt a method like `writeInt()` after it has written some data but before the `written` field has been updated. It would be simple to fix this problem by declaring all methods that update `written` as `synchronized`. However, that would be a huge performance hit, so I've elected to follow the example of `DataOutputStream` and not synchronize these methods.

Example 7-9 is the corresponding `LittleEndianInputStream` class, based on the `DataInputStream` class.

Example 7-9. The LittleEndianInputStream Class

```
/*
 * @(#)LittleEndianInputStream.java  1.0 98/08/29
 */

package com.macfaq.io;
```

Example 7-9. The LittleEndianInputStream Class (continued)

```java
import java.io.*;

/**
 * A little-endian input stream reads two's complement,
 * little-endian integers, floating-point numbers, and characters
 * and returns them as Java primitive types.
 * The standard java.io.DataInputStream class
 * which this class imitates reads big-endian quantities.
 *
 * @author  Elliotte Rusty Harold
 * @version 1.0, 28 Aug 1998
 * @see     com.macfaq.io.LittleEndianOutputStream
 * @see     java.io.DataInputStream
 */
public class LittleEndianInputStream extends FilterInputStream {

  /**
   * Creates a new little-endian input stream and chains it to the
   * input stream specified by the in argument.
   *
   * @param  in   the underlying input stream.
   * @see     java.io.FilterInputStream#out
   */
  public LittleEndianInputStream(InputStream in) {
    super(in);
  }


  /**
   * Reads a <code>boolean</code> from the underlying input stream by
   * reading a single byte. If the byte is zero, false is returned.
   * If the byte is positive, true is returned.
   *
   * @return      b   the <code>boolean</code> value read.
   * @exception  EOFException  if the end of the underlying input stream
   *                has been reached
   * @exception  IOException  if the underlying stream throws an IOException.
   */
  public boolean readBoolean() throws IOException {

    int bool = in.read();
    if (bool == -1) throw new EOFException();
    return (bool != 0);
  }


  /**
   * Reads a signed <code>byte</code> from the underlying input stream
   * with value between -128 and 127.
   *
```

Example 7-9. The LittleEndianInputStream Class (continued)

```
 * @return      the <code>byte</code> value read.
 * @exception  EOFException  if the end of the underlying input stream
 *               has been reached
 * @exception  IOException  if the underlying stream throws an IOException.
 */
public byte readByte(int b) throws IOException {

  int temp = in.read();
  if (temp == -1) throw new EOFException();
  return (byte) temp;
}


/**
 * Reads an unsigned <code>byte</code> from the underlying
 * input stream with value between 0 and 255.
 *
 * @return      the <code>byte</code> value read.
 * @exception  EOFException  if the end of the underlying input
 *               stream has been reached
 * @exception  IOException  if the underlying stream throws an IOException.
 */
public int readUnsignedByte() throws IOException {

  int temp = in.read();
  if (temp == -1) throw new EOFException();
  return temp;
}

/**
 * Reads a two byte signed <code>short</code> from the underlying
 * input stream in little-endian order, low byte first.
 *
 * @return      the <code>short</code> read.
 * @exception  EOFException  if the end of the underlying input stream
 *               has been reached
 * @exception  IOException  if the underlying stream throws an IOException.
 */
public short readShort() throws IOException {

  int byte1 = in.read();
  int byte2 = in.read();
  // may only need to test last byte read, here and similar elsewhere
  // if byte1 is -1 so is byte2
  if (byte2 == -1  || byte2 == -1) throw new EOFException();
  return (short) ((byte2 << 8) + byte1);
}

/**
```

Example 7-9. The LittleEndianInputStream Class (continued)

```
 * Reads a two byte unsigned <code>short</code> from the underlying
 * input stream in little-endian order, low byte first.
 *
 * @return      the int value of the unsigned short read.
 * @exception   EOFException  if the end of the underlying input stream
 *                    has been reached
 * @exception   IOException  if the underlying stream throws an IOException.
 */
public int readUnsignedShort() throws IOException {

  int byte1 = in.read();
  int byte2 = in.read();
  if (byte2 == -1  || byte2 == -1) throw new EOFException();
  return (byte2 << 8) + byte1;
}


/**
 * Reads a two byte Unicode <code>char</code> from the underlying
 * input stream in little-endian order, low byte first.
 *
 * @return      the int value of the unsigned short read.
 * @exception   EOFException  if the end of the underlying input stream
 *                    has been reached
 * @exception   IOException  if the underlying stream throws an IOException.
 */
public char readChar() throws IOException {

  int byte1 = in.read();
  int byte2 = in.read();
  if (byte1 == -1  || byte2 == -1) throw new EOFException();
  return (char) ((byte2 << 8) + byte1);
}


/**
 * Reads a four byte signed <code>int</code> from the underlying
 * input stream in little-endian order, low byte first.
 *
 * @return      the <code>int</code> read.
 * @exception   EOFException  if the end of the underlying input stream
 *                     has been reached
 * @exception   IOException  if the underlying stream throws an IOException.
 */
public int readInt() throws IOException {

  int byte1, byte2, byte3, byte4;

  synchronized (this) {
    byte1 = in.read();
```

Example 7-9. The LittleEndianInputStream Class (continued)

```
    byte2 = in.read();
    byte3 = in.read();
    byte4 = in.read();
  }
  if (byte4 == -1  || byte3 == -1 || byte2 == -1 || byte1 == -1) {
    throw new EOFException();
  }
  return (byte4 << 24) + (byte3 << 16) + (byte2 << 8) + byte1;
}


/**
 * Reads an eight byte signed <code>int</code> from the underlying
 * input stream in little-endian order, low byte first.
 *
 * @return      the <code>int</code> read.
 * @exception  EOFException  if the end of the underlying input stream
 *                has been reached
 * @exception  IOException  if the underlying stream throws an IOException.
 */
public long readLong() throws IOException {

  long byte1 = in.read();
  long byte2 = in.read();
  long byte3 = in.read();
  long byte4 = in.read();
  long byte5 = in.read();
  long byte6 = in.read();
  long byte7 = in.read();
  long byte8 = in.read();
  if (byte4 == -1  || byte3 == -1 || byte2 == -1 || byte1 == -1 ||
    byte8 == -1  || byte7 == -1 || byte6 == -1 || byte5 == -1) {
    throw new EOFException();
  }
  return (byte8 << 56) + (byte7 << 48) + (byte6 << 40) + (byte5 << 32) +
    (byte4 << 24) + (byte3 << 16) + (byte2 << 8) + byte1;
}


/**
 * Reads a string of no more than 65,535 characters
 * from the underlying input stream using little endian UTF-8
 * encoding. This method first reads a two byte short
 * in little-endian order as if by the
 * <code>readShort()</code> method. This gives the number of bytes in
 * the UTF-8 encoded version of the string.
 * Next this many bytes are read and decoded as little-endian UTF-8
 * encoded characters.
 *
 * @return      the decoded string
```

Example 7-9. The LittleEndianInputStream Class (continued)

```
 * @exception  UTFDataFormatException if the string cannot be decoded
 * @exception  IOException  if the underlying stream throws an IOException.
 */
public String readUTF() throws IOException {

  int numbytes = readUnsignedShort();
  char result[] = new char[numbytes];
  int numread = 0;
  int numchars = 0;

  while (numread < numbytes) {

    int c1 = readUnsignedByte();
    int c2, c3;

    // Look at the first four bits of c1 to determine how many
    // bytes in this char.
    int test = c1 >> 4;
    if (test < 8) {  // one byte
      numread++;
      result[numchars++] = (char) c1;
    }
    else if (test == 12 || test == 13) { // two bytes
      numread += 2;
      if (numread > numbytes) throw new UTFDataFormatException();
      c2 = readUnsignedByte();
      if ((c2 & 0xC0) != 0x80) throw new UTFDataFormatException();
      result[numchars++] = (char) (((c1 & 0x1F) << 6) | (c2 & 0x3F));
    }
    else if (test == 14) { // three bytes
      numread += 3;
      if (numread > numbytes) throw new UTFDataFormatException();
      c2 = readUnsignedByte();
      c3 = readUnsignedByte();
      if (((c2 & 0xC0) != 0x80) || ((c3 & 0xC0) != 0x80)) {
        throw new UTFDataFormatException();
      }
      result[numchars++] = (char)
        (((c1 & 0x0F) << 12) | ((c2 & 0x3F) << 6) | (c3 & 0x3F));
    }
    else { // malformed
      throw new UTFDataFormatException();
    }
  }  // end while
  return new String(result, 0, numchars);
}
/**
 *
```

Example 7-9. The LittleEndianInputStream Class (continued)

```
 * @return       the next eight bytes of this input stream, interpreted as a
 *               little-endian <code>double</code>.
 * @exception  EOFException if end of stream occurs before eight bytes
 *               have been read.
 * @exception  IOException   if an I/O error occurs.
 */
public final double readDouble() throws IOException {

  return Double.longBitsToDouble(this.readLong());
}

/**
 *
 * @return       the next four bytes of this input stream, interpreted as a
 *               little-endian <code>int</code>.
 * @exception  EOFException if end of stream occurs before four bytes
 *               have been read.
 * @exception  IOException  if an I/O error occurs.
 */
public final float readFloat() throws IOException {

  return Float.intBitsToFloat(this.readInt());
}

/**
 * Skip exactly <code>n</code> bytes of input in the underlying
 * input stream. This method blocks until all the bytes are skipped,
 * the end of the stream is detected, or an exception is thrown.
 *
 * @param       n   the number of bytes to skip.
 * @return       the number of bytes skipped, generally n
 * @exception  EOFException  if this input stream reaches the end before
 *               skipping all the bytes.
 * @exception  IOException  if the underlying stream throws an IOException.
 */
public final int skipBytes(int n) throws IOException {

  for (int i = 0; i < n; i += (int) skip(n - i));
  return n;
 }
}
```

This class will be used in the last section to view files containing little-endian numbers.

Thread Safety

The `LittleEndianInputStream` class is not perfectly thread-safe. Consider the `readInt()` method:

```
public int readInt() throws IOException {

  int byte1 = in.read();
  int byte2 = in.read();
  int byte3 = in.read();
  int byte4 = in.read();
  if (byte4 == -1  || byte3 == -1 || byte2 == -1 || byte1 == -1) {
    throw new EOFException();
  }
  return (byte4 << 24) + (byte3 << 16) + (byte2 << 8) + byte1;
}
```

If two threads are trying to read from this input stream at the same time, there is no guarantee that bytes 1 through 4 will be read in order. The first thread might read bytes 1 and 2, then the second thread could preempt it and read any number of bytes. When the first thread regained control, it would no longer be able to read bytes 3 and 4, but would read whichever bytes happened to be next in line. It would then return an erroneous result.

A synchronized block would solve this problem neatly:

```
public int readInt() throws IOException {

  int byte1, byte2, byte3, byte4;

  synchronized (this) {
    byte1 = in.read();
    byte2 = in.read();
    byte3 = in.read();
    byte4 = in.read();
  }
  if (byte4 == -1  || byte3 == -1 || byte2 == -1 || byte1 == -1) {
    throw new EOFException();
  }
  return (byte4 << 24) + (byte3 << 16) + (byte2 << 8) + byte1;
}
```

It isn't necessary to synchronize the entire method, only the four lines that read from the underlying stream. However, this solution is still imperfect. It is remotely possible that another thread has a reference to the underlying stream rather than the little-endian input stream and will try to read directly from that. Therefore, you might be better off synchronizing on the underlying input stream `in`:

```
    synchronized (in) {
      byte1 = in.read();
      byte2 = in.read();
      byte3 = in.read();
      byte4 = in.read();
    }
```

`LittleEndianOutputStream` has equally severe problems. I've already noted the problem with keeping the `written` field up to date. Now consider this in the `writeInt()` method:

```
  public void writeInt(int i) throws IOException {

    out.write(i & 0xFF);
    out.write((i >>> 8) & 0xFF);
    out.write((i >>> 16) & 0xFF);
    // What happens if another thread preempts here?
    out.write((i >>> 24) & 0xFF);
    written += 4;
  }
```

Suppose a second thread preempts the running thread where indicated in the previous code and writes unrelated data onto the output stream. The entire stream can be corrupted, because the bytes of the int are separated. The same synchronization tricks work here as well. However, all the problems I've noted here are shared by `DataInputStream` and `DataOutputStream`. Similar problems crop up in other filter stream classes. This leads to the following general principle for thread-safe programming:

Never allow two threads to share a stream.

The principle is most obvious for filter streams, but it applies to regular streams as well. Although writing or reading a single byte can be treated as an atomic operation, many programs will not be happy to read and write individual bytes. They'll want to read or write a particular group of bytes and will not react well to being interrupted.

File Viewer, Part 3

In Chapter 4, *File Streams*, I introduced a `FileDumper` program that could print the raw bytes of a file in ASCII, hexadecimal, or decimal. In this chapter, I'm going to expand that program so that it can interpret the file as containing binary numbers of varying widths. In particular I'm going to make it possible to dump a file as `shorts`, unsigned `shorts`, `ints`, `longs`, `floats`, and `doubles`. Integer types may be either big-endian or little-endian. The main class, `FileDumper3`, is shown in Example 7-10. As in Chapter 4, this program reads a series of filenames and arguments from the command line in the `main()` method. Each filename is passed to a method that opens a file input stream from the file. Depending on the command-line arguments, a particular subclass of DumpFilter from Chapter 4 is selected and chained to the input stream. Finally, the StreamCopier.copy() method pours data from the input stream onto System.out.

Example 7-10. The FileDumper3 Class

```
import java.io.*;
import com.macfaq.io.*;

public class FileDumper3 {

  public static final int ASC = 0;
  public static final int DEC = 1;
  public static final int HEX = 2;
  public static final int SHORT = 3;
  public static final int INT = 4;
  public static final int LONG = 5;
  public static final int FLOAT = 6;
  public static final int DOUBLE = 7;

  public static void main(String[] args) {

    if (args.length < 1) {
      System.err.println(
        "Usage: java FileDumper2 [-ahdsilfx] [-little] file1 file2...");
    }

    boolean bigEndian = true;
    int firstFile = 0;
    int mode = ASC;

    // Process command-line switches.
    for (firstFile = 0; firstFile < args.length; firstFile++) {
      if (!args[firstFile].startsWith("-")) break;
      if (args[firstFile].equals("-h")) mode = HEX;
      else if (args[firstFile].equals("-d")) mode = DEC;
      else if (args[firstFile].equals("-s")) mode = SHORT;
      else if (args[firstFile].equals("-i")) mode = INT;
      else if (args[firstFile].equals("-l")) mode = LONG;
      else if (args[firstFile].equals("-f")) mode = FLOAT;
      else if (args[firstFile].equals("-x")) mode = DOUBLE;
      else if (args[firstFile].equals("-little")) bigEndian = false;
    }

    for (int i = firstFile; i < args.length; i++) {
      try {
        InputStream in = new FileInputStream(args[i]);
        dump(in, System.out, mode, bigEndian);
```

Example 7-10. The FileDumper3 Class (continued)

```java
      if (i < args.length-1) {  // more files to dump
        System.out.println();
        System.out.println("-------------------------------------");
        System.out.println();
      }
    }
    catch (Exception e) {
      System.err.println(e);
      e.printStackTrace();
    }
  }
}


public static void dump(InputStream in, OutputStream out, int mode,
                        boolean bigEndian)
 throws IOException {

  // The reference variable in may point to several different objects
  // within the space of the next few lines. We can attach
  // more filters here to do decompression, decryption, and more.

  if (bigEndian) {
    DataInputStream din = new DataInputStream(in);
    switch (mode) {
      case HEX:
        in = new HexFilter(in);
        break;
      case DEC:
        in = new DecimalFilter(in);
        break;
      case INT:
        in = new IntFilter(din);
        break;
      case SHORT:
        in = new ShortFilter(din);
        break;
      case LONG:
        in = new LongFilter(din);
        break;
      case DOUBLE:
        in = new DoubleFilter(din);
        break;
      case FLOAT:
        in = new FloatFilter(din);
        break;
      default:
    }
  }
```

Example 7-10. The FileDumper3 Class (continued)

```
    else {
      LittleEndianInputStream lin = new LittleEndianInputStream(in);
      switch (mode) {
        case HEX:
          in = new HexFilter(in);
          break;
        case DEC:
          in = new DecimalFilter(in);
          break;
        case INT:
          in = new LEIntFilter(lin);
          break;
        case SHORT:
          in = new LEShortFilter(lin);
          break;
        case LONG:
          in = new LELongFilter(lin);
          break;
        case DOUBLE:
          in = new LEDoubleFilter(lin);
          break;
        case FLOAT:
          in = new LEFloatFilter(lin);
          break;
        default:
      }
    }

    StreamCopier.copy(in, out);
    in.close();
  }
}
```

The `main()` method of this class reads the command-line arguments and uses the switches to determine the format of the input data. The `dump()` method reads the mode and the endianness, selects the appropriate filter, then copies the input onto the output. Table 7-2 shows the command-line switches. Eight of these switches select a particular format. One, -little, is used to determine the endianness of the data. Since there's no difference between big-endian and little-endian ASCII, decimal, and hexadecimal dumps, there are a total of 12 different filters used here. Two, the `HexFilter` and the `DecimalFilter`, were introduced in the last chapter. They haven't changed.

Table 7-2. Command-Line Switches for FileDumper3

Switch	Format
-a	ASCII
-d	decimal dump
-h	hexadecimal
-s	short
-i	int
-l	long
-f	float
-x	double
-little	little-endian

I've introduced ten new filters for big- and little-endian `shorts`, `ints`, `longs`, `floats`, and `doubles`. The big-endian filters read data from a data input stream. The little-endian filters read data from a little-endian input stream. To take advantage of code reuse, the big-endian filters are all subclasses of a new abstract subclass of `DumpFilter` called `DataFilter`, shown in Example 7-11. The little-endian filters are all subclasses of a new abstract subclass of `DumpFilter` called `LEFilter`, shown in Example 7-12. The hierarchy of these filters is shown in Figure 7-1.

Example 7-11. DataFilter

```
package com.macfaq.io;

import java.io.*;

public abstract class DataFilter extends DumpFilter {

  // The use of DataInputStream here is a little forced.
  // It would be more natural (though more complicated)
  // to read the bytes and manually convert them to an int.
  DataInputStream din;

  public DataFilter(DataInputStream din) {
    super(din);
    this.din = din;
  }

  public int available() throws IOException {
    return (buf.length - index) + in.available();
  }
}
```

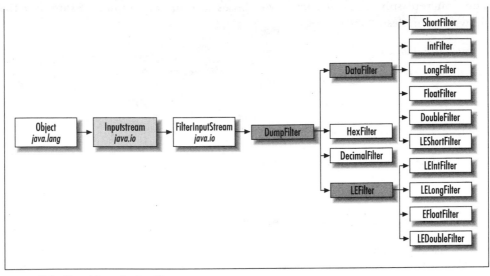

Figure 7-1. Class hierarchy for filters

DataFilter makes sure that a data input stream is available to subclasses to read from. It also has enough information to provide a reasonable available() method. The actual implementation of the fill() method is left to specific subclasses like IntFilter. LEFilter, given in Example 7-12, is identical except for its use of a LittleEndianInputStream in place of a DataInputStream.

Example 7-12. LEFilter

```
package com.macfaq.io;

import java.io.*;

public abstract class LEFilter extends DumpFilter {

  // The use of LittleEndianInputStream here is a little forced.
  // It would be more natural (though more complicated)
  // to read the bytes and manually convert them to an int.
  LittleEndianInputStream lin;

  public LEFilter(LittleEndianInputStream lin) {
    super(lin);
    this.lin = lin;
  }

  public int available() throws IOException {
    return (buf.length - index) + lin.available();
  }
}
```

The concrete subclasses of these two classes are all very similar. Example 7-13 shows the simplest, IntFilter.

Example 7-13. IntFilter

```
package com.macfaq.io;

import java.io.*;

public class IntFilter extends DataFilter {

  public IntFilter(DataInputStream din) {
    super(din);
  }

  protected void fill() throws IOException {

    int number = din.readInt();
    String s = Integer.toString(number)
     + System.getProperty("line.separator", "\r\n");
    byte[] b = s.getBytes("8859_1");
    buf = new int[b.length];
    for (int i = 0; i < b.length; i++) {
      buf[i] = b[i];
    }
  }
}
```

The fill() method reads an integer from the underlying DataInputStream din. That integer is converted to a string using the static Integer.toString() method. The string is then converted to bytes using the ISO 8859-1 (Latin-1) encoding. Encodings will be discussed in more detail in Chapters 14 and 15. For now, all you need to know is that for the characters that appear in a number, Latin-1 is identical to ASCII.

The remaining DataFilter subclasses are very similar. For example, Example 7-14 shows the ShortFilter. Aside from the trivial difference in the class and constructor name, the only real difference is the use of readShort() instead of readInt() in the first line of the fill() method.

Example 7-14. ShortFilter

```
package com.macfaq.io;

import java.io.*;

public class ShortFilter extends DataFilter {

  public ShortFilter(DataInputStream din) {
```

Example 7-14. ShortFilter (continued)

```
    super(din);
  }

  protected void fill() throws IOException {

    int number = din.readShort();
    String s = Integer.toString(number)
     + System.getProperty("line.separator", "\r\n");
    byte[] b = s.getBytes("8859_1");
    buf = new int[b.length];
    for (int i = 0; i < b.length; i++) {
      buf[i] = b[i];
    }
  }
}
```

The `LongFilter`, `FloatFilter`, and `DoubleFilter` are only slightly different, and I haven't put the source code in the book; it's available with the rest of the examples online. Likewise, I've omitted the similar set of filters for little-endian data. The little-endian filters all extend `LEFilter`; they are `LEIntFilter`, `LEShortFilter`, `LELongFilter`, `LEFloatFilter`, and `LEDoubleFilter`.

In later chapters, I'll add support for compressed and encrypted files, a graphical user interface, and various text interpretations of the data in the file. However, none of that will require any changes to any of the filters we've developed here.

8

In this chapter:
- *Sequence Input Streams*
- *Byte Array Streams*
- *Communicating Between Threads with Piped Streams*

Streams in Memory

In the last several chapters, you've learned how to use streams to move data between a running Java program and external programs and stores. Streams can also be used to move data from one part of a Java program to another. This chapter explores three such methods. Sequence input streams chain several input streams together so that they appear as a single stream. Byte array streams allow output to be stored in byte arrays and input to be read from byte arrays. Finally, piped input and output streams allow output from one thread to become input for another thread.

Sequence Input Streams

The `java.io.SequenceInputStream` class connects multiple input streams together in a particular order:

```
public class SequenceInputStream extends InputStream
```

Reads from a `SequenceInputStream` first read all the bytes from the first stream in the sequence, then all the bytes from the second stream in the sequence, then all the bytes from the third stream, and so on. When the end of one of the streams is reached, that stream is closed; the next data comes from the next stream. Of course, this assumes that the streams in the sequence are in fact finite. There are two constructors for this class:

```
public SequenceInputStream(Enumeration e)
public SequenceInputStream(InputStream in1, InputStream in2)
```

The first constructor creates a sequence out of all the elements of the `Enumeration e`. This assumes all objects in the enumeration are input streams. If this isn't the case, a `ClassCastException` will be thrown the first time a read is attempted from an object that is not an `InputStream`. The second constructor

144

creates a sequence input stream that reads first from `in1`, then from `in2`. Note that `in1` or `in2` may themselves be sequence input streams, so repeated application of this constructor allows a sequence input stream with an indefinite number of underlying streams to be created. For example, to read the home pages of both JavaSoft and AltaVista, you might do this:

```
try {
  URL u1 = new URL("http://java.sun.com/");
  URL u2 = new URL("http://www.altavista.com");
  SequenceInputStream sin = new SequenceInputStream(u1.openStream(),
    u2.openStream());
}
catch (IOException e) { //...
```

Example 8-1 reads a series of filenames from the command line, creates a sequence input stream from file input streams for each file named, then copies the contents of all the files onto `System.out`. The `SequenceInputStream` class already provides the necessary layer of abstraction for this problem. There's nothing to be gained by constructing a new object that chains streams together and prints them. Therefore, this class only has a `main()` method that builds a sequence input stream from files named on the command line. This stream is passed into the `StreamCopier` from Chapter 4, *File Streams*, which does the actual copying.

Example 8-1. The SequencePrinter Program

```
import java.io.*;
import java.util.*;
import com.macfaq.io.*;

public class SequencePrinter {

  public static void main(String[] args) {

    Vector theStreams = new Vector();

    for (int i = 0; i < args.length; i++) {
       try {
         FileInputStream fin = new FileInputStream(args[i]);
         theStreams.addElement(fin);
       }
       catch (IOException e) { System.err.println(e); }
    }

    SequenceInputStream sin = new SequenceInputStream(theStreams.elements());
    try {
      StreamCopier.copy(sin, System.out);
    }
```

Example 8-1. The SequencePrinter Program (continued)

```
    catch (IOException e) { System.err.println(e); }
  }
}
```

Byte Array Streams

It's sometimes convenient to use stream methods to manipulate data in byte arrays. For example, you might receive an array of raw bytes that you want to interpret as double-precision, floating-point numbers. (This is common when using UDP to transfer data across the Internet, for one example.) The quickest way to do this is to use a `DataInputStream`. However, before you can create a data input stream, you first need to create a raw, byte-oriented stream. This is what the `java.io.ByteArrayInputStream` class gives you. Similarly, you might want to send a group of double-precision, floating-point numbers across the network with UDP. Before you can do this, you have to convert the numbers into bytes. The simplest solution is to use a data output stream chained to a `java.io.ByteArrayOutputStream`. By chaining the data output stream to a byte array output stream, you can write the binary form of the floating-point numbers into a byte array, then send the entire array in a single packet.

UDP

Byte array input and output streams are commonly used when sending and receiving UDP data over the Internet. Unlike the more common TCP data, which acts like the streams I discuss in this book, UDP data arrives in raw packets of bytes, which do not necessarily have any relation to the previous packet or the next packet. Each packet is just a group of bytes to be processed in isolation from other packets. Thus, you may get nothing for several seconds, or even minutes, and then suddenly have a few hundred numbers to deal with.

In Java, UDP data is sent and received via the `java.net.DatagramSocket` and `java.net.DatagramPacket` classes. The `receive()` method of the `DatagramSocket` class returns its data in a `DatagramPacket`, which is little more than a wrapper around a byte array. This byte array can be easily used as the source of a `ByteArrayInputStream`. UDP is discussed in more detail in Chapter 9 of my book *Java Network Programming* (O'Reilly & Associates, 1997).

Byte Array Input Streams

Th `ByteArrayInputStream` class reads data from a byte array using the methods of `java.io.InputStream`:

```
    public class ByteArrayInputStream extends InputStream
```

There are two `ByteArrayInputStream()` constructors. Both take a byte array as an argument. This byte array is the buffer from which data will be read. The first constructor uses the entire buffer array as an input stream. The second constructor only uses the subarray of `length` bytes of `buffer` starting with the byte at `offset`.

```
public ByteArrayInputStream(byte[] buffer)
public ByteArrayInputStream(byte[] buffer, int offset, int length)
```

Other than these two constructors, the `ByteArrayInputStream` class just has the usual `read()`, `available()`, `close()`, `mark()`, and `reset()` methods. Byte array input streams do support marking and resetting up to the full length of the stream. This is relatively straightforward to implement, because a byte array contains all the data in the stream in memory at any time. There's no need to implement special buffering as with other kinds of streams and no need to worry that you'll try to reset further back than the buffer allows.

Byte Array Output Streams

The `ByteArrayOutputStream` class writes data into the successive components of a byte array using the methods of `java.io.OutputStream`:

```
public class ByteArrayOutputStream extends OutputStream
```

This class has the following two constructors, plus the usual `write()`, `close()`, and `flush()` methods:

```
public ByteArrayOutputStream()
public ByteArrayOutputStream(int size)
```

The no-argument constructor uses a buffer of 32 bytes. The second constructor uses the user-specified buffer size. However, regardless of the initial size, the byte array output stream will expand its buffer as necessary to accommodate additional data.

To return the byte array that contains the written data, use the `toByteArray()` method:

```
public synchronized byte[] toByteArray()
```

There are also `toString()` methods that convert the bytes into a string. The no-argument version uses the platform's default encoding (most commonly ISO Latin-1). The second method allows you to specify the encoding to be used:

```
public String toString()
public String toString(String encoding) throws UnsupportedEncodingException
```

For example, one way to convert a number of doubles to bytes is to chain a DataOutputStream to a ByteArrayOutputStream and write the doubles into the byte array like this:

```
ByteArrayOutputStream bos = new ByteArrayOutputStream(1024);
DataOutputStream dos = new DataOutputStream(bos);
for (int r = 1; i <= 1024; r++) {
  dos.writeDouble(r * 2.0 * Math.PI);
}
```

Example 8-2 uses a byte array output stream to implement a simple form of buffering. An array is created to hold the first n Fibonacci numbers* in binary form, where n is specified on the command line. The array is filled using the methods of java.io.DataOutputStream. Once the array is created, a file is opened, and the data in the array is written into the file. Then the file is closed. This way, the data can be written quickly without requiring the file to be open while the program is calculating.

Example 8-2. The FibonacciFile program

```
import java.io.*;

public class FibonacciFile {

  public static void main(String args[]) {

    String outputFile = "fibonacci.dat";
    if (args.length > 0) outputFile = args[0];
    int howMany;
    try {
      howMany = Integer.parseInt(args[1]);
    }
    catch (Exception e) {
      howMany = 20;
    }

    try {
      // So that the buffer doesn't have to be resized,
      // we calculate in advance the size of the necessary byte array.
      ByteArrayOutputStream bout = new ByteArrayOutputStream(howMany*4);
      DataOutputStream dout = new DataOutputStream(bout);

      // First two Fibonacci numbers must be given
      // to start the process.
      int f1 = 1;
```

---

* The Fibonacci numbers are the sequence 1, 1, 2, 3, 5, 8, . . . where each number except the first two is calculated by adding the previous two numbers in the sequence.

Example 8-2. The FibonacciFile program (continued)

```
        int f2 = 1;
      dout.writeInt(f1);
      dout.writeInt(f2);

      // Now calculate the rest.
      for (int i = 2; i < howMany; i++) {
        int temp = f2;
        f2 = f2 + f1;
        f1 = temp;
        dout.writeInt(f2);
      }

      FileOutputStream fout = new FileOutputStream(outputFile);
      fout.write(bout.toByteArray());
      fout.flush();
      fout.close();
    }
    catch (IOException e) { System.err.println(e); }
  }
}
```

You can use the `FileDumper3` program from the last chapter with the `-i` option to view the output. For example:

```
% java FibonacciFile fibonacci.dat 10
% java FileDumper3 -i fibonacci.dat
1
1
2
3
5
8
13
21
34
55
```

Communicating Between Threads with Piped Streams

The `java.io.PipedInputStream` class and `java.io.PipedOutputStream` class provide a convenient means to move streaming data from one thread to another. Output from one thread becomes input for the other thread, as shown in Figure 8-1.

```
public class PipedInputStream extends InputStream
public class PipedOutputStream extends OutputStream
```

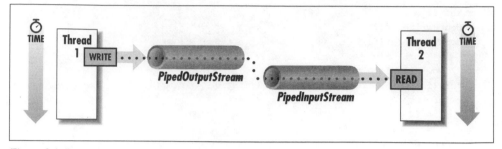

Figure 8-1. Data moving between threads with piped streams

The `PipedInputStream` class has two constructors:

```
public PipedInputStream()
public PipedInputStream(PipedOutputStream source) throws IOException
```

The no-argument constructor creates a piped input stream that is not yet connected to a piped output stream. The second constructor creates a piped input stream that's connected to the piped output stream `source`.

The `PipedOutputStream` class also has two constructors:

```
public PipedOutputStream(PipedInputStream sink) throws IOException
public PipedOutputStream()
```

The no-argument constructor creates a piped output stream that is not yet connected to a piped input stream. The second constructor creates a piped output stream that's connected to the piped input stream `sink`.

Piped streams are normally created in pairs. The piped output stream becomes the underlying source for the piped input stream. For example:

```
PipedOutputStream pout = new PipedOutputStream();
PipedInputStream pin = new PipedInputStream(pout);
```

This simple example is a little deceptive, because these lines of code will normally be in different methods and perhaps even different classes. Some mechanism must be established to pass a reference to the `PipedOutputStream` into the thread that handles the `PipedInputStream`. Or you can create them in the same thread, then pass a reference to the connected stream into a separate thread. Alternately, you can reverse the order:

```
PipedInputStream pin = new PipedInputStream();
PipedOutputStream pout = new PipedOutputStream(pin);
```

Or you can create them both unconnected, then use one or the other's `connect()` method to link them:

```
PipedInputStream pin = new PipedInputStream();
PipedOutputStream pout = new PipedOutputStream();
pin.connect(pos);
```

Otherwise, these classes just have the usual `read()`, `write()`, `flush()`, `close()`, and `available()` public methods like all stream classes.

The piped input stream also has four protected fields and one protected method that are used to implement the piping:

```
protected static final int PIPE_SIZE
protected byte[] buffer
protected int in
protected int out
protected synchronized void receive(int b) throws IOException
```

`PIPE_SIZE` is a named constant for the size of the buffer. It's 1024 in Java 1.1 and 1.2. The buffer is the byte array where the data is stored, and it's initialized to be an array of length `PIPE_SIZE`. When a client class invokes a `write()` method in the piped output stream class, the `write()` method invokes the `receive()` method in the connected piped input stream to place the data in the byte array `buffer`. Data is always written at the position in the buffer given by the field `in` and read from the position in the buffer given by the field `out`.

There are two possible blocking situations here. The first occurs if the writing thread tries to write data while the reading thread's input buffer is full. When this occurs, the output stream enters an infinite loop in which it repeatedly waits for one second until some thread reads some data out of the buffer and frees up space. The second possible block is when the reading thread tries to read and no data is present in the buffer. In this case, the input stream enters an infinite loop in which it repeatedly waits for one second until some thread writes some data into the buffer. If this is likely to be a problem for your application, you should subclass `PipedInputStream` and provide a larger value for `PIPE_SIZE`.

Although piped input streams contain an internal buffer, they do not support marking and resetting. The circular nature of the buffer would make this excessively complicated. You can always chain the piped input stream to a buffered input stream and read from that, if you need marking and resetting.

The following program is a simple and somewhat artificial example that generates Fibonacci numbers in one thread and writes them onto a piped output stream while another thread reads the numbers from a corresponding piped input stream and prints them on `System.out`. There are three classes in this program: `FibonacciWriter` and `FibonacciReader`, which are subclasses of `Thread`, and `FibonacciDriver`, which manages the other two classes. Example 8-3 shows the `FibonacciWriter` class, a subclass of `Thread`. This class does not directly use a piped output stream. It just writes data onto the output stream it's given in the constructor.

Example 8-3. The FibonacciWriter Class

```java
import java.io.*;

public class FibonacciWriter extends Thread {

  DataOutputStream theOutput;
  int howMany;

  public FibonacciWriter(OutputStream out, int howMany)
   throws IOException {
    theOutput = new DataOutputStream(out);
    this.howMany = howMany;
  }

  public FibonacciWriter(OutputStream out) throws IOException {
    this(out, Integer.MAX_VALUE);
  }

  public void run() {

    try {
      int f1 = 1;
      int f2 = 1;
      theOutput.writeInt(f1);
      theOutput.writeInt(f2);

      // Now calculate the rest.
      for (int i = 2; i < howMany; i++) {
        int temp = f2;
        f2 = f2 + f1;
        f1 = temp;
            if (f2 < 0) { // overflow
               break;
            }
        theOutput.writeInt(f2);
      }
    }
    catch (IOException e) { System.err.println(e); }
  }
}
```

Example 8-4 is the `FibonacciReader` class. It could just as well have been called the `IntegerReader` class, since it doesn't know anything about Fibonacci numbers. Its `run()` method merely reads integers from its input stream until the stream is exhausted or an `IOException` is thrown.

Example 8-4. The FibonacciReader Class

```
import java.io.*;

public class FibonacciReader extends Thread {

  DataInputStream theInput;

  public FibonacciReader(InputStream in)
   throws IOException {
    theInput = new DataInputStream(in);
  }

  public void run() {

    try {
      while (true) {
        System.out.println(theInput.readInt());
      }
    }
    catch (IOException e) {
      // probably just an end of stream exception
    }
  }
}
```

Example 8-5 is the `FibonacciDriver` class. It creates a piped output stream and a piped input stream and uses those to construct `FibonacciWriter` and `FibonacciReader` objects. These streams are a channel of communication between the two threads. As data is written by the `FibonacciWriter` thread it becomes available for the `FibonacciReader` thread to read. Both the `FibonacciWriter` and the `FibonacciReader` are run with normal priority so when the `FibonacciWriter` blocks or is preempted, the `FibonacciReader` runs and vice versa.

Example 8-5. The FibonacciDriver Class

```
import java.io.*;

public class FibonacciDriver {

  public static void main (String[] args) {

    int howMany;
    try {
      howMany = Integer.parseInt(args[0]);
```

Example 8-5. The FibonacciDriver Class (continued)

```
    }
    catch (Exception e) {
      howMany = 20;
    }

    try {
      PipedOutputStream pout = new PipedOutputStream();
      PipedInputStream pin = new PipedInputStream(pout);

      FibonacciWriter fw = new FibonacciWriter(pout, howMany);
      FibonacciReader fr = new FibonacciReader(pin);
      fw.start();
      fr.start();
    }
    catch (IOException e) { System.err.println(e);}
  }
}
```

You may be wondering how the piped streams differ from the stream copiers presented earlier in the book. The first difference is that the piped stream moves data from an output stream to an input stream. The stream copier always moves data in the opposite direction, from an input stream to an output stream. The second difference is that the stream copier actively moves the data by calling the `read()` and `write()` methods of the underlying streams. A piped output stream merely makes the data available to the input stream. It is still necessary for some other object to invoke the piped input stream's `read()` method to read the data. If no other object reads from the piped input stream, then after about one kilobyte of data has been written onto the piped output stream, the writing thread will block while it waits for the piped input stream's buffer to empty out.

In this chapter:
- *Inflaters and Deflaters*
- *Compressing and Decompressing Streams*
- *Working with Zip Files*
- *Checksums*
- *JAR Files*
- *File Viewer, Part 4*

9

Compressing Streams

The `java.util.zip` package, shown in Figure 9-1, contains six stream classes and another half dozen assorted classes that read and write data in zip, gzip, and inflate/deflate formats. Java uses these classes to read and write JAR archives and to display PNG images. You can use the `java.util.zip` classes as general utilities for general-purpose compression and decompression. Among other things, these classes make it trivial to write a simple file compression or decompression program.

Inflaters and Deflaters

The `java.util.zip.Deflater` and `java.util.zip.Inflater` classes provide compression and decompression services for all other classes. They are Java's compression and decompression engines. These classes support several related compression formats, including zlib, deflate, and gzip. These formats are documented in RFCs 1950, 1951, and 1952. (See *ftp://ftp.uu.net/graphics/png/documents/zlib/zdoc-index.html*) They all use the Lempel-Ziv 1977 (LZ77) compression algorithm (named after the inventors, Jakob Ziv and Abraham Lempel), though each has a different way of storing metadata that describes an archive's contents. Since compression and decompression are extremely CPU-intensive operations, for the most part these classes are Java wrappers around native methods written in C. More precisely, these are wrappers around the zlib compression library written by Jean-Loup Gailly and Mark Adler. According to Greg Roelofs, writing on the zlib web page at *http://www.cdrom.com/pub/infozip/zlib/*, "zlib is designed to be a free, general-purpose, legally unencumbered—that is, not covered by any patents—lossless data-compression library for use on virtually any computer hardware and operating system."

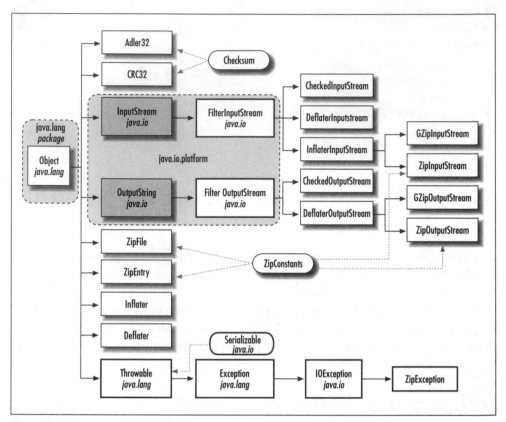

Figure 9-1. The java.util.zip package hierarchy

Without going into excessive detail, zip, gzip, and zlib all compress data in more or less the same way. Repeated bit sequences in the input data are replaced with pointers back to the first occurrence of that bit sequence. Other tricks are used, but this is basically how these compression schemes work and has certain implications for compression and decompression code. First, you can't randomly access data in a compressed file. To decompress the nth byte of data, you must first decompress bytes 1 through $n-1$ of the data. Second, a single twiddled bit doesn't just change the meaning of the byte it's part of. It also changes the meaning of bytes that come after it in the data, since subsequent bytes may be stored as copies of the previous bytes. Therefore, compressed files are much more susceptible to corruption than uncompressed files. For more general information about compression and archiving algorithms and formats, the *comp.compression* FAQ is a good place to start. See *http://www.faqs.org/faqs/compression-faq/part1/preamble.html.*

Deflating Data

The `Deflater` class contains methods to compress blocks of data. You can choose the compression format, the level of compression, and the compression strategy. There are nine steps to deflating data with the `Deflater` class:

1. Construct a `Deflater` object.

2. Choose the strategy (optional).

3. Set the compression level (optional).

4. Preset the dictionary (optional).

5. Set the input.

6. Deflate the data repeatedly until `needsInput()` returns `true`.

7. If more input is available, go back to step 4 to provide additional input data. Otherwise, go to step 8.

8. Finish the data.

9. If there are more streams to be deflated, reset the deflater.

More often than not, you don't use this class directly. Instead, you use a `Deflater` object indirectly through one of the compressing stream classes like `DeflaterInputStream` or `DeflaterOutputStream`. These classes provide more convenient programmer interfaces for stream-oriented compression than the raw `Deflater` methods.

Constructing deflaters

There are three `Deflater()` constructors:

```
public Deflater(int level, boolean useGzip)
public Deflater(int level)
public Deflater()
```

The most general constructor allows you to set the level of compression and the format used. Compression level is specified as an `int` between 0 and 9. 0 is no compression; 9 is maximum compression. Generally, the higher the compression level, the smaller the output will be and the longer the compression will take. Four mnemonic constants are available to select particular levels of compression. These are:

```
public static final int NO_COMPRESSION = 0;
public static final int BEST_SPEED = 1;
public static final int BEST_COMPRESSION = 9;
public static final int DEFAULT_COMPRESSION = -1;
```

If useGzip is true, then gzip compression format is used. Otherwise, the zlib compression format is used. (zlib format is the default.) These formats are essentially the same except that zlib includes some extra header and checksum fields.

In Java 1.1 and 2 the Deflater class only supports a single compression method, deflation. This one method is used by zip, gzip, and zlib. This is represented by the mnemonic constant Deflater.DEFLATED:

```
public static final int DEFLATED = 8;
```

Other methods exist and may be added in the future, such as LZ78 dictionary-based compression, arithmetic compression, wavelet compression, fractal compression, and many more. The design of the java.util.zip package does not allow you to install third-party compression engines easily. Therefore, classes to support these new methods must come from Sun.* In the next chapter, you'll see the Java Cryptography Extension (JCE), which is designed along similar lines. However, because outdated laws prevent Sun from including strong cryptography in the core API, the JCE allows you to plug in third-party engines that support a wide variety of encryption methods.

Choose a strategy

The first step is to choose the strategy. Java 1.1 supports three strategies: filtered, Huffman, and default. These are represented by the mnemonic constants Deflater.FILTERED, Deflater.HUFFMAN_ONLY, and Deflater.DEFAULT_STRATEGY, respectively. The setStrategy() method chooses one of these strategies.

```
public static final int DEFAULT_STRATEGY = 0;
public static final int FILTERED = 1;
public static final int HUFFMAN_ONLY = 2;

public synchronized void setStrategy(int strategy)
```

This method throws an IllegalArgumentException if an unrecognized strategy is passed as an argument. If no strategy is chosen explicitly, then the default strategy is used. The default strategy works well for most data you're likely to encounter. It concentrates primarily on emitting pointers to previously seen data, so it works well in data where runs of bytes tend to repeat themselves. In certain kinds of files where long runs of bytes are uncommon, but where the distribution of bytes is uneven, you may be better off with pure Huffman coding. Huffman coding simply uses fewer bits for more common characters like "e" and more bits

---

* There's no reason a third party can't write compression classes that exist outside the java.util.zip package, of course. However, such classes would not be able to replace Deflater and Inflater in the rest of the core API.

for less common characters like "q." A third situation, common in some binary files, is where all bytes are more or less equally likely. When dealing with these sorts of files, the filtered strategy provides a good compromise with some Huffman coding and some matching of data to previously seen values. Most of the time, the default strategy will do the best job, and even if it doesn't, it will compress within a few percent of the optimal strategy, so it's rarely worth agonizing over which is the best solution.

Set the compression level

The deflater compresses by trying to match the data it's looking at now to data it's already seen earlier in the stream. The compression level determines how far back in the stream the deflater looks for a match. The farther back it looks, the more likely it is to find a match and the larger the run of bytes it can replace with a simple pointer. However, the farther back it looks, the longer it takes as well. Thus, compression level is a trade-off between speed and file size. The tighter you compress, the more time it takes. Generally, the compression level is set in the constructor, but you can change it after the deflater is constructed by using the `setLevel()` method:

```
public synchronized void setLevel(int Level)
```

As with the `Deflater()` constructors, the compression level should be an `int` between 0 and 9 (no compression to maximum compression) or perhaps –1, signifying the default compression level. Any other value will cause an `IllegalArgumentException`. It's good coding style to use one of the mnemonic constants `Deflater.NO_COMPRESSION` (0), `Deflater.BEST_SPEED` (1), `Deflater.BEST_COMPRESSION` (9), or `Deflater.DEFAULT_COMPRESSION` (–1) instead of an explicit value.

In limited testing with small files, I haven't found the difference between best speed and best compression to be noticeable, either in file size or the time it takes to compress or decompress. You may occasionally want to set the level to no compression (0) if you're deflating already compressed files like GIF, JPEG, or PNG images before storing them in an archive. These file formats have built-in compression algorithms specifically designed for the type of data they contain, and the general-purpose deflation algorithm provided here is unlikely to compress them further.* It may even increase their size.

---

* In fact, the deflation algorithm described here is the exact algorithm used by PNG images; it was first invented specifically for the PNG file format.

Set the dictionary

You can think of the deflater as building a dictionary of phrases as it reads the text. The first time it sees a phrase, it puts the phrase in the dictionary. The second time it sees the phrase, it replaces the phrase with its position in the dictionary. However, it can't do this until it's seen the phrase at least once, so data early in the stream isn't compressed very well compared to data that occurs later in the stream. On rare occasion, when you have a good idea that certain byte sequences appear in the data very frequently, you can preset the dictionary used for compression. You would fill the dictionary with the frequently repeated data in the text. For instance, if your text is composed completely of ASCII digits and assorted whitespace (tabs, carriage returns, and so forth) you could put those characters in your dictionary. This allows the early part of the stream to compress as well as later parts.

There are two `setDictionary()` methods. The first uses the entire byte array passed as an argument as the dictionary. The second uses the subarray of data starting at `offset` and continuing for `length` bytes.

```
public void setDictionary(byte[] data)
public native synchronized void setDictionary(byte[] data,
   int offset, int length)
```

TIP

Presetting a dictionary is never necessary and requires detailed understanding of both the compression format used and the data to be compressed. Putting the wrong data in your dictionary can actually increase the file size. Unless you're a compression expert and you really need every last byte of space you can save, I recommend letting the deflater build the dictionary adaptively as the data is compressed.

I started with a highly compressible 44,392-byte text file (the output of running *FileDumper2.java* on itself in decimal mode). Without presetting the dictionary, it deflated to 3,859 bytes. My first attempt to preset the dictionary to the ASCII digits, space, and \r\n actually increased that size to 3,863 bytes. After carefully examining the data and custom-designing a dictionary to fit it, I was able to deflate the data to 3,852 bytes, saving a whopping 7 extra bytes or 0.18%. Of course, the dictionary itself occupied 112 bytes, so it's truly arguable whether I really saved anything.

Exact details are likely to vary from file to file. The only real possible gain is for very short, very predictable files where zlib may not have enough data to build a good dictionary before the end of stream is reached. However, zlib uses a pretty good algorithm for building an adaptive dictionary, and you're unlikely to do significantly better by hand. I recommend you not worry about setting a dictionary, and simply let the deflater build one for you.

If `Inflater.inflate()` decompresses the data later, the `Inflater.getAdler()` method will return the Adler-32 checksum of the dictionary needed for decompression. However, you'll need some other means to pass the dictionary itself between the deflater and the inflater. It is not stored with the deflated file.

Set the input

Next you must set the input data to be deflated with one of the `setInput()` methods:

```
public void setInput(byte[] input)
public synchronized void setInput(byte[] input, int offset, int length)
```

The first method prepares the entire array to be deflated. The second method prepares the specified subarray of data starting at `offset` and continuing for `length` bytes.

Deflate the data repeatedly until needsInput() returns true

Finally, you're ready to deflate the data. Once `setInput()` has filled the input buffer with data, it is deflated through one of two `deflate()` methods:

```
public int deflate(byte[] output)
public native synchronized int deflate(byte[] output, int offset, int length)
```

The first method fills the specified `output` array with the bytes of compressed data. The second fills the specified subarray of `output` beginning at `offset` and continuing for `length` bytes with the compressed data. Both methods return the actual number of compressed bytes written into the array. You do not know in advance how many compressed bytes will actually be written into `output`, because you do not know how well the data will compress. You always have to check the return value. If `deflate()` returns 0, you should check `needsInput()` to see if you need to call `setInput()` again to provide more uncompressed input data:

```
public boolean needsInput()
```

When more data is needed, the `needsInput()` method returns `true`. At this point you should invoke `setInput()` again to feed in more uncompressed input data, call `deflate()`, and repeat the process until `deflate()` returns 0 *and* there is no more input data to be compressed.

Finish the deflation

Finally, when the input data is exhausted, invoke `finish()` to indicate that no more data is forthcoming and the deflater should finish with the data it already has in its buffer:

```
public synchronized void finish()
```

The finished() method returns true when the end of the compressed output has been reached; that is, when all data stored in the input buffer has been deflated:

```
public synchronized boolean finished()
```

After calling finish(), you invoke deflate() repeatedly until finished() returns true. This flushes out any data that remains in the input buffer.

Reset the deflater and start over

This completes the sequence of method invocations required to compress data. If you'd like to use the same strategy, compression level, and other settings to compress more data with the same Deflater, call its reset() method:

```
public native synchronized void reset()
```

Otherwise, call end() to throw away any unprocessed input and free the resources used by the native code:

```
public native synchronized void end()
```

The finalize() method calls end() before the deflater is garbage-collected, if you forget:

```
protected void finalize()
```

An example

Example 9-1 is a simple program that deflates files named on the command line. First a Deflater object, def, is created with the default strategy, method, and compression level. A file input stream named fin is opened to each file. At the same time, a file output stream named fout is opened to an output file with the same name plus the three-letter extension .dfl. The program then enters a loop in which it tries to read 1024-byte chunks of data from fin, though care is taken not to assume that 1024 bytes are actually read. Any data that is successfully read is passed to the deflater's setInput() method. The data is repeatedly deflated and written onto the output stream until the deflater indicates that it needs more input. Then the process repeats itself until the end of the input stream is reached. When no more input is available, the deflater's finish() method is called. Then the deflater's deflate() method is repeatedly invoked until its finished() method returns true. At this point, the program breaks out of the infinite read() loop and moves on to the next file.

Figure 9-2 is a flow chart demonstrating this sequence for a single file. One thing may seem a little fishy about this chart. After the deflater is finished, a repeated check is made to see if the deflater is in fact finished. The finish() method tells the deflater that no more data is forthcoming and it should work with whatever data remains in its input buffer. However, the `finished()` method does not actually return `true` until the input buffer has been emptied by calls to `deflate()`.

Example 9-1. The DirectDeflater

```java
import java.io.*;
import java.util.zip.*;

public class DirectDeflater {

  public final static String DEFLATE_SUFFIX = ".dfl";

  public static void main(String[] args) {

    Deflater def = new Deflater();
    byte[] input = new byte[1024];
    byte[] output = new byte[1024];

    for (int i = 0; i < args.length; i++) {

      try {
        FileInputStream fin = new FileInputStream(args[i]);
        FileOutputStream fout = new FileOutputStream(args[i] + DEFLATE_SUFFIX);

        while (true) { // read and deflate the data

          // Fill the input array.
          int numRead = fin.read(input);
          if (numRead == -1) { // end of stream
            // Deflate any data that remains in the input buffer.
            def.finish();
            while (!def.finished()) {
              int numCompressedBytes = def.deflate(output, 0, output.length);
              if (numCompressedBytes > 0) {
                fout.write(output, 0, numCompressedBytes);
              } // end if
            }  // end while
            break; // Exit while loop.
          } // end if
          else {  // Deflate the input.
            def.setInput(input, 0, numRead);
            while (!def.needsInput()) {
              int numCompressedBytes = def.deflate(output, 0, output.length);
              if (numCompressedBytes > 0) {
                fout.write(output, 0, numCompressedBytes);
              } // end if
            }  // end while
          }  // end else
        } // end while
```

Example 9-1. The DirectDeflater (continued)

```
        fin.close();
        fout.flush();
        fout.close();
        def.reset();
    } // end try
    catch (IOException e) {System.err.println(e);}
  }
 }
}
```

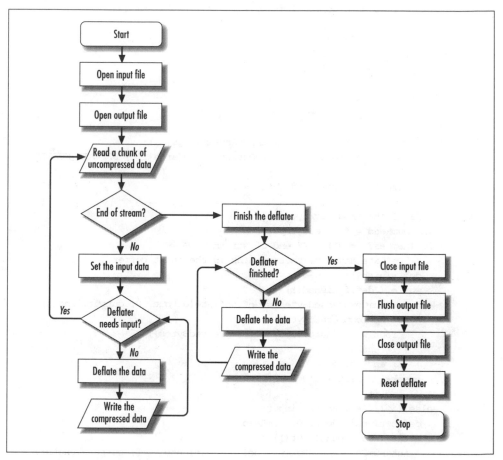

Figure 9-2. The deflation sequence

This program is more complicated than it needs to be, because it has to read the file in small chunks. In Example 9-3, later in this chapter, you'll see a simpler program that achieves the same result using the `DeflaterOutputStream` class.

Checking the state of a deflater

The `Deflater` class also provides several methods that return information about the deflater's state. The `getAdler()` method returns the Adler-32 checksum of the uncompressed data. This is *not* a `java.util.zip.Checksum` object but the actual `int` value of the checksum:

```
public native synchronized int getAdler()
```

The `getTotalIn()` method returns the number of uncompressed bytes passed to the `setInput()` method:

```
public native synchronized int getTotalIn()
```

The `getTotalOut()` method returns the total number of compressed bytes output so far via `deflate()`:

```
public native synchronized int getTotalOut()
```

For example, to print a running total of the compression achieved by the `Deflater` object `def`, you might do something like this:

```
System.out.println((1.0 - def.getTotalOut()/def.getTotalIn())*100.0 +
'% saved');
```

Inflating Data

The `Inflater` class contains methods to decompress blocks of data compressed in the zip, gzip, or zlib formats. This data may have been produced by Java's `Deflater` class or by some other program written in another language entirely, such as PKZip or gzip. Using an inflater is a little simpler than using a deflater, since there aren't a lot of settings to pick. Those were established when the data was compressed. There are seven steps to inflating data:

1. Construct an `Inflater` object.

2. Set the input with the compressed data to be inflated.

3. Call `needsDictionary()` to determine if a preset dictionary is required.

4. If `needsDictionary()` returns `true`, call `getAdler()` to get the Adler-32 checksum of the dictionary. Then invoke `setDictionary()` to set the dictionary data.

5. Inflate the data repeatedly until `inflate()` returns zero.

6. If `needsInput()` returns `true`, go back to step 4 to provide additional input data.

7. The `finished()` method returns `true`.

If you want to decompress more data with this `Inflater` object, reset it.

You rarely use this class directly. Instead, you use an inflater indirectly through one of the decompressing stream classes like `InflaterInputStream` or `InflaterOutputStream`. These classes provide much more convenient programmer interfaces for stream-oriented decompression.

Constructing inflaters

There are two `Inflater()` constructors:

```
public Inflater(boolean zipped)
public Inflater()
```

By passing `true` to the first constructor, you indicate that data to be inflated has been compressed using the zip or gzip format. Otherwise, the constructor assumes the data is in the zlib format.

Set the input

Once you have an `Inflater` to work with, you can start feeding it compressed data with `setInput()`:

```
public void setInput(byte[] input)
public synchronized void setInput(byte[] input, int offset, int length)
```

As usual, the first variant treats the entire `input` array as data to be inflated. The second uses the subarray of `input`, starting at `offset` and continuing for `length` bytes.

Check whether a preset dictionary was used

Next, you can determine whether this block of data was compressed with a preset dictionary. If it was, `needsDictionary()` returns `true`:

```
public synchronized boolean needsDictionary()
```

If `needsDictionary()` does return `true`, you can get the Adler-32 checksum of the requisite dictionary with the `getAdler()` method:

```
public native synchronized int getAdler()
```

This doesn't actually tell you what the dictionary is (which would be a lot more useful); but if you have a list of commonly used dictionaries, you can probably use the Adler-32 checksum to determine which of those was used to compress the data.

Set the dictionary

If `needsDictionary()` returns `true`, you'll have to use one of the `setDictionary()` methods to provide the data for the dictionary. The first uses the entire `dictionary` byte array as the dictionary. The second uses the subarray of `dictionary`, starting at `offset` and continuing for `length` bytes.

```
public void setDictionary(byte[] dictionary)
public native synchronized void setDictionary(byte[] dictionary,
   int offset, int length)
```

The dictionary is not generally available with the compressed data. Whoever writes files using a preset dictionary is responsible for determining some higher-level protocol for passing the dictionary used by the compression program to the decompression program. One possibility is to store the dictionary file, along with the compressed data, in an archive. Another possibility is that programs that read and write many very similar files may always use the same dictionary built into both the compression and decompression programs.

Inflate the data

Once `setInput()` has filled the input buffer with data, it is inflated through one of two `inflate()` methods:

```
public int inflate(byte[] output) throws DataFormatException
public native synchronized int inflate(byte[] output, int offset, int length)
   throws DataFormatException
```

The first method fills the `output` array with the uncompressed data. The second fills the specified subarray, beginning at `offset` and continuing for `length` bytes, with the uncompressed data. The actual number of uncompressed bytes written into the array is returned. If one of these methods returns 0, then you should check `needsInput()` to see if you need to call `setInput()` again to insert more uncompressed input data:

```
public boolean needsInput()
```

When more data is needed, `needsInput()` returns `true`. At this point you call `setInput()` again to feed in more uncompressed input data, then call `inflate()`, then repeat the process until there is no more input data to be decompressed. If more data is not needed after `inflate()` returns zero, this should mean that decompression is finished, and the `finished()` method should return `true`:

```
public synchronized boolean finished()
```

The `inflate()` methods throw a `java.util.zip.DataFormatException` if they encounter invalid data, generally indicating a corrupted input stream. This is a direct subclass of `java.lang.Exception`, not an `IOException`.

Reset the inflater

This completes the sequence of method invocations required to decompress data. If you'd like to use the same settings to decompress more data with the same `Inflater` object, you can invoke its `reset()` method:

```
public native synchronized void reset()
```

Otherwise, you call `end()` to throw away any unprocessed input and free the resources used by the native code:

```
public native synchronized void end()
```

The `finalize()` method calls `end()` before the inflater is garbage-collected, even if you forget to invoke it explicitly:

```
protected void finalize()
```

An example

Example 9-2 is a simple program that inflates files named on the command line. First an `Inflater` object, `inf`, is created. A file input stream named `fin` is opened to each file. At the same time, a file output stream named `fout` is opened to an output file with the same name minus the three-letter extension *.dfl*. The program then enters a loop in which it tries to read 1024-byte chunks of data from `fin`, though care is taken not to assume that 1024 bytes are actually read. Any data that is successfully read is passed to the inflater's `setInput()` method. This data is repeatedly inflated and written onto the output stream until the inflater indicates that it needs more input. Then the process repeats itself until the end of the input stream is reached and the inflater's `finished()` method returns `true`. At this point, the program breaks out of the `read()` loop and moves on to the next file.

Example 9-2. The DirectInflater

```
import java.io.*;
import java.util.zip.*;

public class DirectInflater {

  public static void main(String[] args) {

    Inflater inf = new Inflater();
    byte[] input = new byte[1024];
    byte[] output = new byte[1024];

    for (int i = 0; i < args.length; i++) {

      try {
        if (!args[i].endsWith(DirectDeflater.DEFLATE_SUFFIX)) {
          System.err.println(args[i] + " does not look like a deflated file");
```

Example 9-2. The DirectInflater (continued)

```java
        continue;
      }
    FileInputStream fin = new FileInputStream(args[i]);
    FileOutputStream fout = new FileOutputStream(args[i].substring(0,
     args[i].length() - DirectDeflater.DEFLATE_SUFFIX.length())));

    while (true) { // Read and inflate the data.

      // Fill the input array.
      int numRead = fin.read(input);
      if (numRead != -1) { // End of stream, finish inflating.
        inf.setInput(input, 0, numRead);
      } // end if
      // Inflate the input.

      int numDecompressed = 0;
      while ((numDecompressed = inf.inflate(output, 0, output.length))
       != 0) {
        fout.write(output, 0, numDecompressed);
      }
      // At this point inflate() has returned 0.
      // Let's find out why.
      if (inf.finished()) { // all done
        break;
      }
      else if (inf.needsDictionary()) { // We don't handle dictionaries.
        System.err.println("Dictionary required! bailing...");
        break;
      }
      else if (inf.needsInput()) {
        continue;
      }
    } // end while

    // Close up and get ready for the next file.
    fin.close();
    fout.flush();
    fout.close();
    inf.reset();
  } // end try
  catch (IOException e) {System.err.println(e);}
  catch (DataFormatException e) {
    System.err.println(args[i] + " appears to be corrupt");
    System.err.println(e);
  } // end catch
  }
 }
]
```

Once again, this program is more complicated than it needs to be, because of the necessity of reading the input in small chunks. In Example 9-4, you'll see a much simpler program that achieves the same result via an `InflaterOutputStream`.

Checking the state of an inflater

The `Inflater` class also provides several methods that return information about the `Inflater` object's state. The `getAdler()` method returns the Adler-32 checksum of the uncompressed data. This is *not* a `java.util.zip.Checksum` object but the actual `int` value of the checksum:

```
public native synchronized int getAdler()
```

The `getTotalIn()` method returns the number of compressed bytes passed to the `setInput()` method:

```
public native synchronized int getTotalIn()
```

The `getTotalOut()` method returns the total number of decompressed bytes output via `inflate()`:

```
public native synchronized int getTotalOut()
```

The `getRemaining()` method returns the number of compressed bytes left in the input buffer:

```
public native synchronized int getRemaining()
```

Compressing and Decompressing Streams

The `Inflater` and `Deflater` classes are a little raw for easy digestion. It would be more convenient to write uncompressed data onto an output stream and have it compressed by the stream itself, without having to worry about the mechanics of deflation. Similarly, it would be useful to have an input stream class that could read from a compressed file but return the uncompressed data. Java, in fact, has several classes that do exactly this. The `java.util.zip.DeflaterOutputStream` class is a filter stream that compresses the data it receives in deflated format before writing it out to the underlying stream. The `java.util.zip.Inflater-InputStream` class inflates deflated data before passing it to the reading program. `java.util.zip.GZIPInputStream` and `java.util.zip.GZIPOutputStream` do the same thing except with the gzip format.

The DeflaterOutputStream Class

`DeflaterOutputStream` is a filter stream that deflates data before writing it onto the underlying stream:

```
public class DeflaterOutputStream extends FilterOutputStream
```

Each stream uses a protected `Deflater` object called `def` to compress data stored in a protected internal buffer called `buf`:

```
protected Deflater def;
protected byte[] buf;
```

The same deflater must not be used in multiple streams at the same time, though Java takes no steps to guarantee this.

The underlying output stream that receives the deflated data, the deflater object `def`, and the length of the byte array `buf` are all set by one of the three `DeflaterOutputStream` constructors:

```
public DeflaterOutputStream(OutputStream out, Deflater def, int bufferLength)
public DeflaterOutputStream(OutputStream out, Deflater def)
public DeflaterOutputStream(OutputStream out)
```

The underlying output stream must be specified. The buffer length defaults to 512 bytes, and the `Deflater` defaults to the default compression level, strategy, and method. Of course, the `DeflaterOutputStream` has all the usual output stream methods like `write()`, `flush()`, and `close()`. It overrides three of these methods, but as a client programmer, you don't use them any differently than you would in any other output stream:

```
public void write(int b) throws IOException
public void write(byte[] data, int offset, int length) throws IOException
public void close() throws IOException
```

There's also one new method, `finish()`, which finishes writing the compressed data onto the underlying output stream but does not close the underlying stream. You should call `finish()` instead of `close()` if there are multiple filters chained to the stream:

```
public void finish() throws IOException
```

The `close()` method finishes writing the compressed data onto the underlying stream and then closes it:

```
public void close() throws IOException
```

The protected `deflate()` method sends the compressed data to the underlying stream. You don't invoke it directly. Subclasses that implement different compression formats may override it:

```
protected void deflate() throws IOException
```

Example 9-3 is a simple character-mode program that deflates files. Filenames are read from the command line. A file input stream is opened to each file; a file output stream is opened to that same filename plus *.dfl* (for deflated). Finally, the file output stream is chained to a deflater output stream, then a stream copier pours the data from the input file into the output file.

Example 9-3. The FileDeflater Program

```
import java.io.*;
import java.util.zip.*;
import com.macfaq.io.*;

public class FileDeflater {

  public final static String DEFLATE_SUFFIX = ".dfl";

  public static void main(String[] args) {

    for (int i = 0; i < args.length; i++) {
      try {
        FileInputStream fin = new FileInputStream(args[i]);
        FileOutputStream fout = new FileOutputStream(args[i] + DEFLATE_SUFFIX);
        DeflaterOutputStream dos = new DeflaterOutputStream(fout);
        StreamCopier.copy(fin, dos);
        dos.close();
        fin.close();
      }
      catch (IOException e) {System.err.println(e);}
    }
  }
}
```

This program is a lot simpler than Example 9-1, even though the two programs do the same thing. In general, a `DeflaterOutputStream` is preferable to a raw `Deflater` object for reasons of simplicity and legibility, especially if you want to use the default strategy, algorithm, and compression level. However, using the `Deflater` class directly does give you more control over the strategy, algorithm, and compression level. You can get the best of both worlds by passing a custom-configured `Deflater` object as the second argument to the `DeflaterOutputStream()` constructor.

The InflaterInputStream Class

The `InflaterInputStream` class is a filter stream that inflates data while reading it from the underlying stream.

```
public class InflaterInputStream extends FilterInputStream
```

Each inflater input stream uses a protected `Inflater` object called `inf` to decompress data that is stored in a protected internal byte array called `buf`. There's also a protected int field called len that (unreliably) stores the number of bytes currently in the buffer, as opposed to the length of the buffer itself.

```
protected Inflater inf;
protected byte[] buf;
protected int len;
```

The same $Inflater$ object must not be used in multiple streams at the same time.

The underlying input stream from which deflated data is read, the $Inflater$ object inf, and the length of the byte array buf are all set by one of the three $InflaterInputStream()$ constructors:

```
public InflaterInputStream(InputStream in, Inflater inf, int bufferLength)
public InflaterInputStream(InputStream in, Inflater inf)
public InflaterInputStream(InputStream in)
```

The underlying input stream must be specified, while the buffer length defaults to 512 bytes, and the $Inflater$ defaults to an inflater for deflated streams (as opposed to zipped or gzipped streams). Of course, the $InflaterInputStream$ has all the usual input stream methods like $read()$, $available()$, and $close()$. It overrides the following three methods:

```
public int read() throws IOException
public int read(byte[] data, int offset, int length) throws IOException
public long skip(long n) throws IOException
```

For the most part, you use these the same way you'd use any $read()$ or $skip()$ method. However, it's occasionally useful to know that the read method throws a new subclass of $IOException$, $java.util.zip.ZipException$, if the problem is that the data doesn't adhere to the expected format. You should also know that $read()$, $skip()$, and all other input stream methods count the uncompressed bytes, not the compressed raw bytes that were actually read.

There's also one new protected method, $fill()$, which reads compressed data from the underlying input stream into buf, sets len to the number of bytes read, and then sets inf's input to the appropriate subarray of buf:

```
protected void fill() throws IOException
```

Example 9-4 is a simple character-mode program that inflates files. When it is combined with Example 9-3, you've now got a simple compression system. Filenames are read from the command line. A file input stream is opened from each file that ends in *.dfl*, and this stream is chained to an inflater input stream. A file output stream is opened to that same file minus the *.dfl* extension. Finally, a stream copier pours the data from the input file through the inflating stream into the output file.

Example 9-4. The FileInflater Program

```java
import java.io.*;
import java.util.zip.*;
import com.macfaq.io.*;

public class FileInflater {

  public static void main(String[] args) {

    for (int i = 0; i < args.length; i++) {
      if (args[i].toLowerCase().endsWith(FileDeflater.DEFLATE_SUFFIX)) {
        try {
          FileInputStream fin = new FileInputStream(args[i]);
          InflaterInputStream iis = new InflaterInputStream(fin);
          FileOutputStream fout = new FileOutputStream(
           args[i].substring(0, args[i].length()-4));
          StreamCopier.copy(iis, fout);
          fout.close();
        }
        catch (IOException e) {System.err.println(e);}
      }
      else {
        System.err.println(args[i] + " does not appear to be a deflated file.");
      }
    }
  }
}
```

The GZIPOutputStream Class

Although zip files deflate their entries, raw deflated files are uncommon. More common are gzipped files. These are deflated files with some additional header information attached, which specifies a checksum for the contents, the name of the compressed file, the time the file was last modified, and so on. The `java.util.zip.GZIPOutputStream` class is a subclass of `DeflaterOutputStream` that understands when and how to write this extra information to the output stream.

```java
public class GZIPOutputStream extends DeflaterOutputStream
```

There are two constructors for `GZIPOutputStream`. Since `GZIPOutputStream` is a filter stream, both take an underlying output stream as an argument. The second constructor also allows you to specify a buffer size. (The first uses a default buffer size of 512 bytes.)

```java
public GZIPOutputStream(OutputStream out) throws IOException
public GZIPOutputStream(OutputStream out, int size) throws IOException
```

Data is written onto a gzip output stream as onto any other stream, typically with the `write()` methods. `GZIPOutputStream` only overrides one of these methods:

```
public synchronized void write(byte[] data, int offset, int length)
                        throws IOException
```

However, some of the data may be temporarily stored in the input buffer until more data is available. At that point the data is compressed and written onto the underlying output stream. Therefore, when you are finished writing the data that you want to be compressed onto the stream, you should call `finish()`:

```
public void finish() throws IOException
```

This writes all remaining data in the buffer onto the underlying output stream. Then it writes a trailer containing a CRC value and the number of uncompressed bytes stored in the file onto the stream. This trailer is part of the gzip format specification that's not part of a raw deflated file. If you're through with the underlying stream as well as the gzip output stream, call `close()` instead of `finish()`. If the stream hasn't yet been finished, `close()` finishes it, then closes the underlying output stream. From this point on, data may not be written to that stream.

```
public void close() throws IOException
```

Example 9-5 is a simple command-line program that reads a list of files from the command line and gzips each one. A file input stream is used to read each file. A file output stream chained to a gzip output stream is used to write each output file. The gzipped files have the same name as the input files plus the suffix *.gz*.

Example 9-5. The GZipper

```java
import java.io.*;
import java.util.zip.*;
import com.macfaq.io.*;

public class GZipper {

  public final static String GZIP_SUFFIX = ".gz";

  public static void main(String[] args) {

    for (int i = 0; i < args.length; i++) {
      try {
        FileInputStream fin = new FileInputStream(args[i]);
        FileOutputStream fout = new FileOutputStream(args[i] + GZIP_SUFFIX);
        GZIPOutputStream gzout = new GZIPOutputStream(fout);
        StreamCopier.copy(fin, gzout);
        gzout.close();
      }
      catch (IOException e) {System.err.println(e);}
    }
  }
}
```

If this looks similar to Example 9-3, that's because it is. All that's changed is the compression format (gzip instead of deflate) and the compressed file suffix. However, since *gzip* and *gunzip* are available on virtually all operating systems—unlike raw deflate—you can test this code by unzipping the files it produces with the Free Software Foundation's (FSF) *gunzip* or some other program that handles gzipped files.

The GZIPInputStream Class

The `java.util.zip.GZIPInputStream` class is a subclass of `InflaterInput-Stream` that provides a very simple interface for decompressing gzipped data:

```
public class GZIPInputStream extends InflaterInputStream
```

There are two constructors in this class:

```
public GZIPInputStream(InputStream in) throws IOException
public GZIPInputStream(InputStream in, int bufferLength) throws IOException
```

Since this is a filter stream, both constructors take an underlying input stream as an argument. The second constructor also accepts a length for the buffer into which the compressed data will be read. Otherwise, `GZIPInputStream` has the usual methods of an input stream: `read()`, `skip()`, `close()`, `mark()`, `reset()`, and so on. Marking and resetting are not supported. Two methods are overridden, `read()` and `close()`:

```
public int read(byte[] data, int offset, int length) throws IOException
public void close() throws IOException
```

These methods work exactly like the superclass methods they override. The only thing you need to be aware of is that the `read()` method blocks until sufficient data is available in the buffer to allow decompression.

`GZIPInputStream` has two protected fields that may be accessed from subclasses. The `crc` field provides a cyclic redundancy code for that portion of the data that has been decoded. `CRC32` objects are discussed later in this chapter. The `eos` field is a `boolean` indicating whether the end of the stream has been reached. It's initially set to `false`. It becomes `true` once the end of the compressed data has been reached:

```
protected CRC32 crc;
protected boolean eos;
```

Finally, there's one not very useful mnemonic constant, `GZIPInputStream.GZIP_MAGIC`. All valid gzip files must begin with this number, which helps to identify the file's type:

```
public static final int GZIP_MAGIC = 0x8B1F;
```

Example 9-6 shows how easy it is to decompress gzipped data with GZIPInputStream. The main() method reads a series of filenames from the command line. A FileInputStream object is created for each file and a GZIPInputStream is chained to that. The data is read from the file, and the decompressed data is written into a new file with the same name minus the .gz suffix. (A more robust implementation would handle the case where the suffix is not .gz.) You can test this program with files gzipped by Example 9-5 and with files gzipped by the FSF's *Gzip* program.

Example 9-6. The GUnzipper

```java
import java.io.*;
import java.util.zip.*;
import com.macfaq.io.*;

public class GUnzipper {

  public static void main(String[] args) {

    for (int i = 0; i < args.length; i++) {
      if (args[i].toLowerCase().endsWith(GZipper.GZIP_SUFFIX)) {
        try {
          FileInputStream fin = new FileInputStream(args[i]);
          GZIPInputStream gzin = new GZIPInputStream(fin);
          FileOutputStream fout = new FileOutputStream(
           args[i].substring(0, args[i].length()-3));
          StreamCopier.copy(gzin, fout);
          fout.close();
        }
        catch (IOException e) {System.err.println(e);}
      }
      else {
        System.err.println(args[i] + " does not appear to be a gzipped file.");
      }
    }
  }
}
```

Expanding Output Streams and Compressing Input Streams

You may have noticed that the compression stream classes are not fully symmetrical. You can expand the data being read from an input stream, and you can compress data being written to an output stream, but there are no classes that compress data being read from an input stream or expand data being written to an output stream. Such classes aren't commonly needed. It's possible that you might want to read compressed data from a file and write uncompressed data onto the network, but as long as there are an input stream and an output stream, you can always put the compressor on the output stream or the decompressor on the input stream. In either case, the compressor and decompressor fall between the two underlying streams, so how they're chained doesn't really matter. Alternatively, you may have some reason to work with compressed data in memory; for example, your application might find it more efficient to store large chunks of text in compressed form. In this case, a byte array output stream chained to a deflater output stream will do the trick.

Working with Zip Files

Gzip and deflate are compression formats. Zip is both a compression and an archive format. This means that a single zip file may contain more than one uncompressed file, along with information about the names, permissions, creation and modification dates, and other information about each file in the archive. This makes reading and writing zip archives somewhat more complex and somewhat less amenable to a stream metaphor than reading and writing deflated or gzipped files.

The `java.util.zip.ZipFile` class represents a file in the zip format. Such a file might be created by zip, PKZip, ZipIt, WinZip, or any of the many other zip programs. The `java.util.zip.ZipEntry` class represents a single file stored in such an archive.

```
public class ZipFile extends Object implements ZipConstants
public class ZipEntry extends Object implements ZipConstants
```

NOTE   The `java.util.zip.ZipConstants` interface that both these class-es implement is a rare nonpublic interface that contains constants useful for reading and writing zip files. Most of these constants define the positions in a zip file where particular information, like the compression method used, is found. You don't need to concern yourself with it.

The `ZipFile` class contains two constructors. The first takes a filename as an argument. The second takes a `java.io.File` object as an argument. `File` objects will be discussed in Chapter 12, *Working with Files*; for now, I'll just use the constructor that accepts a filename. Functionally, these two constructors are similar.

```
public ZipFile(String filename) throws IOException
public ZipFile(File file) throws ZipException, IOException
```

`ZipException` is a subclass of `IOException` that generally indicates that data in the zip file doesn't fit the zip format. In this case, the zip exception's message will contain more details, like "invalid END header signature" or "cannot have more than one drive." While these may be useful to a zip expert, in general they indicate that the file is corrupted, and there's not much that can be done about it.

```
public class ZipException extends IOException
```

I can discern no reason why the first constructor is declared to throw IOException, while the second is declared to throw both IOException and ZipException. The second constructor merely invokes the first after converting the File object to a string pathname. Since ZipException extends IOException, your code can catch either ZipException and IOException or just IOException, as your needs dictate.

Both constructors attempt to open the specified file for random access. If the file is opened successfully with no exceptions, the entries() method will return a list of all the files in the archive:

```
public Enumeration entries()
```

The return value is a java.util.Enumeration object containing one java.util.zip.ZipEntry object for each file in the archive. Example 9-7 lists the entries in a zip file specified on the command line. The toString() method is used implicitly to provide the name for each zip entry in the list.

Example 9-7. ZipLister

```
import java.util.*;
import java.util.zip.*;
import java.io.*;

public class ZipLister {

  public static void main(String[] args) {

    for (int i = 0; i < args.length; i++) {
      try {
        ZipFile zf = new ZipFile(args[i]);
        Enumeration e = zf.entries();
        while (e.hasMoreElements()) {
          System.out.println(e.nextElement());
        }
      }
      catch (IOException e) {System.err.println(e);}
    }
  }
}
```

Here are the first few lines that result from running this program on the *classes.zip* file from JDK 1.1.4:

```
% java ZipLister /usr/local/java/lib/classes.zip
sun/net/www/protocol/systemresource/ParseSystemURL.class
java/io/ObjectInputValidation.class
sun/awt/motif/MTextFieldPeer.class
sun/tools/javac/BatchParser.class
sun/rmi/transport/proxy/HttpOutputStream.class
```

To get a single entry in the zip file rather than a list of the entire contents, you pass the name of the entry to the getEntry() method:

```
public ZipEntry getEntry(String name)
```

Of course, this requires you to know the name of the entry in advance. The name is simply the path and filename, like *java/io/ObjectInputValidation.class*. For example, to retrieve the zip entry for *java/io/ObjectInputValidation.class* from the ZipFile zf, you might write:

```
ZipEntry ze = zf.getEntry("java/io/ObjectInputValidation.class");
```

You can also get the name with the getName() method of the ZipEntry class, discussed later in this chapter. This method, however, requires you to have a ZipEntry object already, so there's a little chicken-and-egg problem here.

Most of the time, you'll want more than the names of the files in the archive. You can get the actual contents of the zip entry using getInputStream():

```
public InputStream getInputStream(ZipEntry ze) throws IOException
```

This returns an input stream from which you can read the uncompressed contents of the zip entry (file). Example 9-8 is a simple unzip program that uses this input stream to unpack zip archives named on the command line.

Example 9-8. Unzipper

```
import java.util.*;
import java.util.zip.*;
import java.io.*;
import com.macfaq.io.*;

public class Unzipper {

  public static void main(String[] args) {

    for (int i = 0; i < args.length; i++) {
      try {
        ZipFile zf = new ZipFile(args[i]);
        Enumeration e = zf.entries();
        while (e.hasMoreElements()) {
```

Example 9-8. Unzipper (continued)

```
        ZipEntry ze = (ZipEntry) e.nextElement();
        System.out.println("Unzipping " + ze.getName());
        FileOutputStream fout = new FileOutputStream(ze.getName());
        InputStream in = zf.getInputStream(ze);
        StreamCopier.copy(in, fout);
        in.close();
        fout.close();
      }
    }
    catch (IOException e) {
      System.err.println(e);
      e.printStackTrace();
    }
  }
 }
}
```

This is not an ideal unzip program. For one thing, it blindly overwrites any files that already exist with the same name in the current directory. Before creating a new file, it should check to see if it exists and, if it does, ask whether the user wants to overwrite it. Furthermore, it can only unzip files into existing directories. If the archive contains a file in a directory that does not exist, a `FileNot-FoundException` will be thrown. Both problems are completely fixable, but to fix them, you'll have to learn about the `java.io.File` class. You'll learn about this in Chapter 12.

Finally, there are two utility methods in `java.util.zip.ZipFile` that relate to the "File" part of `ZipFile` rather than the "Zip" part:

```
public String getName()
public void close() throws IOException
```

The `getName()` method returns the full path to the file; for example, */usr/local/java/lib/classes.zip*. The `close()` method closes the zip file (and its associated `RandomAccessFile` object). Even after a file is closed, you can still get an entry or an input stream, because the entries are read and stored in memory when the `ZipFile` object is first constructed. However, you cannot get the actual data associated with the entry. Attempts to do so will throw a `NullPointerException`.

Zip Entries

The `java.util.zip.ZipEntry` class represents a file stored in a zip archive.* A `ZipEntry` object contains information about a file stored in the zip archive but

---

* There's no reason a zip entry has to be a file. It could be a database record, some calculated data that never appeared in the filesystem, or some other sequence of bytes. But it's almost always a file, and it's easiest to visualize if we assume that it is.

not the actual data of the file. Most `ZipEntry` objects are created by non-Java tools and retrieved from zip files using the `getEntry()` or `entries()` methods of the `ZipFile` class. However, if you're writing your own program to write zip files using the `ZipOutputStream` class, you'll need to create new `ZipEntry` objects with this constructor:

```
public ZipEntry(String name)
```

Normally, the `name` argument is the name of the file that's being placed in the archive. It should not be null, or a `NullPointerException` will be thrown. It is also required to be less than 65,536 bytes long (which is plenty long for a file-name). Java 2 adds one more public constructor that copies the name, comment, modification time, CRC checksum, size, compressed size, method, comment, and indeed everything except the actual data of the file from an existing `ZipEntry` object. (It's unclear why you might need this.)

```
public ZipEntry(ZipEntry e) // Java 2
```

There are nine methods that return information about a specific entry in a zip file:

```
public String getName()
public long getTime()
public long getSize()
public long getCompressedSize()
public long getCrc()
public int getMethod()
public byte[] getExtra()
public String getComment()
public boolean isDirectory()
```

The name is simply the relative path and filename stored in the archive, like *sun/ net/www/protocol/systemresource/ParseSystemURL.class* or *java/awt/Dialog.class*. The time is the last time this entry was modified. It is given as a `long`, counting the number of milliseconds since midnight, January 1, 1970, Greenwich Mean Time. (This is not how the time is stored in the zip file, but Java converts the time before returning it.) -1 indicates that the modification time is not specified. The CRC is a 32-bit cyclic redundancy code for the data that's used to determine whether or not the file is corrupt. If no CRC is included, `getCRC()` returns -1.

The size is the original, uncompressed length of the data in bytes. The compressed size is the length of the compressed data in bytes. The `getSize()` and `getCompressedSize()` methods both return -1 to indicate that the size isn't known.

`getMethod()` tells you whether or not the data is compressed; it returns 0 if the data is uncompressed, 8 if it's compressed using the deflation format, and -1 if the compression format is unknown. 0 and 8 are given as the mnemonic constants `ZipEntry.STORED` and `ZipEntry.DEFLATED`:

```
public static final int STORED = 0;
public static final int DEFLATED = 8;
```

Each entry may contain an arbitrary amount of extra data. If so, this data is returned in a byte array by the getExtra() method. Similarly, each entry may contain an optional string comment. If it does, the getComment() method returns it; if it doesn't, getComment() returns null. Finally, the isDirectory() method returns true if the entry is a directory and false if it isn't.

Example 9-9 is an improved ZipLister that prints information about the files in a zip archive.

Example 9-9. FancyZipLister

```
import java.util.*;
import java.util.zip.*;
import java.io.*;

public class FancyZipLister {

  public static void main(String[] args) {

    for (int i = 0; i < args.length; i++) {
      try {
        ZipFile zf = new ZipFile(args[i]);
        Enumeration e = zf.entries();
        while (e.hasMoreElements()) {
          ZipEntry ze = (ZipEntry) e.nextElement();
          String name = ze.getName();
          Date lastModified = new Date(ze.getTime());
          long uncompressedSize = ze.getSize();
          long compressedSize = ze.getCompressedSize();
          long crc = ze.getCrc();
          int method = ze.getMethod();
          String comment = ze.getComment();

          if (method == ZipEntry.STORED) {
            System.out.println(name + " was stored at " + lastModified);
            System.out.println("with a size of  " + uncompressedSize
              + " bytes");
          }
          else if (method == ZipEntry.DEFLATED) {
            System.out.println(name + " was deflated at " + lastModified);
            System.out.println("from  " + uncompressedSize + " bytes to "
              + compressedSize + " bytes, a savings of "
              + 100.0*(1.0 - compressedSize/uncompressedSize) + "%");
          }
          else {
            System.out.println(name
```

Example 9-9. FancyZipLister

```
                + " was compressed using an unrecognized method at "
                + lastModified);
            System.out.println("from  " + uncompressedSize + " bytes to "
                + compressedSize + " bytes, a savings of "
                + 100.0*(1.0 - compressedSize/uncompressedSize) + "%");
          }
          System.out.println("Its CRC is " + crc);
          if (comment != null && !comment.equals("")) {
            System.out.println(comment);
          }
          if (ze.isDirectory()) {
            System.out.println(name + " is a directory");
          }
          System.out.println();
        }
      }
      catch (IOException e) {System.err.println(e);}
    }
  }
}
```

Typical output looks like this:

```
% java FancyZipLister temp.zip
test.txt was deflated at Wed Jun 11 15:57:32 EDT 1997
from  187 bytes to 98 bytes, a savings of 52.406417112299465%
Its CRC is 1981281836

ticktock.txt was deflated at Wed Jun 11 10:42:02 EDT 1997
from  1480 bytes to 405 bytes, a savings of 27.364864864864863%
Its CRC is 4103395328
```

There are also six corresponding set methods, which are used to attach information to each entry you store in a zip archive. However, most of the time it's enough to let the ZipEntry class calculate these for you:

```
public void setTime(long time)
public void setSize(long size)
public void setCrc(long crc)
public void setMethod(int method)
public void setExtra(byte[] extra)
public void setComment(String comment)
```

Finally, there's the toString() method, which was implicitly used in the ZipLister program to print the name of each entry:

```
public String toString()
```

Java 2 adds `hashCode()` and `clone()` methods:

```
public int hashCode()   // Java 2
public Object clone()   // Java 2
```

In Java 1.1, `ZipEntry` simply inherits these methods from `java.lang.Object`. However, `ZipEntry` only implements the `Cloneable` interface in Java 2, not in Java 1.1.

The ZipOutputStream Class

The `java.util.zip.ZipOutputStream` class subclasses `DeflaterOutputStream` and writes compressed data in the zip format. `ZipOutputStream` implements the nonpublic `java.util.zip.ZipConstants` interface.

```
public class ZipOutputStream  extends DeflaterOutputStream
                      implements ZipConstants
```

Java supports two zip formats, uncompressed and compressed. These are slightly less obviously known as *stored* and *deflated.* They correspond to the mnemonic constants `ZipOutputStream.STORED` and `ZipOutputStream.DEFLATED`:

```
public static final int STORED = ZipEntry.STORED;
public static final int DEFLATED = ZipEntry.DEFLATED;
```

Deflated files are compressed by a `Deflater` object using the deflation method. Stored files are copied byte for byte into the archive without any compression. This is the right format for files that are already compressed but still need to go into the archive, like a GIF image or an MPEG movie.

Because zip is not just a compression format like deflation or gzip but an archival format, a single zip file often contains multiple zip entries, each of which contains a deflated or stored file. Furthermore, the zip file contains a header with meta-information about the archive itself, such as the location of the entries in the archive. Therefore, it's not possible to write raw, compressed data onto the output stream. Instead, zip entries must be created for each successive file (or other sequence of data), and data must be written into the entries. The sequence of steps you must follow to write data onto a zip output stream is:

1. Construct a `ZipOutputStream` object from an underlying stream, most often a file output stream.

2. Set the comment for the zip file (optional).

3. Set the default compression level and method (optional).

4. Construct a `ZipEntry` object.

5. Set the meta-information for the zip entry.

6. Put the zip entry in the archive.

7. Write the entry's data onto the output stream.

8. Close the zip entry (optional).

9. Repeat steps 4 through 8 for each entry you want to store in the archive.

10. Finish the zip output stream.

11. Close the zip output stream.

Steps 4 and 6, the creation and closing of zip entries in the archive, are new. You won't find anything like them in other stream classes. However, attempts to write data onto a zip output stream using only the regular `write()`, `flush()`, and `close()` methods are doomed to failure.

Constructing and initializing the ZipOutputStream

There is a single `ZipOutputStream()` constructor that takes as an argument the underlying stream to which data will be written:

```
public ZipOutputStream(OutputStream out)
```

For example:

```
FileOutputStream fout = new FileOutputStream("data.zip");
ZipOutputStream zout = new ZipOutputStream(fout);
```

Set the comment for the zip file

After the zip output stream has been constructed (in fact, at any point before the zip output stream is finished), you can add a single comment to the zip file with the `setComment()` method:

```
public void setComment(String comment)
```

The comment is an arbitrary ASCII string comment of up to 65,535 bytes. For example:

```
zout.setComment("Archive created by Zipper 1.0");
```

All high-order Unicode bytes are discarded before the comment is written onto the zip output stream. Attempts to attach a comment longer than 65,535 characters throw `IllegalArgumentExceptions`. Each zip output stream can have only one comment (though individual entries may have their own comments too). Resetting the comment erases the previous comment.

Set the default compression level and method

Next, you may wish to set the default compression method with `setMethod()`:

```
public void setMethod(int method)
```

You can change the default compression method from stored to deflated or deflated to stored. This default method is used only when the zip entry itself does not specify a compression method. The initial value is `ZipOutputStream.DEFLATED` (compressed); the alternative is `ZipOutputStream.STORED` (uncompressed). An `IllegalArgumentException` is thrown if an unrecognized compression method is specified. You can call this method again at any time before the zip output stream is finished. This sets the default compression method for all subsequent entries in the zip output stream. For example:

```
zout.setMethod(ZipOutputStream.STORED);
```

You can change the default compression level with `setLevel()` at any time before the zip output stream is finished:

```
public void setLevel(int level)
```

For example:

```
zout.setLevel(9);
```

As with the default method, the zip output stream's default level is used only when the zip entry itself does not specify a compression level. The initial value is `Deflater.DEFAULT_COMPRESSION`. Valid levels range from 0 (no compression) to 9 (high compression); an `IllegalArgumentException` is thrown if a compression level outside that range is specified. You can call `setLevel()` again at any time before the zip output stream is finished, which sets the default compression level for all subsequent entries in the zip output stream.

Construct a ZipEntry object and put it in the archive

Data is written into the zip output stream in separate groups called zip entries. These are represented by `ZipEntry` objects. A zip entry must be opened before data is written, and each zip entry must be closed before the next one is opened. The `putNextEntry()` method opens a new zip entry on the zip output stream:

```
public void putNextEntry(ZipEntry ze) throws IOException
```

If a previous zip entry is still open, it's closed automatically. The properties of the `ZipEntry` argument ze specify the compression level and method. If ze leaves those unspecified, then the defaults set by the last calls to `setLevel()` and `setMethod()` are used. The `ZipEntry` object may also contain a CRC checksum, the time the file was last modified, the size of the file, a comment, and perhaps some optional data with an application-specific meaning (for instance, the resource fork of a Macintosh file). These are set by the `setTime()`, `setSize()`, `setCrc()`, `setComment()`, and `setExtra()` methods of the `ZipEntry` class. (These are not set by the `ZipOutputStream` class, as they will be different for each file stored in the archive.)

Write the entry's data onto the output stream

Data is written into the zip entry using the usual `write()` methods of any output stream. Only one `write()` method is overridden in `ZipOutputStream`:

```
public synchronized void write(byte[] data, int offset, int length)
                         throws IOException
```

Close the zip entry

Finally, you may want to close the zip entry to prevent any further data from being written to it. For this, use the `closeEntry()` method:

```
public void closeEntry() throws IOException
```

If an entry is still open when `putNextEntry()` is called or when you finish the zip output stream, this method will be called automatically. Thus, an explicit invocation is usually unnecessary.

Finish the zip output stream

A zip file stores meta-information in both the header and the tail of the file. The `finish()` method writes out this tail information:

```
public void finish() throws IOException
```

Once a zip output stream is finished, no more data may be written to it. However, data may be written to the underlying stream using a separate reference to the underlying stream. In other words, finishing a stream does not close it.

Close the zip output stream

Most of the time you will want to close a zip output stream at the same time you finish it. `ZipOutputStream` overrides the `close()` method inherited from `java.util.zip.DeflaterOutputStream`.

```
public void close() throws IOException
```

This method finishes the zip output stream and then closes the underlying stream.

An example

Example 9-10 uses a zip output stream chained to a file output stream to create a single zip archive from a group of files named on the command line. The name of the output zip file and the files to be stored in the archive are read from the command line. An optional -d command-line flag can be used to set the level of compression from 0 to 9.

Example 9-10. The Zipper Program

```java
import java.util.zip.*;
import java.io.*;
import com.macfaq.io.*;

public class Zipper {

  public static void main(String[] args) {

    if (args.length < 2) {
      System.out.println("Usage: java Zipper [-d level] name.zip"+
                         " file1 file2...");
      return;
    }

    String outputFile = args[0];
    // Maximum compression is our default.
    int level = 9;
    int start = 1;
    if (args[0].equals("-d")) {
      try {
        level = Integer.parseInt(args[1]);
        outputFile = args[2];
        start = 3;
      }
      catch (Exception e) {
        System.out.println("Usage: java Zipper [-d level] name.zip"
                           " file1 file2...");
        return;
      }
    }

    try {
      FileOutputStream fout = new FileOutputStream(outputFile);
      ZipOutputStream zout = new ZipOutputStream(fout);
      zout.setLevel(level);
      for (int i = start; i < args.length; i++) {
        ZipEntry ze = new ZipEntry(args[i]);
        try {
          System.out.println("Compressing " + args[i]);
          FileInputStream fin = new FileInputStream(args[i]);
          zout.putNextEntry(ze);
          StreamCopier.copy(fin, zout);
          zout.closeEntry();
          fin.close();
        }
        catch (IOException e) {System.err.println(e);}
      }
      zout.close();
```

Example 9-10. The Zipper Program (continued)

```
    }
    catch (Exception e) {System.err.println(e);}
  }
}
```

The ZipInputStream Class

Zip input streams read data from zip archives, which are most commonly stored in files. As with output streams, it's generally best not to read the raw data. (If you must read the raw data, you can always use a bare file input stream.) Instead, the input is first parsed into zip entries. Once you've positioned the stream on a particular zip entry, you read decompressed data from it using the normal `read()` methods. Then the entry is closed, and you open the next zip entry in the file. The sequence of steps you must follow to read data from a zip input stream is as follows:

1. Construct a `ZipInputStream` object from an underlying stream, most commonly a file input stream.

2. Open the next zip entry in the archive.

3. Read data from the zip entry using `InputStream` methods like `read()`.

4. Close the zip entry (optional).

5. Repeat steps 2 through 4 as long as there are more entries (files) remaining in the archive.

6. Close the zip input stream.

Steps 2 and 4, the opening and closing of zip entries in the archive, are new; you won't find anything like them in other input stream classes. However, attempts to read data from a zip input stream using only the regular `read()`, `skip()`, and `close()` methods without first opening a zip entry are doomed to failure.

NOTE   You probably noticed that the `ZipInputStream` class provides a second way to decompress zip files. The `ZipFile` class approach shown in the `Unzipper` program of Example 9-8 is the first. `ZipInputStream` uses one input stream to read from successive entries. The `ZipFile` class uses different input stream objects for different entries. Which to use is mainly a matter of aesthetics. There's not a strong reason to prefer one approach over the other, though the `ZipInputStream` is somewhat more convenient in the middle of a sequence of filters.

Construct a ZipInputStream

There is a single `ZipInputStream()` constructor that takes as an argument the underlying input stream:

```
public ZipInputStream(InputStream in)
```

For example:

```
FileInputStream fin = new FileInputStream("data.zip");
ZipInputStream zin = new ZipInputStream(fin);
```

No further initialization or parameter setting are needed. A zip input stream can read from a file regardless of the compression method or level used.

Open the next zip entry

Reads from a zip input stream read successive zip entries from the stream. Zip entries are read in the order in which they appear in the file. You do not need to read each entry in its entirety, however. Instead, you can open an entry, close it without reading it, read the next entry, and repeat until you come to the entry you want. The `getNextEntry()` method opens the next entry in the zip input stream:

```
public ZipEntry getNextEntry() throws IOException
```

If the underlying stream throws an `IOException`, it's passed along by this method. If the stream data doesn't represent a valid zip file, then a `ZipException` is thrown.

Reading from a ZipInputStream

Once the entry is open, you can read from it using the regular `read()`, `skip()`, and `available()` methods of any input stream. (Zip input streams do not support marking and resetting.) Only two of these are overridden:

```
public int read(byte[] data, int offset, int length) throws IOException
public long skip(long n) throws IOException
```

The `read()` method reads and the `skip()` method skips the decompressed bytes of data.

Close the zip entry

When you reach the end of a zip entry, or when you've read as much data as you're interested in, you may call `closeEntry()` to close the zip entry and prepare to read the next one:

```
public void closeEntry() throws IOException
```

Explicitly closing the entry is optional. If you don't close an entry, it will be closed automatically when you open the next entry or close the stream.

These three steps—open the entry, read from the entry, close the entry—may be repeated as many times as there are entries in the zip input stream.

Close the ZipInputStream

When you are finished with the stream, you can close it using the close() method:

```
public void close() throws IOException
```

As usual for filter streams, this method also closes the underlying stream. Unlike zip output streams, zip input streams do not absolutely have to be finished or closed when you're through with them, but it's polite to do so.

An example

Example 9-11 is an alternative unzipper that uses a ZipInputStream instead of a ZipFile. There's not really a huge advantage to using one or the other. Use whichever you find more convenient or aesthetically pleasing.

Example 9-11. Another Unzipper

```java
import java.util.*;
import java.util.zip.*;
import java.io.*;
import com.macfaq.io.*;

public class Unzipper2 {

  public static void main(String[] args) {

    for (int i = 0; i < args.length; i++) {
      try {
        FileInputStream fin = new FileInputStream(args[i]);
        ZipInputStream zin = new ZipInputStream(fin);
        ZipEntry ze = null;
        while ((ze = zin.getNextEntry()) != null) {
          System.out.println("Unzipping " + ze.getName());
          FileOutputStream fout = new FileOutputStream(ze.getName());
          StreamCopier.copy(zin, fout);
          zin.closeEntry();
          fout.close();
        }
        zin.close();
      }
      catch (IOException e) {
```

Example 9-11. Another Unzipper (continued)

```
        System.err.println(e);
        e.printStackTrace();
      }
    }
  }
}
```

Checksums

Compressed files are especially susceptible to corruption. While changing a bit from 0 to 1 or vice versa in a text file generally only affects a single character, changing a single bit in a compressed file often makes the entire file unreadable. Therefore, it's customary to store a checksum with the compressed file so that the recipient can verify that the file is intact. The zip format does this automatically, but you may wish to use manual checksums in other circumstances as well.

There are many different checksum schemes. A particularly simple example adds a parity bit to the data, typically 1 if the number of 1 bits is odd, 0 if the number of 1 bits is even. This checksum can be calculated by summing up the number of 1 bits and taking the remainder when that sum is divided by two. However, this scheme isn't very robust. It can detect single-bit errors, but in the face of bursts of errors as often occur in transmissions over modems and other noisy connections, there's a 50/50 chance that corrupt data will be reported as correct.

Better checksum schemes use more bits. For example, a 16-bit checksum could sum up the number of 1 bits and take the remainder modulo 65,536. This means that in the face of completely random data, there's only 1 in 65,536 chances of corrupt data being reported as correct. This chance drops exponentially as the number of bits in the checksum increases. More mathematically sophisticated schemes can reduce the likelihood of a false positive even further. For more details about checksums, see "Everything you wanted to know about CRC algorithms, but were afraid to ask for fear that errors in your understanding might be detected," by Ross Williams, available from *ftp://ftp.rocksoft.com/clients/rocksoft/papers/crc_v3.txt.* Of course, the advantage of a class library is that you only really need to understand the interface of the classes you use and what they do in broad perspective. You don't necessarily have to know all the technical details of the algorithms used inside the classes.

The `java.util.zip.Checksum` interface defines four methods for calculating a checksum for a sequence of bytes. Implementations of this interface provide specific checksum algorithms.

```
    public abstract void update(int b)
    public abstract void update(byte[] data, int offset, int length)
```

```
public abstract long getValue()
public abstract void reset()
```

The update() methods are used to calculate the initial checksum and to update the checksum as more bytes are added to the sequence. As bytes increase, the checksum changes. For example, using the parity checksum algorithm described earlier, if the byte 255 (binary 11111111) were added to the sequence, then the checksum would not change, because an even number of 1 bits had been added. If the byte 3 (binary 00000011) were added to the sequence, the checksum's value would flip (from 1 to 0 or 0 to 1), because an odd number of ones had been added to the sequence.

The getValue() method returns the current value of the checksum. The reset() method returns the checksum to its initial value. Example 9-12 shows about the simplest checksum class imaginable, one that implements the parity algorithm described earlier.

Example 9-12. The Parity Checksum

```java
import java.util.zip.*;

public class ParityChecksum implements Checksum {

  private long checksum = 0;

  public void update(int b) {

    int numOneBits = 0;
    for (int i = 1; i < 256; i *= 2) {
      if ((b & i) != 0) numOneBits++;
    }
    checksum = (checksum + numOneBits) % 2;
  }

  public void update(byte data[], int offset, int length) {

    for (int i = offset; i < offset+length; i++) {
      this.update(data[i]);
    }
  }

  public long getValue() {
    return checksum;
  }

  public void reset() {
    checksum = 0;
  }
}
```

The `java.util.zip` package provides two concrete implementations of the `Checksum` interface, CRC32 and `Adler32`. Both produce 32-bit checksums. The Adler-32 algorithm is not quite as reliable as CRC-32 but can be computed much faster. Both of these classes have a single no-argument constructor:

```
public CRC32()
public Adler32()
```

They share the same five methods, four implementing the methods of the `Checksum` interface, plus one additional `update()` method that reads an entire byte array:

```
public void update(int b)
public native void update(byte[] data, int offset, int length)
public void update(byte[] data)
public void reset()
public long getValue()
```

Example 9-13, `FileSummer`, is a simple program that calculates and prints a CRC-32 checksum for any file. However, it's structured such that the static `getCRC32()` method can calculate a CRC-32 checksum for any stream.

Example 9-13. FileSummer

```
import java.io.*;
import java.util.zip.*;

public class FileSummer {

  public static void main(String[] args) {

    for (int i = 0; i < args.length; i++) {
      try {
        FileInputStream fin = new FileInputStream(args[i]);
        System.out.println(args[i] + ":\t" + getCRC32(fin));
        fin.close();
      }
      catch (IOException e) {System.err.println(e);}
    }
  }

  public static long getCRC32(InputStream in) throws IOException {

    Checksum cs = new CRC32();

    // It would be more efficient to read chunks of data
    // at a time, but this is simpler and easier to understand.
    int b;
    while ((b = in.read()) != -1) {
      cs.update(b);
```

Example 9-13. FileSummer (continued)

```
    }
    return cs.getValue();
  }
}
```

This isn't as useful as it might appear at first. Most of the time, you don't want to read the entire stream just to calculate a checksum. Instead, you want to look at the bytes of the stream as they go past on their way to some other ultimate destination. You neither want to alter the bytes nor consume them. The CheckedInputStream and CheckedOutputStream filters allow you to do this.

Checked Streams

The java.util.zip.CheckedInputStream and java.util.zip.CheckedOutputStream classes keep a checksum of the data they've read or written.

```
public class CheckedInputStream extends FilterInputStream
public class CheckedOutputStream extends FilterOutputStream
```

These are filter streams, so they're constructed from an underlying stream and an object that implements the Checksum interface.

```
public CheckedInputStream(InputStream in, Checksum cksum)
public CheckedOutputStream(OutputStream out, Checksum cksum)
```

For example:

```
FileInputStream fin = new FileInputStream("/etc/passwd");
Checksum cksum = new CRC32();
CheckedInputStream cin = new CheckedInputStream(fin, cksum);
```

The CheckedInputStream and CheckedOutputStream classes have all the usual read(), write(), and other methods you expect in a stream class. The CheckedInputStream overrides two read() methods and one skip() method so that it can calculate the checksum as the bytes are read or skipped.

```
public int read() throws IOException
public int read(byte[] data, int offset, int length) throws IOException
public long skip(long n) throws IOException
```

Externally, these behave exactly like the methods in the superclass and do not require any special treatment.

Similarly, the CheckedOutputStream class overrides two write() methods from its superclass:

```
public void write(int b) throws IOException
public void write(byte[] data, int offset, int length) throws IOException
```

Again, these do not change the data in any way and may be used exactly like any other `write()` method. They simply update the internal checksum with the bytes written as they're written. Both `CheckedOutputStream` and `CheckedInput-Stream` have a `getChecksum()` method that returns the `Checksum` object for the stream. You can use this `Checksum` object to get the current value of the checksum for the stream.

```
public Checksum getChecksum()
```

These methods return a reference to the actual `Checksum` object that's being used to calculate the checksum. It is not copied first. Thus, if a separate thread is accessing this stream, the value in the checksum may change while you're working with the `Checksum` object. Conversely, if you invoke one of this `Checksum` object's `update()` methods, it affects the value of the checksum for the stream as well.

JAR Files

Java 1.1 added support for Java ARchive files, JAR files for short. JAR files bundle the many different classes, images, and sound files an applet requires into a single file. It is generally faster for a web browser to download one JAR file than to download the individual files the archive contains, since only one HTTP connection is required. An applet stored in a JAR file, instead of as merely loose *.class* files, is embedded in a web page with an `<applet>` tag with an `archive` attribute pointing to the JAR file. For example:

```
<applet code=NavigationMenu archive="NavigationMenu.jar" width=400 height=80>
</applet>
```

The `code` attribute still says that the main class of this applet is called `NavigationMenu`. However, a Java 1.1 web browser, rather than asking the web server for the file *NavigationMenu.class* as a Java 1.0 web browser would, asks the web server for the file *NavigationMenu.jar*. Then the browser looks inside *NavigationMenu.jar* to find the file *NavigationMenu.class*. Only if it doesn't find *NavigationMenu.class* inside *NavigationMenu.jar* does it then go back to the web server and ask for *NavigationMenu.class*. Now suppose the `NavigationMenu` applet tries to load an image called *menu.gif.* The applet will look for this file inside the JAR archive too. It only has to make a new connection to the web server if it can't find *menu.gif* in the archive.

Sun wisely decided not to attempt to define a new file format for JAR files. Instead, they stuck with the tried-and-true zip format. This means that the classes, images, sounds, and other files stored inside a JAR archive can be compressed, making the applet even faster to download. This also means that standard tools like PKZip and standard zip libraries like `java.util.zip` can work with JAR files.

JAR files have also become Java's preferred means of distributing Java Beans and class libraries. For instance, the Java Cryptography Extension, discussed in the next chapter, is mostly a set of classes packed up in the file *jce12-ea-dom.jar*. Since the library is distributed as a single file rather than a collection of nested folders, it's harder for one file to get moved or deleted. The overall system is more robust. To make the files contained in the archive available to Java, the complete path to the archive itself is added to the class path. For example, under Unix, to make the classes in the JAR archive *jce12-rc1-dom.jar* in the directory */usr/local/java/lib* available to your program, you'd use this command:

```
% setenv CLASSPATH $CLASSPATH:/usr/local/java/lib/jce12-rc1-dom.jar
```

The JAR file is treated like a directory in the context of the class path. This is sensible, because although the archive is a file to the file system, it behaves like a directory to Java.

Meta-Infomation: Manifest Files and Signatures

Aside from the three-letter extension, the only distinction between a zip file and a JAR file is that most (though not all) JAR files contain a manifest file that lists the contents of the JAR file as well as various information about those contents. The manifest file is named *MANIFEST.MF* and is stored in the *META-INF* directory at the top of the archive. This file provides meta-information about the contents of the archive in a particular format. This directory and file are not necessarily present in the unarchived collection. Generally, a manifest is added as part of the archiving process. The lefthand side of Figure 9-3 shows a directory structure for the com.macfaq package that can be stored in a JAR archive. The righthand side shows the contents of the corresponding JAR archive.

At a minimum, a manifest file must contain this opening line:

```
Manifest-Version: 1.0
```

A manifest usually contains additional entries for some of the files in the archive. However, the manifest does not necessarily contain an entry for every file in the archive. Entries are separated from each other by a blank line. Each entry is composed of a list of name/value pairs, one to a line. Names are separated from values by colons and whitespace, as in email headers. For example:

```
Name: com/macfaq/awt/Filmstrip.class
Java-Bean: true
Last-modified: 09-07-1998
Depends-On: com/macfaq/io/StreamCopier.class
Brad: Majors
Digest-Algorithms: MD5
MD5-Digest: XD4578YEEIK9MGX54RFGT7UJUI9810
```

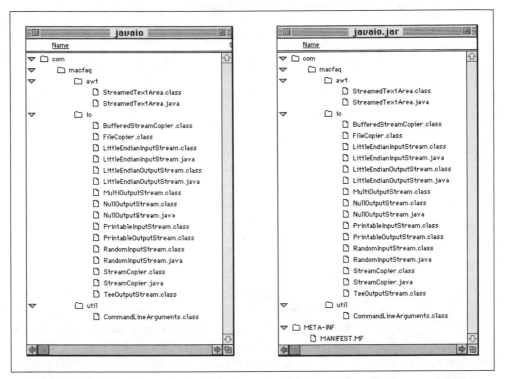

Figure 9-3. JAR archive: before and after

This defines an entry with the name *com/macfaq/awt/Filmstrip.class*. This entry has six attributes: `Java-Bean` with the value `true`, `Last-modified` with the value 09-07-1998, `Brad` with the value `Majors`, `Depends-On` with the value `com/macfaq/io/StreamCopier.class`, and so on. Each of these has a specific meaning in a particular context. For instance, the `Java-Bean` attribute with the value `true` means that this class is a Java Bean that can be loaded into a visual builder tool. `Digest-Algorithms` gives you the types of message digests computed from the file, and `MD5-Digest` gives the value of one particular digest. Most of the attributes have an application-specific meaning. Applications reading a JAR archive that don't understand a particular attribute should simply ignore it.

One possible manifest file for the directory shown in Figure 9-3 looks like this:

```
Manifest-Version: 1.0

Name: com/macfaq/awt/StreamedTextArea.class

Name: com/macfaq/io/BufferedStreamCopier.class

Name: com/macfaq/io/FileCopier.class
```

```
Name: com/macfaq/io/LittleEndianOutputStream.class

Name: com/macfaq/io/MultiOutputStream.class

Name: com/macfaq/io/NullOutputStream.class

Name: com/macfaq/io/PrintableInputStream.class

Name: com/macfaq/io/PrintableOutputStream.class

Name: com/macfaq/io/RandomInputStream.class

Name: com/macfaq/io/StreamCopier.class
Brad: Majors

Name: com/macfaq/io/TeeOutputStream.class
Riff: Raff

Name: com/macfaq/util/CommandLineArguments.class
```

The files in the JAR archive may be signed using a digital signature algorithm. Different individuals may sign different files, and more than one person may sign each file. For each file that's signed, the *META-INF* directory will also contain a signature file. I won't discuss signatures in great detail here; for starters, they're very different in Java 1.1 and Java 2. However, you should realize that signatures can be checked when a file is read from a JAR archive. If the signatures no longer match the files, then an IOException can be thrown (though this behavior is configurable at the programmer level).*

The jar Tool

Sun's JDK contains a simple command-line program called *jar* that packages a set of files or a directory structure into a JAR file. Its syntax is modeled after the Unix *tar* command. For instance, to verbosely compress the directory *com* into the file *javaio.jar* with the manifest file *javaio.mf*, you would type at the command line:

```
% jar cvmf javaio.mf javaio.jar com
added manifest
adding: com/ (in=0) (out=0) (stored 0%)
adding: com/macfaq/ (in=0) (out=0) (stored 0%)
adding: com/macfaq/io/ (in=0) (out=0) (stored 0%)
adding: com/macfaq/io/StreamCopier.class (in=887) (out=552) (deflated 37%)
adding: com/macfaq/io/NullOutputStream.class (in=374) (out=225) (deflated 39%)
adding: com/macfaq/io/RandomInputStream.class (in=792) (out=487) (deflated 38%)
```

---

* If you're interested, the details are available in *Java Security*, by Scott Oaks (O'Reilly & Associates, 1998).

```
adding: com/macfaq/io/NullOutputStream.java (in=263) (out=149) (deflated 43%)
adding: com/macfaq/io/StreamCopier.java (in=764) (out=377) (deflated 50%)
```

Several lines have been deleted to save space. After this, the *javaio.jar* file can be placed in the class path to provide access to all the files and packages it contains. To extract files, change cvmf (*c*reate *v*erbose with *m*anifest *f*ile) to xvf (*ex*tract *v*erbose *f*ile). If you don't care to see each file as it's added or extracted, you can omit the v argument:

```
% jar xf javaio.jar
```

You can also use any other zip tool to create or unpack JAR archives. However, you'll have to include the *META-INF/MANIFEST.MF* file manually. The JDK also includes a *jarsigner* tool that digitally signs JAR archives and verifies JAR archives signed by others using a public key system.

The java.util.jar Package

The java.util.zip package was included in Java 1.1 primarily to support JAR archives. The java.util.jar package, added in Java 2, provides additional support for reading and writing manifests. It contains seven classes and one exception, shown in Figure 9-4. As you can see, almost everything in this package is a subclass of a related class in the java.util.zip package. JAR files are zip files, and they are read and written just like zip files. In fact, you don't have to use the java.util.jar package at all. java.util.zip and the standard I/O and string classes are enough to do anything you need to do, but java.util.jar certainly does make your job easier when you need to read manifest entries.

All of these classes are used much like their superclasses are. For instance, to read a JAR file, follow these steps:

1. Construct a JarInputStream object from an underlying stream, most commonly a file input stream.

2. Open the next JAR entry in the archive.

3. Read data from the JAR entry using InputStream methods like read().

4. Close the JAR entry (optional)

5. Repeat steps 2 through 4 as long as there are more entries (files) remaining in the archive.

6. Close the JAR input stream.

These are the same six steps you use to read a zip file, only with the java.util. zip classes replaced by their counterparts in java.util.jar. Even that much is unnecessary. All the standard zip tools as well the programs developed in this chapter can work equally well with JAR files. However, the java.util.jar classes

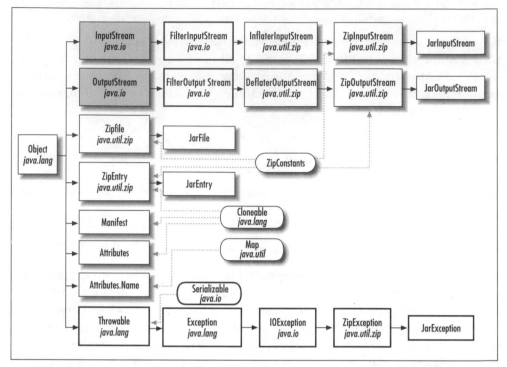

Figure 9-4. The java.util.jar package hierarchy

do provide some extra convenience methods for reading and writing manifest entries.

JarFile

The `java.util.jar.JarFile` class represents a file in the JAR format. It is a subclass of `java.util.zip.ZipFile`, and `JarFile` objects are almost exactly like `ZipFile` objects.

```
public class JarFile extends ZipFile  // Java 2
```

The `JarFile` class has four constructors:

```
public JarFile(String filename) throws IOException                     // Java 2
public JarFile(String filename, boolean verify) throws IOException  // Java 2
public JarFile(File file) throws IOException                          // Java 2
public JarFile(File file, boolean verify) throws IOException         // Java 2
```

The first argument specifies the file to be read, either by name or with a `java.io.File` object. The optional second argument `verify` is important only for signed JAR files. If `verify` is true, signatures will be checked against the file's contents; if `verify` is false, signatures will not be checked against the file's contents. The default is to check signatures. An `IOException` is thrown if an entry does not match its signature when verified.

The `JarFile` class is so similar in interface and behavior to `java.util.zip.ZipFile` that I can spare you a lot of details about most of its methods. It declares only five methods, though of course you shouldn't forget about the others it inherits from its superclass.

```
public ZipEntry getEntry(String name)                                // Java 2
public Enumeration entries()                                         // Java 2
public InputStream getInputStream(ZipEntry ze) throws IOException    // Java 2
public JarEntry getJarEntry(String name)                            // Java 2
public Manifest getManifest() throws IOException                    // Java 2
```

`getEntry()`, `entries()`, and `getInputStream()` are used exactly as they are for zip files. `getJarEntry()` is used almost exactly like `getEntry()`, except that it's declared to return an instance of `JarEntry`, a subclass of `ZipEntry`. Some extra work takes place in these methods to read the manifest file and verify signatures, but unless the signatures don't verify (in which case an `IOException` is thrown), none of this is relevant to the client programmer. The one really interesting new method in this list is `getManifest()`, which returns an instance of the `java.util.jar.Manifest` class. You can use this to read the entries in the manifest file, as described in the section on the `Manifest` class later in this chapter.

JarEntry

`JarEntry` objects represent files stored inside a JAR archive. `JarEntry` is a subclass of `java.util.zip.ZipEntry`, and `JarEntry` objects are almost exactly like `ZipEntry` objects.

```
public class JarEntry extends ZipEntry  // Java 2
```

`JarEntry` has three constructors:

```
public JarEntry(String filename)  // Java 2
public JarEntry(ZipEntry ze)      // Java 2
public JarEntry(JarEntry je)      // Java 2
```

You might use the first one if you were creating a JAR file from scratch, though that's rare. The other two are mainly for Java's internal use to allow the internal state of one `JarEntry` object to be quickly copied to a new one.

`JarEntry` does not override any methods from `ZipEntry`. It inherits all of `ZipEntry`'s assorted getter and setter and utility methods. It also provides two new methods:

```
public Attributes getAttributes() throws IOException  // Java 2
public Certificate[] getCertificates()                // Java 2
```

The getAttributes() method returns the attributes for this entry as documented in the manifest file of the archive. In brief, an Attributes object is a map of the name/value pairs for the entry. This will be discussed further in the next section. The getCertificates() method returns an array of java.security. cert.Certificate objects formed from any signature files for this entry stored in the archive. These can be used to allow some classes more access to the system than they would normally get. I won't go into this possibility here; the details are available in *Java Security*.

Attributes

The java.util.jar.Attributes class is mostly just a concrete implementation of the java.util.Map interface from the Collections API.

```
public class Attributes implements Map, Cloneable  // Java 2
```

An Attributes object is a container for an entry in a manifest file. Recall that the entry is composed of name/value pairs; the keys of the map are the names, while the values of the entries are the values of the map. The Attributes class is accessed almost entirely through the methods of the Map interface and has three public constructors:

```
public Attributes()             // Java 2
public Attributes(int size)     // Java 2
public Attributes(Attributes a) // Java 2
```

However, these are primarily for Java's internal use. Most of the time, you'll simply retrieve Attributes objects from the getAttributes() method of JarEntry or the getAttributes() and getMainAttributes() method of Manifest.

The Attributes class implements all the usual Map methods:

```
public Object get(Object name)                    // Java 2
public Object put(Object name, Object value)      // Java 2
public Object remove(Object name)                 // Java 2
public boolean containsValue(Object value)        // Java 2
public boolean containsKey(Object name)           // Java 2
public void putAll(Map attr)                      // Java 2
public void clear()                               // Java 2
public int size()                                 // Java 2
public boolean isEmpty()                          // Java 2
public Set keySet()                               // Java 2
public Collection values()                        // Java 2
public Set entrySet()                             // Java 2
public boolean equals(Object o)                   // Java 2
public int hashCode()                             // Java 2
```

The key objects for this map should all be `Attributes.Name` objects. `Attributes.Name` is a rare public inner class called `Name` inside the `Attributes` class. However, it's simplest to just think of it as another class in `java.util.jar` with a somewhat funny name. This strangely named class has a single constructor:

```
public Attributes.Name(String name)  // Java 2
```

The `java.util.jar.Attributes.Name` class represents the name half of the name/value pairs in a manifest file. Attribute names are restricted to the upper- and lowercase letters A–Z, the digits 0–9, the underscore, and the hyphen. The `Attributes.Name()` constructor checks to make sure that the name is legal and throws an `IllegalArgumentException` if it isn't.

`Attributes.Name` overrides the three major utility methods but has no other methods. It exists only to be a key in the `Attributes` map.

```
public boolean equals(Object o)   // Java 2
public int hashCode()             // Java 2
public String toString()          // Java 2
```

The `Attributes.Name` class defines some mnemonic constants that identify particular attribute names found in some kinds of JAR files. These are all `Attributes.Name` objects.

```
Attributes.Name.MANIFEST_VERSION        // "Manifest-Version"
Attributes.Name.SIGNATURE_VERSION       // "Signature-Version"
Attributes.Name.CONTENT_TYPE            // "Content-Type"
Attributes.Name.CLASS_PATH              // "Class-Path"
Attributes.Name.MAIN_CLASS              // "Main-Class"
Attributes.Name.SEALED                  // "Sealed"
Attributes.Name.IMPLEMENTATION_TITLE    // "Implementation-Title"
Attributes.Name.IMPLEMENTATION_VERSION  // "Implementation-Version"
Attributes.Name.IMPLEMENTATION_VENDOR   // "Implementation-Vendor"
Attributes.Name.SPECIFICATION_TITLE     // "Specification-Title"
Attributes.Name.SPECIFICATION_VERSION   // "Specification-Version"
Attributes.Name.SPECIFICATION_VENDOR    // "Specification-Vendor"
```

Since `Attributes` implements `Cloneable` as well as `Map`, it also provides a `clone()` method:

```
public Object clone()   // Java 2
```

Unlike maps in general, `Attributes` maps only contain strings, raw strings as values, and strings embedded in an `Attributes.Name` object. Therefore, the `Attributes` class contains three extra map-like methods for getting and putting strings into the map:

```
public String putValue(String name, String value)  // Java 2
public String getValue(String name)                // Java 2
public String getValue(Attributes.Name name)       // Java 2
```

The last one takes an `Attributes.Name` object as an argument. Example 9-14 is a revised version of the `FancyZipLister` from Example 9-9. This program works with JAR files and prints the attributes of each entry as well as the information seen previously.

Example 9-14. JarLister

```java
import java.util.*;
import java.util.zip.*;
import java.util.jar.*;
import java.io.*;

public class JarLister {

  public static void main(String[] args) {

    for (int i = 0; i < args.length; i++) {
      try {
        JarFile jf = new JarFile(args[i]);

        Enumeration e = jf.entries();
        while (e.hasMoreElements()) {
          JarEntry je = (JarEntry) e.nextElement();
          String name = je.getName();
          Date lastModified = new Date(je.getTime());
          long uncompressedSize = je.getSize();
          long compressedSize = je.getCompressedSize();
          long crc = je.getCrc();
          int method = je.getMethod();
          String comment = je.getComment();

          if (method == ZipEntry.STORED) {
            System.out.println(name + " was stored at " + lastModified);
            System.out.println("with a size of  " + uncompressedSize
              + " bytes");
          }
          else if (method == ZipEntry.DEFLATED) {
            System.out.println(name + " was deflated at " + lastModified);
            System.out.println("from  " + uncompressedSize + " bytes to "
              + compressedSize + " bytes, a savings of "
              + 100.0*(1.0 - compressedSize/uncompressedSize) + "%");
          }
          else {
            System.out.println(name
              + " was compressed using an unrecognized method at "
              + lastModified);
            System.out.println("from  " + uncompressedSize + " bytes to "
              + compressedSize + " bytes, a savings of "
              + 100.0*(1.0 - compressedSize/uncompressedSize) + "%");
```

Example 9-14. JarLister (continued)

```
        }
        System.out.println("Its CRC is " + crc);
        if (comment != null && !comment.equals("")) {
          System.out.println(comment);
        }
        if (je.isDirectory()) {
          System.out.println(name + " is a directory");
        }
        Attributes a = je.getAttributes();
        if (a != null) {
          Object[] nameValuePairs = a.entrySet().toArray();
          for (int j = 0; j < nameValuePairs.length; j++) {
            System.out.println(nameValuePairs[j]);
          }
        }
        System.out.println();
      }
    }
    catch (IOException e) {
      System.err.println(e);
      e.printStackTrace();
    }
  }
 }
}
```

Manifest

What the `java.util.jar` classes add to the superclasses in `java.util.zip` is the ability to read the attributes of each JAR entry as well as the manifest for the entire JAR archive. Recall that a JAR archive should have exactly one manifest file. That manifest file has entries that apply to the entire file as well as entries for some (though perhaps not all) of the files stored in the archive. Although physically the manifest file belongs to the entire archive, logically parts of it belong to different entries in the archive. The `java.util.jar.Manifest` class represents this manifest file.

```
    public class Manifest extends Object implements Cloneable  // Java 2
```

It has methods to get the entries and attributes of a manifest, to write the manifest onto an output stream or to read entries from an input stream, and an assortment of utility methods. The `Manifest` class has three constructors:

```
    public Manifest()                                     // Java 2
    public Manifest(InputStream in) throws IOException    // Java 2
    public Manifest(Manifest man)                         // Java 2
```

The first constructor creates an empty manifest (one with no entries); the second reads the manifest from the given stream; the third copies the manifest from the Manifest object passed as an argument. However, all three are mostly for the internal use of Java. Instead, client programmers use the getManifest() method of JarFile to retrieve the Manifest object for the manifest file in a particular archive. For example:

```
JarFile jf = new JarFile("classes.jar");
Manifest m = jf.getManifest();
```

The Manifest class has three methods that return a map of the entries in the manifest. getEntries() returns an unspecified Map (a HashMap object in JDK 1.2beta4) in which the keys are the entry names and the values are the Attributes objects for the entry:

```
public Map getEntries()  // Java 2
```

The getMainAttributes() method returns an Attributes object representing the attributes in the manifest file that apply to the file as a whole rather than to any individual entry in the file, such as Manifest-Version:

```
public Attributes getMainAttributes()  // Java 2
```

The getAttributes() method returns an Attributes object containing the name/value pairs of the named entry. The Name attribute is not included in this list:

```
public Attributes getAttributes(String entryName)  // Java 2
```

The clear() method removes all entries and attributes from the manifest so that it can be reused; client programmers have little reason to call this method:

```
public void clear() // Java 2
```

The Manifest class also contains methods to read a Manifest object from an input stream and write one onto an output stream. These are mostly for Java's private use.

```
public void write(OutputStream out) throws IOException  // Java 2
public void read(InputStream in) throws IOException     // Java 2
```

The write() method is particularly useless, since there's no good way to create a Manifest object and add attributes to it from within Java.* Most commonly, you'll simply work with Manifest objects returned by getManifest().

Finally, the Manifest class overrides the default implementations of equals() and clone():

```
public boolean equals(Object o)  // Java 2
public Object clone()            // Java 2
```

---

* I suppose you could write a manifest file on a byte array output stream, create a byte array input stream from the output stream's byte array, then read it back in, but that's really a kludge.

JarInputStream

JarInputStream is a subclass of ZipInputStream that reads data from JAR archives.

```
public class JarInputStream extends ZipInputStream  // Java 2
```

There are two constructors that chain the JAR input stream to an underlying input stream.

```
public JarInputStream(InputStream in) throws IOException  // Java 2
public JarInputStream(InputStream in, boolean verify)
        throws IOException                                 // Java 2
```

By default, any signatures present in the JAR archive will be verified and an IOException thrown if verification fails. However, you can turn this behavior off by passing false as the second argument to the constructor. For example:

```
FileInputStream fin = new FileInputStream("javaio.jar");
JarInputStream jin = new JarInputStream(fin, false);
```

When the JarInputStream object is constructed, the manifest, if present, is read from the stream and stored inside the class as a Manifest object. You do not get an opportunity to read the manifest from the stream yourself. However, you can retrieve the Manifest object with the getManifest() method:

```
public Manifest getManifest()  // Java 2
```

Otherwise, a JAR input stream is used almost exactly like a zip input stream. You position the stream on a particular entry in the file, then read data from it using the normal read() methods. Any necessary inflation is performed transparently. When you've finished reading an entry, you close it, then position the stream on the next entry. Two methods, getNextEntry() and read(), are overridden so that verification of signatures can be performed. A getNextJarEntry() method that returns a JarEntry instead of ZipEntry is also available. This method can be used in place of getNextEntry(), if you like.

```
public ZipEntry getNextEntry() throws IOException     // Java 2
public int read(byte[] data, int offset, int length)
        throws IOException                             // Java 2
public JarEntry getNextJarEntry() throws IOException  // Java 2
```

JarOutputStream

JarOutputStream is a subclass of ZipOutputStream.

```
public class JarOutputStream extends ZipOutputStream  // Java 2
```

You can specify a manifest for the archive in the constructor, but this is optional. If you don't provide a manifest, none is written onto the stream.

```
public JarOutputStream(OutputStream out, Manifest man) throws IOException
                                                    // Java 2
public JarOutputStream(OutputStream out) throws IOException  // Java 2
```

This class is even closer to `ZipOutputStream` than `JarInputStream` is to `ZipInputStream`. It overrides exactly one method, `putNextEntry()`:

```
public void putNextEntry(ZipEntry ze) throws IOException  // Java 2
```

This is done in order to store the JAR magic number with each entry, but you don't need to know this. Other than the constructor invocation, you use this class exactly like you use `ZipOutputStream`.

JarURLConnection

In Java 2 and later, one of the simplest ways to get information from a JAR file is through the `java.net.JarURLConnection` class. This class represents an active connection to a JAR file, generally either via the HTTP or file protocols.

```
public abstract class JarURLConnection extends URLConnection
```

It provides methods to get the URL, name, manifest, JAR entries, attributes, and certificates associated with the JAR file and its entries. The only constructor in this class is protected:

```
protected JarURLConnection(URL url) throws MalformedURLException
```

As you with most `URLConnection` subclasses, you don't instantiate `JarURLConnection` directly. Instead, you create a `URL` object using a the string form of a JAR URL and invoke its `openConnection()` method. For example:

```
try {
  URL u = new URL(
   "jar:http://www.oreilly.com/javaio.jar!/com/macfaq/io/StreamCopier.class");
  URLConnection juc = u.openConnection();
  // ...
}
catch (MalformedURLException e) {
 // ...
}
```

Notice the strange URL in the previous code. A JAR URL is like a normal HTTP or file URL pointing to a JAR file with the prefix "jar:" added to the URL's scheme (i.e., *jar:http:* or *jar:file:*). After the hostname, you place the pathname to the JAR file on the server. After the JAR filename, you add an exclamation point and a path to the particular entry you want within the JAR archive. For example, to refer to the file *StreamCopier.class* in the *com/macfaq/io* directory of the JAR file *javaio.jar* located at *http://www.oreilly.com/*, you would use the JAR URL *jar:http://www.oreilly. com/javaio.jar!/com/macfaq/io/StreamCopier.class*. If the entry is omitted, then the

URL refers to the JAR archive as a whole; for example, *jar:http://www.oreilly.com/ javaio.jar!/*.

If you only want to read data from the connection using `getInputStream()` from the `URLConnection` superclass, the previous code will suffice. If you want to use the methods of the `JarURLConnection` class directly, then you should cast the object returned from `openConnection()` to `JarURLConnection`. For example:

```
try {
  URL u = new URL(
    "jar:http://www.oreilly.com/javaio.jar!/com/macfaq/io/StreamCopier.class");
  JarURLConnection juc = (JarURLConnection) u.openConnection();
  // ...
}
catch (MalformedURLException e) {
  // ...
}
```

Once you've done this, you can use eight methods that provide easy access to various meta-information about the JAR file and its contents. This meta-information comes from the archive's manifest or certificate files. The `getJarFileURL()` method returns the URL of the JAR file for this connection:

```
public URL getJarFileURL()
```

This is most useful if the URL refers to a particular entry in the file. In that instance, the URL returned by `getJarFileURL()` refers to the URL of the archive. For example:

```
URL u = new URL(
  "jar:http://www.oreilly.com/javaio.jar!/com/macfaq/io/StreamCopier.class");
JarURLConnection juc = (JarURLConnection) u.openConnection();
URL base = juc.getURL();
```

The URL object **base** now refers to *http://www.oreilly.com/javaio.jar*.

The `getEntryName()` method returns the name of the JAR entry this JAR URL refers to. It returns `null` if the JAR URL points to a JAR file as a whole rather than to one of the entries in the file.

```
public String getEntryName()
```

The `getJarFile()` method returns an immutable `JarFile` object for the JAR archive referred to by this URL. You can read the state of this object, but you cannot change it. Attempts to do so throw a `java.lang.Unsupported-OperationException`. This is a runtime exception, so you do not have to catch it.

```
public abstract JarFile getJarFile() throws IOException
```

The `getJarEntry()` method returns an immutable `JarEntry` object for the JAR entry referred to by this URL. You can read the state of this object, but you cannot change it. Attempts to do so throw a `java.lang.UnsupportedOperation-Exception`.

```
public JarEntry getJarEntry() throws IOException
```

The `getManifest()` method returns an immutable `Manifest` object constructed from the manifest file in the JAR archive. It returns `null` if the archive doesn't have a manifest. Again, you cannot modify this `Manifest` object, and any attempt to do so will throw an `UnsupportedOperationException`.

```
public Manifest getManifest() throws IOException
```

The `getAttributes()` method returns an `Attributes` object representing the attributes of the JAR entry this URL refers to. It returns `null` if the URL refers to a JAR file rather than a particular entry. To get the attributes of the entire archive, use the `getMainAttributes()` method instead.

```
public Attributes getAttributes() throws IOException
public Attributes getMainAttributes() throws IOException
```

The `getCertificates()` method returns an array of `java.security.cert.Certificate` objects containing the certificates for the JAR entry this URL refers to (if any). This method returns `null` if the URL refers to a JAR file rather than a JAR entry.

```
public Certificate[] getCertificates() throws IOException
```

File Viewer, Part 4

Because of the nature of filter streams, it is relatively straightforward to add decompression services to the `FileDumper` program last seen in Chapter 7, *Data Streams*. Generally, you'll want to decompress a file before dumping it. Adding decompression does not require a new dump filter. Instead, it simply requires passing the file through an inflater input stream before passing it to one of the dump filters. We'll let the user choose from either gzipped or deflated files with the command-line switches –gz and –deflate. When one of these switches is seen, the appropriate inflater input stream is selected; it is an error to select both. Example 9-15, `FileDumper4`, demonstrates.

Example 9-15. FileDumper4

```
import java.io.*;
import java.util.zip.*;
import com.macfaq.io.*;

public class FileDumper4 {

  public static final int ASC = 0;
```

Example 9-15. FileDumper4 (continued)

```java
public static final int DEC = 1;
public static final int HEX = 2;
public static final int SHORT = 3;
public static final int INT = 4;
public static final int LONG = 5;
public static final int FLOAT = 6;
public static final int DOUBLE = 7;

public static void main(String[] args) {

  if (args.length < 1) {
    System.err.println("Usage: java FileDumper2 [-ahdsilfx] [-little]"+
                                  "[-gzip|-deflated] file1...");
  }

  boolean bigEndian = true;
  int firstFile = 0;
  int mode = ASC;
  boolean deflated = false;
  boolean gzipped = false;

  // Process command-line switches.
  for (firstFile = 0; firstFile < args.length; firstFile++) {
    if (!args[firstFile].startsWith("-")) break;
    if (args[firstFile].equals("-h")) mode = HEX;
    else if (args[firstFile].equals("-d")) mode = DEC;
    else if (args[firstFile].equals("-s")) mode = SHORT;
    else if (args[firstFile].equals("-i")) mode = INT;
    else if (args[firstFile].equals("-l")) mode = LONG;
    else if (args[firstFile].equals("-f")) mode = FLOAT;
    else if (args[firstFile].equals("-x")) mode = DOUBLE;
    else if (args[firstFile].equals("-little")) bigEndian = false;
    else if (args[firstFile].equals("-deflated") && !gzipped) deflated = true;
    else if (args[firstFile].equals("-gzip") && !deflated) gzipped = true;
  }

  for (int i = firstFile; i < args.length; i++) {
    try {
      InputStream in = new FileInputStream(args[i]);
      dump(in, System.out, mode, bigEndian, deflated, gzipped);

      if (i < args.length-1) {  // more files to dump
        System.out.println();
        System.out.println("-------------------------------------");
        System.out.println();
      }
    }
    catch (Exception e) {
```

Example 9-15. FileDumper4 (continued)

```java
      System.err.println(e);
      e.printStackTrace();
    }
  }
}


  public static void dump(InputStream in, OutputStream out, int mode,
   boolean bigEndian, boolean deflated, boolean gzipped) throws IOException {

    // The reference variable in may point to several different objects
    // within the space of the next few lines. We can attach
    //  more filters here to do decompression, decryption, and more.
    if (deflated) {
      in = new InflaterInputStream(in);
    }
    else if (gzipped) {
      in = new GZIPInputStream(in);
    }

    // could really pass to FileDumper3 at this point
    if (bigEndian) {
      DataInputStream din = new DataInputStream(in);
      switch (mode) {
        case HEX:
          in = new HexFilter(in);
          break;
        case DEC:
          in = new DecimalFilter(in);
          break;
        case INT:
          in = new IntFilter(din);
          break;
        case SHORT:
          in = new ShortFilter(din);
          break;
        case LONG:
          in = new LongFilter(din);
          break;
        case DOUBLE:
          in = new DoubleFilter(din);
          break;
        case FLOAT:
          in = new FloatFilter(din);
          break;
        default:
      }
    }
    else {
```

Example 9-15. FileDumper4 (continued)

```
    LittleEndianInputStream lin = new LittleEndianInputStream(in);
    switch (mode) {
      case HEX:
        in = new HexFilter(in);
        break;
      case DEC:
        in = new DecimalFilter(in);
        break;
      case INT:
        in = new LEIntFilter(lin);
        break;
      case SHORT:
        in = new LEShortFilter(lin);
        break;
      case LONG:
        in = new LELongFilter(lin);
        break;
      case DOUBLE:
        in = new LEDoubleFilter(lin);
        break;
      case FLOAT:
        in = new LEFloatFilter(lin);
        break;
      default:
    }
  }
  StreamCopier.copy(in, out);
  in.close();
  }
}
```

Note how little I had to change to add support for compressed files. I simply imported one package and added a couple of command-line switches and six lines of code (which could easily have been two) to test for the command-line arguments and add one more filter stream to the chain. Zip and JAR files would not be hard to support either. You'd just have to iterate through the entries in the archive and dump each entry onto System.out. That's left as an exercise for the reader.

10

In this chapter:
- *Hash Function Basics*
- *The MessageDigest Class*
- *Digest Streams*
- *Encryption Basics*
- *The Cipher Class*
- *Cipher Streams*
- *File Viewer, Part 5*

Cryptographic Streams

This chapter discusses filter streams that implement some sort of cryptography. The Java core API contains two of these in the `java.security` package, `DigestInputStream` and `DigestOutputStream`. There are two more cryptography streams in the `javax.crypto` package, `CipherInputStream` and `CipherOutputStream`. All four of these streams use an engine object to handle the filtering. `DigestInputStream` and `DigestOutputStream` use a `MessageDigest` object, while `CipherInputStream` and `CipherOutputStream` use a `Cipher` object. The streams rely on the programmer to properly initialize and—in the case of the digest streams—clean up after the engines. Therefore, we'll first look at the engine classes, then at the streams built around these engines.

In a sane world, these classes would all be part of the core API in a `java.crypto` package. Regrettably, U.S. export laws prohibit the export of cryptographic software without special permission. Therefore, the cryptography API and associated classes must be downloaded separately from the main JDK. Collectively these are called the Java Cryptography Extension, or JCE for short. To protect national security, you'll have to fill out a form promising you're not an international terrorist before you can download it.* I feel safer already. If you're outside the United States and Canada, and you're one of the three people worldwide who actually respect U.S. export laws or who can't figure out how to penetrate the incredible security Sun has placed around JCE to make sure it doesn't fall into the hands of international terrorists, there are several third-party implementations of the JCE created outside the United States and thus not subject to its laws, including at least two free ones. These may not be completely synced with the beta release of the JCE 1.2 discussed here, but they should be close by the time you read this.

---

* Domestic terrorists may download it freely.

216

Although the initial version of the JCE worked with Java 1.1, the only version available from Sun at the time of this writing, JCE 1.2, requires Java 2 to run. The material in this chapter about message digests, hash functions, and digest streams applies to both Java 1.1 and 2. The remainder of the chapter, encryption and decryption mostly, only works in Java 2.

Hash Function Basics

Sometimes it's essential to know whether data has changed. For instance, crackers invading Unix systems often replace crucial files like *etc/passwd* or *usr/ucb/cc* with their own hacked versions that allow them to regain access to the system if the original hole they entered through is plugged. Therefore, if you discover your system has been penetrated, one of the first things you need to do is to replace any changed files. Of course, this raises the question of how you identify the changed files, especially since anybody who's capable of replacing system executables is more than capable of resetting the last-modified date of the files. You can keep an offline copy of the system files, but this is costly and difficult, especially since multiple copies need to be stored for long periods of time. If you don't discover a penetration until several months after it occurred, you may need to roll back the system files to that point in time. Recent backups are likely to have been made after the penetration occurred and thus are also likely to be compromised.

As a less threatening example, suppose you want to be notified whenever a particular web page changes. It's not hard to write a robot that connects to the site at periodic intervals, downloads the page, and compares it to a previously retrieved copy for changes. However, if you need to do this for hundreds or thousands of web pages, the space to store the pages becomes prohibitive. Email clients have similar needs. Many broken mail clients and mailing list managers send multiple copies of the same message. A mail client should recognize when multiple copies of the same message are being passed through the system and delete them. On an ISP level, it might be possible to use this as a spam filter by comparing messages sent to different customers.

All these tasks need a way to compare files at different times without storing the files themselves. You can write a special kind of method called a hash function that reads an indefinite number of sequential bytes and assigns a number to that sequence of bytes. This number is called a *hash code* or *digest*. The size of the number depends on the hash function. It is not necessarily the same size as any Java primitive data type like `int` or `long`. For instance, digests calculated with the SHA algorithm are 20-byte numbers. You can store the digest of the files, then compare the digests. The digests are generally much smaller than the files themselves.

Hash functions are also used in digital signatures. To indicate that you actually authored a document, you first calculate the hash function for the message, then encrypt the hash code with your private key. To check your signature, the recipient of the message decrypts the hash code with your public key and compares it to the hash function you calculated. If they match, then only someone who knew your private key could have signed the message. Although you could simply encrypt the entire message with your private key rather than a hash code, public key algorithms are rather slow, and encrypting a 20-byte hash code is much faster than encrypting even a short email message. In Java, digital signatures are implemented through the `java.security.Signature` class. We won't talk much about that class in this book, but it is dependent on the `MessageDigest` classes we will discuss.

Requirements for Hash Functions

Hash codes are calculated by hash functions, and there are better and worse hash functions. Good hash functions (also called strong hash functions) make it extremely unlikely that two different documents will share a hash value. Furthermore, hash functions used for cryptography must also be one-way hash functions—that is, given a hash code, you should not be able to create a document with that hash code. A strong one-way hash function must meet several related criteria. Among these criteria are the following:

- Hash functions are deterministic. The same document always has the same hash code. The hash code does not depend on the time it's calculated, a random number, or anything other than the sequence of bytes in the document. Without this requirement, the same document could have different hash codes at different times, thus indicating that documents had changed, when in fact they hadn't.

- Hash codes should be uniformly distributed throughout the available range. Given any sample of the documents you wish to track, all hash codes are equally likely. For instance, given a 64-bit hash code, which might be interpreted as a long integer, it would be an error if even numbers were substantially more likely than odd numbers.

- Hash codes should be extremely difficult to reverse engineer. Given a hash code, there should be no means easier than brute force to produce a document that matches that hash code. For instance, if I know the hash code is 9,423,456,789, I shouldn't be able to then create a file that happens to have that exact hash code.

- It should be difficult to find two documents that share a hash code. You cannot easily find two documents with the same hash code, regardless of what that hash code is. The previous criterion means that you can't change the document to match a hash code. This criterion says you can't change two documents to match each other.

- Small changes in documents produce large changes in the hash code. Mathematicians call this criterion "sensitive dependence on initial conditions." Without this requirement, somebody attempting to create a document with a given hash code could modify the document a little at a time until the hash code matched, much as you might adjust the hot and cold water faucets gradually until the water reaches a desired temperature. A hash function should act more like a faucet that can scald or freeze you after the tiniest nudge.

- The hash code does not say anything about the document it represents. The one-way hash function is not even partially invertible. For instance, knowing that the hash code is even should not suggest that the document being hashed contains an even number of bytes. Nor should it suggest that the document being hashed is 60% more likely to contain an even number of bytes than an odd number. While one-way hash functions need to be reproducible—that is, the same document always has the same hash code—they should otherwise be completely random. It is extremely hard, perhaps impossible, to prove that any function meets this criterion. Nonetheless, stronger functions come closer than weaker functions, and years of experience among cryptographers allow them to make reasonable guesses about what are and are not strong hash functions, even if their hunches can't be proved to a mathematical certainty.

The proper design of one-way hash functions is a well-studied field. It's easy to create weak one-way hash functions. However, it is much harder to create truly strong, reliable, one-way hash functions. Nonexperts tend to make nonobvious but serious mistakes when implementing hash functions. Therefore, this is a task that's best left to the experts. Fortunately, the Java core API contains some hash functions designed by experts that the rest of us can use without earning a Ph.D. in applied mathematics first.

NOTE   The hash codes used by the `java.util.Hashtable` class and returned by the `hashCode()` method of any Java object are only intended to be used as IDs for elements of a hash table, not as cryptographically strong digest. These sorts of hash codes have different requirements for utility. Most of the time, they only need to meet the first two of the six criteria given earlier, and in practice they often don't meet even that. The `hashCode()` method is a hash function but not necessarily a *one-way* hash function.

The MessageDigest Class

The `java.security.MessageDigest` class is an abstract class that represents a hash code and its associated algorithm. Concrete subclasses (actually concrete subclasses of `java.security.MessageDigestSPI`, though the difference isn't relevant from a client's point of view) implement particular, professionally designed, well-known hash code algorithms. Thus, rather than constructing instances of this class directly, you ask the static `MessageDigest.getInstance()` factory method to provide an implementation of an algorithm with a particular name. Table 10-1 lists the standard names for message digest algorithms. Depending on which service providers are installed, you may or may not have all of these. The JDK 1.1 includes SHA-1 (which is the same as SHA) and MD5 but not MD2. RSA's payware JSafe cryptography library also supports MD2. (See *http://www.rsa.com/rsa/products/jsafe/.*)

Table 10-1. Message Digest Algorithms in Java 1.1

Name	Algorithm
SHA-1	The Secure Hash Algorithm, as defined in Secure Hash Standard, NIST FIPS 180-1 (National Institute of Standards and Technology Federal Information Processing Standards Publications 180-1); produces 20-byte digests; see *http://www.itl.nist.gov/div897/pubs/fip180-1.htm*
SHA	Another name for SHA-1
MD2	RSA-MD2 as defined in RFC 1319 and RFC 1423 (RFC 1423 corrects a mistake in RFC 1319); produces 16-byte digests; suitable for use with digital signatures; see *http://www.faqs.org/rfcs/rfc1319.htm* and *http://www.faqs.org/rfcs/rfc1423.txt*
MD5	RSA-MD5 as defined in RFC 1321; produces 16-byte digests; quite fast on 32-bit machines; see *http://www.faqs.org/rfcs/rfc1321.txt*

Calculating Message Digests

There are four steps to calculating a hash code for a file or other sequential set of bytes with a `MessageDigest` object; Figure 10-1 shows a flow chart for this process.

1. Pass the name of the algorithm you want to use to the static `MessageDigest.getInstance()` factory method to get a new `MessageDigest` object.

2. Feed bytes into the `update()` method.

3. If more data remains, repeat step 2.

4. Invoke a `digest()` method to complete computation of the digest and return it as an array of bytes.

Once the `digest()` method has been invoked, the digest is reset. You can begin again at step 1 to calculate a new digest, but you cannot update the digest you've already created.

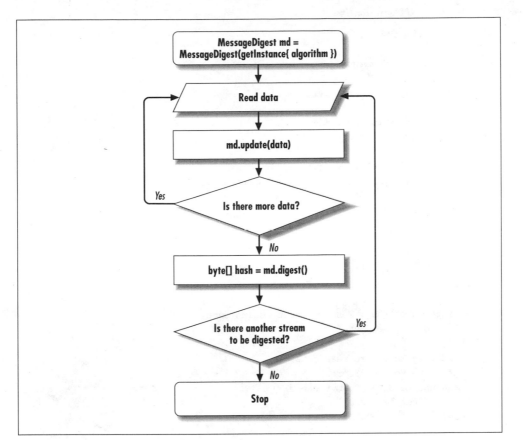

Figure 10-1. The four steps to calculating a message digest

Example 10-1, URLDigest, is a simple program that uses the MessageDigest class to calculate the SHA-1 hash for web pages named on the command line. The main() method gets the input stream from a URL as discussed in Chapter 5, *Network Streams*, and passes it to printDigest(). The printDigest() method gets an SHA MessageDigest object named sha with the getInstance() factory method. Then it repeatedly reads data from the input stream. All bytes read are passed to sha.update(). When the stream is exhausted, the sha.digest() method is called; it returns the SHA hash of the URL as an array of bytes, which is then printed.

Example 10-1. URLDigest

```
import java.net.*;
import java.io.*;
import java.security.*;
import java.math.*;
```

Example 10-1. URLDigest (continued)

```java
public class URLDigest {

  public static void main(String[] args) {

    for (int i = 0; i < args.length; i++) {
      try {
        URL u = new URL(args[i]);
        printDigest(u.openStream());
      }
      catch (MalformedURLException e) {
        System.err.println(args[i] + " is not a URL");
      }
      catch (Exception e) {System.err.println(e);}
    }
  }

  public static void printDigest(InputStream in)
   throws IOException, NoSuchAlgorithmException {

    MessageDigest sha = MessageDigest.getInstance("SHA");
    byte[] data = new byte[128];
    while (true) {
      int bytesRead = in.read(data);
      if (bytesRead < 0) break;
      sha.update(data, 0, bytesRead);
    }
    byte[] result = sha.digest();
    for (int i = 0; i < result.length; i++) {
      System.out.print(result[i] + " ");
    }
    System.out.println();
    System.out.println(new BigInteger(data));
  }
}
```

Here's a sample run. The digest is shown both as a list of bytes and as one very long integer. The `java.math.BigInteger` class converts the bytes to a decimal integer. This class was added to the core API precisely to support cryptography, where arithmetic with very large numbers is common.

```
D:\JAVA\ioexamples\10>java URLDigest http://www.oreilly.com
4 124 -18 84 -96 -20 -87 -65 101 14 47 31 17 -88 38 -98 91 -49 1 -95
591739989697434133978636109723084032701499868257806248107462640051391104470330
951881925189906731448985158407464399141144743516185572360230826270737640774481
322947443424819056185669636681480454022397848287114845876737887882358574012446
917617160663605818778685214389486703113050033009347339540804583204307060080815
```

This output doesn't really mean anything to a human reader. However, if you were to run the program again, you'd get a different result if* the web page had changed in some way. Even a small change that would be unlikely to be noticed by a human or even an HTML parser—for instance, adding an extra space to the end of one line—would be picked up by the digest. If you only want to detect significant changes, you have to first filter the insignificant data from the stream in a predictable fashion before calculating the message digest.

Creating Message Digests

There are no public constructors in `java.security.MessageDigest`. Instead, you generally use one of two `MessageDigest.getInstance()` factory methods to retrieve the appropriate digest for a particular algorithm.

```
public static MessageDigest getInstance(String algorithm)
  throws NoSuchAlgorithmException
public static MessageDigest getInstance(String algorithm, String provider)
  throws NoSuchAlgorithmException, NoSuchProviderException
```

For example:

```
MessageDigest sha = MessageDigest.getInstance("SHA");
MessageDigest md2 = MessageDigest.getInstance("MD2", "Cryptix");
```

Each of these methods returns an instance of a `MessageDigest` subclass that's configured with the requested algorithm. These subclasses and the associated `MessageDigestSPI` classes that actually implement the algorithms are installed when you install a cryptographic provider. JDK 1.2 installs the Sun provider, which supplies implementations of SHA-1 and MD5.

Each provider provides a possibly redundant collection of message digest algorithms. The factory method design pattern used here allows for the possibility that a particular algorithm may be provided by different classes in different environments. For instance, the SHA algorithm may be supplied by the `sun.security.provider.SHA` class in one development environment and by the `cryptix.provider.md.SHA1` class in another. Some standard algorithm names are listed in Table 10-1. If you request an algorithm none of your installed providers can supply, a `NoSuchAlgorithmException` is thrown. Most of the time, you're content to simply request an algorithm and let any provider that can fulfill your request provide it. However, if you want to specify a particular provider by name (for instance, because it's got an especially fast native-code implementation of the algorithm you want), you can pass the provider name as the second argument to

---

* There is an extremely small, though not quite zero, chance that two different pages will show the same message digest. This is true because there are more possible pages than there are message digests. Part of the reason a message digest is used instead of the raw page is that it is smaller than the page itself.

MessageDigest.getInstance(). If the provider you request isn't found, a NoSuchProviderException is thrown.

MessageDigest has a protected constructor for use by subclasses. If you were writing your own provider, with your own message digest algorithms and implementations, you'd use this:

```
protected MessageDigest(String algorithm)
```

However, as I said earlier, the creation of message digest algorithms and implementations is harder than it looks and is a task best left to the experts.*

Feeding Data to the Digest

Once you have a MessageDigest object, you feed data into that digest by passing bytes into one of three update() methods. If you're digesting some other form of data, like Unicode text, you must first convert that data to bytes.

```
public void update(byte input)
public void update(byte[] input)
public void update(byte[] input, int offset, int length)
```

For example:

```
byte[] data = new byte[128];
int bytesRead = in.read(data);
sha.update(data, 0, bytesRead);
```

The first update() method takes a single byte as an argument. The second method takes an entire array of bytes. The third method takes the subarray of input beginning at offset and continuing for length bytes. You can call update() repeatedly, as long as you have more data to feed it. Example 10-1 passed in bytes as they were read from the input stream. The only restriction is that the bytes should not be reordered between calls to update().

Finishing the Digest

Digest algorithms cannot finish the calculation and return the digest until the last byte is received. When you are ready to finish the calculation and receive the digest, you invoke one of three overloaded digest() methods:

```
public byte[] digest()
public byte[] digest(byte[] input)
public int digest(byte[] input, int offset, int length)
   throws DigestException
```

---

* If you want to design your own one-way hash functions, *Applied Cryptography*, by Bruce Schneier (John Wiley & Sons, 1995) is a good place to start. For details about how to implement Java security providers that supply new message digest algorithms, see Chapter 9 of *Java Cryptography*, by Jonathan Knudsen (O'Reilly & Associates, 1998).

The first digest() method simply returns the digest as an array of bytes based on the data that was already passed in through update(). The second digest() method receives one last chunk of data in the input array, then returns the digest. The third digest() method receives one last chunk of data in the subarray of input beginning at offset and continuing for length bytes, then returns the digest. For example:

```
byte[] result = sha.digest();
```

Any error that occurs in the calculation of the digest throws a DigestException. However, errors during the digestion process are rare. After you've called digest(), the MessageDigest object is reset so it can be reused to calculate a new digest.

Reusing Digests

There's some overhead associated with creating a new message digest with MessageDigest.getInstance(). Therefore, if you want to use the same algorithm to calculate digests for many different files, web pages, or other streams, you can reset the digest and reuse it. The reset() method accomplishes this:

```
public void reset()
```

In practice, you rarely call reset() directly, because the digest() method invokes the reset() method after it's through. Once you've reset a message digest, all information you had previously passed into it through update() is lost.

Comparing Digests

It's not all that hard to loop through two byte arrays to see whether or not they're equal. Nonetheless, if you do have two MessageDigest objects, the MessageDigest class does provide the simple static method MessageDigest.isEqual() that does the work for you. As you certainly expect, this method returns true if the two byte arrays are byte-for-byte identical, false otherwise.

```
public static boolean isEqual(byte[] digest1, byte[] digest2)
```

A little surprisingly, MessageDigest does *not* override equals(). Therefore, md1.equals(md2) returns true if, and only if, md1 and md2 are both references to the same MessageDigest object.

Example 10-2 uses this method to compare the byte arrays returned by two SHA digests, one for an original web page and one for a mirror copy of the page. The URLs to compare are passed in from the command line. However, it would not be hard to expand this to a general program that automatically checked a list of mirror sites to determine whether or not they needed to be updated.

Example 10-2. TrueMirror

```java
import java.net.*;
import java.io.*;
import java.security.*;

public class TrueMirror {

  public static void main(String[] args) {

    if (args.length != 2) {
      System.err.println("Usage: java TrueMirror url1 url2");
      return;
    }

    try {
      URL source = new URL(args[0]);
      URL mirror = new URL(args[1]);
      byte[] sourceDigest = getDigestFromURL(source);
      byte[] mirrorDigest = getDigestFromURL(mirror);
      if (MessageDigest.isEqual(sourceDigest, mirrorDigest)) {
        System.out.println(mirror + " is up to date");
      }
      else {
        System.out.println(mirror + " needs to be updated");
      }
    }
    catch (MalformedURLException e) {System.err.println(e);}
    catch (Exception e) {System.err.println(e);}
  }

  public static byte[] getDigestFromURL(URL u)
   throws IOException, NoSuchAlgorithmException {

    MessageDigest sha = MessageDigest.getInstance("MD5");
    InputStream in = u.openStream();
    byte[] data = new byte[128];
    while (true) {
      int bytesRead = in.read(data);
      if (bytesRead < 0) { // end of stream
        break;
      }
      sha.update(data, 0, bytesRead);
    }

    return sha.digest();
  }
}
```

Here's a sample run:

```
% java TrueMirror http://metalab.unc.edu/javafaq/  http://sunsite.uakom.sk/
javafaq/
http://metalab.uakom.sk/javafaq/ is up to date
```

Accessor Methods

The MessageDigest class contains three accessor methods that return information about the digest:

```
public final Provider getProvider()
public final String getAlgorithm()
public final int getDigestLength()
```

The getProvider() method returns a reference to the instance of java.security.Provider that provided this MessageDigest implementation. The getAlgorithm() method returns a string containing the name of the digest algorithm as given in Table 10-1; for example, "SHA" or "MD2". Finally, getDigestLength() returns the length of the digest in bytes. Digest algorithms are supposed to have fixed lengths. For instance, SHA digests are always 20 bytes long. However, this method allows for the possibility of variable length digests. It returns 0 if the length of the digest is not yet available.

Cloning Digests

Some digests allow themselves to be cloned, though not all do. A digest that does not implement cloning throws a CloneNotSupportedException if you attempt to clone it. SHA and MD5 digests from the JDK do support cloning. Cloning a digest is useful if you want to view a series of intermediate digests before the entire data sequence has been read:

```
public Object clone() throws CloneNotSupportedException
```

After each successful call to update(), you can clone the digest and invoke the digest() method on the clone. This lets you inspect the digest without interfering with the data that still needs to be processed. This might be useful if you have an exceptionally large amount of data read from a slow connection, and you don't want to wait for the end of the stream before checking whether or not the data is corrupt. Of course, you would need the intermediate digests for the original data, in addition to the digests for the data you're checking.

toString()

For completeness' sake, I'll note that MessageDigest overrides toString():

```
public String toString()
```

This returns a string in the form *classname Message Digest digest_in_hexadecimal*, for example:

```
java.security.MessageDigest$Delegate Message Digest
A8908E556566000621FFF44FF3
```

Digest Streams

The MessageDigest class isn't particularly hard to use, as I hope Examples 10-1 and 10-2 demonstrated. It's flexible and can be used to calculate a digest for anything that can be converted into a byte array, such as a string, an array of floating point numbers, or the contents of a text area. Nonetheless, the input data almost always comes from streams. Therefore, the java.security package contains an input stream and an output stream class that each possess a MessageDigest object to calculate a digest for the stream as it is read or written. These are DigestInputStream and DigestOutputStream.

DigestInputStream

The DigestInputStream class is a subclass of FilterInputStream:

```
public class DigestInputStream extends FilterInputStream
```

DigestInputStream has all the usual methods of any input stream, like read(), skip(), and close(). It overrides two read() methods to do its filtering. Clients use these methods exactly as they use the read() methods of other input streams:

```
public int read() throws IOException
public int read(byte[] data, int offset, int length) throws IOException
```

DigestInputStream does not change the data it reads in any way. However, as each byte or group of bytes is read, it is fed as input to a MessageDigest object stored in the class as the protected digest field:

```
protected MessageDigest digest;
```

The digest field is normally set in the constructor:

```
public DigestInputStream(InputStream stream, MessageDigest digest)
```

For example:

```
URL u = new URL("http://java.sun.com");
DigestInputStream din = new DigestInputStream(u.openStream(),
        MessageDigest.getInstance("SHA"));
```

The digest is not cloned inside the class. Only a reference to it is stored. Therefore, the message digest used inside the stream should only be used by the stream. Simultaneous or interleaved use by other objects will corrupt the digest.

You can change the `MessageDigest` object used by the stream with the `setMessageDigest()` method:

```
public void setMessageDigest(MessageDigest digest)
```

You can retrieve the message digest at any time by calling `getMessageDigest()`:

```
public MessageDigest getMessageDigest()
```

After you invoke `getMessageDigest()`, the `digest` field of the stream has received all the data read by the stream up to that point. However, it has not been finished. It is still necessary to invoke `digest()` to complete the calculation. For example:

```
MessageDigest md = dis.getMessageDigest();
md.digest();
```

On rare occasion, you may only want to digest part of a stream. You can turn digesting off at any point by passing `false` to the `on()` method:

```
public void on(boolean on)
```

You can turn digesting back on by passing `true` to `on()`. When digest streams are created, they are on by default.

Finally, there's a `toString()` method, which is a little unusual in input streams. It simply returns "[Digest Input Stream]" plus the string representation of the digest.

```
public String toString()
```

Here's a revised `printDigest()` method for Example 10-1 that makes use of a `DigestInputStream`:

```
public static void printDigest(InputStream in)
  throws IOException, NoSuchAlgorithmException {

    MessageDigest sha = MessageDigest.getInstance("SHA");
    DigestInputStream din = new DigestInputStream(in, sha);
    byte[] data = new byte[128];
    while (true) {
      int bytesRead = din.read(data);
        if (bytesRead < 0) break;
    }
    MessageDigest md = din.getMessageDigest();
    byte[] result = md.digest();

    for (int i = 0; i < result.length; i++) {
      System.out.println(result[i]);
    }
}
```

The main purpose of `DigestInputStream` is to be one of a chain of filters. Otherwise, it doesn't really make your work any easier. You still need to construct the `MessageDigest` object by invoking `getInstance()`, pass it to the `DigestInputStream()` constructor, retrieve the `MessageDigest` object from the input stream, invoke its `digest()` method, and retrieve the digest data from that object. I would prefer the `DigestInputStream` to completely hide the `MessageDigest` object. You could pass the name of the digest algorithm to the constructor as a string rather than an actual `MessageDigest` object. The digest would only be made available after the stream was closed, and then only through its data, not through the actual object.

DigestOutputStream

The `DigestOutputStream` class is a subclass of `FilterOutputStream` that maintains a digest of all the bytes it has written:

```
public class DigestOutputStream extends FilterOutputStream
```

`DigestOutputStream` has all the usual methods of any output stream, like `write()`, `flush()`, and `close()`. It overrides two `write()` methods to do its filtering:

```
public void write(int b) throws IOException
public void write(byte[] data, int offset, int length) throws IOException
```

These are used much as they would be for any other output stream. `DigestOutputStream` does not change the data it writes in any way. However, as each byte or group of bytes is written, it is fed as input to a `MessageDigest` object stored in the class as the protected `digest` field:

```
protected MessageDigest digest;
```

This is normally set in the constructor:

```
public DigestOutputStream(OutputStream out, MessageDigest digest)
```

For example:

```
FileOutputStream fout = new FileOutputStream("data.txt");
DigestOutputStream dout = new DigestOutputStream(fout,
           MessageDigest.getInstance("SHA"));
```

The digest is not cloned inside the class. Only a reference to it is stored. Therefore, the message digest used inside the stream should only be used by the stream. Interleaved use by other objects or simultaneous use by other threads will corrupt the digest. You can change the `MessageDigest` object used by the stream with the `setMessageDigest()` method:

```
public void setMessageDigest(MessageDigest digest)
```

You can retrieve the message digest at any time by calling getMessageDigest():

```
public MessageDigest getMessageDigest()
```

After you invoke getMessageDigest(), the digest field contains the digest of all the data written by the stream up to that point. However, it has not been finished. It is still necessary to invoke digest() to complete the calculation. For example:

```
MessageDigest md = dout.getMessageDigest();
md.digest();
```

On rare occasion, you may only want to digest part of a stream. For instance, you might want to calculate the digest of the body of an email message while ignoring the headers. You can turn digesting off at any point by passing false to the on() method:

```
public void on(boolean on)
```

You can turn digesting back on by passing true to on(). When digest output streams are created, they are on by default.

Finally, there's a toString() method, which is a little unusual in output streams. It simply returns "[Digest Output Stream]" plus the string representation of the digest.

```
public String toString()
```

Example 10-3 is a FileDigestOutputStream class that reads data from a specified URL and copies it into a file on the local system. As the file is written, its SHA digest is calculated. When the file is closed, the digest is printed.

Example 10-3. FileDigestOutputStream

```
import java.net.*;
import java.io.*;
import java.security.*;

public class FileDigest {

  public static void main(String[] args) {

    if (args.length != 2) {
      System.err.println("Usage: java FileDigest url filename");
      return;
    }

    try {
      URL u = new URL(args[0]);
      FileOutputStream out = new FileOutputStream(args[1]);
      copyFileWithDigest(u.openStream(), out);
      out.close();
```

Example 10-3. FileDigestOutputStream (continued)

```
    }
    catch (MalformedURLException e) {
      System.err.println(args[0] + " is not a URL");
    }
    catch (Exception e) {System.err.println(e);}
  }

  public static void copyFileWithDigest(InputStream in, OutputStream out)
   throws IOException, NoSuchAlgorithmException {

    MessageDigest sha = MessageDigest.getInstance("SHA");
    DigestOutputStream dout = new DigestOutputStream(out, sha);
    byte[] data = new byte[128];
    while (true) {
      int bytesRead = in.read(data);
      if (bytesRead < 0) break;
      dout.write(data, 0, bytesRead);
    }
    dout.flush();
    byte[] result = dout.getMessageDigest().digest();
    for (int i = 0; i < result.length; i++) {
      System.out.print(result[i] + " ");
    }
    System.out.println();
  }
}
```

A sample run looks like this:

```
% java FileDigest http://www.oreilly.com/ oreilly.html
10 -10 103 -27 -110 3 -2 -115 8 -112 13 19 25 76 -120 31 51 116 -94 -58
```

To be perfectly honest, I'm not sure if `DigestOutputStream` is all that useful. You still need to construct the `MessageDigest` object, pass it to the `DigestOutputStream()` constructor, retrieve the `MessageDigest` object from the output stream, invoke its `digest()` method, and retrieve the digest data from that object. The only real reason I can think of to use `DigestOutputStream` would be if you needed a digest in the middle of a chain of filter streams. For instance, you could write data onto a data output stream chained to a gzip output stream chained to a file output stream. When you had finished writing the data onto the data output stream, you could calculate the digest and write that directly onto the file output stream. When the data was read back in, you could use a digest input stream chained to a data input stream to check that the file had not been corrupted in the meantime. If the digest calculated by the digest input stream matched the digest stored in the file, you'd know the data was OK.

I would prefer the `DigestOutputStream` to completely hide the `MessageDigest` object. You could pass the name of the digest algorithm to the constructor rather than an actual `MessageDigest` object. The digest would only be made available after the stream was closed, and then only through its data, not through the actual object. Example 10-4 demonstrates how such a class might be implemented.

Example 10-4. EasyDigestOutputStream

```java
package com.macfaq.security;

import java.io.*;
import java.security.*;

public class EasyDigestOutputStream extends FilterOutputStream {

  private boolean on = true;
  private boolean closed = false;
  protected byte[] result = null;
  protected MessageDigest digest;

  public EasyDigestOutputStream(OutputStream out, String algorithm)
   throws NoSuchAlgorithmException {
    super(out);
    digest = MessageDigest.getInstance(algorithm);
  }

 public EasyDigestOutputStream(OutputStream out, String algorithm,
   String provider) throws NoSuchAlgorithmException, NoSuchProviderException {
    super(out);
    digest = MessageDigest.getInstance(algorithm, provider);
  }

  public void write(int b) throws IOException {
    if (on) digest.update((byte)b);
    out.write(b);
  }

  public void write(byte[] data, int offset, int length) throws IOException {
    if (on) digest.update(data, offset, length);
    out.write(data, offset, length);
  }

  public void on(boolean on) {
    this.on = on;
  }

  public void close() throws IOException {
    out.close();
    result = digest.digest();
    closed = true;
```

Example 10-4. EasyDigestOutputStream (continued)

```
  }

  public byte[] getDigest() {
    return result;
  }
}
```

Example 10-5 is similar to the `FileDigest` of Example 10-3 rewritten to use the `EasyDigestOutputStream`. This program produces the same digests as Example 10-3, but it's quite a bit shorter and doesn't require any explicit mucking around with `MessageDigest` objects. That's all hidden inside the `EasyDigest-OutputStream` class.

Example 10-5. EasyFileDigest

```
import java.net.*;
import java.io.*;
import com.macfaq.security.*;
import com.macfaq.io.*;

public class EasyFileDigest {

  public static void main(String[] args) {

    if (args.length != 2) {
      System.err.println("Usage: java FileDigest url filename");
      return;
    }

    try {
      URL u = new URL(args[0]);
      FileOutputStream out = new FileOutputStream(args[1]);
      EasyDigestOutputStream edout = new EasyDigestOutputStream(out, "SHA");
      StreamCopier.copy(u.openStream(), edout);
      edout.close();
      byte[] result = edout.getDigest();
      for (int i = 0; i < result.length; i++) {
        System.out.print(result[i] + " ");
      }
      System.out.println();

    }
    catch (MalformedURLException e) {
      System.err.println(args[0] + " is not a URL");
    }
    catch (Exception e) {System.err.println(e);}
  }
}
```

Encryption Basics

In this section we begin discussing cryptography. The packages, classes, and methods discussed in this and following sections are part of Sun's separately available Java Cryptography Extension (JCE). As a standard extension to Java, the JCE cryptography classes live in the `javax` package rather than the `java` package. They are not part of the core API. You will need to download JCE from *http://java. sun.com/products/jdk/1.2/jce/* and install it before continuing.

Because Sun is not legally allowed to export the JCE outside the U.S. and Canada, a number of third parties in other countries have implemented their own versions. In particular, Austria's Institute for Applied Information Processing and Communications has released the IAIK_JCE, which is free for noncommercial use and can be retrieved from *http://wwwjce.iaik.tu-graz.ac.at/IAIK_JCE/jce.htm.* Also notable is the more-or-less open source Cryptix package, which can be downloaded from many mirror sites worldwide. See *http://www.systemics.com/software/cryptix-java/.*

There are many different kinds of codes and ciphers, both for digital and nondigital data. To be precise, a code encrypts data at word or higher levels. Ciphers encrypt data at the level of letters or, in the case of digital ciphers, bytes. Most ciphers replace each byte in the original, unencrypted data, called *plaintext*, with a different byte, thus producing encrypted data, called *ciphertext*. There are many different possible algorithms for determining how plaintext is transformed into ciphertext (encryption) and how the ciphertext is transformed back into plaintext (decryption).

Keys

All the algorithms discussed here, and included in the JCE, are key-based. The key is a sequence of bytes used to parameterize the cipher. The same algorithm will encrypt the same plaintext differently when a different key is used. Decryption also requires a key. Good algorithms make it effectively impossible to decrypt ciphertext without knowing the right key.

One common attack on cryptosystems is an exhaustive search through all possible keys. Therefore, one popular measure of algorithmic security is key length. Shorter keys (56 bits and less) are definitely breakable by brute force search with specialized equipment. Keys of 112 bits are considered to have the minimum key length required for reasonable security. The U.S. government generally only allows the export of cryptography with key lengths of 40 bits or less (easily crackable on commodity hardware) and occasionally allows the export of encryption software that uses 56-bit keys with special permission. However, remember that a reasonable key length is only a necessary condition for security. Long key length is far from a sufficient condition. Long keys do not protect a weak algorithm or implementation.

NOTE   The U.S. government's data encryption standard, DES, specifies a 56-bit key. The first draft of this book stated that "it is widely believed that the United States National Security Agency (NSA) and likely similar organizations in other governments are capable of breaking this encryption scheme" by brute force search through the key space.

While this book was in editing, John Gilmore and the Electronic Frontier Foundation built a custom machine for less than $250,000 that can crack DES encryption in about four days. (See *Cracking DES: Secrets of Encryption Research, Wiretap Politics & Chip Design*, O'Reilly & Associates, 1998.) Now that design costs are covered, future versions can be built for about $50,000, and following Moore's Law* this price should drop by half every 18 months.

Since brute force search depends only on the key length and is more or less independent of the exact algorithm used, this conclusively demonstrated that all encryption algorithms are insecure with key lengths of 56 bits or less. Not surprisingly, the U.S. government has never considered DES sufficient for the protection of its own classified data.

Secret Key Versus Public Key Algorithms

There are two primary kinds of ciphers: symmetric (secret key) ciphers and asymmetric (public key) ciphers. Symmetric ciphers such as DES use the same key to encrypt and decrypt the data. Symmetric ciphers rely on the secrecy of the key for security. Anybody who knows the key can both encrypt and decrypt data. Asymmetric ciphers, also known as public key ciphers, use different keys for encryption and decryption. This makes the problem of key exchange relatively trivial. To allow people to send you encrypted messages, you simply send them your encryption (public) key. Even if the key is intercepted, this only allows the interceptor to send you encrypted messages. It does not allow them to decode encrypted messages intended for you.

The most famous public key cipher is the patented† RSA cipher, named after its inventors, Ronald L. Rivest, Adi Shamir, and Leonard M. Adleman. RSA has the particularly nice property that either key can be used for encryption or decryp-

---

* In 1964 Gordon Moore, who was to co-found Intel four years later, noted that computing power at a fixed price was doubling roughly every year. In the late 1970s, the rate slowed to doubling merely every 18 months.

† The patent expires September 20, 2000.

tion. Generally, you'll keep one key secret (your private key) and publish the corresponding key. People can send encrypted messages to you using your public key that you decrypt with your private key. Furthermore, by encrypting either a message or a hash code of the message with your private key, which may then be decrypted with your public key, you can digitally sign messages. Any message that can be successfully decrypted with your public key may be presumed to have come from you, because only you could have encrypted it with your private key in the first place. (Of course, if someone steals your private key, all bets are off.)

Block Versus Stream Ciphers

Encryption algorithms may also be divided into block and stream ciphers. A block cipher always encrypts a fixed number of bytes with each pass. For example, DES encrypts eight-byte blocks. If the data you're encrypting is not an integral multiple of the block size, the data must be padded with extra bytes to round up to the block size. Stream ciphers, by contrast, act on each bit or byte individually in the order it appears in the stream; padding is not required.

Block ciphers can operate in a variety of modes that use various algorithms to determine how the result of the encryption of one block of data influences the encryption of subsequent blocks. This ensures that identical blocks of plaintext do not produce identical blocks of ciphertext, a weakness code breakers can exploit. To ensure that messages that start with the same plaintext (for example, many email messages or form letters) don't also start with the same ciphertext (also a weakness code breakers can exploit), these modes require a nonsecret initialization vector, generally of the same size as a block, in order to begin the encoding. Initialization vectors are not secret and are generally passed in the clear with the encrypted data.

Key Management

Storing keys securely is a difficult problem. If the key is stored in hardware like a smart card, it can be stolen. If the key is stored in a file on a disk, the disk can be stolen. Many basic PC protection schemes are based on OS- or driver-level operations that refuse to mount the disk without the proper password, but simply using a new OS (or driver or custom hardware) allows the key or unencrypted data to be read off the disk.

Ideally, keys should not be stored anywhere except in a human being's memory. Human beings, however, have a hard time remembering arbitrary 56-bit keys like 0x78A53666090BCC, much less more secure 64-, 112-, or 128-bit keys. Therefore, keys humans have to remember are generally stored as a string of text called a password. Even then, the password is vulnerable to a rubber hose attack. Truly secure systems like those used to protect bank vaults require separate passwords remembered by two or more individuals.

A text password is converted into the raw bits of the key according to some well-known, generally public hash algorithm. The simplest such algorithm is to use the bytes of the password as the key, but this weakens the security, because the bits are somewhat predictable. For instance, the bits 01110001 (q) are very likely to be followed by the bits 01110101 (u). The bits 11111111 (the nonprinting delete character) are unlikely to appear at all. Because of the less than random nature of text, passwords must be longer than the corresponding keys. Unfortunately, little is known (at least outside three-letter agencies) about just how long a password is really required for reliable security.

To make matters worse, humans like passwords that are common words or phrases, like "secret," "password," or "sex." Therefore, one of the most common attacks on password-based systems is to attempt decryption with every word in a dictionary. To make these sorts of attacks harder, passwords are commonly "salted": combined with a random number that's also stored in the ciphertext. Salting can increase the space that a dictionary-based attack must search by several orders of magnitude.

Humans also have an annoying tendency to write passwords down, especially when they need to store many different passwords for different networks, computers, and web sites. These written passwords can then be stolen. In Java 2, the `java.security.KeyStore` class is a simple, password-protected digital lockbox for keys of all sorts. Keys can be stored in the key store, and only the password for the key store needs to be remembered.*

NOTE   This discussion has been necessarily brief. A lot of interesting details have been skimmed over or omitted entirely. For the more complete story, see the Crypt Cabal's Cryptography FAQ at *http://www.faqs.org/faqs/cryptography-faq/* or the books *Java Cryptography*, by Jonathan Knudsen, or *Applied Cryptography*, by Bruce Schneier.

The Cipher Class

The `javax.crypto.Cipher` class is a concrete class that encrypts arrays of bytes. The default implementation performs no encryption, but you'll never see this. You'll only receive subclasses that implement particular algorithms.

```
public class Cipher extends Object
```

---

* For more details, see *Java Security*, by Scott Oaks (O'Reilly & Associates, 1998).

The subclasses of `Cipher` that do real encryption are supplied by providers. Different providers can provide different sets of algorithms. For instance, an authoritarian government might only allow the installation of algorithms it knew how to crack, and create a provider that provided those algorithms and only those algorithms. A corporation might want to install algorithms that allowed for key recovery in the event that an employee left the company or forgot their password.

JDK 1.2 only includes the Sun provider that supplies no encryption schemes, though it does supply several digest algorithms. The JCE adds one more provider, SunJCE, which provides DES, triple DES (DESede), and password-based encryption (PBE). RSA's payware JSafe product has a security provider that provides the RSA, DES, DESede, RC2, RC4, and RC5 cipher algorithms. Ireland's Baltimore Technologies payware J/Crypto software has a security provider that provides the RSA, DES, DESede, RC2, RC4, and PBE cipher algorithms. Table 10-2 lists several of the available security providers and the algorithms they implement.

Table 10-2. Security Providers

Product (Company, Country)	URL	Digests	Ciphers	License
JDK 1.2 (Sun, U.S.)	http://java.sun.com/ products/jdk/1.2/	SHA, MD5	None	Free
JCE (Sun, U.S.)	http://java.sun.com/ products/jdk/1.2/jce/		Blowfish, DESede, DES, PBE	Free
JSafe (RSA Data Security, U.S.)	http://www.rsa.com/ rsa/products/jsafe/	SHA, MD5	DESede, DES, RC2, RC4, RC5	Payware
IAIK-JCE (Institute for Applied Information Processing and Communications, Austria)	http://wwwjce.iaik. tu-graz.ac.at/IAIK_ JCE/jce.htm	SHA, MD5	DESede, DES, IDEA, RC2, RC4	Free for non-commercial use
JCP CDK (JCP Computer Services LTD, U.K.)	http://www.jcp.co. uk/technology/cdk_ index.htm	SHA, MD5	DESede, DES, IDEA, RSA, RC4	Payware
Cryptix (the Internet)	http://www.systemics. com/software/cryptix-java/	Haval, MD2, MD4, MD5, RIPE-MD128, RIPE-MD160, SHA	Blowfish, CAST 5, DES, DESede, El Gamal, IDEA, Loki, RC2, RC4, Safer, Speed, Square	Open source
J/Crypto (Baltimore Technologies, Ireland)	http://www.baltimore. ie/jcrypto.htm	SHA, MD5	DESede, DES, RSA, RC4, PBE	Per-copy or per-user royalty

Most providers provide some unique algorithms. However, providers usually also include some algorithms already supplied by other providers. At compile time, you do not know which providers will be installed at runtime. Indeed, different people running your program are likely to have different providers available, especially if you ship internationally. Therefore, rather than using constructors, the `Cipher` class relies on two static `getInstance()` factory methods that return `Cipher` objects initialized to support particular transformations:

```
public static final Cipher getInstance(String transformation)
  throws NoSuchAlgorithmException, NoSuchPaddingException
public static final Cipher getInstance(String transformation, String provider)
  throws NoSuchAlgorithmException, NoSuchProviderException,
   NoSuchPaddingException
```

The first argument, `transformation`, is a string that names the algorithm, mode, and padding scheme to be used to encrypt or decrypt the data. Examples include "DES", "PBEWithMD5AndDES", and "DES/ECB/PKCS5Padding". The optional second argument to `getInstance()`, `provider`, names the preferred provider for the requested transformation. If more than one installed provider supports the transformation, the one named in the second argument will be used. Otherwise, an implementation will be selected from any available provider that supports the transformation. If you request a transformation from `getInstance()` that the provider does not support, a `NoSuchAlgorithmException` or `NoSuchPadding-Exception` will be thrown. If you request a provider that is not installed, a `NoSuchProviderException` is thrown.

The transformation string always includes the name of a cryptographic algorithm: for example, DES. The standard names for common algorithms are listed in Table 10-3. Not all of these algorithms are guaranteed to be available. In fact, JDK 1.2 doesn't supply any of these. If you install JCE, you get access to Blowfish, DES, Triple DES, and PBEWithMD5AndDES. You'll need a third-party provider to use RSA, IDEA, RC2, or RC4.

Table 10-3. JCE Standard Algorithm Names

Name	Algorithm
DES	The U.S. Federal government's Data Encryption Standard as defined by NIST in FIPS 46-1 and 46-2; a symmetric 64-bit block cipher that uses a 56-bit key; see *http://www.itl.nist.gov/div897/pubs/fip46-2.htm*.
DESede	DES *encryption-decryption-encryption*; triple DES; like DES, a 64-bit symmetric block cipher. DES encryption with one 56-bit key is followed by decryption with a different 56-bit key, which is followed by encryption with a third 56-bit key, effectively providing a 168-bit key space. It is considered possible that the NSA cannot penetrate this algorithm.

Table 10-3. JCE Standard Algorithm Names (continued)

Name	Algorithm
PBEWithMD5 AndDES	Password-Based Encryption as defined in RSA Laboratories, "PKCS #5: Password-Based Encryption Standard," Version 1.5, Nov. 1993; based on DES; also requires a salt; see *http://www.rsa.com/rsalabs/pubs/PKCS/html/pkcs-5.html.*
PBEWithMD5 AndTripleDES	Password-Based Encryption as defined in RSA Laboratories, "PKCS #5: Password-Based Encryption Standard," version 1.5, Nov. 1993; based on DES; also requires a salt and an initialization vector; see *http://www.rsa.com/rsalabs/pubs/PKCS/html/pkcs-5.html.*
RSA	The patented Rivest, Shamir, and Adleman asymmetric cipher algorithm; RSA encryption as defined in the RSA Laboratories Technical Note PKCS#1, *http://www.rsa.com/rsalabs/pubs/PKCS/.* It is considered possible that the NSA cannot penetrate this algorithm.[a] The patent expires in 2000.
IDEA	The International Data Encryption Algorithm developed and patented by Dr. X. Lai and Professor J. Massey of the Federal Institute of Technology in Zurich, Switzerland; a symmetrical 64-bit block cipher with a 128-bit key; the algorithm is published but patented. The patent expires in 2010 in the U.S., 2011 in Europe; see *http://www.ascom.com/systec/idea.html.*
RC2	A variable key-size symmetric 64-bit block cipher designed by Ron Rivest as a drop-in replacement for DES; it is generally allowed to be exported with a 40-bit key size and sometimes with a 56-bit key length (which probably means the NSA doesn't have much trouble breaking it); see IETF RFC 2268, *http://www.faqs.org/rfcs/rfc2268.html.*
RC4	A symmetric stream cipher algorithm proprietary to RSA Data Security, Inc. used in Netscape's Secure Sockets Layer (SSL), among other products. RC4 is a stream cipher designed by Ron Rivest; since the U.S. government occasionally allows this to be exported, the NSA probably knows how to break it. See *ftp://idea.sec.dsi.unimi.it/pub/security/crypt/code/rc4.revealed.gz* and Chapter 17.1 of Bruce Schneier's *Applied Cryptography.*
Blowfish	An unpatented fast, free, symmetric, variable key length (32 to 448 bits) 64-bit block cipher designed by Bruce Schneier as a drop-in replacement for DES; see *http://www.counterpane.com/blowfish.html.*

a I have a hunch (not necessarily shared by experts in the field) that RSA and similar algorithms will be broken someday by means much less computationally intensive than brute force search. RSA's strength rests on the difficulty of factoring a large number into two large primes. However, it is not known whether such factorization is fundamentally hard or whether we just don't yet know the right factoring algorithms. It seems obvious to me that there's a lot of structure in the prime numbers that has yet to be exploited or understood by number theorists. For instance, the Goldbach conjecture and the number of prime pairs are still unsolved questions. Therefore, I would not be surprised if far more efficient factorization algorithms are discovered. Any such algorithm would severely reduce the strength of encryption schemes like RSA. Furthermore, there's been an explosion of interest and research in quantum computing, following the discovery that RSA would be much more easily cracked by a quantum computer than by a traditional one. This does not seem to be the case for public-key encryption schemes based on something other than prime factorization, for instance, discrete logarithms or elliptic curves.

When faced with input longer than its block size, a block cipher must divide and possibly reorder that input into blocks of the appropriate size. The algorithm used to do this is called a *mode*. A mode name may be included in the transformation string separated from the algorithm by a slash. If a mode is not selected, the provider supplies a default. Modes apply to block ciphers in general and DES in particular, though other block ciphers like Blowfish may use some of these modes as well. The named modes in the JCE are listed in Table 10-4. All of these modes are supported by the JCE, but modes are algorithm-specific. If you try to use an unsupported mode or a mode that doesn't match the algorithm, a NoSuch-AlgorithmException is thrown.

Table 10-4. Block Cipher Modes

Name	Mode
ECB	Electronic CodeBook Mode; the 64-bit blocks are encrypted independently of each other and may also be decrypted independently of each other, so this mode is useful when you want random access to an encrypted file but in general is less secure than other modes. It does not require an initialization vector. See "DES Modes of Operation," National Institute of Standards and Technology Federal Information Processing Standards Publication 81, December 1980; see *http://www.itl.nist.gov/div897/pubs/fip81.htm* (NIST FIPS PUB 81).
CBC	Cipher Block Chaining Mode, as defined in NIST FIPS PUB 81; best choice for encrypting files; uses an initialization vector.
CFB	K-bit Cipher FeedBack Mode, as defined in NIST FIPS PUB 81; best choice for real-time encryption of streaming data such as network connections where each byte must be sent immediately rather than being buffered; uses an initialization vector.
OFB	K-bit Output FeedBack Mode, as defined in NIST FIPS PUB 8; designed so that a 1-bit error in the ciphertext only produces a 1-bit error in the plaintext; therefore, the best choice on noisy, error-prone channels; uses an initialization vector.
PCBC	Propagating Cipher Block Chaining, as used in pre-Version 5 Kerberos; similar to the more secure CBC mode used in Kerberos Version 5 and later; uses an initialization vector.

If the algorithm is a block cipher like DES, then the transformation string may include a padding scheme that's used to add extra bytes to the input to fill out the last block. The named padding schemes are shown in Table 10-5. Algorithms that use modes must generally also specify the padding scheme.

Table 10-5. Padding Schemes

Name	Scheme
NoPadding	Do not add any padding bytes.
PKCS5Padding	RSA Laboratories, "PKCS #5: Password-Based Encryption Standard," Version 1.5, Nov. 1993; see *http://www.rsa.com/rsalabs/pubs/PKCS/html/pkcs-5.html.*
SSL3Padding	A slight variation of PKCS5Padding used in Secure Sockets Layer (SSL); see "SSL Protocol Version 3.0, November 18, 1996, section 5.2.3.2 (CBC block cipher)" at *http://home.netscape.com/eng/ssl3/ssl-toc.html.*

There are six steps to encrypting data with a `Cipher` object:

1. Create the key for the cipher.

2. Retrieve the transformation you want to use with the `Cipher.getInstance()` factory method.

3. Initialize the cipher by passing `Cipher.ENCRYPT_MODE` and the key to the `init()` method.

4. Feed data to the `update()` method.

5. While there's more data, repeat step 4.

6. Invoke `doFinal()`.

Steps 1 and 2 can be reversed, as is done in the flow chart for this process, shown in Figure 10-2. Decryption is almost an identical process except that you pass `Cipher.DECRYPT_MODE` to `init()` instead of `Cipher.ENCRYPT_MODE`. The same engine can both encrypt and decrypt data with a given transformation.

Example 10-6 is a simple program that reads a filename and a password from the command line and encrypts the file with DES. The key is generated from the bytes of the password in a fairly predictable and insecure fashion. The cipher is initialized for encryption with the DES algorithm in CBC mode with PKCS5Padding and a random initialization vector. The initialization vector and its length are written at the start of the encrypted file so they'll be conveniently available for decryption.

Data is read from the file in 64-byte blocks. This happens to be an integral multiple of the eight-byte block size used by DES, but that's not necessary. The `Cipher` object buffers as necessary to handle nonintegral multiples of the block size. Each block of data is fed into the `update()` method to be encrypted. `update()` returns either encrypted data or `null` if it doesn't have enough data to fill out a block. If it returns the encrypted data, that's written into the output file. When no more input data remains, the cipher's `doFinal()` method is invoked to pad and flush any remaining data. Then both input and output files are closed.

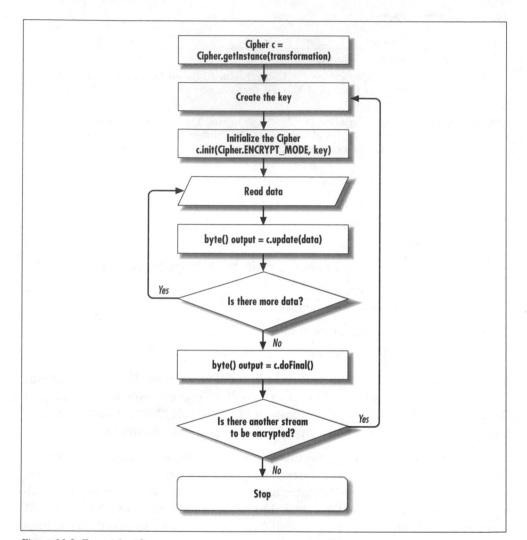

Figure 10-2. Encrypting data

Example 10-6. FileEncryptor

```
import java.io.*;
import java.security.*;
import java.security.spec.*;
import javax.crypto.*;
import javax.crypto.spec.*;

public class FileEncryptor {

  public static void main(String[] args) {
```

Example 10-6. FileEncryptor (continued)

```java
if (args.length != 2) {
  System.err.println("Usage: java FileEncryptor filename password");
  return;
}

String filename = args[0];
String password = args[1];

if (password.length() < 8 ) {
  System.err.println("Password must be at least eight characters long");
}

try {
  FileInputStream fin = new FileInputStream(args[0]);
  FileOutputStream fout = new FileOutputStream(args[0] + ".des");

  // Create a key.
  byte[] desKeyData = password.getBytes();
  DESKeySpec desKeySpec = new DESKeySpec(desKeyData);
  SecretKeyFactory keyFactory = SecretKeyFactory.getInstance("DES");
  SecretKey desKey = keyFactory.generateSecret(desKeySpec);

  // Use Data Encryption Standard.
  Cipher des = Cipher.getInstance("DES/CBC/PKCS5Padding");
  des.init(Cipher.ENCRYPT_MODE, desKey);

  // Write the initialization vector onto the output.
  byte[] iv = des.getIV();
  DataOutputStream dout = new DataOutputStream(fout);
  dout.writeInt(iv.length);
  dout.write(iv);

  byte[] input = new byte[64];
  while (true) {
    int bytesRead = fin.read(input);
    if (bytesRead == -1) break;
    byte[] output = des.update(input, 0, bytesRead);
    if (output != null) dout.write(output);
  }

  byte[] output = des.doFinal();
  if (output != null) dout.write(output);
  fin.close();
  dout.flush();
  dout.close();

}
catch (InvalidKeySpecException e) {System.err.println(e);}
```

Example 10-6. FileEncryptor (continued)

```
    catch (InvalidKeyException e) {System.err.println(e);}
    catch (NoSuchAlgorithmException e) {
      System.err.println(e);
      e.printStackTrace();
    }
    catch (NoSuchPaddingException e) {System.err.println(e);}
    catch (BadPaddingException e) {System.err.println(e);}
    catch (IllegalBlockSizeException e) {System.err.println(e);}
    catch (IOException e) {System.err.println(e);}
  }
}
```

There are a lot of different exceptions that must be caught. Except for the usual `IOException`, these are all subclasses of `java.security.GeneralSecurity-Exception`. You could save some space simply by catching that. For example:

```
      catch (GeneralSecurityException e) {
        System.err.println(e);
        e.printStackTrace();
      }
```

One exception I'll note in particular (because it threw me more than once while writing this chapter): if you should see a `NoSuchAlgorithmException`, it probably means you haven't properly installed the JCE or other provider that supports your algorithm.

```
java.security.NoSuchAlgorithmException: Algorithm DES not available
java.security.NoSuchAlgorithmException: Algorithm DES not available
        at javax.crypto.JceSecurity.getImpl(Compiled Code)
        at javax.crypto.SecretKeyFactory.getInstance(SecretKeyFactory.java:105)
        at FileEncryptor.main(Compiled Code)
```

Adding the JCE classes to your class path is enough to get the program to compile, but to actually run it, you'll need to add the following line to the *java.security* file in the *jre/lib/security* directory in your JDK folder:

```
security.provider.2=com.sun.crypto.provider.SunJCE
```

To be honest, this is far too complicated and error-prone. For one thing, every time you upgrade your JDK, this property will get overwritten and you'll have to do it all over again. Sun really needs a better installer for the JCE that handles the setting of the necessary properties.

Decrypting a file is similar, as Example 10-7 shows. The name of the input and output files and the password are read from the command line. A DES key factory converts the password to a DES secret key. Then both input and output files are opened in file streams, and a data input stream is chained to the input file. The main reason for this is to read the initialization vector. First the integer size is read, then the actual bytes of the vector. The resulting array is used to construct an IvParameterSpec object that will be used along with the key to initialize the cipher. Once the cipher has been initialized, the data is copied from input to output much as before.

Example 10-7. FileDecryptor

```java
import java.io.*;
import java.security.*;
import java.security.spec.*;
import javax.crypto.*;
import javax.crypto.spec.*;

public class FileDecryptor {

  public static void main(String[] args) {

    if (args.length != 3) {
      System.err.println("Usage: java FileDecryptor infile outfile password");
      return;
    }

    String infile = args[0];
    String outfile = args[1];
    String password = args[2];

    if (password.length() < 8 ) {
      System.err.println("Password must be at least eight characters long");
    }

    try {
      FileInputStream fin = new FileInputStream(infile);
      FileOutputStream fout = new FileOutputStream(outfile);

      // Create a key.
      byte[] desKeyData = password.getBytes();
      DESKeySpec desKeySpec = new DESKeySpec(desKeyData);
      SecretKeyFactory keyFactory = SecretKeyFactory.getInstance("DES");
      SecretKey desKey = keyFactory.generateSecret(desKeySpec);

      // Read the initialization vector.
      DataInputStream din = new DataInputStream(fin);
      int ivSize = din.readInt();
      byte[] iv = new byte[ivSize];
      din.readFully(iv);
      IvParameterSpec ivps = new IvParameterSpec(iv);

      // Use Data Encryption Standard.
      Cipher des = Cipher.getInstance("DES/CBC/PKCS5Padding");
```

Example 10-7. FileDecryptor (continued)

```
        des.init(Cipher.DECRYPT_MODE, desKey, ivps);

        byte[] input = new byte[64];
        while (true) {
          int bytesRead = fin.read(input);
          if (bytesRead == -1) break;
          byte[] output = des.update(input, 0, bytesRead);
          if (output != null) fout.write(output);
        }

        byte[] output = des.doFinal();
        if (output != null) fout.write(output);
        fin.close();
        fout.flush();
        fout.close();
      }
    catch (InvalidKeySpecException e) {System.err.println(e);}
    catch (InvalidKeyException e) {System.err.println(e);}
    catch (InvalidAlgorithmParameterException e) {System.err.println(e);}
    catch (NoSuchAlgorithmException e) {
      System.err.println(e);
      e.printStackTrace();
    }
    catch (NoSuchPaddingException e) {System.err.println(e);}
    catch (BadPaddingException e) {System.err.println(e);}
    catch (IllegalBlockSizeException e) {System.err.println(e);}
    catch (IOException e) {System.err.println(e);}
  }
}
```

Let's investigate some of the methods used in Examples 10-6 and 10-7 in more detail.

init()

Before a `Cipher` object can encrypt or decrypt data, it requires four things:

- The mode to operate in*
- A key
- Algorithm parameters, e.g., an initialization vector
- A source of randomness

---

* This is the mode the cipher should operate in; that is, encryption or decryption; this is *not* a block cipher mode.

The `init()` method prepares the cipher by providing these four quantities or reasonable defaults. There are six overloaded variants:

```
public final void init(int opmode, Key key) throws InvalidKeyException
public final void init(int opmode, Key key, SecureRandom random)
    throws InvalidKeyException
public final void init(int opmode, Key key, AlgorithmParameterSpec params)
    throws InvalidKeyException, InvalidAlgorithmParameterException
public final void init(int opmode, Key key, AlgorithmParameterSpec params,
    SecureRandom random) throws InvalidKeyException,
    InvalidAlgorithmParameterException
public final void init(int opmode, Key key, AlgorithmParameters params)
    throws InvalidKeyException, InvalidAlgorithmParameterException
public final void init(int opmode, Key key, AlgorithmParameters params,
    SecureRandom random) throws InvalidKeyException,
    InvalidAlgorithmParameterException
```

You can reuse a cipher object by invoking its `init()` method a second time. If you do, all previous information in the object is lost.

Mode

The mode determines whether this cipher is used for encryption or decryption. The mode argument has two possible values, which are both mnemonic constants defined by the `Cipher` class: `Cipher.ENCRYPT_MODE` and `Cipher.DECRYPT_MODE`.

```
public static final int ENCRYPT_MODE
public static final int DECRYPT_MODE
```

Key

The key is an instance of the `java.security.Key` interface that's used to either encrypt or decrypt the data. Symmetric ciphers like DES use the same key for both encryption and decryption. Asymmetric ciphers like RSA use different keys for encryption or decryption. Keys are generally dependent on the cipher. For instance, an RSA key cannot be used to encrypt a DES file or vice versa. If the key you provide doesn't match the cipher's algorithm, an `InvalidKeyException` is thrown.

To create a key, you first use the bytes of the key to construct a `KeySpec` for the algorithm you're using. Key specs are instances of the `java.security.spec.KeySpec` interface. Algorithm-specific implementations in the `java.security.spec` package include `EncodedKeySpec`, `X509EncodedKeySpec`, `PKCS8EncodedKeySpec`, `DSAPrivateKeySpec`, and `DSAPublicKeySpec`. Algorithm-specific implementations in the `javax.crypto.spec` package include `DESKeySpec`, `DESedeKeySpec`, `DHPrivateKeySpec`, `DHPublicKeySpec`, `PBEKeySpec`, `RSAPrivateKeyCrtSpec`, `RSAPrivateKeySpec`, and `RSAPublicKeySpec`. For example, if password is a string whose bytes are to form a DES key, the following creates a DESKeySpec object that can be used to encrypt or decrypt:

```
byte[] desKeyData = password.getBytes();
DESKeySpec desKeySpec = new DESKeySpec(desKeyData);
```

Once you've constructed a key specification from the raw bytes of the key, you use a key factory to generate the actual key. A key factory is normally an instance of an algorithm-specific subclass of java.security.KeyFactory. It's retrieved by passing the name of the algorithm to the factory method javax.crypto.Secret-KeyFactory.getInstance(). For example:

```
SecretKeyFactory keyFactory = SecretKeyFactory.getInstance("DES");
SecretKey desKey = keyFactory.generateSecret(desKeySpec);
```

Providers should supply the necessary key factories and spec classes for any algorithms they implement.

A few algorithms, most notably Blowfish, use raw bytes as a key without any further manipulations. In these cases there may not be a key factory for the algorithm. Instead, you simply use the key spec as the secret key. For example:

```
byte[] blowfishKeyData = password.getBytes();
SecretKeySpec blowfishKeySpec = new SecretKeySpec(blowfishKeyData,
                                                  "Blowfish");
Cipher blowfish = Cipher.getInstance("Blowfish/ECB/PKCS5Padding");
blowfish.init(Cipher.ENCRYPT_MODE, blowfishKeySpec);
```

Most of the examples in this book use very basic and not particularly secure passwords as keys. Stronger encryption requires more random keys. The javax.crypto.KeyGenerator class provides methods that generate random keys for any installed algorithm. For example:

```
KeyGenerator blowfishKeyGenerator = KeyGenerator.getInstance("Blowfish");
SecretKey blowfishKey = blowfishKeyGenerator.generateKey();
Cipher blowfish = Cipher.getInstance("Blowfish/ECB/PKCS5Padding");
blowfish.init(Cipher.ENCRYPT_MODE, blowfishKey);
```

Generating random keys opens up the issue of how one stores and transmits the secret keys. To my way of thinking, random key generation makes more sense in public key cryptography, where all keys that need to be transmitted can be transmitted in the clear.

Algorithm parameters

The third possible argument to init() is a series of instructions for the cipher contained in an instance of the java.security.spec.AlgorithmParameter-Spec interface or an instance of the java.security.AlgorithmParameters class. The AlgorithmParameterSpec interface declares no methods or constants.

It's simply a marker for more specific subclasses that can provide additional, algorithm-dependent parameters for specific algorithms and modes (for instance, an initialization vector). If the algorithm parameters you provide don't fit the cipher's algorithm, an `InvalidAlgorithmParameterException` is thrown. The JCE provides several `AlgorithmParameterSpec` classes in the `javax.crypto.spec` package, including `IVParameterSpec`, which can set an initialization vector for modes that need it (CBC, CFB, and OFB), and `PBEParameterSpec` for password-based encryption.

Source of randomness

The final possible argument to `init()` is a `SecureRandom` object. This argument is only used when in encryption mode. This is an instance of the `java.security.SecureRandom` class, a subclass of `java.util.Random` that uses a pseudo-random number algorithm based on the SHA-1 hash algorithm instead of `java.util.Random`'s linear congruential formula. `java.util.Random`'s random numbers aren't random enough for strong cryptography. In this book, I will simply accept the default source of randomness.

update()

Once the `init()` method has prepared the cipher for use, the `update()` method feeds data into it, encrypting or decrypting as it goes. There are four overloaded variants of this method. The first two return the encrypted or decrypted bytes:

```
public final byte[] update(byte[] input) throws IllegalStateException
public final byte[] update(byte[] input, int inputOffset, int inputLength)
                    throws IllegalStateException
```

These may return `null` if you're using a block cipher and not enough data has been provided to fill a block. The input data to be encrypted or decrypted is passed in as an array of bytes. Optional offsets and lengths may be used to select a particular subarray to be processed. `update()` throws an `IllegalStateException` if the cipher has not been initialized or it has already been finished with `doFinal()`. In either case, it's not prepared to accept data until `init()` is called.

The second two variants of `update()` store the output in a buffer byte array passed in as the fourth argument and return the number of bytes stored in the buffer:

```
public final int update(byte[] input, int inputOffset, int inputLength,
    byte[] output) throws IllegalStateException, ShortBufferException
public final int update(byte[] input, int inputOffset, int inputLength,
    byte[] output, int outputOffset) throws IllegalStateException,
    ShortBufferException
```

You can also provide an offset into the output array to specify where in the array data should be stored. An offset is useful when you want to repeatedly encrypt/ decrypt data into the same array until the data is exhausted. You cannot, however, specify a length for the output data, because it's up to the cipher to determine how many bytes of data it's willing to provide. The trick here is to make sure your output buffer is big enough to hold the processed output. Most of the time, the number of output bytes is close to the number of input bytes. However, block ciphers sometimes return fewer bytes on one call and more on the next. You can use the getOutputSize() method to determine an upper bound on the amount of data that will be returned if you were to pass in inputLength bytes of data:

```
public final int getOutputSize(int inputLength) throws IllegalStateException
```

If you don't do this and your output buffer is too small, update() throws a ShortBufferException. In this case, the cipher stores the data for the next call to update().

Once you run out of data to feed to update(), invoke doFinal(). This signals the cipher that it should pad the data with extra bytes if necessary and encrypt or decrypt all remaining bytes.

doFinal()

The doFinal() method is responsible for reading one final array of data, wrapping that up with any data remaining in the cipher's internal buffer, adding any extra padding that might be necessary, and then returning the last chunk of encrypted or decrypted data. The simplest implementation of doFinal() takes no arguments and returns an array of bytes containing the encrypted or decrypted data. This is used to flush out any data that still remains in the cipher's buffer.

```
public final byte[] doFinal()
    throws IllegalStateException, IllegalBlockSizeException, BadPaddingException
```

An IllegalStateException means that the cipher is not ready to be finished; it has not been initialized; it has been initialized but no data has been fed into it; or it has already been finished and not yet reinitialized. An Illegal-BlockSizeException is thrown by encrypting block ciphers if no padding has been requested, and the total number of bytes fed into the cipher is not a multiple of the block size. A BadPaddingException is thrown by a decrypting cipher that does not find the padding it expects to see.

There are five overloaded variants of doFinal() that allow you to provide additional input data or to place the result in an output buffer you supply. These variants are:

```
public final int doFinal(byte[] output, int outputOffset)
  throws IllegalStateException, IllegalBlockSizeException,
  ShortBufferException, BadPaddingException
public final byte[] doFinal(byte[] input)
  throws IllegalStateException, IllegalBlockSizeException, BadPaddingException
public final byte[] doFinal(byte[] input, int inputOffset, int inputLength)
  throws IllegalStateException, IllegalBlockSizeException, BadPaddingException
public final int doFinal(byte[] input, int inputOffset, int inputLength,
  byte[] output) throws IllegalStateException, ShortBufferException,
  IllegalBlockSizeException, BadPaddingException
public final int doFinal(byte[] input, int inputOffset, int inputLength,
  byte[] output, int outputOffset) throws IllegalStateException,
  ShortBufferException, IllegalBlockSizeException, BadPaddingException
```

All of the arguments are essentially the same as they are for update(). output is a buffer where the cipher places the encrypted or decrypted data. outputOffset is the position in the output buffer where this data is placed. input is a byte array that contains the last chunk of data to be encrypted. inputOffset and inputLength select a subarray of input to be encrypted or decrypted.

Accessor Methods

As well as the methods that actually perform the encryption, the Cipher class has several accessor methods that provide various information about the cipher. The getProvider() method returns a reference to the Provider that's implementing this algorithm. This is an instance of a subclass of java.security. Provider.

```
public final Provider getProvider()
```

For block ciphers, getBlockSize() returns the number of bytes in a block. For nonblock methods, it returns 0.

```
public final int getBlockSize()
```

The getOutputSize() method tells you how many bytes of output will be produced by this cipher for a given number of bytes of input. You generally use this before calling doFinal() or update() to make sure you provide a large enough byte array for the output, given inputLength additional bytes of data.

```
public final int getOutputSize(int inputLen) throws IllegalStateException
```

The length returned is the maximum number of bytes that may be needed. In some cases fewer bytes may actually be returned when doFinal() is called. An IllegalStateException is thrown if the cipher is not ready to accept more data.

The getIV() method returns a new byte array containing this cipher's initialization vector. It's useful when the system picks a random initialization vector, and you need to find out what that vector is so you can pass it to the decryption program, perhaps by storing it with the encrypted data.

```
public final byte[] getIV()
```

getIV() returns null if the algorithm doesn't use initialization vectors or if the initialization vector isn't yet set.

Cipher Streams

The Cipher class is the engine that powers encryption. Figure 10-2 and Example 10-7 showed how this class could be used to encrypt and decrypt data read from a stream. The javax.crypto package also provides Cipher-InputStream and CipherOutputStream filter streams that use a Cipher object to encrypt or decrypt data passed through the stream. Like DigestInputStream and DigestOutputStream, they aren't a great deal of use in themselves. However, you can chain them in the middle of several other streams. For example, if you chain a GZIPOutputStream to a CipherOutputStream that is chained to a FileOutputStream, you can compress, encrypt and write to a file, all with a single call to write(). This is shown in Figure 10-3. Similarly, you might read from a URL with the input stream returned by openStream(), decrypt the data read with a CipherInputStream, then check the decrypted data with a MessageDigest-InputStream, then finally pass it all into an InputStreamReader for conversion from ISO Latin-1 to Unicode. On the other side of the connection, a web server could read a file from its hard drive, write the file onto a socket with an output stream, calculate a digest with a DigestOutputStream, and encrypt the file with a CipherOutputStream.

Figure 10-3. The CipherOutputStream in the middle of a chain of filters

CipherInputStream

CipherInputStream is a subclass of FilterInputStream.

```
public class CipherInputStream extends FilterInputStream
```

CipherInputStream has all the usual methods of any input stream, like read(), skip(), and close(). It overrides seven of these methods to do its filtering:

```
public int read() throws IOException
public int read(byte[] data) throws IOException
public int read(byte[] data, int offset, int length) throws IOException
public long skip(long n) throws IOException
public int available() throws IOException
public void close() throws IOException
public boolean markSupported()
```

These methods are all invoked much as they would be for any other input stream. However, as the data is read, the stream's `Cipher` object either decrypts or encrypts the data. (Assuming your program wants to work with unencrypted data, as is most commonly the case, the cipher input stream will decrypt the data.)

A `CipherInputStream` object contains a `Cipher` object that's used to decrypt or encrypt all data read from the underlying stream before passing it to the eventual source. This `Cipher` object is set in the constructor. Like all filter stream constructors, this constructor also takes another input stream as an argument:

```
public CipherInputStream(InputStream in, Cipher c)
```

The `Cipher` object used here must be a properly initialized instance of `javax.crypto.Cipher`, most likely returned by `Cipher.getInstance()`. This `Cipher` object must also have been initialized for either encryption or decryption with `init()` before being passed into the constructor. There is also a protected constructor that might be used by subclasses that want to implement their own, non-JCE-based encryption scheme:

```
protected CipherInputStream(InputStream in)
```

`CipherInputStream` overrides most methods declared in `FilterInputStream`. Each of these makes the necessary adjustments to handle encrypted data. For example, `skip()` skips the number of bytes after encryption or decryption, which is important if the ciphertext does not have the same length as the plaintext. The `available()` method also returns the number of bytes available after encryption or decryption. The `markSupported()` method returns `false`; you cannot mark and reset a cipher input stream, even if the underlying class supports marking and resetting. Allowing this would confuse many encryption algorithms. However, you can make a cipher input stream the underlying stream of another class like `BufferedInputStream`, which does support marking and resetting.

Strong encryption schemes have the distinct disadvantage that changing even a single bit in the data can render the entire file unrecoverable gibberish. Therefore, it's useful to combine encryption with a digest so you can tell whether a file has been modified. Example 10-8 uses `CipherInputStream` to DES-encrypt a file named on the command line, but that's not all. The ciphertext is also digested and the digest saved so corruption can be detected.

Example 10-8. DigestEncryptor

```java
import java.io.*;
import java.security.*;
import java.security.spec.*;
import javax.crypto.*;
import javax.crypto.spec.*;

public class DigestEncryptor {

  public static void main(String[] args) {

    if (args.length != 2) {
      System.err.println("Usage: java DigestEncryptor filename password");
      return;
    }

    String filename = args[0];
    String password = args[1];

    if (password.length() < 8 ) {
      System.err.println("Password must be at least eight characters long");
    }

    try {
      FileInputStream fin = new FileInputStream(filename);
      FileOutputStream fout = new FileOutputStream(filename +".des");
      FileOutputStream digest = new FileOutputStream(filename + ".des.digest");

      // Create the key.
      byte[] desKeyData = password.getBytes();
      DESKeySpec desKeySpec = new DESKeySpec(desKeyData);
      SecretKeyFactory keyFactory = SecretKeyFactory.getInstance("DES");
      SecretKey desKey = keyFactory.generateSecret(desKeySpec);

      // Use Data Encryption Standard.
      Cipher des = Cipher.getInstance("DES/ECB/PKCS5Padding");
      des.init(Cipher.ENCRYPT_MODE, desKey);
      CipherInputStream cin = new CipherInputStream(fin, des);

      // Use SHA digest algorithm.
      MessageDigest sha = MessageDigest.getInstance("SHA");
      DigestInputStream din = new DigestInputStream(cin, sha);

      byte[] input = new byte[64];
      while (true) {
        int bytesRead = din.read(input);
        if (bytesRead == -1) break;
        fout.write(input, 0, bytesRead);
      }
```

Example 10-8. DigestEncryptor (continued)

```
        digest.write(sha.digest());
        digest.close();
        din.close();
        fout.flush();
        fout.close();
      }
      catch (InvalidKeySpecException e) {System.err.println(e);}
      catch (InvalidKeyException e) {System.err.println(e);}
      catch (NoSuchAlgorithmException e) {
        System.err.println(e);
        e.printStackTrace();
      }
      catch (NoSuchPaddingException e) {System.err.println(e);}
      catch (IOException e) {System.err.println(e);}
    }
}
```

The file is read with a file input stream chained to a cipher input stream chained to a digest input stream. As the file is read, encrypted, and digested, it's written into an output file. After the file has been completely read, the digest is written into another file so it can later be compared with the first file. Because the cipher input stream appears before the digest input stream in the chain, the digest is of the ciphertext, not the plaintext. If you read the file with a file input stream chained to a digest input stream chained to a cipher input stream, you would digest the plaintext. In fact, you could even use a file input stream chained to a digest input stream chained to a cipher input stream chained to a second digest input stream to get digests of both the plain- and ciphertext, though I won't do that here.

CipherOutputStream

`CipherOutputStream` is a subclass of `FilterOutputStream`.

```
    public class CipherInputStream extends FilterOutputStream
```

Each `CipherOutputStream` object contains a `Cipher` object used to decrypt or encrypt all data passed as arguments to the `write()` method before writing it to the underlying stream. This `Cipher` object is set in the constructor. Like all filter stream constructors, this constructor also takes another input stream as an argument:

```
    public CipherOutputStream(OutputStream out, Cipher c)
```

The `Cipher` object used here must be a properly initialized instance of `javax.crypto.Cipher`, most likely returned by `Cipher.getInstance()`. The `Cipher` object c should be initialized for encryption or decryption by calling init() before being passed to the CipherOutputStream() constructor. There is also a protected constructor that might be used by subclasses that want to implement their own, non-JCE-based encryption scheme:

```
protected CipherOutputStream(OutputStream out)
```

CipherOutputStream has all the usual methods of any output stream, like write(), flush(), and close(). It overrides five of these methods to do its filtering:

```
public void write(int b) throws IOException
public void write(byte[] data) throws IOException
public void write(byte[] data, int offset, int length) throws IOException
public void flush() throws IOException
public void close() throws IOException
```

Clients use these methods the same way they use them in any output stream. Before the data is written, the stream's cipher either decrypts or encrypts the data. Each of these five methods makes the necessary adjustments to handle encrypted data. For example, the flush() method (which is invoked by the close() method as well) calls doFinal() on the Cipher object to make sure it has finished padding and encrypting all the data before it flushes the final data to the underlying stream.

There are no new methods in CipherOutputStream not declared in the super-class. Anything else you need to do, such as getting the cipher's initialization vector, must be handled by the Cipher object.

Example 10-9 uses CipherOutputStream to decrypt files encrypted by the DigestEncryptor of Example 10-8. A digest input stream chained to a file input stream checks the digest of the ciphertext as it's read from the file. If the digest does not match, an error message is printed. The file is still written into the output file, since—depending on the algorithm and mode used—it may be partially legible, especially if the error does not occur until relatively late in the encrypted data.

Example 10-9. DigestDecryptor

```
import java.io.*;
import java.security.*;
import java.security.spec.*;
import javax.crypto.*;
import javax.crypto.spec.*;

public class DigestDecryptor {

  public static void main(String[] args) {
```

Example 10-9. DigestDecryptor (continued)

```
if (args.length != 3) {
  System.err.println("Usage: java DigestDecryptor infile outfile password");
  return;
}

String infile = args[0];
String outfile = args[1];
String password = args[2];

if (password.length() < 8 ) {
  System.err.println("Password must be at least eight characters long");
}

try {
  FileInputStream fin = new FileInputStream(infile);
  FileOutputStream fout = new FileOutputStream(outfile);

  // Get the digest.
  FileInputStream digestIn = new FileInputStream(infile + ".digest");
  DataInputStream dataIn = new DataInputStream(digestIn);
  // SHA digests are always 20 bytes long .
  byte[] oldDigest = new byte[20];
  dataIn.readFully(oldDigest);
  dataIn.close();

  // Create a key.
  byte[] desKeyData = password.getBytes();
  DESKeySpec desKeySpec = new DESKeySpec(desKeyData);
  SecretKeyFactory keyFactory = SecretKeyFactory.getInstance("DES");
  SecretKey desKey = keyFactory.generateSecret(desKeySpec);

  // Use Data Encryption Standard.
  Cipher des = Cipher.getInstance("DES/ECB/PKCS5Padding");
  des.init(Cipher.DECRYPT_MODE, desKey);
  CipherOutputStream cout = new CipherOutputStream(fout, des);

  // Use SHA digest algorithm.
  MessageDigest sha = MessageDigest.getInstance("SHA");
  DigestInputStream din = new DigestInputStream(fin, sha);

  byte[] input = new byte[64];
  while (true) {
    int bytesRead = din.read(input);
    if (bytesRead == -1) break;
    cout.write(input, 0, bytesRead);
  }

  byte[] newDigest = sha.digest();
  if (!MessageDigest.isEqual(newDigest, oldDigest)) {
```

Example 10-9. DigestDecryptor (continued)

```
        System.out.println("Input file appears to be corrupt!");
    }

    din.close();
    cout.flush();
    cout.close();
  }
  catch (InvalidKeySpecException e) {System.err.println(e);}
  catch (InvalidKeyException e) {System.err.println(e);}
  catch (NoSuchAlgorithmException e) {
    System.err.println(e);
    e.printStackTrace();
  }
  catch (NoSuchPaddingException e) {System.err.println(e);}
  catch (IOException e) {System.err.println(e);}
 }
}
```

File Viewer, Part 5

Handling a particular form of encryption in the `FileDumper` program is not hard. Handling the general case is not. It's not that decryption is difficult. In fact, it's quite easy. However, most encryption schemes require more than simply providing a key. You also need to know an assortment of algorithm parameters, like initialization vector, salt, iteration count, and more. Higher-level protocols are usually used to pass this information between the encryption program and the decryption program. The most common type of protocol is to simply store the information unencrypted at the beginning of the encrypted file. You saw an example of this in the `FileDecryptor` and `FileEncryptor` programs. The `FileEncryptor` chose a random initialization vector and placed its length and the vector itself at the beginning of the encrypted file so the decryptor could easily find it.

For the next iteration of the `FileDumper` program, I am going to use the simplest available encryption scheme, DES in ECB mode with PKCS5Padding. Furthermore, the key will simply be the first eight bytes of the password. This is probably the least secure algorithm discussed in this chapter; however, it doesn't require an initialization vector, salt, or other meta-information to be passed between the encryptor and the decryptor. Because of the nature of filter streams, it is relatively straightforward to add decryption services to the `FileDumper` program, assuming you know the format in which the encrypted data is stored. Generally, you'll want to decrypt a file before dumping it. This does not require a new dump filter. Instead, I simply pass the file through a cipher input stream before passing it to one of the dump filters.

When a file is both compressed and encrypted, compression is usually performed first. Therefore, we'll always decompress after decrypting. The reason is twofold. Since encryption schemes make data appear random, and compression works by taking advantage of redundancy in nonrandom data, it is difficult, if not impossible, to compress encrypted files. In fact, one quick test of how good an encryption scheme is checks whether encrypted files are compressible; if they are, it's virtually certain the encryption scheme is flawed and can be broken. Conversely, compressing files before encrypting them removes redundancy from the data that a code breaker can exploit. Therefore, it may serve to shore up some weaker algorithms. On the other hand, some algorithms have been broken by taking advantage of magic numbers and other known plaintext sequences that some compression programs insert into the encrypted data. Thus, there's no guarantee that compressing files before encrypting them will make them harder to penetrate. The best option is simply to use the strongest encryption that's available to you.

We'll let the user set the password with the –password command-line switch. The next argument after –password is assumed to be the password. Example 10-10, FileDumper5, demonstrates.

Example 10-10. FileDumper5

```
import java.io.*;
import java.util.zip.*;
import java.security.*;
import javax.crypto.*;
import javax.crypto.spec.*;
import com.macfaq.io.*;


public class FileDumper5 {

  public static final int ASC = 0;
  public static final int DEC - 1;
  public static final int HEX = 2;
  public static final int SHORT = 3;
  public static final int INT = 4;
  public static final int LONG = 5;
  public static final int FLOAT = 6;
  public static final int DOUBLE = 7;


  public static void main(String[] args) {

    if (args.length < 1) {
      System.err.println(
        "Usage: java FileDumper5 [-ahdsilfx] [-little] [-gzip|-deflated] "
        + "[-password password] file1...");
    }
```

Example 10-10. FileDumper5 (continued)

```java
    boolean bigEndian = true;
    int firstFile = 0;
    int mode = ASC;
    boolean deflated = false;
    boolean gzipped = false;
    String password = null;

    // Process command-line switches.
    for (firstFile = 0; firstFile < args.length; firstFile++) {
      if (!args[firstFile].startsWith("-")) break;
      if (args[firstFile].equals("-h")) mode = HEX;
      else if (args[firstFile].equals("-d")) mode = DEC;
      else if (args[firstFile].equals("-s")) mode = SHORT;
      else if (args[firstFile].equals("-i")) mode = INT;
      else if (args[firstFile].equals("-l")) mode = LONG;
      else if (args[firstFile].equals("-f")) mode = FLOAT;
      else if (args[firstFile].equals("-x")) mode = DOUBLE;
      else if (args[firstFile].equals("-little")) bigEndian = false;
      else if (args[firstFile].equals("-deflated") && !gzipped) deflated = true;
      else if (args[firstFile].equals("-gzip") && !deflated) gzipped = true;
      else if (args[firstFile].equals("-password")) {
        password = args[firstFile+1];
        firstFile++;
      }
    }

    for (int i = firstFile; i < args.length; i++) {
      try {
        InputStream in = new FileInputStream(args[i]);
        dump(in, System.out, mode, bigEndian, deflated, gzipped, password);

        if (i < args.length-1) {  // more files to dump
          System.out.println();
          System.out.println("-------------------------------------");
          System.out.println();
        }
      }
      catch (IOException e) {
        System.err.println(e);
        e.printStackTrace();
      }
    }
  }

  public static void dump(InputStream in, OutputStream out, int mode,
    boolean bigEndian, boolean deflated, boolean gzipped, String password)
    throws IOException {
```

Example 10-10. FileDumper5 (continued)

```
// The reference variable in may point to several different objects
// within the space of the next few lines.
if (password != null) {
  // Create a key.
  try {
    byte[] desKeyData = password.getBytes();
    DESKeySpec desKeySpec = new DESKeySpec(desKeyData);
    SecretKeyFactory keyFactory = SecretKeyFactory.getInstance("DES");
    SecretKey desKey = keyFactory.generateSecret(desKeySpec);

    // Use Data Encryption Standard.
    Cipher des = Cipher.getInstance("DES/ECB/PKCS5Padding");
    des.init(Cipher.DECRYPT_MODE, desKey);

    in = new CipherInputStream(in, des);
  }
  catch (GeneralSecurityException e) {
    throw new IOException(e.getMessage());
  }
}

if (deflated) {
  in = new InflaterInputStream(in);
}
else if (gzipped) {
  in = new GZIPInputStream(in);
}

// could really pass to FileDumper3 at this point
if (bigEndian) {
  DataInputStream din = new DataInputStream(in);
  switch (mode) {
    case HEX:
      in = new HexFilter(in);
      break;
    case DEC:
      in = new DecimalFilter(in);
      break;
    case INT:
      in = new IntFilter(din);
      break;
    case SHORT:
      in = new ShortFilter(din);
      break;
    case LONG:
      in = new LongFilter(din);
      break;
    case DOUBLE:
```

Example 10-10. FileDumper5 (continued)

```
          in = new DoubleFilter(din);
          break;
        case FLOAT:
          in = new FloatFilter(din);
          break;
        default:
      }
    }
    else {
      LittleEndianInputStream lin = new LittleEndianInputStream(in);
      switch (mode) {
        case HEX:
          in = new HexFilter(in);
          break;
        case DEC:
          in = new DecimalFilter(in);
          break;
        case INT:
          in = new LEIntFilter(lin);
          break;
        case SHORT:
          in = new LEShortFilter(lin);
          break;
        case LONG:
          in = new LELongFilter(lin);
          break;
        case DOUBLE:
          in = new LEDoubleFilter(lin);
          break;
        case FLOAT:
          in = new LEFloatFilter(lin);
          break;
        default:
      }
    }
    StreamCopier.copy(in, out);
    in.close();
  }
}
```

Note how little we had to change. I simply imported two more packages and added a command-line switch and about a dozen lines of code (which could easily have been half that) to build a `Cipher` object and add a cipher input stream to the chain. Other encryption schemes, like password-based encryption, would not be hard to support either. The main difficulty lies in deciding exactly how the key would be entered, since not all schemes have keys that map to passwords in a straightforward way. That's left as an exercise for the reader.

IV

ADVANCED AND MISCELLANEOUS TOPICS

11

Object Serialization

The last several chapters have shown you how to read and write Java's fundamental data types (`byte`, `int`, `String`, etc.). However, there's been one glaring omission. Java is a fully object-oriented language; and yet aside from the special case of strings, you haven't seen any general-purpose methods for reading or writing objects.

Object serialization, first used in the context of Remote Method Invocation (RMI) and later for JavaBeans, addresses this need. The `java.io.ObjectOutputStream` class provides a `writeObject()` method you can use to write a Java object onto a stream. The `java.io.ObjectInputStream` class has a `readObject()` method you can use to read an object from a stream. In this chapter you'll learn how to use these two classes to read and write objects as well as how to customize the format used for serialization.

Reading and Writing Objects

Object serialization saves an object's state in a sequence of bytes so that the object can be reconstituted from those bytes at a later time. Serialization in Java was first developed for use in RMI. RMI allows an object in one virtual machine to invoke methods in an object in another virtual machine, possibly in a different computer on the other side of the planet, by sending arguments and return values across the Internet. This requires a way to convert those arguments and return values to and from byte streams. It's a trivial task for primitive data types, but you need to be able to convert objects as well. That's what object serialization provides.

Object serialization is also used in the JavaBeans component software architecture. Bean classes are loaded into visual builder tools like the BeanBox (shown in Figure 11-1) or Borland's JBuilder. The designer then customizes the beans by assigning fonts, sizes, text, and other properties to each bean and connects them together with events. For instance, a button bean generally has a label property that is encoded as a string of text ("Start" in the button in Figure 11-1). The designer can change this text.

Figure 11-1. The BeanBox showing a Juggler bean and an ExplicitButton bean

Once the designer has assembled and customized the beans, the form containing all the beans must be saved. It's not enough to save the bean classes themselves; the customizations that have been applied to the beans must also be saved. That's where serialization comes in: it stores the bean as an object and thus includes any customizations, which are nothing more than the values of the bean's fields. The customized beans are stored in a *.ser* file, which is often placed inside a JAR archive. This JAR archive can then be loaded into web browsers as an applet; then both the classes and the objects used by the applet are loaded into the virtual machine. Thus, instead of having to write long `init()` methods that create and initialize many different components and objects, you can assemble the components in a visual tool, assign properties to them, save the whole group, and then load them back in. None of this requires any extra code.

As long as you're using objects to store your application's state, object serialization provides a predefined format you can use for saving files. For example, suppose you're writing a chess game with a `Board` class that stores the locations of all the pieces on the board. It's not particularly difficult to design a file format that includes the position of every piece on the board and write the code to write the current state of the board into a file. It is, however, time-consuming. With object serialization, you can write the entire board into a file with one method call. All you need to do to save a game is write the `Board` object onto an object output stream chained to a file output stream. To restore the game, read the `Board` object from an object input stream chained to a file input stream. I don't suggest using object serialization for all your file formats. For one thing, current incarnations of object serialization are slow and will be a performance bottleneck for large and complicated files. (If you define your own format, you can save just the information you need; serialization saves the entire object graph for the `Board`, including lots of things that Java needs to know about but that you don't.) Certainly, for small chores, though, object serialization provides a very convenient predefined file format.

Object Streams

Objects are serialized by object output streams. They are deserialized by object input streams. These are instances of `java.io.ObjectOutputStream` and `java.io.ObjectInputStream`, respectively:

```
public class ObjectOutputStream extends OutputStream
    implements ObjectOutput, ObjectStreamConstants
public class ObjectInputStream extends InputStream
    implements ObjectInput, ObjectStreamConstants
```

The `ObjectOutput` interface is a subinterface of `java.io.DataOutput` that declares the basic methods used to write objects and data. The `ObjectInput` interface is a subinterface of `java.io.DataInput` that declares the basic methods used to read objects and data. `java.io.ObjectStreamConstants` is an unimportant interface that merely declares mnemonic constants for "magic numbers" used in the object serialization. (A major goal of the object stream classes is shielding client programmers from details of the format used to serialize objects such as magic numbers.)

Although these classes are not technically filter output streams, since they do not extend `FilterOutputStream` and `FilterInputStream`, they are chained to underlying streams in the constructors:

```
public ObjectOutputStream(OutputStream out) throws IOException
public ObjectInputStream(InputStream in) throws IOException
```

To write an object onto a stream, you chain an object output stream to the stream, then pass the object to the object output stream's `writeObject()` method:

```
public final void writeObject(Object o) throws IOException
```

For example:

```
try {
    Point p = new Point(34, 22);
    FileOutputStream fout = new FileOutputStream("point.ser");
    ObjectOutputStream oout = new ObjectOutputStream(fout);
    oout.writeObject(p);
    oout.close();
}
catch (Exception e) {System.err.println(e);}
```

Later, the object can be read back using the `readObject()` method of the `ObjectInputStream` class:

```
public final Object readObject()
            throws OptionalDataException, ClassNotFoundException, IOException
```

For example:

```
try {
    FileInputStream fin = new FileInputStream("point.ser");
    ObjectInputStream oin = new ObjectInputStream(fin);
    Object o = oin.readObject();
    Point p = (Point) o;
    oin.close();
}
catch (Exception e) {System.err.println(e);}
```

The reconstituted point has the same values as the original point. Its x is 34 and its y is 22, just like the `Point` object that was written. However, since `readObject()` is only declared to return an `Object`, you usually need to cast the deserialized object to a more specific type.

Both `writeObject()` and `readObject()` throw `IOException` for all the usual reasons an I/O operation can fail (disk filling up, network connection being severed, etc.). The `readObject()` method also throws `OptionalDataException` if the stream doesn't appear to contain an object in the proper format or a `ClassNotFoundException` if a definition for the class of the object read from the input stream is not available in the current VM.

How Object Serialization Works

Objects possess state. This state is stored in the values of the nonstatic, nontransient fields of an object's class. Consider this `TwoDPoint` class:

```
public class TwoDPoint {
    public double x;
    public double y;
}
```

Every object of this class has a state defined by the values of the double fields x and y. If you know the values of those fields, you know the value of the TwoDPoint. Nothing changes if you add some methods to the class or make the fields private, as in Example 11-1.

Example 11-1. The TwoDPoint Class

```
public class TwoDPoint {
  private double x;
  private double y;

  public TwoDPoint(double x, double y) {
    this.x = x;
    this.y = y;
  }

  public double getX() {
    return x;
  }

  public double getY() {
    return y;
  }

  public void setX(double x) {
    this.x = x;
  }

  public void setY(double y) {
    this.y = y;
  }

  public String toString() {
    return "[TwoDPoint:x=" + this.x + ", y=" + y +"]";
  }
}
```

The object information, the information stored in the fields, is still the same. If you know the values of x and y, you know everything there is to know about the state of the object. The methods only affect the actions an object can perform. They do not change what an object is. Now suppose you wanted to save the state of a particular point object by writing a sequence of bytes onto a stream. This process is called *serialization*, since the object is serialized into a sequence of bytes. You could add a `writeState()` method to your class that looked something like this:

```
public void writeState(OutputStream out) throws IOException {
  DataOutputStream dout = new DataOutputStream(out);
  dout.writeDouble(x);
  dout.writeDouble(y);
}
```

To restore the state of a `Point` object, you could add a `readState()` method like this:

```
public void readState(InputStream in) throws IOException {
  DataInputStream din = new DataInputStream(in);
  this.x = din.readDouble();
  this.y = din.readDouble();
}
```

Needless to say, this is a lot of work. You would have to define `readState()` and `writeState()` methods for every class whose instances you wanted to serialize. Furthermore, you would have to track where in the byte stream particular values were stored, to make sure that you didn't accidentally read the y coordinate of one point as the x coordinate of the next. You'd also have to make sure you could serialize the object's superclasses, if the superclass contained a relevant state. Classes composed of other classes would cause a lot of trouble, since you'd need to serialize each object the first object contained, then each object those objects contained, then the objects those objects contained, and so forth. Finally, you'd need to avoid circular references that could put you in an infinite loop.

Fortunately, Sun's done all the work for you. Java 1.1 and later virtual machines possess code that allows them to read the nonstatic, nontransient fields of an object and write them out in a well-specified format. All you have to do is chain object output streams to an underlying stream where you want the object to be written and call `write()`; you do not have to add any new methods. Reading objects in from an object input stream is only slightly more complicated; as well as reading the object from the stream, you also need to cast the object to the correct type.

Performance

Serialization is often the easiest way to save the state of your program. You simply write out the objects you're using, then read them back in when you're ready to restore the document. There is a downside, however. First of all, serialization is slow. If you can define a custom file format for your application's documents, using that format will almost certainly be much faster than object serialization.

Second, serialization can slow or prevent garbage collection. Every time an object is written onto an object output stream, the stream holds on to a reference to the object. Then, if the same object is written onto the same stream again, it can be replaced with a reference to its first occurrence in the stream. However, this means that your program holds on to live references to the objects it has written until the stream is reset or closed—which means these objects won't be garbage-collected. The worst-case scenario is when you keep a stream open as long as your program runs and write every object you create onto the stream. This prevents any objects from being garbage-collected.

The easy solution is to avoid keeping a running stream of the objects you create. Instead, save the entire state only when the entire state is available, and then close the stream immediately.

If this isn't possible, you have the option to reset the stream by invoking its `reset()` method:

```
public void reset() throws IOException
```

`reset()` flushes the `ObjectOutputStream` object's internal cache of the objects it has already written so they can be garbage-collected. However, this also means that an object may be written onto the stream more than once, so use this method with caution.

The Serializable Interface

Unlimited serialization would introduce some security problems. For one thing, it allows unrestricted access to an object's private fields. By chaining an object output stream to a byte array output stream, a hacker can convert an object into a byte array. The byte array can be manipulated and modified without any access protection or security manager checks. Then the byte array can be reconstituted into a Java object by using it as the source of a byte array input stream.

Security isn't the only potential problem. Some objects exist only as long as the current program is running. A `java.net.Socket` object represents an active connection to a remote host. Suppose a socket is serialized to a file, and the program exits. Later the socket is deserialized from the file in a new program—but the connection it represents no longer exists. Similar problems arise with file descriptors, I/O streams, and many more classes.

For these and other reasons, Java does not allow instances of arbitrary classes to be serialized. You can only serialize instances of classes that implement the `java.io.Serializable` interface. By implementing this interface, a class indicates that it may be serialized without undue problems.

```
public interface Serializable
```

This interface does not declare any methods or fields; it serves purely to indicate that a class may be serialized. You should recall, however, that subclasses of a class that implements a particular interface also implement that interface by inheritance. Thus, many classes that do not explicitly declare that they implement Serializable are in fact serializable. For instance, java.awt.Component implements Serializable. Therefore, its direct and indirect subclasses, including Button, Scrollbar, TextArea, List, Container, Panel, java.applet.Applet, all subclasses of Applet, and all Swing components may be serialized. java.lang. Throwable implements Serializable. Therefore, all exceptions and errors are serializable.

Table 11-1 lists the classes in the Java 2 core API that directly implement Serializable. Instances of these classes or their subclasses are serializable. Many packages not listed here do contain serializable classes. However, these are only serializable because their superclasses in another package are serializable. For example, java.applet.Applet is serializable because java.awt.Component is serializable. Some of the unfamiliar names in Table 11-1 are inner classes you don't normally see, like java.text.UnicodeClassMapping. Inner classes are only serializable if they are declared to implement Serializable. That their outer class implements Serializable is not enough to make the inner class serializable.

Table 11-1. Serializable Classes in the java Packages

Package	Serializable
java.awt	BorderLayout, CardLayout, CheckboxGroup, Color, Component, ComponentOrientation, Cursor, Dimension, Event, FlowLayout, FocusManager, Font, FontMetrics, GraphicsConfigTemplate, GridBagConstraints, GridBagLayout, GridBagLayoutInfo, GridLayout, ImageMediaEntry, Insets, LightweightDispatcher, MediaTracker, MenuComponent, MenuShortcut, Point, Polygon, Rectangle, ScrollPaneAdjustable, SystemColor
java.awt.dnd	DropTarget
java.awt.font	TransformAttribute
java.awt.geom	AffineTransform
java.awt.image.renderable	ParameterBlock
java.beans	PropertyChangeSupport, VetoableChangeSupport
java.beans.beancontext	BeanContextChildSupport, BeanContextSupport
java.io	Externalizable, File, FilePermission, FilePermissionCollection, ObjectStreamClass
java.net	InetAddress, SocketPermission, SocketPermissionCollection, URL
java.rmi	MarshalledObject

Table 11-1. Serializable Classes in the java Packages (continued)

Package	Serializable
java.rmi.activation	ActivationDesc, ActivationGroupDesc, ActivationGroupID, ActivationID
java.rmi.dgc	Lease, VMID
java.rmi.server	ObjID, RemoteObject, UID
java.security	AllPermissionCollection, BasicPermission, BasicPermissionCollection, CodeSource, GuardedObject, Identity, Key, KeyPair, Permission, PermissionCollection, Permissions, PermissionsHash, SecureRandomSpi, SignedObject, UnresolvedPermission, UnresolvedPermissionCollection
java.text	BreakIterator, Collator, DateFormatSymbols, DecimalFormatSymbols, Format, SpecialMapping, TextBoundaryData, UnicodeClassMapping, WordBreakTable
java.util	ArrayList, BitSet, Calendar, Date, EventObject, HashMap, HashSet, Hashtable, LinkedList, Locale, PropertyPermissionCollection, Random, TimeZone, TreeMap, TreeSet, Vector
javax.swing.table	AbstractTableModel, DefaultTableCellRenderer, DefaultTableColumnModel, DefaultTableModel, TableColumn
javax.swing.text	AbstractDocument, EditorKit, GapContent, SimpleAttributeSet, StringContent, StyleContext, TabSet, TabStop
javax.swing.tree	DefaultMutableTreeNode, DefaultTreeModel, DefaultTreeSelectionModel, TreePath

You can glean some general principles about what classes are and are not likely to be serializable. Exceptions, errors, and other throwable objects are always serializable. Streams, readers and writers, and most other I/O classes are not serializable. Beyond these general rules, you can look at specific packages. AWT components, containers, and events are serializable, but event adapters, image filters, and AWT classes that abstract OS-dependent features are not. java.beans classes are not serializable. Type wrapper classes are serializable except for Void; most other java.lang classes are not. Reflection classes are not serializable. java.math classes are serializable. URLs are serializable. Socket, URLConnection, and most other java.net classes are not. Container classes are serializable (though see the next section). Compression classes are not serializable.

Overall, there are five reasons why a class may not be serializable:

1. It is too closely tied to native code (`java.util.zip.Deflater`).

2. The object's state depends on the internals of the virtual machine or the runtime environment and thus may change from run to run. (`java.lang.Thread`, `java.io.InputStream`, `java.io.FileDescriptor`, `java.awt.PrintJob`).

3. Serializing it is a potential security risk (`java.lang.SecurityManager`, `java.security.MessageDigest`).

4. The class is mostly a holder for static methods without any real internal state (`java.beans.Beans`, `java.lang.Math`).

5. The person who wrote the class simply didn't think about serialization.

Classes That Implement Serializable but Aren't

Just because a class *may* be serialized does not mean that it *can* be serialized. Several problems can prevent a class that implements `Serializable` from actually being serialized. Attempting to serialize such a class throws a `NotSerializableException`, a kind of `IOException`:

```
public class NotSerializableException extends ObjectStreamException
```

Problem 1: References to nonserializable objects

The first common problem that prevents a serializable class from being serialized is that its graph contains objects that do not implement `Serializable`. The graph of an object is the collection of all objects that the object holds references to, and all the objects those objects hold references to, and all the objects those objects hold references to, and so on, until there are no more connected objects that haven't appeared in the collection. For an object to be serialized, all the objects it holds references to must also be serializable, and all the objects they hold references to must be serializable, and so on. For instance, consider this skeleton of a class:

```
import java.applet.*;
import java.net.*;

public class MyNetworkingApplet extends Applet {

  Socket theConnection;
  //...
}
```

`MyNetworkingApplet` extends `Applet`, which extends `Panel`, which extends `Container`, which extends `Component`, which implements `Serializable`. Thus,

`MyNetworkingApplet` should be serializable. However, `MyNetworkingApplet` contains a reference to a `java.net.Socket` object. `Socket` is not a serializable class. Therefore, if you try to pass a `MyNetworkingApplet` instance to `writeObject()`, a `NotSerializableException` will be thrown.

The situation is even worse for container classes like `Hashtable` and `Vector`. Since serialization performs a deep copy to the output stream, storing even a single nonserializable class inside a vector or hash table prevents it from being serialized. Since the objects stored in a container can vary from program to program or run to run, there's no sure-fire way to know whether or not a particular instance of a container class can be serialized, short of trying it.

The same problem commonly occurs in applets and other GUI programs that use a `Container` to hold many different components connected by events. If any of the objects in the container are not serializable, then the container won't be, either. Most Sun-supplied components are serializable, but third-party components often aren't.

Problem 2: Missing a no-argument constructor in superclass

The second common problem that prevents a serializable class from being deserialized is that a superclass of the class is not serializable *and* does not contain a no-argument constructor. `java.lang.Object` does not implement `Serializable`, so all classes have at least one superclass that's not serializable. When an object is deserialized, the no-argument constructor of the closest superclass that does not implement `Serializable` is invoked to establish the state of the object's nonserializable superclasses. If that class does not have a no-argument constructor, then the object cannot be deserialized. For example, consider the `java.io.ZipFile` class introduced in Chapter 9, *Compressing Streams*. It does not implement `Serializable`:

```
public class ZipFile extends Object implements java.util.zip.ZipConstants
```

Furthermore, it has only these two constructors, both of which take arguments:

```
public ZipFile(String filename) throws IOException
public ZipFile(File file) throws ZipException, IOException
```

Suppose you want to subclass it to allow the class to be serialized, as shown in Example 11-2.

Example 11-2. A SerializableZipFileNot

```
import java.io.*;
import java.util.zip.*;

public class SerializableZipFileNot extends ZipFile
  implements Serializable {
```

Example 11-2. A SerializableZipFileNot (continued)

```java
public SerializableZipFileNot(String filename) throws IOException {
  super(filename);
}

public SerializableZipFileNot(File file) throws IOException {
  super(file);
}

public static void main(String[] args) {

  try {
    SerializableZipFileNot szf = new SerializableZipFileNot(args[0]);
    ByteArrayOutputStream bout = new ByteArrayOutputStream();
    ObjectOutputStream oout = new ObjectOutputStream(bout);
    oout.writeObject(szf);
    oout.close();
    System.out.println("Wrote object!");

    ByteArrayInputStream bin = new
     ByteArrayInputStream(bout.toByteArray());
    ObjectInputStream oin = new ObjectInputStream(bin);
    Object o = oin.readObject();
    System.out.println("Read object!");
  }
  catch (Exception e) {e.printStackTrace();}
  }
}
```

The `main()` method attempts to create an instance of this class, serialize it to a byte array output stream, then read it back in from a byte array input stream. However, here's what happens when you run it:

```
D:\JAVA>java SerializableZipFileNot test.zip
Wrote object!
java.io.InvalidClassException: java.util.zip.ZipFile; <init>
        at java.io.ObjectInputStream.inputObject(Compiled Code)
        at java.io.ObjectInputStream.readObject(ObjectInputStream.java:363)
        at java.io.ObjectInputStream.readObject(ObjectInputStream.java:226)
        at SerializableZipFileNot.main(SerializableZipFileNot.java:28)
```

Since the superclass, `ZipFile`, is not itself serializable and cannot be instantiated with a no-argument constructor, the subclass cannot be deserialized. It can be serialized, but that isn't much use unless you can get the object back again. Later, you'll see how to make a `SerializableZipFile` class that can be both written and read. However, to do this, you'll have to give up something else, notably the `ZipFile` type.

Problem 3: Deliberate throwing of NotSerializableException

A few classes appear to be not serializable out of pure spite (though normally there's more reason to it than that). Sometimes it's necessary, for security or other reasons, to make a class not serializable, even though one of its superclasses does implement `Serializable`. Since a subclass can't unimplement an interface implemented in its superclass, the subclass may choose to deliberately throw a `NotSerializableException` when you attempt to serialize it. You'll see exactly how this is done shortly.

Locating the offending object

When you encounter a class that you think should be serializable but isn't (and this happens all too frequently, often after you've spent two hours adjusting and customizing several dozen beans in a builder tool that now can't save your work), you'll need to locate the offending class. The `detailMessage` field of the `NotSerializableException` contains the name of the unserializable class. This can be retrieved with the `getMessage()` method of `java.lang.Throwable` or as part of the string returned by `toString()`:

```
try {
  out.writeObject(unserializableObject);
}
catch (NotSerializableException e) {
  System.err.println(e);
  System.err.println(e.getMessage() + " could not be serialized");
}
```

It is not always obvious where the offending class sneaked in. For example, if you're trying to serialize a hash table that contains seven vectors, each of which contains many different objects of different classes, a single nonserializable object in one of the vectors will cause a `NotSerializableException`. You'll need to explore the source code to determine which object caused the problem.

Making nonserializable fields transient

Once you've identified the problem object, the simplest solution to is to mark the field that contains the object `transient`. For example, we can mark the `Socket` field `transient` in our networking applet:

```
import java.applet.*;
import java.net.*;

public class MyNetworkingApplet extends Applet {

  transient Socket theConnection;  //...
}
```

The `transient` keyword tells the `writeObject()` method not to serialize the `Socket` object `theConnection` onto the underlying output stream. Instead, it's just skipped. When the object is deserialized, you may need to ensure that the state is consistent with what you expect. You'll learn how to do this in the section "Customizing the Serialization Format." It may be enough to make sure `theConnection` is non-null before accessing it.

The ObjectInput and ObjectOutput Interfaces

As well as the `ObjectInputStream` and `ObjectOutputStream` classes, the `java.io` package also provides `ObjectInput` and `ObjectOutput` interfaces:

```
public interface ObjectInput extends DataInput
public interface ObjectOutput extends DataOutput
```

These interfaces are not much used in Java 1.1 and 2. The only classes in the core API that actually implement them are `ObjectInputStream` and `ObjectOutput-Stream`. However, several methods used for customization of the serialization process are declared to accept `ObjectInput` or `ObjectOutput` objects as arguments, rather than specifically `ObjectInputStream` or `ObjectOutputStream` objects. This provides a little wiggle room for Java to grow in unforeseen ways.

The `ObjectInput` interface declares seven methods, all of which `ObjectInputStream` faithfully implements:

```
public abstract Object readObject()
  throws ClassNotFoundException, IOException
public abstract int read() throws IOException
public abstract int read(byte[] data) throws IOException
public abstract int read(byte[] data, int offset, int length)
  throws IOException
public abstract long skip(long n) throws IOException
public abstract int available() throws IOException
public abstract void close() throws IOException
```

The `readObject()` method has already been discussed in the context of object input streams. The other six methods behave exactly as they do for all input streams. In fact, at first glance, all these methods except `readObject()` appear superfluous, since any `InputStream` subclass will possess `read()`, `skip()`, `available()`, and `close()` methods with these signatures. However, this interface may be implemented by classes that aren't subclasses of `InputStream`.

The `ObjectOutput` interface declares the following six methods, all of which `ObjectOutputStream` faithfully implements. Except for `writeObject()`, which has already been discussed in the context of object output streams, these methods should behave exactly as they do for all output streams:

```
public abstract void writeObject(Object o) throws IOException
public abstract void write(int b) throws IOException
public abstract void write(byte data[]) throws IOException
public abstract void write(byte[] data, int offset, int length)
   throws IOException
public abstract void flush() throws IOException
public abstract void close() throws IOException
```

ObjectInput and ObjectOutput extend DataInput and DataOutput. Thus, as well as the methods declared outright, classes that implement ObjectInput must provide these additional methods as well:

```
public abstract void readFully(byte data[]) throws IOException
public abstract void readFully(byte data[], int offset, int length)
   throws IOException
public abstract int skipBytes(int n) throws IOException
public abstract boolean readBoolean() throws IOException
public abstract byte readByte() throws IOException
public abstract int readUnsignedByte() throws IOException
public abstract short readShort() throws IOException
public abstract int readUnsignedShort() throws IOException
public abstract char readChar() throws IOException
public abstract int readInt() throws IOException
public abstract long readLong() throws IOException
public abstract float readFloat() throws IOException
public abstract double readDouble() throws IOException
public abstract String readLine() throws IOException
public abstract String readUTF() throws IOException
```

Classes that implement ObjectOutput must provide these additional methods:

```
public abstract void write(int b) throws IOException
public abstract void write(byte[] data) throws IOException
public abstract void write(byte[] data, int offset, int length)
   throws IOException
public abstract void writeBoolean(boolean v) throws IOException
public abstract void writeByte(int b) throws IOException
public abstract void writeShort(int s) throws IOException
public abstract void writeChar(int c) throws IOException
public abstract void writeInt(int i) throws IOException
public abstract void writeLong(long l) throws IOException
public abstract void writeFloat(float f) throws IOException
public abstract void writeDouble(double d) throws IOException
public abstract void writeBytes(String s) throws IOException
public abstract void writeChars(String s) throws IOException
public abstract void writeUTF(String s) throws IOException
```

As I noted back in Chapter 7, *Data Streams*, there's a bit of asymmetry between the `DataInput` and `DataOutput` interfaces. `DataOutput` declares the three `write()` methods you expect to find in output streams, but `DataInput` does not declare the three corresponding `read()` methods you expect to find in input streams. This asymmetry does not carry over into the `ObjectInput` and `ObjectOutput` interfaces where `ObjectInput` has `read()` methods and `ObjectOutput` has `write()` methods.

By extending `DataInput` and `DataOutput`, `ObjectInput` and `ObjectOutput` guarantee that their implementers are able to read and write both objects and primitive types like `int` and `double`. Since an object may contain fields of primitive types, anything that has to read or write the state of an object also has to be able to read or write the primitive fields the object contains.

Versioning

When an object is written onto a stream, only the state of the object and the name of the object's class are stored; the byte codes for the object's class are not stored with the object. There's no guarantee that a serialized object will be deserialized into the same environment from which it was serialized. It's possible for the class definition to change between the time the object is written and the time it's read. For instance, a `Component` object may be written in Java 1.1 but read in Java 2. However, in Java 2 the `Component` class has three nonstatic, nontransient fields the 1.1 version of `Component` does not:

```
boolean inputMethodsEnabled;
DropTarget dropTarget;
private PropertyChangeSupport changeSupport;
```

There are even more differences when methods, constructors, and static and transient fields are considered. Not all changes, however, prevent deserialization. For instance, the values of static fields aren't saved when an object is serialized. Therefore, you don't have to worry about adding or deleting a static field to or from a class. Similarly, serialization completely ignores the methods in a class, so changing method bodies or adding or removing methods does not affect serialization. However, removing an instance field does affect serialization, because deserializing an object saved by the earlier version of the class will result in an attempt to set the value of a field that no longer exists.

Compatible and Incompatible Changes

Changes to a class are divided into two groups: compatible changes and incompatible changes. Compatible changes are those that do not affect the serialization format of the object, like adding a method or deleting a static field. Incompatible changes are those that do prevent a previously serialized object from being restored. Examples include deleting an instance field or changing the type of a field. As a general rule, any change that affects the signatures of the nontransient instance fields of a class is incompatible, while any change that does not affect the signatures of the nontransient instance fields of a class is compatible. However, there are a couple of exceptions. The following is a complete list of compatible changes:

- Most changes to constructors and methods, whether instance or static. Serialization doesn't touch the methods of a class. The exceptions are those methods directly involved in the serialization process, particularly `writeObject()` and `readObject()`.

- All changes to static fields—changing their type, their names, adding or removing them, etc. Serialization ignores all static fields.

- All changes to transient fields—changing their type, their names, adding or removing them, etc. Serialization ignores all transient fields.

- Adding an instance field. When an instance of the older version of the class is deserialized, the new field will merely be set to its default value (0 for numeric types, `false` for booleans, `null` for object types) when an object in that class is deserialized.

- Adding or removing an interface (except the `Serializable` interface) from a class. Interfaces say nothing about the instance fields of a class.

- Adding or removing inner classes, provided no nontransient instance field has the type of the inner class.

- Changing the access specifiers of a field. Serialization does not respect access protection.

- Changing a field from static to nonstatic or transient to nontransient. This is the same as adding a field.

The following incompatible changes prevent deserialization of serialized objects:

- Changing the name of a class.

- Changing the type of an instance field.

- Changing the name of an instance field. This is the same as removing the field with the old name.

- Changing a field from nonstatic to static or nontransient to transient. This is the same as removing the field.

- Changing the superclass of a class. This may affect the inherited state of an object.

- Changing the `writeObject()` or `readObject()` method (discussed later) in an incompatible fashion.

- Changing a class from `Serializable` to `Externalizable` (discussed later) or `Externalizable` to `Serializable`.

Version IDs

To help identify compatible or incompatible classes, each class may have a *stream unique identifier*, SUID for short. This is a `long` calculated by a special hash function and stored in the class in a static field called `serialVersionUID` like this:

```
public class UnicodeApplet extends Applet {

    static final long serialVersionUID = 5913267123532863320L;
    // ...
```

Every time you release a new version of a class that features an incompatible change, you should change the `serialVersionUID` field. The hash function only depends on the same things the serialization depends on, so making a compatible change won't change the SUID. The *serialver* tool, included with the JDK, calculates the appropriate hash of the class's name and fields. For example:

```
% serialver UnicodeApplet
UnicodeApplet:    static final long serialVersionUID = 5913267123532863320L;
```

There's also a GUI interface available with the `-show` flag, as shown in Figure 11-2.

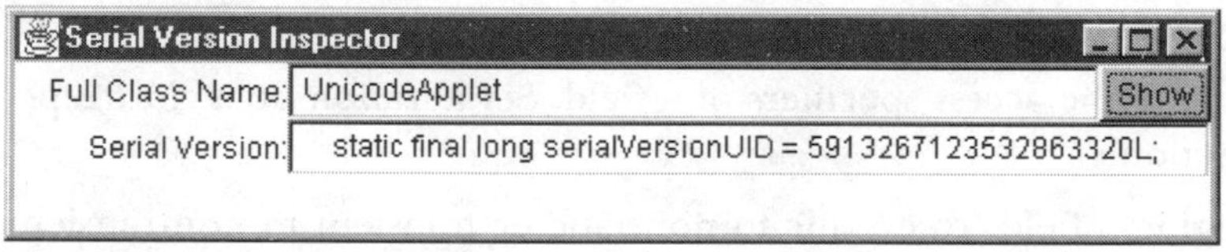

Figure 11-2. The serialver GUI

You are not limited to the values that *serialver* calculates. You can use your own version-numbering scheme. The simplest such scheme would be to give the first version of your applet SUID 1, the second version SUID 2, and so forth. However, if you do this, you will be completely responsible for making sure that all classes with the same version number are in fact compatible. One reason for developing your own version scheme is that you're customizing the serialization format, so that either normally incompatible changes become compatible or normally compatible changes become incompatible.

Customizing the Serialization Format

The default serialization procedure does not always produce the results you want. Most often, a nonserializable field like a `Socket` or a `FileOutputStream` needs to be excluded from serialization. Sometimes, a class may contain data in nonserializable fields like a `Socket` that you nonetheless want to save—for example, the host that the socket's connected to. Or perhaps a singleton object wants to verify that no other instance of itself exists in the virtual machine before it's reconstructed.* Or perhaps an incompatible change to a class (such as changing a `Font` field to three separate fields storing the font's name, style, and size) can be made compatible with a little programmer-supplied logic. Or perhaps you want an exceptionally large array of image data to be compressed before being written to disk. For these or many other reasons, you're allowed to customize the serialization process.

The simplest way to customize serialization is to declare certain fields transient. The values of transient fields will not be written onto the underlying output stream when an object in the class is serialized. However, this only goes as far as excluding certain information from serialization; it doesn't help you change the format that's used to store the data or take action on deserialization or ensure that no more than one instance of a singleton class is created.

For more control over the details of your class's serialization, you can provide custom `readObject()` and `writeObject()` methods. These are private methods that the virtual machine uses to read and write the data for your class. This gives you complete control over how objects in your class are written onto the underlying stream but does not require you to handle data stored in your objects' superclasses.

If you need even more control over the superclasses and everything else, you can implement the `java.io.Externalizable` interface, a subinterface of `java.io.Serializable`. When serializing an externalizable object, the virtual machine does almost nothing except identify the class. The class itself is completely responsible for reading and writing its state and its superclass's state in whatever format it chooses.

The readObject() and writeObject() Methods

The code that serializes objects is built into the virtual machine and is not part of the `ObjectInputStream` and `ObjectOutputStream` classes. This allows the

---

* Singleton is a popular design pattern that uses a private constructor to prevent instances of itself from being created. A single instance of the class is created in a static block when the class is loaded, and references to this one instance of the class are returned by a public static get method. For more details, see *Design Patterns*, Erich Gamma, et al., pp. 127–134, Addison-Wesley, 1995.

private data of an object to be read and written. If serialization was written in pure Java without any special access to the internals of all the different classes, it wouldn't be able to get at the private, internal state of most objects. However, as long as serialization is allowed to access private members of an object, that might as well be taken advantage of to customize the serialization process without affecting the picture of a class shown to the rest of the world.

By default, serialization takes place as previously described. When an object is passed to an `ObjectOutput`'s `writeObject()` method, the `ObjectOutput` reads the data in the object and writes it onto the underlying output stream in a specified format. Data is written starting with the highest serializable superclass of the object and continuing down through the hierarchy. However, before the data of each class is written, the virtual machine checks to see if the class in question has methods with these two signatures:

```
private void writeObject(ObjectOutputStream out) throws IOException
private void readObject(ObjectInputStream in)
   throws IOException, ClassNotFoundException
```

(Actually, an `ObjectOutput` only checks to see if the object has a `writeObject()` method, and an `ObjectInput` only checks for a `readObject()` method, but it's rare to implement one of these methods without implementing the other.) If the appropriate method is present, it is used to serialize the fields of this class rather than writing them directly. The object stream still handles serialization for any superclass or subclass fields.

For example, let's return to the issue of making a `SerializableZipFile`. Previously it wasn't possible, because the superclass, `ZipFile`, didn't have a no-argument constructor. In fact, because of this problem, no subclass of this class can be serializable. However, it is possible to use composition rather than inheritance to make our zip file serializable.* Example 11-3 shows a `SerializableZipFile` class that does *not* extend `java.util.zip.ZipFile`. Instead, it stores a `ZipFile` object in a transient field in the class called `zf`. The `zf` field is initialized either in the constructor or in the `readObject()` method. Invocations of the normal `ZipFile` methods, like `entries()` or `getInputStream()` methods, are merely passed along to the `zf` field `java.io`.

Example 11-3. SerializableZipFile

```
import java.io.*;
import java.util.*;
import java.util.zip.*;
```

---

* Design pattern aficionados may recognize what's about to happen as an application of the Decorator pattern so common in the `java.io` package. For more details, see *Design Patterns*, Erich Gamma, et al., pp. 179–184, Addison-Wesley, 1995.

Example 11-3. SerializableZipFile (continued)

```java
public class SerializableZipFile implements Serializable {

  ZipFile zf;

  public SerializableZipFile(String filename) throws IOException {
    this.zf = new ZipFile(filename);
  }

  public SerializableZipFile(File file) throws IOException {
    this.zf = new ZipFile(file);
  }

  private void writeObject(ObjectOutputStream out) throws IOException {
    out.writeObject(zf.getName());
  }

  private void readObject(ObjectInputStream in)
    throws IOException, ClassNotFoundException {

    String filename = (String) in.readObject();
    zf = new ZipFile(filename);
  }

  public ZipEntry getEntry(String name) {
    return zf.getEntry(name);
  }

  public InputStream getInputStream(ZipEntry entry) throws IOException {
    return zf.getInputStream(entry);
  }

  public String getName() {
    return zf.getName();
  }

  public Enumeration entries() {
    return zf.entries();
  }

  public int size() {
    return zf.size();
  }

  public void close() throws IOException {
    zf.close();
  }

  public static void main(String[] args) {
```

Example 11-3. SerializableZipFile (continued)

```
    try {
      SerializableZipFile szf = new SerializableZipFile(args[0]);
      ByteArrayOutputStream bout = new ByteArrayOutputStream();
      ObjectOutputStream oout = new ObjectOutputStream(bout);
      oout.writeObject(szf);
      oout.close();
      System.out.println("Wrote object!");

      ByteArrayInputStream bin = new ByteArrayInputStream(bout.toByteArray());
      ObjectInputStream oin = new ObjectInputStream(bin);
      Object o = oin.readObject();
      System.out.println("Read object!");
    }
    catch (Exception e) {e.printStackTrace();}
  }
}
```

Let's look closer at the serialization parts of this program. What does it mean to serialize `ZipFile`? Internally a `ZipFile` object is a filename and a `long` integer that serves as a native file descriptor to interface with the native zlib library. File descriptors have no state that would make sense across multiple runs of the same program or from one machine to the next. This is why `ZipFile` is not itself declared serializable. However, if you know the filename, you can create a new `ZipFile` object that is the same for all practical purposes.

This is the approach Example 11-3 takes. To serialize an object, the `writeObject()` method writes the filename onto the output stream. The `readObject()` method reads this name back in and recreates the object. When `readObject()` is invoked, the virtual machine creates a new `ZipFile` object out of thin air; no constructor is invoked. The `zf` field is set to `null`. Next, the private `readObject()` method of this object is called. The value of `filename` is read from the stream. Finally, a new `ZipFile` object is created from the filename and assigned to `zf`.

This scheme isn't perfect. In particular, the whole thing may come crashing down if the actual file that's referred to isn't present when the object is deserialized. This might happen if the actual file was deleted in between the time the object was written and the time it was read, for example. However, this will only result in an `IOException`, which the client programmer should be ready for in any case.

The `main()` method tests this scheme by creating a serializable zip file with a name passed in from the command line. Then the serializable zip file is serialized. Next the `SerializableRandomAccessFile` object is deserialized from the same byte array it was previously written into. Here's the result:

```
D:\JAVA>java SerializableZipFile test.zip
Wrote object!
Read object!
```

The defaultWriteObject() and defaultReadObject() Methods

Sometimes rather than changing the format of an object that's serialized, all you want to do is add some additional information, perhaps something that isn't normally serialized, like a static field. In this case, you can use `ObjectOutput-Stream`'s `defaultWriteObject()` method to write the state of the object, then use `ObjectOutputStream`'s `defaultReadObject()` method to read the state of the object. After this is done, you can perform any custom work you need to do on serialization or deserialization.

```
public final void defaultReadObject()
    throws IOException, ClassNotFoundException, NotActiveException
public final void defaultWriteObject() throws IOException
```

For example, let's suppose an application that would otherwise be serializable contains a `Socket` field. As well as this field, assume it contains more than a few other complex fields, so that serializing it by hand, while possible, would be onerous. It might look something like this:

```
public class NetworkWindow extends Frame implements Serializable {

  private Socket theSocket;

  // several dozen other fields and methods
}
```

You could make this class fully serializable by merely declaring `theSocket` transient:

```
private transient Socket theSocket;
```

Let's assume you actually do want to restore the state of the socket when the object is deserialized. In this case, you can use private `readObject()` and `write-Object()` methods as in the last section. You can use `defaultReadObject()` and `defaultWriteObject()` methods to handle all the normal, nontransient fields; then handle the socket specifically. For example:

```
private void writeObject(ObjectOutputStream out) throws IOException {

  out.defaultWriteObject();
  out.writeObject(theSocket.getInetAddress());
  out.writeInt(theSocket.getPort());
}
```

```
    private void readObject(ObjectInputStream in)
      throws IOException, ClassNotFoundException {

      in.defaultReadObject();
      InetAddress ia = (InetAddress) in.readObject();
      int thePort = in.readInt();

      this.theSocket = new Socket(ia, thePort);
    }
```

It isn't even necessary to know what the other fields are to make this work. The only extra work that has to be done is for the transient fields. This technique applies far beyond this one example. It can be used anytime when you're happy with the default behavior and merely want to do additional things on serialization or deserialization. For instance, it can be used to set the values of static fields or to execute additional code when deserialization is complete. However, if the latter is your intent, you might be better served by validation, discussed later in the chapter. For example, let's suppose you have a `Die` class that must have a value between 1 and 6, as shown in Example 11-4.

Example 11-4. A Six-Sided Die

```
import java.util.*;
import java.io.*;

public class Die implements Serializable {

  private int face = 1;
  Random shooter = new Random();

  public Die(int face) {
    this.face = (int) (Math.abs(face % 6) + 1);
  }

  public int getFace() {
    return this.face;
  }

  public void setFace(int face) {
    this.face = (int) (Math.abs(face % 6) + 1);
  }

  public int roll() {
    this.face = (int) ((Math.abs(shooter.nextInt()) % 6) + 1);
    return this.face;
  }

  public static void main(String[] args) {
```

Example 11-4. A Six-Sided Die (continued)

```
    Die d = new Die(2);
    for (int i = 0; i < 10; i++) {
      d.roll();
      System.out.println(d.getFace());
    }
  }
}
```

Obviously, this class, simple as it is, goes to a lot of trouble to ensure that the die always has a value between 1 and 6. Every method that can possibly set the value of the private field `face` carefully checks to make sure the value is between 1 and 6. However, serialization provides a back door through which the value of `face` can be changed, because default serialization uses neither constructors nor set methods but accesses the private field directly. To close the door, you can provide a `readObject()` method that performs the necessary check:

```
    private void readObject(ObjectInputStream in)
      throws IOException, ClassNotFoundException {

      in.defaultReadObject();
      this.face = (int) (Math.abs(this.face % 6) + 1);
    }
```

In this example, the normal serialization format is perfectly acceptable, so that's completely handled by `defaultReadObject()`. It's just that a little more work is required than merely restoring the fields of the object.

Preventing Serialization

On occasion, you need to prevent a normally serializable subclass from being serialized. This most commonly occurs with components that are serializable, because `java.awt.Component` is serializable. You can prevent an object from being serialized, even though it or one of its superclasses implements `Serializable`, by throwing a `NotSerializableException` from `writeObject()`.`NotSerializableException` is a subclass of `java.io.ObjectStreamException`, which is itself a kind of `IOException`:

```
    public class NotSerializableException extends ObjectStreamException
```

For example:

```
    private void writeObject(ObjectOutputStream out) throws IOException {
      throws new NotSerializableException();
    }

    private void readObject(ObjectInputStream in) throws IOException {
      throws new NotSerializableException();
    }
```

Externalizable

Sometimes customization requires you to manipulate the values stored for the superclass of an object as well as for the object's class. In these cases, you should implement the `java.io.Externalizable` interface instead of `Serializable`. `Externalizable` is a subinterface of `Serializable`:

```
public interface Externalizable extends Serializable
```

This interface declares two methods, `readExternal()` and `writeExternal()`:

```
public void writeExternal(ObjectOutput out) throws IOException
public void readExternal(ObjectInput in)
    throws IOException, ClassNotFoundException
```

Unlike `writeObject()` and `readObject()`, `readExternal()` and `writeExternal()` are public. This allows the possibility of violating access protection by using these methods to access the private fields of an object. `Externalizable` should therefore be used with caution. The implementation of its methods is completely responsible for saving the object's state, including the state stored in its superclasses. This is the primary difference between implementing `Externalizable` and providing private `readObject()` and `writeObject()` methods. Since some of the superclass's state may be stored in private or friendly fields that are not accessible to the `Externalizable` object, saving and restoring can be a tricky proposition. Furthermore, externalizable objects are responsible for tracking their own versions; the virtual machine assumes that whatever version of the externalizable class is available when the object is deserialized is the correct one. It does not check the `serialVersionUID` field as it does for merely serializable objects. If you want to check for different versions of the class, you must write your own code to do the checks.

For example, suppose you want a vector that can be serialized no matter what it contains; that is, that will never throw a `NotSerializableException` even if it contains objects that aren't serializable. You can do this by creating a subclass of `Vector` that implements `Externalizable`, as in Example 11-5. The `writeExternal()` method uses `instanceof` to test whether each element is or is not serializable before writing it onto the output. If the element does not implement `Serializable`, then `writeExternal()` writes `null` in its place. We'll start by peeking at the source code for `java.util.Vector`. (Source for the core API is included with the JDK in a file called *src.zip*.) It contains three nonstatic, nontransient fields:

```
protected Object elementData[];
protected int elementCount;
protected int capacityIncrement;
```

These are all protected so subclasses can access them directly. (The key criterion for being able to use `Externalizable` is that there are enough get and set methods to read and write all necessary fields in the superclasses. If this isn't the case, often your only recourse is to use the `Decorator` pattern to wrap a class to which you do have complete access around the original class. This was the tack taken in Example 11-3 for `SerializableZipFile`.)

Example 11-5. SerializableVector

```java
import java.util.*;
import java.io.*;
import java.net.*;

public class SerializableVector extends Vector
 implements Externalizable {

  public void writeExternal(ObjectOutput out) throws IOException {

    out.writeInt(capacityIncrement);
    out.writeInt(elementCount);
    for (int i = 0; i < elementCount; i++) {
      if (elementData[i] instanceof Serializable) {
        out.writeObject(elementData[i]);
      }
      else {
        out.writeObject(null);
      }
    }
  }

  public void readExternal(ObjectInput in)
    throws IOException, ClassNotFoundException {

    this.capacityIncrement = in.readInt();
    this.elementCount = in.readInt();
    this.elementData = new Object[elementCount];
    for (int i = 0; i < elementCount; i++) {
      elementData[i] = in.readObject();
    }
  }

  public static void main(String[] args) throws Exception {

    SerializableVector sv1 = new SerializableVector();
    sv1.addElement("Element 1");
    sv1.addElement(new Integer(9));
    sv1.addElement(new URL("http://www.oreilly.com/"));

    // not Serializable
```

Example 11-5. SerializableVector (continued)

```
    sv1.addElement(new Socket("www.ora.com", 80));

    sv1.addElement("Element 1");
    sv1.addElement(new Integer(9));
    sv1.addElement(new URL("http://www.oreilly.com/"));

    ByteArrayOutputStream bout = new ByteArrayOutputStream();
    ObjectOutputStream temp = new ObjectOutputStream(bout);
    temp.writeObject(sv1);
    temp.close();

    ByteArrayInputStream bin = new ByteArrayInputStream(bout.toByteArray());
    ObjectInputStream oin = new ObjectInputStream(bin);
    Vector v = (Vector) oin.readObject();
    Enumeration e = v.elements();
    while (e.hasMoreElements()) {
      System.out.println(e.nextElement());
    }
  }
}
```

You may argue with my choice of name here; `ExternalizableVector` may seem more accurate. However, from the perspective of a programmer using a class, it doesn't matter whether a class is serializable or externalizable. In either case, instances of the class are merely passed to the `writeObject()` method of an object output stream or read by the `readObject()` method of an object input stream. The difference between `Serializable` and `Externalizable` is hidden from the end user.

The `writeExternal()` method first writes `capacityIncrement` and `element-Count` onto the stream using `writeInt()`. It then loops through all the elements in the vector, testing each one with `instanceof` to see whether or not it's serializable. If the element is serializable, it's written with `writeObject()`; otherwise, `null` is written instead. The `readExternal()` method simply reads in the data and sets the appropriate fields in `Vector`. `capacityIncrement` is read first, then `elementCount`. The `elementData` array was not directly written onto the output in `writeExternal()`; instead, its individual elements were written. Thus, a new `elementData` array is created with length `elementCount`. Finally, the individual elements are read out and stored in `elementData` in the same order they were written.

The `main()` method tests the program by serializing and deserializing a `SerializableVector` that contains assorted serializable and nonserializable elements. Its output is:

```
D:\JAVA>java SerializableVector
Element 1
9
http://www.oreilly.com/
null
Element 1
9
http://www.oreilly.com/
```

Other schemes are possible and might be useful in some circumstances. Since `elementData` itself isn't stored but only recreated from its length, one obvious possibility is to omit the nonserializable elements when writing the vector and to adjust the `elementCount` accordingly. For example:

```
public void writeExternal(ObjectOutput out) throws IOException {

  out.writeInt(capacityIncrement);
  int numSerializable = 0;
  for (int i = 0; i < elementCount; i++) {
    if (elementData[i] instanceof Serializable) {
      numSerializable++;
    }
  }
  // when deserialized elementCount will be set to numSerializable
  out.writeInt(numSerializable);

  for (int i = 0; i < elementCount; i++) {
    if (elementData[i] instanceof Serializable) {
      out.writeObject(elementData[i]);
    }
  }
}
```

This still isn't a perfect solution. The vector may contain an object that implements `Serializable` but isn't serializable: for example, a hash table that contains a socket. It seems as if it would be a better solution to catch any such `NotSerializableExceptions` inside the `readExternal()` method, then write `null`, possibly after backing the stream up to the beginning of the element that threw the exception (using `mark()` and `reset()` and an extra buffered stream if necessary). However, my tests showed that you cannot catch a `NotSerializable-Exception` inside the `writeExternal()` method. I can see no reason why this should be the case. It's probably a result of how serialization is implemented by native code in the virtual machine, so the exception isn't thrown exactly where the Java code indicates it is. (I suspect this should be classified as a bug.)

Resolving Classes

The `readObject()` method of `java.io.ObjectInputStream` only creates new objects from known classes. It doesn't load classes. If a class for an object can't be found, `readObject()` throws a `ClassNotFoundException`. It specifically does not attempt to read the class data from the object stream. This is limiting for some things you might want to do, particularly RMI. Therefore, trusted subclasses of `ObjectInputStream` may be allowed to load classes from the stream or some other source like a URL. Specifically, a class is trusted if, and only if, it was loaded from the local class path; that is, the `ClassLoader` object returned by `getClassLoader()` is `null`.

Two protected methods are involved. The first is the `annotateClass()` method of `ObjectOutputStream`:

```
protected void annotateClass(Class c) throws IOException
```

In `ObjectOutputStream` this is a do-nothing method. A subclass of `ObjectOutputStream` can provide a different implementation that provides data for the class. For instance, this might be the byte code of the class itself or a URL where the class can be found.

Standard object input streams cannot read and resolve the class data written by `annotateClass()`. For each subclass of `ObjectOutputStream` that overrides `annotateClass()`, there will normally be a corresponding subclass of `ObjectInputStream` that implements the `resolveClass()` method:

```
protected Class resolveClass(ObjectStreamClass v)
    throws IOException, ClassNotFoundException
```

In `java.io.ObjectInputStream`, this is a do-nothing method. A subclass of `ObjectInputStream` can provide an implementation that loads a class based on the data read from the stream. For instance, if `annotateClass()` wrote byte code to the stream, then the `resolveClass()` method would need to have a class loader that read the data from the stream. If `annotateClass()` wrote the URL of the class to the stream, then the `resolveClass()` method would need a class loader that read the URL from the stream and downloaded the class from that URL.

The `resolveClass()` method is called exactly once for each class encountered in the stream (not just those written by `annotateClass()`). `resolveClass()` is responsible for knowing what sort of data needs to be read to reconstruct the class and for reading it from the input stream. `resolveClass()` should then load and return the class. If it can't do so, it should throw a `ClassNotFoundException`. If it returns a class, but that class's SUID does not match the SUID of the class in the stream, then the runtime throws a `ClassNotFoundException`.

Resolving Objects

There may be occasions where you want to replace the objects read from the stream with other, alternative objects. Perhaps an old version of a program whose data you need to read used `Franc` objects, but the new version of the program uses `Euro` objects. The `ObjectInputStream` can replace each `Franc` object read with the equivalent `Euro` object.

Only trusted subclasses of `ObjectInputStream` may replace objects. A class is only trusted if it was loaded from the local class path; that is, the class loader returned by `getClassLoader()` is `null`. To make it possible for a trusted subclass to replace objects, you must first pass `true` to its `enableResolveObject()` method:

```
protected final boolean enableResolveObject(boolean enable)
    throws SecurityException
```

Generally, you would do this in the constructor of any class that needed to replace objects. Once object replacement is enabled, whenever an object is read, it is passed to the `ObjectInputStream` subclass's `resolveObject()` method before `readObject()` returns:

```
protected Object resolveObject(Object o) throws IOException
```

The `resolveObject()` method may return the object itself (the default behavior) or return a different object. Resolving objects is a tricky business. The substituted object must be compatible with the use of the original object, or errors will soon surface as the program tries to invoke methods or access fields that don't exist. Most of the time, the replacing object is an instance of a subclass of the class of the replaced object. Another possibility is that the replacing object and the object it replaces are both instances of different subclasses of a common superclass or interface, where the original object was only used as an instance of that superclass or interface.

Validation

It is not always enough to merely restore the state of a serialized object. You may need to verify that the value of a field still makes sense, you may need to notify another object that this object has come into existence, or you simply may need to have the entire graph of the object available before you can finish initializing it.

For example, valid XML documents are essentially trees of elements combined with a document type definition (DTD). The DTD defines a grammar the document must follow.* The Document Object Model (DOM) defines a means of representing XML (and HTML) documents as instances of Java classes and interfaces,

---

* For more details, see *XML: Extensible Markup Language,* by Elliotte Rusty Harold, IDG Books, 1998.

including `XMLNode`, `EntityReference`, `EntityDeclaration`, `DocumentType`, `ElementDefinition`, `AttributeDefinition`, and others.

An XML document could be saved as a set of these serialized objects. In that case, when you deserialized the document, you would want to check that the deserialized document is still valid; that is, that the document adheres to the grammar given in the DTD. You can't do this until the entire document—all its elements, and its entire DTD—has been read. There are also a number of smaller checks you might want to perform. For instance, well-formedness (well-formedness is a slightly less stringent requirement than validity) requires that all entity references like `&date;` be defined in the DTD. To check this, it's not enough to have deserialized the `EntityReference` object. You must also have deserialized the corresponding `DocumentType` object that contains the necessary `Entity-Declaration` objects.

You can use the `ObjectInputStream` class's `registerValidation()` method to specify an `ObjectInputValidation` object that will be notified of the object after its entire graph has been reconstructed but before `readObject()` has returned it. This gives the validator an opportunity to make sure that the object doesn't violate any implicit assertions about the state of the system.

```
public synchronized void registerValidation(ObjectInputValidation oiv,
    int priority) throws NotActiveException, InvalidObjectException
```

This method is invoked inside the `readObject()` method of the object that needs to be validated. Every time the `readObject()` method is called to read an object, that object is registered with the stream as needing to be validated when the rest of the graph is available. Invoking the `registerValidation()` method from anywhere except the `readObject()` method throws a `NotActiveException`. The `oiv` argument is the object that implements the `ObjectInputValidation` interface and that will validate deserialized objects. Most of the time, this is the object that has the `readObject()` method; that is, objects tend to validate themselves. The `priority` argument determines the order in which objects will be validated if there's more than one registered `ObjectInputValidation` object for the class. Validators with higher priorities are invoked first.

The `ObjectInputValidation` interface declares a single method, `validateObject()`:

```
public abstract void validateObject() throws InvalidObjectException
```

If the object is invalid, `validateObject()` throws an `InvalidObjectException`.

For example, let's suppose an application maintains a linked list of `Person` objects, each of which is identified primarily by its Social Security Number. Let's further suppose that the application doesn't allow two `Person` objects with the same Social Security Number to exist at the same time. You can use an `ObjectInputValidation` to ensure that this doesn't happen. Example 11-6 demonstrates.

Example 11-6. Person

```java
import java.util.*;
import java.io.*;

public class Person implements Serializable, ObjectInputValidation {

  Hashtable thePeople;

  String name;
  String ss;

  public Person(String name, String ss) {
    this.name = name;
    this.ss = ss;
    thePeople = new Hashtable();
    thePeople.put(ss, name);
  }

  public Person(Hashtable thePeople, String name, String ss)
   throws IllegalArgumentException {

    this.name = name;
    this.ss = ss;
    this.thePeople = thePeople;
    thePeople.put(ss, name);
  }

  private void readObject(ObjectInputStream in)
   throws IOException, ClassNotFoundException {

    in.registerValidation(this, 5);
    in.defaultReadObject();
  }

  public void validateObject() throws InvalidObjectException {

    if (this.thePeople.containsKey(this.ss)) {
      throw new InvalidObjectException(this.name + " already exists");
    }
  }
}
```

Sealed Objects

The JCE standard extension to Java 2, discussed in the last chapter, provides a SealedObject class that lets you encrypt objects written onto an object output stream using any available cipher. Most of the time, I suspect, you'll either encrypt the entire object output stream by chaining it to a cipher output stream, or you won't encrypt anything at all. However, if there's some reason to encrypt only some of the objects you're writing to the stream, you can make them sealed objects.

The javax.crypto.SealedObject class wraps a serializable object in an encrypted digital lockbox. The sealed object is serializable so it can be written onto object output streams and read from object input streams as normal. However, the object inside the sealed object can only be deserialized by someone who knows the key.

```
public class SealedObject extends Object implements Serializable
```

The big advantage to using sealed objects rather than encrypting the entire output stream is that the sealed objects contain all necessary parameters for decryption (algorithm used, initialization vector, salt, iteration count). All the receiver of the sealed object needs to know is the key. Thus, there doesn't necessarily have to be any prior agreement about these other aspects of encryption.

You seal an object with the SealedObject() constructor. The constructor takes as arguments the object to be sealed, which must be serializable, and the properly initialized Cipher object with which to encrypt the object:

```
public SealedObject(Serializable object, Cipher c)
    throws IOException, IllegalBlockSizeException
```

Inside the constructor, the object is immediately serialized by an object output stream chained to a byte array output stream. The byte array is then stored in a private field that is encrypted using the Cipher object c. The cipher's algorithms and parameters are also stored. Thus, the state of the original object written onto the ultimate object output stream is the state of the object when it was sealed; subsequent changes it may undergo between being sealed and being written are not reflected in the sealed object. Since serialization takes place immediately inside the constructor, the constructor throws a NotSerializableException if the object argument cannot be serialized. It throws an IllegalBlockSize-Exception if c is a block cipher with no padding and the length of the serialized object's contents is not an integral multiple of the block size.

You unseal an object by first reading the sealed object from an object input stream, then invoking one of the three getObject() methods to return the original object. All of these methods require you to supply a key and an algorithm.

Example 11-7 is a very simple program that writes an encrypted java.awt.Point object into the file *point.des*. First a file output stream is opened to the file *point.des*. Next this is chained to the ObjectOutputStream oin. As in the last chapter, a fixed DES key called desKey is built from a fixed array of bytes and used to construct a Cipher object called des. des is initialized in encryption mode with the key. Finally both the des Cipher object and the Point object tdp are passed into the SealedObject() constructor to create a SealedObject so. Since SealedObject implements Serializable, this can be written on the Object-OutputStream oout as any other serializable object. At this point, this program closes oout and exits. However, the same Cipher object des could be used to create more sealed objects from serializable objects, and these could also be written onto the stream, if you had more objects you wanted to serialize.

Example 11-7. SealedPoint

```java
import java.security.*;
import java.io.*;
import javax.crypto.*;
import javax.crypto.spec.*;
import java.awt.*;

public class SealedPoint {

  public static void main(String[] args) {

    String filename = "point.des";
    Point tdp = new Point(32, 45);

    try {
      FileOutputStream fout = new FileOutputStream(filename);
      ObjectOutputStream oout = new ObjectOutputStream(fout);

      // Create a key.
      byte[] desKeyData = {(byte) 0x90, (byte) 0x67, (byte) 0x3E, (byte) 0xE6,
        (byte) 0x42, (byte) 0x15, (byte) 0x7A, (byte) 0xA3 };
      DESKeySpec desKeySpec = new DESKeySpec(desKeyData);
      SecretKeyFactory keyFactory = SecretKeyFactory.getInstance("DES");
      SecretKey desKey = keyFactory.generateSecret(desKeySpec);

      // Use Data Encryption Standard.
      Cipher des = Cipher.getInstance("DES/ECB/PKCS5Padding");
      des.init(Cipher.ENCRYPT_MODE, desKey);

      SealedObject so = new SealedObject(tdp, des);
      oout.writeObject(so);
      oout.close();
    }
    catch (IOException e) { System.err.println(e); }
```

Example 11-7. SealedPoint (continued)

```
    catch (GeneralSecurityException e) { System.err.println(e); }
  }
}
```

Reading a sealed object from an object input stream is easy. You read it exactly as you read any other object from an object input stream. For example:

```
FileInputStream fin = new FileInputStream(filename);
ObjectInputStream oin = new ObjectInputStream(fin);
SealedObject so = (SealedObject) oin.readObject();
```

Once you've read the object, unsealing it to retrieve the original object is straightforward, provided you know the key. There are three `getObject()` methods that return the original object:

```
public final Object getObject(Key key) throws IOException,
   ClassNotFoundException, NoSuchAlgorithmException, InvalidKeyException
public final Object getObject(Cipher c) throws IOException,
   ClassNotFoundException, IllegalBlockSizeException, BadPaddingException
public final Object getObject(Key key, String provider) throws IOException,
   ClassNotFoundException, NoSuchAlgorithmException, NoSuchProviderException,
   InvalidKeyException
```

The first variant is the most useful, since it only requires the key. It does not require you to create and initialize a `Cipher` object. You will in general need to know the algorithm used in order to know what kind of key to create, but that information is available from the `getAlgorithm()` method:

```
public final String getAlgorithm()
```

For example:

```
if (so.getAlgorithm().startsWith("DES")) {
   byte[] desKeyData = {(byte) 0x90, (byte) 0x67, (byte) 0x3E, (byte) 0xE6,
     (byte) 0x42, (byte) 0x15, (byte) 0x7A, (byte) 0xA3, };
   DESKeySpec desKeySpec = new DESKeySpec(desKeyData);
   SecretKeyFactory keyFactory = SecretKeyFactory.getInstance("DES");
   SecretKey desKey = keyFactory.generateSecret(desKeySpec);
   Object o = so.getObject(desKey);
}
```

Example 11-8 reads the sealed object from the *point.des* file written by Example 11-7, unseals the object, then prints it on `System.out`.

Example 11-8. UnsealPoint

```
import java.security.*;
import java.io.*;
import javax.crypto.*;
import javax.crypto.spec.*;
```

Example 11-8. UnsealPoint (continued)

```java
import java.awt.*;

public class UnsealPoint {

  public static void main(String[] args) {

    String filename = "point.des";

    try {
      FileInputStream fin = new FileInputStream(filename);
      ObjectInputStream oin = new ObjectInputStream(fin);

      // Create a key.
      byte[] desKeyData = { (byte) 0x90, (byte) 0x67, (byte) 0x3E, (byte) 0xE6,
        (byte) 0x42, (byte) 0x15, (byte) 0x7A, (byte) 0xA3 };
      DESKeySpec desKeySpec = new DESKeySpec(desKeyData);
      SecretKeyFactory keyFactory = SecretKeyFactory.getInstance("DES");
      SecretKey desKey = keyFactory.generateSecret(desKeySpec);

      SealedObject so = (SealedObject) oin.readObject();

      Point p = (Point) so.getObject(desKey);
      System.out.println(p);
      oin.close();
    }
    catch (ClassNotFoundException e) {System.err.println(e);}
    catch (IOException e) {System.err.println(e);}
    catch (GeneralSecurityException e) {System.err.println(e);}
  }
}
```

12

In this chapter:
- *Understanding Files*
- *Directories and Paths*
- *The File Class*
- *Filename Filters*
- *File Filters*
- *File Descriptors*
- *Random-Access Files*
- *General Techniques for Cross-Platform File Access Code*

Working with Files

You've already learned how to read and write data in files using file input streams and file output streams. That's not all there is to files. Files can be created, moved, renamed, copied, deleted, and otherwise manipulated without respect to their contents. Files are also often associated with meta-information that's not strictly part of the contents of the file, such as the time the file was created, the icon for the file, the permissions that determine which users can read or write to the file, and even the name of the file.

While the abstraction of the contents of a file as an ordered sequence of bytes used by file input and output streams is almost standard across platforms, the meta-information is not. The `java.io.File` class attempts to provide a platform-independent abstraction for common file operations and meta-information. Unfortunately, this class really shows its Unix roots. It works well on Unix, adequately on Windows and OS/2—with a few caveats—and fails miserably on the Macintosh. Java 2 improves things, but there's still a lot of history—and coming up with something that genuinely works on all platforms is an extremely difficult problem.

File manipulation is thus one of the real difficulties of cross-platform Java programming. Before you can hope to write truly cross-platform code, you need a solid understanding of the filesystem basics on all the target platforms. This chapter tries to cover those basics for the major platforms that support Java—Unix; DOS/Windows 3.*x*; Windows 95, 98, and NT; OS/2; and the Mac—then it shows you how to write your file code so that it's as portable as possible.

Understanding Files

As far as a Java program knows, a file is a sequential set of bytes stored on a disk like a hard drive or a CD-ROM. There is a first byte in the file, a second byte, and so on, until the end of the file. In this way a file is similar to a stream. However, a program can jump around in a file, reading first one part of a file, then another. This isn't possible with a stream.

Macintosh files are a little different. Mac files are divided into two *forks*, each of which is equivalent to a separate file on other platforms. The first part of a Mac file is called the *data fork* and contains the text, image data, or other basic information of the file. The second part of the file is called the *resource fork* and typically contains localizable strings, pictures, icons, graphical user interface components like menubars and dialogs, executable code, and more. On a Macintosh, all the standard `java.io` classes work exclusively with the data fork.

Filenames

Every file has a name. The format of the filename is determined by the operating system. For example, in DOS and Windows 3.1, filenames are case-insensitive, (though generally rendered as all capitals), eight ASCII characters long with a three-letter extension. *README.TXT* is a valid DOS filename, but *Read me before you run this program or your hard drive will get trashed* is not. All ASCII characters from 32 up (that is, noncontrol characters), except for the 15 punctuation characters (+=/] [":;,?*\<>|) and the space character, may be used in filenames. A period may be used only as a separator between the eight-character name and the three-letter extension. Furthermore, the complete path to the file, including the disk drive and all directories, may not exceed 80 characters in length.

On the other hand, *Read me before you run this program or your hard drive will get trashed* is a valid Win32 (Windows 95, 98, and NT) filename. On those systems filenames may contain up to 255 characters, though room also has to be left for the path to the file. The full pathname may not exceed 255 characters. Furthermore, Win32 filenames are stored in Unicode, though in most circumstances only the ISO Latin-1 character set is actually used to name files. Win32 systems allow any Unicode character with value 32 or above to be used, except \/*<>:?" and |. In particular, the +,;=] [characters, forbidden in DOS and Windows 3.1, are legal in Win32 filenames.

NOTE   Windows 95, 98, and NT also make short versions of the filename
              that conform to the DOS 8.3 format available to non-32-bit applica-
              tions that don't understand the long filenames. Java understands the
              long filenames and uses them in preference to the short form.

Read me before you run this program or your hard drive will get trashed is not a valid
Macintosh filename because Mac filenames cannot be longer than 32 characters.
Read me or your HD will be trashed contains only 27 letters and is a valid Macintosh
filename. Directory names are limited to 27 characters, but there's no fixed length
to a full pathname. Macintosh filenames can contain slashes and backslashes
(unlike Windows filenames) but may not contain colons. Furthermore, while
Macintosh filenames can and often do contain periods, it is an *extremely* bad idea to
begin a Macintosh file name with a period. On occasion the Mac interprets filenames beginning with a period as being device drivers rather than ordinary files,
and this can lead to corrupted filesystems. Otherwise, any ASCII characters, as well
as eight-bit MacRoman characters like ® and π, can be used in a Mac filename.

By way of contrast, many standard Unix files have names that begin with periods.
.cshrc and *.login* are just two of the most common examples. Beginning a file with a
period is Unix's way of telling that a file should be hidden. (FTPing a directory of
Unix files to the Mac without accounting for this can lead to a trashed Mac filesystem.) Most modern Unix systems allow at least 255 characters in a filename,*
and none of those 255 characters needs to be left for a path. Just about any ASCII
character except the forward slash (/) and the null (ASCII 0) is valid in a Unix
filename. However, because Unix makes heavy use of a command line, filenames
containing spaces, single quotation marks, double quotes, hyphens, or other characters interpreted by the Unix shell are often inconvenient. Underscores (which
aren't interpreted by the Unix shell) are safe and often used in place of problematic characters; for example, *Read_me_or_your_HD_will_be_trashed*.

OS/2 filenames depend on the filesystem being used. If a disk is formatted using
the DOS FAT filesystem, then OS/2 filenames are limited to DOS's 8.3 format filenames. Files may have a title as well as a name, and the title may contain up to 254
printable characters. Any character with value from 32 up may be used in the title,
except \-/&<>:?" and |. Titles may not begin with an @. Under OS/2's High
Performance File System (HPFS), filenames are the same as titles, and full paths
may have indefinite length.

---

* Extremely early versions of Unix on which Java doesn't run (and probably never will) limit filenames
to 14 characters in length.

Character sets are a problem for filenames too. American Macintosh filenames are given in the eight-bit MacRoman character set, but there are many internationalized versions of the MacOS that use different character sets. The same is true for OS/2. Windows 95 and NT filenames use Unicode characters. Some Unix versions use ISO Latin-1, some use ASCII only, and some use Unicode (but only if optional software is installed). The lowest common denominator character set for filenames is ASCII.

Case sensitivity is a problem too. *Readme.txt* and *README.TXT* are the same file on the Mac and Windows, but represent two different files on Unix.

Handling different filename conventions is one of the difficulties of doing real cross-platform work. For best results:

- Use only printable ASCII characters, periods, and underscores in filenames.

- Avoid punctuation characters in filenames where possible.

- Never begin a filename with a period, a hyphen, or an @.

- Avoid extended character sets and accented characters like ü, ç, and é.

- Use mixed-case filenames (since they're easier to read), but do not assume case alone will distinguish between filenames.

- Try to keep your filenames to 32 characters or less so Macs won't have to truncate the name and Windows PCs will be able to store them reasonably deep in a directory hierarchy.

- If a filename can be stored in a DOS-compatible 8.3 format without excessive effort, you might as well do so. However, Java itself assumes a system on which files have long names with four- and five-character extensions, so don't go out of your way to do this.

File Attributes

Most operating systems also store a series of attributes describing each file. The exact attributes a file possesses are platform-dependent. For example, on Unix a file has an owner ID, a group ID, a modification time, and a series of read, write, and execute flags that determine who is allowed to do what with the file. If an operating system supports multiple types of filesystems, as does Windows NT, the attributes of a file may vary depending on what kind of filesystem it resides on.

The Macintosh has no concept of file ownership, since Macs aren't multiuser systems; but most Mac files have a type code and a creator code as well as 12 boolean attributes that determine whether a file is invisible or not, is on the desktop or not, is an alias or not, has a custom icon or not, and eight other characteristics mostly unique to the Mac platform.

Windows and DOS systems store a file's last modification date, the actual size of the file, the number of allocation blocks the file occupies, and essentially boolean information about whether or not a file is hidden, read-only, a system file, or whether the file has been modified since it was last backed up.

Windows NT supports multiple kinds of filesystems, including FAT (the basic DOS-compatible filesystem) and NTFS (NT File System). NT 3.5.1 and earlier (but not NT 4.0 and later) support OS/2's HPFS. Each of these filesystems supports a slightly different set of attributes. They all support a superset of the basic DOS/Windows file attributes, including creation time, modification time, access time, allocation size, file size, and whether the file is read-only, system, hidden, archive, or control.

On Unix, file attributes may be viewed by using the -1 switch to the ls command:

```
% ls -l
total 3408
-r--r--r--    1 root      other         89795 Aug 30 14:41 CHANGES
-r--r--r--    1 root      other           896 Aug 30 14:41 COPYRIGHT
-r--r--r--    1 root      other          5994 Aug 30 14:41 LICENSE
-r--r--r--    1 root      other         34689 Aug 30 14:41 README
drwxr-xr-x    3 root      other           512 Oct 17 10:31 bin
drwxr-xr-x   24 root      other           512 Oct 16 21:07 demo
drwxr-xr-x    4 root      other          1024 Oct 17 10:31 include
-r--r--r--    1 root      other          2497 Aug 30 14:41 index.html
drwxr-xr-x    4 root      other          1024 Oct 17 10:32 lib
-rw-r--r--    1 root      other       1593763 Aug 30 14:40 src.zip
```

The first column is a series of character flags indicating, respectively, the type of the file; the owner's read, write, and execute permissions; the group's read, write and execute permissions; and the world's read, write, and execute permissions. The number following that is the number of links to this file. The next word, root in all these cases, is the username of the owner of the file. The second word, other in this example, is the group associated with the file. The following number is the size of the file in bytes. This is followed by the last modification date of the file. The last column contains the name of the file itself.

The attributes of a Windows file may be viewed from a DOS window with the DIR command:

```
C:> DIR/X
 Volume in drive C has no label.
 Volume Serial Number is 9460-4CAA

 Directory of C:\

12/31/96  04:03p                   0              AUTOEXEC.BAT
12/31/96  04:03p                   0              CONFIG.SYS
```

```
12/31/96  04:48p      <DIR>                      MSOffice
11/12/97  11:28a           45,088,768           pagefile.sys
11/05/97  08:13p      <DIR>                      Pro18
12/31/96  03:54p      <DIR>         PROGRA~1     Program Files
12/31/96  04:03p      <DIR>                      TEMP
11/12/97  11:29a      <DIR>                      WINNT
              8 File(s)      45,088,768 bytes
                            640,570,880 bytes free
```

This shows the file's name, optionally its short name, the size of the file in bytes (if it's not a directory), and the date and time when the file was created. With the /T:A or /T:W flags, you would see the time the file was last accessed or written (modified), respectively. DOS won't show you the archive, hidden, system, or read-only flags directly, but by using the /A:A, /A:H, /A:S, or /A:R flags, you can list only those files that have the specified attributes. By placing a minus sign before the flag—e.g., /A:-S—you can see all files that do not have the specified attributes.

The Macintosh has a different set of file attributes, which are not meant to be viewed as such by the end user. However, a number of developers' tools, like ResEdit and Disktop, make them explicit. Figure 12-1 shows the File Info screen of ResEdit listing the attributes of a typical Macintosh file.

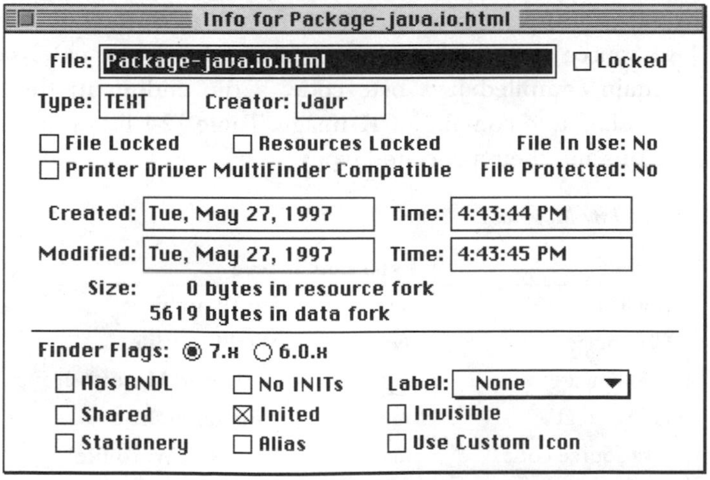

Figure 12-1. The File Info screen in ResEdit on the Macintosh

You see that the file has a name, a creation time and date, a four-letter type code, a four-letter creator code, a last-modified time and date, sizes for both the resource and data forks, a label, and various boolean flags, some whose meaning is obvious (shared, alias, invisible, use custom icon, file locked, file in use, file protected), and some whose meaning is a little more obscure (has BNDL, stationery, no INITs, inited, 7.x or 6.0.x, resources locked, printer driver MultiFinder compatible). Some of these attributes, like modification date and time, are common across most platforms, but many, like "Inited" and "Use Custom Icon," are unique to the Macintosh.

Any cross-platform library like the `java.io` package is going to have trouble supporting all these attributes. Java allows you to test a fairly broad cross-section of these possible attributes for which most platforms have some reasonable equivalent. It does not allow you easy access to platform-specific attributes, like Mac file types and creator codes, Windows' archive attributes, or Unix group IDs.

TIP — The `com.apple.mrj.MRJOSType` and `com.apple.mrj.MRJFile-Utils` classes included in Macintosh Runtime for Java provide access to some of the unique Macintosh file attributes. See *http://developer. apple.com/techpubs/mac/ProgMRJToolkit/MRJToolBook-2.html* for more details.

Filename Extensions and File Types

Filename extensions are often used to indicate the type of a file. For example, a file that ends with the four-letter extension *.java* is presumed to be a text file containing Java source code; a file ending in the five-letter extension *.class* is assumed to contain compiled Java byte code; a file ending in the three-letter extension *.gif* is assumed to contain a GIF image. Table 12-1 lists some of the more common extensions and their associated types.

Table 12-1. Extension Type Mappings

Extension	Type	Extension	Type
.txt	ASCII text	*.sit*	StuffIt archive
.gif	GIF image	*.bin*	MacBinary file
.jpg, .jpeg	JPEG image	*.hqx*	BinHexed Macintosh file
.htm, .html	HTML text	*.tar*	Unix tar archive
.java	Java source code	*.doc*	Microsoft Word file
.class	compiled Java class	*.c*	C source code
.jar	JAR archive	*.pl*	Perl program
.zip	Zip archive	*.cc, .cpp*	C++ source code
.Z	Unix compressed file	*.o*	Prelinked native object code
.gz	gzipped file	*.exe*	DOS/Windows executable

What does your computer do when you double-click on the file *panther.gif*? If your computer is a Macintosh, it opens the file in the program that created the file. That's because the MacOS stores a four-letter creator code in the resource fork of every file. Assuming the application associated with that creator code can be found (it can't always, though), the file *panther.gif* is opened in the creating program. On the other hand, if your computer is a Windows PC or a Unix workstation, the creating program is not necessarily opened. Instead, whichever program is registered as the viewer of *.gif* files is launched and used to view the file. In command-line environments, like the Unix shell, this isn't really an issue, because you begin by specifying the program to run; that is, you type *xv panther.gif*, not simply *panther.gif*. But in GUI environments, the program that's opened may not be the program you want to use.

File extensions have the further disadvantage that they do not really guarantee the content type of their document and are an unreliable means of determining the type of a file. Users can easily change them. For example, the simple command `copy HelloWorld.java HelloWorld.gif` causes an ASCII text file to be misinterpreted as a GIF image. Filename extensions are only as reliable as the user that assigned them. What's more, it's hard to distinguish between files that belong to different applications that have the same type. For instance, many users are surprised to discover that after installing Internet Explorer, all their HTML files appear to belong to Explorer instead of Netscape.

The Macintosh solved this problem over a decade ago. Almost every Mac file has a four-letter type code like "TEXT" and a four-letter creator code like "R*ch". Since each file has both a type code *and* a creator code, a Mac can distinguish between files that belong to different applications but have the same type. Installing Internet Explorer doesn't mean that IE suddenly thinks it owns all your Netscape documents, as is the case when you install IE on Windows. Software vendors register codes with Apple so companies don't accidentally step on each other's toes; and since codes are almost never seen by end users, there's not a huge rush to snap up all the good ones like "TEXT" and "HTML". The list of codes that a particular Macintosh understands is stored in the Desktop database, a file users never see and only rarely have to worry about. Overall, this is a pretty good system that's worked incredibly well for more than a decade. Neither Windows nor Unix has anything nearly as simple and trouble-free. Because Windows and Unix have not adopted Mac-style type and creator codes, Java does not have any standard means for accessing them.

None of these solutions is perfect. On a Mac you're likely to want to use Photoshop to create GIF files but use JPEGView or Netscape to view them. You can drag and drop the file onto the desired application, but only if both the file and the application you want to view it with are on the screen at the same time, which is not necessarily true if both are stored several folders deep. Furthermore, it's relatively hard to say that you want all text files opened in BBEdit. On the other hand, the Windows solution is prone to user error; filename extensions are too exposed. For example, novice HTML coders often can't understand why their HTML files painstakingly crafted in Notepad open as plaintext in Navigator. Notepad surreptitiously inserts a *.txt* extension on all the files it saves unless the filename is enclosed in double quote marks. For instance, a file saved as *HelloWorld.html* actually becomes *HelloWorld.html.txt*, while a file saved as *"HelloWorld.html"* is saved with the expected name. Furthermore, filename extensions make it easy for a user to lie about the contents of a file, potentially confusing and crashing applications. (You can lie about a file type on a Mac too, but it takes a lot more work.) Finally, Windows provides absolutely no support for saying that you want one group of GIF images opened in Photoshop and another group opened in DeBabelizer.

There are some algorithms that can attempt to determine a file's type from its contents, though these are also error-prone. Many file formats require files to begin with a particular *magic number* that uniquely identifies the format. For instance, all compiled Java class files begin with the number 0xCAFEBABE (in hexadecimal). If the first four bytes of a file aren't 0xCAFEBABE, then it's definitely not a Java class file. Furthermore, barring deliberate fraud, there's only about a one in four billion chance that a random, non-Java file will begin with those four bytes. Unfortunately, only a few file formats require magic numbers. Text files, for instance, can begin with any four ASCII characters. There are some heuristics you can apply to identify such files. For example, a file of pure ASCII should not contain any bytes with values between 128 and 255 and should have a limited number of control characters with values less than 32. But such algorithms are complicated to devise and far from reliable. Even if you are able to identify a file as ASCII text, how would you determine whether it contains Java source code or a letter to your mother? Worse yet, how could you tell whether it contains Java source code or C source code? It's not impossible, barring deliberately perverse files like a concatenation of a C program with a Java program, but it's difficult and often not worth your time.

One possible solution to the problem of identifying file types across platforms is using MIME. The file-extension-content type mappings listed in Table 12-1 are *de facto* standards. MIME, the Multipurpose Internet Mail Extensions, is a *de jure* (RFCs 2045–2049) specification for embedding and identifying arbitrary data types in Internet email. MIME is also used by HTTP servers that want to identify the kinds of data they're sending to a client. And, in the BeOS, it's used as a Mac-like means of identifying file types. A MIME type consists of a primary type like "text" or "image," followed by a forward slash, followed by a subtype like "html" or "gif." "text/html" is a typical MIME content type that indicates a file of textual information in the HTML format. MIME also uses x-types, like "application/x-tar" and "application/x-mif," to allow ad hoc extensions to the standard. There may be more than one x-type referring to the same basic type (for instance, "application/x-pict" and "application/x-macpict" both refer to Macintosh PICT images), and the same x-type may be used for different purposes by different programs. Nonetheless, since new MIME types are adopted rather slowly, the x-types are important as well.

Directories and Paths

Modern operating systems organize files into hierarchical directories. Each directory contains zero or more files or other directories. Like files, directories have names and attributes, though—depending on the operating system—those names and attributes may be different from the attributes allowed for files. For example, on the Macintosh, a filename can be up to 32 characters long, but a directory name can be no more than 27 characters long.

Paths and Separators

To specify a file completely, you don't just give its name. You also give the directory the file lives in. Of course, that directory may itself be inside another directory, which may be in another directory, until you reach the *root* of the filesystem. The complete list of directories from the root to a specified file plus the name of the file itself is called the *absolute path* to the file. The exact syntax of absolute paths varies from system to system. Here are a few examples:

DOS	*C:\PUBLIC\HTML\JAVAFAQ\INDEX.HTM*
Win32	*C:\public\html\javafaq\index.html*
MacOS	*Macintosh HD:public:html:javafaq:index.html*
Unix	*/public/html/javafaq/index.html*

All three strings reference a file named *index.html* on the primary hard drive in the *javafaq* directory, which is itself in the *html* directory, which is in the *public* directory. One obvious difference is the file separator character. Unix uses a forward slash (/) to separate directories; DOS-based filesystems, including the variants of Windows and OS/2, use a backslash (\); Macs use a colon (:). Other platforms may use something completely different.

The separator used on a given system is available from the mnemonic constants `java.io.File.separator` and `java.io.File.separatorChar`. `File.separatorChar` is the first character of the string `File.separator`. All operating systems I'm familiar with use a single character separator string, so these two variables are essentially the same. The `File.separator` variable is set from the system property `file.separator`; that is:

```
public static final String separator = System.getProperty("file.separator");
public static final char separatorChar = separator.charAt(0);
```

System Properties

System properties are a cross-platform abstraction of environment variables. Some properties, like *user.dir*, are set directly from environment variables by the Java runtime. Others are read from configuration files. Regardless of where system properties come from, they're available to you from the static `System.getProperty()` methods:

```
public static String getProperty(String name)
public static String getProperty(String name, String default)
```

The first version returns the value of the named property or `null` if the property isn't found. The second returns the value of the named property or `default` if the property isn't found. Property reads are subject to security manager checks. Generally, applets are allowed to read properties that reveal information about the runtime environment, like `file.separator`, but not ones that reveal information about the host running the applet, such as `user.home`.

Many of these properties provide useful information about the host system in which your program is running. For instance, the `os.name` property returns a string like "Windows NT", "Solaris", or "MacOS" that tells you the operating system your program is running on. The `java.vendor` property tells you who wrote this VM. No matter how hard you try to write 100% pure Java, there are times when you simply have to adjust your code to match a particular operating system or virtual machine.

Several properties provide full paths to directories according to the local filesystem conventions. The security manager permitting, you can use these to construct cross-platform filenames. Such properties include:

`java.home`
> The directory where Java is installed; e.g., */usr/local/java* on many Unix systems.

`java.class.path`
> The class path contains many directories separated by the path separator character.

`user.home`
> The user's home directory.

`user.dir`
> The current working directory.

There may be others, but these four are guaranteed to have values.

There are also two unrelated mnemonic constants, `File.pathSeparator` and `File.pathSeparatorChar`. The path separator string is set from the system property `path.separator`. As with the separator character, `File.pathSeparatorChar` is the first character in `File.pathSeparator`.

```
public static final String pathSeparator =
System.getProperty("path.separator");
public static final char pathSeparatorChar = pathSeparator.charAt(0);
```

The path separator is used to separate two files (generally with complete pathnames) in a list of paths such as a class path. For example, with a separator of a slash and a path separator of a colon, my class path looks like this:

```
.:/usr/local/java/lib:/home/users/elharo/:/home/users/elharo/JavaDis/
```

NOTE   These four mnemonic constants are one of the few instances in the core API where JavaSoft violates its convention of using all caps for public final static fields. You'd expect these constants to be named `File.SEPARATOR`, `File.SEPARATOR_CHAR`, `File.PATH_SEPARATOR`, and `File.PATH_SEPARATOR_CHAR`. Perhaps a future version of Java will conform to the standard naming conventions.

Now the bad news: although JavaSoft has provided a fairly powerful abstraction layer so that programmers don't need to hardcode explicit separators and path separators, few programmers actually use this. Many programmers simply assume that the file separator is a slash and the path separator is a colon and hardcode those constants as `"/"` and `":"` or `'/'` and `':'`. Therefore, to avoid breaking all this third-party code, Java 1.1 VMs on the Mac and Windows generally use a slash for the separator and a colon for the path separator, then make the appropriate conversions in the native code that underlies Java. Java 2 VMs pass pathnames through a normalization phase that attempts to recognize the separator conventions and convert those to the conventions of the local platform.

This isn't a big problem for Windows, since both the slash and the backslash are illegal characters in filenames. However, on the Mac a filename can contain both a slash and a backslash. Macintosh virtual machines have adopted a number of different and incompatible schemes to distinguish between slashes that are part of filenames and slashes that represent separators. One early scheme was to replace slashes by colons and colons by slashes. However, all but one of the alternative Mac VM vendors have canceled their own VM efforts in favor of Apple's own Macintosh Runtime for Java (MRJ), and thus the scheme that MRJ uses seems likely to become the standard way to handle unusual filenames on the Mac.

Apple's translation scheme is loosely based on the x-www-form-urlencoded format for encoding URLs. Any characters that are likely to cause problems in a filename are replaced by a percent sign (%) followed by the two hexadecimal digits corresponding to the ASCII value of that character. For example, the space is ASCII 32 (decimal) or 20 (hexadecimal). Thus, it's encoded as %20. The forward slash is ASCII 47 (decimal) or 2f (hexadecimal). Thus, it's encoded as %2f. The pathname for this chapter, *Macintosh HD:Java:Java I/O:12 Working with Files/12 Working with Files.doc*, would be encoded as */Macintosh%20HD/Java/Java%20I%2fO/ 12%20Working%20with%20Files/12%20Working%20with%20Files.doc*. Table 12-2 gives a complete list of the ASCII characters between 32 and 127 that must be encoded. For readers not familiar with Macintosh files, let me emphasize that this is purely for use inside Java. Native Macintosh code and the native Mac interface use the actual characters. As well as the characters listed here, all the upper 128 characters with their high bit set—that is, characters like • and © and é—must be encoded. A little surprisingly, control characters between 0 and 31 are not encoded.

Table 12-2. Hex-Encoded Characters in Macintosh Filenames

Character	Encoded As	Decimal Value
space	%20	32
#	%23	35
%	%25	37
/	%2f	47
<	%3c	60
=	%3d	61
>	%3e	62
?	%3f	63
@	%40	64
[	%5b	91
\	%5c	92
]	%5d	93
^	%5e	94
`	%60	96
{	%7b	123
|	%7c	124
}	%7d	125
~	%7e	126

You probably don't need to know about the encoding at this level of detail unless you're trying to manipulate filenames manually—for example, walking directories by looking for separator characters rather than calling `getParent()`. The more you let Java do the work for you, the better off you'll be. As long as you use the methods of the `File` class rather than parsing pathnames directly as strings, this encoding scheme should be transparent.

Relative Versus Absolute Paths

There are two ways to reference a file, relative and absolute. Absolute addressing gives a complete path to a file, starting with the disk or root of the filesystem and working its way down. *C:\PUBLIC\HTML\JAVAFAQ\INDEX.HTM*, *Macintosh HD: public:html:javafaq:index.htm*, and */public/html/javafaq/index.htm* are all examples of absolute paths. Relative addressing does not use a complete path to a file; instead, it specifies the path relative to the current working directory. A relative pathname may point to a file in the current working directory by giving its name alone; other times it may point to a file in a subdirectory of the current working directory by giving the name of the subdirectory and the name of the file, and it may point to the parent of the current working directory with the double period (..).

Absolute paths

On Unix all mounted disks, whether local or mounted over the network, are combined into a single virtual filesystem. The *root* of this filesystem is the directory called /. You generally do not need to concern yourself with which physical disk any particular directory resides on, as long as that disk has sufficient space. Absolute paths always begin with the root directory, /.

On Windows and the Mac, there is no root directory. Each mounted disk partition or network server is a separate and independent filesystem. On Windows, these disks are assigned drive letters. A: is normally the floppy drive. B: is the second floppy drive (less common these days, since fewer systems have multiple floppy drives.) C: is the primary boot disk. D: is often reserved for a CD-ROM, though it can be an additional hard disk or partition as well. E: through Z: can be used for further disks, partitions, or network servers. A full pathname begins with the drive letter where the file resides, e.g., *C:\PUBLIC\HTML\JAVAFAQ\INDEX.HTM*.

On Windows 95, 98 and NT, an additional level is possible by specifying remote machines on the network like this: *\\BIO\C\PUBLIC\HTML\JAVAFAQ\INDEX.HTM*. This path refers to a file called *INDEX.HTM* in the directory *JAVAFAQ* in the directory *HTML* in the directory *PUBLIC* on the *C* drive of the machine *BIO*. Java 1.1 does not provide a pure Java means to get a list of all the available volumes on Windows; the best you can do is check all possible drive letters and catch any `IOExceptions` that occur. Java 2 does add a `File.listRoots()` method that returns all the roots of the local system.

Like Windows, the Macintosh does not have a true root from which all mounted disks and servers can be accessed. Each disk or disk partition and each server appear as a separate volume, though the names are generally a little more descriptive than A, B, C, and D. Macintosh virtual machines interpret a request to list the contents of the directory "/" as a request for a list of all mounted volumes. You should be warned, however, that a single Macintosh can have several volumes with the same name. This is rare on a single-user Mac but relatively common in networked environments where file sharing can mount volumes on other Macs with common names like *Macintosh HD* or *untitled* or *Public Folder*. This isn't a problem for native code, which doesn't use names to identify volumes, but it's a real showstopper for pure Java programs. To further complicate matters, the Mac's primary hard drive may not be named *Macintosh HD*.

For these reasons and more, absolute pathnames are a royal pain to work with across platforms. You should avoid hardcoding them in your programs whenever possible. Instead, you should calculate them at runtime from system properties and user input.

Relative paths

The following are some examples of relative paths:

Unix	*html/index.html*
DOS	*HTML\INDEX.HTM*
Win32	*html\index.html*
MacOS	*html:index.html*
Unix	*index.html*
DOS	*INDEX.HTM*
Win32	*index.html*
MacOS	*index.html*

Note that a filename in isolation constitutes a relative path on all platforms.

Generally, the running application identifies one directory as the current working directory. Relative pathnames are interpreted relative to the working directory. Normally, this is the directory in which the application was launched. For example, if you started your program from the command line in the */home/users/elharo* directory, then a relative path of *classes/juggler.class* would point to a file with the absolute path */home/users/elharo/classes/juggler.class*. On the Macintosh, the current working directory is generally whichever one the application lives in. If you're using JBindery to run your app, then the current working directory will be the folder JBindery is in. If you launch a standalone Java application, the current working directory will be the folder in which that application is.

On Unix and the Mac, the current working directory is fixed once a program starts running. Java provides no means to change it. However, Windows with the JDK 1.1 is annoyingly different. If you bring up a file dialog (discussed in the next chapter), then the current working directory is changed to the directory in which the user selects a file. The current working directory is fixed on all platforms under Java 2.

You *must* not assume that your *.class* file and any associated support files are necessarily in the current working directory. For example, suppose I'm in the */home/users/elharo* directory, and I run the Java program *Trivia* which is located in the */home/users/bfrank* directory, like this:

```
% java /home/users/bfrank/Trivia
```

Although *Trivia.class* is located in the */home/users/bfrank* directory, the current working directory for this run of the *Trivia* program is */home/users/elharo*. Suppose the *Trivia* program expects to find support files—*Trivia.gif*, for example—in the current working directory. If those files are in */home/users/bfrank* along with *Trivia.class*, they won't be found, and the program probably won't run. I've used full paths to make the cause of the problem more obvious, but the problem would still occur if I used a relative path from the */home/users/elharo* directory:

```
% java ../bfrank/Trivia
```

If I first changed to the */home/users/bfrank/* directory, then the support files will be found and the program will run. For example:

```
% cd /home/users/bfrank
% java Trivia
```

Java provides no reliable means to get the path of the currently running program's *.class* file. Because the current working directory is unpredictable, you must not hardcode relative pathnames into your application. You must place any data files your program requires in a location that can be found independently of the location of the *.class* files for your program. One possibility is to place the files on a web server accessible through a known URL. An even better solution is to distribute your program as a JAR archive, store the data files in the JAR file, then retrieve them with the various getResource(), getResourceAsStream(), and findResource() methods of java.lang.Class or java.lang.ClassLoader. This works irrespective of the current working directory as long as the JAR archive has been placed somewhere in the class path.

NOTE   When you consider all the difficulties of writing file access code that works on all the platforms Java supports, you can become grateful that applets aren't allowed to write files. Although this limits the sort of applets you can write, perhaps what's really needed is not unlimited (or even limited) file access but some non-file-oriented persistent storage mechanism, probably some sort of database, that hides the idiosyncrasies of each individual platform. JavaSoft is now working on exactly such a mechanism called JavaSpaces, though it probably won't appear in web browsers for some time

The File Class

Instances of the `java.io.File` class represent *filenames* on the local system, not actual files. Occasionally, this distinction is crucial. For instance, `File` objects can represent directories as well as files. Also, you cannot assume that a file exists just because you have a `File` object for a file.

```
public class File extends Object implements Serializable
```

In Java 2, the `File` class also implements the `java.lang.Comparable` interface:

```
public class File extends Object implements Serializable, Comparable // Java 2
```

Although there are no guarantees that a file named by a `File` object actually exists, the `File` class does contain many methods for getting information about the attributes of a file and for manipulating those files. The `File` class attempts to account for system-dependent features like the file separator character and file attributes, though in practice it doesn't do a very good job, especially in Java 1.0 and 1.1.

Each `File` object contains a single `String` field called `path` that contains either a relative or absolute path to the file, including the name of the file or directory itself:

```
private String path
```

Many methods in this class work solely by looking at this string. They do not necessarily look at any part of the filesystem.

Constructing File Objects

The `java.io.File` class has three constructors. Each accepts some variation of a filename as an argument. This one is the simplest:

```
public File(String path)
```

The `path` argument should be either an absolute or relative path to the file in a format understood by the host operating system. For example, using Unix filename conventions:

```
File uf1 = new File("25.html");
File uf2 = new File("course/week2/25.html");
File uf3 = new File("/public/html/course/week2/25.html");
```

Much poorly written Java code (including large parts of the Java 1.0 and Java 1.1 class libraries) implicitly assumes Unix filename conventions, and most VMs take this into account. Therefore, code that assumes Unix conventions is likely to produce reasonable results on most operating systems. Windows VMs generally allow you to use Windows conventions instead. For example:

```
File wf1 = new File("25.htm");
File wf2 = new File("course\\week2\\25.html");
File wf3 = new File("D:\\public\\html\\course\\week2\\25.htm");
```

The double backslashes are merely the escape sequence for the single backslash in a string literal. Otherwise, attempts to compile this code would generate an "Invalid escape character" error message. Remember that \t is a tab, \n a line-feed, and so on. Here, however, we need a backslash to simply be a backslash.

Macintosh VMs use Unix conventions with the modifications noted previously in Table 12-2. For example:

```
File mf1 = new File("25.html");
File mf2 = new File("course/week2/25.html");
File mf3 = new File("/Macintosh%20HD/public/html/course/week2/25.html");
```

The second `File` constructor specifies an absolute or relative pathname and a filename:

```
public File(String directory, String filename)
```

For cxample:

```
File f2 = new File("course/week2", "25.html");
```

This produces a `File` object with the `path` field set to *course/week2/25.htm*. The constructor is smart enough to handle the case of directories with and without trailing separators. The third constructor is identical to the second, except that the first argument is a `File` object instead of a string.

```
public File(File directory, String filename)
```

This third constructor is the most robust of the lot, provided the filename is only a filename like *readme.txt* and not a relative path like *cryptozip/readme.txt*. The reason is that this constructor guarantees the use of the local path separator character and is thus more platform-independent. You can use this to build a file structure that works on all platforms regardless of path separators or normalization routines. For example, suppose you want to build a `File` object that points to the file *com/macfaq/io/StreamCopier.class*. The following four lines do this without reference to the file separator character:

```
File temp = new File("com");
temp = new File(temp, "macfaq");
temp = new File(temp, "io");
File scfile = new File(temp, "StreamCopier.class");
```

None of these constructors throw any exceptions. All the constructor does is set the `path` field; Java never checks to see whether the file named by `path` actually exists or even whether the name passed to the constructor is a valid filename. For example, the following `File` object will cause problems on Unix, OS/2, the Mac, and Windows; but you can still construct it:

```
File f = new File("-This is not a /nice\\ file:\r\nno it isn't");
```

Some methods in other classes also return `File` objects, most notably the `java.awt.FileDialog` and `javax.awt.swing.JFileChooser` methods discussed in the next chapter. Using file dialogs or choosers to ask the user for a filename is preferable to hardcoding them or reading them from the command line, because file dialogs properly handle cross-platform issues and the distinctions between relative and absolute paths.

TIP　　　　One thing you may not have noticed about these constructors: since a `File` object does not represent a file as much as a filename, these constructors do not actually create files. To create a new file with Java, you can open a file output stream to the file or invoke the `createNewFile()` method. The latter only works in Java 2 and later.

In Java 2 and later, construction of a `File` object includes normalization. This process reads hardcoded pathnames and attempts to convert them to the conventions of the local platform. This improves compatibility with code that's making assumptions about filenames. For instance, if a Windows VM is asked to create a `File` object with the path */public/html/javafaq/course/week2/index.html*, it will actually set the `path` field to *\public\html\javafaq\course\week2\index.html*. The reverse process happens on Unix; backslashes are converted to forward slashes. Java 2 is not available for the Mac at the time of this writing, so it remains to be seen how the Mac will normalize filenames. Because it can only really normalize separators, not filesystem roots, this scheme works better for relative pathnames than absolute ones.

Listing the Roots

Java 2 provides a static `File.listRoots()` method that returns an array of all the available roots of the filesystem as `File` objects:

```
public static File[] listRoots()  // Java 2
```

On Unix, this array is likely to have length 1 and contain the single root /. On Windows, it will probably contain all the drive letters mapped to one device or another, whether or not there's actually any media in the drive; e.g., `A:\`, `C:\`, `D:\`, `E:\`, `F:\`, `G:\`. On the Mac, the list will likely contain only the currently mounted drives, and these are likely to have somewhat more descriptive names than `C:\`. If the security manager does not allow the program to read a particular root, then that root is not included in the returned list. If the security manager does not allow the program to read any root, then the returned list will have length zero. Do not assume the array returned by `listRoots()` necessarily has any members! `null` is returned if the list can't be determined at all. This is not the same thing as a zero-length array.

The list of roots may or may not contain drives that are mounted over the network. If the drive is mounted in such a fashion that it pretends to be a local drive, it probably will be in the list. If the filesystem does not look like a local drive, it probably won't appear in the list. For instance, on Windows, network drives mapped to letters appear, but drives with UNC pathnames do not. Example 12-1 is a very simple program to list the roots and print them.

Example 12-1. RootLister

```
import java.io.*;

public class RootLister {

  public static void main(String[] args) {

    File[] roots = File.listRoots();
    for (int i = 0; i < roots.length; i++) {
      System.out.println(roots[i]);
    }
  }
}
```

Here's the output produced by `RootLister` on my Windows NT system. `A:` is the floppy drive. This system doesn't have a second floppy, which would normally be `B:`. `C:`, `D:`, `E:`, and `F:` are all partitions of the primary hard drive that appear to be separate drives. `G:` is the Zip drive, and `H:` is the CD-ROM. `I:` is a Macintosh drive mounted over the LAN.

```
D:\JAVA\ioexamples\12>java RootLister
A:\
C:\
D:\
E:\
F:\
G:\
H:\
I:\
```

The output on Unix is much simpler and is virtually guaranteed to look like this:

```
% java RootLister
/
```

Since Java 2 isn't available for the Mac at the time of this writing, I can only specu-late about what the output is likely to be on that platform. However, it will probably look something like this:

```
Macintosh HD
System 8
Drive D
Drive F
```

The exact names would depend on the names the user gave to the individual hard drives and network servers.

Listing Information About a File

The `File` class contains many methods that return particular information about the file. Most of this information can be gleaned from the `path` field alone without accessing the filesystem. Therefore, most of these methods do not throw `IOExceptions`.

Does the file exist? Is it a normal file? Is it a directory?

Since a `File` object does not necessarily correspond to a real file on the disk, the first question you'll probably want to ask is whether the file corresponding to the `File` object actually exists. This is especially important if you're relying on a user to type a filename rather than select it from a dialog, because users routinely mistype filenames. The `exists()` method returns `true` if the file named in this file object's `path` field exists, `false` if it doesn't:

```
public boolean exists()
```

There are two other ways to ask this question. The `isFile()` method returns `true` if the file exists and is not a directory. On the other hand, the `isDirectory()` method returns `true` if the file exists and is a directory.

```
public boolean isFile()
public boolean isDirectory()
```

The isDirectory() method does consider Unix symbolic links and Mac aliases to directories to be directories themselves; it does *not* consider Windows shortcuts to directories to be directories. All three of these methods throw a security exception if security manager does not allow the specified file to be read. In fact, if the file couldn't be read if it did exist, then this exception is thrown whether or not the file actually exists. Even determining whether or not certain files exist can be considered to be a security violation. Like most security issues, this is primarily a problem for applets, not applications.

Filename and path

The getName() method takes no arguments and returns the name of the file as a string:

```
public String getName()
```

The name does not include any part of the directory in which the file lives. That is, you get back *index.html* instead of */public/html/javafaq/index.html.* If the file is a directory like */public/html/javafaq/*, only the last name is returned (*javafaq* in this example).

The getPath() method returns the complete path to the file as stored in the File object's path field:

```
public String getPath()
```

This is merely a get method that returns the path field. Therefore, the path is relative if the File object was constructed with a relative path and absolute if the File object was constructed with an absolute path. Furthermore, this method never throws IOExceptions. Consider Example 12-2. This simple program constructs two File objects, one with a relative path and one with an absolute path, then prints the name and path of each object.

Example 12-2. Paths

```
import java.io.*;

public class Paths {

  public static void main(String[] args) {

    File absolute = new File("/public/html/javafaq/index.html");
    File relative = new File("html/javafaq/index.html");

    System.out.println("absolute: ");
    System.out.println(absolute.getName());
```

Example 12-2. Paths (continued)

```
    System.out.println(absolute.getPath());

    System.out.println("relative: ");
    System.out.println(relative.getName());
    System.out.println(relative.getPath());
  }
}
```

When the program is run on Unix, here's the output:

```
% java Paths
absolute:
index.html
/public/html/javafaq/index.html
relative:
index.html
html/javafaq/index.html
```

On Windows with Java 2, the output's a little different, because the `File` constructor normalizes the file separator character to the backslash:

```
D:\JAVA\ioexamples\12>java Paths
absolute:
index.html
\public\html\javafaq\index.html
relative:
index.html
html\javafaq\index:html
```

Absolute paths

The `getAbsolutePath()` method returns the complete path to the file starting from a filesystem root:

```
public String getAbsolutePath()
```

Examples of absolute paths include */public/html/javafaq/index.html* and *D:\JAVA\ ioexamples\12* but not *html/javafaq/index.html* or *ioexamples\12*. If the `File` object's `path` field is already an absolute path, then its value is returned. Otherwise, a separator character and the value of the `path` field are appended to the value of the system property `user.dir`, which refers to the current working directory. This method throws a security exception in most applet environments, because applets are usually not allowed to read the `user.dir` property.

If you need to know whether a file is specified by a relative or absolute path, you can call `isAbsolute()`:

```
public boolean isAbsolute()
```

This does not throw any security exceptions, because it does not need to go outside the class to determine whether or not a pathname is absolute. Instead, the check is performed by looking at the first few characters of the path field. On Unix or the Mac an absolute path begins with a /. On Windows or OS/2 an absolute path begins with a capital letter followed by a colon and a backslash, like C:\.

Canonical paths

Exactly what a canonical path is, and how it differs from an absolute path, is system-dependent, but it tends to mean that the path is somehow more real than the absolute path. Typically, if the full path contains aliases, shortcuts, shadows, or symbolic links of some kind, the canonical path resolves those aliases to the actual directories they refer to. The canonical path is returned by the getCanonicalPath() method:

```
public String getCanonicalPath() throws IOException
```

For example, on Unix when getAbsolutePath() is invoked on a symbolic link or a file that has a symbolic link (an alias or shortcut) in its path, the symbolic link is included in the path that getAbsolutePath() returns. However getCanonicalPath() returns the path with all symbolic links resolved. For example, suppose */bin/perl* is a link to the real file at */usr/local/bin/perl*, and you construct a File object perlLink like this:

```
File perlLink = new File("/bin/perl");
```

perlLink.getAbsolutePath() returns */bin/perl*, but perlLink.getCanonicalPath() returns */usr/local/bin/perl*.

On Windows and the Macintosh, getAbsolutePath() and getCanonicalPath() both resolve shortcuts and aliases. Suppose */Macintosh%20HD/Desktop%20Folder/javac* is an alias to */Macintosh%20HD/Java/MRJ%202.0% 20Early%20Access% 20Rel%202/MRJ%20SDK%202.0/Tools/javac*, and a File object named alias is constructed like this:

```
File alias = new File("/Macintosh%20HD/Desktop%20Folder/javac");
```

Both alias.getAbsolutePath() and alias.getCanonicalPath() return */Macintosh%20HD/Java/MRJ%202.0%20Early%20Access%20Rel%202/MRJ%20SDK%202. 0/Tools/javac*, not */Macintosh%20HD/Desktop%20Folder/javac*. getCanonicalPath() throws a security exception in most applet environments, because it reveals too much information about the host the applet is running on. getCanonicalPath() also removes relative references like the double period (..), which refers to the parent directory in many command-line environments and in URLs. For instance, suppose the current working directory is */home/users/elharo/javaio/ioexamples/12*. Then you create a `File` object like this:

```
File f = new File("../11/index.html");
String absolutePath = f.getAbsolutePath();
String canonicalPath = f.getCanonicalPath();
```

`absolutePath` is now */home/users/elharo/javaio/ioexamples/12/../11/index.html*. However, `canonicalPath` is */home/users/elharo/javaio/ioexamples/11/index.html*.

One use for canonical paths is to test whether two files are the same. You might need to do this if you're reading from an input file and writing to an output file. While it might occasionally be possible to read from and write to the same file, doing so always requires special care. For example, the `FileCopier` program from Example 4-2 in Chapter 4, *File Streams*, failed when the source and destination were the same file. Now we can use canonical paths to correct that flaw by testing whether two files are the same before copying, as shown in Example 12-3. If the files are the same, no copy needs to take place.

Example 12-3. SafeFileCopier

```
import java.io.*;
import com.macfaq.io.*;

public class SafeFileCopier {

  public static void main(String[] args) {

    if (args.length != 2) {
      System.err.println("Usage: java FileCopier infile outfile");
    }
    try {
      copy(new File(args[0]), new File(args[1]));
    }
    catch (IOException e) {System.err.println(e);}
  }

  public static void copy(File inFile, File outFile) throws IOException {

    if (inFile.getCanonicalPath().equals(outFile.getCanonicalPath())) {
      // inFile and outFile are the same,
      // hence no copying is required.
      return;
    }

    FileInputStream fin = new FileInputStream(inFile);
    FileOutputStream fout = new FileOutputStream(outFile);
    StreamCopier.copy(fin, fout);
    fin.close();
```

Example 12-3. SafeFileCopier (continued)

```
    fout.close();
  }
}
```

I could test the files themselves, but since a single file may have multiple paths through aliases or parent links, I'm still not guaranteed that the `inFile` and `outFile` aren't the same. But each file has exactly one unique canonical path, so if `inFile`'s canonical path is not equal to `outFile`'s canonical path, then they can't possibly be the same file. Conversely, if `inFile`'s canonical path is equal to `outFile`'s canonical path, then they must be the same file.

The `getCanonicalFile()` method, new in Java 2, acts just like `getCanonical-Path()`, except that it returns a new `File` object instead of a string:

```
    public File getCanonicalFile() throws IOException  //  Java 2
```

The `File` object returned has a `path` field that's the canonical path of the file. In Java 1.1 you can get the same effect for a `File` object f by calling new `File(f.getCanonicalPath())`. Both `getCanonicalPath()` and `getCanonicalFile()` can throw `IOExceptions`, because both need to read the filesystem to resolve aliases, shadows, symbolic links, shortcuts, and parent directory references.

Parents

The `getParent()` method returns a string containing everything before the last file separator in the `path` field:

```
    public String getParent()
```

For example, if a `File` object's `path` field is */home/users/elharo/javaio/ioexamples/11/index.html*, then `getParent()` returns `/home/users/elharo/javaio/ioexamples/11`. If a `File` object's `path` field is *11/index.html*, then `getParent()` returns 11. If a `File` object's `path` field is *index.html*, then `getParent()` returns `null`. Files at the top level of the disk have no parent directories. For these files, `getParent()` returns `null`.

In Java 2 the `getParentFile()` method does the same thing, except that it returns the parent as a new `File` object instead of a string:

```
    public File getParentFile()  // Java 2
```

File attributes

The `File` class has several methods that return assorted information about the file, such as its length, the time it was last modified, whether it's readable, whether it's writable, and whether it's hidden.

The canWrite() method indicates whether the program can write into the file referred to by this File object. The canRead() method indicates whether the program can read from the file.

```
public boolean canRead()
public boolean canWrite()
```

Both these methods perform two checks. The first check determines whether Java's security manager allows the file in question to be read or written; the second determines whether the operating system allows the file to be read or written. If Java's security manager disallows the access, a security exception is thrown. If the OS disallows the access, then the method returns false but does not throw any exceptions. However, attempting to read from or write to such a file will probably throw an IOException.*

The isHidden() method, only available in Java 2 and later, returns true if the file exists but is hidden; that is, it does not appear in normal displays or listings. It returns false if the file isn't hidden or doesn't exist.

```
public boolean isHidden()  // Java 2
```

Exactly how a file is hidden varies from platform to platform. On Unix, any file whose name begins with a period is hidden. On Windows and the Mac, hidden files are identified by particular attributes. This method throws a security exception if the security manager doesn't allow the file to be read.

The lastModified() method returns a long indicating the last time this file was modified:

```
public long lastModified()
```

Java 2 specifies that the long returned is the number of milliseconds since midnight, January 1, 1970, Greenwich Mean Time. However, in earlier VMs the conversion between this long and a real date is platform-dependent, so it's only useful for comparing the modification dates of different files, not for determining the absolute time a file was modified. This method throws a security exception if the security manager doesn't allow the file to be read. It returns 0 if the file doesn't exist or the last modified date can't be determined.

Finally, the length() method returns the number of bytes in the file or 0 if the file does not exist:

```
public long length()
```

---

* If the attempt to read from or write to a file does not closely follow on the call to canRead() or canWrite(), it's theoretically possible the file will have become readable or writable in the meantime. However, this is unusual, and you certainly shouldn't count on it.

This method throws a security exception if the security manager doesn't allow the file to be read.

An example

Example 12-4 is a character-mode program that lists all the available information about files named on the command line. Names may be given as absolute or relative paths.

Example 12-4. The FileSpy Program

```java
import java.io.*;
import java.util.*;

public class FileSpy {

  public static void main(String[] args) {

    for (int i = 0; i < args.length; i++) {
      File f = new File(args[i]);
      if (f.exists()) {
        System.out.println("Name: " + f.getName());
        System.out.println("Absolute path: " + f.getAbsolutePath());
        try {
          System.out.println("Canonical path: " + f.getCanonicalPath());
        }
        catch (IOException e) {
          System.out.println("Could not determine the canonical path.");
        }

        String parent = f.getParent();
        if (parent != null) {
          System.out.println("Parent: " + f.getParent());
        }

        if (f.canWrite()) System.out.println(f.getName() + " is writable.");
        if (f.canRead()) System.out.println(f.getName() + " is readable.");

        if (f.isFile()) {
          System.out.println(f.getName() + " is a file.");
        }
        else if (f.isDirectory()) {
          System.out.println(f.getName() + " is a directory.");
        }
        else {
          System.out.println("What is this?");
        }

        if (f.isAbsolute()) {
```

Example 12-4. The FileSpy Program (continued)

```
        System.out.println(f.getPath() + " is an absolute path.");
      }
      else {
        System.out.println(f.getPath() + " is not an absolute path.");
      }

      long lm = f.lastModified();
      if (lm != 0) System.out.println("Last Modified at " + new Date(lm));

      long length = f.length();
      if (length != 0) {
        System.out.println(f.getName() + " is " + length + " bytes long.");
      }
    }
    else {
      System.out.println("I'm sorry. I can't find the file " + args[i]);
    }
  }
 }
}
```

Here's the result of running `FileSpy` on itself:

```
D:\JAVA\ioexamples\12>java FileSpy FileSpy.java
Name: FileSpy.java
Absolute path: D:\JAVA\ioexamples\12\FileSpy.java
Canonical path: D:\Java\ioexamples\12\FileSpy.java
FileSpy.java is writable.
FileSpy.java is readable.
FileSpy.java is a file.
FileSpy.java is not an absolute path.
Last Modified at Fri Sep 11 15:11:24 PDT 1998
FileSpy.java is 1846 bytes long.
```

Manipulating Files

The `File` class has methods to create, move, rename, and delete files. A method to copy files is a noticeable omission.

Creating files

Java 1.1 provides no method to create a new file. Opening a file output stream to the file you want to create, then immediately closing it, has the same effect. For example, the following method creates a file if, and only if, it doesn't already exist. Otherwise, it throws an `IOException`:

```
public static void createFileSafely(File f) throws IOException {
```

```
    if (f.exists()) {
      throw new IOException(f.getName() + " already exists.");
    }
    FileOutputStream fout = new FileOutputStream(f);
    fout.close();
  }
```

Java 2 adds the `createNewFile()` method:

```
public boolean createNewFile()  throws IOException  // Java 2
```

This method checks to see whether the file exists and creates the file if it doesn't already exist. It returns `true` if the file was created and `false` if it wasn't created, either because it couldn't be created or because the file already existed. For example:

```
File f = new File("output.dat");
boolean success = f.createNewFile();
if (success) {
  //...
}
else { //...
```

This method throws an `IOException` if an I/O error occurs. It throws a security exception if the security manager vetoes the creation of the file.

Moving and renaming files

The `renameTo()` method changes the name of a file:

```
public boolean renameTo(File destination)
```

For example, to change the name of the file *src.txt* in the current working directory to *dst.txt*, you would write:

```
File src = new File("src.txt");
File dst = new File("dst.txt");
src.renameTo(dst);
```

As well as renaming the source file, `renameTo()` moves the source file from its original directory to the directory specified by the `destination` argument if the destination file is in a different directory than the source file. For example, to move a file *src* to the directory */usr/tmp* on a Unix system without changing the file's name, do this:

```
File dest = new File("/usr/tmp/" + src.getName());
src.renameTo(dest);
```

If `dest` already exists, then it is overwritten by the source file (permissions permitting; otherwise, an exception is thrown). If `src` is successfully renamed, the method returns `true`. If the security manager doesn't allow the program to write to both the source file and the destination file, a security exception is thrown. Otherwise, the method returns `false`. However, this behavior is unreliable and platform-dependent. For instance, `renameTo()` moves files if, and only if, the directory structure specified in the `dest File` object already exists. I've also seen this code work on some Unix versions with some versions of the JDK and fail on others. It's best not to rely on this method for more than renaming a file in the same directory.

Copying files

There is no `copy()` method that merely copies a file to a new location without removing the original. However, you can open a file output stream to the copy, open a file input stream from the original file, then copy the data byte by byte from the original into the copy. For example, to copy the file `src` to the file `dst`:

```
FileInputStream fin = new FileInputStream(src);
FileOutputStream fout = new FileOutputStream(dst);
StreamCopier.copy(fin, fout);
fin.close();
fout.close();
```

There are some serious problems with this code. First of all, it assumes that both `src` and `dst` refer to files, not directories. Second, it only copies the contents of the files. If the file is associated with meta-information or extra data, that data is lost. Macintosh files are most vulnerable to this problem, since resource forks are lost in the copy operation. However, Windows and Unix files also have permissions and other meta-information that will not necessarily be maintained by the copy. Third, file copies can take nontrivial amounts of time. It's rude to tie up the user's system without at least putting up some sort of progress bar.

Deleting files

The `delete()` method removes files from the filesystem permanently:

```
public boolean delete()
```

This method returns `true` if the file existed and was deleted. (You can't delete a file that doesn't exist.) If the security manager disallows this action, a security exception is thrown. Otherwise, `delete()` returns false. You can move a file by copying it then deleting the original. For example, to move the file `src` to the file `dst`:

```
FileInputStream fin = new FileInputStream(src);
FileOutputStream fout = new FileOutputStream(dst);
StreamCopier.copy(fin, fout);
fout.close();
fin.close();
src.delete();
```

The warnings about copying files (meta-information and resource forks not maintained, copies file-to-file only supported) go double for this sort of move, because after the move is complete, the original file and all its data and meta-information are deleted. Any information that wasn't copied is lost.

Changing file attributes

Java 2 allows an application to change a file's last modified time:

```
public boolean setLastModified(long time)  // Java 2
```

The `time` argument is the number of milliseconds since midnight, GMT, January 1, 1970. This will be converted to the format necessary for a particular platform's file modification times. If the platform does not support millisecond-accurate file modification times, then the time will be rounded to the nearest time the host platform does support. An `IllegalArgumentException` is thrown if `time` is negative; a `SecurityException` is thrown if the security manager disallows write access to the file.

The `setReadOnly()` method marks the file so that only reading of the file is allowed. Any form of writing to the file is disallowed.

```
public boolean setReadOnly()  // Java 2
```

It may be an oversight, but Java provides no way to undo the effects of this method and allow a file to be written. To accomplish that, you'll need to use `chmod` (Unix), the Properties window (Windows), the Get Info window (Mac), or whatever facility your platform provides for locking and unlocking files. A `SecurityException` is thrown if the security manager disallows write access to the file.

Temporary Files

Java 2 adds support for temporary files: files that only exist as long as the program runs. The `File` class provides two methods that create temporary files and one method to mark a file to be deleted when the program exits.

```
public static File createTempFile(String prefix, String suffix)
   throws IOException                 // Java 2
public static File createTempFile(String prefix, String suffix,
   File directory) throws IOException  // Java 2
```

The `createTempFile()` methods create a file with a name that begins with the specified prefix and ends with the specified suffix. The prefix is a string used at the beginning of all temporary file names; the suffix is appended to the end of all temporary file names. The suffix may be null. If so, *.tmp* will be used as the suffix.

The same run of the same VM will not create two files with the same name. For example, consider this for loop:

```
for (int i=0; i < 10; i++) {
  File f1 = File.createTempFile("mail", ".tem");
}
```

When run, it creates files named *mail30446.tem, mail30447.tem,* etc. through *mail30455.tem.*

By default, temporary files are placed in the directory named by the java.io. tmpdir property. On Unix, this is likely to be */tmp* or */var/tmp*. On Windows, it's probably *C:\temp* or *C:\Windows\Temp*. On the Mac, it's probably the invisible *Temporary Items* folder on the startup drive. You can specify a different directory using the third argument to createTempFile(). For instance, to create a temporary file in the current working directory:

```
File cwd = new File(System.getProperty("user.dir"));
File temp = File.createTempFile("rus", ".tmp", cwd);
```

You often want to delete temporary files when your program exits. You can accomplish this by passing them to the deleteOnExit() method:

```
public void deleteOnExit() // Java 2
```

For example:

```
File temp = File.createTempFile("mail", ".tem");
temp.deleteOnExit();
```

This method works on any File object, not just temporary files. Be careful, because there's no good way to cancel a request to delete files when your program exits.

Temporary files are useful when you need to operate on a file in place. You can do this in two passes. In the first pass, you read from the file you're converting and write into the temporary file. In the second pass, you read from the temporary file and write into the file you're converting. Here's an example:

```
try {
  File infile = new File(args[2]);
  File outfile = new File(args[3]);
  boolean usingTempFile = false;

  if (infile.getCanonicalPath().equals(outfile.getCanonicalPath())) {
    outfile = File.createTempFile("temp", null);
    outfile.deleteOnExit();
    usingTempFile = true;
  }

  // perform operations as normal, then close both files...
```

```
    if (usingTempFile) {
      FileInputStream fin = new FileInputStream(outfile);
      FileOutputStream fout = new FileOutputStream(infile);
      StreamCopier.copy(fin, fout);
      fin.close();
      fout.close();
    }
  }
  catch (IOException e) {System.err.println(e);}
```

Utility Methods

The `File` class also contains the usual `equals()`, `hashCode()`, and `toString()` methods, which behave exactly as you would expect. It does not contain a `clone()` method.

```
public int hashCode()
public boolean equals(Object o)
public String toString()
```

In Java 2, the `File` class implements the `java.lang.Comparable` interface so that two pathnames may be compared to each other. This requires these two `compareTo()` methods:

```
public int compareTo(File pathname)   // Java 2
public int compareTo(Object o)        // Java 2
```

For example:

```
File f1 = new File("readme.txt");
File f2 = new File("README.TXT");
int result = f1.compareTo(f2);
```

This method returns a number less than zero if `f1` is less than `f2`, zero if they're the same, and a positive number if `f1` is greater than `f2`. The comparison is made against the `path` fields of `f1` and `f2`. The algorithm used for comparison is more or less alphabetical. On case-insensitive platforms like Windows and the Mac, case is not considered. For instance, the previous `result` would be zero on the Mac or Windows but positive on Unix.

Working with Directories

A `File` object can represent a directory as easily as a file. Most of the `File` methods, like `getName()`, `canWrite()`, and `getPath()`, behave exactly the same for a directory as they do for a file. However, there are a couple of methods in the `File` class that behave differently when they operate on directories than they do when operating on ordinary files.

The delete() method only works on empty directories. If a directory contains even one file, it can't be easily deleted. If you attempt to delete a nonempty directory, delete() fails and returns false. No exception is thrown.

The renameTo() method works on both empty and nonempty directories. However—whether a directory is empty or not—renameTo() can only rename it, not move it to a different directory. If you attempt to move a directory into another directory, renameTo() fails and returns false. No exception is thrown.

The File class also has several methods that just work with directories, not with regular files.

Creating directories

To create a file, you open a FileOutputStream to it (Java 1.0 and 1.1) or call createNewFile() (Java 2). This doesn't work for directories, though. For that purpose, the File class has a mkdir() method:

```
public boolean mkdir()
```

The mkdir() method attempts to create a directory with the path specified in the path field. If the directory is created, the method returns true. For example:

```
File f = new File("tmp/");
f.mkdir();
```

The trailing slash is optional, but it helps you to remember that you're dealing with a directory rather than a plain file. If the security manager does not allow the directory to be created, a security exception is thrown. If the directory cannot be created for any other reason, mkdir() returns false. The mkdir() method only works for single directories. Trying to create a directory like *com/macfaq/io/* with mkdir() only works if *com/macfaq* already exists.

The mkdirs() method creates every directory in a path that doesn't already exist:

```
public boolean mkdirs()
```

For example:

```
File f = new File("com/macfaq/io/");
f.mkdirs();
```

mkdirs() returns true if all directories in this path are created or already exist and false if only some or none of them are created. If mkdirs() returns false, you need to test each directory in the path to see whether it was created, because the invocation could have been partially successful.

One reason mkdir() and mkdirs() may return false (fail to create a directory) is that a file already exists with the name the directory has. Neither mkdir() nor mkdirs() will overwrite an existing file or directory.

Listing directories

The list() method returns an array of strings containing the names of each file in the directory referred to by the File object:

```
public String[] list()
```

This method returns null if the File object doesn't point to a directory. It throws a security exception if the program isn't allowed to read the directory being listed. An alternative version of list() uses a FilenameFilter object (discussed later in the chapter) to restrict which files are included in the list:

```
public String[] list(FilenameFilter filter)
```

Example 12-5 is a simple character-mode program that recursively lists all the files in a directory, and all the files in directories in the directory, and all the files in directories in the directory, and so on. Files are indented two spaces for each level deep they are in the hierarchy.

Example 12-5. The DirList Program

```
import java.io.*;
import java.util.*;

public class DirList {

  File directory;
  int indent = 2;
  static Vector seen = new Vector();

  public static void main(String[] args) {
    try {
      for (int i = 0; i < args.length; i++) {
        DirList dl = new DirList(args[i]);
        dl.list();
      }
    }
    catch (IOException e) {System.err.println(e);}
  }

  public DirList(String s) throws IOException {
    this(new File(s), 2);
  }

  public DirList(File f) throws IOException {
    this(f, 2);
  }

  public DirList(File directory, int indent) throws IOException {
    if (directory.isDirectory()) {
```

Example 12-5. The DirList Program (continued)

```
        this.directory = new File(directory.getCanonicalPath());
    }
    else {
      throw new IOException(directory.toString() + " is not a directory");
    }
    this.indent = indent;
    String spaces = "";
    for (int i = 0; i < indent-2; i++) spaces += " ";
    System.out.println(spaces + directory + File.separatorChar);
  }

  public void list() throws IOException {

    if (!seen.contains(this.directory)) {
      seen.addElement(this.directory);
      String[] files = directory.list();
      String spaces = "";
      for (int i = 0; i < indent; i++) spaces += " ";
      for (int i = 0; i < files.length; i++) {
        File f = new File(directory, files[i]);
        if (f.isFile()) {
          System.out.println(spaces + f.getName());
        }
        else { // it's another directory
          DirList dl = new DirList(f, indent + 2);
          dl.list();
        }
      }
    }
  }
}
```

Special care has to be taken to make sure this program doesn't get caught in an infinite recursion. If a directory contains an alias, shadow, shortcut, or symbolic link that points to one of its own parents, there's potential for infinite recursion. To avoid this possibility, all paths are converted to canonical paths in the constructor, and these paths are stored in the static vector seen. A directory is listed only if it has not yet been traversed by this program.

The listFiles() methods

The two list() methods return arrays of strings. The strings contain the names of files. You can use these to construct File objects. Java 2 allows you to eliminate the intermediate step of creating File objects by providing two listFiles() methods that return arrays of File objects instead of arrays of strings.

```
public File[] listFiles()                          // Java 2
public File[] listFiles(FilenameFilter filter)     // Java 2
public File[] listFiles(FileFilter filter)         // Java 2
```

The no-argument variant of `listFiles()` simply returns an array of all the files in the given directory. The other two variants return the files that pass through their filters. File and filename filters will be discussed shortly.

File URLs

File URLs are used inside web browsers to refer to a file on the local hard drive.[*] They have the basic form:

```
file://<host>/<path>
```

`<host>` should be the fully qualified domain name of the system on which the `<path>` is found, though if it's omitted, the local host is assumed. `<path>` is the hierarchical path to the file, using a forward slash as a directory separator (regardless of host filename conventions) and URL encoding of any special characters in filenames that would normally be encoded in a URL. Examples of file URLs include:

```
file:///C|/docs/JCE%201.2%20beta%201/guide/API_users_guide.html
file:///usr/local/java/docs/JCE%201.2%20beta%201/guide/API_users_guide.html
file:///D%7C/JAVA/
file:///Macintosh%20HD/Java/Cafe%20%au%20%Lait/course/week4/01.5.html
```

Many web browsers allow other, nonstandard formats like:

```
file:///D:/JAVA/
file:///usr/local/java/docs/JCE 1.2 beta 1/guide/API_users_guide.html
file:///C|/jdk2beta4/docs/JCE 1.2 beta 1/guide/API_users_guide.html
file:///C:\jdk1.2beta4\docs\JCE 1.2 beta 1\guide\API_users_guide.html
file:/D:/Java/ioexamples/12/FileDialogApplet.html
```

Because of the differences between file, and directory names from one computer to the next, the exact syntax of file URLs is unpredictable from platform to platform and web browser to web browser. In Java 2 the `File` class has a `toURL()` method that returns a file URL that's appropriate for the local platform:

```
public URL toURL() throws MalformedURLException  // Java 2
```

---

[*] Very early web browsers used file URLs to refer to FTP sites. However, that usage has mostly disappeared now.

Filename Filters

You often want to look for a particular kind of file—for example, text files. To do this, you need a `FilenameFilter` object that specifies which files you'll accept. `FilenameFilter` is an interface in the `java.io` package:

```
public interface FilenameFilter
```

This interface declares a single method, `accept()`:

```
public abstract boolean accept(File directory, String name);
```

The `directory` argument is a `File` object pointing to a directory, and the `name` argument is the name of a file. The method should return `true` if a file with this name in this directory passes through the filter and `false` if it doesn't. Because `FilenameFilter` is an interface, it must be implemented in a class. Example 12-6 is a class that filters out everything that is not an HTML file.

Example 12-6. HTMLFilter

```
import java.io.*;

public class HTMLFilter implements FilenameFilter {

 public boolean accept(File directory, String name) {

   if (name.endsWith(".html")) return true;
   if (name.endsWith(".htm")) return true;
   return false;
 }
}
```

Files can be filtered using any criteria you like. An `accept()` method may test modification date, permissions, file size, and any attribute Java supports. (You can't filter by attributes Java does not support, like Macintosh file and creator codes, at least not without native methods or some sort of access to the native API.) This `accept()` method tests whether the file ends with *.html* and is in a directory where the program can read files:

```
public boolean accept(File directory, String name) {

  if (name.endsWith(".html") && directory.canRead()) {
    return true;
  }
  return false;
}
```

Filename filters are primarily intended for the use of file dialogs, which will be discussed in the next chapter. However, in Java 2 the File class has a listFiles() method that takes a FilenameFilter as an argument:

```
public File[] listFiles(FilenameFilter filter)  // Java 2
```

This method assumes that the File object represents a directory. The array of File objects returned by listFiles() only contains those files that passed the filter. For example, the following lines of code list HTML files in the */public/html/javafaq* directory using the HTMLFilter of Example 12-5.

```
File dir = new File("/public/html/javafaq");
File[] htmlFiles = dir.listFiles(new HTMLFilter());
for (int i = 0; i < htmlFiles.length; i++) {
  System.out.println(htmlFiles[i]);
}
```

File Filters

Java 2 adds a new java.io.FileFilter interface that's very similar to FilenameFilter:

```
public abstract interface FileFilter  // Java 2
```

The accept() method of FileFilter takes a single File object as an argument, rather than two strings giving the directory and path:

```
public boolean accept(File pathname)  // Java 2
```

Example 12-7 is a filter that only passes HTML files. Its logic is essentially the same as the filter of Example 12-6.

Example 12-7. HTMLFileFilter

```
import java.io.*;

public class HTMLFileFilter implements FileFilter {

 public boolean accept(File pathname) {

   if (pathname.getName().endsWith(".html")) return true;
   if (pathname.getName().endsWith(".htm")) return true;
   return false;
 }
}
```

This class appears as an argument in one of the listFiles() methods of java.io.File:

```
public File[] listFiles(FileFilter filter)      // Java 2
```

Example 12-8 uses the HTMLFileFilter to list the HTML files in the current working directory.

Example 12-8. List HTML Files

```
import java.io.*;

public class HTMLFiles {

  public static void main(String[] args) {

    File cwd = new File(System.getProperty("user.dir"));
    File[] htmlFiles = cwd.listFiles(new HTMLFileFilter());
    for (int i = 0; i < htmlFiles.length; i++) {
      System.out.println(htmlFiles[i]);
    }
  }
}
```

NOTE   There's a nasty name conflict between the java.io.FileFilter interface and the abstract javax.swing.filechooser.FileFilter class discussed in the next chapter. I would not be surprised if this interface were replaced by a new abstract FileFilter class more like javax.swing.filechooser.FileFilter.

File Descriptors

As I've said several times so far, the existence of a java.io.File object doesn't imply the existence of the file it represents. A java.io.FileDescriptor object does, however, refer to an actual file:

```
    public final class FileDescriptor extends Object
```

A FileDescriptor object is an abstraction of an underlying machine-specific structure that represents an open file. While file descriptors are very important for the underlying OS and filesystem, their only real use in Java is to guarantee that data that's been written to a stream is in fact committed to disk; that is, to synchronize between the program and the hardware.

In addition to open files, file descriptors can also represent open sockets, though this use won't be emphasized in this book. There are also three file descriptors for the console: System.in, System.out, and System.err. These are available as the three mnemonic constants FileDescriptor.in, FileDescriptor.out, and FileDescriptor.err:

```
public static final FileDescriptor in
public static final FileDescriptor out
public static final FileDescriptor err
```

Because file descriptors are very closely tied to the native operating system, you never construct your own file descriptors. Various methods in other classes that refer to open files or sockets may return them. Both the `FileInputStream` and `FileOutputStream` classes and the `RandomAccessFile` class have a `getFD()` method that returns the file descriptor associated with the open stream or file:

```
public final FileDescriptor getFD() throws IOException
```

The `java.net.SocketImpl` class stores the file descriptor for a socket in a protected field called `fd`:

```
protected FileDescriptor fd
```

This field is returned by `SocketImpl`'s protected `getFileDescriptor()` method:

```
protected FileDescriptor getFileDescriptor()
```

Since file descriptors are only associated with *open* files and sockets, they become invalid as soon as the file or socket is closed. You can test whether a file descriptor is still valid with the `valid()` method:

```
public native boolean valid()
```

This returns `true` if the descriptor is still valid, `false` if it isn't.

The one real use to which a client programmer can put a file descriptor object is to sync a file. This is accomplished with the aptly named `sync()` method:

```
public native void sync() throws SyncFailedException
```

The `sync()` method forces the system buffers to write all the data they contain to the actual hardware. Generally, you'll want to flush the stream before syncing it. Flushing clears out Java's internal buffers. Syncing clears out the operating system's, device driver's, and hardware's buffers. If synchronization does not succeed, then `sync()` throws a `java.io.SyncFailedException`, a subclass of `IOException`.

Random-Access Files

File input and output streams require you to start reading or writing at the beginning of a file and then read or write the file in order, possibly skipping over some bytes or backing up but more or less moving from start to finish. Sometimes, however, you need to read parts of a file in a more or less random order, where the data near the beginning of the file isn't necessarily read before the data nearer the end. Other times you need to both read and write the same file. For example, in record-oriented applications like databases, the actual data may be indexed; you would use the index to determine where in the file to find the record you need to read or write. While you could do this by constantly opening and closing the file and skipping to the point where you needed to read, this is far from efficient. Writes are even worse, since you would need to read and rewrite the entire file, even to change just one byte of data.

Random-access files can be read from or written to or both from a particular byte position in the file. A single random-access file can be both read and written without first being closed. The position in the file where reads and writes start from is indicated by an integer called the file pointer. Each read or write advances the file pointer by the number of bytes read or written. Furthermore, the programmer can reposition the file pointer at different bytes in the file without closing the file.

In Java, random file access is performed through the `java.io.RandomAccess-File` class. This is *not* a subclass of `java.io.File`:

```
public class RandomAccessFile extends Object implements DataInput, DataOutput
```

Among other differences between `File` objects and `RandomAccessFile` objects, the `RandomAccessFile` constructors actually open the file in question and throw an `IOException` if it doesn't exist:

```
public RandomAccessFile(String filename, String mode) throws
FileNotFoundException
public RandomAccessFile(File file, String mode) throws IOException
```

The first argument to the constructor is the file you want to access. The second argument is the mode for access. The mode should be either the string literal `"r"` for read-only access or the string `"rw"` for read/write access. Java does not support write-only access. For example:

```
RandomAccessFile raf = new RandomAccessFile("29.html", "r");
```

An `IllegalArgumentException` is thrown if anything other than the strings `"rw"` or `"r"` is passed as the second argument to this constructor. A security exception is thrown if the security manager does not allow the requested file to be read. A security exception is also thrown if you request read/write access, but only read access is allowed. Security checks are made only when the object is constructed. It is assumed that the security manger's policy won't change while the program is running. Finally, an `IOException` is thrown if the operating system doesn't allow the file to be accessed or some other I/O problem occurs.

The `getFilePointer()` and `seek()` methods allow you to determine and modify the position in the file at which reads and writes occur. Attempts to seek (position the file pointer) past the end of the file just move the file pointer to the end of the file. Attempts to write from the end of the file extend the file.

```
public native long getFilePointer() throws IOException
public native void seek(long pos) throws IOException
```

Attempts to read from the end of the file throw an `EOFException` (a subclass of `IOException`). You can determine the length of the file with the `length()` method:

```
public native long length() throws IOException
```

The `RandomAccessFile` class implements both the `DataInput` and `DataOutput` interfaces. Therefore, reads and writes use methods exactly like the methods of the `DataInputStream` and `DataOutputStream` classes, such as `read()`, `readFully()`, `readBoolean()`, `writeBoolean()`, and so on.

```
public native int read() throws IOException
public int read(byte[] data, int offset, int length) throws IOException
public int read(byte[] data) throws IOException
public final void readFully(byte[] data) throws IOException
public final void readFully(byte[] data, int offset, int length)
                throws IOException
public native void write(int b) throws IOException
public void write(byte[] data) throws IOException
public void write(byte[] data, int offset, int length) throws IOException
public final boolean readBoolean() throws IOException
public final byte readByte() throws IOException
public final int readUnsignedByte() throws IOException
public final short readShort() throws IOException
public final int readUnsignedShort() throws IOException
public final char readChar() throws IOException
public final int readInt() throws IOException
public final long readLong() throws IOException
public final float readFloat() throws IOException
public final double readDouble() throws IOException
public final String readLine() throws IOException
public final String readUTF() throws IOException
public final void writeBoolean(boolean b) throws IOException
public final void writeByte(int b) throws IOException
public final void writeShort(int s) throws IOException
public final void writeChar(int c) throws IOException
public final void writeInt(int i) throws IOException
public final void writeLong(long l) throws IOException
public final void writeFloat(float f) throws IOException
public final void writeDouble(double d) throws IOException
public final void writeBytes(String s) throws IOException
public final void writeChars(String s) throws IOException
public final void writeUTF(String s) throws IOException
```

Finally, there are a few miscellaneous methods. The `getFD()` method simply returns the file descriptor for this file:

```
public final FileDescriptor getFD() throws IOException
```

The `skipBytes()` method attempts to reposition the file pointer n bytes further in the file from where it is now. It returns the number of bytes actually skipped, which may be less than n:

```
public int skipBytes(int n) throws IOException
```

The `seek()` method jumps to an absolute position in the file starting from 0, whereas `skipBytes()` moves n bytes past wherever the file pointer is now:

```
public void seek(long position) throws IOException
```

Finally, the `close()` method closes the file:

```
public native void close() throws IOException
```

Once the file is closed, it may not be read from, though a new `RandomAccessFile` object that refers to the same file can be created.

General Techniques for Cross-Platform File Access Code

File manipulation vies with AWT for being the part of Java where it's hardest to write truly cross-platform, robust code. Until Java 2, Sun really didn't pay a lot of attention to differences between filesystems on different platforms. The situation is getting better, however. The `java.io.File` class does work much more reliably across Windows and Unix in Java 2 and has hooks to allow it to work more naturally on other platforms as well. Of course, Java 1.1 is still the primary delivery platform for most Java applications that work with files. To help you achieve greater serenity and overall cross-platform nirvana, I've summarized some basic rules from this chapter to help you write file manipulation code that's robust across a multitude of platforms:

- Never, never, never hardcode pathnames in your application.

- Ask the user to name your files. If you must provide a name for a file, try to make it fit in an 8.3 DOS filename with only pure ASCII characters.

- Do not assume the file separator is "/" (or anything else). Use `File.separatorChar` instead.

- Do not parse pathnames to find directories. Use the methods of the `java.io.File` class instead.

- Do not use `renameTo()` for anything except renaming a file. In particular, do not use it to move a file.

- Try to avoid moving and copying files from within Java programs if at all possible.

- Do not use . to refer to the current directory. Use `System.getProperty ("user.dir")` instead.

- Do not use .. to refer to the parent directory. Use `getParent()` instead.

- Do not assume the current working directory is the one where your .*class* files live. It almost certainly won't be that directory on the Mac, and it may not be on other platforms, including Windows and Unix.

- Place any data files your program requires in JAR archives rather than directly in the filesystem, then load them as resources from the class path.

- When in doubt, it never hurts to convert filenames to canonical form.

- Do not assume anything about filesystem conventions. Some platform somewhere will surprise you. (Have you tested your program on BeOS yet?)

- Test your code on as many different filesystems as you can get your hands on.

Despite all the problems I've pointed out, it is mostly possible to write robust file access code that works across all platforms where Java runs. But doing so requires understanding, effort, and thought. You cannot simply write for Windows or Unix and hope things will work out for the best on other platforms. You must plan to handle a wide range of filesystems and filename conventions.

13

File Dialogs and Choosers

Filenames are problematic, even if you don't have to worry about cross-platform idiosyncrasies. Users forget filenames, mistype them, can't remember the exact path to files they need, and more. The proper way to ask a user to select a file is to show them a list of the files in the current directory and get them to select from that list. You also need to allow them to navigate between directories, insert and remove floppy disks, mount network servers, and more.

Most graphical user interfaces (and not a few nongraphical ones) provide standard widgets for selecting a file. In Java the platform's native file selector widget is exposed through the `java.awt.FileDialog` class. Like many native peer-based classes, however, `FileDialog` doesn't behave exactly the same on all platforms. Therefore, Swing (part of the Java Foundation Classes) provides a pure Java implementation of a file dialog, the `javax.swing.JFileChooser` class.* `JFileChooser` (and Swing in general) has much more reliable cross-platform behavior.

File Dialogs

I'm going to jump out of the `java.io` package for a minute to pick up one file-related class from the AWT, `java.awt.FileDialog`. File dialogs are the standard open and save dialogs provided by the host GUI. Users use them to pick a directory and a name under which to save a file or to choose a file to open. The appearance varies from platform to platform, but the intent is the same.

---

* The package name for Swing has changed several times since its first early access release. `javax.swing` is its final home—this package name is used in Swing 1.1 (for use with JDK 1.1) and Java 2 (which includes Swing and the rest of JFC). For more information about Swing, see *Java Swing*, by Robert Eckstein, Marc Loy, and Dave Wood (O'Reilly & Associates, 1998).

Figure 13-1 shows a standard Save dialog on the Mac; Figure 13-2 shows a standard open dialog on Solaris.

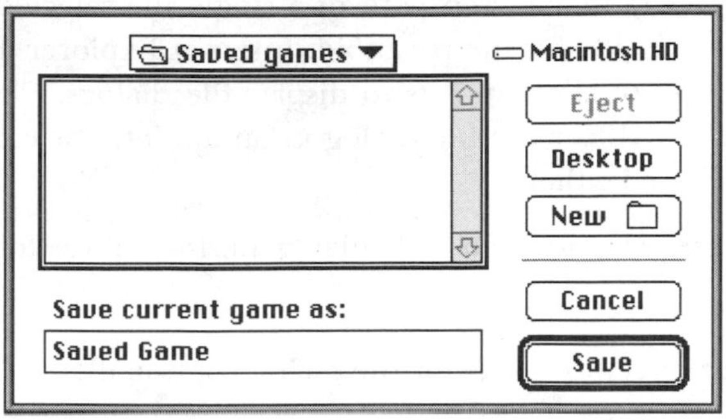

Figure 13-1. The Mac's standard Save dialog

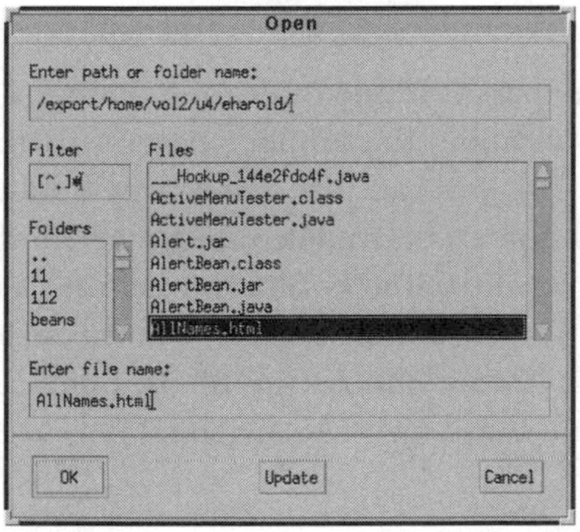

Figure 13-2. Motif standard Open dialog

FileDialog is a subclass of java.awt.Dialog that represents the native save and open dialog boxes:

```
public class FileDialog extends Dialog
```

A file dialog is almost completely implemented by a native peer. Your program doesn't add components to a file dialog or handle user interaction with event listeners. It just displays the dialog and retrieves the name and directory of the file the user chose after the dialog is dismissed.

Since applets normally can't read or write files, file dialogs are primarily useful only in applications. Nonetheless, there is no specific security manager check to see whether file dialogs are allowed. Sun's applet viewer, HotJava, and some recent versions of Netscape Navigator do allow untrusted applets to display file dialogs, retrieve the name and path of the file selected, and send that information back to the originating host over the network. Although this is a very minor security hole, since it only exposes the name and path of a single file selected by the user, it's still on the worrisome side for the paranoid. Internet Explorer 4.0 and Navigator 4.0.3 and earlier do not allow applets to display file dialogs. Certainly, you can't count on being allowed to use a file dialog in an applet, nor can you be guaranteed that it isn't allowed either.

To ask the user to select a file from a file dialog, perform these four steps:

1. Construct a `FileDialog` object.

2. Set the default directory or file for the dialog (optional).

3. Make the dialog visible.

4. Get the name and directory of the file the user chose.

There is one `FileDialog` constructor:

```
public FileDialog(Frame parent, String title, int mode)
```

The first argument is the parent frame of this file dialog. This will normally be the main window of the application, the applet's parent, or the frontmost window of the application. Conversely, you can just create a new frame; you're not required to show the frame if you don't want to. File dialogs are modal. While the file dialog is shown, input to the parent frame is blocked, as with the parent frame of any modal dialog. The `title` argument is the prompt string for the file dialog, normally something like "Please choose the file to open:". The `mode` argument is one of the two mnemonic constants `FileDialog.LOAD` or `FileDialog.SAVE`:

```
public static final int LOAD = 0;
public static final int SAVE = 1;
```

Use `FileDialog.LOAD` if you want the user to choose a file to open. Use `FileDialog.SAVE` if you want the user to choose a file to save the data into. A typical use of this constructor might look like this:

```
FileDialog fd = new FileDialog(new Frame("Dummy frame"),
  "Please choose the file to open:", FileDialog.LOAD);
```

To specify that the file dialog should appear with a particular directory opened or a particular file in that directory selected, you can invoke the `setDirectory()` and `setFile()` methods:

```
public synchronized void setDirectory(String directory)
public synchronized void setFile(String file)
```

For example:

```
fd.setDirectory("/etc");
fd.setFile("passwd");
```

You make the file dialog visible by invoking the file dialog's show() method, just like any other window:

```
fd.show();
```

As soon as the file dialog becomes visible, the calling thread stops and waits for the user to choose a file. The operating system takes over and handles user interaction until the user chooses a file or presses the Cancel button. At this point, the file dialog disappears from the screen, and normal program execution resumes.

Once the dialog has been dismissed, you can find out which file the user chose by using the file dialog's getDirectory() and getFile() methods:

```
public String getFile()
public String getDirectory()
```

For example:

```
FileDialog fd = new FileDialog(new Frame(), "Please choose a file:",
FileDialog.LOAD);
fd.setVisible(true);
File f = new File(fd.getDirectory(), fd.getFile());
```

If the user cancels the file dialog without selecting a file, getFile() and getDirectory() return null. You should be ready to handle this, or you'll bump into a NullPointerException in short order.

Example 13-1 is a program that presents an open file dialog to the user, then writes the contents of the file they selected on System.out. There are many good ways to do this. I chose to write a static getFile() method that returns a File object; then open and print this file back in the main() method.

Example 13-1. The FileTyper Program

```
import java.io.*;
import java.awt.*;
import com.macfaq.io.*;

public class FileChooser {

  public static void main(String[] args) {

    try {
      File f = getFile();
      if (f == null) return;
      FileInputStream fin = new FileInputStream(f);
```

Example 13-1. The FileTyper Program (continued)

```
      StreamCopier.copy(fin, System.out);
    }
    catch (IOException e) {System.err.println(e);}

    // Work around annoying AWT non-daemon thread bug.
    System.exit(0);
  }

  public static File getFile() throws IOException {

    // dummy Frame, never shown
    Frame parent = new Frame();
    FileDialog fd = new FileDialog(parent, "Please choose a file:",
     FileDialog.LOAD);
    fd.show();

    // Program stops here until user selects a file or cancels.

    String dir = fd.getDirectory();
    String file = fd.getFile();

    // Clean up our windows, they won't be needed again.
    parent.dispose();
    fd.dispose();

    if (dir == null || file == null) { // user cancelled the dialog
      return null;
    }
    return new File(dir, file);
  }
}
```

File dialogs only allow the user to select ordinary files, never directories. If you want to ask users to pick a directory, you have to ask them to choose a file in that directory, then call `getDirectory()`. (This workaround fails with empty directories.) Here's an alternative `main()` method for the `DirList` program given in Example 12-5 that uses a file dialog to select the directory to list rather than command-line arguments:

```
  public static void main(String[] args) {

    try {
      FileDialog fd = new FileDialog(new Frame("Not important"),
       "Please select a file in the directory you want to list:",
       FileDialog.LOAD);
      fd.setVisible(true);
      if (fd.getDirectory() == null) return;
```

```
      DirList dl = new DirList(fd.getDirectory());
      dl.list();
      fd.dispose();
    }
    catch (IOException e) {System.err.println(e);}
  }
```

A filename filter can be attached to a file dialog via the dialog's
`setFilenameFilter()` method:

```
public synchronized void setFilenameFilter(FilenameFilter filter)
```

Once a file dialog's filename filter is set, it should only display files that pass
through the filter. In practice, however, filename filters in file dialogs are only
truly reliable on Unix. Many early Mac VMs do not really support this feature,
though some of the more recent ones do. And Windows is almost congenitally
unable to support it, because Windows' native file chooser dialog can only filter by
file extension. The problem is that filename filters are designed for the Motif API.
The Windows and Macintosh APIs provide different ways of achieving the same
effect.

Example 13-2 demonstrates the use of a filename filter in a file dialog. The
`TextChooser` class implements the `FilenameFilter` interface. The `main()`
method calls the `getFile()` method to load a file. Once a file is loaded, it's
written on `System.out`. The `getFile()` method uses a file dialog to ask the user
what file should be written. A new `TextChooser` object is passed to the file
dialog's `setFilter()` method to indicate that this class's `accept()` method
should be used to filter files. The `accept()` method accepts files ending in *.text*,
.txt, *.java*, *.jav*, *.html*, and *.htm*; all others are rejected.

Example 13-2. The TextChooser Program

```
import java.io.*;
import java.awt.*;
import com.macfaq.io.*;

public class TextChooser implements FilenameFilter {

  public static void main(String[] args) {

    try {
      File f = getFile();
      if (f == null) return;
      FileInputStream fin = new FileInputStream(f);
      StreamCopier.copy(fin, System.out);
    }
    catch (IOException e) {System.err.println(e);}
```

Example 13-2. The TextChooser Program (continued)

```
    // Work around annoying AWT non-daemon thread bug.
    System.exit(0);
  }

  public boolean accept(File dir, String name) {

    if (name.endsWith(".java")) return true;
    else if (name.endsWith(".jav")) return true;
    else if (name.endsWith(".html")) return true;
    else if (name.endsWith(".htm")) return true;
    else if (name.endsWith(".txt")) return true;
    else if (name.endsWith(".text")) return true;
    return false;
  }

  public static File getFile() throws IOException {

    // dummy Frame, never shown
    Frame parent = new Frame();
    FileDialog fd = new FileDialog(parent, "Please choose a file:",
     FileDialog.LOAD);
    fd.setFilenameFilter(new TextChooser());
    fd.show();

    // Program stops here until user selects a file or cancels.

    String dir = fd.getDirectory();
    String file = fd.getFile();

    // Clean up our windows, they won't be needed again.
    parent.dispose();
    fd.dispose();

    if (dir == null || file == null) { // User cancelled the dialog.
      return null;
    }
    return new File(dir, file);
  }
}
```

This program demonstrates one problem of relying on file extensions to determine file type. There are many other file extensions that indicate text files; for example, *.c*, *.cc*, *.pl*, *.f*, and many more. Furthermore, there are a lot of text files, especially on Macintoshes, that don't have any extension at all. This program completely ignores all those files.

You do not necessarily have to write a new subclass for each different file filter. Example 13-3 demonstrates a class that can be configured with different lists of filename extensions. Every file with an extension in the list passes the filter. Others don't.

Example 13-3. ExtensionFilenameFilter

```java
package com.macfaq.io;

import java.awt.*;
import java.util.*;
import java.io.*;

public class ExtensionFilenameFilter implements FilenameFilter  {

  Vector extensions = new Vector();

  public ExtensionFilenameFilter(String extension) {

    if (extension.indexOf('.') != -1) {
      extension = extension.substring(extension.lastIndexOf('.')+1);
    }
    extensions.addElement(extension);
  }

  public void addExtension(String extension) {

    if (extension.indexOf('.') != -1) {
      extension = extension.substring(extension.lastIndexOf('.')+1);
    }
    extensions.addElement(extension);
  }

  public boolean accept(File directory, String filename) {

    String extension = filename.substring(filename.lastIndexOf('.')+1);
    if (extensions.contains(extension)) {
      return true;
    }
    return false;
  }
}
```

This class is designed to filter files by extension. You configure which extensions pass the filter when you create the object or by calling addExtension(). This avoids excessive proliferation of classes. Here's a method that can be used to test the extension filter:

```java
public static void main(String[] args) {
```

```java
ExtensionFilenameFilter ef = new ExtensionFilenameFilter("txt");
ef.addExtension(".pl");
ef.addExtension(".c");
ef.addExtension("c");
ef.addExtension("h");
ef.addExtension("cpp");
ef.addExtension(".cc");
ef.addExtension(".java");
ef.addExtension(".html");
ef.addExtension("htm");
ef.addExtension(".c++");

// dummy Frame, never shown
Frame parent = new Frame();
FileDialog fd = new FileDialog(parent, "Please choose a file:",
 FileDialog.LOAD);
fd.setFilenameFilter(ef);
fd.show();

// Program stops here until user selects a file or cancels.

String dir = fd.getDirectory();
String file = fd.getFile();

// Clean up our windows, they won't be needed again.
parent.dispose();
fd.dispose();

if (dir == null || file == null) { // User cancelled the dialog.
   ;
}
else {
  File f = new File(dir, file);
}
System.exit(0);
}
```

JFileChooser

Swing, part of the Java Foundation Classes, provides a much more sophisticated and useful file chooser component written in pure Java, `javax.swing.JFileChooser`:

```java
public class JFileChooser extends JComponent implements Accessible
```

JFileChooser is not an independent, free-standing window like FileDialog. Instead, it is a component you can add to your own frame, dialog, or other container or window. You can, however, ask the JFileChooser class to create a modal dialog just for your file chooser. Figure 13-3 shows a file chooser embedded in a `JFrame` window with the Metal look and feel.* Of course, like all Swing components, the exact appearance depends on the look and feel currently selected.

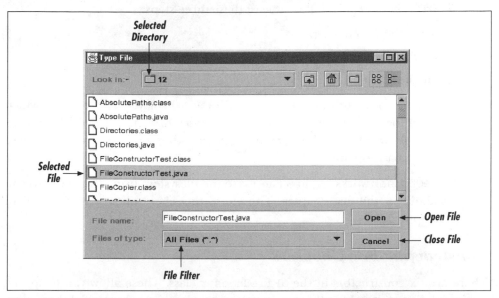

Figure 13-3. A JFileChooser with the Metal look and feel

For the most part, the file chooser works as you expect, especially if you're accustomed to Windows. You select a file with the mouse. Double-clicking the filename or pressing the Open button returns the currently selected file. You can change which files are displayed by selecting different filters from the pop-up list of choosable file filters. All the components have tooltips to help users who are a little thrown by an unfamiliar look and feel. One difference between a Swing file chooser and a standard, native chooser may surprise you. While double-clicking on a directory will open the directory as you expect, selecting a directory and then pressing the Open button returns the selected directory as a `File` object.

The `JFileChooser` class relies on support from several classes in the `javax.swing.filechooser` package, including:

```
public abstract class FileFilter
public abstract class FileSystemView
public abstract class FileView
```

---

* Metal is a new look and feel designed specifically for Java.

Unfortunately, these classes still have a few rough edges as of Java 2. They still don't support the Macintosh (though an early access release is available), and they have to jump through some hoops to account for the different levels of support for I/O in Java 1.1 and Java 2.

To use JFileChooser, you follow at least these three steps:

1. Construct the file chooser.

2. Display the file chooser.

3. Get the files the user selected.

You can also set a lot of options for how files are displayed and chosen, which directory and file are selected when the file chooser first appears, which files are and are not shown in the choosers, and several other options. However, these three are your basic operations.

The JFileChooser works via direct access to the filesystem using the methods you learned about in the last chapter. Therefore, this class will not work at all in untrusted applets.

Constructing File Choosers

There are six constructors in the JFileChooser class. These allow you to specify the initial directory and file that appear when the chooser is shown and the view of the filesystem.

```
public JFileChooser()
public JFileChooser(String initialDirectoryPath)
public JFileChooser(File initialDirectory)
public JFileChooser(FileSystemView fileSystemView)
public JFileChooser(File initialDirectory, FileSystemView fileSystemView)
public JFileChooser(String initialDirectoryPath,
                    FileSystemView fileSystemView)
```

Most of the time the no-argument constructor is sufficient. The first time a particular JFileChooser object is shown, it brings up the user's home directory, at least on platforms where the concept of a home directory makes sense. If you'd like it to appear somewhere else, you can pass the directory to the constructor. For example, the following two lines construct a file chooser that will appear with the Java home directory shown:

```
String javahome = System.getProperty("java.home");
JFileChooser chooser = new JFileChooser(javahome);
```

If you reuse the same file chooser repeatedly by showing and hiding it, every time it's shown, it will initially display the last directory where the user chose a file.

Displaying File Choosers

Although JFileChooser is a component, not a window, you usually want to display a modal dialog containing a JFileChooser component that asks the user to save or open a file. There are two methods that do this without requiring you to construct a dialog or frame explicitly:

```
public int showOpenDialog(Component parent)
public int showSaveDialog(Component parent)
```

Although one method is for saving and one is for opening, you use them the same way. Both of these methods display a modal dialog. This dialog will block input to all of the application's windows and will block the current thread until the user either selects a file or cancels the dialog. If the user did choose a file, both these methods return JFileChooser.APPROVE_OPTION. If the user did not choose a file, both these methods return JFileChooser.CANCEL_OPTION.

Getting the User's Selection

If showOpenDialog() or showSaveDialog() returns JFileChooser.APPROVE_OPTION, the getSelectedFile() method returns a File object pointing to the file the user chose; otherwise, it returns null:

```
public File getSelectedFile()
```

If the file chooser allows multiple selections, getSelectedFiles() returns an array of all the files the user chose:

```
public File[] getSelectedFiles()
```

You can get a File object for the directory in which the selected file lives by calling getCurrentDirectory():

```
public File getCurrentDirectory()
```

Example 13-4 is a program that uses JFileChooser to ask the user to select a file and then prints the file's contents on System.out. This example is essentially the same as Example 13-1, except that it uses JFileChooser instead of FileDialog.

Example 13-4. JFileTyper

```
import java.io.*;
import javax.swing.*;
import com.macfaq.io.*;

public class JFileTyper {

  public static void main(String[] args) {

    JFileChooser fc = new JFileChooser();
```

Example 13-4. JFileTyper (continued)

```
    int result = fc.showOpenDialog(new JFrame());
    if (result == JFileChooser.APPROVE_OPTION) {
      try {
        File f = fc.getSelectedFile();
        if (f != null) { // Make sure the user didn't choose a directory.
          FileInputStream fin = new FileInputStream(f);
          StreamCopier.copy(fin, System.out);
          fin.close();
        }
      }
      catch (IOException e) {System.err.println(e);}
    }

    // Work around annoying AWT non-daemon thread bug.
    System.exit(0);
  }
}
```

This program is shorter and simpler than Example 13-1. It's also more reliable across different platforms. The only downside is that it's noticeably slower to start up. However, that's because it must load the entire Swing package. A program that's using many Swing classes won't have to pay that penalty more than once. The only other disadvantage is that standard file extenders like Action Files or Super Boomerang won't notice a file chooser, whereas they will work inside a file dialog brought up by a Java program.

Programmatically Manipulating the JFileChooser

The `JFileChooser` class includes several methods to specify which files and directories are selected and displayed when the chooser is shown. These include:

```
    public void changeToParentDirectory()
    public void rescanCurrentDirectory()
    public void ensureFileIsVisible(File f)
```

The `changeToParentDirectory()` method simply displays the parent directory of the directory currently displayed; that is, it moves one level up in the directory hierarchy. The `rescanCurrentDirectory()` method refreshes the list of files shown. Use it when you have reason to believe a file may have been added to or deleted from the directory. `ensureFileIsVisible()` scrolls the list up or down until the specified file is shown.

Three methods allow you to specify which directory and file are selected in the file chooser:

```
public void setSelectedFile(File selectedFile)
public void setSelectedFiles(File[] selectedFiles)
public void setCurrentDirectory(File dir)
```

You can use these to point the user at a particular file. For instance, a Java source code editor might like to set the filename to the title of the class being edited plus the customary *.java* extension. Another common example: if the user opens a file, edits it, then selects Save As... from the File menu, it's customary to bring up the save dialog with the previous location of the file already selected. The user can change this if they like.

Custom Dialogs

File choosers support three dialog types: open, save, and custom. The type is indicated by one of these three mnemonic constants:

```
FileChooser.OPEN_DIALOG
FileChooser.SAVE_DIALOG
FileChooser.CUSTOM_DIALOG
```

You set the type with the setDialogType() method or, less commonly, retrieve it with getDialogType():

```
public int getDialogType()
public void setDialogType(int dialogType)
```

If you use a custom dialog, you should also set the dialog title, the text of the Approve button's label, the text of the Approve button's tooltip, and the Approve button mnemonic (shortcut key). Setting the Approve button's text automatically sets the dialog to custom type. There are five set and four get methods to handle these tasks:

```
public void setDialogTitle(String dialogTitle)
public String getDialogTitle()
public void setApproveButtonToolTipText(String toolTipText)
public String getApproveButtonToolTipText()
public int getApproveButtonMnemonic()
public void setApproveButtonMnemonic(int mnemonic)
public void setApproveButtonMnemonic(char mnemonic)
public void setApproveButtonText(String approveButtonText)
public String getApproveButtonText()
```

Use these methods sparingly. If you use them, you'll probably want to store the exact strings you use in a resource bundle so your code is easily localizable.

When you're showing a custom dialog, you'll simply use the showDialog() method rather than showOpenDialog() or showSaveDialog() (since a custom dialog is neither):

```
public int showDialog(Component parent, String approveButtonText)
```

Suppose you want a file chooser that allows you to gzip files, then exit when the user presses the Cancel button. You can set the Approve button text to "GZIP," the Approve button tooltip to "Select a file, then press this button to gzip it," the Approve button mnemonic to the letter "g" (for gzip), and the dialog title to "Please choose a file to gzip:," as Example 13-5 demonstrates. The chosen file is read from a file input stream. StreamCopier.copy() copies this file onto a file output stream chained to a gzip output stream that compresses the data. After both input and output streams are closed, the directory is rescanned so the compressed file will appear in the list.

Example 13-5. GUIGZipper

```java
import java.io.*;
import java.util.zip.*;
import javax.swing.*;
import com.macfaq.io.*;

public class GUIGZipper {

  public final static String GZIP_SUFFIX = ".gz";

  public static void main(String[] args) {

    JFrame parent = new JFrame(); // never shown
    JFileChooser fc = new JFileChooser();
    fc.setDialogTitle("Please choose a file to gzip: ");
    fc.setApproveButtonToolTipText(
     "Select a file, then press this button to gzip it");
    fc.setApproveButtonMnemonic('g');

    while (true) {
      int result = fc.showDialog(parent, "GZIP" );
      if (result == JFileChooser.APPROVE_OPTION) {
        try {
          File f = fc.getSelectedFile();
          if (f == null) {
            System.out.println("Can only gzip files, not directories");
            break;
          }
          FileInputStream fin = new FileInputStream(f);
          FileOutputStream fout = new FileOutputStream(f.getAbsolutePath()
           + GZIP_SUFFIX);
          GZIPOutputStream gzout = new GZIPOutputStream(fout);
          StreamCopier.copy(fin, gzout);
          gzout.close();
          fin.close();
          fc.rescanCurrentDirectory();
        }
```

Example 13-5. GUIGZipper (continued)

```
        catch (IOException e) {System.err.println(e);}
    }
    else {
      parent.dispose();
      break;
      // exit
    }
  }

  // Work around annoying AWT non-daemon thread bug.
  System.exit(0);
  }
}
```

Filters

A filename filter affects which files a file dialog shows to the user. The user cannot change this list. For instance, a user can't switch from displaying HTML files to displaying Java source code. However, a `FileFilter` in combination with a `JFileChooser` allows programmers to give users a choice about which files are filtered by providing users with a series of different file filters. By choosing a file filter from the pop-up menu in a file chooser dialog, the user can adjust which files are and are not shown. Figure 13-4 shows a file chooser that allows the user to select text files, all files, C and C++ files, Perl files, HTML files, or Java source code files.

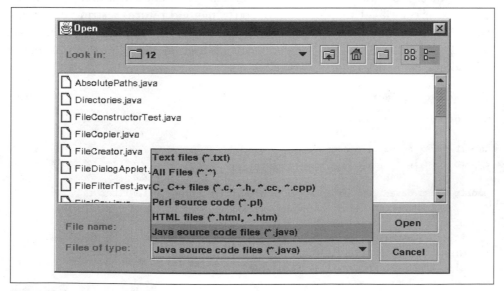

Figure 13-4. The choosable file filters pop-up in a file chooser

Annoyingly, these file filters are not instances of the `java.io.FileFilter` interface you're already familiar with. Instead, they're instances of a new abstract class in the `javax.swing.filechooser` package. Because of name conflicts with the `java.io.FileFilter` interface, any file that imports both packages will have to use the fully qualified name.

```
public abstract class javax.swing.filechooser.FileFilter
```

NOTE   I would not be surprised to see these replaced by a `java.io.FileFilter` objects in a future release. `javax.swing.filechooser.FileFilter` is an abstract class instead of an interface, and it declares a `getDescription()` method as well as an `accept()` method; but other than these minor differences, the two versions of `FileFilter` are identical in all important respects. Another possibility is that the `javax.swing.filechooser.FileFilter` class will be renamed `javax.swing.filechooser.ChoosableFileFilter` to avoid the annoying name conflict.

This class declares two methods, both abstract:

```
public abstract boolean accept(File f);
public abstract String getDescription();
```

The `accept()` method returns `true` if the file passes the filter and should be displayed in the chooser, `false` if it shouldn't be. Unlike the `accept()` method `java.io.FilenameFilter`, this `accept()` method is called to filter directories as well as files. Most filters will accept all directories to allow the user to navigate between directories. The `getDescription()` method returns a string describing the filter to be shown to the user in the chooser's pop-up menu; for example, `Text files (*.txt, *.text)`. Example 13-6 is a simple file filter that only passes Java source code files:

Example 13-6. JavaFilter

```
package com.macfaq.swing.filechooser;

import javax.swing.filechooser.*;
import java.io.*;

public class JavaFilter extends javax.swing.filechooser.FileFilter {

  public boolean accept(File f) {
    if (f.getName().endsWith(".java")) return true;
    else if (f.getName().endsWith(".jav")) return true;
    else if (f.isDirectory()) return true;
    return false;
  }
```

Example 13-6. JavaFilter (continued)

```
  public String getDescription() {
    return "Java source code (*.java)";
  }
}
```

Each file chooser stores a list of `javax.swing.filechooser.FileFilter` objects. The `JFileChooser` class has methods for setting and getting the list of file filters"

```
    public void addChoosableFileFilter(FileFilter filter)
    public boolean removeChoosableFileFilter(FileFilter f)
    public FileFilter[] getChoosableFileFilters()
```

You can add a file filter to the list with `addChoosableFileFilter()`. You can remove a file filter from the list with `removeChoosableFileFilter()`. You can retrieve the current list of file filters with `getChoosableFileFilters()`.

At any given time, exactly one file filter is selected and active. In Figure 13-4, the Java filter is active. That one file filter is returned by the `getFileFilter()` method and can be changed by the `setFileFilter()` method:

```
    public void setFileFilter(FileFilter filter)
    public FileFilter getFileFilter()
```

By default, a `JFileChooser` object includes a file filter that accepts all files (*.*). A reference to this object is returned by the `getAcceptAllFileFilter()` method:

```
    public FileFilter getAcceptAllFileFilter()
```

The `resetChoosableFileFilters()` method removes all file filters from the list, except the *.* filter:

```
    public void resetChoosableFileFilters()
```

It is not possible to remove the *.* filter from the list. Example 13-7 uses the `JavaFilter` class of Example 13-6 to set up a file chooser that passes Java source code files or all files.

Example 13-7. JavaChooser

```
import java.io.*;
import javax.swing.*;
import javax.swing.filechooser.*;
import com.macfaq.swing.filechooser.*;
import com.macfaq.io.*;

public class JavaChooser {
```

Example 13-7. JavaChooser (continued)

```
  public static void main(String[] args) {

    JFileChooser fc = new JFileChooser();
    fc.addChoosableFileFilter(new JavaFilter());
    int result = fc.showOpenDialog(new JFrame());
    if (result == JFileChooser.APPROVE_OPTION) {
      try {
        File f = fc.getSelectedFile();
        if (f != null) {
          FileInputStream fin = new FileInputStream(f);
          StreamCopier.copy(fin, System.out);
          fin.close();
        }
      }
      catch (IOException e) {System.err.println(e);}
    }

    System.exit(0);
  }
}
```

The `JFileChooser` class also a related `accept()` method:

```
  public boolean accept(File f)
```

This passes the `File` object f through the file chooser's currently selected file filter. You'll have little reason to call this method directly, and it's unclear why it's even public.

You do not need to construct a new subclass of `FileFilter` to create a new filter. Often it's more convenient to encapsulate some algorithm in a subclass than parameterize the algorithm in particular objects. For instance, Example 13-8 is an `ExtensionFilter` that extends `FileFilter`. It's similar to the `ExtensionFile-nameFilter` of Example 13-3. However, this class also needs to store a description for each extension. Furthermore, the extensions are used one at a time, not all at once. This reflects the difference between `JFileChooser` and `FileDialog`.

Example 13-8. ExtensionFilter

```
package com.macfaq.swing.filechooser;

import java.io.*;
import javax.swing.filechooser.*;
import javax.swing.*;

public class ExtensionFilter extends javax.swing.filechooser.FileFilter {

  String extension;
```

Example 13-8. ExtensionFilter (continued)

```java
  String description;

  public ExtensionFilter(String extension, String description) {

    if (extension.indexOf('.') == -1) {
      extension = "." + extension;
    }
    this.extension = extension;
    this.description = description;
  }

  public boolean accept(File f) {

    if (f.getName().endsWith(extension)) {
      return true;
    }
    else if (f.isDirectory()) {
      return true;
    }
    return false;
  }

  public String getDescription() {
    return this.description + "(*" + extension + ")";
  }
}
```

Here's a `main()` method that tests this class. `ExtensionFilter` is used in several of the examples yet to come.

```java
  public static void main(String[] args) {

    JFrame parent = new JFrame(); // never shown
    JFileChooser fc = new JFileChooser();
    fc.setDialogTitle("Please choose a file: ");
    fc.addChoosableFileFilter(new ExtensionFilter("txt", "Text Files"));
    fc.addChoosableFileFilter(new ExtensionFilter("java",
                                              "Java Source Code"));
    fc.addChoosableFileFilter(new ExtensionFilter(".c", "C Source Code"));
    fc.addChoosableFileFilter(new ExtensionFilter(".pl",
                                              "Perl Source Code"));
    fc.addChoosableFileFilter(new ExtensionFilter(".html", "HTML Files"));

    fc.showOpenDialog(parent);
    parent.dispose();

    // Work around annoying AWT non-daemon thread bug.
    System.exit(0);
  }
```

The Swing source code contains hints that a class like this may be added to a future release of Swing.

Selecting Directories

A common complaint about `FileDialog` is that it doesn't provide a good way to select directories instead of files. `JFileChooser`, by contrast, can have a selection mode that allows the user to select files, directories, or both. The selection mode is set by `setFileSelectionMode()` and returned by `getFileSelectionMode()`:

```
public void setFileSelectionMode(int mode)
public int getFileSelectionMode()
```

The selection mode should be one of the three mnemonic constants `JFileChooser.FILES_ONLY`, `JFileChooser.DIRECTORIES_ONLY`, or `JFile-Chooser.FILES_AND_DIRECTORIES`:

```
public static final int FILES_ONLY = 0;
public static final int DIRECTORIES_ONLY = 1;
public static final int FILES_AND_DIRECTORIES = 2;
```

For example:

```
JFileChooser fc = new JFileChooser();
fc.setFileSelectionMode(JFileChooser.DIRECTORIES_ONLY);
```

NOTE   You would expect that you could use `setFileSelection-Mode(JFileChooser.FILES_ONLY)` to allow for selection only of files, thus avoiding all the tests as to whether the user selected a file or a directory. Regrettably, this appears not to be the case. This should probably be classified as a bug.

The `isFileSelectionEnabled()` method returns `true` if the selection mode allows files to be selected—that is, the selection mode is either `FILES_ONLY` or `FILES_AND_DIRECTORIES`.

```
public boolean isFileSelectionEnabled()
```

The `isDirectorySelectionEnabled()` method returns `true` if the selection mode allows directories to be selected—that is, the selection mode is either `DIRECTORIES_ONLY` or `FILES_AND_DIRECTORIES`.

```
public boolean isDirectorySelectionEnabled()
```

Example 13-9 is a simple program that lets the user pick a directory from the file chooser. The contents of that directory are then listed.

Example 13-9. DirectoryChooser

```
import java.io.*;
import javax.swing.*;
import javax.swing.filechooser.*;

public class DirectoryChooser {

  public static void main(String[] args) {

    JFileChooser fc = new JFileChooser();
    fc.setFileSelectionMode(JFileChooser.DIRECTORIES_ONLY);

    int result = fc.showOpenDialog(new JFrame());
    if (result == JFileChooser.APPROVE_OPTION) {
      File dir = fc.getSelectedFile();
      String[] contents = dir.list();
      for (int i = 0; i < contents.length; i++) {
        System.out.println(contents[i]);
      }
    }
    System.exit(0);
  }
}
```

Multiple Selections

JFileChooser also allows you to permit users to choose more than one file. To enable this ability, pass `true` to `setMultiSelectionEnabled()`:

```
public void setMultiSelectionEnabled(boolean b)
```

NOTE   As of Java 2 and Swing 1.1, this functionality isn't yet available.

The `isMultiSelectionEnabled()` method returns `true` if the file chooser allows multiple files to be selected at one time, `false` otherwise:

```
public boolean isMultiSelectionEnabled()
```

Hidden Files

Most operating systems have ways of hiding a file. By default, hidden files are not shown in file choosers. However, you can change this by passing `false` to the `setFileHidingEnabled()` method. You can check whether or not hidden files are shown with the `isFileHidingEnabled()` method:

```
public boolean isFileHidingEnabled()
public void setFileHidingEnabled(boolean b)
```

File Views

A `javax.swing.filechooser.FileView` object determines how files are shown in the file chooser. For example, it's responsible for finding the icon to represent each file. At the time of this writing, this class is mostly undocumented and seems likely to change before final release, so I won't say a lot about it. However, I will mention that you can change the file view with the `JFileChooser`'s `setFileView()` method or get the current view with the `getFileView()` method:

```
public void setFileView(fileView)
public FileView getFileView()
```

The current file view determines how information about files is interpreted and displayed to the user. For instance, you can use a file view to display names but not extensions, icons for files, last-modified dates of files, file sizes, and more. In general, the more information you choose to display in the file chooser, the slower your choosers are to display and the longer it takes to switch directories.

The `JFileChooser` class has five methods that return information about a file. These methods are used to display the list of files from which the user can select:

```
public String getName(File f)
public String getDescription(File f)
public String getTypeDescription(File f)
public Icon getIcon(File f)
public boolean isTraversable(File f)
```

Each of these methods delegates its work to the file chooser's internal `FileView` object. Most of the time the default file view is enough. However, you can write your own subclass of `FileView` that implements all five of these methods, then install it in the file chooser with `setFileView()`. The `getName()` method should return the name of the file to be displayed to the user. The `getDescription()` method returns a short description of the file, generally not shown to the user. `getTypeDescription()` should return a short description of the general kind of file, also generally not shown to the user. The `getIcon()` method returns a `javax.swing.ImageIcon` object for the type of file, which is generally shown to the user to the left of the filename. Finally, `isTraversable()` should return `true` for directories the user can enter; returning `false` for a directory prevents the user from opening it. Example 13-10 is a `FileView` class that describes compressed files.

Example 13-10. CompressedFileView

```java
import java.io.*;
import javax.swing.*;
import javax.swing.filechooser.*;

public class CompressedFileView extends FileView {

    ImageIcon zipIcon = new ImageIcon("images/zipIcon.gif");
    ImageIcon gzipIcon = new ImageIcon("images/gzipIcon.gif");
    ImageIcon deflateIcon = new ImageIcon("images/deflateIcon.gif");

    public String getName(File f) {
        return f.getName();
    }

    public String getTypeDescription(File f) {

        if (f.getName().endsWith(".zip")) return "Zip archive";
        if (f.getName().endsWith(".gz")) return "Gzipped file";
        if (f.getName().endsWith(".dfl")) return "Deflated file";
        return null;
    }

    public Icon getIcon(File f) {

        if (f.getName().endsWith(".zip")) return zipIcon;
        if (f.getName().endsWith(".gz")) return gzipIcon;
        if (f.getName().endsWith(".dfl")) return deflateIcon;
        return null;
    }

    public String getDescription(File f) {
        return null;
    }

    public Boolean isTraversable(File f) {
        return null;
    }
}
```

Two methods in this class, `getDescription()` and `isTraversable()`, always return `null`. The other three methods can return `null` if they don't recognize the file's extension. Returning `null` in this context means that the look and feel should figure out the details for itself. Using this class is easy once you've written it.

Simply pass an instance of it to the file chooser's `setFileView()` method like this:

```
fc.setFileView(new CompressedFileView());
```

You will also need to make sure that the GIF files *images/zipIcon.gif*, *images/gzipIcon.gif*, and *images/deflateIcon.gif* exist in the current working directory. In practice, it would probably be more reliable to place these files in a JAR archive and load them from there, perhaps through a JAR URL.

Filesystem Views

`javax.swing.FileSystemView` is an abstract class that attempts to abstract differences between platforms. For example, it's responsible for deciding whether a file is hidden if it begins with a period. On Unix the answer is yes; on other platforms the answer is no. Currently Unix and Windows are supported. Programmers porting Swing to new platforms like the Mac or BeOS will need to implement their own subclasses that recognize those platforms' filesystem conventions. These programmers can use either the constructor or the `setFileSystemView()` method to set the filesystem view. They can use `getFileSystemView()` to determine what view is in effect:

```
public void setFileSystemView(FileSystemView fileSystemView)
public FileSystemView getFileSystemView()
```

The rest of us can safely ignore this class.

Handling Events

`FileDialog` is difficult to work with because of its synchronous nature. When a file dialog is shown, it blocks execution of the calling thread and all input to the parent frame. A raw `JFileChooser`, by contrast, (*not* a `JFileChooser` embedded in a modal dialog by `showOpenDialog()`, `showSaveDialog()`, or `showDialog()`) is asynchronous. It follows the standard 1.1 AWT event model and can fire action and property change events.

Action events

When the user hits the Approve button, the chooser fires an action event with the action command `JFileChooser.APPROVE_SELECTION`. When the user hits the Cancel button, the chooser fires an action event with the action command `JFileChooser.CANCEL_SELECTION`.

```
public static final String CANCEL_SELECTION  = "CancelSelection";
public static final String APPROVE_SELECTION = "ApproveSelection";
```

You register and remove action listeners with the file chooser in the usual fashion using `addActionListener()` and `removeActionListener()`:

```
public void addActionListener(ActionListener l)
public void removeActionListener(ActionListener l)
```

The `approveSelection()` and `cancelSelection()` methods are called by the user interface when the user hits the Approve or Cancel button, respectively. You can call them yourself if you're driving the selection directly:

```
public void approveSelection()
public void cancelSelection()
```

Each of these methods fires an action event to all the registered action listeners by invoking the `fireActionPerformed()` method:

```
protected void fireActionPerformed(String command)
```

I'll show you how to do this when we write a graphical frontend for the `FileViewer` program.

Property change events

When the state of a file chooser changes, the file chooser fires a property change event (an instance of `java.beans.PropertyChangeEvent`). Property changes are triggered by file selections, changing directories, hitting the Approve or Cancel button, and many more actions. The event fired has its own name property set to one of the following constants in the `JFileChooser` class:

```
public static final String CANCEL_SELECTION = "CancelSelection";
public static final String APPROVE_SELECTION = "ApproveSelection";
public static final String APPROVE_BUTTON_TEXT_CHANGED_PROPERTY =
    "ApproveButtonTextChangedProperty";
public static final String APPROVE_BUTTON_TOOL_TIP_TEXT_CHANGED_PROPERTY =
    "ApproveButtonToolTipTextChangedProperty";
public static final String APPROVE_BUTTON_MNEMONIC_CHANGED_PROPERTY =
    "ApproveButtonMnemonicChangedProperty";
public static final String DIRECTORY_CHANGED_PROPERTY = "directoryChanged";
public static final String SELECTED_FILE_CHANGED_PROPERTY =
    "ApproveSelection";
public static final String MULTI_SELECTION_ENABLED_CHANGED_PROPERTY =
    "fileFilterChanged";
public static final String FILE_SYSTEM_VIEW_CHANGED_PROPERTY =
    "FileSystemViewChanged";
public static final String FILE_VIEW_CHANGED_PROPERTY = "fileViewChanged";
public static final String FILE_HIDING_CHANGED_PROPERTY =
    "FileHidingChanged";
public static final String FILE_FILTER_CHANGED_PROPERTY =
    "fileFilterChanged";
public static final String FILE_SELECTION_MODE_CHANGED_PROPERTY =
```

```
    "fileSelectionChanged";
public static final String ACCESSORY_CHANGED_PROPERTY =
    "AccessoryChangedProperty";
public static final String DIALOG_TYPE_CHANGED_PROPERTY =
    "DialogTypeChangedProperty";
public static final String CHOOSABLE_FILE_FILTER_CHANGED_PROPERTY =
    "ChoosableFileFilterChangedProperty";
```

You listen for and respond to property change events through an instance of the `java.beans.PropertyChangeListener` interface. This interface declares a single method, `propertyChange()`. However, it's relatively rare to use a property change listener with a file chooser. Most of the time, you don't need to do anything as a result of a state change in the file chooser. You might want to respond to a property change event fired by a file chooser if you're using an accessory to preview the selected file. In this case, you'll watch for changes in the `SELECTED_FILE_CHANGED_PROPERTY`, as demonstrated in the next section.

Accessory

An accessory is an optional component you can add to the `JFileChooser`. The most common use of this is to show a preview of the file. For example, a file chooser used to select an image file might provide an accessory that shows a thumbnail of the picture. The `setAccessory()` method adds an accessory to the file chooser, while the `getAccessory()` method returns a reference to it:

```
public JComponent getAccessory()
public void setAccessory(JComponent newAccessory)
```

A `JFileChooser` object can have at most one accessory and does not need to have any.

Example 13-11 is a chooser that uses a `JTextArea` as an accessory to show the first few lines of the selected text file. This `TextFilePreview` class extends `JTextArea` so it can easily display text. It implements the `PropertyChangeListener` interface so it can be notified through its `propertyChange()` method when the user changes the selected file and the preview needs to be changed. The `loadText()` method reads in the first few hundred bytes of the selected file and stores that data in the `preview` field. Finally, the `main()` method tests this class by displaying a file chooser with this accessory. Figure 13-5 shows the result.

Example 13-11. TextFilePreview

```
import javax.swing.*;
import java.beans.*;
import java.io.*;
import java.awt.*;
import com.macfaq.io.*;
```

Example 13-11. TextFilePreview (continued)

```java
public class TextFilePreview extends JTextArea
 implements PropertyChangeListener {

  File selectedFile = null;
  String preview = "";
  int previewLength = 250;

  public TextFilePreview(JFileChooser fc) {
    super(10, 20);
    this.setEditable(false);
    this.setPreferredSize(new Dimension(150, 150));
    this.setLineWrap(true);
    fc.addPropertyChangeListener(this);
  }

  void loadText() {

    if (selectedFile != null) {
      try {
        FileInputStream fin = new FileInputStream(selectedFile);
        byte[] data = new byte[previewLength];
        int bytesRead = 0;
        for (int i = 0; i < previewLength; i++) {
          int b = fin.read();
          if (b == -1) break;
          bytesRead++;
          data[i] = (byte) b;
        }
        preview = new String(data, 0, bytesRead);
        fin.close();
      }
      catch (IOException e) {
        // File preview is not an essential operation so
        // we'll simply ignore the exception and return.
      }
    }
  }

  public void propertyChange(PropertyChangeEvent e) {

    if (e.getPropertyName().equals(JFileChooser.SELECTED_FILE_CHANGED_PROPERTY))
{
      selectedFile = (File) e.getNewValue();
      if(isShowing()) {
        loadText();
        this.setText(preview);
      }
    }
```

Example 13-11. TextFilePreview (continued)

```
  }

  public static void main(String[] args) {

    JFileChooser fc = new JFileChooser();
    fc.setAccessory(new TextFilePreview(fc));
    int result = fc.showOpenDialog(new JFrame());
    if (result == JFileChooser.APPROVE_OPTION) {
      try {
        File f = fc.getSelectedFile();
        if (f != null) {
          FileInputStream fin = new FileInputStream(f);
          StreamCopier.copy(fin, System.out);
          fin.close();
        }
      }
      catch (IOException e) {System.err.println(e);}
    }

    System.exit(0);
  }
}
```

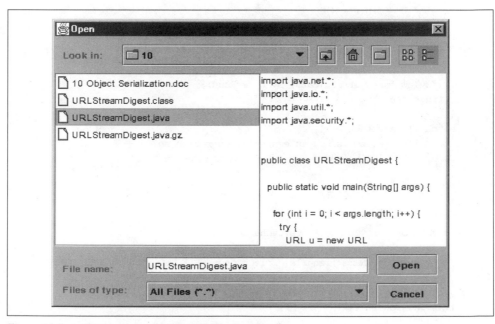

Figure 13-5. A JFileChooser with a TextFilePreview accessory

Swing Methods

Like most Swing components, `JFileChooser` has several methods for working with the look and feel. The `updateUI()` method is invoked if the look and feel has changed, to tell the component to redraw itself:

```
public void updateUI()
```

The `getUIClassID()` method returns the name of the look-and-feel class that drew this file chooser:

```
public String getUIClassID()
```

The `getUI()` method returns the actual object that implements the particular look and feel:

```
public FileChooserUI getUI()
```

It's unlikely you'll need to call any of these three methods directly.

`getAccessibleContext()` returns the `com.sun.java.accessibility.AccessibleContext` object used to provide handicapped accessibility for the component:

```
public AccessibleContext getAccessibleContext()
```

File Viewer, Part 6

We've now got the tools needed to put a graphical user interface onto the `FileViewer` application we've been developing. The back end doesn't need to change at all. It's still based on the same filter streams we've used for the last several chapters. However, instead of reading filenames from the command line, we can get them from a file chooser. Instead of dumping the files on `System.out`, we can display them in a text area. And instead of relying on the user remembering a lot of confusing command-line switches, we can provide simple radio buttons for the user to choose from. This has the added advantage of making it easy to repeatedly interpret the same file according to different filters.

Figure 13-6 shows the finished application. This will give you some idea of what the code is aiming at. Initially, I started with a pencil-and-paper sketch, but I'll spare you my inartistic renderings. The single `JFrame` window is organized with a border layout. The west panel contains various controls for determining how the data is interpreted. The east panel contains the `JFileChooser` used to select the file. Notice that the Approve button has been customized to say "View File" rather than "Open". Ideally, I'd like to make the Cancel button say "Quit" instead, but the `JFileChooser` class doesn't allow you to do that without using resource bundles, a subject I would prefer to leave for another book. The south panel contains a scroll pane. Inside the scroll pane is a streamed text area.

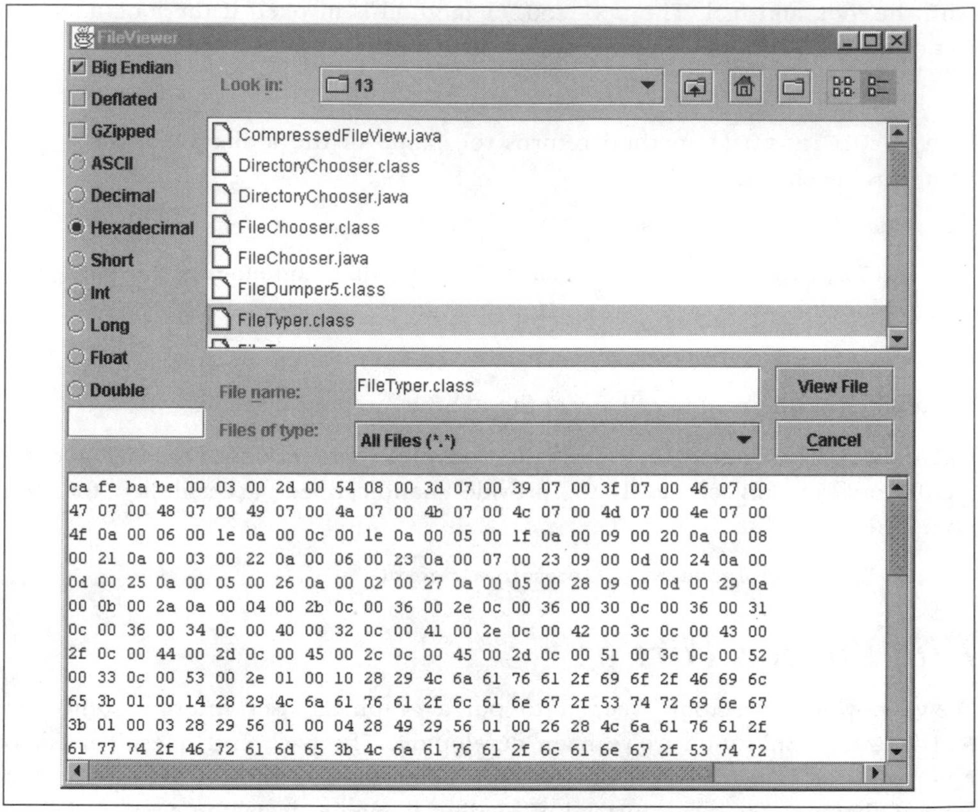

Figure 13-6. The FileViewer

One fact I discovered while developing this application was that Swing components don't get along well with standard AWT components like `Frame` and `TextArea`. My initial attempts that mixed AWT components with the Swing `JFileChooser` rapidly crashed the VM. Replacing all components with their Swing equivalents solved the problem.

Let's begin the exegesis of the code where I began writing it, with the user interface. The main driver class is `FileViewer`, shown in Example 13-12. This class extends `JFrame`. Its constructor doesn't do a lot. Most of the work is relegated to the `init()` method, which sets up the user interface composed of the three parts previously described, then centers the whole frame on the primary display.

Example 13-12. FileViewer

```
import javax.swing.*;
import java.io.*;
```

Example 13-12. FileViewer (continued)

```java
import com.macfaq.io.*;
import com.macfaq.swing.*;
import java.awt.*;
import java.awt.event.*;

public class FileViewer extends JFrame
 implements WindowListener, ActionListener {

  JFileChooser fc = new JFileChooser();
  JStreamedTextArea theView = new JStreamedTextArea();
  ModePanel mp = new ModePanel();

  public FileViewer() {
    super("FileViewer");
  }

  public void init() {

    this.addWindowListener(this);

    fc.setApproveButtonText("View File");
    fc.setApproveButtonMnemonic('V');
    fc.addActionListener(this);

    this.getContentPane().add("Center", fc);
    JScrollPane sp = new JScrollPane(theView);
    this.getContentPane().add("South", sp);
    this.getContentPane().add("West", mp);
    this.pack();

    // Center on display.
    Dimension display = getToolkit().getScreenSize();
    Dimension bounds = this.getSize();

    int x = (display.width - bounds.width)/2;
    int y = (display.height - bounds.height)/2;
    if (x < 0) x = 10;
    if (y < 0) y = 15;
    this.setLocation(x, y);
  }

  public void actionPerformed(ActionEvent e) {

    if (e.getActionCommand().equals(JFileChooser.APPROVE_SELECTION)) {
      File f = fc.getSelectedFile();
      if (f != null) {
        theView.setText("");
        OutputStream out = theView.getOutputStream();
```

Example 13-12. FileViewer (continued)

```
        try {
          FileInputStream in = new FileInputStream(f);
          FileDumper5.dump(in, out, mp.getMode(), mp.isBigEndian(),
           mp.isDeflated(), mp.isGZipped(), mp.getPassword());
        }
        catch (IOException ex) {
        }
      }
    }
    else if (e.getActionCommand().equals(JFileChooser.CANCEL_SELECTION)) {
      this.closeAndQuit();
    }
  }


  public void windowClosing(WindowEvent e) {
    this.closeAndQuit();
  }


  // Do-nothing methods for WindowListener.
  public void windowOpened(WindowEvent e) {}

  public void windowClosed(WindowEvent e) {}
  public void windowIconified(WindowEvent e) {}
  public void windowDeiconified(WindowEvent e) {}
  public void windowActivated(WindowEvent e) {}
  public void windowDeactivated(WindowEvent e) {}

  private void closeAndQuit() {

    this.setVisible(false);
    this.dispose();

    System.exit(0);
  }


  public static void main(String[] args) {

    FileViewer fv = new FileViewer();
    fv.init();
    fv.show();
  }
}
```

FileViewer implements the WindowListener interface simply so that it will be closed when the user clicks the Close box. It also implements the ActionListener interface. However, the action events that its actionPerformed() method responds to are fired by the file chooser, indicating that the user pressed the View File button.

When the user presses the View File button, the mode panel is read to determine exactly how the file is to be interpreted. These parameters and the selected file are fed to the static `FileDumper5.dumpFile()` method from Chapter 10, *Cryptographic Streams*.

The next new class in this application is the `ModePanel`, shown in Example 13-13. This class provides a simple user interface to allow the user to specify the format the file is in, whether and how it's compressed, and the password, if any. This part of the GUI is completely contained inside this class. Other methods that need access to this information can query the `ModePanel` for it through any of several public get methods. They do not need to concern themselves with the internal details of the `ModePanel` GUI.

Example 13-13. ModePanel

```
import java.awt.*;
import javax.swing.*;

public class ModePanel extends JPanel {

  JCheckBox bigEndian = new JCheckBox("Big Endian", true);
  JCheckBox deflated = new JCheckBox("Deflated", false);
  JCheckBox gzipped = new JCheckBox("GZipped", false);

  ButtonGroup dataTypes = new ButtonGroup();
  JRadioButton asciiRadio   = new JRadioButton("ASCII");
  JRadioButton decimalRadio = new JRadioButton("Decimal");
  JRadioButton hexRadio     = new JRadioButton("Hexadecimal");
  JRadioButton shortRadio   = new JRadioButton("Short");
  JRadioButton intRadio     = new JRadioButton("Int");
  JRadioButton longRadio    = new JRadioButton("Long");
  JRadioButton floatRadio   = new JRadioButton("Float");
  JRadioButton doubleRadio  = new JRadioButton("Double");

  JTextField password = new JTextField();

  public ModePanel() {

    this.setLayout(new GridLayout(13, 1));
    this.add(bigEndian);
    this.add(deflated);
    this.add(gzipped);

    this.add(asciiRadio);
    asciiRadio.setSelected(true);
```

Example 13-13. ModePanel (continued)

```java
    this.add(decimalRadio);
    this.add(hexRadio);
    this.add(shortRadio);
    this.add(intRadio);
    this.add(longRadio);
    this.add(floatRadio);
    this.add(doubleRadio);

    dataTypes.add(asciiRadio);
    dataTypes.add(decimalRadio);
    dataTypes.add(hexRadio);
    dataTypes.add(shortRadio);
    dataTypes.add(intRadio);
    dataTypes.add(longRadio);
    dataTypes.add(floatRadio);
    dataTypes.add(doubleRadio);

  this.add(password);
  }

public boolean isBigEndian() {
  return bigEndian.isSelected();
}

public boolean isDeflated() {
  return deflated.isSelected();
}

public boolean isGZipped() {
  return gzipped.isSelected();
}

public int getMode() {

  if (asciiRadio.isSelected()) return FileDumper6.ASC;
  else if (decimalRadio.isSelected()) return FileDumper6.DEC;
  else if (hexRadio.isSelected()) return FileDumper6.HEX;
  else if (shortRadio.isSelected()) return FileDumper6.SHORT;
  else if (intRadio.isSelected()) return FileDumper6.INT;
  else if (longRadio.isSelected()) return FileDumper6.LONG;
  else if (floatRadio.isSelected()) return FileDumper6.FLOAT;
  else if (doubleRadio.isSelected()) return FileDumper6.DOUBLE;
  else return FileDumper6.ASC;
}

public String getPassword() {
  return password.getText();
}
}
```

One final class is needed. The StreamedTextArea of Chapter 2, *Output Streams*, turned out to be inadequate here because of its apparent incompatibility with Swing components. Example 13-14 is a new JStreamedTextArea class that's based on Swing's JTextArea rather than the AWT's TextArea class.

Example 13-14. JStreamedTextArea

```
package com.macfaq.swing;

import javax.swing.*;
import java.io.*;
import java.awt.*;

public class JStreamedTextArea extends JTextArea {

  OutputStream theOutput = new TextAreaOutputStream();

  public JStreamedTextArea() {
    this("", 12, 20);
  }

  public JStreamedTextArea(String text) {
    this(text, 12, 20);
  }

  public JStreamedTextArea(int rows, int columns) {
    this("", rows, columns);
  }

  public JStreamedTextArea(String text, int rows, int columns) {
    super(text, rows, columns);
    this.setEditable(false);
    this.setFont(new Font("Monospaced", Font.PLAIN, 12));
  }

  public OutputStream getOutputStream() {
    return theOutput;
  }

  public Dimension getMinimumSize() {
    return new Dimension(72, 200);
  }

  public Dimension getPreferredSize() {
    return new Dimension(60*12, getLineCount()*12);
  }

  class TextAreaOutputStream extends OutputStream {
```

Example 13-14. JStreamedTextArea (continued)

```java
    public void write(int b) {

        // Recall that the int should really just be a byte.
        b &= 0x000000FF;

        // Must convert byte to a char in order to append it.
        char c = (char) b;
        append(String.valueOf(c));
    }

    public void write(byte[] b, int offset, int length) {

        append(new String(b, offset, length));
    }
  }
}
```

And there you have it: a graphical file viewer application. The I/O code hasn't changed at all, but the resulting application is much easier to use. One final piece remains before we can say the file viewer is complete. In Chapter 15, *Readers and Writers*, we will add support for many additional text encodings besides the ASCII used here.

14

In this chapter:
- *Unicode*
- *Displaying Unicode Text*
- *Unicode Escapes*
- *UTF-8*
- *The char Data Type*
- *Other Encodings*
- *Converting Between Byte Arrays and Strings*

Multilingual Character Sets and Unicode

We live on a planet on which many languages are spoken. I can walk out my front door in Brooklyn on any given day and hear people conversing in French, Creole, Hebrew, Arabic, Spanish, and languages I don't even recognize. And the Internet is even more diverse than Brooklyn. A local doctor's office that sets up a storefront on the Web to sell vitamins may soon find itself shipping to customers whose native language is Chinese, Gujarati, Turkish, German, Portuguese, or something else. There's no such thing as a local business on the Internet.

However, the first computers and the first programming languages were mostly designed by English-speaking programmers in countries where English was the native language. These programmers designed character sets that worked well for English text, though not much else. The preeminent such set is ASCII. Since ASCII is a seven-bit character set, each ASCII character can easily be represented as a single byte, signed or unsigned. Thus, it's natural for ASCII-based programming languages to equate the character data type with the byte data type. In these languages, such as C, the same operations that read and write bytes also read and write characters.

Unfortunately, ASCII is inadequate for almost all non-English languages. It contains no cedillas, umlauts, betas, thorns, or any of the other thousands of non-English characters that are used to read and write text around the world. Fairly shortly after the development of ASCII, there was an explosion of extended character sets around the world, each of which encoded the basic ASCII characters as well as the additional characters needed for another language like Greek, Turkish, Arabic, Chinese, Japanese, or Russian. Many of these character sets are still used today, and much existing data is encoded in them.

However, these character sets are still inadequate for many needs. For one thing, most assume that you only want to encode English plus one other language. This makes it difficult for a Russian classicist to write a commentary on an ancient Greek text, for example. Furthermore, documents are limited by their character sets. Email sent from Morocco may become illegible in India if the sender is using an Arabic character set but the recipient is using Devanagari.

Unicode is an international effort to provide a single character set that everyone can use. Unicode supports the characters needed for English, Arabic, Cyrillic, Greek, Devanagari, and many others. Unicode isn't perfect. There are some omissions, especially in the ideographic character sets for Chinese and Japanese, but it is the most comprehensive character set yet devised for all the languages of planet Earth.

Java is one of the first programming languages to explicitly address the need for non-English text. It does this by adopting Unicode as its native character set. All Java chars and strings are given in Unicode. However, since there's also a lot of non-Unicode legacy text in the world, in a dizzying array of encodings, Java also provides the classes you need to read and write text in these encodings as well.

Unicode

Unicode is Java's native character set. Each Unicode character is a two-byte, unsigned number with a value between 0 and 65,535. This provides enough space for characters from all the world's alphabetic scripts and the most common characters from the ideographic scripts of Chinese and Japanese. The current version of Unicode (2.1) defines 38,887 different characters from many languages, including English, Russian, Arabic, Hebrew, Greek, Thai, Korean, and Sanskrit. The most common ideographic characters from Japanese and Chinese are also included. However, Chinese alone contains over 80,000 different ideograms, so it's impossible to include them all in a two-byte set. A four-byte Universal Character Set (UCS) that will include the full Chinese and Japanese scripts is under development. Java does not yet support UCS.

The first 128 Unicode characters (characters 0 through 127) are identical to the ASCII character set. 32 is the ASCII space; therefore, 32 is the Unicode space. 33 is the ASCII exclamation point, so 33 is the Unicode exclamation point, and so on. Table B-1, in Appendix B, *Character Sets*, shows this character set. The next 128 Unicode characters (characters 128 through 255) have the same values as the equivalent characters in the Latin-1 character set defined by ISO standard 8859-1. Latin-1, a slight variation of which is used by Windows, adds the various accented characters, umlauts, cedillas, upside-down question marks, and other characters needed to write text in most Western European languages. Table B-2 shows these characters. The first 128 characters in Latin-1 are identical to the ASCII character set.

Values beyond 255 encode characters from various other character sets. Where possible, character blocks describing a particular group of characters map onto established encodings for that set of characters by simple transposition. For instance, Unicode characters 884 through 1011 encode the Greek alphabet and associated characters like the Greek question mark (;).* This is a direct transposition by 756 of characters 128 through 255 of the ISO 8859-7 character set, which is in turn based on the Greek national standard ELOT 928. For example, the small letter delta, δ, ISO 8859-7 character 228, is Unicode character 984. A small epsilon, ε, ISO 8859-7 character 229, is Unicode character 985. In general, the Unicode value for a Greek character equals the ISO 8859-7 value for the character plus 756. Other character sets are included in Unicode in a similar fashion whenever possible.†

NextStep, BeOS, MacOS X Server, Bell Labs' Plan 9, and Windows NT 4.0 all support Unicode to some extent. Unicode support in MacOS and Windows 98 is more nascent, but it's coming. Application software is a little slower to appear, but Microsoft Word 97 and 98, Netscape Navigator 4.0, and Internet Explorer 4.0 all support Unicode. The big hold-up on most systems is fonts and input methods. Windows NT 5.0 will include fonts covering most of the defined Unicode characters as well as input methods for most major languages.

Displaying Unicode Text

Although internally Java can handle full Unicode data (it's just numbers, after all), not all Java environments can display all Unicode characters. In fact, I'll go so far as to say none of the current Java environments, whether standalone virtual machines or web browsers, can display all Unicode characters.

Unicode is divided into blocks. For example, characters 0 through 127 are the Basic Latin block and contain ASCII. Characters 128 through 255 are the Latin Extended-A block and contain the upper 128 characters of the Latin-1 character set. Characters 9984 through 10,175 are the Dingbats block and contain the characters in the popular Zapf Dingbats font. Characters 19,968 through 40,959 are the unified Chinese-Japanese-Korean ideograph block. Each block represents a script or a subset of a script. As a rule of thumb, most runtime environments can display only some of these blocks. Occasionally, a particular runtime may be able

---

* Indeed, the Greek question mark is nearly identical to a Latin semicolon; this is not a mistranslation of the character.

† As much as I'd like to include complete tables for all Unicode characters, if I did so, this book would be little more than that table. For complete lists of all the Unicode characters and associated glyphs, the canonical reference is *The Unicode Standard Version 2.0*, by the Unicode Consortium, ISBN 0-201-48345-9. Online versions of the character tables can be found at *http://charts.unicode.org/*.

to display some characters from a block but not others. For instance, most Macintoshes can display the entire Latin Extended-A block except for the Icelandic characters þ, Þ, ý, Ý, ð, and Ð.

The biggest problem is the lack of fonts. Few computers have fonts for all the scripts Java supports. Even computers that possess the necessary fonts can't install a lot of them because of their size. A normal, 8-bit outline font ranges from about 30–60K. A Unicode font that omits the Han ideographs will be about 10 times that size. And a full Unicode font that includes the full range of Han ideographs will occupy between five and seven megabytes. Furthermore, text display algorithms based on English often break down when faced with right-to-left languages like Hebrew and Arabic, vertical languages like the traditional Chinese still used in Taiwan, or context-sensitive languages like Arabic.

Finally, even web browsers that can handle Chinese, Cyrillic, Arabic, Japanese, or other non-Roman scripts in HTML don't necessarily support those same scripts in applets. (HotJava 1.1 and earlier is a notable offender here.) It's even sometimes the case that characters an applet can draw directly using a `java.awt.Graphics` object may not be able to be drawn by peer-based components like text areas, labels, and buttons. However, all runtimes do support some subset of full Unicode. It's not hard to write an applet that allows you to test a web browser's support. Figure 14-1 shows such an applet. By selecting different character blocks, you'll see which characters in those blocks your web browser can and cannot draw.

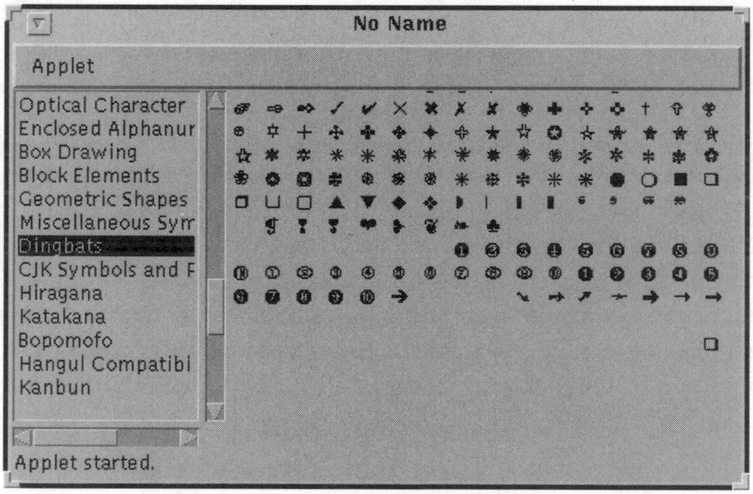

Figure 14-1. The UnicodeApplet showing the Dingbats character block

This applet is built from three new classes. The first is the `CharacterBlock` class, shown in Example 14-1, which represents a character block, including its name, the start character in the block, and the end character in the block. The constructor enforces restrictions on the valid values for start and end. They must be greater than or equal to Character.MIN_VALUE (0) and less than or equal to Character.MAX_VALUE (65,535). Furthermore, the start character must be less than or equal to the end character. Since the constructor is private and only accessed from inside the class with established values, these checks are not absolutely necessary; but they did help me catch several data entry errors as this class was developed.

A private constructor is unusual but not unheard of, especially when there are only a finite number of valid objects. There are only a few dozen character blocks defined in Unicode 2.0, each with a precise range. Declaring the constructor private prevents arbitrary blocks from being created. Instead, a Java static block initializes all possible character blocks the first time the class is loaded and stores them in a Hashtable called blocks. From this point forward, the static getBlock() method can retrieve a particular block by its name. The names of the blocks are used as keys in the hash table. The static getNames() method returns a list of the available blocks, and the static getNumBlocks() method returns the number of blocks stored in the hash table. There are several instance methods as well. The getStart(), getEnd(), and getName() methods are accessors that return the values of the respective fields. Finally, getCharactersInBlock() returns an array of chars containing each of the defined characters in the block in sequence. However, many of the blocks contain undefined empty spaces. For example, characters 983, 984, and 985 in the middle of the Greek block are not defined. Testing each character in the range with the static method Character. isDefined() weeds out undefined characters.

Example 14-1. The CharacterBlock Class

```
import java.util.*;

public class CharacterBlock {

   String name;
   int start;
   int end;

   private static Hashtable blocks = new Hashtable(66);

   /* The blocks given here are as listed in The Unicode Standard,
      Version 2.0. Ranges are given in hexadecimal as in that
      document. It is not difficult to add additional blocks to this
      list as they're defined.
   */
   static {
```

Example 14-1. The CharacterBlock Class (continued)

```
// General Scripts
makeBlock("Basic Latin", 0x0000, 0x007F);
makeBlock("Latin-1 Supplement", 0x0080, 0x00FF);
makeBlock("Latin Extended-A", 0x0100, 0x017F);
makeBlock("Latin Extended-B", 0x0180, 0x024F);
makeBlock("IPA Extensions", 0x0250, 0x02AF);
makeBlock("Spacing Modifier Letters", 0x02B0, 0x02FF);
makeBlock("Combining Diacritical Marks", 0x0300, 0x036F);
makeBlock("Greek", 0x0370, 0x03FF);
makeBlock("Cyrillic", 0x0400, 0x04FF);
makeBlock("Armenian", 0x0530, 0x058F);
makeBlock("Hebrew", 0x0590, 0x05FF);
makeBlock("Arabic", 0x0600, 0x06FF);
makeBlock("Devanagari", 0x0900, 0x097F);
makeBlock("Bengali", 0x0980, 0x09FF);
makeBlock("Gurmukhi", 0x0A00, 0x0A7F);
makeBlock("Gujarati", 0x0A80, 0x0AFF);
makeBlock("Oriya", 0x0B00, 0x0B7F);
makeBlock("Tamil", 0x0B80, 0x0BFF);
makeBlock("Telugu", 0x0C00, 0x0C7F);
makeBlock("Kannada", 0x0C80, 0x0CFF);
makeBlock("Malayalam", 0x0D00, 0x0D7F);
makeBlock("Thai", 0x0E00, 0x0E7F);
makeBlock("Lao", 0x0E80, 0x0EFF);
makeBlock("Tibetan", 0x0F00, 0x0FBF);
makeBlock("Georgian", 0x10A0, 0x10FF);
makeBlock("Hangul Jamo", 0x1100, 0x11FF);
makeBlock("Latin Extended Additional", 0x1E00, 0x1EFF);
makeBlock("Greek Extended", 0x1F00, 0x1FFF);

// Symbols
makeBlock("General Punctuation", 0x2000, 0x206F);
makeBlock("Superscripts and Subscripts", 0x2070, 0x209F);
makeBlock("Currency Symbols", 0x20A0, 0x20CF);
makeBlock("Combining Marks for Symbols", 0x20D0, 0x20FF);
makeBlock("Letterlike Symbols", 0x2100, 0x214F);
makeBlock("Number Forms", 0x2150, 0x218F);
makeBlock("Arrows", 0x2190, 0x21FF);
makeBlock("Mathematical Operators", 0x2200, 0x22FF);
makeBlock("Miscellaneous Technical", 0x2300, 0x234F);
makeBlock("Control Pictures", 0x2400, 0x243F);
makeBlock("Optical Character Recognition", 0x2440, 0x245F);
makeBlock("Enclosed Alphanumerics", 0x2460, 0x24FF);
makeBlock("Box Drawing", 0x2500, 0x257F);
makeBlock("Block Elements", 0x2580, 0x259F);
makeBlock("Geometric Shapes", 0x25A0, 0x25FF);
makeBlock("Miscellaneous Symbols", 0x2600, 0x26FF);
makeBlock("Dingbats", 0x2700, 0x27BF);
```

Example 14-1. The CharacterBlock Class (continued)

```
   // Chinese-Japanese-Korean Phonetics and Symbols
   makeBlock("CJK Symbols and Punctuation", 0x3000, 0x303F);
   makeBlock("Hiragana", 0x3040, 0x309F);
   makeBlock("Katakana", 0x30A0, 0x30FF);
   makeBlock("Bopomofo", 0x3100, 0x312F);
   makeBlock("Hangul Compatibility Jamo", 0x3130, 0x318F);
   makeBlock("Kanbun", 0x3190, 0x319F);
   makeBlock("Enclosed CJK Letters and Months", 0x3200, 0x32FF);
   makeBlock("CJK Compatibility", 0x3300, 0x33FF);

   // Chinese-Japanese-Korean Ideographs
   makeBlock("CJK Unified Ideographs", 0x4E00, 0x9FFF);

   // Hangul Syllables
   makeBlock("Hangul Syllables", 0xAC00, 0xD7A3);

   // Surrogates
   makeBlock("Surrogates", 0xD800, 0xDFFF);

   // Private Use
   makeBlock("Private Use", 0xE000, 0xF8FF);

   // Compatibility and Specials
   makeBlock("CJK Compatibility Ideographs", 0xF900, 0xFAFF);
   makeBlock("Alphabetic Presentation Forms", 0xFB00, 0xFB4F);
   makeBlock("Arabic Presentation Forms", 0xFB50, 0xFDFF);
   makeBlock("Combining Half Marks", 0xFE20, 0xFE2F);
   makeBlock("CJK Compatibility Forms", 0xFE30, 0xFE4F);
   makeBlock("Small Form Variants", 0xFE50, 0xFE6F);
   makeBlock("More Arabic Presentation Forms", 0xFE70, 0xFEFF);
   makeBlock("Halfwidth and Fullwidth Forms", 0xFF00, 0xFFEF);
   makeBlock("Specials", 0xFEFF, 0xFFFF);

 }


 /* Originally I inlined this method from the static block where it's invoked.
    However, that produced excessively long lines in the static block that
    wouldn't look good in the printed book. So I split out this common
    invocation here. Since it's final, a good compiler can optimize it away
    anyway.
 */
 private final static void makeBlock(String name, int start, int end) {
   blocks.put(name, new CharacterBlock(name, start, end));
 }

 private CharacterBlock(String name, int start, int end) {
   this.name = name;
   if (start < Character.MIN_VALUE || start > Character.MAX_VALUE
```

Example 14-1. The CharacterBlock Class (continued)

```java
      || end < Character.MIN_VALUE || end > Character.MAX_VALUE) {
        throw new IllegalArgumentException("Ranges must fall between 0 and 65,535");
      }
      if (end < start) {
        throw new IllegalArgumentException("End must come after start");
      }
      this.start = start;
      this.end = end;
  }

  public static CharacterBlock getBlock(String name) {
    return (CharacterBlock) blocks.get(name);
  }

  public static int getNumBlocks() {
    return blocks.size();
  }

  public static String[] getBlockNames() {

    CharacterBlock[] cb = new CharacterBlock[blocks.size()];
    Enumeration e = blocks.elements();
    for (int i = 0; e.hasMoreElements(); i++) {
      cb[i] = ((CharacterBlock) e.nextElement());
    }

    // bubble sort based on start
    boolean sorted = false;
    while (!sorted) {
      sorted = true;
      for (int i = 0; i < cb.length-1; i++) {
        if (cb[i].start > cb[i+1].start) {
          sorted = false;
          CharacterBlock temp = cb[i+1];
          cb[i+1] = cb[i];
          cb[i] = temp;
        }
      }
    }

    String[] names = new String[blocks.size()];
    for (int i = 0; i < names.length; i++) names[i] = cb[i].name;
    return names;
  }

  public char[] getCharactersInBlock() {

    char[] block = new char[end-start+1];
```

Example 14-1. The CharacterBlock Class (continued)

```
    int j = 0;
    for (int i = start; i <= end; i++) {
      if (Character.isDefined((char) i)) {
        block[j++] = (char) i;
      }
    }
    char[] result = new char[j];
    System.arraycopy(block, 0, result, 0, j);
    return result;
  }

  public String getName() {
    return this.name;
  }

  public int getStart() {
    return this.start;
  }

  public int getEnd() {
    return this.end;
  }
}
```

Example 14-2 shows the `BlockCanvas` class, a custom component that is initialized with a particular character block and draws all characters in that block. The block of characters it draws may be changed with the `setBlock()` method or inspected with the `getBlock()` method. The `paint()` method merely tries to fit a grid of characters into the allotted space.

Example 14-2. The BlockCanvas Class

```
import java.awt.*;

public class BlockCanvas extends Canvas {

  CharacterBlock block = CharacterBlock.getBlock("Basic Latin");

  int charWidth = 20;
  int charHeight = 15;
  int hgap = 5;
  int vgap = 0;

  public BlockCanvas() {
    setFont(new Font("Monospaced", Font.BOLD, 12));
  }

  public void setBlock(CharacterBlock block) {
```

Example 14-2. The BlockCanvas Class (continued)

```java
      this.block = block;
      this.repaint();
  }

  public CharacterBlock getBlock() {
    return block;
  }

  public void paint(Graphics g) {

    char[] charsOnPage = block.getCharactersInBlock();
    int charsPerRow = (getSize().width - 2*hgap)/charWidth;
    if (charsPerRow <= 0) charsPerRow = 1;

    for (int i = 0; i < charsOnPage.length; i++) {
      int x = i % charsPerRow;
      int y = i / charsPerRow + 1;
      g.drawChars(charsOnPage, i, 1, hgap + charWidth*x, vgap + charHeight*y);
    }
  }
}
```

Finally, Example 14-3 is an applet that allows the user to select a character block from a list box and have it displayed in a block canvas. This applet was shown in Figure 14-1. The `init()` method sets up the user interface. The list box is filled with the names returned from `CharacterBlock`'s `getNames()` method. `UnicodeApplet` implements `ItemListener` and registers itself as the listener with the list box. When an item is selected from the list, `UnicodeApplet` sets the block of the `BlockCanvas` to the chosen selection.

Example 14-3. The UnicodeApplet

```java
import java.awt.*;
import java.awt.event.*;
import java.applet.*;

public class UnicodeApplet extends Applet implements ItemListener {

  List scripts = new List(CharacterBlock.getNumBlocks());
  BlockCanvas theChart = new BlockCanvas();

  public void init() {

    setLayout(new BorderLayout());
    String[] names = CharacterBlock.getBlockNames();
    for (int i = 0; i < names.length; i++) {
      scripts.add(names[i]);
    }
```

Example 14-3. The UnicodeApplet (continued)

```
    scripts.addItemListener(this);
    scripts.select(0);
    this.add("West", scripts);
    this.add("Center", theChart);
  }

  public void itemStateChanged(ItemEvent ie) {

    if (ie.getStateChange() == ItemEvent.SELECTED) {
      String selected = scripts.getSelectedItem();
      if (!selected.equals(theChart.getBlock().getName())) {
        theChart.setBlock(CharacterBlock.getBlock(selected));
      }
    }
  }
}
```

Unicode Escapes

Currently, there isn't a large installed base of Unicode text editors. There's an even smaller installed base of machines with full Unicode fonts installed. Therefore, it's essential that all valid Java programs can be written using nothing more than ASCII characters.

All Java keywords and operators as well as the names of all the classes, methods, and fields in the core API may be written in pure ASCII. This is by deliberate design on the part of JavaSoft. However, Unicode characters are explicitly allowed in comments, string and `char` literals, and identifiers. The following, the opening line from Homer's *Odyssey,* should be legal Java:

ἄνδρα μοι ἔννεπε Μοῦσα πολύτροπον ὃς μάλα πολλὰ

To enable statements like that in Java source, non-ASCII characters are embedded through Unicode escape sequences. The escape sequence for a character is a backslash (\) followed by a small u, followed by the four-digit hexadecimal code for the character. For example:

```
    char tab = '\u0009';
    char softHyphen = '\u00AD';
    char sigma = '\u03C3';
    char squareKeesu = '\u30B9';.
```

Using Unicode escapes, the opening line from Homer's *Odyssey* would be rendered as:

```
    /* \u039F\u03B4\u03C5\u03C3\u03C3\u03B5\u03B9\u03B1 */
    String \u03B1\u03C1\u03C7\u03B7 =
```

```
  "\u0386\u03BD\u03B4\u03C1\u03B1 \u03BC\u03BF\u03B9 "
+ "\u03AD\u03BD\u03BD\u03B5\u03C0\u03B5, "
+ "\u039C\u03BF\u03C5\u03C3\u03B1, "
+ " \u03BF\u03C2 \u03BC\u03AC\u03BB\u03B1 \u03C0\u03BF\u03BB\u03BB\u03B1";
```

Obviously, this is horribly inconvenient for anything more than an occasional non-ASCII character.

Many Java compilers assume that source files are written in ASCII and that the only Unicode characters present are Unicode escapes. During a single-pass preprocessing phase, the compiler converts each raw ASCII character or Unicode escape sequence to a two-byte Unicode character it stores in memory. Only after preprocessing is complete and the ASCII file has been converted to in-memory Unicode, is the file actually compiled. Some compilers and runtimes will also compile the upper 128 characters of the ISO Latin-1 character set. However, some do not. Worse yet, some Java virtual machines can compile files containing non-ASCII, ISO Latin-1 characters but can't run the files they've compiled. For safety's sake and maximum portability, you should escape all non-ASCII characters.

Version 1.1 and later of Sun's *javac* compiler assumes a *.java* file is written in the platform's default encoding, which is Latin-1 on Solaris and Windows, MacRoman on the Mac. However, this produces incorrect results on Windows, because Windows does not use true Latin-1 but a modified version that includes fewer control characters and more printing characters.

Text editors that work with non-ASCII character sets like MacRoman, Arabic, or Big-5 Chinese can integrate with existing Java compilers by providing a preprocessing phase where the natively encoded data is translated to Unicode-escaped ASCII before being passed to Sun's *javac* compiler. Alternately, they can hand off the translation work to *javac* (1.1 and later) by using its -encoding flag. For example, to specify that the file *MyClass.java* is written in the ISO 8859-9 character set (essentially Latin-1 with the Turkish characters ş, Ş, 1, İ, ğ, and Ğ replacing the Icelandic characters þ, Þ, ý, Ý, ð, and Ð) you would type:

```
% javac -encoding 8859_9 MyClass.java
```

Table B-4 lists the encodings that Java 1.1 understands.

UTF-8

Since every Unicode character is encoded in exactly two bytes, Unicode is a fairly simple encoding. The first two bytes of a file are the first character. The next two bytes are the second character, and so on. This makes parsing Unicode data relatively simple compared to schemes that use variable-width characters. The downside is that Unicode is far from the most efficient encoding possible. In a file containing mostly English text, the high bytes of almost all the characters will be 0.

These 0 bytes can occupy as much as half of the file. If you're sending data across the network, Unicode data can take twice as long.

A more efficient encoding can be achieved for files that are composed primarily of ASCII text by encoding the more common characters in fewer bytes. UTF-8 is one such format that encodes the non-null ASCII characters in a single byte, characters between 128 and 2047 and ASCII null in two bytes, and the remaining characters in three bytes. While theoretically this encoding might expand a file's size by 50%, because most text files contain primarily ASCII, in practice it's almost always a huge savings. Therefore, Java uses UTF-8 in string literals, identifiers, and other text data in compiled byte code. UTF-8 is also a common encoding for XML files and the native encoding of Bell Labs' experimental Plan 9 operating system.

To better understand UTF-8, consider a typical Unicode character as a sequence of 16 bits:

x15	x14	x13	x12	x11	x10	x9	x8
x7	x6	x5	x4	x3	x2	x1	x0

Each ASCII character except the null character (each character between 1 and 127) has its upper nine bits equal to 0:

0	0	0	0	0	0	0	0
0	x6	x5	x4	x3	x2	x1	x0

Therefore, it's easy to encode an ASCII character as a single byte. Just drop the high-order byte:

0	x6	x5	x4	x3	x2	x1	x0

Now consider characters between 128 and 2047. These all have their top five bits equal to 0, as shown here:

0	0	0	0	0	x10	x9	x8
x7	x6	x5	x4	x3	x2	x1	x0

These characters are encoded into two bytes, but not in the most obvious fashion. The 11 significant bits of the character are broken up:

1	1	0	x10	x9	x8	x7	x6
1	0	x5	x4	x3	x2	x1	x0

Neither of the bytes that make up this number begins with a 0 bit. Thus, you can distinguish between bytes that are part of a two-byte character and bytes that represent one-byte characters (which all begin with 0).

The remaining characters have values between 2048 and 65,535. Any or all of the bits in these characters may take on either value 0 or 1. Thus, they are encoded in three bytes, like this:

1	1	1	0	x15	x14	x13	x12
1	0	x11	x10	x9	x8	x7	x6
1	0	x5	x4	x3	x2	x1	x0

Within this scheme, any byte beginning with a 0 bit must be a single-byte ASCII character between 1 and 127. Any byte beginning with the three bits 110 must be the first byte of a two-byte character. Any byte beginning with the four bits 1110 must be the first byte of a three-byte character. Finally, any byte beginning with the two bits 10 must be the second or third byte of a multibyte character.

The `DataOutputStream` class provides a `writeUTF()` method that encodes a string into UTF-8 format. It first writes the number of encoded bytes in the string (as an unsigned `short`) followed by the UTF-8 encoded format of the string onto the underlying output stream:

```
public final void writeUTF(String s) throws IOException
```

The `DataInputStream` class provides two corresponding `readUTF()` methods to read a UTF-8 encoded string from its underlying input stream:

```
public final String readUTF() throws IOException
public static final String readUTF(DataInput in) throws IOException
```

Each of these first reads a two-byte, unsigned `short` that tells it how many more bytes to read. These bytes are then read and decoded from UTF-8 into a Java Unicode string. An `EOFException` is thrown if the stream ends before all the expected bytes have been read. If the bytes read cannot be interpreted as a valid UTF-8 string, then a `UTFDataFormatException` is thrown.

`DataInputStream` and `DataOutputStream` actually read and write a slight modification of the official UTF-8 format. They encode the null character (0x00) in two bytes rather than one. This makes it slightly easier for C code that expects null-terminated strings to parse Java *.class* files. The `Reader` and `Writer` classes discussed in the next chapter read and write true UTF-8 with one-byte nulls.

The char Data Type

The `char` primitive data type in Java is a two-byte unsigned integer whose values range from 0 to 65,535. `char` variables may be assigned from `int` literals, like this:

```
char exclamationPoint = 33;
```

In the virtual machine, `chars` are promoted to `ints` in arithmetic operations like addition and multiplication. Therefore, operations more complicated than a simple assignment require an explicit cast to `char`, like this:

```
char a = 97;
char b = (char) (a + 1);
```

In practice, `chars` are rarely used in arithmetic operations. Instead, they're given symbolic meanings through mappings to particular elements of the Unicode character set. For instance, 33 is the Unicode (and ASCII) character for the exclamation point (!). 97 is the Unicode (and ASCII) character for the small letter a. When the Unicode and printable ASCII characters converge, as they do for values between 32 and 127, a `char` may be written in Java source code as a `char` literal. This is the desired ASCII character between single quote marks, like this:

```
char exclamationPoint = '!';
char a = 'a';
char b = 'b';
```

For characters outside this range, you can assign values to `chars` using Unicode escape sequences, like this:

```
char tab = '\u0009';
char softHyphen = '\u00AD';
char sigma = '\u03C3';
char squareKeesu = '\u30B9';
```

The java.lang.Character Class

As for the other primitive data types, the core API includes a type wrapper class for `char` values. This is `java.lang.Character`:

```
public final class Character implements Serializable
```

In Java 2 `Character` also implements `Comparable`:

```
public final class Character implements Serializable, Comparable // Java 2
```

Constructor

This class has a single constructor:

```
public Character(char value)
```

For example:

```
Character g = new Character('g');
Character ya = new Character('\u0BAF');
```

Instance methods

There aren't many instance methods in this class. charValue() returns the char primitive that this object wraps:

```
public char charValue()
```

There's also the usual trio of hashCode(), equals(), and toString() methods:

```
public int hashCode()
public boolean equals(Object obj)
public String toString()
```

The equals() method returns true if the compared object is a Character object wrapping the same primitive char value. The hashCode() method returns the primitive value of this object cast to an int. The toString() method returns a length 1 string containing the character that this object wraps. In Java 2 you have two methods to implement the Comparable interface:

```
public int compareTo(Character c) // Java 2
public int compareTo(Object o)    // Java 2
```

The comparison is performed numerically. Both methods return −1 if the lefthand side of compareTo() is less than the argument, 0 if they're the same, and a positive number if the lefthand side is greater than the argument. The second variant throws a ClassCastException if its argument is not an instance of java.lang.Character.

That's pretty much all there is to say about the instance methods in the java.lang.Character class. The only real purpose of Character objects is to wrap char values for the Reflection API and other places where primitive data types must be embedded in objects. However, this class has some interesting static utility methods.

Character types

Unicode defines 29 mutually exclusive categories or types of Unicode characters. The Character class associates mnemonic byte constants with each of these types. The type of a character is returned by the static getType() method:

```
public static int getType(char ch)
```

The possible types are:

```
public static final byte UNASSIGNED = 0;
public static final byte UPPERCASE_LETTER = 1;
public static final byte LOWERCASE_LETTER = 2;
public static final byte TITLECASE_LETTER = 3;
public static final byte MODIFIER_LETTER  = 4;
public static final byte OTHER_LETTER = 5;
```

```
public static final byte NON_SPACING_MARK = 6;
public static final byte ENCLOSING_MARK = 7;
public static final byte COMBINING_SPACING_MARK = 8;
public static final byte DECIMAL_DIGIT_NUMBER = 9;
public static final byte LETTER_NUMBER = 10;
public static final byte OTHER_NUMBER = 11;
public static final byte SPACE_SEPARATOR = 12;
public static final byte LINE_SEPARATOR = 13;
public static final byte PARAGRAPH_SEPARATOR = 14;
public static final byte CONTROL = 15;
public static final byte FORMAT = 16;
public static final byte PRIVATE_USE = 18;
public static final byte SURROGATE = 19;
public static final byte DASH_PUNCTUATION = 20;
public static final byte START_PUNCTUATION = 21;
public static final byte END_PUNCTUATION = 22;
public static final byte CONNECTOR_PUNCTUATION = 23;
public static final byte OTHER_PUNCTUATION = 24;
public static final byte MATH_SYMBOL = 25;
public static final byte CURRENCY_SYMBOL = 26;
public static final byte MODIFIER_SYMBOL = 27;
public static final byte OTHER_SYMBOL = 28;
```

Every defined Unicode character is exactly one of these types. The isDefined()
method returns true if the specified character is a valid Unicode character.
Although Unicode has space for more than 65,000 different characters, only a few
more than 38,000 are currently defined. The rest are reserved for expansion or
private use.

```
public static boolean isDefined(char c)
```

Unlike ASCII, Unicode does not suggest an easy algorithm for testing facts about
particular characters, such as whether the character is upper- or lowercase or
whether it's a digit. The following test determines whether an ASCII character is
upper- or lowercase:

```
public static boolean isUpper(char c) {
  return char >= 'A' && char <= 'Z';
}
```

This test fails for the full Unicode character set, because uppercase characters are
spread throughout the full range. It gives incorrect results for Ð, Ý, Á, Œ, and
many other uppercase characters from non-ASCII character sets. A true test for
whether or not a Unicode character is uppercase must take into account all the
different scripts Unicode encompasses. Needless to say, this is a daunting
proposition.

Fortunately, the Character class provides a number of static utility methods for
determining precisely this sort of information about Unicode characters. The

isLetter() method returns true if the specified character is a letter in one of the scripts Unicode supports; Chinese and Japanese ideographs are generally considered letters:

```
public static boolean isLetter(char c)
```

Letters are divided into uppercase, lowercase, title case, modifiers, and "other." Lowercase includes letters like a, b, c, d, e, ä, ð, ğ, æ, and so on. Uppercase includes letters like A, B, C, D, E, Ä, Đ, Ğ, Æ, etc. For almost all characters, upper case and title case are the same. For instance, an uppercase "a" is "A." A title case "a" is also "A." However, there are four exceptions. Unicode characters 453, 456, 459, and 498 are all single characters that appear as two Latin letters. In uppercase they are DŽ, LJ, NJ, and DZ. In lowercase they are dž, lj, nj, and dz. In title case they are Dž, Lj, Nj, and Dz. The isUpperCase() method returns true if the specified character is defined as uppercase; isLowerCase() returns true if the specified character is defined as lowercase; and isTitleCase() returns true if the specified character is defined as title case by the Unicode specification.

```
public static boolean isLowerCase(char c)
public static boolean isUpperCase(char c)
public static boolean isTitleCase(char c)
```

Many characters are neither uppercase nor lowercase. For instance, both Character.isLowerCase('7') and Character.isUpperCase('7') return false. The Devanagari script used for Hindi, Sanskrit, and some other languages of the Indian subcontinent does not have upper- and lowercases. The toUpperCase(), toLowerCase(), and toTitleCase() methods return the upper-, lower-, and title case equivalents of the specified character:

```
public static char toLowerCase(char c)
public static char toUpperCase(char c)
public static char toTitleCase(char c)
```

For example:

```
character upperA = Character.toUpperCase('a');
```

Not all letters and certainly not all characters have upper-, lower-, or title case equivalents. If the specified character does not have an upper-, lower-, or title case equivalent, then the unmodified character itself is returned.

The isDigit() method returns true if its argument is a digit in any character set. This includes not just the usual ASCII digits 0 through 9 but digits from Arabic, Devanagari, Bengali, Gurmukhi, Gujarati, Oriya, Tamil, Telugu, Kannada, Lao, Malayalam, Thai, and Tibetan.

```
public static boolean isDigit(char ch)
```

The `isLetterOrDigit()` method returns `true` if the specified character is either a Unicode letter or a Unicode digit as determined by the `isLetter()` and `isDigit()` methods:

```
public static boolean isLetterOrDigit(char c)
```

The `isSpaceChar()` method returns `true` if Unicode defines the specified character as a space character:

```
public static boolean isSpaceChar(char c)
```

Space characters include ASCII spaces (32) but do not include some characters you might expect, like carriage returns, tabs, or linefeeds.

The `isWhitespace()` method returns `true` if a character is a Unicode space separator character other than a nonbreaking space (160 and 65,279). It also returns `true` if the specified character is a line separator, a paragraph separator, a horizontal tab (\t, ASCII 9), a vertical tab (ASCII 11), a formfeed (ASCII 12), a carriage return (\r, ASCII 13), a linefeed (\n, ASCII 10), a file separator (ASCII 28), a group separator (ASCII 29), a record separator (ASCII 30), or a unit separator (ASCII 31).

```
public static boolean isWhitespace(char ch)
```

The `isSpace()` method is a less accurate version of `isWhitespace()` held over from Java 1.0. It returns `true` if its argument is a carriage return, linefeed, horizontal tab, formfeed, or ASCII space. Otherwise, it returns `false`. It's deprecated and should not be used in new code.

```
public static boolean isSpace(char c)
```

The `isISOControl()` method returns `true` if the specified character is an ISO Latin-1 control character; in other words, if it's in the range 0 to 31 or 127 to 159.

```
public static boolean isISOControl(char c)
```

Identifiers

Until Java, most programming languages were explicitly based on ASCII. Identifiers—e.g., variable names, class names, method names, and so forth—were defined as being composed of some particular subset of these characters, generally allowing alphanumeric characters and some punctuation marks like the underscore but excluding the rest of ASCII. Furthermore, some languages distinguish between characters allowed in the middle of an identifier and characters that may start an identifier.

The Unicode standard makes some suggestions for which Unicode characters should be allowed in programming language identifiers. Generally, all the alphanumeric characters from any script as well as certain joining characters and bidirectional indicators are allowed in identifiers, while most other characters are not. However, programming language designers are free to accept or reject the Unicode standard's suggestions in these matters. `Character.isUnicodeIdentifierStart()` returns `true` if the specified character may be the first character of an identifier; that is, if it is a Unicode letter. `Character.isUnicodeIdentifierPart()` returns `true` if the specified character may be part of the interior of a Unicode identifier; that is, the specified character is a letter, a digit, a numeric letter like a Roman numeral, a combining mark, an underscore, a nonspacing mark, or an ignorable control character.

```
public static boolean isUnicodeIdentifierStart(char c)
public static boolean isUnicodeIdentifierPart(char c)
```

Java's identifier syntax is not exactly the same as the Unicode identifier syntax, though they are similar; the Java identifier characters are a superset of the Unicode identifier characters. As well as the Unicode identifier characters, Java identifiers include currency symbols ($, £, ¢, ¥, ¤, the Bengali rupee sign, the Thai currency symbol baht, the EC sign, the colon sign, the cruzeiro sign, the French franc sign, the lira sign, the mill sign, the naira sign, the peseta sign, the Indian rupee sign, the won sign, the new shekel sign, the dong sign, etc.). Java start identifiers also include the connecting punctuation characters underscore, undertie, character tie, and a few similar characters that may be included in the interior of a Unicode identifier but may not start it.

The `isJavaIdentifierStart()` method returns `true` if the specified character is a valid beginning of an identifier in Java source code; that is, if it's a letter as determined by `isLetter()`, or if it's a currency indicator like $ or £, or if it's a connecting punctuation character like the underscore (_).

```
public static boolean isJavaIdentifierStart(char c)
```

This method might be used by Java compilers and similar tools.

The `isJavaIdentifierPart()` method is similar but also returns `true` if the specified character is a digit in any of Unicode's supported scripts. Digits are legal parts of Java identifiers but may not begin an identifier.

```
public static boolean isJavaIdentifierPart(char c)
```

Numeric letters like Roman numerals, combining marks, nonspacing marks, and ignorable control characters are also allowed in Java identifiers as long as they aren't the first characters of the identifier. `isJavaIdentifierStart()` and `isJavaIdentifierPart()` are new in Java 1.1. Java 1.0 had identical methods, now deprecated, called `isJavaLetter()` and `isJavaLetterOrDigit()`:

```
public static boolean isJavaLetter(char c)
public static boolean isJavaLetterOrDigit(char c)
```

Certain Unicode characters are classified as ignorable within the context of Unicode and Java identifiers. The name is something of a misnomer, since these characters aren't ignored. A better name would be "illegal," since they can't be used in Java or Unicode identifiers. Nonetheless, the word is ignorable; and the `isIdentifierIgnorable()` method returns `true` if the character is ignorable:

```
public static boolean isIdentifierIgnorable(char c)
```

Ignorable characters include the nonwhitespace ASCII control characters 0 through 8 and 14 through 27; the Latin-1 control characters 127 through 159; the joining characters 8024 through 8027; the bidirectional controls 8202 through 8206; the format controls 8298 through 8303; and the zero-width nonbreaking space 65,279.

Numeric values

`java.lang.Character` also has several methods for interpreting characters as numbers. The `digit()` method returns the numeric value of the character c in the specified base:

```
public static int digit(char c, int base)
```

For example, `Character.digit('A', 16)` returns 10, because in hexadecimal (base 16) the letter A is used as a digit with the value 10. This method handles bases between 2 and 36. (The latter is 10 plus the 26 letters in the Roman alphabet.) These limits are available in the mnemonic constants `Character.MIN_RADIX` and `Character.MAX_RADIX` respectively:

```
public static final int MIN_RADIX = 2;
public static final int MAX_RADIX = 36;
```

This method works for digit characters in any script (that is, characters for which `Character.isDigit()` returns `true`) as well as for Roman letters A–Z and a–z, as long as the base is large enough to include the specified digit. Most Unicode characters are not valid digits in any base. If such a character or a character outside the range of the base (e.g., 9 in base 8) is passed to `digit()`, `digit()` returns –1.

`forDigit()` reverses the procedure. It returns the `char` corresponding to a specified `int` in a given base.

```
public static char forDigit(int digit, int base)
```

For example, `Character.forDigit(11, 16)` returns b. If the specified `int` is not available as a character in the given base, `forDigit()` returns the null character \u0000. This is not the same thing as the null reference provided by the Java keyword `null`. The null character is also returned if the base is not inside the range `Character.MIN_RADIX` to `Character.MAX_RADIX`.

The getNumericValue() method returns the value of the specified character as a number:

```
public static int getNumericValue(char c)
```

For example, Character.getNumericValue('4') has the value 4. Unlike the digit() method, getNumericValue() does not work in bases other than 10. However, it interprets characters like \u217F, the Roman numeral for 1000, properly. If the specified character does not have a numeric value, getNumericValue() returns –1. If the character has a numeric value that cannot be represented as a nonnegative integer, getNumericValue() returns –2. For example, Unicode character 189 is the fraction 1⁄2. Thus, Character.getNumericValue('\u00BD') returns –2.

Character subsets

In Java 2, java.lang.Character contains two unusual public static inner classes, Subset and UnicodeBlock:

```
public static class Character.Subset extends Object
public static class Character.UnicodeBlock extends Character.Subset
```

Each character subset represents a particular block of the complete Unicode character set. This class has a single protected constructor:

```
protected Character.Subset(String name)
```

The only methods in the Character.Subset class are the standard utility methods equals(), hashCode(), and toString():

```
public final boolean equals(Object o)
public final int hashCode()
public final String toString()
```

The most common type of character subset is a Unicode block. A Unicode block is a character subset that maps onto one of the blocks defined by the Unicode consortium for the characters in a particular script. Several more character subsets are defined in the java.awt.im.InputSubset class for use with input methods for various languages.

Unicode blocks

You don't create instances of the Character.UnicodeBlock class directly. Instead, the Character class preforms several dozen subsets:

```
Character.UnicodeBlock.BASIC_LATIN
Character.UnicodeBlock.LATIN_1_SUPPLEMENT
Character.UnicodeBlock.LATIN_EXTENDED_A
Character.UnicodeBlock.LATIN_EXTENDED_B
```

```
Character.UnicodeBlock.IPA_EXTENSIONS
Character.UnicodeBlock.SPACING_MODIFIER_LETTERS
Character.UnicodeBlock.COMBINING_DIACRITICAL_MARKS
Character.UnicodeBlock.GREEK
Character.UnicodeBlock.CYRILLIC
Character.UnicodeBlock.ARMENIAN
Character.UnicodeBlock.HEBREW
Character.UnicodeBlock.ARABIC
Character.UnicodeBlock.DEVANAGARI
Character.UnicodeBlock.BENGALI
Character.UnicodeBlock.GURMUKHI
Character.UnicodeBlock.GUJARATI
Character.UnicodeBlock.ORIYA
Character.UnicodeBlock.TAMIL
Character.UnicodeBlock.TELUGU
Character.UnicodeBlock.KANNADA
Character.UnicodeBlock.MALAYALAM
Character.UnicodeBlock.THAI
Character.UnicodeBlock.LAO
Character.UnicodeBlock.TIBETAN
Character.UnicodeBlock.GEORGIAN
Character.UnicodeBlock.HANGUL_JAMO
Character.UnicodeBlock.LATIN_EXTENDED_ADDITIONAL
Character.UnicodeBlock.GREEK_EXTENDED
Character.UnicodeBlock.GENERAL_PUNCTUATION
Character.UnicodeBlock.SUPERSCRIPTS_AND_SUBSCRIPTS
Character.UnicodeBlock.CURRENCY_SYMBOLS
Character.UnicodeBlock.COMBINING_MARKS_FOR_SYMBOLS
Character.UnicodeBlock.LETTERLIKE_SYMBOLS
Character.UnicodeBlock.NUMBER_FORMS
Character.UnicodeBlock.ARROWS
Character.UnicodeBlock.MATHEMATICAL_OPERATORS
Character.UnicodeBlock.MISCELLANEOUS_TECHNICAL
Character.UnicodeBlock.CONTROL_PICTURES
Character.UnicodeBlock.OPTICAL_CHARACTER_RECOGNITION
Character.UnicodeBlock.ENCLOSED_ALPHANUMERICS
Character.UnicodeBlock.BOX_DRAWING
Character.UnicodeBlock.BLOCK_ELEMENTS
Character.UnicodeBlock.GEOMETRIC_SHAPES
Character.UnicodeBlock.MISCELLANEOUS_SYMBOLS
Character.UnicodeBlock.DINGBATS
Character.UnicodeBlock.CJK_SYMBOLS_AND_PUNCTUATION
Character.UnicodeBlock.HIRAGANA
Character.UnicodeBlock.KATAKANA
Character.UnicodeBlock.BOPOMOFO
Character.UnicodeBlock.HANGUL_COMPATIBILITY_JAMO
Character.UnicodeBlock.KANBUN
Character.UnicodeBlock.ENCLOSED_CJK_LETTERS_AND_MONTHS
Character.UnicodeBlock.CJK_COMPATIBILITY
```

```
Character.UnicodeBlock.CJK_UNIFIED_IDEOGRAPHS
Character.UnicodeBlock.HANGUL_SYLLABLES
Character.UnicodeBlock.SURROGATES_AREA
Character.UnicodeBlock.PRIVATE_USE_AREA
Character.UnicodeBlock.CJK_COMPATIBILITY_IDEOGRAPHS
Character.UnicodeBlock.ALPHABETIC_PRESENTATION_FORMS
Character.UnicodeBlock.ARABIC_PRESENTATION_FORMS_A
Character.UnicodeBlock.COMBINING_HALF_MARKS
Character.UnicodeBlock.CJK_COMPATIBILITY_FORMS
Character.UnicodeBlock.SMALL_FORM_VARIANTS
Character.UnicodeBlock.ARABIC_PRESENTATION_FORMS_B
Character.UnicodeBlock.HALFWIDTH_AND_FULLWIDTH_FORMS
Character.UnicodeBlock.SPECIALS
Character.UnicodeBlock.LATIN
Character.UnicodeBlock.LATIN_DIGITS
Character.UnicodeBlock.TRADITIONAL_HANZI
Character.UnicodeBlock.SIMPLIFIED_HANZI
Character.UnicodeBlock.KANJI
Character.UnicodeBlock.HANJA
Character.UnicodeBlock.HALFWIDTH_KATAKANA
```

You can find out to which block a particular character belongs with the static `Character.UnicodeBlock.of()` method:

```
public static Character.UnicodeBlock of(char c)
```

This returns one of the named constants in the previous list or `null` if the character doesn't belong to any of those blocks.

Other Encodings

Although Unicode is the most advanced and comprehensive character set yet designed on this planet, it has not taken the world by storm. Compared to the vast quantities of ASCII data, there are virtually no Unicode files on today's computers. Although Unicode support is growing, there will doubtless be legacy data in other encodings that must be read for centuries to come. A lot of it is in the Unicode subsets ASCII and ISO Latin-1, but a lot of it is also in less popular encoding schemes like EBCDIC and MacRoman. Those only cover English and a few Western European languages. There are multiple encodings in use for Arabic, Turkish, Hebrew, Greek, Cyrillic, Chinese, Japanese, Korean, and many other languages and scripts. The `Reader` and `Writer` classes (discussed in the next chapter) allow you to read and write data in these different character sets. The `String` class also has a number of methods that convert between different encodings (though a `String` object itself is always represented in Unicode). Furthermore, the JDK includes a character mode tool based on these classes called *native2ascii* that performs such conversions on existing files.

The name *native2ascii* is a misnomer. Rather than converting to ASCII, it converts to ISO Latin-1 with Unicode characters embedded with Unicode escape sequences like \u020F. It can also work in reverse, converting an ISO Latin-1 file with embedded Unicode to a native character set. For example, to copy the contents of the file *macdata.txt* from the MacRoman encoding into a new file called *isodata.txt* encoded with ISO Latin-1 with Unicode escapes, you would type:

```
% native2ascii -encoding MacRoman macdata.txt isodata.txt
```

You can convert it back with the -reverse option:

```
% native2ascii -encoding MacRoman -reverse isodata.txt macdata.txt
```

If you don't specify a particular encoding, *native2ascii* makes its best guess as to the platform's native encoding. This best guess is read from the system property file.encoding. On American Macs, the default is MacRoman. On American Solaris, the default is 8859_1 (ISO Latin-1). On American Windows, the default is also 8859_1. However, you shouldn't rely on these values. Instead, check the property directly. Systems configured for other countries are likely to have different default encodings. Table B-4 lists the many encodings that Java, *javac*, and *native2ascii* understand. As extensive as this list is, there are a few missing pieces. In particular, ISO 8859-10, a.k.a. Latin-6, includes ASCII plus various characters used for Lappish, Nordic, and Inuit languages in the upper 128 places. Java cannot currently convert characters in this set to Unicode.

Work is continuing on both Unicode and other character sets. ISO 8859-11 will provide a standard encoding for Thai. ISO 8859-12, also known as Latin-7, will use the upper 128 characters past ASCII for Celtic. ISO 8859-13, also known as Latin-8, will use them for the Baltic Rim languages. ISO 8859-14, also known as Latin-9, will encode ASCII plus Sami. Eventually, converters will be needed for these encodings as well.

Converting Between Byte Arrays and Strings

The java.lang.String class has several constructors that form strings from byte arrays and several methods that return a byte array corresponding to a given string. Anytime a Unicode string is converted to bytes or vice versa, that conversion happens according to one of the encodings listed in Table B-4. The same string can produce different byte arrays if different encodings are used. Six constructors form a new String object from a byte array:

```
public String(byte[] ascii, int highByte)
public String(byte[] ascii, int highByte, int offset, int length)
public String(byte[] data, String encoding)
```

```
  throws UnsupportedEncodingException
public String(byte[] data, int offset, int length, String encoding)
  throws UnsupportedEncodingException
public String(byte[] data)
public String(byte[] data, int offset, int length)
```

The first two constructors, the ones with the highByte argument, are leftovers from Java 1.0 that are deprecated in Java 1.1. These two constructors do not accurately translate non-Latin-1 character sets into Unicode. Instead, they read each byte in the ascii array as the low-order byte of a two-byte character, then fill in the high-order byte with the highByte argument. For example:

```
byte[] isoLatin1 = new byte[256];
for (int i = 0; i < 256; i++) isoLatin1[i] = (byte) i;
String s = new String(isoLatin1, 0);
```

Frankly, this is a kludge; it's deprecated for good reason. This scheme works quite well for Latin-1 data with a high byte of 0. However, it's extremely difficult to use for character sets where different characters need to have different high bytes, and it's completely unworkable for character sets like MacRoman that also need to adjust bits in the low-order byte to conform to Unicode. The only approach that genuinely works for the broad range of character sets Java programs may be asked to handle is table lookup. Each character set in Table B-4 is associated with a table mapping characters in the set to Unicode characters. These tables are hidden inside the sun.io package, but they are present; and they are how the next four constructors translate from various encodings to Unicode.

The third and fourth constructors allow the client programmer to specify not only the byte data but also the encoding table to be used when converting these bytes to Unicode chars. The third constructor converts the entire array from the specified encoding into Unicode. The fourth one only converts the specified subarray of data starting at offset and continuing for length bytes. Otherwise, they're identical. The first argument is the data to be converted. The final argument is the encoding scheme used to perform the conversion. For example:

```
byte[] isoLatin1 = new byte[256];
for (int i = 0; i < 256; i++) isoLatin1[i] = (byte) i;
String s = new String(isoLatin1, "8859_1");
```

The fifth and sixth constructors are similar to the third and fourth. However, they always use the host platform's default encoding as specified by the system property file.encoding. If this is ISO 8859-1, then you may write:

```
byte[] isoLatin1 = new byte[256];
for (int i = 0; i < 256; i++) isoLatin1[i] = (byte) i;
String s = new String(isoLatin1);
```

This code fragment produces different results on a platform with a different default encoding.

Three instance methods go the other direction, converting the Unicode string into an array of bytes in a particular non-Unicode encoding:

```
public void getBytes(int srcBegin, int srcEnd, byte[] dst, int dstBegin)
public byte[] getBytes()
public byte[] getBytes(String encoding) throws UnsupportedEncodingException
```

Once again, the first method is deprecated. The byte array it returns only contains the low-order bytes of the two-byte characters in the string (starting at `srcBegin` and continuing through `srcEnd`). This works well enough for ASCII and ISO Latin-1 but fails miserably for pretty much all other character sets. The no-argument `getBytes()` method properly converts the Unicode characters in the string into a byte array in the platform's default encoding—assuming a full conversion is possible (and it isn't always; you cannot, for example, convert a string of Chinese ideographs into ISO Latin-1). The byte array returned contains the converted characters. The third and final `getBytes()` method specifies the encoding to be used to make the conversion. For example:

```
String openingLineInUnicode =
  "\u03B1\u03BD\u03B4\u03C1\u03B1 \u03BC\u03BF\u03B9 " +
  "\u03B5\u03BD\u03BD\u03B5\u03C0\u03B5, " +
  "\u03BC\u03BF\u03C5\u03C3\u03B1, " +
  "\u03C0\u03BF\u03BB\u03C5\u03C4\u03C1\u03BF\u03C0\u03BF\u03BD," +
  "\u03B7\u03BF\u03C2 \u03BC\u03B1\u03BB\u03B1\u03C0\u03BF\u03BB\u03BB\u03B1";
byte[] openingLineInMacGreek = openingLineInUnicode.getBytes("MacGreek");
```

This method throws an `UnsupportedEncodingException` if the requested encoding is not understood by the Java virtual machine.

15

Readers and Writers

In this chapter:
- *The java.io.Writer Class*
- *The OutputStream-Writer Class*
- *The java.io.Reader Class*
- *The InputStream-Reader Class*
- *Character Array Readers and Writers*
- *String Readers and Writers*
- *Reading and Writing Files*
- *Print Writers*
- *Filtered Readers and Writers*
- *File Viewer Finis*

A language that supports international text must separate the reading and writing of raw bytes from the reading and writing of characters, since in an international system they are no longer the same thing. Classes that read characters must be able to parse a variety of character encodings, not just ASCII, and translate them into the language's native character set. Classes that write characters must be able to translate the language's native character set into a variety of formats and write those. In Java this task is performed by the Reader and Writer classes.

You're probably going to experience a little *déjà vu*. The java.io.Writer class is modeled on the java.io.OutputStream class. The java.io.Reader class is modeled on the java.io.InputStream class. The names and signatures of the members of the Reader and Writer classes are similar (sometimes identical) to the names and signatures of the members of the InputStream and Output-Stream classes. The patterns these classes follow are similar as well. Filtered input and output streams are chained to other streams in their constructors. Similarly, filtered readers and writers are chained to other readers and writers in their constructors. InputStream and OutputStream are abstract superclasses that identify common functionality in the concrete subclasses. Likewise, Reader and Writer are abstract superclasses that identify common functionality in the concrete subclasses. The difference between readers and writers and input and output streams is that streams are fundamentally byte based, while readers and writers are fundamentally character based. Where an input stream reads a byte, a reader reads a character; where an output stream writes a byte, a writer writes a character.

While bytes are a more or less universal concept, characters are not. As you learned in the last chapter, the same character can be encoded differently in different character sets. Different character sets encode different characters. Characters can even have different widths in different character sets. For example, ASCII and ISO Latin-1 use one-byte characters. Unicode uses two-byte characters. UTF-8 uses characters of varying width between one and three bytes. Concrete subclasses of the Reader and Writer classes convert between different character sets and Java's internal Unicode character set

The java.io.Writer Class

The Writer class is abstract, just like OutputStream is abstract. You won't have any pure instances of Writer that are not also instances of some concrete subclass of Writer. However, many of the subclasses of Writer differ primarily in the targets of the text they write, just as many concrete subclasses of OutputStream differ only in the targets of the data they write. Most of the time you don't care about the difference between FileOutputStream and ByteArrayOutputStream. Similarly, most of the time you won't care about the differences between FileWriter and StringWriter. You'll just use the methods of the common superclass, java.io.Writer.

You use a writer almost exactly as you use an output stream. Rather than writing bytes, you write chars. The write() method writes a subarray from the char array text starting at offset and continuing for length characters:

```
public abstract void write(char[] text, int offset, int length)
    throws IOException
```

For example, given some Writer object w, you can write the string Testing 1-2-3 like this:

```
char[] test = {'T', 'e', 's', 't', 'i', 'n', 'g', ' ',
               '1', '-', '2', '-', '3'};
w.write(test, 0, test.length);
```

This method is abstract. Concrete subclasses that convert chars into bytes according to a specified encoding and write those bytes onto an underlying stream must override this method. An IOException may be thrown if the underlying stream's `write()` method throws an `IOException`. You can also write a single character, an entire array of characters, a string, or a substring:

```
public void write(int c) throws IOException
public void write(char[] text) throws IOException
public void write(String s) throws IOException
public void write(String s, int offset, int length) throws IOException
```

The default implementations of these four methods convert their first argument into an array of `chars` and pass that to `write(char[] text, int offset, int length)`. Specific subclasses may provide more efficient implementations of these methods.

NOTE   This is one of the few instances where the general structure of the `Writer` and the `OutputStream` classes diverge, though not in a very significant way. In `OutputStream` the fundamental, abstract method that must be overridden by subclasses is the `write()` method that writes a single byte. `OutputStream`'s multibyte `write()` methods are implemented in terms of the single-byte `write()` method, whereas `Writer`'s single-character `write()` method is implemented in terms of a multicharacter `write()` method.

Like output streams, writers may be buffered, precisely because their underlying output stream is buffered. To force the write to take place, call `flush()`:

```
public abstract void flush() throws IOException
```

The `close()` method closes the writer and releases any resources associated with it:

```
public abstract void close() throws IOException
```

This flushes the writer, then closes the underlying output stream.

The OutputStreamWriter Class

`java.io.Writer` is an abstract class. Its most basic concrete subclass is `OutputStreamWriter`:

```
public class OutputStreamWriter extends Writer
```

Its constructor connects a character writer to an underlying output stream:

```
public OutputStreamWriter(OutputStream out)
public OutputStreamWriter(OutputStream out, String encoding) throws
  UnsupportedEncodingException
```

The first constructor assumes that the text in the stream is to be written using the platform's default encoding. The second constructor specifies an encoding. There's no easy way to determine which encodings are supported, but the ones listed in Table B-4 in Appendix B, *Character Sets*, are supported by most VMs. For example, this code attaches an OutputStreamWriter to System.out with the default encoding:

```
OutputStreamWriter osw = new OutputStreamWriter(System.out);
```

The default encoding is normally ISO Latin-1, except on Macs, where it is MacRoman. Whatever it is, you can find it in the system property file.encoding:

```
String defaultEncoding = System.getProperty("file.encoding");
```

On the other hand, if you want to write a file encoded in ISO 8859-7 (ASCII plus Greek) you might do this:

```
FileOutputStream fos = new FileOutputStream("greek.txt");
OutputStreamWriter greekWriter = new OutputStreamWriter(fos, "8859_7");
```

The write() methods convert characters to bytes according to a specified character encoding and write those bytes onto the underlying output stream:

```
public void write(int c) throws IOException
public void write(char[] text, int offset, int length) throws IOException
public void write(String s, int offset, int length) throws IOException
```

Once the Writer is constructed, writing the characters is easy. For example:

```
String  arete = "\u03B1\u03C1\u03B5\u03C4\u03B7";
greekWriter.write(arete, 0, arete.length());
```

The String variable arete is the Unicode-escaped encoding of αρετη, the Greek word for excellence. The second line writes this word in the ISO 8859-7 character set. In this encoding, these five Unicode characters (10 bytes) become the five bytes 225, 241, 229, 244, 231, which encode the word αρετη in ISO 8859-7. You don't have to worry about exactly how this conversion is performed. You just have to construct the writer, write the string, and let Java do the grunt work of figuring out which Unicode characters map to which externally encoded characters.

Unicode is a fairly large character set; most other character sets don't have all the characters in Unicode. Attempts to write characters that don't exist in a given set instead produce a substitution character, generally a question mark.

The getEncoding() method returns a string containing the name of the encoding used by this writer:

```
public String getEncoding()
```

The flush() and close() methods flush and close the underlying output stream.

```
public void flush() throws IOException
public void close() throws IOException
```

Example 15-1 loops through all 65,536 Unicode characters and writes them into the file given on the command line, using the specified character encoding. If no character encoding is specified, the platform's default encoding is used. If no file is specified, System.out is used.

Example 15-1. UnicodeTable

```
import java.io.*;

public class UnicodeTable {

  public static void main(String[] args) {

    String encoding = System.getProperty("font.encoding", "8859_1");
    String lineSeparator = System.getProperty("line.separator", "\r\n");

    OutputStream target = System.out;
    try {
      if (args.length > 0) target = new FileOutputStream(args[0]);
    }
    catch (IOException e) {System.err.println("Sending text to System.out");}
    if (args.length > 1) encoding = args[1];

    OutputStreamWriter osw = null;
    try {
      osw = new OutputStreamWriter(target, encoding);
    }
    catch (UnsupportedEncodingException e) {
      osw = new OutputStreamWriter(target);
    }

    try {
      for (int i = Character.MIN_VALUE; i < Character.MAX_VALUE; i++) {
        char c = (char) i;
        osw.write(i + ":\t" + c + lineSeparator);
      }
      osw.close();
    }
    catch (IOException e) {
      System.err.println(e);
      e.printStackTrace();
    }
  }
}
```

The java.io.Reader Class

You use a reader almost exactly as you use an input stream. Rather than reading bytes, you read characters. The basic `read()` method reads a specified number of characters from the underlying input stream into an array starting at a given offset:

```
public abstract int read(char[] buffer, int offset, int length)
  throws IOException
```

This `read()` method returns the number of characters actually read. As with input streams reading bytes, there may not be as many characters available as you requested. Also like the `read()` method of an input stream, it returns −1 when it detects the end of the data.

This `read()` method is abstract. Concrete subclasses that read bytes from some source must override this method. An `IOException` may be thrown if the underlying stream's `read()` method throws an `IOException` or an encoding error is detected.

You can also fill an array with characters using this method:

```
public int read(char[] buffer) throws IOException
```

This is equivalent to invoking `read(buffer, 0, buffer.length)`. Thus, it also returns the number of characters read and throws an `IOException` when the underlying stream throws an `IOException` or when an encoding error is detected. The following method reads a single character and returns it:

```
public int read() throws IOException
```

Although an `int` is returned, this `int` is always between 0 and 65,535 and may be cast to a `char` without losing information. All three `read()` methods block until some input is available, an I/O error occurs, or the end of the stream is reached.

You can skip a certain number of characters. This method also blocks until some characters are available. It returns the number of characters skipped or −1 if the end of stream is reached.

```
public long skip(long n) throws IOException
```

The `ready()` method returns `true` if the reader is ready to be read from, `false` if it isn't. Generally, this means the underlying stream has available data.

```
public boolean ready() throws IOException
```

This is not quite the same as `InputStream`'s `available()` method. `available()` returns an `int` specifying how many bytes are available to be read. However, it's not always possible to tell how many characters are available in a stream without actually reading them, particularly with encodings that use characters of different widths (such as UTF-8, where a character may be one, two, or three bytes).

Readers may or may not support marking and resetting, like input streams. The markSupported() method returns true if the underlying stream supports marking and resetting, false if it doesn't.

```
public boolean markSupported()
public void mark(int readAheadLimit) throws IOException
public void reset() throws IOException
```

The close() method closes the reader and its underlying input stream and releases any resources the reader held:

```
public abstract void close() throws IOException
```

The InputStreamReader Class

The most basic concrete subclass of Reader is InputStreamReader:

```
public class InputStreamReader extends Reader
```

The constructor connects a character reader to an underlying input stream:

```
public InputStreamReader(InputStream in)
public InputStreamReader(InputStream in, String encoding)
  throws UnsupportedEncodingException
```

The first constructor uses the platform's default encoding, as given by the system property file.encoding. The second one uses the specified encoding. For example, to attach an InputStreamReader to System.in with the default encoding (generally ISO Latin-1):

```
InputStreamReader isr = new InputStreamReader(System.in);
```

If you want to read a file encoded in Latin-5 (ASCII plus Turkish, as specified by ISO 8859-9), you might do this:

```
FileInputStream fin = new FileInputStream("symbol.txt");
InputStreamReader isr = new InputStreamReader(fin, "8859_9");
```

There's no easy way to determine which encodings are supported, but the ones listed in Table B-4 are supported by most VMs.

The read() methods read bytes from an underlying input stream and convert those bytes to characters according to the specified encoding:

```
public int read() throws IOException
public int read(char c[], int off, int length) throws IOException
```

The getEncoding() method returns a string containing the name of the encoding used by this reader:

```
public String getEncoding()
```

The remaining two methods just override methods from `java.io.Reader` but behave identically from the perspective of the programmer:

```
public boolean ready() throws IOException
public void close() throws IOException
```

Example 15-2 uses an `InputStreamReader` to read a file in a user-specified encoding. The `FileConverter` reads the name of the input file, the name of the of the output file, the input encoding, and the output encoding. Characters that are not available in the output character set are replaced by the substitution character, generally the question mark.

Example 15-2. CharacterSetConverter

```java
import java.io.*;

public class CharacterSetConverter {

  public static void main(String[] args) {

    if (args.length < 2) {
      System.err.println(
        "Usage: java CharacterSetConverter "
        + "infile_encoding outfile_encoding infile outfile");
      return;
    }

    try {
      File infile = new File(args[2]);
      File outfile = new File(args[3]);

      if (infile.getCanonicalPath().equals(outfile.getCanonicalPath())) {
        System.err.println("Can't convert file in place");
        return;
      }

      FileInputStream fin = new FileInputStream(infile);
      FileOutputStream fout = new FileOutputStream(outfile);
      InputStreamReader isr = new InputStreamReader(fin, args[0]);
      OutputStreamWriter osw = new OutputStreamWriter(fout, args[1]);

      while (true) {
        int c = isr.read();
        if (c == -1) break;  // end of stream
        osw.write(c);
      }
      osw.close();
      isr.close();
    }
```

Example 15-2. CharacterSetConverter (continued)

```
   catch (IOException e) {System.err.println(e);}
  }
}
```

Since this is just a simple example, I haven't put a lot of effort into the user interface. A more realistic command-line interface would provide a set of flags and sensible defaults. Even better would be a graphical user interface. I'll demonstrate that at the end of the chapter, when we return to the file viewer program.

Character Array Readers and Writers

The `java.io.ByteArrayInputStream` and `java.io.ByteArrayOutputStream` classes let programmers use stream methods to read and write arrays of bytes. The `java.io.CharArrayReader` and `java.io.CharArrayWriter` classes allow programmers to use `Reader` and `Writer` methods to read and write arrays of `char`s. Since `char` arrays are purely internal to Java and thus composed of true Unicode characters, this is one of the few uses of readers and writers where you don't need to concern yourself with conversions between different encodings. If you want to read arrays of text encoded in some non-Unicode encoding, you should chain a `ByteArrayInputStream` to an `InputStreamReader` instead. Similarly, to write text into a byte array in a non-Unicode encoding, just chain an `OutputStreamWriter` to a `ByteArrayOutputStream`.

The CharArrayWriter Class

The `CharArrayWriter` maintains an internal array of `char`s into which successive characters are written. The array is expanded as needed. This array is stored in a protected field called `buf`:

```
   protected char[] buf
```

For efficiency, the array generally contains more components than characters. The number of characters actually written is stored in a protected `int` field called `count`:

```
   protected int count
```

The value of the `count` field is always less than or equal to `buf.length`.

The no-argument constructor creates a `CharArrayWriter` object with a 32-character buffer. This is on the small side, so you can expand it with the second constructor:

```
   public CharArrayWriter()
   public CharArrayWriter(int initialSize)
```

The `write()` methods write their characters into the buffer. If there's insufficient space in `buf` to hold the characters, its size is doubled.*

```
public void write(int c)
public void write(char[] text, int offset, int length)
public void write(String s, int offset, int length)
```

There is a `flush()` method, but it doesn't do anything, as `CharArrayWriters` operate completely internally to Java and don't require flushing:

```
public void flush()
```

The `close()` method prevents further writes from taking place. Attempts to write to a `CharArrayWriter` after it's been closed throw `IOExceptions`.

```
public void close()
```

However, even after the writer is closed, its buffer may be read in one of several ways. The `writeTo()` method copies the text in the buffer onto another `Writer` object:

```
public void writeTo(Writer out) throws IOException
```

The `toCharArray()` method returns a copy of the text in the buffer:

```
public char[] toCharArray()
```

Changes to the copy do not affect the `CharArrayWriter`'s internal data and vice versa.

The `toString()` method returns a string initialized from the characters stored in the buffer:

```
public String toString()
```

The `size()` method returns the number of characters currently stored in the buffer (i.e., the value of `count`):

```
public int size()
```

Finally, the `reset()` method sets `count` back to 0, effectively emptying the buffer. However, it may still be used for new data written to the `CharArrayWriter`:

```
public void reset()
```

For example, the following code fragment fills a `char` array with the complete Unicode character set:

```
CharArrayWriter caw = new CharArrayWriter(65536);
for (int i = 0; i < 65536; i++) {
```

---

* In other words, a new array is created of twice the length; the old text is copied into the new array; and the `buf` field is then set to the new array. This is the same scheme used for growable arrays by the `java.util.Vector` class.

```
    caw.write(i);
}
caw.close();
char[] unicode = caw.toCharArray();
```

The CharArrayReader Class

A `CharArrayReader` uses an array of `char`s as the underlying source of text to be read. It is one of the few readers that does not have an underlying input stream; it has an underlying `char` array instead. This array is set in the constructor. Either an entire array may be used or a specified subarray beginning at `offset` and continuing for `length` characters:

```
public CharArrayReader(char[] text)
public CharArrayReader(char[] text, int offset, int length)
```

The `CharArrayReader` class stores a reference to the `text` array in a protected field called `buf[]`. A separate copy is not made. Thus, if the array is changed by another thread while the reader is being read, synchronization problems can occur. The reader also stores the current position in the array (the index of the next array component that will be returned by `read()`), the number of `char`s in the array, and the current mark, if any.

```
protected char buf[]
protected int pos
protected int count
protected int markedPos
```

The `read()` methods read text from the `buf` array, updating the `pos` field as they do so:

```
public int read() throws IOException
public int read(char[] buffer, int offset, int length) throws IOException
```

These methods behave like any other reader's `read()` methods. If the end of the array is reached, they return –1.

The `skip()` method skips `char`s in the `buf` array by advancing `pos` without actually returning any characters:

```
public long skip(long n) throws IOException
```

The `ready()` method returns `true` if `pos` is less than `count`; that is, if any unread characters remain in the array:

```
public boolean ready() throws IOException
```

`CharArrayReader`s support marking and resetting to the limit of the length of the array. `markSupported()` returns `true`. `mark()` marks the current position in the stream by setting `markedPos` equal to `pos`. The `readAheadLimit` argument is for compatibility; its value is ignored. The `reset()` method sets `pos` equal to `markedPos`.

```
public boolean markSupported()
public void mark(int readAheadLimit) throws IOException
public void reset() throws IOException
```

Finally, the `close()` method sets `buf` to `null`. Attempts to read from a `CharArrayReader` after it's been closed throw `IOExceptions`.

```
public void close()
```

String Readers and Writers

The `java.io.StringReader` and `java.io.StringWriter` classes allow programmers to use `Reader` and `Writer` methods to read and write strings. Like `char` arrays, Java strings are also composed of pure Unicode characters. Therefore, they're good sources of data for readers and good targets for writers. This is the other common case where readers and writers don't need to convert between different encodings.

String Writers

This class would more accurately be called `StringBufferWriter`, but `StringWriter` is more poetic. A `StringWriter` maintains an internal `java.lang.StringBuffer` object to which written characters are appended. This buffer can easily be converted to a string as necessary.

```
public class StringWriter extends Writer
```

There is a single public constructor:

```
public StringWriter()
```

There is also a constructor that allows you to specify the initial size of the internal string buffer. This isn't too important, because string buffers (and, by extension, string writers) are expanded as necessary. Still, if you can estimate the size of the string in advance, it's marginally more efficient to select a size big enough to hold all characters that will be written. The constructor is protected in Java 1.1 and public in Java 2:

```
protected StringWriter(int initialSize)
public StringWriter(int initialSize)  // Java 2
```

The `StringWriter` class has the usual collection of `write()` methods, all of which just append their data to the `StringBuffer`:

```
public void write(int c)
public void write(char[] text, int offset, int length)
```

```
public void write(String s)
public void write(String s, int offset, int length)
```

There are flush() and close() methods, but both have empty method bodies, as string writers operate completely internal to Java and do not require flushing or closing:

```
public void flush()
public void close()
```

You can continue to write to a string writer even after it's been closed. This should probably be classified as a bug, and I don't recommend that you write code that relies on this behavior.

There are two ways to get the current contents of the StringWriter's internal buffer. The toString() method returns it as a new String object, while the getBuffer() method returns the actual buffer:

```
public String toString()
public StringBuffer getBuffer()
```

Strings are immutable, but changes to the buffer object returned by getBuffer() change the state of the StringWriter.

The following code fragment creates a string containing the printable ASCII character set:

```
StringWriter sw = new StringWriter(128);
for (int i = 32; i < 127; i++) {
  sw.write(i);
}
String ascii = sw.toString();
```

String Readers

A StringReader uses the methods of the Reader class to get characters from a string. This is useful when you want to process each character in a string in sequential order. This class replaces the deprecated StringBufferInputStream class from Java 1.0:

```
public class StringReader extends Reader
```

The single constructor sets the string that's the source of data for this reader:

```
public StringReader(String s)
```

Since string objects are immutable, the data in the string may not be changed after the StringReader is constructed. The current position from which characters are read is stored in a private field. Synchronization and thread safety are thus not major problems for this class. Of course, the class has the usual read() methods, all of which read as many characters as requested from the string:

```
public int read() throws IOException
public int read(char[] buffer, int offset, int length) throws IOException
```

These methods return –1 if the end of the string has been reached. They throw an IOException if the reader has been closed.

The skip() method skips forward in the string the specified number of places and returns the number of characters skipped. It throws an IOException if the reader is closed.

```
public long skip(long n) throws IOException
```

The ready() method returns true. Strings are always ready to be read.

```
public boolean ready() throws IOException
```

String readers support marking and resetting to the limit of the string's length. markSupported() returns true. mark() marks the current position in the stream. (The readAheadLimit argument is for compatibility only; its value is ignored.) The reset() method moves backward in the string to the marked position.

```
public boolean markSupported()
public void mark(int readAheadLimit) throws IOException
public void reset() throws IOException
```

Finally, the close() method sets the internal string data to null. Attempts to read from a StringReader after it's been closed throw IOExceptions.

```
public void close()
```

Here's a simple method that uses StringReader to break a string into its separate characters and print them:

```
public static void printCharacters(String s) {

    StringReader sr = new StringReader(s);
    try {
      int c;
      while ((c = sr.read()) != -1) {
        System.out.println((char) c);
      }
    }
    catch (IOException e) {System.err.println(e);}
    return;
  }
```

Admittedly, this is a contrived example. If you really needed to do this, you could just call the string's `toCharArray()` method and loop through that (or even the string itself) using its `charAt()` method.

Reading and Writing Files

You've already learned how to chain an `OutputStreamWriter` to a `FileOutputStream` and an `InputStreamReader` to a `FileInputStream`. Although this isn't hard, Java provides two simple utility classes that take care of the details, `java.io.FileWriter` and `java.io.FileReader`.

FileWriter

The `FileWriter` class is a subclass of `OutputStreamWriter` that writes text files using the platform's default character encoding and buffer size. If you need to change these values, construct an `OutputStreamWriter` on a `FileOutputStream` instead.

```
public class FileWriter extends OutputStreamWriter
```

This class has four constructors:

```
public FileWriter(String fileName) throws IOException
public FileWriter(String fileName, boolean append) throws IOException
public FileWriter(File file) throws IOException
public FileWriter(FileDescriptor fd)
```

The first constructor opens a file and positions the file pointer at the beginning of the file. Any text in the file is overwritten. For example:

```
FileWriter fw = new FileWriter("36.html");
```

The second constructor allows you to specify that new text is appended to the existing contents of the file rather than overwriting them by setting the second argument to true. For example:

```
FileWriter fw = new FileWriter("36.html", true);
```

The third and fourth constructors use a `File` object and a `FileDescriptor`, respectively, instead of a filename to identify the file to be written to. Any pre-existing contents in a file so opened are overwritten.

No methods other than the constructors are declared in this class. You use the standard `Writer` methods like `write()`, `flush()`, and `close()` to write the text in the file.

FileReader

The `FileReader` class is a subclass of `InputStreamReader` that reads text files using the platform's default character encoding. If you need to change the encoding, construct an `InputStreamReader` chained to a `FileInputStream` instead.

```
public class FileReader extends InputStreamReader
```

This class has three constructors that differ only in how the file to be read is specified:

```
public FileReader(String fileName) throws FileNotFoundException
public FileReader(File file) throws FileNotFoundException
public FileReader(FileDescriptor fd)
```

Only the constructors are declared in this class. You use the standard `Reader` methods like `read()`, `ready()`, and `close()` to read the text in the file. For example:

```
try {
  FileReader fr = new FileReader("36.html");
  while (true) {
    int i = fr.read();
    if (i == -1) break;
    // ...
  }
}
catch (IOexception e) {System.err.println(e);}
```

Example 15-3 copies text from the file named in the first command-line argument to the file named in the second command-line argument using a `FileReader` and a `FileWriter`. This assumes both the input and output files are written using the platform's default encoding.

Example 15-3. TextFileCopier

```
import java.io.*;

public class TextFileCopier {

  public static void main(String[] args) {

    if (args.length != 2) {
      System.err.println("Usage: java TextFileCopier file1 file2");
    }
    try {
      copyFile(args[0], args[1]);
    }
    catch (IOException e) {System.err.println(e);}
```

Example 15-3. TextFileCopier (continued)

```
  }

  public static void copyFile(String file1, String file2) throws IOException {

    File infile = new File(file1);
    File outfile = new File(file2);

    if (infile.getCanonicalPath().equals(outfile.getCanonicalPath())) {
      return;
    }

    FileReader fr = new FileReader(infile);
    FileWriter fw = new FileWriter(outfile);

    while (true) {
      int i = fr.read();
      if (i == -1) break;
      fw.write(i);
    }
    fw.close();
    fr.close();
  }
}
```

Buffered Readers and Writers

Input and output can be time-consuming operations. It's often quicker to read or write text in large chunks rather than in many separate smaller pieces, even when you only process the text in the smaller pieces. The `java.io.BufferedReader` and `java.io.BufferedWriter` classes provide internal character buffers. Text that's written to a buffered writer is stored in the internal buffer and only written to the underlying writer when the buffer fills up or is flushed. Likewise, reading text from a buffered reader may cause more characters to be read than were requested; the extra characters are stored in an internal buffer. Future reads first access characters from the internal buffer and only access the underlying reader when the buffer is emptied.

Buffering Writes for Better Performance

The `java.io.BufferedWriter` class is a subclass of `java.io.Writer` that you chain to another `Writer` class to buffer characters. This allows more efficient writing of text.

```
    public class BufferedWriter extends Writer
```

There are two constructors. One has a default buffer size (8192 characters); the other lets you specify the buffer size:

```
public BufferedWriter(Writer out)
public BufferedWriter(Writer out, int size)
```

Each time you write to an unbuffered writer, there's a matching write to the underlying output stream. Therefore, it's a good idea to wrap a BufferedWriter around each writer whose write() operations are expensive, such as a FileWriter. For example:

```
BufferedWriter bw = new BufferedWriter(new FileWriter("37.html"));
```

BufferedWriter overrides most of its superclass's methods, including:

```
public void write(int c) throws IOException
public void write(char[] text,int offset, int length) throws IOException
public void write(String s, int offset, int length) throws IOException
public void flush() throws IOException
public void close() throws IOException
```

These methods are used exactly as they are for any writer object. The differences are purely internal.

The one new method in this class is newLine(). This method writes a platform-dependent line terminator string: \n on Unix, \r on the Mac, \r\n on Windows. The value of this string is taken from the system property line.separator.

```
public String newLine() throws IOException
```

TIP   Do not use the newLine() method if you're writing network code like an HTTP server. Instead, explicitly write the carriage return/ linefeed pair. Most network protocols specify a \r\n line separator, regardless of host-platform conventions.

Example 15-4 is a revised version of Example 15-1 that uses a BufferedWriter to increase efficiency and handle platform-dependent line separators.

Example 15-4. BufferedUnicodeTable

```
import java.io.*;

public class BufferedUnicodeTable {

  public static void main(String[] args) {

    String encoding = System.getProperty("font.encoding", "8859_1");
    OutputStream target = System.out;
    try {
```

Example 15-4. BufferedUnicodeTable (continued)

```
      if (args.length > 0) target = new FileOutputStream(args[0]);
    }
    catch (IOException e) {
      System.err.println("Sending text to System.out");
    }
    if (args.length > 1) encoding = args[1];

    OutputStreamWriter osw = null;
    try {
      osw = new OutputStreamWriter(target, encoding);
    }
    catch (UnsupportedEncodingException e) {
      osw = new OutputStreamWriter(target);
    }

    BufferedWriter bw = new BufferedWriter(osw);
    try {

      for (int i = Character.MIN_VALUE; i < Character.MAX_VALUE; i++) {
        char c = (char) i;
        bw.write(i + ":\t" + c);
        bw.newLine();
      }
      bw.close();
    }
    catch (IOException e) {System.err.println(e);}
  }
}
```

Buffering Reads for Better Performance

The `java.io.BufferedReader` class is a subclass of `java.io.Reader` that is chained to another `Reader` class to buffer input. This allows more efficient reading of characters and lines.

```
    public class BufferedReader extends Reader
```

`BufferedReader` is notable for its `readLine()` method that allows you to read text a line at a time. This replaces the common but deprecated `readLine()` method in `DataInputStream`.

Each time you read from an unbuffered reader, there's a matching read from the underlying input stream. Therefore, it's a good idea to wrap a `BufferedReader` around each reader whose `read()` operations are expensive, such as a `FileReader`. For example:

```
    BufferedReader br = new BufferedReader(new FileReader("37.html"));
```

There are two constructors. One has a default buffer size (8192 characters); the other requires the programmer to specify the buffer size:

```
public BufferedReader(Reader in, int buffer_size)
public BufferedReader(Reader in)
```

$BufferedReader$ overrides most of its superclass's methods, including:

```
public int read() throws IOException
public int read(char[] text, int offset, int length) throws IOException
public long skip(long n) throws IOException
public boolean ready() throws IOException
```

In Java 2 and later, the two multicharacter $read()$ methods try to completely fill the specified array or subarray of text by reading repeatedly from the underlying reader. They return only when the requested number of characters have been read, the end of the data is reached, or the underlying reader would block. This is not the case for most readers (including buffered readers in Java 1.1.x), which only attempt one read from the underlying data source before returning.

$BufferedReader$ does support marking and resetting, at least up to the length of the buffer:

```
public boolean markSupported()
public void mark(int readAheadLimit) throws IOException
public void reset() throws IOException
```

The one new method in this class is $readLine()$:

```
public String readLine() throws IOException
```

This method returns a string that contains a line of text from a text file. \r, \n, and \r\n are assumed to be line breaks and are not included in the returned string. This method is often used when reading user input from $System.in$, since most platforms only send the user's input to the running program after the user has typed a full line (that is, hit the Return key). $readLine()$ has the same problem with line ends that $DataInputStream$'s $readLine()$ method has; that is, the potential to hang on a lone carriage return that ends the stream. This problem is especially acute on networked connections, where $readLine()$ should never be used.

Example 15-5 uses a $BufferedReader$ and $readLine()$ to read all files named on the command line, line by line, and copy them to $System.out$. In essence it implements the Unix *cat* or the DOS *type* utility.

Example 15-5. The cat Program

```
import java.io.*;

class Cat {
```

Example 15-5. The cat Program (continued)

```java
public static void main (String[] args) {

  String thisLine;

  // Loop across the arguments.
  for (int i=0; i < args.length; i++) {

   // Open the file for reading.
   try {
     BufferedReader br = new BufferedReader(new FileReader(args[i]));
     while ((thisLine = br.readLine()) != null) {
       System.out.println(thisLine);
     } // end while
   } // end try
   catch (IOException e) {System.err.println("Error: " + e);}
  } // end for
 } // end main
}
```

Line Numbering

The `java.io.LineNumberReader` class is a subclass of `java.io.Buffered-Reader` that keeps track of which line you're currently reading. It has all the methods of `BufferedReader`, including `readLine()`. It also has methods to get and set the line number. This class replaces the deprecated `java.io.Line-NumberInputStream` class.

```java
public class LineNumberReader extends BufferedReader
```

There are two constructors in this class. Both chain this reader to an underlying reader; the second also sets the size of the buffer.

```java
public LineNumberReader(Reader in)
public LineNumberReader(Reader in, int size)
```

The `LineNumberReader` class overrides these six methods from its superclass, `BufferedReader`:

```java
public int read() throws IOException
public int read(char[] text, int offset, int length) throws IOException
public long skip(long n) throws IOException
public void mark(int readAheadLimit) throws IOException
public void reset() throws IOException
public String readLine() throws IOException
```

However, the changes are solely for the purpose of keeping track of the line number. They do not change the semantics of these methods at all. This class also introduces two methods:

```
public void setLineNumber(int lineNumber)
public int getLineNumber()
```

The `setLineNumber()` method does not change the line that you're reading in the file. It just changes the value `getLineNumber()` returns. For example, it would allow you to start counting from –5 if you knew there were six lines of header data you didn't want to count.

Example 15-6 uses a `LineNumberReader` and `readLine()` to read all files named on the command line, line by line, and copy them to `System.out`, prefixing each line with its line number.

Example 15-6. The LineCat Program

```java
import java.io.*;

public class LineCat  {

  public static void main (String args[]) {

    String thisLine;

    // Loop across the arguments.
    for (int i=0; i < args.length; i++) {

     //Open the file for reading.
     try {
       LineNumberReader br = new LineNumberReader(new FileReader(args[i]));
       while ((thisLine = br.readLine()) != null) {
         System.out.println(br.getLineNumber() + ": " + thisLine);
        } // end while
      } // end try
      catch (IOException e) {System.err.println("Error: " + e);}
    } // end for
  } // end main
}
```

Print Writers

The `java.io.PrintWriter` class is a subclass of `java.io.Writer` that contains the familiar `print()` and `println()` methods from `System.out` and other instances of `PrintStream`. It's deliberately similar to the `java.io.PrintStream` class. In Java 1.0 `PrintStream` was used for text-oriented output, but it didn't handle multiple-byte character sets particularly well (or really at all). In Java 1.1 and later, streams are only for byte-oriented and numeric output; writers should be used when you want to output text.

The main difference between `PrintStream` and `PrintWriter` is that `PrintWriter` handles multiple-byte and other non-ISO Latin-1 character sets properly. The other, more minor difference is that automatic flushing is performed only when `println()` is invoked, not every time a newline character is seen. Sun would probably like to deprecate `PrintStream` and use `PrintWriter` instead, but that would break too much existing code. (In fact, Sun did deprecate the `PrintStream()` constructors in 1.1, but they undeprecated them in Java 2.)

There are four constructors in this class:

```
public PrintWriter(Writer out)
public PrintWriter(Writer out, boolean autoFlush)
public PrintWriter(OutputStream out)
public PrintWriter(OutputStream out, boolean autoFlush)
```

The `PrintWriter` can send text either to an output stream or to another writer. If `autoFlush` is set to `true`, the `PrintWriter` is flushed every time `println()` is invoked.

The `PrintWriter` class implements the abstract `write()` method from `java.io.Writer` and overrides five other methods:

```
public void write(int c)
public void write(char[] text)
public void write(String s)
public void write(String s, int offset, int length)
public void flush()
public void close()
```

These methods are used almost identically to their equivalents in any other `Writer` class. The one difference is that none of them throw `IOExceptions`; in fact, no method in the `PrintWriter` class ever throws an `IOException`. If the underlying output stream or writer throws an `IOException`, it's caught inside `PrintWriter` and an error flag is set. Read the status of this flag with the `checkError()` method:

```
public boolean checkError()
```

Since `checkError()` returns a `boolean`, it only tells you that an I/O error has occurred; it does not tell you what that error was. Furthermore, once an error has occurred, `checkError()` always returns `true`—there is no way to reset it so you can test for later errors. On the other hand, you can indicate that an error has occurred with `setError()`:

```
protected void setError()
```

The main advantages of the `PrintWriter` class are the nine-way overloaded `print()` method and the 10-way overloaded `println()` method. Any Java object, variable, or literal can be printed by passing it to a `print()` or `println()`

method. The `println()` method follows its argument with a platform-dependent line separator (such as `\r\n`) and then flushes the output if `autoFlush` is enabled. The `print()` method does not. Otherwise, these methods are the same.

```
public void print(boolean b)
public void print(char c)
public void print(int i)
public void print(long l)
public void print(float f)
public void print(double d)
public void print(char[] text)
public void print(String s)
public void print(Object obj)
public void println()
public void println(boolean b)
public void println(char c)
public void println(int i)
public void println(long l)
public void println(float f)
public void println(double d)
public void println(char[] c)
public void println(String s)
public void println(Object o)
```

You should never use `println()`, either the `PrintWriter` or the `PrintStream` version, in networking code. Most network protocols like HTTP expect to see a carriage return/linefeed pair as the line separator character. If you use `println()`, your network programs may run on Windows, but they'll have problems on most other platforms. Furthermore, these problems can be hard to diagnose, because some servers and clients are more forgiving of improper line-ending conventions than others.

Piped Readers and Writers

Piped readers and writers do for character streams what piped input and output streams do for byte streams: they allow two threads to communicate. Character output from one thread becomes character input for the other thread:

```
public class PipedWriter extends Writer
public class PipedReader extends Reader
```

The `PipedWriter` class has two constructors. The first constructs an unconnected `PipedWriter` object. The second constructs one that's connected to the `PipedReader` object sink:

```
public PipedWriter()
public PipedWriter(PipedReader sink) throws IOException
```

The `PipedReader` class also has two constructors. Again, the first constructor creates an unconnected `PipedReader` object. The second constructs one that's connected to the `PipedWriter` object source:

```
public PipedReader()
public PipedReader(PipedWriter source) throws IOException
```

Piped readers and writers are normally created in pairs. The piped writer becomes the underlying source for the piped reader. This is one of the few cases where a reader does not have an underlying input stream. For example:

```
PipedWriter pw = new PipedWriter();
PipedReader pr = new PipedReader(pw);
```

This simple example is a little deceptive, because these lines of code will normally be in different methods and perhaps even different classes. Some mechanism must be established to pass a reference to the `PipedWriter` into the thread that handles the `PipedReader`, or you can create them in the same thread, then pass a reference to the connected stream into a separate thread.

Alternately, you can start with a `PipedReader` and then wrap it with a `PipedWriter`:

```
PipedReader pr = new PipedReader();
PipedWriter pw = new PipedWriter(pr);
```

Or you can create them both unconnected, then use one or the other's `connect()` method to link them:

```
public void connect(PipedReader sink) throws IOException
public void connect(PipedWriter source) throws IOException
```

`PipedWriter`'s `connect()` method takes as an argument the `PipedReader` to connect to. `PipedReader`'s `connect()` argument takes as an argument the `PipedWriter` to connect to:

```
PipedReader pr = new PipedReader();
PipedWriter pw = new PipedWriter();
pr.connect(pw);
```

or:

```
PipedReader pr = new PipedReader();
PipedWriter pw = new PipedWriter();
pw.connect(pr);
```

Neither a `PipedWriter` nor a `PipedReader` may be connected to more than one reader or writer. Attempts to do so throw `IOExceptions`. Furthermore, once connected, a `PipedWriter`/`PipedReader` pair may not be disconnected. Otherwise, these classes have the usual `read()`, `write()`, `flush()`, `close()`, and `ready()` methods like all reader and writer classes. These are the remaining declared methods in `PipedWriter`:

```
public void write(char[] text, int offset, int length) throws IOException
public void flush() throws IOException
public void close() throws IOException
```

When characters are written on the `PipedWriter`, that text becomes available as input to be read by the connected `PipedReader`. If a `PipedReader` tries to read characters, but its connected `PipedWriter` hasn't yet provided it with any, the `PipedReader` blocks.

These are the remaining declared methods in `PipedReader`:

```
public int read(char[] text, int offset, int length) throws IOException
public void close() throws IOException
```

Closing either a `PipedReader` or a `PipedWriter` also closes the reader or writer it's connected to.

Filtered Readers and Writers

The `java.io.FilterReader` and `java.io.FilterWriter` classes are abstract classes that read characters and filter them in some way before passing the text along. You can imagine a `FilterReader` that converts all characters to uppercase.

```
public abstract class FilterReader extends Reader
public abstract class FilterWriter extends Writer
```

Although `FilterReader` and `FilterWriter` are modeled after `java.io.FilterInputStream` and `java.io.FilterOutputStream`, they are much less commonly used than those classes. There are no concrete subclasses of `FilterWriter` in the java packages and only one concrete subclass of `FilterReader` (`PushbackReader` discussed later). These classes exist so you can write your own filters.

The FilterReader Class

`FilterReader` has a single constructor, which is protected:

```
protected FilterReader(Reader in)
```

The `in` argument is the `Reader` to which this filter is chained. This reference is stored in a protected field called `in` from which text for this filter is read and is `null` after the filter has been closed.

```
protected Reader in
```

Since `FilterReader` is an abstract class, only subclasses may be instantiated. Therefore, it doesn't matter that the constructor is protected, since it may only be invoked from subclass constructors.

`FilterReader` provides the usual collection of `read()`, `skip()`, `ready()`, `markSupported()`, `mark()`, `reset()`, and `close()` methods:

```
public int read() throws IOException
public int read(char[] text, int offset, int length) throws IOException
public long skip(long n) throws IOException
public boolean ready() throws IOException
public boolean markSupported()
public void mark(int readAheadLimit) throws IOException
public void reset() throws IOException
public void close() throws IOException
```

These all simply invoke the equivalent method in the in field with the same arguments. For example:

```
public long skip(long n) throws IOException {
  return in.skip(n);
}
```

Java source code is written in pure ASCII with Unicode characters written as a \u followed by the four-hexadecimal-digit equivalent of the Unicode character. As an example, I'll write a `FilterReader` subclass that reads a \u-escaped file and converts it to pure Unicode. This is a much trickier problem than it first appears. First, there's not a fixed ratio between the number of bytes and number of characters. Most of the time one byte is one character, but some of the time five bytes are one character. The second difficulty is ensuring that \u09EF is recognized as Unicode escape, while \\u09EF is not. In other words, only a u preceded by an odd number of slashes is a valid Unicode escape. A u preceded by an even number of slashes should be passed along unchanged. Example 15-7 shows a solution.

Example 15-7. SourceReader

```
package com.macfaq.io;

import java.io.*;

public class SourceReader extends FilterReader {

  public SourceReader(InputStream in) {
    this(new InputStreamReader(in));
  }

  public SourceReader(Reader in) {
    super(new BufferedReader(in));
  }
```

Example 15-7. SourceReader (continued)

```java
private int backslashParity = 1;

public int read() throws IOException {

  int c = in.read();
  if (c != '\\') return c;

  backslashParity *= -1;
  // If there are an even number of backslashes,
  // this is not a Unicode escape.
  if (backslashParity == 1) return c;

  // Mark is supported because I used
  // a BufferedReader in the constructor.
  in.mark(1);
  int next = in.read();
  if (next != 'u' ) { // This is not a Unicode escape
    in.reset();
    return c;
  }
  // Read next 4 hex digits.
  // If the next four chars do not make a valid hex digit
  // this is not a valid .java file and you need a compiler error.
  StringBuffer sb = new StringBuffer();
  sb.append((char) in.read());
  sb.append((char) in.read());
  sb.append((char) in.read());
  sb.append((char) in.read());
  String hex = sb.toString();
  try {
    return Integer.valueOf(hex, 16).intValue();
  }
  catch (NumberFormatException e) {
    throw new IOException("Bad Unicode escape");
  }
}

public int read(char[] text, int offset, int length) throws IOException {

  int numRead = 0;
  for (int i = offset; i < offset+length; i++) {
    int temp = this.read();
    if (temp == -1) break;
    text[i] = (char) temp;
    numRead++;
  }
  return numRead;
}
```

Example 15-7. SourceReader (continued)

```
public long skip(long n) throws IOException {

  char[] c = new char[(int) n];
  int numSkipped = this.read(c);
  return numSkipped;
}
}
```

The FilterWriter Class

The `FilterWriter` class has a single constructor and no other unique methods:

```
protected FilterWriter(Writer out)
```

The `out` argument is the writer to which this filter is chained. This reference is stored in a protected field called `out`, to which text sent through this filter is written.

```
protected Writer out
```

Since `FilterWriter` is an abstract class, only subclasses may be instantiated. Therefore, it doesn't matter that the constructor is protected, since it may only be invoked from subclass constructors anyway. `FilterWriter` provides the usual collection of `write()`, `close()`, and `flush()` methods:

```
public void write(int c) throws IOException
public void write(char[] text, int offset, int length) throws IOException
public void write(String s, int offset, int length) throws IOException
public void flush() throws IOException
public void close() throws IOException
```

These all simply invoke the equivalent method in the `out` field with the same arguments. For example:

```
public void close() throws IOException {
  out.close();
}
```

In general, each subclass will have to override at least the three `write()` methods to perform the filtering.

There are no subclasses of `FilterWriter` in the core API. Example 15-8, `SourceWriter`, is an example of a `FilterWriter` that converts Unicode text to \u-escaped ASCII. The big question is what to do if the input text contains an unescaped backslash. The easiest and most robust solution is to replace it with \u005C, the Unicode escape for the backslash itself.

Example 15-8. SourceWriter

```java
package com.macfaq.io;

import java.io.*;

public class SourceWriter extends FilterWriter {

  public SourceWriter(Writer out) {
    super(out);
  }

  public void write(char[] text, int offset, int length) throws IOException {

    for (int i = offset; i < offset+length; i++) {
      this.write(text[i]);
    }
  }

  public void write(String s, int offset, int length) throws IOException {

    for (int i = offset; i < offset+length; i++) {
      this.write(s.charAt(i));
    }
  }

  public void write(int c) throws IOException {

    // We have to escape the backslashes below.
    if (c == '\\') out.write("\\u005C");
    else if (c < 128) out.write(c);
    else {
      String s = Integer.toHexString(c);
      // Pad with leading zeroes if necessary.
      if (c < 256) s = "00" + s;
      else if (c < 4096) s = "0" + s;
      out.write("\\u");
      out.write(s);
    }
  }
}
```

PushbackReader

The PushbackReader class is a filter that provides a pushback buffer around a given reader. This allows a program to "unread" the last character it read. It's similar to PushbackInputStream, discussed in Chapter 6, *Filter Streams*, but instead of pushing back bytes, it pushes back chars. Both PushbackReader and BufferedReader use buffers, but only PushbackReader allows unreading and only BufferedReader allows marking and resetting. The difference is that pushing back characters allows you to unread characters after the fact. Marking and resetting requires you to mark in advance the location you want to reset to.

PushbackReader has two constructors, both of which take an underlying reader as an argument. The first uses a one-character pushback buffer; the second sets the pushback buffer to a specified size:

```
public PushbackReader(Reader in)
public PushbackReader(Reader in, int size)
```

The PushbackReader class has the usual collection of read() methods. These methods first try to read the requested characters from the pushback buffer and only read from the underlying reader if the pushback buffer is empty or has too few characters.

```
public int read() throws IOException
public int read(char[] text, int offset, int length) throws IOException
```

PushbackReader also has ready(), markSupported(), and close() methods:

```
public boolean ready() throws IOException
public boolean markSupported()
public void close() throws IOException
```

The ready() and close() methods merely invoke the ready() and close() methods of the underlying reader. The markSupported() method returns false; pushback readers do not support marking and resetting.

Three unread() methods push back specific characters. The first pushes back the character c; the second pushes back the text array; the third pushes back the sub-array of text beginning at offset and continuing for length chars.

```
public void unread(int c) throws IOException
public void unread(char[] text) throws IOException
public void unread(char[] text, int offset, int length) throws IOException
```

The unread characters aren't necessarily the same as the characters that were read. It would be nicer if the PushbackReader itself kept track of which characters had been read, and all you had to tell it was how many characters to unread. However, this approach does give the client programmer the option of inserting tags or other data as the stream is read. The number of characters you can push back onto the stream is limited by the size of the buffer set in the constructor. Attempts to unread more characters than can fit in the buffer cause an IOException to be thrown. An IOException is also thrown if you try to unread a closed reader; once a PushbackReader has been closed, it can be neither read nor unread.

File Viewer Finis

As a final example of working with readers and writers, we return for the last time to the `FileDumper` application last seen in Chapter 13, *File Dialogs and Choosers*. At that point, we had a GUI program that allowed any file to be opened and interpreted in one of several formats, including ASCII, decimal, hexadecimal, short, regular, and long integers in both big- and little-endian formats, floating point, and double-precision floating point.

In this section we expand the program to read many different text formats besides ASCII. The user interface must be adjusted to allow a binary choice of whether the file contains text or numeric data. If they choose text, you'll need to use a reader to read the file instead of an input stream. You'll also need to provide some means for the user to pick the encoding they want text read in (e.g., MacRoman, ISO Latin-1, Unicode, etc). Since there are several dozen text encodings, the best choice is a list box. All of this can be integrated into the mode panel. Figure 15-1 shows the revised `ModePanel2` class. The code is given in Example 15-9. Two new public methods are added, `isText()` and `getEncoding()`. The rest of the changes are fairly minor ones to set up the GUI.

Example 15-9. ModePanel2

```
import java.awt.*;
import javax.swing.*;

public class ModePanel2 extends JPanel {

    JCheckBox bigEndian = new JCheckBox("Big Endian", true);
    JCheckBox deflated  = new JCheckBox("Deflated", false);
    JCheckBox gzipped   = new JCheckBox("GZipped", false);

    ButtonGroup dataTypes      = new ButtonGroup();
    JRadioButton asciiRadio    = new JRadioButton("Text");
    JRadioButton decimalRadio  = new JRadioButton("Decimal");
    JRadioButton hexRadio      = new JRadioButton("Hexadecimal");
    JRadioButton shortRadio    = new JRadioButton("Short");
    JRadioButton intRadio      = new JRadioButton("Int");
    JRadioButton longRadio     = new JRadioButton("Long");
    JRadioButton floatRadio    = new JRadioButton("Float");
    JRadioButton doubleRadio   = new JRadioButton("Double");

    JTextField password = new JTextField();

    final static String[] encodings = {"8859_1", "8859_2", "8859_3", "8859_4",
      "8859_5", "8859_6", "8859_7", "8859_8", "8859_9", "Big5", "CNS11643",
      "Cp037", "Cp273", "Cp277", "Cp278", "Cp280", "Cp284", "Cp285", "Cp297",
      "Cp420", "Cp424", "Cp437", "Cp500", "Cp737", "Cp775", "Cp850", "Cp852",
```

Example 15-9. ModePanel2 (continued)

```
    "Cp855", "Cp856", "Cp857", "Cp860", "Cp861", "Cp862", "Cp863", "Cp864",
    "Cp865", "Cp866", "Cp868", "Cp869", "Cp870", "Cp871", "Cp874", "Cp875",
    "Cp918", "Cp921", "Cp922", "Cp1006", "Cp1025", "Cp1026", "Cp1046",
    "Cp1097", "Cp1098", "Cp1112", "Cp1122", "Cp1123", "Cp1124", "Cp1250",
    "Cp1251", "Cp1252", "Cp1253", "Cp1254", "Cp1255", "Cp1256", "Cp1257",
    "Cp1258", "EUCJIS", "GB2312", "JIS", "JIS0208", "KSC5601", "MacArabic",
    "MacCentralEurope", "MacCroatian", "MacCyrillic", "MacDingbat", "MacGreek",
    "MacHebrew", "MacIceland", "MacRoman", "MacRomania", "MacSymbol", "MacThai",
    "MacTurkish", "MacUkraine", "SJIS", "UTF8", "Unicode" };

  JList theEncoding = new JList(encodings);

  public ModePanel2() {

    this.setLayout(new GridLayout(1, 2));

    JPanel left = new JPanel();
    JScrollPane right = new JScrollPane(theEncoding);
    left.setLayout(new GridLayout(13, 1));
    left.add(bigEndian);
    left.add(deflated);
    left.add(gzipped);

    left.add(asciiRadio);
    asciiRadio.setSelected(true);
    left.add(decimalRadio);
    left.add(hexRadio);
    left.add(shortRadio);
    left.add(intRadio);
    left.add(longRadio);
    left.add(floatRadio);
    left.add(doubleRadio);

    dataTypes.add(asciiRadio);
    dataTypes.add(decimalRadio);
    dataTypes.add(hexRadio);
    dataTypes.add(shortRadio);
    dataTypes.add(intRadio);
    dataTypes.add(longRadio);
    dataTypes.add(floatRadio);
    dataTypes.add(doubleRadio);

    left.add(password);
    this.add(left);
    this.add(right);
  }

  public boolean isBigEndian() {
```

Example 15-9. ModePanel2 (continued)

```java
    return bigEndian.isSelected();
  }

  public boolean isDeflated() {
    return deflated.isSelected();
  }

  public boolean isGZipped() {
    return gzipped.isSelected();
  }

  public boolean isText() {
    if (this.getMode() == FileDumper6.ASC) return true;
    return false;
  }

  public String getEncoding() {
    return (String) theEncoding.getSelectedValue();
  }

  public int getMode() {

    if (asciiRadio.isSelected()) return FileDumper6.ASC;
    else if (decimalRadio.isSelected()) return FileDumper6.DEC;
    else if (hexRadio.isSelected()) return FileDumper6.HEX;
    else if (shortRadio.isSelected()) return FileDumper6.SHORT;
    else if (intRadio.isSelected()) return FileDumper6.INT;
    else if (longRadio.isSelected()) return FileDumper6.LONG;
    else if (floatRadio.isSelected()) return FileDumper6.FLOAT;
    else if (doubleRadio.isSelected()) return FileDumper6.DOUBLE;
    else return FileDumper6.ASC;
  }

  public String getPassword() {
    return password.getText();
  }

  // A simple test method.
  public static void main(String[] args) {

    JFrame jf = new JFrame("Test Mode Panel");
    ModePanel2 mp2 = new ModePanel2();
    jf.getContentPane().add(mp2);
    jf.pack();
    jf.show();
    System.out.println("done");
  }
}
```

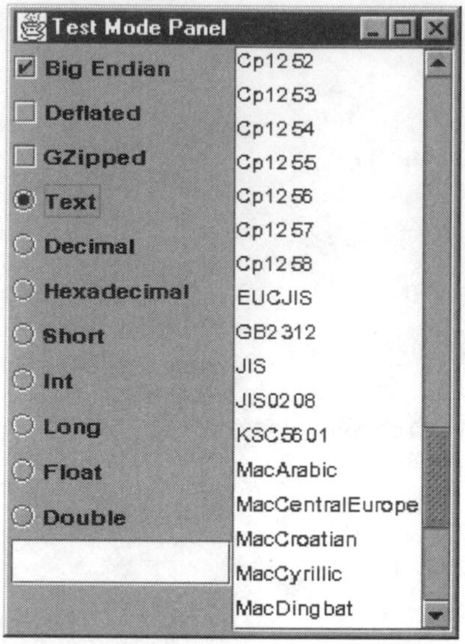

Figure 15-1. A mode panel with a list box for encodings

Next we need to expand the `FileDumper` class to read and write text in a variety of encodings. This is straightforward and only requires one new overloaded `dump()` method, as shown in Example 15-10.

Example 15-10. FileDumper6

```
import java.io.*;
import java.util.zip.*;
import java.security.*;
import javax.crypto.*;
import javax.crypto.spec.*;
import com.macfaq.io.*;


public class FileDumper6 {

  public static final int ASC    = 0;
  public static final int DEC    = 1;
  public static final int HEX    = 2;
  public static final int SHORT  = 3;
  public static final int INT    = 4;
  public static final int LONG   = 5;
  public static final int FLOAT  = 6;
  public static final int DOUBLE = 7;


  public static void dump(InputStream in, OutputStream out, int mode,
    boolean bigEndian, boolean deflated, boolean gzipped, String password)
```

Example 15-10. FileDumper6 (continued)

```
    throws IOException {

  // The reference variable in may point to several different objects
  // within the space of the next few lines.

  if (password != null && !password.equals("")) {
    // Create a key.
    try {
      byte[] desKeyData = password.getBytes();
      DESKeySpec desKeySpec = new DESKeySpec(desKeyData);
      SecretKeyFactory keyFactory = SecretKeyFactory.getInstance("DES");
      SecretKey desKey = keyFactory.generateSecret(desKeySpec);

      // Use Data Encryption Standard.
      Cipher des = Cipher.getInstance("DES/ECB/PKCS5Padding");
      des.init(Cipher.DECRYPT_MODE, desKey);

      in = new CipherInputStream(in, des);
    }
    catch (GeneralSecurityException e) {
      throw new IOException(e.getMessage());
    }
  }

  if (deflated) {
    in = new InflaterInputStream(in);
  }
  else if (gzipped) {
    in = new GZIPInputStream(in);
  }

  // Could really pass to FileDumper3 at this point.
  if (bigEndian) {
    DataInputStream din = new DataInputStream(in);
    switch (mode) {
      case HEX:
        in = new HexFilter(in);
        break;
      case DEC:
        in = new DecimalFilter(in);
        break;
      case INT:
        in = new IntFilter(din);
        break;
      case SHORT:
        in = new ShortFilter(din);
        break;
      case LONG:
```

Example 15-10. FileDumper6 (continued)

```java
          in = new LongFilter(din);
          break;
        case DOUBLE:
          in = new DoubleFilter(din);
          break;
        case FLOAT:
          in = new FloatFilter(din);
          break;
        default:
      }
    }
    else {
      LittleEndianInputStream lin = new LittleEndianInputStream(in);
      switch (mode) {
        case HEX:
          in = new HexFilter(in);
          break;
        case DEC:
          in = new DecimalFilter(in);
          break;
        case INT:
          in = new LEIntFilter(lin);
          break;
        case SHORT:
          in = new LEShortFilter(lin);
          break;
        case LONG:
          in = new LELongFilter(lin);
          break;
        case DOUBLE:
          in = new LEDoubleFilter(lin);
          break;
        case FLOAT:
          in = new LEFloatFilter(lin);
          break;
        default:
      }
    }
    StreamCopier.copy(in, out);
    in.close();
  }

  public static void dump(InputStream in, OutputStream out,
   String inputEncoding, String outputEncoding, boolean deflated,
   boolean gzipped, String password) throws IOException {

    if (inputEncoding == null || inputEncoding.equals("")) {
      dump(in, out, ASC, true, deflated, gzipped, password);
```

Example 15-10. FileDumper6 (continued)

```
      return;
    }

    if (outputEncoding == null || outputEncoding.equals("")) {
      outputEncoding = System.getProperty("file.encoding", "8859_1");
    }

    // Note that the reference variable in
    // may point to several different objects
    // within the space of the next few lines.
    if (password != null && !password.equals("")) {
      try {
        // Create a key.
        byte[] desKeyData = password.getBytes();
        DESKeySpec desKeySpec = new DESKeySpec(desKeyData);
        SecretKeyFactory keyFactory = SecretKeyFactory.getInstance("DES");
        SecretKey desKey = keyFactory.generateSecret(desKeySpec);

        // Use Data Encryption Standard.
        Cipher des = Cipher.getInstance("DES/ECB/PKCS5Padding");
        des.init(Cipher.DECRYPT_MODE, desKey);
        in = new CipherInputStream(in, des);
      }
      catch (GeneralSecurityException e) {
        throw new IOException(e.getMessage());
      }
    }

    if (deflated) {
      in = new InflaterInputStream(in);
    }
    else if (gzipped) {
      in = new GZIPInputStream(in);
    }

    InputStreamReader isr = new InputStreamReader(in, inputEncoding);
    OutputStreamWriter osw = new OutputStreamWriter(out, outputEncoding);

    int c;
    while ((c = isr.read()) != -1) {
      osw.write(c);
    }
    isr.close();
    osw.close();
  }
}
```

There's one new method in this class. An overloaded variant of dump() can be invoked to dump a text file in a particular encoding. This method accepts an input encoding string and an output encoding string as arguments. These are used to form readers and writers that interpret the bytes read from the file and written onto the output stream. Output encoding is optional. If it's omitted, the platform's default encoding is used.

The FileViewer2 class is straightforward. Aside from using a ModePanel2 instead of a ModePanel, the only change it really requires is in the actionPerformed() method. Here you have to test whether the format is text or numeric and select the dump() method accordingly. Example 15-11 illustrates.

Example 15-11. FileViewer2

```java
import javax.swing.*;
import java.io.*;
import com.macfaq.io.*;
import com.macfaq.swing.*;
import java.awt.*;
import java.awt.event.*;

public class FileViewer2 extends JFrame
 implements WindowListener, ActionListener {

  JFileChooser fc = new JFileChooser();
  JStreamedTextArea theView = new JStreamedTextArea();
  ModePanel2 mp = new ModePanel2();

  public FileViewer2() {
    super("FileViewer");
  }

  public void init() {

    this.addWindowListener(this);

    fc.setApproveButtonText("View File");
    fc.setApproveButtonMnemonic('V');
    fc.addActionListener(this);

    this.getContentPane().add("Center", fc);
    JScrollPane sp = new JScrollPane(theView);
    this.getContentPane().add("South", sp);
    this.getContentPane().add("West", mp);
    this.pack();

    // Center on display.
    Dimension display = getToolkit().getScreenSize();
```

Example 15-11. FileViewer2 (continued)

```java
    Dimension bounds = this.getSize();

    int x = (display.width - bounds.width)/2;
    int y = (display.height - bounds.height)/2;
    if (x < 0) x = 10;
    if (y < 0) y = 15;
    this.setLocation(x, y);
}

public void actionPerformed(ActionEvent e) {

  if (e.getActionCommand().equals(JFileChooser.APPROVE_SELECTION)) {
    File f = fc.getSelectedFile();
    if (f != null) {
      theView.setText("");
      try {
        InputStream in = new FileInputStream(f);
        OutputStream out = theView.getOutputStream();
        if (!mp.isText()) {
          FileDumper6.dump(in, out, mp.getMode(), mp.isBigEndian(),
            mp.isDeflated(), mp.isGZipped(), mp.getPassword());
        }
        else {
          FileDumper6.dump(in, out, mp.getEncoding(), null,
            mp.isDeflated(), mp.isGZipped(), mp.getPassword());
        }
      }
      catch (IOException ex) {}
    }
  }
  else if (e.getActionCommand().equals(JFileChooser.CANCEL_SELECTION)) {
    this.closeAndQuit();
  }
}

public void windowClosing(WindowEvent e) {
  this.closeAndQuit();
}

// Do-nothing methods for WindowListener
public void windowOpened(WindowEvent e) {}

public void windowClosed(WindowEvent e) {}
public void windowIconified(WindowEvent e) {}
public void windowDeiconified(WindowEvent e) {}
public void windowActivated(WindowEvent e) {}
public void windowDeactivated(WindowEvent e) {}
```

Example 15-11. FileViewer2 (continued)

```
private void closeAndQuit() {

  this.setVisible(false);
  this.dispose();
  System.exit(0);

}
public static void main(String[] args) {

  FileViewer2 fv = new FileViewer2();
  fv.init();
  fv.show();
}
}
```

Figure 15-2 shows the completed `FileViewer` application displaying a file full of Unicode text. Unfortunately, the `JTextArea` component doesn't yet do a great job of handling international characters so there are a lot of question marks serving as substitution characters.

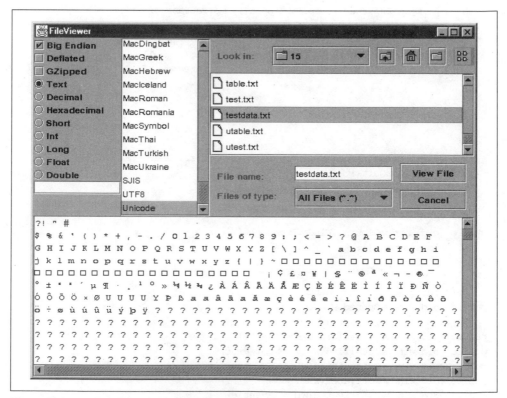

Figure 15-2. The final FileViewer application

This completes this program, at least as far as it will be taken in this book. You could certainly extend it further. For example, the program can be quite slow as it reads large files, so both optimization and a progress bar are called for. Still larger files may cause out-of-memory errors, so some sort of paging scheme is suggested. And it would be a nice touch to add support for various image formats and perhaps even formatted text like HTML files. However, this would take us too far afield from the topic of this book, so I leave further improvements as exercises for the motivated reader.

16

In this chapter:
- *The Old Way*
- *Choosing a Locale*
- *Number Formats*
- *Specifying Width with FieldPosition*
- *Parsing Input*
- *Decimal Formats*
- *An Exponential Number Format*

Formatted I/O with java.text

One of the most obvious differences between Java and C is that Java has no equivalent of `printf()` or `scanf()`. Part of the reason is that Java doesn't support the variable length argument lists on which these functions depend. However, the real reason Java doesn't have equivalents to C's formatted I/O routines is a difference in philosophy. C's `printf()` and the like combine number formatting with I/O in an inflexible manner. Java separates number formatting and I/O into separate packages and by so doing produces a much more general and powerful system.

More than one programmer has attempted to recreate `printf()` and `scanf()` in Java. This task is difficult, since those functions are designed around variable length argument lists, which Java does not support. However, overloading the + signs for string concatenation is easily as effective, probably more so, since it doesn't share the problems of mismatched argument lists. For example, which is clearer to you? This:

```
printf("%s worked %d hours at $%d per/hour for a total of %d dollars.\n",
  hours, salary, hours*salary);
```

or this:

```
System.out.println(employee + " worked " + hours + " hours at $" + salary
 + "per/hour for a total of $%d.");
```

I'd argue that the second is clearer. Among other advantages, it avoids problems with mismatched format strings and argument lists. (Did you notice that an argument is missing from the previous `printf()` statement?) On the flip side, the format string approach is a little less prone to missing spaces. (Did you notice that the `println()` statement would print pay scales as "$5.35per/hour" rather than "$5.35 per/hour"?) However, this is only a cosmetic problem and is easily fixed. A mismatched argument list in a `printf()` or `scanf()` statement may crash the computer, especially if pointers are involved.

The real advantage of the `printf()`/`scanf()` family of functions is not the format string. It's number formatting:

```
printf(
"%s worked %4.1d hours at $%6.2d per/hour for a total of %8.2d dollars.\n",
 employee, hours, salary, hours*salary);
```

Java 1.0 did not provide classes for specifying the width, precision, and alignment of numeric strings. Java 1.1 and later make these available as subclasses of `java.text.NumberFormat`. As well as handling the traditional formatting achieved by languages like C and Fortran, `NumberFormat` also internationalizes numbers with different character sets, thousands separators, decimal points, and digit characters.

The Old Way

Traditional computer languages have combined input of text with the parsing of numeric strings. For example, to read a decimal number into the variable `x`, programmers are accustomed to writing C code like this:

```
scanf("%d", &x);
```

In C++, that line would become:

```
cin >> x;
```

In Pascal:

```
READLN (X);
```

In Fortran:

```
      READ 2, X
   2 FORMAT (F5.1)
```

Similarly, formatting numeric strings for output tends to be mixed up with writing the string to the screen. For instance, consider the simple task of writing the `double` variable `salary` with two decimal digits of precision. In C, you'd write this:

```
printf("%.2d", salary);
```

In C++:

```
cout.precision(2);
cout << salary;
```

In Fortran:

```
      PRINT 20, SALARY
   20 FORMAT(F10.2)
```

This conflation of basic input and output with number formatting is so ingrained in most programmers today that we rarely stop to think whether it actually makes sense. What, precisely, does the formatting of numbers as text strings have to do with input and output? It's certainly true that you often need to format numbers to print numbers on the console, but you also need to format numbers to write data in files, to include numbers in text fields and text areas, and to send data across the network. What makes the console so special that it has to have a group of number-formatting routines all to itself? In C, the `printf()` and `scanf()` functions are supplemented by `fprintf()` and `fscanf()` for formatted I/O to files and by `sprintf()` and `sscanf()` for formatted I/O to strings. Perhaps the conflation of I/O with number formatting is really a relic of a time when command-line interfaces were a lot more important than they are today, and it's simply that nobody's thought to challenge this assumption, at least until Java. When you think about it, there's no fundamental connection between converting a binary number like 11010100110110100100011101011011 to a text string like " −7.500E+12" and writing that string onto an output stream. These are two different operations, and in Java they're handled by separate classes. Input and output are handled by all the streams and readers and writers I've been discussing, while number formatting is handled by a few `NumberFormat` classes from the `java.text` package I'll introduce in this chapter.

In Java you don't just say, "Print the `double` variable `salary` 12 places wide with three decimal places of precision." Instead, you say "First, make a string variable from the `double` variable `salary` 12 places wide with three decimal places of precision. Then print that string." Similarly, when doing input, you first read the string, then convert it to a number. You don't read the number directly. This really isn't very different from the programs you're used to writing in other languages; it adds a step, but the benefit is enhanced flexibility, particularly in regard to internationalization. It's easy to add new `NumberFormat` classes and locales that handle different kinds of formatting—much easier than reinventing all this from scratch, because the formatting is too tightly coupled to I/O, as it is in traditional languages and APIs.

In this chapter, we'll explore how to use the `java.text.NumberFormat` and `java.text.DecimalFormat` classes to format integers and floating point numbers. You'll also learn how the `java.util.Locale` class lets you select number formats matched to different languages, cultures, and countries. And you'll see how to write your own subclasses of `NumberFormat` that provide alternative formats such as exponential notation. There's more in the `java.text` package I won't cover. In particular, `java.text` includes classes for formatting dates, and sorting and collating text. These classes can also be customized to different locales. The date formats in particular work very similarly to the number formats discussed in this chapter and should not be hard to pick up from Sun's class library documentation once you understand `NumberFormat`.

Choosing a Locale

Number formats are dependent on the *locale*; that is, the country/language/ culture group of the local operating system. The number formats most English-speaking Americans are accustomed to use are a period as a decimal point, a comma to separate every three orders of magnitude, a dollar sign for currency, and numbers in base 10 that read from left to right. In this locale, Bill Gates's personal fortune,* in Microsoft stock alone as of January 12, 1998, is represented as $74,741,086,650.

However, in Egypt this number would be written as:

$$\$ \vee\xi\, ,\vee\xi\, \backslash\, ,\cdot\, \wedge\daleth\, ,\daleth\mathsf{o}\cdot$$

The primary difference here is that Egyptians use a different set of glyphs for the digits 0 through 9. For example, in Egypt zero is a ˙ and the ¶ glyph means 6. There are other differences in how Arabic and English treat numbers, and these vary from country to country. In most of the rest of North Africa, this number would be $74,741,086,650 as it is in the U.S. These are just two different scripts; there are several dozen more to go!

Java encapsulates many of the common differences between language/script/ culture/country combinations in a loosely defined group called a locale. There's really no better word for it. You can't just rely on language or country or culture alone. Many languages are shared between countries (English is only the most obvious example) but with subtle differences between how they are used in different places: Do commas and periods belong inside or outside of quotation marks? Is it color or colour? Many countries have no clearly dominant tongue: Is Canada an English- or a French-speaking nation? Switzerland has four official languages.† Almost all countries have significant minority populations with their own languages. The New York City public school system has to hire teachers fluent in over 100 different languages.

---

* See *http://www.webho.com/WealthClock* for up-to-date figures. It's a little depressing that between the first draft of this chapter and the copyedit phase this figure more than doubled. If, like me, you have a little trouble visualizing what this all means, you might want to check out the Bill Gates Wealth Index, by Brad Templeton, at *http://www.templetons.com/brad/billg.html* or the Bill Gates Net Worth Page at *http://www. quuxuum.org/~evan/bgnw.html.*

† Three of the four are German, French, and Italian. Can you identify the fourth? I'll give you a hint: it's not English.

Java isn't quite ready for use in New York City public schools. Sun's JDK 1.1 and most derivatives, such as Apple's Macintosh Runtime for Java 2.0, only support the 50 locales listed in Table 16-1. The first three columns are self-explanatory. The fourth is the ISO 639 two-letter language code, and the fifth is the ISO 3166 two-letter country code. These are used when constructing new `Locale` objects. If a locale doesn't have a country code, you can construct it with the language code. The last column is the mnemonic constant (public final static variable) that refers to a `Locale` object for a given locale. Not all locales supported are associated with such constants. Microsoft's Java virtual machine adds about 50 locale constants to those in Table 16-1 and includes support for several dozen additional locales.

Table 16-1. The Locales Supported in Java 1.1

Language	Script	Country	Language Code	Country Code	Constant
Albanian	Roman	Albania	sq		
Arabic	Arabic	Egypt	ar		
Byelorus-sian	Cyrillic	Belarus	be		
Bulgarian	Cyrillic	Bulgaria	bg		
Catalan	Roman	Spain	ca		
Chinese	Chinese	China	zh		`Locale.SIMPLIFIED_CHINESE` `Locale.CHINA` `Locale.PRC`
Chinese	Chinese	Taiwan	zh	TW	`Locale.TRADITIONAL_CHINESE` `Locale.TAIWAN`
Croatian	Roman	Croatia	hr		
Czech	Roman	Czech Republic	cs		
Danish	Roman	Denmark	da		
Dutch	Roman	Netherlands	nl		
Dutch	Roman	Belgium	nl	BE	
English	Roman	Canada	en	CA	`Locale.CANADA`
English	Roman	United Kingdom	en	GB	`Locale.UK`
English	Roman	Ireland	en	IE	
English	Roman	United States	en		`Locale.US`
Estonian	Roman	Estonia	et		
Finnish	Roman	Finland	fi		

Table 16-1. The Locales Supported in Java 1.1 (continued)

Language	Script	Country	Language Code	Country Code	Constant
French	Roman	France	fr		Locale.FRANCE
French	Roman	Belgium	fr	BE	
French	Roman	Canada	fr	CA	Locale.CANADA_FRENCH
French	Roman	Switzerland	fr	CH	
German	Roman	Germany	de		Locale.GERMANY
German	Roman	Austria	de	AT	
German	Roman	Switzerland	de	CH	
Greek	Greek	Greece	el		
Hebrew	Hebrew	Israel	iw		
Hungarian	Roman	Hungary	hu		
Icelandic	Roman	Iceland	is		
Italian	Roman	Italy	it		Locale.ITALY
Italian	Roman	Switzerland	it	CH	
Japanese	Japanese	Japan	ja		Locale.JAPAN
Korean	Korean	Korea	ko		Locale.KOREA
Latvian	Roman	Latvia	lv		
Lithuanian	Roman	Lithuania	lt		
Macedonian	Cyrillic	Macedonia	mk		
Norwegian (Bokmål)	Roman	Norway	no		
Norwegian (Nynorsk)	Roman	Norway	no	NO	
Polish	Roman	Poland	pl		
Portuguese	Roman	Portugal	pt		
Romanian	Roman	Romania	ro		
Russian	Cyrillic	Russia	ru		
Serbian	Cyrillic	Serbia	sr		
Serbian	Roman	Serbia	sh		
Slovak	Roman	Slovakia	sk		
Slovene	Roman	Slovenia	sl		
Spanish - Modern Sort	Roman	Spain	es		
Swedish	Roman	Sweden	sv		
Turkish	Roman	Turkey	tr		
Ukrainian	Cyrillic	Ukraine	uk		

In addition to the constants shown in Table 16-1, there are seven constants that refer only to a language, not to a specific country or region:

```
Locale.ENGLISH
Locale.FRENCH
Locale.GERMAN
Locale.ITALIAN
Locale.JAPANESE
Locale.KOREAN
Locale.CHINESE
```

If there isn't a mnemonic constant for the locale you need, you can create your own using the constructors in `java.util.Locale`:

```
public Locale(String languageCode, String countryCode)
public Locale(String languageCode, String countryCode, String variantCode)
```

The language and country codes are the two-letter codes given in Table 16-1. If no two-letter country code is listed for the locale in Table 16-1, just pass in the empty string instead. For example:

```
Locale turkey = new Locale("tr", "");
Locale swissItalian = new Locale("it", "CH");
```

The variant is for vendor-specific extensions and is rarely used. The only encodings in Table 16-1 that list variants are the two Norwegian encodings, Norwegian (Bokmål) and Norwegian (Nynorsk). The Nynorsk encoding has a variant code of "NY". It is permissible to provide Java more information than it needs. If Java cannot find the variant locale you request, it provides a locale that only matches the language and country. If it cannot find a locale that matches the language and the country, it will settle for one that matches the language.

Number Formats

To print a formatted number in Java, perform these two steps:

1. Format the number as a string.

2. Print the string.

Simple, right? Of course, this is a little like the old recipe for rabbit stew:

1. Catch a rabbit.

2. Boil rabbit in pot with vegetables and spices.

Obviously, step 1 is the tricky part. Fortunately, formatting numbers as strings is somewhat easier than catching a rabbit. The key class that formats numbers as strings is `java.text.NumberFormat`. This is an abstract subclass of `java.text.Format`. Concrete subclasses such as `java.text.DecimalFormat` implement formatting policies for particular kinds of numbers.

```
public abstract class NumberFormat extends Format implements Cloneable
```

The static `NumberFormat.getAvailableLocales()` method returns a list of all locales installed that provide number formats. (There may be a few locales installed that only provide date or text formats, not number formats.)

```
public static Locale[] getAvailableLocales()
```

You can request a `NumberFormat` object for the default locale of the host computer or for one of the specified locales in Table 16-1 using the static `NumberFormat.getInstance()` method. For example:

```
NumberFormat myFormat = NumberFormat.getInstance();
NumberFormat canadaFormat = NumberFormat.getInstance(Locale.CANADA);
Locale turkey = new Locale("tr", "");
NumberFormat turkishFormat = NumberFormat.getInstance(turkey);
Locale swissItalian = new Locale("it", "CH");
NumberFormat swissItalianFormat = NumberFormat.getInstance(swissItalian);
```

The number format returned by `NumberFormat.getInstance()` should do a reasonable job of formatting most numbers. However, there's at least a theoretical possibility that the instance returned will format numbers as currencies or percentages. Therefore, it wouldn't hurt to use `NumberFormat.getNumberInstance()` instead:

```
public static final NumberFormat getNumberInstance()
public static NumberFormat getNumberInstance(Locale inLocale)
```

For example:

```
NumberFormat myFormat = NumberFormat.getNumberInstance();
NumberFormat canadaFormat = NumberFormat.getNumberInstance(Locale.CANADA);
```

Formatting Numbers

Once you've got a `NumberFormat` object, you can convert integers and floating point numbers into formatted strings using one of `NumberFormat`'s five overloaded format methods:

```
public final String format(long number)
public final String format(double number)
public abstract StringBuffer format(long number, StringBuffer toAppendTo,
   FieldPosition pos)
public abstract StringBuffer format(double number, StringBuffer toAppendTo,
   FieldPosition pos)
public final StringBuffer format(Object number, StringBuffer toAppendTo,
   FieldPosition pos)
```

These methods all read the number and return a string or a modified string buffer based on that number using the number format's default formatting rules. These rules generally specify:

- Maximum and minimum integer width

- Maximum and minimum fraction width (precision, number of decimal places)

- Whether or not digits are grouped (e.g., 2,109,356 versus 2109356)

For any given number format, these rules can be quite complex. For instance, they may or may not take into account different digit sets, exponential or scientific notation, Roman numerals, or more. By creating new subclasses of NumberFormat, you can specify arbitrarily complex rules for converting binary numbers into strings. Regardless of exactly how a number format formats numbers, they are all manipulated the same way.

The last three format() methods append the string to the specified StringBuffer toAppendTo. They then return that modified string buffer. They use a java.text.FieldPosition object to provide information to the client programmer about where the different parts of the number fall. This will be discussed later. The final format() method is used to format instances of the numeric type wrapper classes; that is, java.lang.Double, java.lang.Float, java.lang.Long, java.lang.Integer, java.lang.Short, java.lang.Character, and java.lang.Byte. It merely determines the type of the argument and passes either the double or long value of the argument to the format() method. Passing any other kind of object to this method will cause an IllegalArgumentException.

Example 16-1 is about the simplest use of NumberFormat imaginable. It uses the default number format for the default locale to print multiples of π. For comparison, both the formatted and unformatted numbers are printed.

Example 16-1. Multiples of π

```
import java.text.*;

public class FormatTest {

  public static void main(String[] args) {

    NumberFormat nf = NumberFormat.getInstance();
    for (double x = Math.PI; x < 100000; x *= 10) {
      String formattedNumber = nf.format(x);
      System.out.println(formattedNumber + "\t" + x);
    }
  }
}
```

On my U.S. English system, the results look like this:

```
3.141        3.14159265358979
31.415       31.4159265358979
314.159      314.159265358979
3,141.592    3141.5926535897897
31,415.926   31415.926535897896
```

The formatted numbers don't use a ridiculous number of decimal places and group the integer part with commas when it becomes large. Of course, the exact formatting depends on the default locale. For instance, when I changed the locale to French, I encountered this result:

```
3,141        3.14159265358979
31,415       31.4159265358979
314,159      314.159265358979
3 141,592    3141.5926535897897
31 415,926   31415.926535897896
```

The French locale uses a decimal comma instead of a decimal point and separates every three digits in the integer part with a space. This may be confusing to an American, but seems perfectly normal to a Parisian. One of the advantages of number formats is that by using the default number format for the system, much of your program is automatically localized. No extra code is required to do the right thing on French systems, on Canadian systems, on Japanese systems, and so on.

Specifying Precision

Number formats have both a maximum and a minimum number of integer and fraction digits that are presented in each number. For instance, in the number 31.415 there are two integer digits and three fraction digits. If the maximum number of digits in a part is less than the number actually present, the number is truncated (integer part) or rounded (fraction part). If the minimum is greater than the number of digits actually present, then extra zeros are added at the beginning of the integer part or after the fraction part. For example, with a minimum of three integer digits and a maximum of two fraction digits, 31.415 would be formatted as 031.42.

You specify the minimum and maximum of each type you want in each number using these four methods:

```
public void setMaximumIntegerDigits(int newValue)
public void setMinimumIntegerDigits(int newValue)
public void setMaximumFractionDigits(int newValue)
public void setMinimumFractionDigits(int newValue)
```

For example, to specify that myFormat should format numbers with at least 10 digits before the decimal point and at most 3 digits after, you would type:

```
myFormat.setMinimumIntegerDigits(10);
myFormat.setMaximumFractionDigits(3);
```

Setting the minimum digits guarantees that those digits will be printed, filled with zeros if necessary. Setting the maximum digits allows the digits to be printed if they're nonzero or a place-holding zero (i.e., not the leftmost or rightmost digit). Leftmost and rightmost strings of zeros will only be printed if it's required to meet the minimum number of digits. If you try to set a maximum below a minimum or a minimum above a maximum, the last one set takes precedence. Java raises the maximum to meet the minimum or lowers the minimum to meet the maximum.

Specifying the number of digits is useful when printing many columns of numbers in a tabular format to the console or in a monospaced font. Example 16-2 prints a three-column table of the angles between 0 and 360 degrees in degrees, radians and grads without any formatting.

Example 16-2. UglyTable

```
public class UglyTable {

  public static void main(String[] args) {

    System.out.println("Degrees \tRadians \tGrads");
    for (double degrees = 0.0; degrees < 360.0; degrees++) {
      double radians = Math.PI * degrees / 180.0;
      double grads = 400 * degrees / 360;
      System.out.println(degrees + "\t" + radians + "\t" + grads);
    }
  }
}
```

Its output looks like this (not very pretty):

```
300.0 5.2359877559829835 333.3333333333333
301.0 5.253441048502927 334.44444444444446
302.0 5.27089434102287 335.55555555555554
303.0 5.288347633542813 336.6666666666667
304.0 5.305800926062757 337.77777777777777
305.0 5.3232542185827 338.8888888888889
306.0 5.340707511102643 340.0
```

Example 16-3 prints the same table with each number formatted to at least three integer digits and exactly two fraction digits (both minimum and maximum set to 2).

Example 16-3. PrettyTable

```
import java.text.*;

public class PrettyTable {

  public static void main(String[] args) {

    System.out.println("Degrees Radians Grads");
    NumberFormat myFormat = NumberFormat.getInstance();
    myFormat.setMinimumIntegerDigits(3);
    myFormat.setMaximumFractionDigits(2);
    myFormat.setMinimumFractionDigits(2);
    for (double degrees = 0.0; degrees < 360.0; degrees++) {
      String radianString = myFormat.format(Math.PI * degrees / 180.0);
      String gradString = myFormat.format(400 * degrees / 360);
      String degreeString = myFormat.format(degrees);
      System.out.println(degreeString + "  " + radianString
        + "  " + gradString);
    }
  }
}
```

Its output looks like this (much nicer):

```
300.00  005.23  333.33
301.00  005.25  334.44
302.00  005.27  335.55
303.00  005.28  336.66
304.00  005.30  337.77
305.00  005.32  338.88
306.00  005.34  340.00
...
```

Note that the extra integer digits are padded with zeros rather than spaces. You'll learn how to fix that shortly.

There are `getMinimumIntegerDigits()` and `getMaximumIntegerDigits()` methods that let you inspect the minimum and maximum number of digits provided by any number format, including the default:

```
public int getMaximumIntegerDigits()
public int getMinimumIntegerDigits()
public int getMaximumFractionDigits()
public int getMinimumFractionDigits()
```

Grouping

How big is 299792500? You can't easily tell because the number is hard to read. It's obviously a pretty big number, but at a glance most people can't tell whether it's in the ballpark of 3 million, 30 million, 300 million, or 3 billion. On the other hand, if it's written as 299,792,500, it's a lot more obvious that the number is about 300 million. The commas group different parts of the number. By counting the groups, you get a quick idea of the number's order of magnitude.

Like other aspects of text formatting, different locales use different grouping conventions. In Belgium, Denmark, Holland, Spain, and Germany, a period groups thousands and a comma is used as the "decimal point." Thus, the U.S. number 2,365,335.32 is equivalent to the Danish/Dutch number 2.365.335,32. Finnish uses an English-style decimal point but separates characters with a space rather than a comma. Thus, 2,365,335.32 is, in Finnish, 2 365 335.32. France, Sweden, and Norway also separate thousands with spaces but use a decimal comma: 2 365 335,32. Francophone Canada follows France's convention, but Canadian Anglophones use the American-British convention. And in Switzerland, an apostrophe is used to separate thousands in all four languages: 2'365'335.32

Most number formats support grouping, and some use it by default. You may inquire whether a particular `NumberFormat` uses grouping with the `isGrouping-Used()` method:

```
public boolean isGroupingUsed()
```

This method returns `true` if the format groups numbers, `false` if it doesn't. You can turn grouping on or off for a number format with the `setGroupingUsed()` method:

```
public void setGroupingUsed(boolean groupNumbers)
```

Passing `true` turns grouping on. Passing `false` turns it off. You'll usually want to use grouping in strings that will be read by human beings and not use grouping in strings that will be parsed by computers.

Currency Formats

It's not hard to tack on a dollar sign before a decimal number with two digits of precision. The `NumberFormat` class does a little more, handling international currencies with relative ease. If you know you're going to be working with money, you can request the default locale's currency formatter with the static `NumberFormat.getCurrencyInstance()` method:

```
public static final NumberFormat getCurrencyInstance()
```

To get a currency formatter for a different locale, pass the locale to `Number-Format.getCurrencyInstance()`:

```
public static NumberFormat getCurrencyInstance(Locale inLocale)
```

Example 16-4 calculates the annual earnings of a worker making minimum wage in U.S. dollars. A currency format returned by `NumberFormat.getCurrency-Instance(Locale.ENGLISH)` formats the monetary quantities.

Example 16-4. Currency Formats

```
import java.text.*;
import java.util.*;

public class MinimumWage {

  public static void main(String[] args) {

    NumberFormat dollarFormat = NumberFormat.getCurrencyInstance(Locale.ENGLISH);
    double minimumWage = 5.15;

    System.out.println("The minimum wage is "
      + dollarFormat.format(minimumWage));
    System.out.println("A worker earning minimum wage and working for forty");
    System.out.println("hours a week, 52 weeks a year, would earn "
      + dollarFormat.format(40*52*minimumWage));
  }
}
```

This program prints:

```
The minimum wage is $5.15
A worker earning minimum wage and working for forty
hours a week, 52 weeks a year, would earn $10,712.00
```

Notice how nicely the numbers are formatted. Nowhere did I add dollar signs, say that I wanted exactly two numbers after the decimal point, or say that I wanted to separate the thousands with commas. The `NumberFormat` class took care of that.

There are limits to how far currency formatting goes. Currency formats may change the currency sign in different locales, but they won't convert the values (between U.S. and Canadian dollars or between U.S. dollars and British pounds, for example). Since conversion rates float from day to day and minute to minute, that's a bit much to ask of a static class. If you want to do this, you need to provide some source of the conversion rate information, either from user input or pulled off the network.

Percent Formats

Number formats can also handle percentages in a variety of international formats. In grammar school math you learned that a number followed by a percent sign is really one-hundredth of its apparent value. Thus, 50% is really decimal 0.5, 100% is 1.0, 10% is 0.1, and so on. Percent formats allow you to use the actual decimal values in your code but print out the hundred-times larger percent values in the output. You request the default locale's percentage formatter with the static method `NumberFormat.getPercentInstance()`:

```
public static final NumberFormat getpercentInstance()
```

To get a percentage formatter for a different locale, pass the locale to `Number-Format.getPercentInstance()`:

```
public static NumberFormat getPercentInstance(Locale inLocale)
```

Example 16-5 prints a table of percents between 1% and 100%. Notice that `doubles` are used in the code, but integral percents appear in the output.

Example 16-5. PercentTable

```java
import java.text.*;
import java.util.*;

public class PercentTable {

  public static void main(String[] args) {

    NumberFormat percentFormat = NumberFormat.getPercentInstance(Locale.ENGLISH);

    for (double d = 0.0; d <= 1.0; d += 0.005) {
      System.out.println(percentFormat.format(d));
    }
  }
}
```

Here's some of the output:

```
0%
0%
1%
1%
2%
2%
3%
3%
4%
4%
...
```

Notice that all percentage values are rounded to the nearest whole percent. This could be a problem if you need to format something like a tax rate. There is no 0.5% or 8.25% as you might need when describing sales tax. If you want to include fractional percents, you can use the same `setMinimumFractionDigits()` and `setMaximumFractionDigits()` methods you'd use for any `NumberFormat` object. For example:

```
NumberFormat percentFormat = NumberFormat.getPercentInstance(Locale.ENGLISH);
percentFormat.setMaximumFractionDigits(2);
```

Utility Methods

For completeness, I'll note that `NumberFormat` overrides the usual three utility methods from `java.lang.Object`, `hashCode()`, `clone()`, and `equals()`:

```
public int hashCode()
public boolean equals(Object obj)
public Object clone()
```

One `NumberFormat` equals another `NumberFormat` if they're instances of the same subclass of `NumberFormat` (`NumberFormat` is abstract, so there aren't any pure instances of it), and the two objects specify the same maximum and minimum number of integer digits, the same maximum and minimum number of fraction digits, and both either can or cannot only parse integers.

Specifying Width with FieldPosition

The Java core API does not include any classes that pad numbers with spaces like the traditional I/O APIs in Fortran, C, and other languages. Part of the reason is that it's no longer a valid assumption that all output is written in a monospaced font on a VT-100 terminal. Therefore, spaces are insufficient to line up numbers in tables. Ideally, if you're writing tabular data in a GUI, you can use a real table component like `JTable` in the Java foundation classes. If that's not possible, you can measure the width of the string using a `FontMetrics` object and offset the position at which you draw the string. And if you are outputting to a terminal or a monospaced font, then you can manually prefix the string with the right number of spaces.

The `java.text.FieldPosition` class separates strings into their component parts, called *fields*. (This is another unfortunate example of an overloaded term. These fields have nothing to do with the fields of a Java class.) For example, a typical date string can be separated into 18 fields including era, year, month, day, date, hour, minute, second, and so on. Of course, not all of these may be present in any given string. For example, 1999 CE includes only a year and an era field. The different fields that can be parsed are represented as `public final static int` fields (there's that annoying overloading again) in the corresponding format class. The `java.text.DateFormat` class defines these kinds of fields as mnemonic constants:

```
public static final int ERA_FIELD
public static final int YEAR_FIELD
```

```
public static final int MONTH_FIELD
public static final int DATE_FIELD
public static final int HOUR_OF_DAY1_FIELD
public static final int HOUR_OF_DAY0_FIELD
public static final int MINUTE_FIELD
public static final int SECOND_FIELD
public static final int MILLISECOND_FIELD
public static final int DAY_OF_WEEK_FIELD
public static final int DAY_OF_YEAR_FIELD
public static final int DAY_OF_WEEK_IN_MONTH_FIELD
public static final int WEEK_OF_YEAR_FIELD
public static final int WEEK_OF_MONTH_FIELD
public static final int AM_PM_FIELD
public static final int HOUR1_FIELD
public static final int HOUR0_FIELD
public static final int TIMEZONE_FIELD
```

Number formats are a little simpler. They are divided into only two fields, the integer field and the fraction field. These are represented by the mnemonic constants `NumberFormat.INTEGER_FIELD` and `NumberFormat.FRACTION_FIELD`:

```
public static final int INTEGER_FIELD
public static final int FRACTION_FIELD
```

The integer field is everything before the decimal point. The fraction field is everything after the decimal point. For instance, the string "–156.32" has an integer field of "–156" and a fraction field of "32".

The `java.text.FieldPosition` class identifies the boundaries of each field in the numeric string. You can then manually add the right number of monospaced characters or pixels to align the decimal points in a column of numbers. You create a `FieldPosition` object by passing one of these numeric constants into the `FieldPosition()` constructor:

```
public FieldPosition(int field)
```

For example, to get the integer field:

```
FieldPosition fp = new FieldPosition(NumberFormat.INTEGER_FIELD);
```

There's a `getField()` method that returns this constant:

```
public int getField()
```

Next you pass this object into one of the `format()` methods that takes a `FieldPosition` object as an argument:

```
NumberFormat nf = NumberFormat().getNumberInstance();
StringBuffer sb = nf.format(2.71828, new StringBuffer(), fp);
```

When `format()` returns, the `FieldPosition` object contains the beginning and ending index of the field in the string. These methods return those items:

```
public int getBeginIndex()
public int getEndIndex()
```

You can subtract getBeginIndex() from getEndIndex() to find the number of characters in the field. If you're working with a monospaced font, this may be all you need to know. If you're working with a proportionally spaced font, you'll probably use java.awt.FontMetrics to measure the exact width of the field instead. Example 16-6 shows how to work in a monospaced font. This is essentially another version of the angle table. Now a FieldPosition object is used to figure out how many spaces to add to the front of the string; the getSpaces() method is simply used to build a string with a certain number of spaces.

Example 16-6. PrettierTable

```
import java.text.*;

public class PrettierTable {

  public static void main(String[] args) {

    NumberFormat myFormat = NumberFormat.getNumberInstance();
    FieldPosition fp = new FieldPosition(NumberFormat.INTEGER_FIELD);
    myFormat.setMaximumIntegerDigits(3);
    myFormat.setMaximumFractionDigits(2);
    myFormat.setMinimumFractionDigits(2);

    System.out.println("Degrees  Radians  Grads");
    for (double degrees = 0.0; degrees < 360.0; degrees++) {
      String radianString = myFormat.format(
          Math.PI * degrees / 180.0, new StringBuffer(), fp).toString();
      radianString = getSpaces(3 - fp.getEndIndex()) + radianString;
      String gradString = myFormat.format(
          400 * degrees / 360, new StringBuffer(), fp).toString();
      gradString = getSpaces(3 - fp.getEndIndex()) + gradString;
      String degreeString = myFormat.format(
          degrees, new StringBuffer(), fp).toString();
      degreeString = getSpaces(3 - fp.getEndIndex()) + degreeString;
      System.out.println(degreeString + "  " + radianString + "  " + gradString);
    }
  }

  public static String getSpaces(int n) {

    StringBuffer sb = new StringBuffer(n);
    for (int i = 0; i < n; i++) sb.append(' ');
    return sb.toString();
  }
}
```

Here's some sample output. Notice the alignment of the decimal points:

```
% java PrettierTable
Degrees  Radians  Grads
  0.00    0.00    0.00
  1.00    0.02    1.11
  2.00    0.03    2.22
  3.00    0.05    3.33
  4.00    0.07    4.44
  5.00    0.09    5.56
  6.00    0.10    6.67
  7.00    0.12    7.78
  8.00    0.14    8.89
  9.00    0.16   10.00
 10.00    0.17   11.11
 11.00    0.19   12.22
 12.00    0.21   13.33
 13.00    0.23   14.44
```

This technique only works with monospaced fonts. In GUI environments, you'll need to work with pixels instead of characters. Instead of prefixing a string with spaces, you adjust the position where the pen starts drawing each string. The `getBeginIndex()` and `getEndIndex()` methods, along with `substring()` in `java.lang.String` can be used to get the actual field, and the `stringWidth()` method in the `java.awt.FontMetrics` class can tell you how wide the field is.

Example 16-7 is yet another variant of the angle table. This one draws the angles in an applet. Figure 16-1 shows a screen shot of the running applet. This technique works equally well in a panel, frame, scroll pane, canvas, or other drawing environment with a `paint()` method.

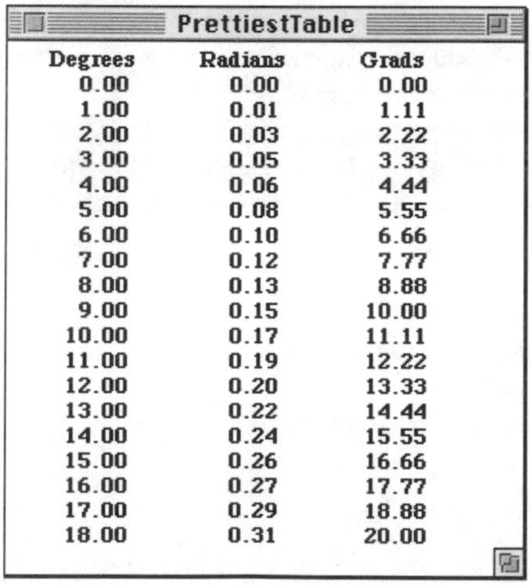

Degrees	Radians	Grads
0.00	0.00	0.00
1.00	0.01	1.11
2.00	0.03	2.22
3.00	0.05	3.33
4.00	0.06	4.44
5.00	0.08	5.55
6.00	0.10	6.66
7.00	0.12	7.77
8.00	0.13	8.88
9.00	0.15	10.00
10.00	0.17	11.11
11.00	0.19	12.22
12.00	0.20	13.33
13.00	0.22	14.44
14.00	0.24	15.55
15.00	0.26	16.66
16.00	0.27	17.77
17.00	0.29	18.88
18.00	0.31	20.00

Figure 16-1. The PrettiestTable applet

Example 16-7. PrettiestTable

```java
import java.text.*;
import java.applet.*;
import java.awt.*;

public class PrettiestTable extends Applet {

  NumberFormat myFormat = NumberFormat.getNumberInstance();
  FieldPosition fp = new FieldPosition(NumberFormat.INTEGER_FIELD);

  public void init() {

    this.setFont(new Font("Serif", Font.BOLD, 12));
    myFormat.setMaximumIntegerDigits(3);
    myFormat.setMaximumFractionDigits(2);
    myFormat.setMinimumFractionDigits(2);
  }

  public void paint(Graphics g) {

    FontMetrics fm = this.getFontMetrics(this.getFont()) ;
    int xmargin = 5;
    int lineHeight = fm.getMaxAscent() + fm.getMaxDescent();
    int y = lineHeight;
    int x = xmargin;
    int desiredPixelWidth = 3 * fm.getMaxAdvance();
    int fieldWidth = 6 * fm.getMaxAdvance();
    int headerWidth = fm.stringWidth("Degrees");
    g.drawString("Degrees", x + (fieldWidth - headerWidth)/2, y);
    headerWidth = fm.stringWidth("Radians");
    g.drawString("Radians", x + fieldWidth + (fieldWidth - headerWidth)/2, y);
    headerWidth = fm.stringWidth("Grads");
    g.drawString("Grads", x + 2*fieldWidth + (fieldWidth - headerWidth)/2, y);

    for (double degrees = 0.0; degrees < 360.0; degrees++) {
      y += lineHeight;
      String degreeString = myFormat.format(degrees, new StringBuffer(),
          fp).toString();
      String intPart = degreeString.substring(0, fp.getEndIndex());
      g.drawString(degreeString, xmargin + desiredPixelWidth
          - fm.stringWidth(intPart), y);
      String radianString = myFormat.format(Math.PI*degrees/180.0,
          new StringBuffer(), fp).toString();
      intPart = radianString.substring(0, fp.getEndIndex());
      g.drawString(radianString,
          xmargin + fieldWidth + desiredPixelWidth - fm.stringWidth(intPart), y);
      String gradString = myFormat.format(400 * degrees / 360,
          new StringBuffer(), fp).toString();
      intPart = gradString.substring(0, fp.getEndIndex());
```

Example 16-7. PrettiestTable (continued)

```
    g.drawString(gradString,
      xmargin + 2*fieldWidth + desiredPixelWidth - fm.stringWidth(intPart), y);
  }
 }
}
```

Parsing Input

Number formats also handle input. When used for input, a number format converts a string in the appropriate format to a binary number, achieving more flexible conversions than you can get with the methods in the type wrapper classes (like `Integer.parseInt()`). For instance, a percent format `parse()` method can interpret 57% as 0.57 instead of 57. A currency format can read (12.45) as –12.45.

There are three `parse()` methods in the `NumberFormat` class. All do roughly the same thing:

```
public Number parse(String text) throws ParseException
public abstract Number parse(String text, ParsePosition parsePosition)
public final Object parseObject(String source, ParsePosition parsePosition)
```

The first `parse()` method attempts to parse a number from the given text. If the text represents an integer, it's returned as an instance of `java.lang.Long`. Otherwise, it's returned as an instance of `java.lang.Double`. If a string contains multiple numbers, only the first one is returned. For instance, if you parse "32 meters" you'll get the number 32 back. Java throws away everything after the number finishes. If the text cannot be interpreted as a number in the given format, a `ParseException` is thrown. The second `parse()` method specifies where in the text parsing starts. The position is given by a `ParsePosition` object. This is a little more complicated than using a simple `int` but does have the advantage of allowing one to read successive numbers from the same string. The third `parse()` method merely invokes the second. It's declared to return `Object` rather than `Number` so that it can override the method of the same signature in `java.text.Format`. If you know you're working with a `NumberFormat` rather than a `DateFormat` or some other nonnumeric format, there's no reason to use it.

The `java.text.ParsePosition` class has one constructor and two public methods:

```
public ParsePosition(int index)
public int getIndex()
public void setIndex(int index)
```

This whole class is just a wrapper around an `int` position, which is set by the constructor and the `setIndex()` mutator method. It's returned by the getIndex() method. As a NumberFormat parses a string, it updates the associated ParsePosition's index. Thus, when passed into a parse() method, the ParsePosition contains the index where parsing will begin. When the parse() method returns, the ParsePosition contains the index immediately after the last character parsed. If parsing fails, the parse position is unchanged.

Some number formats can only read integers, not floating point numbers. The isParseIntegerOnly() method returns true if this is the case, false otherwise.

```
public boolean isParseIntegerOnly()
public void setParseIntegerOnly(boolean value)
```

The setParseInteger() method lets you specify that the format should only parse integers. If a decimal point is encountered, then parsing should stop.

Example 16-8 is a simple program of the sort that's common in CS 101 courses. The assignment is to write a program that reads a number entered from the command line and prints its square root. Successive numbers are read until a negative number is entered, at which point the program halts. Although this is a very basic exercise, it's relatively complex in Java, because Java separates string parsing from basic I/O. Nonetheless, while it may not be suitable for the first week's homework, students should be able to handle it by the end of the semester.

Example 16-8. RootFinder

```
import java.text.*;
import java.io.*;

public class RootFinder {

  public static void main(String[] args) {

    Number input = null;

    try {
      BufferedReader br = new BufferedReader(new InputStreamReader(System.in));
      NumberFormat nf = NumberFormat.getInstance();
      while (true) {
        System.out.println("Enter a number (-1 to quit): ");
        String s = br.readLine();
        try {
          input = nf.parse(s);
        }
        catch (ParseException e) {
          System.out.println(s + " is not a number I understand.");
          continue;
        }
        double d = input.doubleValue();
        if (d < 0) break;
```

Example 16-8. RootFinder (continued)

```
        double root = Math.sqrt(d);
        System.out.println("The square root of " + s + " is " + root);
      }
    }
    catch (IOException e) {System.err.println(e);}
  }
}
```

Here's a sample run:

```
% java RootFinder
Enter a number (-1 to quit):
87
The square root of 87 is 9.327379053088816
Enter a number (-1 to quit):
3.151592
The square root of 3.151592 is 1.7752723734683644
Enter a number (-1 to quit):
2,345,678
The square root of 2,345,678 is 1531.5606419596973
Enter a number (-1 to quit):
2.998E+8
The square root of 2.998E+8 is 1.7314733610425546
Enter a number (-1 to quit):
299800000
The square root of 299800000 is 17314.733610425545
Enter a number (-1 to quit):
0.0
The square root of 0.0 is 0.0
Enter a number (-1 to quit):
four
four is not a number I understand.
Enter a number (-1 to quit):
4
The square root of 4 is 2.0
Enter a number (-1 to quit):
(12)
(12) is not a number I understand.
Enter a number (-1 to quit):
-1
```

These results tell you a few things about the default number format on the platform where I ran it (U.S. English Solaris, JDK 1.1.4). First, it doesn't understand exponential notation. The square root of 2.998E+8 is not 1.7314733610425546; it's 1.7314733610425546E+4. The number format parsed up to the first character it didn't recognize (E) and stopped, thus returning the square root of 2.998 instead. You can also see that this number format doesn't understand negative numbers represented by parentheses or words like "four." On the other hand, it can parse numbers with thousands separators like 2,345,678. This is more than the I/O libraries in most other languages can do. With the appropriate, nondefault number format, Java could parse (12), four, and 2.998E+8 as well.

Decimal Formats

The `java.text` package contains a single concrete subclass of `NumberFormat`, `DecimalFormat`. The `DecimalFormat` class provides even more control over how floating point numbers are formatted:

```
public class DecimalFormat extends NumberFormat
```

Most number formats are in fact decimal formats. Generally, you can simply cast any number format to a decimal format, like this:

```
DecimalFormat df = (DecimalFormat) NumberFormat.getCurrencyInstance();
```

At least in theory, you might encounter a nondecimal format. Therefore, you should use `instanceof` to test whether or not you've got a `DecimalFormat`:

```
NumberFormat nf = NumberFormat.getCurrencyInstance();
if (nf instanceof DecimalFormat) {
  DecimalFormat df = (DecimalFormat) NumberFormat.getCurrencyInstance();
  //...
}
```

Alternately, you can place the cast and associated operations in a `try`/`catch` block that catches `ClassCastExceptions`:

```
try {
  DecimalFormat df = (DecimalFormat) NumberFormat.getCurrencyInstance();
  //...
}
catch (ClassCastException e) {System.err.println(e);}
```

Decimal Format Patterns and Symbols

Every `DecimalFormat` object has a pattern that describes how numbers are formatted and a list of symbols that describes with which characters they're formatted. This allows the single `DecimalFormat` class to be parameterized so that it can handle many different formats for different kinds of numbers in many locales. The pattern is given as an ASCII string. The symbols are provided by a `DecimalFormatSymbols` object. These are accessed and manipulated through the following six methods:

```
public DecimalFormatSymbols getDecimalFormatSymbols()
public void setDecimalFormatSymbols(DecimalFormatSymbols newSymbols)
public String toPattern()
public String toLocalizedPattern()
```

```
public void applyPattern(String pattern)
public void applyLocalizedPattern(String pattern)
```

The decimal format symbols specify the characters or strings used for the zero digit, the grouping separator, the decimal sign, the percent sign, the mille percent sign, infinity (IEEE 754 Inf), not a number (IEEE 754 NaN), and the minus sign. In American English these are 0, ,, ., %, ‰, Inf, NaN, and -, respectively. They may be other things in different locales.

The `pattern` specifies whether leading and trailing zeros are to be printed, whether the fractional part of the number is printed, the number of digits in a group (three in American English), and the leading and trailing suffixes for negative and positive numbers. Patterns are described using an almost Backus-Naur Form (BNF) grammar, given here:

```
pattern      ->  subpattern{;subpattern}
subpattern   ->  {prefix}integer{.fraction}{suffix}
prefix       ->  '\\u0000'..'\\uFFFD' - specialCharacters
suffix       ->  '\\u0000'..'\\uFFFD' - specialCharacters
integer      ->  '#'* '0'* '0'
fraction     ->  '0'* '#'*
```

The first line is not pure BNF. The first subpattern is used for positive numbers. The second subpattern, which may not be present, is used for negative numbers. If it's not present, negative numbers use the positive format but are prefixed with a minus sign. Table 16-2 defines the symbols used in the grammar.

Table 16-2. Symbols Used in Decimal Format Patterns

Symbol	Meaning
0	A digit, including leading or trailing zeros
#	A digit, except for leading or trailing zero
.	Decimal separator
,	Grouping separator
;	Separates formats
-	Default negative prefix
%	Divide by 100 and show as percentage
X	Any other characters can be used in the prefix or suffix
'	Used to quote special characters in a prefix or suffix
X*	Zero or more occurrences of X
(X | Y)	Either X or Y
X..Y	Any character from X through Y inclusive
S - T	Characters in S but not in T

This results in patterns like those seen in Table 16-3 for various locales. For instance, #,##0.### is the decimal format pattern for U.S. English and most other non-Arabic-speaking locales. The # mark means any digit character except a leading or trailing zero. The comma is the grouping separator, the period is the decimal point separator, and the 0 is a digit that will be printed even if it's a nonsignificant zero. You interpret this pattern as follows:

1. The integer part contains as many digits as necessary.

2. These are separated every three digits with the grouping separator.

3. If the integer part contains only zeros, there is a single zero before the decimal separator.

4. Up to three digits are printed after the decimal separator. However, they are not printed if they are trailing zeros.

5. No separate pattern is included for negative numbers. Therefore, they will be printed the same as a positive number but prefixed with a minus sign.

It's relatively painful to work with this grammar directly. Fortunately, there are methods that allow you to get and set the values of these individual pieces directly, and I recommend that you use them:

```
public String getPositivePrefix()
public void setPositivePrefix(String newValue)
public String getPositiveSuffix()
public void setPositiveSuffix(String newValue)
public String getNegativePrefix()
public void setNegativePrefix(String newValue)
public String getNegativeSuffix()
public void setNegativeSuffix(String newValue)
public int getMultiplier()
public void setMultiplier(int newValue)
public int getGroupingSize()
public void setGroupingSize(int newValue)
public boolean isDecimalSeparatorAlwaysShown()
public void setDecimalSeparatorAlwaysShown(boolean newValue)
```

I can only guess why the patterns and the decimal format symbols themselves are exposed as much as they are in the java.text package. In my opinion, this is poor design, since it ties the interface too closely to the implementation of the class. The get and set methods are fully adequate for manipulating the formatting. Since you probably won't be setting a pattern more than once or twice in a program (how many different formats does one program need?), there's no significant performance gain by using a pattern instead of the get and set methods. And there is a significant cost in complexity. Allowing direct setting of patterns requires the class to check that the patterns are valid and throw a ParseException if they're not. The only advantage I can see to manipulating number formats as pattern strings is that it makes them easy to store in resource bundles. However, I'm not sure this ability really needs to be public.

The positive prefix is the string prefixed to positive numbers. Most of the time this is the empty string "", but in some circumstances you might want to use a plus sign (+). In currency formats, the positive prefix is often set to the currency sign, like $ or £, depending on the locale. You can also set a positive suffix; that is, a string that is appended to all positive numbers. I'm not aware of any number formats that use positive suffixes, but if you need to, you can. The negative prefix is the minus sign (–). However, in accounting and other financial applications it may be an open parenthesis instead. In these applications, there's also a negative suffix, generally a closing parenthesis. Thus, –12 might be formatted as (12).

The multiplier is an integer by which the number is multiplied before being formatted. This is commonly used in percent formats. This allows a number like 0.85 to be formatted as 85% instead of 0.85%. 1, 100, and 1000 are the only common values of this number. Grouping size is the number of digits between grouping separators, commas in English. This is how 75365 becomes 75,365. Most locales, including English, break every three digits; a few break every four, formatting 75365 as 7,5365. Finally, you can specify whether or not the decimal separator (decimal point) is shown in numbers without fractional parts. By default, a number like 1999 does not have a decimal point. However, there are situations (C source code, for example) where the difference between 1999 and 1999. is significant.

You also have access to the following methods, inherited from `java.text.NumberFormat`, which allow you to set and get the minimum and maximum number of integer and fraction digits and control whether or not grouping is used at all. These work just as well with decimal formats as they do with regular number formats.

```
public boolean isGroupingUsed()
public void setGroupingUsed(boolean useGrouping)
public int getMaximumIntegerDigits()
public void setMaximumIntegerDigits(int maxDigits)
public int getMinimumIntegerDigits()
public void setMinimumIntegerDigits(int minDigits)
public int getMaximumFractionDigits()
public void setMaximumFractionDigits(int maxDigits)
public int getMinimumFractionDigits()
public void setMinimumFractionDigits(int minDigits)
```

Table 16-3 lists the default patterns used by different locales' decimal formats. For the basic decimal format shown in columns 2 and 3, most of the locales use the same pattern as the U.S. English locale. The notable exceptions are the Arabic-speaking countries and Macedonia. The primary difference between locales comes in the decimal format symbols, not the pattern. The percent formats, (not shown) all round down to the nearest integer. With one exception, all locales share the percent format #,##0%. The one exception is the #,##0‰ used in the mainland China locale. This uses a per mille (per thousand), as opposed to the more common percent (per hundred).

The currency formats, shown in columns 4 and 5, are a lot more interesting, because most countries have their own currencies with their own unique symbols. Even when countries share a symbol and a name for the currency, such as the dollar ($), it's still important to distinguish between Canadian, American, and Australian dollars. Many of the currencies in Table 16-3, especially for country-independent language locales, use the ¤ symbol, which refers to a currency of indeterminate type. The [RLM] you'll see in many of the Arabic formats stands for the non-printing Unicode character \u200f, the right-to-left marker, used to ensure proper directionality in the number in Arabic's right-to-left system. Hebrew is also a right-to-left script, but in modern Hebrew numbers are generally written in the European fashion from left to right.

Table 16-3. Decimal Format Patterns

Language (Country)	Decimal Pattern	Example: -1234.56	Currency Pattern	Example: -1,234.56
Albanian	#,##0.###	-1,234,56	¤ #,##0.00	-¤ 1.234,56
Albanian (Albania)	#,##0.###	-1,234,56	Lek#,##0.###	-Lek1.234,56
Arabic	#,##0.###	-1,234,56	¤ #,##0.00	-¤ 1,234.56
Arabic (Algeria)	#,##0.###; #,##0.###	1,234.56-	ج.د [RLM] #,##0.###; ج.د [RLM] #,##0.###	ج.د [RLM] 1,234.56-
Arabic (Bahrain)	#,##0.###; #,##0.###	1,234.56-	د.ب [RLM] #,##0.###; د.ب [RLM] #,##0.###	د.ب [RLM] 1,234.56-
Arabic (Egypt)	#,##0.###; #,##0.###	1,234.56-	ج.م [RLM] #,##0.###; ج.م [RLM] #,##0.###	ج.م [RLM] 1,234.56-
Arabic (Iraq)	#,##0.###; #,##0.###	1,234.56-	ع.د [RLM] #,##0.###; ع.د [RLM] #,##0.###	ع.د [RLM] 1,234.56-
Arabic (Jordan)	#,##0.###; #,##0.###	1,234.56-	د.أ [RLM] #,##0.###; د.أ [RLM] #,##0.###	د.أ [RLM] 1,234.56-
Arabic (Kuwait)	#,##0.###; #,##0.###	1,234.56-	د.ك [RLM] #,##0.###; د.ك [RLM] #,##0.###	د.ك [RLM] 1,234.56-
Arabic (Lebanon)	#,##0.###; #,##0.###	1,234.56-	ل.ل [RLM] #,##0.###; ل.ل [RLM] #,##0.###	ل.ل [RLM] 1,234.56-
Arabic (Libyan Arab Jamahiriya)	#,##0.###; #,##0.###	1,234.56-	د.ل [RLM] #,##0.###; د.ل [RLM] #,##0.###	د.ل [RLM] 1,234.56-
Arabic (Morocco)	#,##0.###; #,##0.###	1,234.56-	م.د [RLM] #,##0.###; م.د [RLM] #,##0.###	م.د [RLM] 1,234.56-
Arabic (Oman)	#,##0.###; #,##0.###	1,234.56-	ر.ع [RLM] #,##0.###; ر.ع [RLM] #,##0.###	ر.ع [RLM] 1,234.56-
Arabic (Qatar)	#,##0.###; #,##0.###	1,234.56-	ر.ق [RLM] #,##0.###; ر.ق [RLM] #,##0.###	ر.ق [RLM] 1,234.56-

Table 16-3. Decimal Format Patterns (continued)

Language (Country)	Decimal Pattern	Example: -1234.56	Currency Pattern	Example: -1,234.56
Arabic (Saudi Arabia)	#,##0.###; #,##0.###-	1,234.56-	ـس [RLM] #,##0.###; ـس [RLM] #,##0.###-	ـس [RLM] 1,234.56-
Arabic (Sudan)	#,##0.###; #,##0.###-	1,234.56-	ـج [RLM] #,##0.###; ـج [RLM] #,##0.###-	ـج [RLM] 1,234.56-
Arabic (Syria)	#,##0.###; #,##0.###-	1,234.56-	ـل.س [RLM] #,##0.###; ـل.س [RLM] #,##0.###-	ـل.س [RLM] 1,234.56-
Arabic (Tunisia)	#,##0.###; #,##0.###-	1,234.56-	د.ت [RLM] #,##0.###; د.ت [RLM] #,##0.###-	د.ت [RLM] 1,234.56-
Arabic (United Arab Emirates)	#,##0.###; #,##0.###-	1,234.56-	د.إ [RLM] #,##0.###; د.إ [RLM] #,##0.###-	د.إ [RLM] 1,234.56-
Arabic (Yemen)	#,##0.###; #,##0.###-	1,234.56-	ـر [RLM] #,##0.###; ـر [RLM] #,##0.###-	ـر [RLM] 1,234.56-
Bulgarian	#,##0.###	-1 234,56	¤ #,##0.00	-¤ 1 234,56
Bulgarian (Bulgaria)	#,##0.###	-1 234,56	ЛВ #,##0.##	-ЛВ 1 234,56
Byelorussian	#,##0.###	-1 234,56	¤ #,##0.00	-¤ 1 234,56
Byelorussian (Belarus)	#,##0.###	-1 234,56	Руб #,##0.##	-Руб 1 234,56
Catalan	#,##0.###	-1.234,56	¤ #,##0.00	-¤ 1.234,56
Catalan (Spain)	#,##0.###	-1.234,56	Pts #,##0	-Pts 1.235
Chinese	#,##0.###	-1,234.56	¤ #,##0.00	-¤ 1,234.56
Chinese (China)	#,##0.###	-1,234.56	¥#,##0.00	-¥1,234.56
Chinese (Taiwan)	#,##0.###	-1,234.56	NT$#,##0.00	-NT$1,234.56
Croatian	#,##0.###	-1.234,56	¤ #,##0.00	-¤ 1.234,56
Croatian (Croatia)	#,##0.###	-1.234,56	Kn #,##0.##	-Kn 1.234,56
Czech	#,##0.###	-1.234,56	¤ #,##0.00	-¤ 1.234,56

Table 16-3. Decimal Format Patterns (continued)

Language (Country)	Decimal Pattern	Example: -1234.56	Currency Pattern	Example: -1,234.56
Czech (Czech Republic)	#,##0.###	-1,234,56	Kč #,##0.##; -#,##0.## Kč	-1.234,56 Kč
Danish	#,##0.###	-1.234,56	¤ #,##0.00	-¤ 1.234,56
Danish (Denmark)	#,##0.###	-1.234,56	kr #,##0.00; kr -#,##0.00	kr -1.234,56
Dutch	#,##0.###	-1.234,56	¤ #,##0.00	-¤ 1.234,56
Dutch (Belgium)	#,##0.###	-1.234,56	#,##0.00 BF	-1.234,56 BF
Dutch (Netherlands)	#,##0.###	-1.234,56	fl #,##0.00; fl #,##0.00-	fl 1.234,56-
English	#,##0.###	-1,234.56	¤ #,##0.00	-¤ 1,234.56
English (Australia)	#,##0.###	-1,234.56	$#,##0.00	-$1,234.56
English (Canada)	#,##0.###	-1,234.56	$#,##0.00	-$1,234.56
English (Ireland)	#,##0.###	-1,234.56	IR£#,##0.00	-IR£1,234.56
English (New Zealand)	#,##0.###	-1,234.56	$#,##0.00	-$1,234.56
English (South Africa)	#,##0.###	-1,234.56	R #,##0.00; R-#,##0.00	R-1,234.56
English (United Kingdom)	#,##0.###	-1,234.56	£#,##0.00	-£1,234.56
English (United States)	#,##0.###	-1,234.56	$#,##0.00; ($#,##0.00)	($1,234.56)
Estonian	#,##0.###	-1 234,56	¤ #,##0.00	-¤ 1 234,56
Estonian (Estonia)	#,##0.###	-1 234,56	#,##0.## kr	-1 234,56 kr
Finnish	#,##0.###	-1 234,56	¤ #,##0.00	-¤ 1 234,56
Finnish (Finland)	#,##0.###	-1 234,56	#,##0.00 mk	-1 234,56 mk
French	#,##0.###	-1,234,56	¤ #,##0.00	-¤ 1,234,56
French (Belgium)	#,##0.###	-1.234,56	#,##0.00 FB	-1.234,56 FB

Table 16-3. Decimal Format Patterns (continued)

Language (Country)	Decimal Pattern	Example: -1234.56	Currency Pattern	Example: -1,234.56
French (Canada)	#,##0.###	-1 234,56	#,##0.00 $; (#,##0.00$)	(1 234,56$)
French (France)	#,##0.###	-1 234,56	#,##0.00 F	-1 234,56 F
French (Switzerland)	#,##0.###	-1'234.56	SFr. #,##0.00; SFr.-#,##0.00	SFr.-1'234.56
German	#,##0.###	-1.234,56	¤ #,##0.00	-¤ 1.234,56
German (Austria)	#,##0.###	-1.234,56	öS #,##0.00	-öS 1.234,56
German (Germany)	#,##0.###	-1.234,56	#,##0.00 DM	-1.234,56 DM
German (Switzerland)	#,##0.###	-1'234.56	SFr. #,##0.00; SFr.-#,##0.00	SFr.-1'234.56
Greek	#,##0.###	-1.234,56	¤ #,##0.00	-¤ 1.234,56
Greek (Greece)	#,##0.###	-1.234,56	#,##0.00 Δρχ	-1.234,56 Δρχ
Hebrew	#,##0.###	-1,234.56	¤ #,##0.00	-¤ 1,234.56
Hebrew (Israel)	#,##0.###	-1,234.56	#,##0.## ‏ש"ח	-1,234.56 ‏ש"ח
Hungarian	#,##0.###	-1 234,56	¤ #,##0.00	-¤ 1 234,56
Hungarian (Hungary)	#,##0.###	-1 234,56	Ft#,##0.##	-Ft1 234,56
Icelandic	#,##0.###	-1.234,56	¤ #,##0.00	-¤ 1.234,56
Icelandic (Iceland)	#,##0.###	-1.234,56	#,##0.## kr.	-1.234,56 kr.
Italian	#,##0.###	-1.234,56	¤ #,##0.00	-¤ 1.234,56
Italian (Italy)	#,##0.###	-1.234,56	L. #,##0	-L. 1.235
Italian (Switzerland)	#,##0.###	-1'234.56	SFr. #,##0.00; SFr.-#,##0.00	SFr.-1'234.56
Japanese	#,##0.###	-1.234,56	¤ #,##0.00	-¤ 1,234.56
Japanese (Japan)	#,##0.###	-1,234.56	¥#,##0.00	-¥1,234.56
Korean	#,##0.###	-1,234.56	¤ #,##0.00	-¤ 1,234.56
Korean (South Korea)	#,##0.###	-1,234.56	₩ #,##0	-₩ 1,235
Latvian (Lettish)	#,##0.###	-1 234,56	¤ #,##0.00	-¤ 1 234,56

Table 16-3. Decimal Format Patterns (continued)

Language (Country)	Decimal Pattern	Example: -1234.56	Currency Pattern	Example: -1,234.56
Latvian (Lettish) (Latvia)	#,##0.###	-1 234,56	#,##0.## Ls	-1 234,56 Ls
Lithuanian	#,##0.###	-1.234,56	¤ #,##0.00	-¤ 1.234,56
Lithuanian (Lithuania)	#,##0.##	-1.234,56	#,##0.## Lt	-1.234,56 Lt
Macedonian	#,##0.###	-1.234,56	¤ #,##0.00	-¤ 1.234,56
Macedonian (Macedonia)	#,##0.###; (#,##0.###)	(1.234,56)	Den #,##0.#	-Den 1.234,56
Norwegian	#,##0.###	-1 234,56	¤ #,##0.00	-¤ 1 234,56
Norwegian (Norway)	#,##0.###	-1 234,56	kr #,##0.00; kr -#,##0.00	kr -1 234,56
Norwegian (Norway)	#,##0.###	-1 234,56	kr #,##0.00; kr -#,##0.00	kr -1 234,56
Polish	#,##0.###	-1 234,56	¤ #,##0.00	-¤ 1 234,56
Polish (Poland)	#,##0.###	-1 234,56	#,##0.## zł	-1 234,56 zł
Portuguese	#,##0.###	-1.234,56	¤ #,##0.00	-¤ 1.234,56
Portuguese (Brazil)	#,##0.###	-1.234,56	R$ #,##0.##	-R$ 1.234,56
Portuguese (Portugal)	#,##0.###	-1.234,56	#,##0.00 Esc.	-1.234,56 Esc.
Romanian	#,##0.###	-1.234,56	¤ #,##0.00	-¤ 1.234,56
Romanian (Romania)	#,##0.###	-1.234,56	#,##0.00 LEI	-1.234,56 LEI
Russian	#,##0.###	-1 234,56	¤ #,##0.00	-¤ 1 234,56
Russian (Russian Federation)	#,##0.###	-1 234,56	#,##0.##р	-1 234,56р
Serbian	#,##0.###	-1 234,56	¤ #,##0.00	-¤ 1 234,56
Serbian (Yugoslavia)	#,##0.###	-1 234,56	Дн #,##0.00	-Дн 1 234,56
Serbo-Croatian	#,##0.###	-1.234,56	¤ #,##0.00	-¤ 1.234,56

Table 16-3. Decimal Format Patterns (continued)

Language (Country)	Decimal Pattern	Example: -1234.56	Currency Pattern	Example: -1,234.56
Serbo-Croatian (Yugoslavia)	#,##0.###	-1.234,56	Din #,##0.00	-Din 1.234,56
Slovak	#,##0.###	-1 234,56	¤ #,##0.00	-¤ 1 234,56
Slovak (Slovakia)	#,##0.###	-1 234,56	Sk #,##0.00 ; -#,##0.00 Sk	-1 234,56 Sk
Slovenian	#,##0.###	-1.234,56	¤ #,##0.00	-¤ 1.234,56
Slovenian (Slovenia)	#,##0.###	-1.234,56	tol #,##0.##	-tol 1.234,56
Spanish	#,##0.###	-1.234,56	¤ #,##0.00	-¤ 1.234,56
Spanish (Argentina)	#,##0.###	-1.234,56	$#,##0.00; ($#,##0.00)	($1.234,56)
Spanish (Bolivia)	#,##0.###	-1.234,56	B$#,##0.00; (B$#,##0.00)	(B$1,234.56)
Spanish (Chile)	#,##0.###	-1.234,56	Ch$#,##0.00; Ch$-#,##0.00	Ch$-1.234,56
Spanish (Colombia)	#,##0.###	-1.234,56	C$#,##0.00; (C$#,##0.00)	(C$1,234.56)
Spanish (Costa Rica)	#,##0.###	-1.234,56	C#,##0.00; (C#,##0.00)	(C1,234.56)
Spanish (Dominican Republic)	#,##0.###	-1.234,56	RD$#,##0.00; (RD$#,##0.00)	(RD$1,234.56)
Spanish (Ecuador)	#,##0.###	-1.234,56	S/#,##0.00; S/-#,##0.00	S/-1,234.56
Spanish (El Salvador)	#,##0.###	-1.234,56	C#,##0.00; (C#,##0.00)	(C1,234.56)
Spanish (Guatemala)	#,##0.###	-1.234,56	Q#,##0.00; (Q#,##0.00)	(Q1,234.56)
Spanish (Honduras)	#,##0.###	-1.234,56	L#,##0.00; (L#,##0.00)	(L1,234.56)
Spanish (Mexico)	#,##0.###	-1,234.56	$#,##0.00; ($#,##0.00)	($1,234.56)
Spanish (Nicaragua)	#,##0.###	-1,234.56	$C#,##0.00; ($C#,##0.00)	($C1,234.56)
Spanish (Panama)	#,##0.###	-1,234.56	B#,##0.00; (B#,##0.00)	(B1,234.56)
Spanish (Paraguay)	#,##0.###	-1.234,56	G#,##0.00; (G#,##0.00)	(G1.234,56)
Spanish (Peru)	#,##0.###	-1,234.56	S/#,##0.00; S/-#,##0.00	S/-1,234.56

Table 16-3. Decimal Format Patterns (continued)

Language (Country)	Decimal Pattern	Example: -1234.56	Currency Pattern	Example: -1,234.56
Spanish (Puerto Rico)	#,##0.###	-1,234.56	$#,##0.00; ($#,##0.00)	($1,234.56)
Spanish (Spain)	#,##0.###	-1.234,56	#,##0.00 Pts	-1.234,56 Pts
Spanish (Uruguay)	#,##0.###	-1.234,56	NU$ #,##0.00; (NU$#,##0.00)	(NU$1.234,56)
Spanish (Venezuela)	#,##0.###	-1.234,56	Bs#,##0.00; Bs -#,##0.00	Bs -1.234,56
Swedish	#,##0.###	-1 234,56	¤ #,##0.00	-¤ 1 234,56
Swedish (Sweden)	#,##0.###	-1 234,56	#,##0.00 kr	-1 234,56 kr
Thai	#,##0.###	-1,234.56	¤ #,##0.00	-¤ 1,234.56
Thai (Thailand)	#,##0.###	-1,234.56	#,##0.00; -#,##0.00	-1,234.56
Turkish	#,##0.###	-1.234,56	¤ #,##0.00	-¤ 1.234,56
Turkish (Turkey)	#,##0.###	-1.234,56	#,##0.00 TL	-1.234,56 TL
Ukrainian	#,##0.###	-1.234,56	¤ #,##0.00	-¤ 1.234,56
Ukrainian (Ukraine)	#,##0.###	-1.234,56	#,##0.## грв	-1.234,56 грв

DecimalFormatSymbols

Each `DecimalFormat` object has a `DecimalFormatSymbols` object that contains a list of the different symbols used by decimal number formats in a particular locale. The decimal format symbols specify the characters or strings used for the zero digit, the grouping separator, the decimal sign, the percent sign, the mille percent sign, infinity (IEEE 754 Inf), not a number (IEEE 754 NaN), and the minus sign. `DecimalFormatSymbols` has two constructors, but they're rarely used:

```
public DecimalFormatSymbols()
public DecimalFormatSymbols(Locale locale)
```

Instead, the `DecimalFormatSymbols` object is retrieved from a particular `DecimalFormat` object using its `getDecimalFormatSymbols()` method:

```
public DecimalFormatSymbols getDecimalFormatSymbols()
```

If you create your own `DecimalFormatSymbols` object, perhaps for a locale Java doesn't support, you can make a `DecimalFormat` use it by passing it to `DecimalFormat`'s `setDecimalFormatSymbols()` method:

```
public void setDecimalFormatSymbols(DecimalFormatSymbols newSymbols)
```

The `DecimalFormatSymbols` class contains mostly `get` and `set` methods for inspecting and setting the values of the different symbols:

```
public char getZeroDigit()
public void setZeroDigit(char zeroDigit)
public char getGroupingSeparator()
public void setGroupingSeparator(char groupingSeparator)
public char getDecimalSeparator()
public void setDecimalSeparator(char decimalSeparator)
public char getPercent()
public void setPercent(char percent)
public char getPerMill()
public void setPerMill(char perMill)
public String getInfinity()
public void setInfinity(String infinity)
public String getNaN()
public void setNaN(String NaN)
public char getMinusSign()
public void setMinusSign(char minusSign)
```

The zero digit is the character used for zero. This is 0 in most Western languages but is different in Arabic and a few other locales. The grouping separator is the character used to split groups; a comma is used in the U.S., but a period is used in some other countries that use a comma as the decimal separator. The decimal separator is a decimal point (a period) in English but a comma in some other locales. The percent and per mille characters are % and ‰ in English, occasionally other things in other locales. The infinity and not-a-number strings are rarely changed. They're Inf and NaN as specified by IEEE 754, generally even in non-English languages like German, where the word for infinity is Unbegrenztheit and "not a number" translates as "nicht eine Zahl." Finally, the minus sign is the default character used for negative numbers that do not have a specific prefix. It's a hyphen (-) in English. This character is not used if the associated pattern has set a negative prefix.

The DecimalFormatSymbols class also lets you set two of the characters used in patterns. The digit character, # by default, and the pattern separator character, a semicolon by default, can be changed if you want to use one of those characters as a literal in the pattern; for example, by using a # instead of a period for the decimal separator.

```
public char getDigit()
public void setDigit(char digit)
public char getPatternSeparator()
public void setPatternSeparator(char patternSeparator)
```

The pattern separator is used to separate positive from negative patterns. If no explicit negative pattern is given, then a minus sign is simply prefixed onto the positive pattern instead.

Utility methods

For completeness, I'll note that DecimalFormatSymbols overrides the usual three utility methods from java.lang.Object, hashCode(), clone(), and equals():

```
public int hashCode()
public boolean equals(Object obj)
public Object clone()
```

One DecimalFormatSymbols object is equal to another DecimalFormatSymbols object if they're instances of the same class and all their symbols are the same.

Constructing Decimal Formats with Patterns and Symbols

Most of the time, you use the factory methods in NumberFormat to get DecimalFormat instances. However, there are three public DecimalFormat constructors you can use to create DecimalFormat instances directly:

```
public DecimalFormat()
public DecimalFormat(String pattern)
public DecimalFormat(String pattern, DecimalFormatSymbols symbols)
```

The no-argument constructor creates a decimal format that uses the default pattern and symbols for the default locale. The second constructor creates a decimal format that uses the specified pattern and the default symbols for the default locale. The third constructor creates a decimal format that uses the specified pattern and the specified symbols for the default locale. These are useful for special cases that aren't handled by the default patterns and symbols.

An Exponential Number Format

The `DecimalFormat` class is useful for medium-sized numbers, but it doesn't work very well for exceptionally large numbers like Avogadro's number (6,022,094,300,000,000,000,000,000) or exceptionally small numbers like Planck's constant (0.00000000000000000000000000625 erg-seconds). These are traditionally written in scientific notation as a decimal number times 10 to a certain power, positive or negative; for example, 6.0220943×10^{23} and 6.25×10^{-27} erg-seconds. In most programming languages, including Java, an E followed by either a + or a – is used to represent "$\times 10$ to the power"; for example, 6.0220943E+23 or 6.25E–27 erg-seconds.

The `java.text` package does not provide support for formatting numbers in scientific notation,* so as the final example of this chapter, I'll develop a new subclass of `NumberFormat` that does use scientific notation. Technically, scientific notation requires exactly one nonzero digit before the decimal point, but I'll be a little more general than that, providing for numbers like 13.2E-8 as well.

The `NumberFormat` class is abstract. It declares three abstract methods any subclass must implement:

```
public abstract StringBuffer format(double number, StringBuffer toAppendTo,
                                    FieldPosition pos)
public abstract StringBuffer format(long number, StringBuffer toAppendTo,
                                    FieldPosition pos)
public abstract Number parse(String text, ParsePosition parsePosition)
```

The two format methods must format a `long` and a `double` respectively, update the `FieldPosition` object with the locations of the different fields, append the formatted string to the string buffer `toAppendTo`, and return that same string buffer. The `parse()` method must read a number in scientific notation, convert it to a `java.lang.Number` (that is, a `java.lang.Long` or a `java.lang.Double`) and return that.

The concrete formatting methods in `NumberFormat` all invoke these methods, so they may be kept as is rather than being overridden. However, it would not hurt to override `clone()`, `hashCode()`, and `equals()`. You could also add some additional methods to specify formatting of the exponent. However, to keep this

---

* The `java.lang.Double` class's `toString()` methods do format numbers less than 0.001 or greater than 10 million in scientific notation.

example reasonably compact, I'll assume that the exponent is only as wide as it needs to be with either a + or a − prefix. This is large enough to handle both the largest and the smallest double values in Java (1.79769313486231570e+308 and 4.94065645841246544e–324, respectively).

A typical exponential number has three fields: the integer, the fraction, and the exponent. It would be nice to define constants for these fields and use the FieldPosition object passed to format() to identify the locations of these fields in the formatted output. Regrettably, the java.text API does not provide adequate support for third-party formatting classes. The FieldPosition set methods are "friendly"—that is, accessible only to other classes in the same package—so our class can't use them.

```
void setBeginIndex(int bi)
void setEndIndex(int ei)
```

Similarly, there's no way to add extra field definitions, such as an exponent field. Therefore, any user-created Format subclass will be crippled relative to the ones JavaSoft provides.

Example 16-9 shows the code for the ExponentialFormat class. There are at least three different ways to parse and format exponential numbers. The simplest, and the one I've used here, is to treat an exponential number as a combination of a decimal number plus the letter "e" or "E" plus an integer. Then use DecimalFormat to format or parse those parts. It would be slightly more efficient to do all formatting directly, but the benefits of code reuse more than offset a small increase in efficiency. Internationalization comes for free, since the DecimalFormat class handles internationalization. A DecimalFormat object for a given locale may be passed to the constructor. Otherwise, the format for the default locale is selected.

Example 16-9. ExponentialFormat

```
import java.text.*;
import java.io.*;
import java.util.*;

/**
 * Concrete class for formatting large and small numbers, allowing a variety
 * of exponential/scientific notation
 * @see        java.util.Format
 * @see        java.text.NumberFormat
 * @version    1.0 25 Jan 1998
 * @author     Elliotte Rusty Harold
 */
public class ExponentialFormat extends NumberFormat {
```

Example 16-9. ExponentialFormat (continued)

```java
// might make this only a number format
DecimalFormatSymbols symbols;
DecimalFormat parser;

public ExponentialFormat() {
  this(new DecimalFormat());
}


/**
 * Create an ExponentialFormat from the given format and the symbols
 * for the default locale.
 * <p>
 * @param format The decimal format that parses the parts of the exponential.
 */
public ExponentialFormat(DecimalFormat format) {
  this.parser = format;
  this.symbols = format.getDecimalFormatSymbols();
  this.parser.setGroupingUsed(false);
}


public StringBuffer format(double number, StringBuffer toAppendTo,
    FieldPosition pos) {

  if (Double.isNaN(number)) {
    toAppendTo.append(symbols.getNaN());
  }
  else if (number < 0) {
    toAppendTo.append(symbols.getMinusSign());
    number = -number;
  }
  // Now we just have to format a nonnegative number.
  if (Double.isInfinite(number)) {
     toAppendTo.append(symbols.getInfinity());
  }
  else {
    int maxFractionDigits = this.getMaximumFractionDigits();
    if (maxFractionDigits <= 0) maxFractionDigits = 1;
    int maxIntegerDigits = this.getMaximumIntegerDigits();
    if (maxIntegerDigits <= 0) maxIntegerDigits = 1;
    int minIntegerDigits = this.getMinimumIntegerDigits();
    if (minIntegerDigits <= 0) minIntegerDigits = 1;
    int minFractionDigits = this.getMinimumFractionDigits();
    if (minFractionDigits <= 0) minFractionDigits = 1;
    if (number == 0.0) {
      for (int i = 0; i < minIntegerDigits; i++) {
          toAppendTo.append(symbols.getZeroDigit());
            }
        toAppendTo.append(symbols.getDecimalSeparator());
```

Example 16-9. ExponentialFormat (continued)

```java
          for (int i = 0; i < minFractionDigits; i++){
              toAppendTo.append(symbols.getZeroDigit());
                }
          toAppendTo.append("E+000");
      }
      else { // positive number
        // Find integer, fraction, and exponent.
        // This method creates some round-off error but is relatively easy
        // to understand. If round-off is a concern, an alternative method
        // that treats the double as a binary number may be seen in the
        // source code for java.lang.FloatingDecimal.
        double exponent = Math.floor(Math.log(number) / Math.log(10));
        double normalized = number / Math.pow(10, exponent);
        for (int i = 1; i < minIntegerDigits; i++) {
          normalized *= 10;
          exponent--;
        }
        parser.setMinimumFractionDigits(minFractionDigits);
        parser.format(normalized, toAppendTo, pos);
        toAppendTo.append('E');
        if (exponent >= 0) toAppendTo.append('+');
        toAppendTo.append((int) exponent);
      }
    }
    return toAppendTo;
}


public StringBuffer format(long number, StringBuffer toAppendTo,
    FieldPosition pos) {

  if (number < 0) {
    toAppendTo.append(symbols.getMinusSign());
    number = -number;
  }


  int maxFractionDigits = this.getMaximumFractionDigits();
  if (maxFractionDigits <= 0) maxFractionDigits = 1;
  int maxIntegerDigits = this.getMaximumIntegerDigits();
  if (maxIntegerDigits <= 0) maxIntegerDigits = 1;
  int minIntegerDigits = this.getMinimumIntegerDigits();
  if (minIntegerDigits <= 0) minIntegerDigits = 1;
  int minFractionDigits = this.getMinimumFractionDigits();
  if (minFractionDigits <= 0) minFractionDigits = 1;
  if (number == 0) {
    for (int i = 0; i < minIntegerDigits; i++) {
        toAppendTo.append(symbols.getZeroDigit());
            }
    toAppendTo.append(symbols.getDecimalSeparator());
```

Example 16-9. ExponentialFormat (continued)

```java
            for (int i = 0; i < minFractionDigits; i++) {
                toAppendTo.append(symbols.getZeroDigit());
                }
            toAppendTo.append("E+000");
            }
        else { // positive number
          // Find integer, fraction, and exponent.

            int exponent = (int) Math.floor(Math.log(number) / Math.log(10));
            exponent -= minIntegerDigits - 1;
            String digits = Long.toString(number);
            while (digits.length() < minIntegerDigits + maxFractionDigits)  {
                digits += '0';
                }
            String integerField = digits.substring(0, minIntegerDigits);
            String fractionField = digits.substring(minIntegerDigits,
                minIntegerDigits+maxFractionDigits);

            toAppendTo.append(integerField);
            toAppendTo.append(symbols.getDecimalSeparator());
            toAppendTo.append(fractionField);
            toAppendTo.append('E');
            if (exponent > 0) toAppendTo.append('+');
            toAppendTo.append(exponent);
        }
      return toAppendTo;
    }


  public Number parse(String text, ParsePosition parsePosition) {

    int oldIndex = parsePosition.getIndex();

    try {
      double result = parser.parse(text, parsePosition).doubleValue();
      int eposition = text.toUpperCase().indexOf('E');
      if (eposition != -1) {
        // Advance past the E.
        parsePosition.setIndex(parsePosition.getIndex() + 1);
        int exponent = parser.parse(text, parsePosition).intValue();
        result *= Math.pow(10, exponent);
      }
      return new Double(result);
    }
    catch (Exception e) {
      parsePosition.setIndex(oldIndex);
      return null;
    }
  }
```

Example 16-9. ExponentialFormat (continued)

```java
  public Object clone() {

    ExponentialFormat theClone = (ExponentialFormat) super.clone();
    theClone.parser = (DecimalFormat) parser.clone();
    theClone.symbols = (DecimalFormatSymbols)
            theClone.parser.getDecimalFormatSymbols();
    return theClone;
  }


  /**
   * Overrides equals
   */
  public boolean equals(Object o) {

    if (!super.equals(o)) return false;
    ExponentialFormat other = (ExponentialFormat) o;
    other.symbols = other.parser.getDecimalFormatSymbols();
    if (!this.parser.equals(other.parser)) return false;
    if (!this.symbols.equals(other.symbols)) return false;
    return true;
  }


  /**
   * Overrides hashCode
   */
  public int hashCode() {
    return super.hashCode() * 31 + parser.getNegativePrefix().hashCode();
  }
}
```

Aside from special cases like `Inf` and `NaN`, the big trick in formatting both `longs` and `doubles` is to separate the mantissa from the exponent. The mantissa is the set of digits that comes before the E. For example, in 6.0220943E+23 the mantissa is 6.0220943. (Technically, the mantissa is 60220943 without a decimal point, but for reasons you'll see shortly, I need to hang onto it.) By separating the mantissa from the exponent, we can format each one separately, then concatenate them together with an "E" in between. The problem is that Java doesn't have any real concept of mantissa or exponent, especially in base 10. We find the exponent by taking the $\log_{10}$ of the number and rounding toward zero to the nearest integer. (`Math.floor(Math.log(number) / Math.log(10))`). Dividing the loose line number by `Math.pow(10, exponent)`, we get a mantissa between 1 and 9. 999999999.

For true scientific notation, this is exactly what you want. However, this program is a little more general and allows programmers to choose to format numbers as 13.24E+12 instead of the equivalent 1.324E+13. Therefore, if the programmer sets the minimum integer digits higher than 1, we shift the mantissa to the left (multiply by 10) and subtract 1 from the exponent for each shift. In exponential notation, unlike regular decimal notation, a minimum number of integer digits greater than the available number of integer digits does not lead to insignificant zeros.

Parsing is easier. All we have to do is read the exponential string, like 6.345E–1, twice. The first time you read, you get the mantissa (6.345). The parse() method automatically stops when it encounters the nonnumeric character E. Advance the parse position one space to skip past the E and read the exponent. Then multiply the mantissa by Math.pow(10, exponent), convert that into a Double object, and return it. If there's a problem parsing the exponent, then we reset parse-Position back to its original value and return null.

By the way, in case you were wondering, the fourth official language of Switzerland is Romansh, also known as Rhaeto-Romanic. Romansh is spoken by about 1.5% of Switzerland's population and survives the onslaught of German/French/English/Italian by virtue of being prevalent in many isolated mountain communities in the Alps.

17

In this chapter:
- *The Architecture of the Java Communications API*
- *Identifying Ports*
- *Communicating with a Device on a Port*
- *Serial Ports*
- *Parallel Ports*

The Java Communications API

This chapter covers the Java Communications API 2.0, a standard extension available in Java 1.1 and later that allows Java applications (but not applets) to send and receive data to and from the serial and parallel ports of the host computer. The Java Communications API allows Java programs to communicate with essentially any device connected to a serial or parallel port, like a printer, a scanner, a modem, a tape backup unit, and so on. The Comm API operates at a very low level. It only understands how to send and receive bytes to these ports. It does not understand anything about what these bytes mean. Doing useful work generally requires not only understanding the Java Communications API (which is actually quite simple) but also the protocols spoken by the devices connected to the ports (which can be almost arbitrarily complex).

The Architecture of the Java Communications API

Because the Java Communications API is a standard extension, it is not installed by default with the JDK. You have to download it from *http://java.sun.com/products/javacomm/* and install it separately.

NOTE This chapter is based on the first beta of the Java Communications API. It is almost certain that some parts of this chapter will become inaccurate by the time you read this. Indeed, throughout the process of writing this chapter, I identified a number of bugs and inconsistencies that I forwarded to Sun. They even fixed a few in between early access 3 and beta 1. If you have trouble with anything you see here, cross-check it with the most up-to-date documentation from Sun. I'll also try to post minor corrections on my web site at *http://metalab.unc.edu/javafaq/books/javaio/*.

The Java Communications API contains a single package, `javax.comm`, which holds a baker's dozen of classes, exceptions, and interfaces. Because the Comm API is a standard extension, the `javax` prefix is used instead of the `java` prefix. The Java Comm API also includes a DLL, or shared library, containing the native code to communicate with the ports, and a few driver classes in the `com.sun.comm` package that mostly handle the vagaries of Unix or Wintel ports. Other vendors may need to muck around with these if they're porting the Comm API to another platform (e.g., the Mac or OS/2), but as a user of the API, you'll only concern yourself with the documented classes in `javax.comm`.

`javax.comm` is divided into high-level and low-level classes. High-level classes are responsible for controlling access to and ownership of the communication ports and performing basic I/O. The `CommPortIdentifier` class lets you find and open the ports available on a system. The `CommPort` class provides input and output streams connected to the ports. Low-level classes—`javax.comm.SerialPort` and `javax.comm.ParallelPort`, for example—manage interaction with particular kinds of ports and help you read and write the control wires on the ports. They also provide event-based notification of changes to the state of the port.

Version 2.0 of the Java Comm API understands RS-232 serial ports and IEEE 1284–type parallel ports. Future releases may add support for other kinds of ports, like the Universal Serial Bus (USB), FireWire, or SCSI.

Identifying Ports

The `javax.comm.CommPortIdentifier` class is the control room for the ports on a system. It has methods that list the available ports, figure out which program owns them, take control of a port, and open a port so you can perform I/O with it. The actual I/O, stream-based or otherwise, is performed through an instance of `javax.comm.CommPort` that represents the port in question. The purpose of

CommPortIdentifier is to mediate between different programs, objects, or threads that want to use the same port.

Finding the Ports

Before you can use a port, you need a port identifier for the port. Because the possible port identifiers are closely tied to the physical ports on the system, you cannot simply construct an arbitrary CommPortIdentifier object. (For instance, Macs have no parallel ports, and iMacs don't have serial or parallel ports.) Instead, you use one of several static methods in javax.comm.CommPortIdentifier that use native methods and nonpublic constructors to find and create the right port. These include:

```
public static Enumeration getPortIdentifiers()
public static CommPortIdentifier getPortIdentifier(String portName)
        throws NoSuchPortException
public static CommPortIdentifier getPortIdentifier(CommPort port)
        throws NoSuchPortException
```

The most general of these is CommPortIdentifier.getPortIdentifiers(), which returns a java.util.Enumeration containing one CommPortIdentifier for each of the ports on the system. Example 17-1 uses this method to list all the ports on the system.

Example 17-1. PortLister

```
import javax.comm.*;
import java.util.*;

public class PortLister {

  public static void main(String[] args) {

    Enumeration e = CommPortIdentifier.getPortIdentifiers();
    while (e.hasMoreElements()) {
      System.out.println((CommPortIdentifier) e.nextElement());
    }
  }
}
```

Here's the output I got when I ran PortLister on my fairly stock Wintel PC:

```
D:\JAVA\17\>java PortLister
javax.comm.CommPortIdentifier@be3c9581
javax.comm.CommPortIdentifier@be209581
javax.comm.CommPortIdentifier@be489581
javax.comm.CommPortIdentifier@be4c9581
```

This shows you that my system has four ports, though it doesn't tell you what those ports are. Of course, the output will vary depending on how many serial and parallel ports your system possesses, and those first few lines are liable to disappear in the release version of the Comm API. Clearly, a better toString() method is needed. (CommPortIdentifier merely inherits java.lang.Object's toString() method.) You'll see how to work around this in the next section.

You can also get a CommPortIdentifier by using the static method getPortIdentifier() to request a port identifier, either by name or by the actual port object. The latter assumes that you already have a reference to the relevant port, which usually isn't the case. The former allows you to choose from Windows standard names like "COM1" and "LPT2" or Unix names like "Serial A" and "Serial B." The exact format of a name is highly platform- and implementation-dependent. If you ask for a port that doesn't exist, a NoSuchPortException is thrown. Example 17-2 looks for serial and parallel ports by starting with COM1 and LPT1 and counting up until one is missing. Be warned that this code is highly platform-dependent and probably won't work on Unix or the Mac.

Example 17-2. NamedPortLister

```
import javax.comm.*;

public class NamedPortLister {

  public static void main(String[] args) {

    // List serial (COM) ports.
    try {
      int portNumber = 1;
      while (true) {
        CommPortIdentifier.getPortIdentifier("COM" + portNumber);
        System.out.println("COM" + portNumber);
        portNumber++;
      }
    }
    catch (NoSuchPortException e) {
      // Break out of loop.
    }

    // List parallel (LPT) ports.
    try {
      int portNumber = 1;
      while (true) {
        CommPortIdentifier.getPortIdentifier("LPT" + portNumber);
        System.out.println("LPT" + portNumber);
        portNumber++;
      }
    }
```

Example 17-2. NamedPortLister (continued)

```
    catch (NoSuchPortException e) {
      // Break out of loop.
    }
  }
}
```

Once again, here's the output from a stock Wintel box:

```
D:\JAVA\16>java NamedPortLister
COM1
COM2
LPT1
LPT2
```

Now you can see that I have two serial and two parallel ports. However, this same program would fail on Unix, because it relies on hard-wired port names.

Getting Information About a Port

Once you have a `CommPortIdentifier` identifying a particular port, you can discover information about the port by calling several accessor methods. These include:

```
    public String getName()
    public int getPortType()
    public String getCurrentOwner()
    public boolean isCurrentlyOwned()
```

The `getName()` method returns the platform-dependent name of the port, such as "COM1" (Windows) "Serial A" (Solaris) or "modem" (Mac).* The `getPortType()` method returns one of the two mnemonic constants `CommPortIdentifier.PORT_SERIAL` or `CommPortIdentifier.PORT_PARALLEL`:

```
    public static final int PORT_SERIAL = 1;
    public static final int PORT_PARALLEL = 2;
```

The `isCurrentlyOwned()` method returns `true` if some process, thread, or application currently has control of the port. It returns `false` otherwise. If a port is owned by another Java program, the `getCurrentOwner()` returns the name supplied by the program that owns it; otherwise, it returns `null`. This isn't too useful, because it doesn't handle the much more likely case that a non-Java program like Dial-Up Networking or PPP is using the port. A comment in the source code indicates that this should be fixed so that non-Java programs can also be identified; this limitation may not exist by the time you read this. Example 17-3

---

* That last one is hypothetical. The Comm API hasn't been ported to the Mac as of the time of this writing.

is a revision of the `PortLister` in Example 17-1 that uses these four accessor methods to provide information about each port rather than relying on the inherited `toString()` method.

Example 17-3. PrettyPortLister

```java
import javax.comm.*;
import java.util.*;

public class PrettyPortLister {

  public static void main(String[] args) {

    Enumeration e = CommPortIdentifier.getPortIdentifiers();
    while (e.hasMoreElements()) {
      CommPortIdentifier com = (CommPortIdentifier) e.nextElement();
      System.out.print(com.getName());

      switch(com.getPortType()) {
        case CommPortIdentifier.PORT_SERIAL:
          System.out.print(", a serial port, ");
          break;
        case CommPortIdentifier.PORT_PARALLEL:
          System.out.print(", a parallel port, ");
          break;
        default:
          // Important since other types of ports like USB
          // and firewire are expected to be added in the future.
          System.out.print(" , a port of unknown type, ");
          break;
      }
      if (com.isCurrentlyOwned()) {
        System.out.println("is currently owned by "
          + com.getCurrentOwner() + ".");
      }
      else {
        System.out.println("is not currently owned.");
      }
    }
  }
}
```

Here's the output when run on a stock Wintel box:

```
D:\JAVA\16>java PrettyPrintLister
COM1, a serial port, is not currently owned.
COM2, a serial port, is not currently owned.
LPT1, a parallel port, is not currently owned.
LPT2, a parallel port, is not currently owned.
```

This output originally confused me, because I expected one of the COM ports to be occupied by the Dial-Up Networking PPP connection on the internal modem (COM2). However, the `isCurrentlyOwned()` method only notices other Java programs in the same VM occupying ports. To detect whether a non-Java program is controlling a port, you must try to open the port and watch for `PortInUse-Exceptions`, as discussed in the next section.

Opening Ports

Before you can read from or write to a port, you have to open it. Opening a port gives your application exclusive access to the port until you give it up or the program ends. (Two different programs should not send data to the same modem or printer at the same time, after all.) Opening a port is not guaranteed to succeed. If another program (Java or otherwise) is using the port, a `PortInUseException` will be thrown when you try to open the port. Surprisingly, this is not a subclass of `IOException`.

```
public class PortInUseException extends Exception
```

`CommPortIdentifier` has two `open()` methods; they return a `javax.comm.CommPort` object you can use to read data from and write data to the port. The first variant takes two arguments, a name and a time-out value:

```
public synchronized CommPort open(String name, int timeout)
                    throws PortInUseException
```

The `name` argument is a name for the program that wants to use the port and will be returned by `getCurrentOwner()` while the port is in use. The `timeout` argument is the maximum number of milliseconds this method will block while waiting for the port to become available. If the operation does not complete within that time, a `PortInUseException` is thrown. Example 17-4 is a variation of the `PortLister` program that attempts to open each unowned port.

Example 17-4. PortOpener

```
import javax.comm.*;
import java.util.*;

public class PortOpener {

  public static void main(String[] args) {

    Enumeration thePorts = CommPortIdentifier.getPortIdentifiers();
    while (thePorts.hasMoreElements()) {
      CommPortIdentifier com = (CommPortIdentifier) thePorts.nextElement();
      System.out.print(com.getName());
```

Example 17-4. PortOpener (continued)

```java
    switch(com.getPortType()) {
      case CommPortIdentifier.PORT_SERIAL:
        System.out.print(", a serial port, ");
        break;
      case CommPortIdentifier.PORT_PARALLEL:
        System.out.print(", a parallel port, ");
        break;
      default:
        // important since other types of ports like USB
        // and firewire are expected to be added in the future
        System.out.print(" , a port of unknown type, ");
        break;
    }
    try {
      CommPort thePort  = com.open("PortOpener", 10);
      System.out.println("is not currently owned.");
      thePort.close();
    }
    catch (PortInUseException e) {
      String owner = com.getCurrentOwner();
      if (owner == null) owner = "unknown";
      System.out.println("is currently owned by " + owner + ".");
    }
   }
  }
}
```

Here's the output:

```
D:\JAVA\16>java PortOpener
COM1, a serial port, is not currently owned.
COM2, a serial port, is not currently owned.
LPT1, a parallel port, is not currently owned.
LPT2, a parallel port, is not currently owned.
```

In this example, you see that COM2 is occupied, though by a non-Java program that did not register its name. You also see that LPT2 is occupied, which was something of a surprise to me—I didn't think I was using any parallel ports.

The second `open()` method takes a file descriptor as an argument:

```java
public CommPort open(FileDescriptor fd) throws
UnsupportedCommOperationException
```

This may be useful on operating systems like Unix, where all devices, serial ports included, are treated as files. On all other platforms, this method throws an `UnsupportedCommOperationException`:

```java
public class UnsupportedCommOperationException extends Exception
```

There is no corresponding close() method in the CommPortIdentifier class. The necessary close() method is included in the CommPort class itself. You should close all ports you've opened when you're through with them.

Waiting for a Port with Port Ownership Events

The CommPortIdentifier class has two methods that are used to receive notification of changes in the ownership of the port. These are:

```
public void addPortOwnershipListener(CommPortOwnershipListener listener)
public void removePortOwnershipListener(CommPortOwnershipListener listener)
```

Port ownership events are fired to signal that a port has been opened, a port has been closed, or another application wants to take control of the port. To listen for ownership changes on a particular port, you must register a CommPort-OwnershipListener object with the CommPortIdentifier object representing the port using the addPortOwnershipListener() method:

```
public void addPortOwnershipListener(CommPortOwnershipListener listener)
```

You can deregister the port ownership listener by passing it to removePort-OwnershipListener():

```
public void removePortOwnershipListener(CommPortOwnershipListener listener)
```

The javax.comm.CommPortOwnershipListener is a subinterface of java.util. EventListener that declares the single method ownershipChange():

```
public abstract void ownershipChange(int type)
```

The CommPortOwnershipListener interface is unusual; unlike other event listener interfaces, the listener method is passed an int rather than an event. This int will generally have one of three values that indicate particular changes in the ownership of the port. All three values are defined as mnemonic constants in javax.comm.CommPortOwnershipListener:

```
CommPortOwnershipListener.PORT_OWNED
CommPortOwnershipListener.PORT_UNOWNED
CommPortOwnershipListener.PORT_OWNERSHIP_REQUESTED
```

PORT_OWNED means some application has taken ownership of the port. PORT_UNOWNED means some application has released ownership of the port. Finally, PORT_OWNERSHIP_REQUESTED means some application has requested ownership of the port but does not yet have it, because another application owns it. If the owner of the port hears the event, it can close the port to give it up to the requesting application. Example 17-5 is a program that watches for port ownership changes. It's of limited use, since these events only appear to be fired when a Java program takes over or releases a port, not when other programs do.

Example 17-5. PortWatcher

```java
import javax.comm.*;

public class PortWatcher implements CommPortOwnershipListener {

  String portName;

  public PortWatcher(String portName) throws NoSuchPortException {
    this.portName = portName;
    CommPortIdentifier portIdentifier =
     CommPortIdentifier.getPortIdentifier(portName);
    portIdentifier.addPortOwnershipListener(this);
  }

  public void ownershipChange(int type) {

    switch (type) {

      case CommPortOwnershipListener.PORT_OWNED:
        System.out.println(portName + " has become unavailable");
        break;
      case CommPortOwnershipListener.PORT_UNOWNED:
        System.out.println(portName + " has become available");
        break;
      case CommPortOwnershipListener.PORT_OWNERSHIP_REQUESTED:
        System.out.println("An application has requested onwership of "
                           + portName);
        break;
      default:
        System.out.println("Unknown port ownership event, type " + type);
    }
  }

  public static void main(String[] args) {

    try {
      PortWatcher pw = new PortWatcher(args[0]);
    }
    catch (Exception e) {
      System.err.println("Usage: java PortWatcher port_name");
    }
  }
}
```

Registering Ports

For completeness, I'll note the static `CommPortIdentifier.addPortName()` method:

```
public static void addPortName(String portName, int portType, CommDriver driver)
```

This method registers a particular name, type, and driver with the Comm API so that it can be returned by `CommPortIdentifier.getPortIdentifiers()` and similar methods. Like the `javax.comm.CommDriver` class that `addPortName()` takes as its third argument, this method is intended only for implementers of the Java Comm API, not for application programmers.

Communicating with a Device on a Port

The `open()` method of the `CommPortIdentifier` class returns a `CommPort` object. The `javax.comm.CommPort` class has methods for getting input and output streams from a port and for closing the port. There are also a number of driver-dependent methods for adjusting the properties of the port.

Communicating with a Port

There are five basic steps to communicating with a port:

1. Open the port using the `open()` method of `CommPortIdentifier`. If the port is available, this returns a `CommPort` object. Otherwise, a `PortInUseException` is thrown.

2. Get the port's output stream using the `getOutputStream()` method of `CommPort`.

3. Get the port's input stream using the `getInputStream()` method of `CommPort`.

4. Read and write data onto those streams as desired.

5. Close the port using the `close()` method of `CommPort`.

Steps 2 through 4 are new. However, they're not particularly complex. Once the connection has been established, you simply use the normal methods of any input or output stream to read and write data. The `getInputStream()` and `getOutputStream()` methods of `CommPort` are similar to the methods of the same name in the `java.net.URL` class. The primary difference is that with Comm ports, you're completely responsible for understanding and handling the data that's sent to you. There are no content or protocol handlers that perform any manipulation of the data. If the device attached to the port requires a complicated protocol—for example, a fax modem—then you'll have to handle the protocol manually.

```
public abstract InputStream getInputStream() throws IOException
public abstract OutputStream getOutputStream() throws IOException
```

Although these methods are declared abstract in `CommPort`, any instance of `CommPort` you retrieve from `open()` will naturally be a concrete subclass of `CommPort` in which these methods are implemented.

Some ports are unidirectional. In other words, the port hardware only supports writing or reading, not both. For instance, early PC parallel ports only allowed the computer to send data to the printer but could only send a small number of precisely defined signals back to the computer. This was fine for a printer, but it meant that the parallel port wasn't useful for a device like a CD-ROM or a Zip drive. If the port you've opened doesn't allow writing, `getOutputStream()` returns `null`. If the port doesn't allow reading, `getInputStream()` returns `null`.

Example 17-6 is a simple character-mode program that allows you to type back and forth with a port. If a modem is attached to the port, you can use it as an extremely rudimentary terminal emulator. Two separate threads handle input and output so that input doesn't get blocked waiting for output and vice versa.

Example 17-6. PortTyper

```
import javax.comm.*;
import java.util.*;
import java.io.*;

public class PortTyper {

  public static void main(String[] args) {

    if (args.length < 1) {
      System.out.println("Usage: java PortTyper portName");
      return;
    }

    try {
      CommPortIdentifier com = CommPortIdentifier.getPortIdentifier(args[0]);
      CommPort thePort  = com.open("PortOpener", 10);
      CopyThread input = new CopyThread(System.in, thePort.getOutputStream());
      CopyThread output = new CopyThread(thePort.getInputStream(), System.out);
      input.start();
      output.start();
    }
    catch (Exception e) {System.out.println(e);}
  }
}
```

Example 17-6. PortTyper (continued)

```
class CopyThread extends Thread {

  InputStream theInput;
  OutputStream theOutput;

  CopyThread(InputStream in) {
    this(in, System.out);
  }

  CopyThread(OutputStream out) {
    this(System.in, out);
  }

  CopyThread(InputStream in, OutputStream out) {
    theInput = in;
    theOutput = out;
  }

  public void run() {

    try {
      byte[] buffer = new byte[256];
      while (true) {
        int bytesRead = theInput.read(buffer);
        if (bytesRead == -1) break;
        theOutput.write(buffer, 0, bytesRead);
      }
    }
    catch (IOException e) {System.err.println(e);}
  }
}
```

Here's a sample session where I used this program to connect to my ISP. After I logged out, the incoming line rang three times, which you also see:

```
D:\JAVA\16>java PortTyper COM2
at&f
at&f

OK
atdt 321-1444
atdt 321-1444

CONNECT 9600/ARQ
Welcome to Cloud 9 Internet!

If you're already a user, please login below.
```

```
To sign up for an account, type 'new', with no password.

If you have trouble logging in, please call (914)696-4000.

login: elharo
elharo
Password: **********

Password: **********

Last login: Thu May 28 18:26:14 from 168.100.253.71
Copyright (c) 1980, 1983, 1986, 1988, 1990, 1991, 1993, 1994
        The Regents of the University of California.  All rights reserved.

FreeBSD 2.2.6-RELEASE (EARL-GREY) #0: Tue May 19 10:39:36 EDT 1998

You have new mail.
> logout
logo
Connection closed.

NO CARRIER

RING

RING

RING
```

This program would have been state of the art in 1978. These days, it's rather crude, and you'd have to do a lot of work to develop it further. For one thing, local echo mode should be turned off in the modem so that you don't see duplicates of everything you type. (Even my password originally appeared on the screen in clear text. I replaced it with asterisks manually.) And no effort at all is made to perform terminal emulation of any sort. Furthermore, there's no way to exit the program and close the port. Terminating it with a Ctrl-C forces abnormal execution that fails to release control of the port. Nonetheless, it's amazing just how quick and easy it is to write a program that communicates with a simple serial port device. Communicating with a basic daisy-wheel printer would be no harder.

Port Properties

The `javax.comm.CommPort` class has a number of driver-dependent methods for adjusting the properties of the port. These properties are mostly generic characteristics, like buffer size, that may be implemented in software. More specific properties of a particular type of port, like the baud rate of a serial port or the mode of the parallel port, must be set using a more specific subclass, like `javax.comm.SerialPort` or `javax.comm.ParallelPort`.

The five generic properties are receive threshold, time-out value, receive framing byte, input buffer size, and output buffer size. Four of these properties—receive threshold, receive time-out, receive framing and input buffer size—determine exactly how and when the input stream blocks. The receive threshold specifies the number of bytes that must be available before a call to `read()` returns. The receive time-out specifies the number of milliseconds that must pass before a call to `read()` returns. The input buffer size specifies how large a buffer will be provided for the serial port. If the buffer fills up, the `read()` method returns.

For instance, if the receive threshold is set to 5, `read()` won't return until at least 5 bytes are available. If the receive timeout is set to 10 milliseconds, `read()` will wait 10 milliseconds before returning. However, if data becomes available before 10 milliseconds are up, `read()` returns immediately. For example, if the receive threshold is set to 5 bytes *and* the receive time-out is set to 10 milliseconds, then `read()` will wait until either 10 milliseconds pass *or* 5 bytes are available before returning. If the input buffer size is set and the receive threshold is set, the lower of the two values must be reached before `read()` will return. Finally, if receive framing is enabled, all reads return immediately, regardless of the other values. Table 17-1 summarizes.

Table 17-1. When Does read() Return?

Receive Threshold	Receive Time-out	Receive Framing	Input Buffer Size	read() Returns When
disabled	disabled	disabled	b bytes	Returns when any data is available.
n bytes	disabled	disabled	b bytes	Returns when either n or b bytes are available, whichever is less.
disabled	t ms	disabled	b bytes	Returns after t milliseconds or when any data is available.
n bytes	t ms	disabled	b bytes	Returns after t milliseconds or when either n or b bytes are available, whichever is less.
disabled	disabled	enabled	b bytes	Returns immediately.
n bytes	disabled	enabled	b bytes	Returns immediately.
disabled	t ms	enabled	b bytes	Returns immediately.
n bytes	t ms	enabled	b bytes	Returns immediately.

The output buffer size is the number of bytes the driver can store for the output stream before it can write to the port. This is important, because it's easy for a fast program to write data faster than the port can send it out. Buffer overruns are a common problem, especially on older PCs with slower serial ports.

Each of these properties has four methods: one enables the property, one disables it, one checks whether the property is enabled, and one returns the current value. For instance, the receive threshold is adjusted by these four methods:

```
public abstract void enableReceiveThreshold(int size)
    throws UnsupportedCommOperationException
public abstract void disableReceiveThreshold()
public abstract boolean isReceiveThresholdEnabled()
public abstract int getReceiveThreshold()
```

The other three properties follow the same naming conventions. These four methods adjust the receive time-out:

```
public abstract void enableReceiveTimeout(int rcvTimeout)
    throws UnsupportedCommOperationException
public abstract void disableReceiveTimeout()
public abstract boolean isReceiveTimeoutEnabled()
public abstract int getReceiveTimeout()
```

These four methods adjust the receive framing property:

```
public abstract void enableReceiveFraming(int framingByte)
    throws UnsupportedCommOperationException
public abstract void disableReceiveFraming()
public abstract boolean isReceiveFramingEnabled()
public abstract int getReceiveFramingByte()
```

These four methods adjust the input and output buffer sizes:

```
public abstract void setInputBufferSize(int size)
public abstract int getInputBufferSize()
public abstract void setOutputBufferSize(int size)
public abstract int getOutputBufferSize()
```

All drivers must support input and output buffers, so there are no isInput-BufferEnabled() or disableOutputBuffer() methods. However, other than the input and output buffer sizes, drivers are not required to support these properties. If a driver does not support the given property, then enabling it will throw an UnsupportedCommOperationException. You can determine whether or not a driver supports a property by trying to enable it and seeing whether or not an exception is thrown. Example 17-7 uses this scheme to test the properties for the ports of the host system.

Example 17-7. PortTester

```
import javax.comm.*;
import java.util.*;
```

Example 17-7. PortTester (continued)

```java
public class PortTester {

  public static void main(String[] args) {

    Enumeration thePorts = CommPortIdentifier.getPortIdentifiers();
    while (thePorts.hasMoreElements()) {
      CommPortIdentifier com = (CommPortIdentifier) thePorts.nextElement();
      System.out.print(com.getName());

      switch(com.getPortType()) {
        case CommPortIdentifier.PORT_SERIAL:
          System.out.println(", a serial port: ");
          break;
        case CommPortIdentifier.PORT_PARALLEL:
          System.out.println(", a parallel port: ");
          break;
        default:
          // important since other types of ports like USB
          // and firewire are expected to be added in the future
          System.out.println(" , a port of unknown type: ");
          break;
      }

      try {
        CommPort thePort = com.open("Port Tester", 20);
        testProperties(thePort);
        thePort.close();
      }
      catch (PortInUseException e) {
        System.out.println("Port in use, can't test properties");
      }
      System.out.println();
    }
  }

  public static void testProperties(CommPort thePort) {

    try {
      thePort.enableReceiveThreshold(10);
      System.out.println("Receive timeout supported");
    }
    catch (UnsupportedCommOperationException e) {
      System.out.println("Receive timeout not supported");
    }

    try {
      thePort.enableReceiveTimeout(10);
      System.out.println("Receive framing supported");
    }
```

Example 17-7. PortTester (continued)

```
  catch (UnsupportedCommOperationException e) {
    System.out.println("Receive framing not supported");
  }

  try {
    thePort.enableReceiveFraming(10);
    System.out.println("Receive threshold supported");
  }
  catch (UnsupportedCommOperationException e) {
    System.out.println("Receive threshold not supported");
  }
 }
}
```

Here's the results for both serial and parallel ports from a Windows NT box running the Comm API 2.0:

```
D:\JAVA\16>java PortTester
COM1, a serial port:
Receive threshold supported
Receive timeout supported
Receive framing supported

COM2, a serial port:
Port in use, can't test properties

LPT1, a parallel port:
Receive threshold supported
Receive timeout supported
Receive framing supported

LPT2, a parallel port:
Port in use, can't test properties
```

Serial Ports

The javax.comm.SerialPort class is an abstract subclass of CommPort that provides various methods and constants useful for working with RS-232 serial ports and devices. The main purposes of the class are to allow the programmer to inspect, adjust, and monitor changes in the settings of the serial port. Simple input and output is accomplished with the methods of the superclass, CommPort. SerialPort has a public constructor, but that shouldn't be used by applications. Instead, you should call the open() method of a CommPortIdentifier that maps to the port you want to communicate with, then cast the result to SerialPort. For example:

```
CommPortIdentifier cpi = CommPortIdentifier.getPortIdentifier("COM2");
```

```
if (cpi.getType() == CommPortIdentifier.PORT_SERIAL) {
  try {
    SerialPort modem = (SerialPort) cpi.open();
  }
  catch (PortInUseException e) {}
}
```

Methods in the `SerialPort` class fall into roughly three categories:

- Methods that return the state of the port

- Methods that set the state of the port

- Methods that listen for the changes in the state of the port

Control Functions

Data cannot simply be sent over a wire; you need to deal with many issues, like timing, noise, and the fundamentally analog nature of electronics. Therefore, there's a host of layered protocols so that the receiving end can recognize when data is being sent, whether the data was received correctly, and more.

Serial communication uses some very basic, simple protocols. Sending between 3 and 25 volts across the serial cable for a number of nanoseconds inversely proportional to the baud rate of the connection is a one bit. Sending between –3 and –25 volts for the same amount of time is a 0 bit.* These bits are grouped into serial data units, SDUs for short. Common SDU lengths are 8 (used for binary data) and 7 (used for basic ASCII text). Most modern devices use eight data bits per SDU. However, some older devices use seven, six, or even five data bits per SDU. Once an SDU is begun, the rest of the SDU follows in close order. However, there may be gaps of indeterminate length between SDUs.

One of the problems faced by asynchronous serial devices is determining SDU boundaries. If a modem receives eight data bits, how is it to tell whether that's an entire SDU or the last four bits of one SDU and the first four bits of another, especially if the connection has some noise and isn't particularly reliable? To assist with this, each SDU is preceded by a single start bit that's always 0, and followed by between one and two stop bits. Stop bits last longer than data bits so they can always be identified.

In addition to the data and the start and stop bits, an SDU may have a parity bit. Parity is a very simple error detection scheme that can detect (but not correct) single bit errors in an SDU. There are two basic parity schemes. Even parity adds an extra one bit to the end of the SDU if there are an even number of one bits in the data. Odd parity adds an extra one bit to the end of the SDU if there are an

---

* Sending between 3 and -3 volts is a hardware error.

odd number of one bits in the data.* No parity simply omits the parity bit. The combination of data bits, parity scheme, and stop bits is abbreviated in forms like 8N1 or 7E1. 8N1 means a connection uses eight data bits, no parity, and one stop bit; 7E1 means seven data bits, even parity, and one stop bit. Virtually all modern systems use 8N1.

The baud rate is the number of times per second the state of the communication channel changes. This is *not* the same as bits per second. Modern modems send multiple bits per baud. Most U.S. phone lines, configured primarily for voice calls, have a maximum baud rate of 3200. Modems that send higher bit rates send multiple bits with each baud. A 28,800 bps modem is a 3200 baud modem with nine states, for example. In fact, a standard 2400 bps modem is really a 600 baud modem with four states.

The Java Comm API lets you set all of these parameters, including baud rate, data bits, stop bits, and parity. They should all be familiar to anyone who's struggled with modem init strings and terminal software in the bad old days before the Internet separated connectivity from content. Four methods in the `SerialPort` class return the values of these settings. They are:

```
public abstract int getBaudRate()
public abstract int getDataBits()
public abstract int getStopBits()
public abstract int getParity()
```

A little surprisingly, you can't set these values independently. Instead, all four values (baud, data bits, stop bits, and parity) are set at once with the `setSerialPortParams()` method:

```
public abstract void setSerialPortParams(int baud, int dataBits, int
    stopBits, int parity) throws UnsupportedCommOperationException
```

If the requested values are not supported by the driver (e.g., a 240,000 baud connection), an `UnsupportedCommOperationException` is thrown. Except for the baud rate, these arguments should be one of several mnemonic constants in the `SerialPort` class:

```
SerialPort.DATABITS_5     // 5 data bits per byte
SerialPort.DATABITS_6     // 6 data bits per byte
SerialPort.DATABITS_7     // 7 data bits per byte
SerialPort.DATABITS_8     // 8 data bits per byte
SerialPort.STOPBITS_1     // 1 stop bit
SerialPort.STOPBITS_2     // 2 stop bits
SerialPort.STOPBITS_1_5   // 1.5 stop bits†
```

---

* There are two more parity schemes you may encounter in brain-damaged hardware. Mark parity always adds a one bit for the parity; space parity always adds a zero bit. These convey no useful information and are almost never used.

```
SerialPort.PARITY_NONE    // no parity
SerialPort.PARITY_ODD     // odd parity
SerialPort.PARITY_EVEN    // even parity
```

Flow Control

Serial ports and the devices connected to them need a protocol to determine when the port is sending and the device is receiving, when the device is sending and the port is receiving, and how to switch between the two states. There are two main protocols that are used: XON/XOFF and RTS/CTS. They are not mutually exclusive, though it's rare to use both at the same time, and nothing is gained by doing so. XON/XOFF is a software-based protocol; it works by sending special characters down the communication line to tell the other end when to stop and start sending. RTS/CTS is implemented in hardware and requires a special hardware handshaking cable that supports it. Almost all modern hardware, including all modems faster than 2400 bps, supports hardware flow control.

The Java Comm API contains two methods to get and set the flow-control protocol:

```
public abstract int getFlowControlMode()
public abstract void setFlowControlMode(int protocol)
  throws UnsupportedCommOperationException
```

The `int` returned by `getFlowControlMode()` and the argument passed to `setFlowControlMode()` should be a bitwise AND of the following constants:

```
SerialPort.FLOWCONTROL_NONE         // no flow control
SerialPort.FLOWCONTROL_RTSCTS_IN    // RTS/CTS for input
SerialPort.FLOWCONTROL_RTSCTS_OUT   // RTS/CTS for output
SerialPort.FLOWCONTROL_XONXOFF_IN   // XON/XOFF for input
SerialPort.FLOWCONTROL_XONXOFF_OUT  // XON/XOFF for output
```

To set the flow control of the `SerialPort` object `com1` to RTS/CTS for both input and output, you would write:

```
com1.setFlowControlMode(SerialPort.FLOWCONTROL_RTSCTS_IN
                  & SerialPort.FLOWCONTROL_RTSCTS_OUT);
```

Control Wires

A serial port sends data one bit at a time, but it actually uses eight wires to do it. One wire is used for sending, one for receiving, and the other six for various

---

† If one and a half stop bits sounds a little funny to you, just remember that serial communications is ultimately an analog procedure, digital abstractions like bits not withstanding. A bit on a serial line is simply a raised or lowered voltage for a given unit of time. One and a half stop bits is simply a raised or lowered voltage for 150% of the normal time used to transfer a bit.

control information. One or two more pins are connected to ground. Modern serial ports generally come in a nine-pin configuration that reflects this, though most modems and some older PCs and terminals use a 25-pin connector. Table 17-2 shows the "pin-outs" of the standard nine-pin serial port you're likely to find on the back of a PC. Table 17-3 shows the "pin-outs" of the standard 25-pin serial port you're likely to find on a modem.

Table 17-2. Nine-Pin Serial Port Pin-outs

Pin	Name	Code	Direction
1	Carrier Detect	CD	Device → Computer
2	Receive Data	RD	Device → Computer
3	Transmit Data	TD	Computer → Device
4	Data Terminal Ready	DTR	Computer → Device
5	Signal Ground	GND	
6	Data Set Ready	DSR	Device → Computer
7	Request To Send	RTS	Computer → Device
8	Clear To Send	CTS	Device → Computer
9	Ring Indicator	RI	Device → Computer

Table 17-3. 25-pin Serial Port Pin-outs

Pin	Name	Code	Direction
1	Chassis ground		
2	Transmit Data	TD	Computer → Device
3	Receive Data	RD	Device → Computer
4	Request To Send	RTS	Computer → Device
5	Clear To Send	CTS	Device → Computer
6	Data Set Ready	DSR	Device → Computer
7	Signal Ground	GND	
8	Carrier Detect	CD	Device → Computer
20	Data Terminal Ready	DTR	Computer → Device
22	Ring Indicator	RI	Device → Computer

The 15 extra pins on the 25-pin port are generally not connected to anything; Java does not provide methods for manipulating them even if they are.*

On a straight DB-25-to-DB-25 connection, about the simplest connection imaginable, used on some early PCs and some current Unix workstations, the serial cable

---

* The other 15 pins are actually assigned meanings in the RS-232 standard. However, almost no hardware uses those pins, and the Java Communications API does not provide methods for reading or writing the state of those pins.

that connects the PC to the modem runs wires between the corresponding pins. That is, the CD pin is connected to the CD pin, the TD pin is connected to the TD pin, and so forth. Figure 17-1 shows the connection from a PC DB-25 serial port to a DB-25 modem.

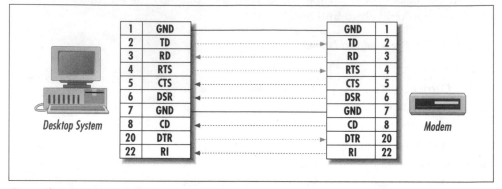

	PC			Modem	
1	GND		GND	1	
2	TD		TD	2	
3	RD		RD	3	
4	RTS		RTS	4	
5	CTS		CTS	5	
6	DSR		DSR	6	
7	GND		GND	7	
8	CD		CD	8	
20	DTR		DTR	20	
22	RI		RI	22	

Figure 17-1. PC DB-25 serial port to a DB-25 modem

The computer and the modem communicate with each other by raising or lowering voltages on these lines. Each line is one-way. A device reads from or writes to that line but never both. The computer sends data to the modem across the TD line. The modem sends data to the computer across the RD line. The computer tells the modem its ready to send by raising the voltage on the RTS line. The modem says its OK for the PC to send using the CTS line. The modem indicates to the computer its ready using the DSR line and that it's detected a carrier by using the DCD line. If the modem loses the carrier signal (e.g., the phone hangs up), it lowers the voltage on the DCD line. Finally, the computer indicates it's ready by raising the voltage on the DTR line.

These cables can get a little more complicated as different kinds of ports get connected. However, the main reason for the complexity is that not all ports put the same pins in the same positions. For example, Figure 17-2 shows a standard DB-9 PC port connected to a standard DB-25 modem port. It looks hairier, but if you look closer, you'll see that all that happened was that the pins swapped positions, taking their connections with them. The TD pin is still connected to the TD pin; the RD pin is still connected to the RD pin; and so forth. The only changes are the numbers of the pins and the omission of one ground pin from the DB-9 port.

A standard modem cable connects the same pin on one end of the wire to the corresponding pin on the other end of the wire (e.g., DTR to DTR), as shown in Figure 17-1 and Figure 17-2. Cables for connecting other kinds of devices often deliberately cross or split wires. For instance, in a null modem cable, shown in

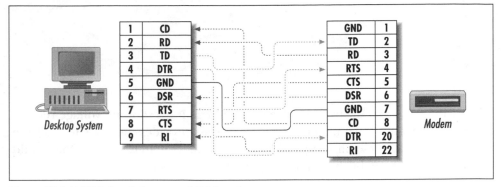

Figure 17-2. PC DB-9 serial port to a DB-25 modem

Figure 17-3, used for direct connections between PCs, the TD pins are connected to the RD pins; the RTS pin is connected to the CTS pin; and the DTR pin is connected to the DCD and DSR pins. This allows two PCs to communicate using a communications program and a direct serial connection without any modem. This is why not all serial cables are created equal, and the cable that works for one device may not work for another.

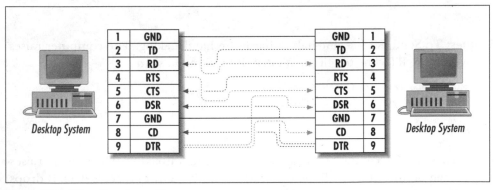

Figure 17-3. PC null modem cable

Data is sent from computer to device across the TD line and from device to computer across the RD line. You access these lines through the output and input streams returned by CommPort's getOutputStream() and getInputStream() methods. You do not directly manipulate these pins. The ground pins are used only to maintain a common reference voltage between the devices. No program ever sends voltage over these lines. This leaves six pins you may want to read or write. These are:

• DTR

- RTS
- CTS
- DSR
- RI
- CD

Each of these has an effectively boolean value: `true` if it's showing voltage relative to ground, `false` if it isn't. The `SerialPort` class provides methods to read the current state of all these pins. It provides methods to write to those pins that would normally be written to by the computer end of the connection.

DTR

Data Terminal Ready, DTR, means the computer is ready to send or receive data. CR, Computer Ready, would be more likely true nowadays, but the RS-232 standard was developed in the days of dumb terminals, when personal computers were still an oddity.

```
public abstract void setDTR(boolean dtr)
public abstract boolean isDTR()
```

RTS

Request To Send, RTS, is one-half of hardware handshaking. The computer raises voltage on the RTS line to tell the modem it's waiting to send.

```
public abstract void setRTS(boolean rts)
public abstract boolean isRTS()
```

CTS

Clear To Send, CTS, is the other half of hardware handshaking. The modem raises the voltage on this wire to tell the computer that it's ready to receive data. It drops the voltage when it's no longer ready to receive data.

```
public abstract boolean isCTS()
```

You cannot set the Clear To Send wire directly. Only the serial device can tell you when it is ready to receive. You cannot force it to be ready.

DSR

The modem raises the voltage on the DSR line, Data Set Ready, to indicate that it's turned on and operating. This line is also read-only.

```
public abstract boolean isDSR()
```

RI

The modem raises the voltage on the RI wire, Ring Indicator, to tell the computer that the phone is ringing.

```
public abstract boolean isRI()
```

You cannot set the Ring Indicator bit directly. This is used only for one-way communication from the device back to the computer, not for the computer to send information to the device. (In other words, the computer can't tell the modem the phone is ringing.)

CD

The modem uses the CD wire, Carrier Detect, to tell the computer that it has successfully negotiated the low-level modem protocols with the modem on the other end of the connection.

```
public abstract boolean isCD()
```

You cannot set the Carrier Detect bit directly. This is used only for one-way communication from the device back to the computer, not for the computer to send information to the device.

Serial Port Events

The examples shown so far all depended on the computer taking the initiative. The computer tells the modem when to dial, the printer when to print, and so on. By analogy with network programming, this is client-based. However, there's another model for port programs, the server-based program. Just as an Internet server waits for an incoming connection, a program can wait for incoming faxes through a fax modem, incoming BBS connections through a modem, notifications of impending shutdown from an uninterruptable power supply, paper-empty messages from a printer on a parallel port, and more. However, unlike the abstract network ports of Chapter 5, *Network Streams*, computers have no concept of binding to a serial port, at least within the Java Comm API. Although you can check the various pins used to send information from a modem or other serial port device to the computer whenever you want to, it's more convenient to do it asynchronously.

Incoming port access relies on an event-based model; in fact, the same model used by JavaBeans and the AWT 1.1 and later. When the runtime detects a change in state at a monitored serial port, it fires a serial port event to the registered serial port listener. The `SerialPortEvent` class has a public constructor, but you shouldn't use it. Instead, the VM creates and fires serial port events to indicate a change on one of the standard serial port lines:

```
public SerialPortEvent (SerialPort src, int type, boolean oldValue,
                        boolean newValue)
```

The `javax.comm.SerialPortEvent` class declares these three public methods:

```
public int getEventType()
public boolean getNewValue()
public boolean getOldValue()
```

The `getEventType()` method returns a named constant from the `SerialPort-Event` class that specifies what caused the event to be fired. There are 10 possibilities:

```
SerialPortEvent.DATA_AVAILABLE       // Data has arrived at the port.
SerialPortEvent.OUTPUT_BUFFER_EMPTY  // Output buffer on the port is empty.
SerialPortEvent.CTS                  // The Clear To Send pin has changed state.
SerialPortEvent.DSR                  // The Data Set Ready pin has changed state.
SerialPortEvent.RI                   // The Ring Indicator pin has changed state.
SerialPortEvent.CD                   // The Carrier Detect pin has changed state.
SerialPortEvent.OE                   // An overrun error occurred.
SerialPortEvent.PE                   // A parity error occurred.
SerialPortEvent.FE                   // A framing error occurred.
SerialPortEvent.BI                   // A break interrupt was detected.
```

`SerialPortEvent.DATA_AVAILABLE` and `SerialPortEvent.OUTPUT_BUFFER_ EMPTY` are enough information all by themselves. The other eight possible types, however, represent a boolean change from one state to another, from on to off or off to on. Therefore, there are also `getNewValue()` and `getOldValue()` methods to tell you what the state of the pin was before and after the event:

```
public boolean getNewValue()
public boolean getOldValue()
```

Serial Port Event Listeners

There are three steps to respond to serial port events:

1. Implement the `SerialPortEventListener` interface.

2. Register your `SerialPortEventListener` object with the `SerialPort` object representing the serial port you want to monitor.

3. Tell the `SerialPort` object the types of events you want to be notified of.

Steps 1 and 2 should be familiar from JavaBeans and the Java 1.1 AWT. Step 3 is used to avoid getting notifications of events you're not interested in.

Step 1

As you might guess, you listen for serial port events with a `SerialPortEvent-Listener`:

```
public interface SerialPortEventListener extends EventListener
```

This interface declares a single method, `serialEvent()`:

```
public abstract void serialEvent(SerialPortEvent spe)
```

Inside this method, you would generally use the `getEventType()` method of `SerialPortEvent` to determine exactly what caused the serial port event and to respond appropriately.

Step 2

Once you've constructed a `SerialPortEventListener`, you need to pass it to the `SerialPort` object's `addEventListener()` method:

```
public abstract void addEventListener(SerialPortEventListener listener)
   throws TooManyListenersException
```

You are limited to one event listener per port. Adding a second event listener throws a `java.util.TooManyListenersException`. If this is a problem, you can install an intermediate event listener directly with the `SerialPort` object. This listener could keep a list of other `SerialPortEventListener` objects and dispatch the events it receives to the other event listeners.

Should you need to, you can remove a listener from the port with the `SerialPort` object's `removeEventListener()` method. This method takes no arguments, because there's never more than one event listener registered directly with the port.

```
public abstract void removeEventListener()
```

Step 3

In many circumstances you may not be interested in some or all of these events. By default, none of these events are fired unless you first enable them with one of the 10 notify methods in `javax.comm.SerialPort`:

```
public abstract void notifyOnDataAvailable(boolean enable)
public abstract void notifyOnOutputEmpty(boolean enable)
public abstract void notifyOnCTS(boolean enable)
public abstract void notifyOnDSR(boolean enable)
public abstract void notifyOnRingIndicator(boolean enable)
public abstract void notifyOnCarrierDetect(boolean enable)
public abstract void notifyOnOverrunError(boolean enable)
public abstract void notifyOnParityError(boolean enable)
public abstract void notifyOnFramingError(boolean enable)
public abstract void notifyOnBreakInterrupt(boolean enable)
```

By default, no events are fired when the serial port's state changes. If you pass `true` to any of these methods, the VM will fire a serial port event when the matching state changes. Example 17-8 activates the Ring Indicator and prints a message on System.out when the modem tells the computer the phone is ringing.

Example 17-8. PhoneListener

```java
import javax.comm.*;
import java.util.TooManyListenersException;

public class PhoneListener implements SerialPortEventListener {

  public static void main(String[] args) {

    String portName = "COM1";
    if (args.length > 0) portName = args[0];

    PhoneListener pl = new PhoneListener();

    try {
      CommPortIdentifier cpi = CommPortIdentifier.getPortIdentifier(portName);
      if (cpi.getPortType() == CommPortIdentifier.PORT_SERIAL) {
        SerialPort modem = (SerialPort) cpi.open("Phone Listener", 1000);
        modem.notifyOnRingIndicator(true);
        modem.addEventListener(pl);
      }
    }
    catch (NoSuchPortException e) {
      System.err.println("Usage: java PhoneListener port_name");
    }
    catch (TooManyListenersException e) {
      // shouldn't happen in this example
    }
    catch (PortInUseException e) {System.err.println(e);}
  }

  public void serialEvent(SerialPortEvent evt) {

    System.err.println(evt.getEventType());
    if (evt.getEventType() == SerialPortEvent.RI) {
      System.out.println("The phone is ringing");
    }
  }
}
```

Parallel Ports

Parallel ports are most common on PCs. Sun SparcStations from the Sparc V on also have them. However, Macs do not have them, nor do many non-x86 workstations. Parallel ports are sometimes called printer ports, because their original purpose was to support printers. The names of the parallel ports—"LPT1," "LPT2," etc.—stand for "Line PrinTer," reflecting this usage. Nowadays, parallel ports are also used for Zip drives, tape drives, and various other devices. However, parallel ports are still largely limited by their original goal of providing simple printing. A parallel port sends data eight bits at a time on eight wires. These bits are sent at the same time in parallel, hence the name. The original parallel ports only allowed data to flow one way, from the PC to the printer. The printer could only respond by sending a few standard messages on other wires. Each return wire corresponded to a particular message, like "Out of paper" or "Printer busy." Modern parallel ports allow full, bidirectional communication.

The `javax.comm.ParallelPort` class is a concrete subclass of `javax.comm.CommPort` that provides various methods and constants useful for working with parallel ports and devices. The main purposes of the class are to allow the programmer to inspect, adjust, and monitor changes in the settings of the parallel port. Simple input and output are accomplished with the methods of the superclass, `CommPort`. `ParallelPort` has a single public constructor, but that shouldn't be used by applications. Instead, you should simply call the `open()` method of a `CommPortIdentifier` that maps to the port you want to communicate with, then cast it to `ParallelPort`:

```
CommPortIdentifier cpi = CommPortIdentifier.getPortIdentifier("LPT2");
if (cpi.getType() == CommPortIdentifier.PORT_PARALLEL) {
  try {
    ParallelPort printer = (ParallelPort) cpi.open ();
  }
  catch (PortInUseException e) {}
}
```

Methods in the `ParallelPort` class fall into roughly four categories:

- Methods that adjust the port mode
- Methods to control the port
- Methods to inspect the state of the port
- Methods that listen for changes in the state of the port

Parallel Port Modes

Like most other computer hardware, parallel ports have evolved over the last two decades. Modern parallel ports support bidirectional communication and other features never envisioned for the original parallel port that was only supposed to send data to a daisy-wheel printer. However, older peripherals may not work with newer parallel ports, so they can, if necessary, be downgraded to any of several various compatibility modes. All of these are available as named `int` constants in the `javax.comm.ParallelPort` class:

```
ParallelPort.LPT_MODE_ANY     // Use the most advanced mode possible.
ParallelPort.LPT_MODE_SPP     // Original lineprinter mode. Unidirectional
                              // transfer from PC to printer. Most compatible
                              // with older peripherals.
ParallelPort.LPT_MODE_PS2     // Byte at a time, bidirectional mode as
                              // introduced in the IBM PS/2 family.
ParallelPort.LPT_MODE_EPP     // Extended parallel port.
ParallelPort.LPT_MODE_ECP     // Enhanced capabilities port.
ParallelPort.LPT_MODE_NIBBLE  // Nibble (4 bits, half a byte) at a time mode,
                              // bidirectional, used by some Hewlett Packard
                              // equipment.
```

The mode the parallel port uses is returned by the `getMode()` method and set by passing the appropriate constant to the `setMode()` method:

```
public abstract int getMode()
public abstract int setMode(int mode) throws
UnsupportedCommOperationException
```

Attempts to set the port to an unsupported mode will throw an `Unsupported-CommOperationException`.

Controlling the Parallel Port

Data is sent to the parallel port and its attached device using the output stream returned by the `CommPort` class's `getOutputStream()` method. You can interrupt this data by sending the appropriate signals out the parallel port to the printer. The `suspend()` and `restart()` methods send these signals:

```
public abstract void restart()
public abstract void suspend()
```

These are generally interpreted as stopping and restarting printing. You normally suspend and restart printing if the printer reports an error. These methods do not automatically start a print job over from the beginning. You are still responsible for sending the printer whatever data it needs to print from whatever point it was printing or from the point where you want to restart printing.

Checking the State of the Port

The original parallel port allowed printers to send only a few predefined messages. Each message was sent by raising the voltage on a specific wire connecting the port to the printer. These messages are always sent from the printer to the CPU, never in the other direction. Therefore, Java only allows you to check the state of each of these pins, not to set them. The methods are:

```
public abstract boolean isPaperOut()
public abstract boolean isPrinterBusy()
public abstract boolean isPrinterSelected()
public abstract boolean isPrinterTimedOut()
public abstract boolean isPrinterError()
```

Each of these methods returns `true` if the matching wire is showing voltage relative to ground, `false` if it isn't.

There is also a `getOutputBufferFree()` method that returns the number of bytes currently available in the parallel port's output buffer—in other words, the number of bytes you can write before the buffer fills up:

```
public abstract int getOutputBufferFree()
```

Parallel Port Events

Although you can check the various pins used to send information from a printer to the computer whenever you want to, it's more convenient to be able to do it asynchronously. The Java Comm API supports asynchronous notification of activity occurring on parallel ports. The model used for notification is the same one used for JavaBeans, the Java 1.1 AWT, and serial port events: when the runtime detects a change in state at a monitored parallel port, it fires a parallel port event to the registered parallel port listener. A parallel port event signals some sort of activity on the parallel port, either an error or an empty output buffer. Parallel port events are represented by instances of the `javax.comm.ParallelPortEvent` class, a subclass of `java.util.EventObject`:

```
public class ParallelPortEvent extends EventObject
```

The `ParallelPortEvent` class has a single public constructor, but you shouldn't use it. Instead, the runtime creates and fires parallel port events when it wants to indicate a change on one of the standard parallel port pins.

```
public ParallelPortEvent(ParallelPort src, int type, boolean oldValue,
boolean newValue)
```

The `javax.comm.ParallelPortEvent` class declares these three public methods:

```
public int getEventType()
public boolean getNewValue()
public boolean getOldValue()
```

The `getEventType()` method returns a named constant from the `ParallelPortEvent` class that specifies what caused the event to be fired. There are two possibilities: an error and an empty output buffer. Each parallel port event has an `eventType` field; its value should be one of these mnemonic constants:

```
ParallelPortEvent.PAR_EV_ERROR    // An error occurred on the port.
```

```
ParallelPortEvent.PAR_EV_BUFFER   // The output buffer is empty.
```

These represent a change from one state to another, from on to off or off to on. Therefore, there are also getNewValue() and getOldValue() methods to tell you the state of the pin before and after the event:

```
public boolean getNewValue()
public boolean getOldValue()
```

Parallel Port Event Listeners

There are three steps to respond to parallel port events:

1. Implement the ParallelPortEventListener interface.

2. Register your ParallelPortEventListener object with the ParallelPort object representing the parallel port you want to monitor.

3. Tell the parallel port the types of events you want to be notified of.

Steps 1 and 2 should be familiar from JavaBeans and the Java 1.1 AWT. Step 3 is used to avoid getting notifications of events you're not interested in and is similar to the same step for serial port events.

Step 1

As you would probably guess, you listen for parallel port events with a Parallel-PortEventListener:

```
public interface ParallelPortEventListener extends EventListener
```

This interface declares a single method, parallelEvent():

```
public abstract void parallelEvent(ParallelPortEvent ppe)
```

Inside this method, you generally use the getEventType() method of Parallel-PortEvent to determine exactly what caused the parallel port event:

```
public int getEventType()
```

This should return ParallelPortEvent.PAR_EV_BUFFER to signal an empty output buffer or ParallelPortEvent.PAR_EV_ERROR to signal some other sort of error.

The getNewValue() and getOldValue() methods tell you what the state of the parallel port was before and after the event:

```
public boolean getNewValue()
public boolean getOldValue()
```

Step 2

Once you've constructed a `ParallelPortEventListener`, you need to pass it to the `ParallelPort` object's `addEventListener()` method:

```
public abstract void addEventListener(ParallelPortEventListener listener)
  throws TooManyListenersException
```

You are limited to one event listener per port. Attempting to add a second event listener throws a `java.util.TooManyListenersException`. If this is a problem, you can install a single intermediate event listener directly with the `ParallelPort` object, which keeps a list of `ParallelPortEventListener` objects and dispatches events it receives to the other event listeners.

Should you need to, you can remove a listener from the port with the `Parallel-Port` object's `removeEventListener()` method:

```
public abstract void removeEventListener()
```

This method takes no arguments, because there's never more than one event listener registered directly with the port.

Step 3

In many circumstances, you may not be interested in both of these events. By default, neither of these events is fired unless you first enable them with the right notify method in `javax.comm.ParallelPort`:

```
public abstract void notifyOnError(boolean notify)
public abstract void notifyOnBuffer(boolean notify)
```

By default no events are fired when the parallel port's state changes. However, if you pass `true` to either of these methods, it will fire a parallel port event when the matching state changes.

V

APPENDIXES

A

Additional Resources

When I began work on this book, I thought it would take me about 200 pages and about two months. Now, more than a year and 500 pages later, I can see that I/O is a far larger, more important, and more encompassing topic than I originally guessed. Many chapters could easily lead to books of their own. Indeed, several (Chapter 5, *Network Streams*, and Chapter 10, *Cryptographic Streams*) already are other books.

Since I can't possibly say everything there is to say about all these fascinating topics I've touched on in one page or another in this tome, I'd like to point you to several books, mailing lists, and web sites that explore some of the issues raised in this book in greater detail. Some of these are I/O-specific; some are mostly tangential. However, they're all interesting and worthy of further study and thought.

Digital Think

Digital Think (*http://www.digitalthink.com/*) offers web-based training courses for programmers, developers, system administrators, and end users in C, C++, Java, Windows, web development, object-oriented programming, and more. This book grew out of two web-based courses I wrote for Digital Think, Java Streams (*http://www.digitalthink.com/catalog/cs/cs108/*) and Java Readers and Writers (*http://www.digitalthink.com/catalog/cs/cs208/*). Although this book is far more comprehensive than those two courses, they're a good way to get started with this material, especially if you think you need a personal helping hand or a leg up. Each course includes graded exercises, a hands-on course project, and tutors to answer your questions and assist you with the difficult parts.

537

Design Patterns

At the time I was writing the first draft of this book, I also happened to be learning about design patterns. Gradually, it became obvious that much of the AWT was written by programmers who had patterns on the brain. The `java.awt.Toolkit` class is a textbook example of the "abstract factory" pattern. The `URL` class's `openConnection()` method is a factory method. The `Reader` and `Writer` classes are decorators on top of `InputStream` and `OutputStream`. The engine classes in the JCE are proxies, and I could cite many more examples. Much of the class library—including the `java.io` package—has been designed with design patterns, and it will all make a lot more sense if you're familiar with the standard patterns.

The seminal text on the subject is *Design Patterns*, by Erich Gamma, Richard Helm, Ralph Johnson, and John Vlissides (Addison-Wesley, 1995). The four authors are colloquially known as the "Gang of Four," and the book is often cited informally as "GoF." The 23 patterns covered in GoF are rapidly becoming part of the vocabulary of the object-oriented programming community. Design patterns are also beginning to be covered in many more introductory books about object-oriented programming and Java.

There are also several extremely active mailing lists and web sites devoted to design patterns. To subscribe to the *patterns@cs.uiuc.edu* list send email to *patterns-request@cs.uiuc.edu* with the word "subscribe" in the Subject: field. Archives of this and several related lists may be perused at *http://www.DistributedObjects.com/portfolio/archives/patterns/index.html*.

The java.io Package

The original source for much of the information contained herein about I/O is the *javadoc* documentation for the `java.io` package. You should have downloaded this with the JDK, but it's also available online at:

http://java.sun.com/products/jdk/1.2/docs/api/package-java.io.html (Java 1.2)
http://java.sun.com/products/jdk/1.1/docs/api/Package-java.io.html (Java 1.1)
http://java.sun.com/products/jdk/1.0.2/api/Package-java.io.html (Java 1.0)

The class library documentation is, however, woefully incomplete. While it explains what each method does, it often fails to explain how, why, or when you should use those methods. Furthermore, it only occasionally discusses assumptions about the behavior of those methods—assumptions that are crucial for anyone not merely using but also subclassing particular classes. There are many implicit assumptions about what particular methods should do (for instance, that a `close()` method of a filter input stream also closes any other streams it's connected to), and these are generally not documented anywhere (or at least they weren't until I wrote this book).

I've tried to document all of these assumptions in this book, but if you're faced with a new class not covered here, the canonical reference is the source code itself. The JDK includes Java source code for the java packages. You'll find it in a file called *src.zip* in your JDK distribution. Sometimes the only way to figure out exactly what Sun intended particular classes to do or how they expected them to do it is to read the source code for those classes.

Network Programming

In many ways this book is a prequel to my previous book with O'Reilly, *Java Network Programming*. Although written first, *Java Network Programming* presumes a solid familiarity with input and output, streams, and readers and writers as discussed in this book. *Java Network Programming* explains the fundamental protocols and technology that underlie the Internet, shows you how to communicate with sockets, provides detailed examples of working network clients and servers, and even develops content and protocol handlers. If you want to learn more about TCP/IP, HTTP, URLs, sockets and server sockets, and other elements of Internet programming in Java, you should definitely pick up *Java Network Programming*. (There's probably an ad for it in the back of this very book.)

The Centre for Distance-spanning Technology (CDT) runs the unmoderated *java-networking@cdt.luth.se* list for informal discussion of Java network programming, which I participate in. To subscribe, send an email containing the word "subscribe" in the body of the message to *java-networking-request@cdt.luth.se*. An archive of the list and complete instructions are available from *http://www.cdt.luth. se/~peppar/java/java-networking-list/*.

Data Compression

Java supports several related compression formats, including zlib, deflate, and gzip. These formats are documented in RFCs 1950, 1951, and 1952, and are available wherever RFCs are found, including *http://www.faqs.org/rfcs/*. The master site for these particular RFCs is *ftp://ftp.uu.net/graphics/png/documents/zlib/zdoc-index. html*.

Java's compression classes are native wrappers around the ZLIB compression library written by Jean-Loup Gailly and Mark Adler. You can learn about this library at *http://www.cdrom.com/pub/infozip/zlib/*.

For more general information about compression and archiving algorithms and formats, the *comp.compression* FAQ is a good place to start. See *http://www.faqs.org/ faqs/compression-faq/part1/preamble.html*. More technical details and sample code in C for a variety of algorithms are available in *The Data Compression Book*, by Mark Nelson and Jean-Loup Gailly (M&T Books, 1996, ISBN 1-55851-434-1).

The JAR file format was developed by Sun for Java. The full specification can be found at *http://java.sun.com/products/jdk/1.2/docs/guide/jar/jarGuide.html* (Java 2) or *http://java.sun.com/products/jdk/1.1/docs/guide/jar/jarGuide.html* (Java 1.1). Aside from the name, the only thing that really distinguishes a JAR file from a zip file is the optional manifest of the contents. The manifest format specification can be found at *http://java.sun.com/products/jdk/1.2/docs/guide/jar/manifest.html*.

Encryption and Related Technology

Chapter 10 only began to explore the fascinating subject of cryptography. The JCE is explicated in much more detail by Jonathan Knudsen in *Java Cryptography* (O'Reilly & Associates, 1998) *Java Cryptography* expands on the coverage of the `Cipher` and `MessageDigest` classes you'll find in this book. It also includes thorough discussions of the `java.security` package and the Java Cryptography Extension (JCE), showing you how to use security providers and even implement your own provider. It discusses authentication, key management, and public and private key encryption and includes a secure talk application that encrypts all data sent over the network. If you write Java programs that communicate sensitive data, you'll find this book indispensable.

For a more in-depth look at the mathematics and protocols that underlie the JCE, you'll want to check out Bruce Schneier's *Applied Cryptography* (John Wiley & Sons, 1995). This is the standard practical text on cryptographic protocols and algorithms, and the attacks on them. Schneier discusses a wide range of cryptographic algorithms, key management and exchange schemes, one-way hash functions, signature algorithms, and many other problems in sufficient detail to allow a competent programmer to implement them. Although Schneier's language of choice is C, the techniques discussed are applicable in any language.

The formal specification of the Java Cryptography API is available from Sun at *http://java.sun.com/products/jdk/1.2/docs/guide/security/CryptoSpec.html*. The actual implementation is in beta at the time of this writing and can be downloaded from *http://developer.javasoft.com/developer/earlyAccess/jdk12/jce.html*.

Object Serialization

Sun's serialization web page at *http://java.sun.com/products/jdk/1.2/docs/guide/serialization/* includes a FAQ list, sample code, and the complete object serialization specification. The specification covers serialization as implemented in Java 1.2, which is mostly upward-compatible with the Java 1.1 serialization discussed in Chapter 11, *Object Serialization*. An earlier prebeta specification that covers Java 1.0.2 serialization is posted at *http://java.sun.com/products/jdk/rmi/doc/serial-spec/serialTOC.doc.html*. A formal specification of Java 1.1 serialization was never published. However, the Java 1.2 spec is mostly the same, with the addition of a few extra features like the `readResolve()` method.

Sun's formal specification for object serialization is not always clear, especially when it comes to motivating the more esoteric areas of serialization like `ObjectInputValidation`. However, it is complete and does add some to what I discussed in Chapter 11, including the binary protocol for serialized objects and *.ser* files.

Object serialization was originally developed to support Remote Method Invocation (RMI), an architecture that allows Java objects in one virtual machine to invoke methods on objects in another virtual machine, possibly running on a different computer somewhere else on the Internet. RMI is discussed briefly in Chapter 14 of my *Java Network Programming* and at great length in Jim Farley's *Java Distributed Computing* (O'Reilly & Associates, 1998, ISBN 1-56592-206-9).

Object serialization is also used extensively as part of the JavaBeans component software architecture, a standard part of Java 1.1 and later. To learn more about this, I recommend you pick up Robert Englander's *Developing Java Beans* (O'Reilly & Associates, 1997, ISBN 1-56592-289-1) or my own *JavaBeans: Developing Component Software in Java* (IDG Books, 1997, ISBN 0-76458-052-3).

International Character Sets and Unicode

The canonical reference to Unicode is *The Unicode Specification 2.0* (Addison-Wesley, 1996, ISBN 0-201-48345-9). This book features detailed analysis of the Unicode standard as well as discussion of the difficulties of defining character sets for all the world's different languages. It's also got tables of almost all the defined characters in Unicode, including about 20,000 Han ideographs. The size of the book and the large number of interesting tables of different scripts from around the world make it a good choice for a techie coffee-table book that can even amuse your liberal arts friends. Updates, corrections, and errata to that volume are available on the Web at *http://www.unicode.org/*.

There's no single source of information for all the different non-Unicode character sets Java readers and writers can translate. However, most of the Windows character sets are enumerated in *Developing International Software for Windows 95 and NT*, by Nadine Kano (Microsoft Press, 1995, ISBN 1-55615-840-8). Kano ignores non-Windows platforms, and she does occasionally sound too much like a Microsoft press release. Nonetheless, this book contains a lot of useful details about how various localized versions of Windows operate. This book is also available on the MSDN Online Library web site at *http://premium.microsoft.com/msdn/*

library/. Registration is required, but otherwise it's free. Assuming Microsoft hasn't added an actually navigable interface to MSDN by the time you read this, you'll find it by clicking on "Books" in the lefthand frame, then clicking on "Developing International Software." (I normally wouldn't bother you with such details, but the interface really is painfully obscure.)

Roman Czyborra maintains a lot of useful information about various ISO 8859 and Cyrillic character sets on his web site at *http://czyborra.com/*, including charts of a wide range of character sets and code pages.

Ken Lunde's *CJKV Information Processing: Chinese, Japanese, Korean & Vietnamese Computing* (O'Reilly & Associates, 1999, ISBN 1-56592-224-7) is the most comprehensive English language reference to developing code for ideographic and other Far Eastern languages and scripts. To some extent this book is based on his free *CJK.INF* file available from *ftp://ftp.ora.com/pub/examples/nutshell/ujip/doc/cjk.inf*.

Finally, for a fascinating look at about 500 of the world's languages and the scripts they use, check out Kenneth Katzner's *Languages of the World* (Routledge, 1995). This small paperback describes and provides samples of about 500 of the world's languages, from the extremely popular (English and Chinese) to the painfully obscure (Romansh, Komi, Ostyak).

Java Communications API

This may well be the first book to cover the Java Communications API. Sun includes a limited amount of documentation with the Java Communications API itself, mostly *javadoc* class library documentation. The latter is also available from Sun's web site at *http://java.sun.com/products/javacomm/javadoc/Package-javax.comm. html*.

The RS-232 serial port and IEEE 1284 parallel port standards predate the Web and widespread use of the Internet. Thus, these standards are still available only on dead trees for the moment. A number of books do cover them in reasonable detail, including Scott Mueller's *Upgrading and Repairing PCs, 10th edition* (Que, 1998, ISBN 0-7897-1636-4).

Several books discuss writing port-aware programs in a variety of languages. Although none yet use Java, it's generally not hard to translate from the low-level C or Basic code to the equivalent code that uses the Java Communications API. The best book I've found for parallel ports is Jan Axelson's *Parallel Port Complete* (Lakeview Research, 1996, ISBN 096508191-5).

There are more choices for serial port books, but the most comprehensive one is certainly Joe Campbell's *C Programmer's Guide to Serial Communications* (Sams, 1993, ISBN 0-672-30286-1). Despite the title, the first half of this 900-page tome is an exhaustive treatment of more or less language-independent serial communication hardware and protocols from 19th-century telegraphy to the present day.

Updates and Breaking News

In the fast-moving world of Java, it's an effort to publish a book that isn't out of date by the time it reaches store shelves. Most of what I've written about in this book seems fairly stable. However, there will undoubtedly by many new developments after publication. The following three web sites can help you stay abreast of new technologies and strategies for Java I/O.

Café au Lait

My Café au Lait site at *http://metalab.unc.edu/javafaq/* features almost daily news updates about Java topics. I pay special attention to new material that's closely related to my books, like I/O and networking libraries. Café au Lait also features many resources to help you develop your Java programming skills, including FAQ lists, tutorials, course notes, examples, exercises, book reviews, and more. Of particular interest will be the Java I/O page at *http://metalab.unc.edu/javafaq/books/ javaio/.* I'll post corrections and updates to this book there as necessary.

java.oreilly.com

O'Reilly's official Java site at *http://java.oreilly.com/* contains feature articles and links to the official O'Reilly sites for all our Java books. You can peruse the rather impressive O'Reilly Java catalog (18 books and counting) and view descriptions, author bios, tables of contents, indexes, reviews, exercises, examples, errata, and reader comments for all the books (including this one).

JavaWorld

I/O isn't the sexiest topic in the programming community, but it is one of the most important. IDG's JavaWorld (*http://www.javaworld.com/*) is to be commended for treating I/O on an equal footing with sexier topics like JavaBeans and the Java Media APIs. JavaWorld publishes monthly how-to articles, book reviews, news, and more. They're particularly notable for providing short, technical articles that show you how to do things Sun's only hinted at and how to work around common problems programmers face.

B

Character Sets

The first 128 Unicode characters—that is, characters 0 through 127—are identical to the ASCII character set. 32 is the ASCII space; therefore, 32 is the Unicode space. 33 is the ASCII exclamation point; therefore, 33 is the Unicode exclamation point, and so on. Table B-1 lists this character set.

Table B-1. The first 128 Unicode Characters, Also Known as the ASCII Character Set

Code	Character	Code	Character	Code	Character	Code	Character
0	nul (null)	32	space	64	@	96	`
1	soh (start of header)	33	!	65	A	97	a
2	stx (start of text)	34	"	66	B	98	b
3	etx (end of text)	35	#	67	C	99	c
4	eot (end of transmission)	36	$	68	D	100	d
5	enq (enquiry)	37	%	69	E	101	e
6	ack (acknowledge)	38	&	70	F	102	f
7	bel (bell)	39	'	71	G	103	g
8	bs (backspace)	40	(	72	H	104	h
9	tab (tab)	41	)	73	I	105	i
10	lf (linefeed)	42	*	74	J.	106	j
11	vtb (vertical tab)	43	+	75	K	107	k
12	ff (formfeed)	44	,	76	L	108	l
13	cr (carriage return)	45	-	77	M	109	m

Table B-1. The first 128 Unicode Characters, Also Known as the ASCII Character Set (continued)

Code	Character	Code	Character	Code	Character	Code	Character
14	so (shift out)	46	.	78	N	110	n
15	si (shift in)	47	/	79	O	111	o
16	dle (data link escape)	48	0	80	P	112	p
17	dc1 (device control 1, XON)	49	1	81	Q	113	q
18	dc2 (device control 2)	50	2	82	R	114	r
19	dc3 (device control 3, XOFF)	51	3	83	S	115	s
20	dc4 (device control 4)	52	4	84	T	116	t
21	nak (negative acknowledge)	53	5	85	U	117	u
22	syn (synchronous idle)	54	6	86	V	118	v
23	etb (end of transmission block)	55	7	87	W	119	w
24	can (cancel)	56	8	88	X	120	x
25	em (end of medium)	57	9	89	Y	121	y
26	sub (substitute)	58	:	90	Z	122	z
27	esc (escape)	59	;	91	[	123	{
28	is4 (file separator)	60	<	92	\	124	|
29	is3 (group separator)	61	=	93	]	125	}
30	is2 (record separator)	62	>	94	^	126	~
31	is1 (unit separator)	63	?	95	_	127	del (delete)

In the first column, characters 0 through 31 are referred to as control characters, because they're traditionally entered by holding down the control key and a letter key (on at least some dumb terminals). For instance Ctrl-H is often ASCII 8, backspace. Ctrl-S is often mapped to ASCII 19, DC3 or XOFF. Ctrl-Q is often mapped to ASCII 17, DC1 or XON. Generally, each control character is entered by pressing the Control key and the printable character whose ASCII value is the ASCII value of the character you want plus 64 (or 96, if you count from the capitals). Character 127, delete, is also a control character.

The common abbreviation for the character is given first, followed by its common meaning. Some of these codes are pretty much obsolete. For instance, I'm not aware of any modern OS that actually uses characters 28 through 31 as file, group, record, and unit separators. Those control codes that are still used often have different meanings on different platforms. For example, character 10, the line-feed, originally meant move the platen on the printer up one line, while character 13, the carriage return, meant return the print-head to the beginning of the line. On paper-based teletype terminals, this could be used to position the print-head anywhere on a page and perhaps overtype characters that had already been typed. This no longer makes sense in an era of glass terminals and GUIs, so linefeed has come to mean a generic end-of-line character.

The next 128 Unicode characters—that is 128 through 255—have the same values as the equivalent characters in the Latin-1 character set defined in ISO standard 8859-1. Latin-1, a slight variation of which is used by Windows, adds the various accented characters, umlauts, cedillas, upside-down question marks, and other characters needed to write text in most Western European languages. Table B-2 shows these characters. The first 128 characters in Latin-1 are the ASCII charac-ters shown in Table B-1.

Table B-2. Unicode Characters Between 128 and 255, Also the Second Half of the ISO 8859-1 Latin-1 Character Set

Code	Character	Code	Character	Code	Character	Code	Character
128	pad (padding character)	160	non-breaking space	192	À	224	à
129	hop (high octet preset)	161	¡	193	Á	225	á
130	bph (break permitted here)	162	¢	194	Â	226	â
131	nbh (no break here)	163	£	195	Ã	227	ã
132	ind (index)	164	¤	196	Ä	228	ä
133	nel (next line)	165	¥	197	Å	229	å
134	ssa (start of selected area)	166	¦	198	Æ	230	æ
135	esa (end of selected area)	167	§	199	Ç	231	ç
136	hts (char-acter tabula-tion set)	168	¨	200	È	232	è

Table B-2. Unicode Characters Between 128 and 255, Also the Second Half of the ISO 8859-1 Latin-1
Character Set (continued)

Code	Character	Code	Character	Code	Character	Code	Character
137	htj (character tabulation with justification)	169	©	201	É	233	é
138	vts (line tabulation set)	170	ª	202	Ê	234	ê
139	pld (partial line forward)	171	«	203	Ë	235	ë
140	plu (partial line backward)	172	¬	204	Ì	236	ì
141	ri (reverse line feed)	173	soft (optional) hyphen	205	Í	237	í
142	ss2 (single-shift two)	174	®	206	Î	238	î
143	ss3 (single-shift three)	175	¯	207	Ï	239	ï
144	dcs (device control string)	176	° (degree)	208	Đ	240	ð
145	pu1 (private use one)	177	±	209	Ñ	241	ñ
146	pu2 (private use two)	178	²	210	Ò	242	ò
147	sts (set transmit state)	179	³	211	Ó	243	ó
148	cch (cancel character)	180	´	212	Ô	244	ô
149	mw (message waiting)	181	µ	213	Õ	245	õ
150	spa (start of guarded area)	182	¶	214	Ö	246	ö
151	epa (end of guarded area)	183	·	215	×	247	÷
152	sos (start of string)	184	, (cedilla)	216	Ø	248	ø
153	sgi (single graphic character introducer)	185	¹	217	Ù	249	ù

Table B-2. Unicode Characters Between 128 and 255, Also the Second Half of the ISO 8859-1 Latin-1 Character Set (continued)

Code	Character	Code	Character	Code	Character	Code	Character
154	sci (single character introducer)	186	º	218	Ú	250	ú
155	csi (control sequence introducer)	187	»	219	Û	251	û
156	st (string terminator)	188	1/4	220	Ü	252	ü
157	osc (operating system command)	189	1/2	221	Ý	253	ý
158	pm (privacy message)	190	3/4	222	Þ	254	þ
159	apc (application program command)	191	¿	223	ß	255	ÿ

Characters 128 through 159 are nonprinting control characters, much like characters 0 through 31 of the ASCII set. Unicode does not specify any meanings for these 32 characters, but their common interpretations are listed in the table. On Windows most of these positions are used for noncontrol characters not normally included in Latin-1. These alternate interpretations are given in Table B-3.

Table B-3. Windows Characters Between 128 and 159

Code	Character	Code	Character	Code	Character	Code	Character
128	undefined	136	ˆ	144	undefined	152	˜
129	undefined	137	‰	145	'	153	™
130	,	138	Š	146	'	154	š
131	ƒ	139	‹	147	"	155	›
132	„	140	Œ	148	"	156	œ
133	...	141	undefined	149	•	157	undefined
134	†	142	Ž [a]	150	–	158	ž [a]
135	‡	143	undefined	151	—	159	Ÿ

[a] These values are true for some, but not all, Windows systems. They are otherwise undefined.

Values beyond 255 encode characters from various other character sets. Where possible, character blocks describing a particular group of characters map onto established encodings for that set of characters by simple transposition. For instance, Unicode characters 884 through 1011 encode the Greek alphabet and associated characters like the Greek question mark (;). This is a direct transposition by 756 of characters 128 through 255 of the ISO 8859-7 character set, which is in turn based on the Greek national standard ELOT 928. For example, the small letter delta, δ, Unicode character 984, is ISO 8859-7 character 228. A small epsilon, ε, Unicode character 985, is ISO 8859-7 character 229. In general, the Unicode value for a Greek character equals the ISO 8859-7 value for the character plus 756. Other character sets are included in Unicode in a similar fashion whenever possible.

As much as I'd like to include complete tables for all Unicode characters, if I did so, this book would be little more than that table. For complete lists of all the Unicode characters and associated glyphs, the canonical reference is *The Unicode Standard Version 2.0,* by the Unicode Consortium, ISBN 0-201-48345-9. Updates to that book can be found at *http://www.unicode.org/.* Online charts can be found at *http://charts.unicode.org/.*

Table B-4 lists the encodings that Java, javac, and native2ascii understand. Detailed information about how these character sets map to Unicode can be found in the various files at *ftp://ftp.unicode.org/Public/MAPPINGS/.*

Table B-4. Available Encodings in Java 1.1

Name	Encoding
8859_1	ISO Latin-1, ASCII plus the characters needed for most Western European languages, including Danish, Dutch, English, Faroese, Finnish, Flemish, German, Icelandic, Irish, Italian, Norwegian, Portuguese, Spanish, and Swedish. Some non-European languages are also sometimes written with these characters, including Hawaiian, Indonesian, and Swahili.
8859_2	ISO Latin-2, ASCII plus the characters needed for most Central European languages, including Croatian, Czech, Hungarian, Polish, Romanian, Slovak, and Slovenian.
8859_3	ISO Latin-3, ASCII plus the characters needed for Esperanto, Maltese, Turkish, and Galician, though Latin-5, ISO 8859-9, is now preferred for Turkish.
8859_4	ISO Latin-4, ASCII plus the characters needed for the Baltic languages Latvian, Lithuanian, Greenlandic, and Lappish
8859_5	ASCII plus variant forms of Cyrillic characters used for Byelorussian, Bulgarian, Macedonian, Russian, Serbian, and Ukrainian.
8859_6	ASCII plus Arabic.
8859_7	ASCII plus modern Greek.
8859_8	ASCII plus Hebrew.
8859_9	ISO Latin-5. This is essentially the same as Latin-1 (ASCII plus Western Europe) except that the Icelandic letters Ý, ý, Ð, ð, þ, and þ are replaced with the Turkish letters İ, ı, Ğ, ğ, Ş, and ş.
Big5	Big5, traditional Chinese.
CNS11643	CNS 11643, the Han character standard interchange code for general use, traditional Chinese.

Table B-4. Available Encodings in Java 1.1 (continued)

Name	Encoding
Cp037	EBCDIC, a non-ASCII-based character set, primarily used on IBM mainframes. This version includes characters for U.S., Australian, and Canadian English, Canadian French, Dutch, and Portuguese.
Cp273	EBCDIC for German.
Cp277	EBCDIC for Danish and Norwegian.
Cp278	EBCDIC for Finnish and Swedish.
Cp280	EBCDIC for Italian.
Cp284	EBCDIC for Spanish and Catalan.
Cp285	EBCDIC for British English (also used in Ireland).
Cp297	EBCDIC for French.
Cp420	EBCDIC for Arabic.
Cp424	EBCDIC for Hebrew.
Cp437	DOS English character set for the United States, Australia, New Zealand, South Africa, ASCII plus various accented characters. Furthermore, like most DOS-based character sets, this includes a number of line and corner characters commonly used to display spreadsheets and tables. These are called *box-drawing characters*.
Cp500	EBCDIC International, essentially a reordered set of the same characters in Latin-1.
Cp737	DOS ASCII plus Greek and various box-drawing characters in the upper 128 places.
Cp775	DOS ASCII plus Baltic and various box-drawing characters in the upper 128 places.
Cp838	EBCDIC for Thai.
Cp850	DOS ASCII plus Western European and various box-drawing characters in the upper 128 places.
Cp852	DOS ASCII plus Central European and various box-drawing characters in the upper 128 places.
Cp855	DOS ASCII plus Cyrillic and various box-drawing characters in the upper 128 places.
Cp857	DOS ASCII plus Turkish and various box-drawing characters in the upper 128 places.
Cp860	DOS ASCII plus Portuguese and various box-drawing characters in the upper 128 places.
Cp861	DOS ASCII plus Icelandic and various box-drawing characters in the upper 128 places.
Cp862	DOS ASCII plus Hebrew and various box-drawing characters in the upper 128 places.
Cp863	DOS ASCII plus Canadian French and various box-drawing characters in the upper 128 places.
Cp864	DOS ASCII plus Arabic characters in the upper 128 places.
Cp865	DOS ASCII plus Nordic and various box-drawing characters in the upper 128 places.

Table B-4. Available Encodings in Java 1.1 (continued)

Name	Encoding
Cp866	DOS ASCII plus Cyrillic and various box-drawing characters in the upper 128 places.
Cp868	DOS Arabic used in Pakistan for the Urdu language plus various box-drawing characters.
Cp869	DOS ASCII plus modern Greek and various box-drawing characters in the upper 128 places.
Cp870	ASCII plus most of the Central European characters found in Latin-2.
Cp871	EBCDIC for Icelandic.
Cp874	DOS ASCII plus Thai and various box-drawing characters in the upper 128 places.
Cp875	EBCDIC for Greek.
Cp918	DOS ASCII plus Arabic as used in Pakistan for the Urdu language plus various box-drawing characters.
Cp921	DOS/AIX ASCII plus the characters needed for Latvian and Lithuanian in the upper 128 places.
Cp922	DOS/AIX ASCII plus the characters needed for Estonian in the upper 128 places.
Cp930	Japanese Katakana-Kanji mixed with 4,370 user-defined characters, a superset of 5026.
Cp933	Korean mixed with 1,880 user-defined characters, a superset of 5029.
Cp935	Simplified Chinese Host mixed with 1,880 user-defined characters, superset of 5031.
Cp937	Traditional Chinese Host mixed with 6,204 user-defined characters, superset of 5033.
Cp939	Japanese Latin Kanji mixed with 4,370 user-defined characters, superset of 5035.
Cp942	Japanese encoding used by OS/2, a superset of the SJIS Japanese Windows encoding.
Cp948	Chinese encoding used by Taiwanese localized OS/2, a superset of Cp938.
Cp949	Windows Unified Hangul (Extended Wansung) Korean.
Cp950	Windows ASCII plus Big5 Chinese, used in Hong Kong and Taiwan.
Cp964	AIX Chinese used in Taiwan.
Cp970	AIX Korean.
Cp1006	AIX Arabic used in Pakistan for Urdu.
Cp1025	EBCDIC Multilingual Cyrillic used in Bulgaria, Bosnia, Herzegovina, Macedonia.
Cp1026	EBCDIC plus Turkish.
Cp1046	"IBM Open Edition US EBCDIC," ASCII plus Arabic.
Cp1097	EBCDIC plus Farsi, a.k.a. Persian (Iran).

Table B-4. Available Encodings in Java 1.1 (continued)

Name	Encoding
Cp1098	ASCII plus Farsi, a.k.a. Persian and various box-drawing characters (Iran).
Cp1112	EBCDIC plus the characters needed for Latvian and Lithuanian.
Cp1122	EBCDIC plus the characters needed for Estonian.
Cp1123	EBCDIC plus the characters needed for Ukrainian.
Cp1124	AIX ASCII plus the characters needed for Ukrainian.
Cp1250	Windows, 3.1 Central European, identical with Latin-2 except for some additional noncontrol characters in the positions 128 to 159, as shown in Table B-3.
Cp1251	Windows, ASCII plus Cyrillic in the upper 128 characters.
Cp1252	Windows, Western European, identical with Latin-1 except for some additional noncontrol characters in the positions 128 to 159, as shown in Table B-3.
Cp1253	Windows, ASCII plus Greek in the upper 128 characters.
Cp1254	Windows, ASCII plus Turkish in the upper 128 characters.
Cp1255	Windows, ASCII plus Hebrew in the upper 128 characters.
Cp1256	Windows, ASCII plus Arabic in the upper 128 characters.
Cp1257	Windows, ASCII plus Baltic in the upper 128 characters.
Cp1258	Windows, ASCII plus Vietnamese in the upper 128 characters.
Cp1381	OS/2, DOS Chinese encoding used in the People's Republic of China.
Cp1383	AIX, Chinese encoding used in the People's Republic of China.
Cp33722	IBM-eucJP, Japanese (superset of 5050).
EUCJIS	Unix, JIS, EUC encoding, Japanese.
GB2312	GB2312, EUC encoding, simplified Chinese.
GBK	GBK, simplified Chinese.
ISO2022CN	ISO 2022, a standard for encoding multibyte characters in seven and eight-bit character sets, as used to encode Chinese.
ISO2022CN_CNS	CNS 11643 in ISO-2022-CN form, traditional Chinese.
ISO2022CN_GB	GB 2312 in ISO-2022-CN form, simplified Chinese.
ISO2022KR	ISO 2022 Korean.
JIS	One of four Japanese Industrial Standards for encoding Japanese text; the exact encoding is auto-detected as the file is read.
JIS0208	Japanese Industrial Standard X 0208 for encoding Japanese.
KOI8_R	ASCII plus various box-drawing characters, a few mathematical symbols, and Cyrillic characters, generally used for Russian.
KSC5601	KSC 5601, Korean.
MS874	Windows Thai.
MacArabic	Macintosh Arabic.
MacCentralEurope	Macintosh Latin-2.
MacCroatian	Macintosh Croatian.

Table B-4. Available Encodings in Java 1.1 (continued)

Name	Encoding
MacCyrillic	Macintosh Cyrillic.
MacDingbat	Zapf Dingbats.
MacGreek	Macintosh Greek.
MacHebrew	Macintosh Hebrew.
MacIceland	Macintosh Icelandic.
MacRoman	Macintosh Roman, the basic eight-bit character set used on most Macs in English-speaking countries and Western Europe. This character set has almost all the characters in Latin-1 with the notable exception of the lower- and uppercase thorn. However, characters are assigned different numeric values than they are in Latin-1.
MacRomania	Macintosh Romanian.
MacSymbol	The Macintosh Symbol font, essentially a MacRoman font that uses Greek glyphs in place of English ones.
MacThai	Macintosh Thai.
MacTurkish	Macintosh Turkish.
MacUkraine	Macintosh Ukrainian.
SJIS	Shift-JIS, same as JIS X 0208 but with the high bit set and no escape sequences, the standard Windows encoding of Japanese.
Unicode	Unicode with a byte order mark. This conversion determines whether the file is big-endian or little-endian by reading the first two bytes. If they are 0xFEFF, the file is assumed to contain big-endian data. If they are 0xFFFE, the file is assumed to contain little-endian data. If the first two bytes are anything else, a `MalformedInputException` is thrown.
UnicodeBig	Unicode with big-endian byte order.
UnicodeLittle	Unicode in little endian byte order.
UTF8	The UTF-8 encoding of full Unicode.

As extensive as this list is, there are a few missing pieces. ISO 8859-10, a.k.a. Latin-6, includes ASCII plus various characters used for Lappish, Nordic, and Inuit languages in the upper 128 places. Java cannot currently convert characters in this set to Unicode.

Work is ongoing on both Unicode and other character sets. ISO 8859-11 will provide a standard encoding for Thai. ISO 8859-12, also known as Latin-7, will use the upper 128 characters past ASCII for Celtic. ISO 8859-13, also known as Latin-8, will use them for the Baltic Rim languages. ISO 8859-14, also known as Latin-9, will encode ASCII plus Sami. Eventually, converters will be needed for these encodings as well.

Index

V

validation (object serialization), 297–299
    ObjectInputValidation interface, 298
    Person (example), 299
versioning, 282–284
    changes, compatible, incompatible, 282
    IDs, 284

W

web sites, 538
    articles, links, 543
    Digital Think (training), 537
    Java topics, 543
    object serialization, 540
WebCat program (example), 63
When Does read( ) Return? (table), 514
Win32 systems
    absolute paths, 317, 327
    canonical paths, 327
    characters (128-159), 548
    file attributes, 308
    file extensions, types, 311
    filenames, 305
    paths, separators, 313
    relative paths, 319
writeBoolean( ) (data stream), 115
writeChar( ), 116
writeObject( ), 285–288
Writer class, 16, 415
writer classes, 16
writeUTF( ), 116, 117
writing doubles with a DataOutputStream
        (example), 113
writing files, 50–53
    FileCopier program (example), 52
    FileOutputStream class, 50

Z

zip files
    defined, 178
    FancyZipLister (example), 183
    JAR files, versus, 198
    nine methods, 182
    set methods, 184
    steps for writing output stream, 185
    Unzipper (example), 180
    utility methods, 181
    ZipEntry object, 181
    ZipInputStream class, 190–193
    ZipLister (example), 179
    ZipOutputStream class, 185
    Zipper program (example), 188
ZipConstants class, 178
ZipEntry objects, 187
ZipInputStream class
    another Unzipper (example), 192
    closing, 192
    constructing, 191
    JarInputStream, 209
    opening, 191
    reading, 191
    steps of, 190
ZipLister (example), 179
ZipOutputStream class, 185
    close( ), 188
    closeEntry( ), 188
    constructing, initializing, 186
    default compression, 186
    finish( ), 188
    JarOutputStream, 209
    setComment( ), 186
    steps for writing to, 185
    write output, 188
    ZipEntry object, 187
Zipper program (example), 189
zlib compression, 155

About the Author

Elliotte Rusty Harold is a noted writer and programmer, both on and off the Internet. He started by writing FAQ lists for the Macintosh newsgroups on Usenet, and has since branched out into books, Web sites, and newsletters. He's currently fascinated by Java, which is beginning to consume his life. His Cafe Au Lait Web site at *http://sunsite.unc.edu/javafaq/* is one of the most popular independent Java sites on the Net.

Elliotte resides in New York City with his wife Beth and cats Charm (named after the quark) and Marjorie (named after his mother-in-law). When not writing about Java, he enjoys genealogy, mathematics, and quantum mechanics, and has been known to try to incorporate these subjects into his computer books (when he can slip them past his editors). So far he hasn't been able to, but he suspects that a short, last-minute biography might not be inspected as closely as the rest of a manuscript. His other books include *The Java Developer's Resource* (Prentice Hall), *Java Network Programming* (O'Reilly), *Java Secrets* (IDG Books), and *JavaBeans* (IDG Books)

Colophon

Our look is the result of reader comments, our own experimentation, and feedback from distribution channels. Distinctive covers complement our distinctive approach to technical topics, breathing personality and life into potentially dry subjects.

Hanna Dyer designed the cover of this book, based on a series design by Edie Freedman. The image was photographed by Kevin Thomas and manipulated in Adobe Photoshop by Michael Snow. The cover layout was produced with Quark XPress 3.3 using the Bodoni Black font from URW Software and BT Bodoni Bold Italic from Bitstream. The inside layout was designed by Nancy Priest. The heading font is Bodoni BT; the text font is New Baskerville. Whenever possible, our books use RepKover™, a durable and flexible lay-flat binding. If the page count exceeds RepKover's limit, perfect binding is used.

Clairemarie Fisher O'Leary was the production editor and copyeditor for *Java I/O*; Sheryl Avruch was the production manager; Madeleine Newell, Ellie Cutler, and Debby English provided quality control. Ruth Rautenberg wrote the index. Robert Romano created the illustrations using Adobe Photoshop 4 and Macromedia Free-Hand 7. Text was prepared by Mike Sierra in FrameMaker 5.5.

More Titles from O'Reilly

Java

Java in a Nutshell, DELUXE EDITION

By David Flanagan, et al.
1st Edition June 1997
628 pages, includes CD-ROM & book
ISBN 1-56592-304-9

Java in a Nutshell, Deluxe Edition, brings together on CD-ROM five volumes for Java developers and programmers, linking related info across books. *Exploring Java, 2nd Edition*, covers Java basics. *Java Language Reference, 2nd Edition, Java Fundamental Classes Reference*, and *Java AWT Reference* provide a definitive set of documentation on the Java language and the Java 1.1 core API. *Java in a Nutshell, 2nd Edition*, our bestselling quick reference, is included both on the CD-ROM and in a companion desktop edition. This deluxe library is an indispensable resource for anyone doing serious programming with Java 1.1.

Java Cryptography

By Jonathan B. Knudsen
1st Edition May 1998
362 pages, ISBN 1-56592-402-9

Java Cryptography teaches you how to write secure programs using Java's cryptographic tools. It includes thorough discussions of the java.security package and the Java Cryptography Extensions (JCE), showing you how to use security providers and even implement your own provider. It discusses authentication, key management, public and private key encryption, and includes a secure talk application that encrypts all data sent over the network. If you work with sensitive data, you'll find this book indispensable.

Java Language Reference, Second Edition

By Mark Grand
2nd Edition July 1997
492 pages, ISBN 1-56592-326-X

This book helps you understand the subtle nuances of Java—from the definition of data types to the syntax of expressions and control structures—so you can ensure your programs run exactly as expected. The second edition covers the new language features that have been added in Java 1.1, such as inner classes, class literals, and instance initializers.

Java Virtual Machine

By Jon Meyer & Troy Downing
1st Edition March 1997
452 pages, includes diskette
ISBN 1-56592-194-1

This book is a comprehensive programming guide for the Java Virtual Machine (JVM). It gives readers a strong overview and reference of the JVM so that they may create their own implementations of the JVM or write their own compilers that create Java object code. A Java assembler is provided with the book, so the examples can all be compiled and executed.

Java Swing

By Robert Eckstein, Marc Loy & Dave Wood
1st Edition September 1998
1252 pages, ISBN 1-56592-455-X

The Swing classes eliminate Java's biggest weakness: its relatively primitive user interface toolkit. Java Swing helps you to take full advantage of the Swing classes, providing detailed descriptions of every class and interface in the key Swing packages. It shows you how to use all of the new components, allowing you to build state-of-the-art user interfaces and giving you the context you need to understand what you're doing. It's more than documentation; Java Swing helps you develop code quickly and effectively.

Java Network Programming

By Elliotte Rusty Harold
1st Edition February 1997
442 pages, ISBN 1-56592-227-1

The network is the soul of Java. Most of what is new and exciting about Java centers around the potential for new kinds of dynamic, networked applications. *Java Network Programming* teaches you to work with Sockets, write network clients and servers, and gives you an advanced look at the new areas like multicasting, using the server API, and RMI. Covers Java 1.1.

Java

Java Examples in a Nutshell

By David Flanagan
1st Edition September 1997
414 pages, ISBN 1-56592-371-5

From the author of *Java in a Nutshell*, this companion book is chock full of practical real-world programming examples to help novice Java programmers and experts alike explore what's possible with Java 1.1. If you learn best by example, this is the book for you.

Java Threads

By Scott Oaks and Henry Wong
1st Edition January 1997
268 pages, ISBN 1-56592-216-6

With this book, you'll learn how to take full advantage of Java's thread facilities: where to use threads to increase efficiency, how to use them effectively, and how to avoid common mistakes like deadlock and race conditions. Covers Java 1.1.

Java in a Nutshell, Second Edition

By David Flanagan
2nd Edition May 1997
628 pages, ISBN 1-56592-262-X

This second edition of the bestselling Java book describes all the classes in the Java 1.1 API, with the exception of the still-evolving Enterprise APIs. And it still has all the great features that have made this the Java book most often recommended on the Internet: practical real-world examples and compact reference information. It's the only quick reference you'll need.

Java Security

By Scott Oaks
1st Edition May 1998
474 pages, ISBN 1-56592-403-7

This essential Java 1.2 book covers Java's security mechanisms and teaches you how to work with them. It discusses class loaders, security managers, access lists, digital signatures, and authentication and shows how to use these to create and enforce your own security policy.

Java Fundamental Classes Reference

By Mark Grand & Jonathan Knudsen
1st Edition May 1997
1114 pages, ISBN 1-56592-241-7

The *Java Fundamental Classes Reference* provides complete reference documentation on the core Java 1.1 classes that comprise the *java.lang, java.io, java.net, java.util, java.text, java.math, java.lang.reflect,* and *java.util.zip* packages. Part of O'Reilly's Java documentation series, this edition describes Version 1.1 of the Java Development Kit. It includes easy-to-use reference material and provides lots of sample code to help you learn by example.

Java Servlet Programming

By Jason Hunter with William Crawford
1st Edition November 1998
528 pages, ISBN 1-56592-391-X

Java servlets offer a fast, powerful, portable replacement for CGI scripts. *Java Servlet Programming* covers everything you need to know to write effective servlets. Topics include: serving dynamic Web content, maintaining state information, session tracking, database connectivity using JDBC, and applet-servlet communication.

Java Distributed Computing

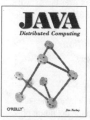

By Jim Farley
1st Edition January 1998
384 pages, ISBN 1-56592-206-9

Java Distributed Computing offers a general introduction to distributed computing, meaning programs that run on two or more systems. It focuses primarily on how to structure and write distributed applications and, therefore, discusses issues like designing protocols, security, working with databases, and dealing with low bandwidth situations.

How to stay in touch with O'Reilly

1. Visit Our Award-Winning Web Site

http://www.oreilly.com/

★ "Top 100 Sites on the Web" —*PC Magazine*
★ "Top 5% Web sites" —*Point Communications*
★ "3-Star site" —*The McKinley Group*

Our web site contains a library of comprehensive product information (including book excerpts and tables of contents), downloadable software, background articles, interviews with technology leaders, links to relevant sites, book cover art, and more. File us in your Bookmarks or Hotlist!

2. Join Our Email Mailing Lists

New Product Releases

To receive automatic email with brief descriptions of all new O'Reilly products as they are released, send email to:
listproc@online.oreilly.com
Put the following information in the first line of your message (*not* in the Subject field):
subscribe oreilly-news

O'Reilly Events

If you'd also like us to send information about trade show events, special promotions, and other O'Reilly events, send email to:
listproc@online.oreilly.com
Put the following information in the first line of your message (*not* in the Subject field):
subscribe oreilly-events

3. Get Examples from Our Books via FTP

There are two ways to access an archive of example files from our books:

Regular FTP

- ftp to:
  ftp.oreilly.com
  (login: anonymous
  password: your email address)
- Point your web browser to:
  ftp://ftp.oreilly.com/

FTPMAIL

- Send an email message to:
  ftpmail@online.oreilly.com
  (Write "help" in the message body)

4. Contact Us via Email

order@oreilly.com
To place a book or software order online. Good for North American and international customers.

subscriptions@oreilly.com
To place an order for any of our newsletters or periodicals.

books@oreilly.com
General questions about any of our books.

software@oreilly.com
For general questions and product information about our software. Check out O'Reilly Software Online at **http://software.oreilly.com/** for software and technical support information. Registered O'Reilly software users send your questions to: **website-support@oreilly.com**

cs@oreilly.com
For answers to problems regarding your order or our products.

booktech@oreilly.com
For book content technical questions or corrections.

proposals@oreilly.com
To submit new book or software proposals to our editors and product managers.

international@oreilly.com
For information about our international distributors or translation queries. For a list of our distributors outside of North America check out:
http://www.oreilly.com/www/order/country.html

O'Reilly & Associates, Inc.
101 Morris Street, Sebastopol, CA 95472 USA
TEL 707-829-0515 or 800-998-9938
    (6am to 5pm PST)
FAX 707-829-0104

International Distributors

UK, EUROPE, MIDDLE EAST AND AFRICA (EXCEPT FRANCE, GERMANY, AUSTRIA, SWITZERLAND, LUXEMBOURG, LIECHTENSTEIN, AND EASTERN EUROPE)

INQUIRIES
O'Reilly UK Limited
4 Castle Street
Farnham
Surrey, GU9 7HS
United Kingdom
Telephone: 44-1252-711776
Fax: 44-1252-734211
Email: josette@oreilly.com

ORDERS
Wiley Distribution Services Ltd.
1 Oldlands Way
Bognor Regis
West Sussex PO22 9SA
United Kingdom
Telephone: 44-1243-779777
Fax: 44-1243-820250
Email: cs-books@wiley.co.uk

FRANCE

ORDERS
GEODIF
61, Bd Saint-Germain
75240 Paris Cedex 05, France
Tel: 33-1-44-41-46-16 (French books)
Tel: 33-1-44-41-11-87 (English books)
Fax: 33-1-44-41-11-44
Email: distribution@eyrolles.com

INQUIRIES
Éditions O'Reilly
18 rue Séguier
75006 Paris, France
Tel: 33-1-40-51-52-30
Fax: 33-1-40-51-52-31
Email: france@editions-oreilly.fr

GERMANY, SWITZERLAND, AUSTRIA, EASTERN EUROPE, LUXEMBOURG, AND LIECHTENSTEIN

INQUIRIES & ORDERS
O'Reilly Verlag
Balthasarstr. 81
D-50670 Köln
Germany
Telephone: 49-221-973160-91
Fax: 49-221-973160-8
Email: anfragen@oreilly.de (inquiries)
Email: order@oreilly.de (orders)

CANADA (FRENCH LANGUAGE BOOKS)
Les Éditions Flammarion ltée
375, Avenue Laurier Ouest
Montréal (Québec) H2V 2K3
Tel: 00-1-514-277-8807
Fax: 00-1-514-278-2085
Email: info@flammarion.qc.ca

HONG KONG
City Discount Subscription Service, Ltd.
Unit D, 3rd Floor, Yan's Tower
27 Wong Chuk Hang Road
Aberdeen, Hong Kong
Tel: 852-2580-3539
Fax: 852-2580-6463
Email: citydis@ppn.com.hk

KOREA
Hanbit Media, Inc.
Sonyoung Bldg. 202
Yeksam-dong 736-36
Kangnam-ku
Seoul, Korea
Tel: 822-554-9610
Fax: 822-556-0363
Email: hant93@chollian.dacom.co.kr

PHILIPPINES
Mutual Books, Inc.
429-D Shaw Boulevard
Mandaluyong City, Metro
Manila, Philippines
Tel: 632-725-7538
Fax: 632-721-3056
Email: mbikikog@mnl.sequel.net

TAIWAN
O'Reilly Taiwan
No. 3, Lane 131
Hang-Chow South Road
Section 1, Taipei, Taiwan
Tel: 886-2-23968990
Fax: 886-2-23968916
Email: benh@oreilly.com

CHINA
O'Reilly Beijing
Room 2410
160, FuXingMenNeiDaJie
XiCheng District
Beijing, China PR 100031
Tel: 86-10-86631006
Fax: 86-10-86631007
Email: frederic@oreilly.com

INDIA
Computer Bookshop (India) Pvt. Ltd.
190 Dr. D.N. Road, Fort
Bombay 400 001 India
Tel: 91-22-207-0989
Fax: 91-22-262-3551
Email: cbsbom@giasbm01.vsnl.net.in

JAPAN
O'Reilly Japan, Inc.
Kiyoshige Building 2F
12-Bancho, Sanei-cho
Shinjuku-ku
Tokyo 160-0008 Japan
Tel: 81-3-3356-5227
Fax: 81-3-3356-5261
Email: japan@oreilly.com

ALL OTHER ASIAN COUNTRIES
O'Reilly & Associates, Inc.
101 Morris Street
Sebastopol, CA 95472 USA
Tel: 707-829-0515
Fax: 707-829-0104
Email: order@oreilly.com

AUSTRALIA
WoodsLane Pty., Ltd.
7/5 Vuko Place
Warriewood NSW 2102
Australia
Tel: 61-2-9970-5111
Fax: 61-2-9970-5002
Email: info@woodslane.com.au

NEW ZEALAND
Woodslane New Zealand, Ltd.
21 Cooks Street (P.O. Box 575)
Waganui, New Zealand
Tel: 64-6-347-6543
Fax: 64-6-345-4840
Email: info@woodslane.com.au

LATIN AMERICA
McGraw-Hill Interamericana
Editores, S.A. de C.V.
Cedro No. 512
Col. Atlampa
06450, Mexico, D.F.
Tel: 52-5-547-6777
Fax: 52-5-547-3336
Email: mcgraw-hill@infosel.net.mx

O'REILLY®

TO ORDER: **800-998-9938** • **order@oreilly.com** • **http://www.oreilly.com/**
OUR PRODUCTS ARE AVAILABLE AT A BOOKSTORE OR SOFTWARE STORE NEAR YOU.
FOR INFORMATION: **800-998-9938** • **707-829-0515** • **info@oreilly.com**